POWER
AND EVERYDAY
PRACTICES

POWER AND EVERYDAY PRACTICES

edited by

DEBORAH BROCK
York University

REBECCA RABY
Brock University

MARK P. THOMAS
York University

NELSON / EDUCATION

NELSON / EDUCATION

Power and Everyday Practices

by Deborah Brock, Rebecca Raby, and Mark P. Thomas

**Vice President,
Editorial Director:**
Evelyn Veitch

**Editor-in-Chief,
Higher Education:**
Anne Williams

Acquisitions Editor:
Maya Castle

Marketing Manager:
Terry Fedorkiw

Senior Developmental Editor:
Elke Price

Photo Researcher:
Kristiina Paul

Permissions Coordinator:
Kristiina Paul

Content Production Manager:
Jennifer Hare

Production Service:
KnowledgeWorks Global Limited

Copy Editor:
Rodney Rawlings

Proofreader:
Senthil

Indexer:
Kevin Broccoli

Production Coordinator:
Ferial Suleman

Design Director:
Ken Phipps

Managing Designer:
Franca Amore

Interior Design:
Olena Sullivan

Cover Design:
Gaye Chan

Cover Image:
Gaye Chan

Compositor:
KnowledgeWorks Global Limited

Printer:
RR Donnelley

**Library and Archives Canada
Cataloguing in Publication Data**

Power and everyday practices / edited by Deborah Brock, Rebecca Raby, Mark P. Thomas.

Includes bibliographical references and index.
ISBN 978-0-17-650203-4

1. Power (Social sciences). 2. Equality. I. Brock, Deborah R. (Deborah Rose), 1956– II. Raby, Rebecca, 1968– III. Thomas, Mark P. (Mark Preston), 1969–

HN49.P6P69 2011   303.3
C2011-901215-4

ISBN-13: 978-0-17-650203-4
ISBN-10: 0-17-650203-3

■ CONTENTS

PREFACE

We are pleased to present you—both students and colleagues—with this first edition of *Power and Everyday Practices*. We have prepared an unconventional textbook: one that takes up sociological theory and methods in the context of everyday objects and practices.

One objective of this text is to enrich students' appreciation of the uses of theory for exploring the everyday world. However, this text is intended to complement, rather than replace, courses in sociological theory. We do not present the range of theoretical approaches available through the study of sociology. Rather, we demonstrate the simultaneous relevance of two major—and often competing—streams of inquiry, which are generally known as materialism and poststructuralism. A second objective is to "trouble" normative assumptions about the everyday world; to question the seemingly taken for granted, commonsense social relations that shape our lives. We ask students to explore not only *why* questions, but also *how* questions; to make visible not only why things are as they are, but how they have come to be historically, socially, and culturally organized. A third objective of this text is to enhance their ability to be critical consumers of information, and to explore the links between the production of knowledge and the circulation of power in contemporary Western societies.

The themes, topics, and organization of this text owe much to an undergraduate foundations course in sociology at York University in Toronto. Social Organization/Social Order was designed to take students who had succeeded in their Introduction to Sociology course to the next level of analytic complexity and critical thinking. In this course we turn the analytic lens toward sites of privilege and the production of power. So, for example, rather than focusing on particular groups as objects of empirical investigation (such as the impact of racism on people of colour, the marginalization of gay, lesbian, and transgendered people, or the problems of the poor), we interrogate the centrality of whiteness, heterosexuality, and consumption practices in contemporary Western societies. Students think about how that cup of coffee they are drinking was produced, how their own deeply personal efforts for self-improvement are connected to a particular therapeutic ethos that characterizes our time and place, and why so many people will now list "shopping" as one of their favourite activities. We have been consistently pleased with the high level of enthusiasm for this course among students and teaching assistants, and we thought it a worthwhile endeavour to make the thematic and substantive approach of this course more widely available. To this end, we have managed to recruit an impressive collection of scholars who are similarly enthusiastic about the project, and keen to contribute their expertise.

FEATURES OF THE TEXT

There are four major parts to *Power and Everyday Practices*:

- **Part I** introduces students to the thematic, theoretical, and methodological approaches of the textbook.

- **Part II** is organized to deepen students' comprehension of some key thematic concepts of the book: the centre, normalization, and power. Appreciation of these concepts is gained through an exploration of bodies, genders, and sexualities; whiteness; social class, the state, and power; and age relations.

- **Part III** shifts the analytic lens to a selection of everyday images and practices. Here students engage with the meanings of scientific knowledge, the pervasiveness of therapeutic culture, consumption practices, and the logic of finance for Western industrialized societies.

- **Part IV** broadens the scope of analysis still further in order to make links between everyday images and practices in the West and global relations of power. Here students will examine the social construction of the "Indian" in the West, the power relations embedded in a cup of coffee, and the significance of tourism and the tourist experience both for local and global economies and for tourists themselves. Finally, students will engage with a critical analysis of nation states, citizenship and borders.

Each chapter concludes with a series of exercises and questions that will assist students with their review and comprehension of the material. Some of these exercises and questions are designed for students to undertake on their own, and some are designed for groups. Accompanying each chapter is a bibliography of sources that were important in its construction.

Throughout the text, key concepts are shown in **bold text**. Typically those concepts are defined at first mention. Also, each definition is found in the Glossary at the end of the book. Keep in mind, however, that the definitions are abbreviated versions of the explanations provided by our authors, and that they are not a substitute for the fuller explanation and analyses to be found in the chapters themselves. Some authors may take up the same concept in a somewhat different way, so it is important to understand the meaning and context for concepts in relation to specific chapters and issues.

ONLINE RESOURCES
www.powerandeverydaypractices.nelson.com

This book's supporting website contains resources that complement the text. Students and instructors can link directly to relevant sites associated with each of the book's chapters, and they can also access the Glossary online.

ACKNOWLEDGEMENTS

We wish to express our heartfelt thanks to the many people who provided the labour, support, guidance, and inspiration that made this textbook possible.

Laura Macleod of Nelson Canada was an early champion of this project. We have greatly appreciated her support and enthusiasm, and equal appreciation goes to Maya Castle for energetically carrying this project forward. Elke Price from Nelson Education has been a terrific guide for us throughout, pulling everything together behind the scenes. We are particularly grateful for her keen attention to detail. Thank you also to Kristiina Paul (Photo Researcher) and Terry Fedorkiw (Marketing Manager), and especially to the excellent Rodney Rawlings, our eagle-eyed copy editor.

York University Graduate Assistants Gopal Bandyopadhyay and Jennifer Proc were a great help compiling the Glossary and skillfully compiling and reviewing bibliographic entries. An enormous thank-you also goes out to Gaye Chan for the intriguing and beautiful cover design.

Our reviewers provided valuable feedback that allowed us to smooth out some of the textbook's rough edges. We are grateful to the following, and to many others who choose to remain anonymous: Seema Ahluwalia at Kwantlen Polytechnic University, Silvia Bartolic at University of British Columbia, Xiaobei Chen at Carleton University, Mara Fridell at University of Manitoba, Melanie Heath at McMaster University, Mervyn Horgan at Acadia University, Agnes Macdonald at University of British Columbia, Mary-Jo Nadeau at University of Toronto, Richard Nimijean at Carleton University, Robin Ostow at Wilfrid Laurier University, Rhonda Sandberg at George Brown College, Sarita Srivastava at Queen's University, and Tamy Superle at Carleton University. A special thank-you also to David Butz who provided us with crucial feedback, on very short notice, at a difficult time of the academic year.

The many, many past students of Sociology 2070: Social Organization/Social Order at York University provided enthusiastic feedback along the way that ultimately convinced us to produce this textbook. Big thanks to all of them! We would like similarly to thank past teaching assistants for their pedagogical commitment to the approach of 2070, and for making it work so well. Particular mention goes to former TAs Lachlan Story and Andie Noack for their dedication to the course and their participation in envisioning the possibility of this textbook.

And now for personal thanks from each of us:

Deborah sends bouquets of thanks to Gerard de Witt for providing a supportive home and an inviting work space under the eaves throughout this book's production. She is enormously grateful to her sister, Janet Brock, for serving as de facto administrative assistant in Canada while Deborah was out of the country on sabbatical. Finally, big, warm thanks to the network of friends and family, both in Canada and the Netherlands, who sustain her and help make her life such a wonderful adventure.

Rebecca would like to specifically thank Shauna Pomerantz, Mary Beth Raddon, and Helen McFadden for editorial feedback and cheerleading; Holly Patterson for unflagging support; and Levi Patterson-Raby for just being himself.

Mark would like to thank Justin Panos for research assistance with Chapter 6, David Camfield for very helpful comments on an early draft of the chapter, and as always, his parents, Mary and Pat Thomas, for their constant support throughout the project.

PART 1

SETTING THE STAGE

Unpacking the Centre[1]

Deborah Brock, Rebecca Raby, and Mark P. Thomas

Jasmine is on vacation with her family. Her parents have found a last-minute, discounted tourist package for a city they have always wanted to see. Jas has stuffed her handbag with the tourist brochures displayed in the lobby of their Sleep Well hotel. So many choices.... She pulls on her Euro Trend hoodie and her DZY sunglasses, grabs her voluminous handbag, and goes out the door. She wonders what new shops she will encounter, and soon finds herself drawn in to the Urban Paradise Shopping and Entertainment Complex. Her excitement soon dissipates. The stores are all exactly the same as the ones at home. There doesn't seem to be anything new here at all. Just then she spies a window display at one of her favourite fashion chains, She's All Mall. The fall season clothing has begun to arrive, and there are designs similar to those featured in her favourite online fashion column, "Chic and Trendy: Choose Your Individual Style." Jasmine's disappointment starts to shift.

Jasmine decides on Khaki pants and a fine cotton T-shirt, and eventually locates the sizes and colours she wants among the packed shelves. She hesitates only a second before handing her brand new credit card to the clerk at the desk. She doesn't have quite enough money to cover the bill, but ... isn't that what credit cards are for? The sales associate asks whether she has found everything that she wanted today and compliments her choices as he folds and bags her new purchases in a reusable logo shopping bag, and passes her a coupon for 10 percent off her next purchase of $100 or more. Jasmine happily takes the coupon. She may have spent too much in the shop this time, but she rationalizes that she will save some money next time!

But now it is time for a coffee break. It does not take long to find a kiosk for her favourite coffee chain. Jas orders a low-fat foamy café latte, her daily treat that she swears she cannot live without, and hands over $4.75. She perches on a tall stool, sips her drink, and checks her new messages on her cell phone. Jas has a new app for another of her favourite magazines, *You're Super!* She is a bit annoyed by all the skinny white women in the advertisements, but she likes the makeup and fashion tips, and thinks the magazine offers good advice columns on self-improvement. Sure enough, Jasmine locates a quiz in the download: "Are you true to yourself or are you a fake?" Perfect. Jasmine loves quizzes and she starts to do it right away. "Question one: You are working on a presentation for school, and you have been teamed up with a really cute guy you have been wanting to get to know. You get ready by: (a) applying cosmetics, (b) reviewing the homework assignment, or (c) practising opening lines in the mirror in the girl's bathroom." Jasmine hesitates for a while and then finally circles "(a)" and

---

1 Some of the issues raised in this chapter were also discussed in "Moving Beyond Deviance: Power, Regulation and Governmentality," in Deborah Brock, ed., *Making Normal: Social Regulation in Canada* (Toronto: Nelson, 2003). This material has been substantially revised for *Power and Everyday Practices*.

moves on. At the end she tallies her score. "You're modest and humble but perhaps a little too modest. Don't be afraid to speak up sometimes about your accomplishments." Jasmine agrees that she needs to improve her self-esteem, but what is more natural than a girl wanting to impress a guy by looking her best? Jas finds a second quiz, "Are your sexual feelings normal?" She decides that she will do that one later. She wishes some of her friends were here at the mall with her—it just doesn't feel quite the same on her own. So Jasmine picks up her bags, throws her coffee cup in the recycle bin and heads back to the Sleep Well Hotel.

Jasmine's story is fictional; but in it we can find many **everyday practices** that are familiar and that might, at first glance, seem benign: staying in a familiar hotel chain, shopping, using a credit card, enjoying a cup of coffee, even taking a quiz. By "everyday" we mean the practices that are a part of people's commonplace and taken-for-granted activities. But people's everyday activities reflect, reproduce, and sometimes challenge a wide range of **power relations**. Through this textbook we will encourage you to ask questions about these kinds of practices. We ask *how*: How are everyday occurrences connected to the social organization of power? How are gender, class, race, and age shaped and reflected in many such taken-for-granted practices? How are the goods that we buying produced? How do practices such as travelling, shopping, and getting a credit card reflect and reproduce power, even creating our very sense of who we are? We also address the *why* questions that these examples will no doubt bring to mind: Why are certain patterns of consumption encouraged and facilitated? And who benefits from this organization of consumerism?

For example, even that café latte some cherish as an everyday ritual reflects a geography, history, and economy of power relations. These relations become visible when we begin to study where coffee beans come from, who grows and harvests them, how they come to be ground and sold in drinks, and how they are marketed to the North American shopper seeking a treat. Chapter 13 thus explores how the choice to buy a cup of coffee— including what kind of coffee and where it is bought—is a practice embedded in a global web of power relations. The places we sleep, the places we shop, the products we buy, and the magazines we read are all a part of a system of corporate consumerism.

Another of Jasmine's everyday practices is to seek out fashion tips and self-improvement advice. The magazines and other popular media she consults are embedded in power relations: selling images, promoting individualized self-improvement, cultivating desires that support a consumer culture, and through these practices, reproducing power relations of race, gender, heterosexuality, and a narrow conceptualization of beauty. The quiz she takes could just have easily been about her fashion style, maturity, likeability, fitness routine, money management, or success with boys. In any of these cases, part of the imperative within the quiz is to encourage Jasmine to reflect upon herself and to try to shape herself to better fit a presumed ideal.

The chapters in this textbook address the diverse power relations embedded in such everyday objects and practices. They complicate objects and practices that many of us take for granted and offer new, sometimes unsettling ways of thinking about them. They illustrate how a cup of coffee is never *just* a cup of coffee and why a magazine is never *just* a magazine. When we begin to examine everyday objects and practices in this way, we also begin a process of "unpacking the centre."

UNPACKING THE CENTRE

Most sociological textbooks do not directly investigate what we will refer to here as the **centre**. It is much more common for them to analyze **social deviance** through the lens of the normative social order, for instance, and thus to focus on what happens to people who exist at the margins: the racialized, the colonized, the so-called sexual "minorities," the poor, and so on. Some scholars have instead focused on studying the centre, in order to develop a more comprehensive understanding of how social relations are organized. They "unpack" the centre—just like taking apart a piece of mechanical equipment—in order to find out how it works. To focus almost exclusively on the marginalized without interrogating the centre is to risk reproducing a pattern that defines the margins as the location of *the problem*.

For example, we think it imperative to conduct sociological research on same-gender sexuality in order to document the forms of systemic and attitudinal inequality that marginalize people because of their homosexual identity and practices. However, when scholars focus on homosexuality while ignoring the social construction of **heterosexuality**, we continue to name homosexuality as, in effect, the problem *for* sociological inquiry, even though our objective may be to explain why homosexuality should not be considered a problem. Heterosexuality is able to maintain its privileged position as the normal and natural sexual expression. **Whiteness** is another social characteristic that occupies the centre. Academic and public accounts of racism commonly focus on the impact of racism on people of colour, and ignore the social construction of whiteness and the relations of power and privilege connected to whiteness. The social organization of whiteness, however, is an important part of the problems of racism.

This approach to studying the social organization of everyday objects and practices draws attention to what sociologists have long referred to as patterns of social inequality. We are interested in power primarily because of the ways it is linked to inequalities between social groups. We do not, however, simply focus on patterns of social inequality as the outcome of power. While themes of inequality are certainly present in the chapters in this book, our approach seeks to understand the social organization of dominant power relations in terms of the ways in which these power relations shape *both* broad patterns of inequality *and* everyday experiences. In other words, we do not simply aim to document different levels of socioeconomic status, as stratification theorists often do (Aronowitz 2003); rather, we are interested in the social relations that produce and reproduce the "normal," the dominant, and the "centre." This means our analysis focuses on understanding relationships between social processes, social groups, *and* individuals as they live their daily lives. For example, in Chapter 6 Mark P. Thomas writes about the need to understand class as a social relation rather than a social position. This means seeking out the ways the economic system we live in—**capitalism**—brings people into social relationships with one another shaped by the distribution and control of economic resources. In order to understand "class" we need to look not simply at one's income level, but at the deeper social organization of the "everyday experience" of going to work.

To unpack the centre is to explore the taken for granted features of dominant forms of social organization. It is the most difficult to see that a centre exists when you occupy it—for example, when you are white, heterosexual, a citizen, or someone with money in your pocket. It is not so difficult when you occupy a position of other—for example, when you are a non-citizen, do not identify as straight, are racialized, or are in some way minoritized. In Chapter 15, Nandita Sharma writes about how non-citizens such as migrant workers make the taken-for-granted character of nationalist narratives visible. The experiences of migrant workers reveal how citizenship and national belonging are part of the centre, even while they might wish such acceptance for themselves.

To further understand the centre, it is helpful here to borrow from Ruth Frankenberg's (1993) words on whiteness, which you will read more about in Chapter 5 by Cynthia Levine Rasky. Here we can begin to apply them to the centre more generally. The centre is

- a position of social advantage;

- a standpoint from which those who occupy the centre see the world; and

- sustained through what are typically unmarked and unnamed cultural practices.

Yet this analysis is not as simple as naming some people insiders and others outsiders. For example, while we might occupy the centre in one respect (such as through an identification as white) we might not in others (such as an identification as queer), as we all have many dimensions and attachments. Furthermore, we are always negotiating, and sometimes even reframing these, according to the distinct composition of various social locations we occupy. As a result, we might simultaneously occupy the centre and the margins.

When we negotiate these multiple locations we exercise **agency**: a capacity to make choices within the frames of reference and possibilities available to us, and to act on those choices. So, we are not one-dimensional people leading prepackaged lives. We are not simply stamped from a mould by processes of **socialization** (see Chapter 7) to be cookie-cutter people created by powerful social institutions. Indeed, we would argue that "socialization" should only be used as a verb, to describe a practice of social learning; it should not imply the predetermination of who we are by social forces. We are complex and thinking subjects. At the same time, *who* we are and how we know ourselves to be, is very much linked to power: the power relations that shape our everyday practices, create the centre, and also create our notions of what is normal. Occupying the centre is a lot like being considered normal. Both are largely taken for granted by the people who occupy the centre, and both reproduce the kinds of comparisons, hierarchies, and exclusions between groups of people that are examined throughout this textbook and that invariably reflect and reproduce relations of power.

THINKING ABOUT POWER

What comes to mind when you think about power? A corporate boardroom? Political office? A fist raised? A gun? Less often does the everyday social world come to mind. How did that T-shirt make its way to your local mall? What does it mean to be responsible for your own economic well-being? Why do you prefer to kiss women rather than men (or vice versa) and why does it matter? Comprehending power, not only in significant world events or in schoolyard fights, but in our everyday, often mundane social worlds, is an important task and is central to this textbook. And because the mundane language and activities of everyday life often reproduce the centre, those who are at the centre often do not see power at work.

Usually we only think of power when it involves visible coercion. For example, sociologist Max Weber (1947: 152) defined power as "the probability that one actor in a social relationship will be in a position to carry out his [*sic*] will despite resistance." Yet power is also being exercised when we are so entrenched within a particular way of "seeing" that we cannot imagine alternatives to it. It is exercised when our thoughts, preferences, and acceptance of ourselves have been established within the taken-for-granted order of things. We might think that this "way" has been designed by God or by the natural order, and is therefore unchangeable. Yet power includes the ability of a person, group, organization, discourse, etc., to put into place the definition of a situation. This entails establishing the terms through which events will be understood and through which one can discuss the pertinent issues. Also, power involves the creation of ideals which people and organizations then endeavour to achieve. So power often entails the ability to define morality (McDowell & Sharp, 1999). In examining these complexities of power, part of our task is to explore how power is socially organized, who is advantaged or disadvantaged, what factors need to be in place for this to happen, when and where the exercise of power is most likely to occur, and ultimately, why power happens. It is also necessary to explore why and how dominant power relations come to be challenged, contested, or resisted, and how such resistance can, in turn, create new social relations and organization. These are daunting tasks, because power is one of the most complex concepts in the social sciences.

Let's think about two very different examples of how power works, each of which will be examined further in this textbook. We'll begin with a discussion of medical science, which one would think is foremost engaged with identifying and explaining naturally occurring phenomena. What is the relation between the professional knowledge of medical science and power? If your answer is that medical experts are powerful, you will find that this textbook requires you to dig much deeper. Scientists and physicians do not simply discover and name diseases that affect human populations; they also make decisions within certain contexts (as outlined in Chapter 8) about what it means to be sick or healthy (as outlined in Chapter 9). Such decisions can, in turn, categorize entire groups of people. The implications of this are enormously significant. Certain populations of people (for example, HIV-positive people, sex workers, and "lepers") become associated with contagion, regardless of their individual likelihood to transmit disease. These populations then become a source of public anxiety, and at times are subject to social rejection and isolation. Heidi Rimke and Deborah Brock develop this topic in Chapter 9, where they address the rise of therapeutic culture.

Another example of how power works can be found in Chapter 11, "Financial Fitness" by Mary Beth Raddon. Discussions of "the market" have dominated the public agenda for decades, and are commonly framed as if market forces have a self-regulating logic of their own. Adam Smith (1723–1790) first introduced this notion of the "invisible hand" in his treatise on the birth of capitalism, *The Wealth of Nations* (1776). **Neoliberal** rationalities similarly attribute to the market the dimensions of a natural force, existing independent of human activity. Problems with this conceptualization of the market became clear in 2008, when global markets that had been most vigorously pursuing the neoliberal agenda began to unravel. Not only did this crisis require the rapid intervention of nation states in order to save their national economies from bankruptcy; it exposed something of the organization of power behind the myth of the self-regulating market. Despite this exposure, the neoliberal conceptualization of social life as governed by natural economic rationalities remains in place and permeates our everyday financial decisions and practices, as Chapter 11 explores.

In this textbook, we do *not* intend to provide a comprehensive survey of the study of power in the social sciences. However, we do want to provoke you to think more about how power works, and to complicate your perceptions of what power is, where it comes from, how it is expressed, and how it is resisted. We offer you some clues, debates, and examples in order to get you started in your own thinking about power. The chapters that follow engage with a range of sociological theorists and perspectives that will assist you in thinking about power in relation to everyday practices. While you will encounter a variety of approaches to the study of power and everyday practices in this textbook, the works of Karl Marx and Michel Foucault are particularly influential to our overall approach, as Deborah Brock explains in detail in Chapter 2.

Karl Marx (1818–1883) was a German political economist who spent his life writing about the economics of capitalism. His aim was to understand both its social organization and the ways in which it could be transformed. For Marx, capitalism is an economic system inherently defined by antagonistic class relations between two fundamental classes—the capitalist class and the working class. He understood class as primarily defined by ownership of and control over economic resources within society, such as capital and business infra-structure (which he termed the **means of production**). Those who own these resources—the capitalist class—are able to generate more capital (profits) by exploiting those who do not—the working class. For Marx, power in capitalist society stems from these fundamental relationships of control over economic resources. The class system of capitalism—in Marx's terms—is explored by Mark P. Thomas in Chapter 6. Marx's ideas about power are reflected in chapters that connect individual everyday objects and practices—for example, drinking a cup of coffee—to broader economic processes rooted in the exploitation of labour that pro-duced that cup of coffee. Marx was not only interested in understanding capitalism. He was also committed to an analysis that would advance social change, arguing that the exploita-tion that he identified as inherent to capitalism must be countered by social movements that aim to create an economic system based on democratic control over economic produc-tion. This being so, various chapters in this text examine alternative social movements and politics, including slow money (Chapter 11) and fair trade purchasing (Chapter 13).

Michel Foucault (1926–1984) was a French social theorist who believed that one of the most pervasive forms of power that is present in contemporary societies comes through proc-esses of **normalization**. Foucault was interested in how we come to understand what is consid-ered to be "normal." This is not an innocent or random process; for Foucault, the "normal" is a form of social regulation that pervades institutions and everyday practices. Following Foucault, chapters in this book seek to understand ways in which discourses about "normal" behav-iour (for example, sexual orientation or age) are connected to the power relations that repro-duce "the centre." We employ the definition of **discourse** provided by Mary Louise Adams: "Organized systems of knowledge that make possible what can be spoken about, and how one can speak about it" (Adams, 1997: 6). The concept of discourse is important for making sense of power and everyday practices; you will encounter it frequently throughout this text.

In shaping our lives through these discourses, by governing ourselves in accordance with principles of "normal" behaviour, we contribute to the reproduction of social inequality. Foucault's approach—explained in more detail in Chapter 2—helps us understand both the connections between discourse and power and how dominant discourses serve to shape our understanding of the "normal," hiding alternative ways of seeing the world. Far from regarding this as an iron cage of social control, Foucault also explored some of the ways in which counter-discourses emerged to produce social change, and new understandings of social life.

We find that the approaches of Foucault and Marx combined can provide valuable insights into the social organization of power in any specific occurrence. For example, throughout this textbook you will find frequent references to neoliberalism. Here we will see Marx's ideas about power expressed in analyses of neoliberalism as the now-dominant economic rationality for Western capitalism. We will also see how Foucault's ideas about discourse, power, and knowledge are helpful for understanding the production of meaning, so that neoliberalism comes to appear as the normal and natural approach to organizing economies. Both approaches therefore assist us in understanding how political institutions and social policies come to prioritize economic logic over the social welfare of people, in ways that normalize this economic logic as "the centre."

As you can see from the example of neoliberalism, the study of Marx and Foucault reveals very different approaches to how power may operate in and through social relations: one focusing on material production and the other on normalizing practices. It is at times a challenge to bring these frameworks into alignment with one another. In order to develop a more integrative approach—one that brings together analyses of discourses (building from Foucault) with analyses of material conditions (building from Marx)—we can also look to the work of social theorists who have themselves sought such integration, such as Stuart Hall. As discussed in the introduction to Part III, Stuart Hall developed his analysis of "The West and the rest" in order to understand the ways the forms of economic and political exploitation inherent to European colonialism were both connected to *and made possible by* discourses of Western cultural superiority. This book aims to build on this kind of theoretical integration. The aim of *Power and Everyday Practices* is not to resolve all the tensions that may exist between these different perspectives, but rather to draw from them so as to help us understand the many ways power is produced, reproduced, and contested in relation to a wide range of everyday practices. While individual chapters utilize different aspects of these approaches, the overarching analysis of the textbook is brought together through the focus on unpacking the centre, particularly the everyday practices and processes so often unquestioned and therefore taken for granted as "normal."

WHAT IS TO COME

The book is divided into four parts. In this section, Part I, "Setting the Stage," we present the general theoretical and methodological approach of this textbook. In Part II, "The Centre, Normalization, and Power," we outline key social relationships that we see as constitutive of "the centre": gender, whiteness, class, and age—and we identify the ways all are present within many everyday practices. The chapters in this section explore the connections of these social relations to the production and reproduction of "normal" through dominant discourses and through the social relations of contemporary capitalism. Building from C. W. Mills' idea of the "sociological imagination," which connects individuals to the wider social context within which they live, the authors in this section introduce ways of making connections between our everyday social locations and the larger events that shape the social world by revealing how the centre is created and reproduced. These chapters frame the case studies of "the everyday" that follow.

In Part III, "Everyday Images and Practices," we introduce examples of practices that illustrate these social relations at work in everyday contexts. These include the pervasive influence of both scientific and economic discourses, our consumption of strategies for "self-help," and the shopping trip to the mall. While this is a diverse collection of case studies, one of the threads running through this section is the emphasis on the influence of experts. Our reliance on experts is sometimes well recognized, such as when we hire a financial advisor to help "get our house in order." In such cases, we may seek expert advice to make sense of the world. Other times, however, this advice may be invisible and unwanted, for example in the strategically designed layout in a big box retailer that requires you to navigate an entire store before finding the checkout and exit. In deferring to experts to help plan our lives, or in accepting the road map of the shopping mall or big box store, we may inadvertently (and overtly) reproduce the centre. Chapters in this section also discuss how such expertise has been challenged through alternative histories, discourses and social movements.

Finally, in Part IV, "Thinking Global: 'The West and the Rest,'" we introduce practices that tie the everyday to the dynamics of international **political economy** through representations of Indigenous peoples, the commodification of coffee, the production of the tourist experience, processes of nation-state building, and the regulation of migrant labour. The section begins by introducing Stuart Hall's writing on "the West and the rest," using Hall's work as a way to study how discourse, systems of **representation**, and political economy connect with one another in organizing power and shaping everyday practices. Following Hall, we see that discourses produce knowledge by shaping how we understand the world; but discourses cannot be separated from economic and political institutions in the production of systems of power. For example, the "escape" to an "exotic" location promoted through all-inclusive vacation packages is produced by both a discourse of "the other" (an exotic location) *and* a political economy of poverty and global inequality that enables some to *become* tourists while others *serve* tourists. Of course—as Margot Francis reminds us in her chapter "The Imaginary Indian: Unpacking the Romance of Domination"—"the West and the Rest" is not just about the global economy; the discursive production of "the other" links to histories of colonialism in Canada as well, through the marginalization of Indigenous populations in North America. Thus, although Hall did not coin the term, through his exploration of the West and the rest, we see varied examples of the production of power through everyday practices in local, national, and global settings.

CONCLUSION

We conclude this chapter by returning you to the shopping mall, where Jasmine has just made her purchases. These she will likely enjoy and then discard at the end of the season. Her café latte is already consumed and forgotten. In "The Silence of the Lambswool Cardigans," Rebecca Solnit (2007: 323) reminds us of the following:

> There was a time not so long ago when everything was recognizable not just as a cup or a coat, but as a cup made by so-and-so out of clay from this bank on the local river or a coat woven by the guy in that house out of wool from the sheep visible on the hills. Then, objects were not purely material, mere commodities, but signs of processes, human and natural, pieces of a story, and both the story and the stuff sustained life. It's as though every object spoke—some of them must have sung out—in a language everyone could hear, a language that surrounded every object in an aura of its history.

Solnit's purpose here is not to suggest that we must return to a more perfect and simple past. Like us, she seeks to foster in you the skills and vision to explore everyday objects, lives, and practices, and to recognize your part in shaping and reshaping social life. Understanding power begins to make that possible.

REFERENCES

Adams, Mary Louise. 1997. *The Trouble with Normal: Postwar Youth and the Making of Heterosexuality*. Toronto: University of Toronto Press.

Aronowitz, Stanley. 2003. *How Class Works: Power and Social Movement*. New Haven: Yale University Press.

Frankenberg, Ruth. 1993. *White Women, Race Matters: The Social Construction of Whiteness*. Minnesota: University of Minnesota Press.

McDowell, Linda, and Joanne Sharp. 1999. *A Feminist Glossary of Human Geography*. London: Arnold.

Solnit, Rebecca. 2007. The silence of the lambswool cardigans (2003). *Storming the Gates of Paradise: Landscapes for Politics*. Berkeley: University of California Press.

Weber, Max. 1947. Sociological categories of economic action. *The Theory of Social and Economic Organization*. New York: Oxford University Press. 158–323.

2

THINKING ABOUT POWER: EXPLORING THEORIES OF DOMINATION AND GOVERNANCE[1]

Deborah Brock *York University*

❚ The first wisdom of sociology is this: Things are not what they seem.

Peter Berger, Invitation to Sociology (New York: Doubleday, 1963), 34.

As you read in Chapter 1, the contributors to *Power and Everyday Practices* want you to find something surprising and enlightening in seemingly mundane everyday activities, such as paying your bills and your taxes, watching Oprah or Dr. Phil on television, drinking a cup of coffee, or applying for a passport. Clearly, however, we don't want you to dismiss, as unworthy of your attention, anything that does *not* impact upon your personal experience. Sociologists are not navel gazers; we are always looking beyond our own lives and own experiences for clues about the organization of the social world. In other words, we want you to connect your everyday experiences to larger social, political, and economic processes. We want you to gain an appreciation for the uses of theory for making sense of *your* everyday world, while encouraging you to develop the skills of abstract and critical thinking to take you *beyond* the bounds of your actual everyday lives. This requires you to interrogate your own practices of looking, listening, and thinking. In Chapter 3, you will learn more about different approaches to knowledge, how to be critical in your consumption of information, and how to familiarize yourself with some strategies for undertaking analytic work. You will find that your methodology is in some way linked to theory, which is the focus of Chapter 2, because there are connections between what we choose to study, why we elect to study it, how we elect to study it, and the lens through which we study it.

Theorists and theories often appear to be abstract and far removed from the world that we know. But it is theorists who help to make the social world more visible, from the everyday activities that people engage in to analyses of historic events. In this chapter, we give particular attention to how some prominent theorists conceptualize the organization of power. In presenting some of their ideas, our aim is to complicate your perception of where power comes from, how it is expressed, and how it is resisted.

In Chapter 1, you were introduced to a basic definition of power. However, this basic definition does not explain *how* power is socially organized, *who* is advantaged or disadvantaged, *what* factors need to be in place for this to happen, *when* and *where* the exercise

---

1 An earlier version of portions of this chapter was published as "Moving Beyond Deviance: Power, Regulation and Governmentality" in Deborah Brock, ed., *Making Normal: Social Regulation in Canada* (Toronto: Nelson, 2003).

of power is most likely to occur, or *why* power happens. You can therefore appreciate the reasons why there is not one single definition of, or approach to, power. You were also introduced to two examples for thinking about how power works in contemporary Western industrialized societies: (1) the organization and significance of medical science and (2) financial markets. You found that there are different means through which theorists can explain these occurrences. These means are not necessarily incompatible, although a preliminary analysis might suggest that the key theories that inform this textbook are far apart on many issues. One key reason for this potential gulf is that some theorists and researchers align their scholarship with **modernism**, while others are more readily located within **postmodernism** or **poststructuralism**. Before we give more attention to our key theorists, Karl Marx, Michel Foucault, and Stuart Hall, we want to explain these distinct **epistemological** (theories of knowledge) and **ontological** (studies of being or reality) approaches.

MODERNISM AND POSTMODERNISM

Modernist thought had its beginnings in the **Enlightenment** (literally meaning, to shed light upon) period that was under way in Europe by the late 17th century. Enlightenment thought posed the radical new idea that people could use human reason to shape history. This ran contrary to accepted wisdom, because it challenged the certainty that God alone was responsible for all creation. In other words, scientific knowledge production began to challenge religious "truths." Enlightenment thinkers embraced the hope that science could be a tool for human progress. Through modernist scientific exploration, it was (and is) believed that we can measure and understand not only the natural environment but also human behaviour. Scientific method is used to try to identify underlying structures or foundations that shape the organization of social life. Enlightenment thought therefore produced a revolution in knowledge, one that challenged the primacy of the church over social life, and, relatedly, the "natural rights" of the aristocracy, which were based on the certainty that these rights had been ordained by God. This was to open the way for new forms of political rights, based upon notions of individualism and freedom (a matter that we will return to toward the conclusion of this chapter). However, Enlightenment knowledge remained constrained by the time and location of its production. Few of its premises were extended beyond the lives of Europeans. Instead, much of Enlightenment thought proposed a new system of natural hierarchy that justified colonial expansion, slavery, and other means of subordinating non-European peoples as lesser or non-people. You will read more about the legacy of these processes throughout this book.

Postmodernism began to emerge toward the end of the 20th century, at a time in history when established truths had possibly never been so quickly and extensively shaken through rapid changes in technology, material life, and meaning. The liberation struggles and social movements of the 1960s, such as anti-colonial (including Third World and aboriginal peoples) liberation struggles, anti-racism movements, workers' movements, the women's liberation movement, and the lesbian and gay liberation movements, had challenged prevailing hierarchical orders, and this challenge also permeated and intersected with new developments in theory. There were more stories to be told, and more truths to be claimed. Postmodernists contest what they refer to as **grand narratives**: grand or sweeping claims or stories about history, such as those developed by Christianity, or the advocates of political and economic systems such as capitalism and socialism. Postmodernists dismiss these narratives as totalizing, because they purport to be comprehensive explanations of history and of knowledge. Moreover, postmodernists refuse (not always successfully) to replace these existing grand narratives with new ones. Part of the rationale for contesting grand narratives was to account what Foucault referred to as **subjugated knowledges** (Foucault, 1989), which are hidden, disqualified, or masked by dominant knowledges. Subjugated knowledges are found among those who were socially positioned as **other**, including the racialized, the colonized, and the sexually marginalized. The production of knowledge itself, rather than only knowledge claims, came under greater scrutiny than possibly ever before.

Postmodernism rejects the Enlightenment belief that, through human reason and research, humanity is on the road of progress. Instead, history has been reconceptualized as fragmented, discontinuous, and without a larger purpose. From this perspective, while history should indeed be studied, researchers should pursue smaller-scale, localized studies in order to piece together the history of ideas and events, rather than making claims about broad swatches of human history and consciousness through the construction of grand narratives. Similarly, **humanism** posits essential, inviolable truths about people, most notably that individual consciousness and will shape human understanding and action. Postmodernism, however, challenges the belief that there are core truths or laws that could be applied to all people, or specific groups of people (for example, racialized groups). For postmodernists, people are made up, or constituted, through the social relations of their time and place, and in a continuous process.

Postmodernism is strongly linked to poststructuralism, which rejects the belief (not surprisingly known as **structuralism**) that there are stable underlying, unifying structures, or rules, shaping social life and communication, and that these structures can be studied through objective scientific method. It also rejects the belief that knowledge constructed through binary oppositions, offering either/or choices can provide sufficient explanation of the nuances of social and material life. "Either/or" choices, such as between bad and good, irrational and rational, black and white, woman and man, or child and adult are **deconstructed** and replaced by "both/and" in poststructuralist thought.

Poststructuralism is also somewhat linked to **postcolonialism**, because postcolonial theorists complicate and disrupt Enlightenment and modernist narratives, particularly those that assume the ascendancy and superiority of European thought and activity. While there is no agreed-upon definition of postcolonialism, it is generally used to describe critical, scholarly research about the history and legacy of European colonialism, most typically by scholars with origins within those former colonies. Postcolonial scholars are thus interested in deconstructing the language and practices of colonialism and their material consequences. In doing so, many working in this area, such as Gayatri Spivak, prioritize the voices of those traditionally silenced by colonialism and debate how this might best be accomplished (Spivak, 1988). Others, such as Homi K. Bhabha, are interested in spaces of **hybridity**, where dominant and marginalized forms of knowledge mix and transform into new ways of being (Bhabha, 1994).

Postcolonial theorists have contributed significantly to the development of poststructuralist thought by introducing multiple and counter narratives that describe and challenge the ongoing effects of colonial rule. However, postcolonial theorists such as Gayatri Spivak have questioned whether the **subaltern**, those who possess the knowledges subordinated by European colonial history and science, could actually be spoken for by European theorists such as Foucault.

By now, you can appreciate that the differences between modernism and postmodernism or poststructuralism can significantly impact the study of power and everyday practices. However, we do not intend to provide a debate between modernists and postmodernists. Instead, we attempt to reconcile some of the tensions between these views through our pragmatic use of theory and through the attempts by numerous scholars to render this division less significant, if not bridgeable.

We will now continue our discussion of the respective ideas of two influential theorists you were introduced to in Chapter 1: the materialist analysis of Karl Marx and the discourse analysis and **genealogical** approach of Michel Foucault. We will discuss their ongoing influence on scholars whose work bridges their analyses, most notably the work of Stuart Hall. We will then conclude this chapter by contrasting the approaches of these theorists to the political and economic philosophy of liberalism and neoliberalism. This exercise is important because it is now liberalism and neoliberalism that occupy the **centre** of political and economic life in most Western industrialized nations.

KARL MARX: HISTORICAL MATERIALISM AND THE CLASS SYSTEM

The legacy of 19th-century philosopher Karl Marx (1818–1883) can be found throughout the discipline of sociology, and certainly here in this textbook. Marx was a typical modernist theorist, because he believed that scientific knowledge could lead to the exposure of truth, and ultimately to people challenging the false belief systems that ruled over them. Marx is best known for his critique of capitalism as an economic and social system. He is also known for his expectation (and indeed, hope)

FIGURE 2.1 ■ Karl Marx.

Wikimedia Commons

that capitalism would eventually be replaced by a more egalitarian system (first by socialism, and then by pure communism), in which class inequalities and inequalities between nations would be eliminated. This new revolutionary phase of history would usher in a more just distribution of wealth and social resources. But how was this to be achieved? Marx believed that it is the responsibility of people not only to understand the world, but also to change it. Power, particularly as exercised through the domination of one class over others, must be made visible, critiqued, resisted, and transformed. For Marx, power must be challenged, and *social change* must be pursued.

In the words of Marx and Engels... The history of all hitherto existing society is the history of class struggles.

Freeman and slave, patrician and plebian, lord and serf, guild-master and journeyman, in a word, oppressor and oppressed, stood in constant opposition to one another, carried on an uninterrupted, now hidden, now open fight, a fight that each time ended, either in a revolutionary reconstitution of society at large, or in the common ruin of the contending classes.... The modern bourgeois society that has sprouted from the ruins of feudal society has not done away with class antagonisms. It has but established new classes, new conditions of oppression, new forms of struggle in place of the old ones.

Source: From Karl Marx and Friedrich Engels, *The Communist Manifesto* (Harmondsworth, UK: Penguin, 1848; 1985).

Marx developed a theory and a methodology called **historical materialism**, which he considered to be a scientific study of the stages of human history and development. Historical materialism was based on two essential beliefs, which together reveal the foundations for his approach to power. First, the word *historical* indicates that this approach emphasizes that social structures, social relationships, and social change can only be understood in historical context. While Marx regarded conflict and struggle, such as those between classes, as present throughout human history, he believed that the specific form these social relationships may take varied considerably across different historical periods. Second, he believed that to understand this, we must study the material conditions under which people live. In other words, we must look at how humans produce and reproduce themselves through their labour (Marx & Engels, 1969). As you read in Chapter 1, it was from this starting point that Marx developed his analysis of the specific class relations within capitalism. You will learn more about class analysis in Chapter 6, where Mark P. Thomas will deepen your engagement with Marx's work.

For Marx, capitalism was defined by two fundamental classes: the capitalist class— those who own and control the productive resources of a society—and the working class—those who must sell their labour power for a wage in order to survive. While the system of wage labour is often viewed as an equal and fair exchange, Marx saw this relationship as inherently exploitative due to the fact that wages paid to the working class are less than the value of the commodities they produce or the services they provide while employed by capitalists. This condition of exploitation, for Marx, results from the power of the capitalist class, power derived through control over economic resources. Marx also believed that this condition of exploitation would eventually lead the working class into struggle toward social transformation.

—*Mark P. Thomas*

When we analyze power as Marx understood it, we see that it is maintained through a system of domination, in which control is exercised by the ruling class over land, labour, and capital. Power therefore rests primarily in the possession of economic resources. It is exercised in order to maintain and reproduce a system of social inequality; indeed, when capitalist economic power is most successful, these inequalities will be deepened. To exercise power is an act of social control, because power means having the ability to organize social, economic, and political relations in a way that benefits the possessors of power (in this case those who control economic wealth), and subordinates those who do not hold it. This means that within a capitalist economy, the **state** (that is, the political and administrative apparatus that claims legitimacy to manage or rule the affairs of a geographical and political territory) is fundamentally a *capitalist* state. It ultimately works in the interest of preserving a particular economic order that benefits foremost the owners of economic wealth.

You would be right to question how a system predicated on social inequality could be maintained, if it indeed works against the best interests of the majority of people. Often, it is an awareness of ordinary everyday issues and problems that compels people to act. For example, sharp increases in the price of bread, a staple food of the working class and poor, has in many times and places instigated women to take to the streets in protest. Resistance to the rising cost of bread (which have also been referred to, perhaps erroneously, as "bread riots") was a contributing factor to the French Revolution. Similar actions by women have been documented in Boston during the early 18th century, in the American South during the 1860s, and in Britain during the late 18th century, among other global locations. Anger about food shortages is again leading to public protests around the world, for reasons we hope will become clear to you as you read this textbook.

Two years after the last food crisis, food inflation is back as a global issue. As in 2008, rocketing prices are the result of rising demand and supply shortages caused by freak weather and poor harvests. Moreover, these conditions are exacerbated by speculation on commodity markets and changing diets in fast-growing Asian countries.

The UN's Food and Agriculture Organization (FAO) last week called an emergency meeting for 24 September to discuss the food crisis. In Mozambique, riots broke out following the government's decision to raise bread prices by 30%, following double-digit hikes in the price of energy and water.

The unrest left seven people dead and hundreds injured. Mozambicans spend an average of three-quarters of their household budget on food and half of Mozambique's poor already suffer from acute malnutrition, according to the FAO.

Source: Julia Kollewe, "UN Calls Special Meeting to Address Food Shortages amid Predictions of Riots," *The Observer*, September 5, 2010; Raj Patel, "Mozambique's Food Riots—The True Face of Global Warming," *The Observer*, September 5, 2010. Copyright Guardian News & Media Ltd 2010.

FIGURE 2.2 ■ Antonio Gramsci.

Wikimedia Commons

Antonio Gramsci: Hegemony

Clearly, people do rise up in protest when they perceive that they are being oppressed by a higher master. These protests have almost always been quelled, sometimes through violent means and sometimes through a renegotiation of the terms between, for example, capitalists and labourers. This kind of resistance can be daunting in the face of a complex nexus of power relations that appear to exclude ordinary people from decision-making processes of any larger social significance. In Western capitalist nations, power is still maintained through coercion when nation states, acting in the interests of preserving the economic order, enact measures for suppressing resistance to domination. However, the exercise of power in Western, capitalist, and formally democratic countries is much more effective when derived from the **organization of consent**, through which people come to identify the interests of the ruling class as synonymous with their own. This is evident in the belief that what is good for the corporation is good for the workers, because a corporation that is doing well will provide more and better jobs for workers. The Italian Marxist Antonio Gramsci (1891–1937) named this dynamic between coercion and consent **hegemony**, and more specifically, **cultural hegemony**.

Gramsci extended the conceptualization of power in capitalism to encompass a range of cultural practices that served to keep the mode of production and the class structure in place. By focusing on how a complex and contradictory web of cultural practices contributes to the organization of consent, Gramsci reveals how domination can be accomplished without direct authoritarian rule. At the same time, by demonstrating how the maintenance of hegemony is an uneven and difficult process, depending on the balance of social forces at a given time and place, Gramsci's notion of hegemony also suggests possibilities for resistance through the emergence of counter-hegemonic forces (Gramsci, 1971). In this way, the concept of hegemony offers something of a bridge between Karl Marx's conceptualization of power and the alternative approach to power offered by Michel Foucault, because it provides a means of identifying a complex, diffuse, and dynamic network of power in capitalist societies.[2]

MICHEL FOUCAULT: GENEALOGY, DISCOURSE, AND THE PRODUCTIVITY OF POWER

When we began our study of power in this chapter, you will have noticed a formula for investigation that is a staple of intellectual inquiry: *Who? What? When? Where? Why? How? How* questions have certainly risen to the forefront in sociology in recent years, because there has been a loss of confidence in **grand theories** or

---

2   Thanks to Ruthann Lee for her discussion of hegemony (Lee, 2010).

FIGURE 2.3 ■ Michel Foucault.

AFP/Getty Images

narratives that attempt to explain the world through sweeping claims about the condition of social and material life. That does not mean we have to dismiss the important research, and often groundbreaking findings, of theorists whose work is given to grand sweeps of social explanation. The foundational work of Karl Marx, which we have just explored, is a case in point. However, while Marx's approach to power can be said to focus mainly on addressing *why* questions, Michel Foucault insisted on shifting the analytic lens to *how* questions through his **genealogical method**,[3] which he used to interrogate the historical constitution (or making) of discourses, knowledges, and objects, and the meanings associated with them. He was concerned with revealing the complexity and contingency of historical events, as well as their often mundane, everyday character. Foucault's work therefore challenged the modernist belief that history and society followed a rational course of development. Foucault developed his genealogical method as he mapped the emergence of different forms of knowledge and power. He explored how knowledge and power are themselves historically produced and reflective of the ethical and political values of their time. Far from revealing a linear course toward progress, as Enlightenment thought had proposed and as Marx had charted in his mapping of historical stages, Foucault's genealogical method presented history as fractured, discontinuous, and contingent on a broad array of circumstances and possibilities. In Chapter 9 you will find an example of how Foucault's genealogical approach can be applied to the history of madness and mental illness.[4]

In his work, Foucault avoids making universal claims, for example, that there is such a thing as "truth" or "human nature." Instead, he undertakes an analysis of how we come to believe in universal claims, seeking to discover how particular discourses come to be regarded as "truth." That is why Foucault's work is associated with postmodernism. Through a genealogical approach, the social construction of what comes to be understood as "truth" is revealed, and so this method has significant implications for the study of power. Like Marx, Foucault directed his life's work toward the investigation of domination. However, while Marx conceptualized domination as the exercise of power, Foucault considered domination to be an effect, or outcome, of power.

---

3   Foucault's genealogical method was preceded by his focus on the **archaeology** of knowledge. In his early writings, Foucault talked about the importance of developing a **history of the present** by uncovering, or excavating, earlier patterns of thought and knowledge that guided people and shaped the times in which they occurred, but which people had remained unconscious of. Foucault's notion of genealogy carried on and deepened his engagement with the history of the present.

4   As you will see, Foucault himself published two books about the history of madness and mental illness during his earlier archaeological period, and this work has made an enormous contribution to more recent genealogical studies of the topic.

As an intellectual who was associated with the French Left during the 1960s, Foucault was very much concerned about social inequality. He aimed to explore how domination was secured, as an end result and effect of power. However, he was not satisfied with the analysis of power provided by the Marxist approach. He believed that modern power was much more complicated, difficult to detect, and therefore more effective in accomplishing domination than could be derived from Marx's conceptualization of power as something possessed by the ruling class.

To understand this, we need to distinguish Foucault's linking of power and knowledge from the popular formulation that "knowledge is power." Foucault investigated how notions of "truth" are created, and how the ability to define truth is inevitably a practice of power. For example, in his investigation of the history of sexuality, Foucault explored how people came to be categorized into distinct sexual categories, such as heterosexual and homosexual, through the development of scientific, and particularly psychological knowledge. A system of classification was developed that differentiated the normal from the "perverse" and the "pathological." This **taxonomy** became the basis for the diagnosis and treatment of an expanding array of perceived illnesses.

Foucault believed that power and knowledge exist in a circular relationship, as power–knowledge. As Foucault comments, "the exercise of power creates and causes to emerge new objects of knowledge and accumulates new bodies of information.... The exercise of power perpetually creates knowledge and, conversely, knowledge constantly induces effects of power" (Foucault, 1995: 194). Referring back to the example of the production of sexual categories, we can see how bodies were produced as objects of knowledge, which could be studied and understood with the aid of research and medical technologies, producing new scientific evidence. These new knowledges in turn induce new forms of power, new ways of classifying and treating people. A number of examples of this process will be provided in various chapters of this textbook.

Now that we have introduced you to Foucault's formulation of the primary means through which power flows in contemporary Western societies, we need to broaden our study, because other forms of power have historical precedence, and continue to exert their influence. Just as Foucault suggested that certain ways of thinking are historically contingent, he also suggested that different forms of power can be similarly **historicized**. Foucault identified and historicized a number of forms of power by situating their emergence within specific conditions, giving particular attention to the **micro-processes** (the detailed, contextual, contingent, and specific circulation) of power. We will discuss each of his approaches in turn, beginning with sovereign power and juridical power, then describing the emergence of disciplinary power and biopower, and finally, the form that Foucault finds most in evidence in contemporary Western industrialized societies, governmental power.

Sovereign Power

Foucault referred to the oldest and most immediately recognized form of power as **sovereign power**. Sovereign power is exercised through direct political rule, most notably the rule over subjects by a monarch, or the representatives of the monarch. It might also include other asymmetrical relationships, such as the patriarchal authority of men over their wives, children, and servants. Sovereign power can be best described as power *over* groups and individuals, and it is generally negative and prohibitive (that is, you must *not*). Sovereign power is expansive, and can be exercised as total control. For example, the sovereign has direct power over the life and death of its subjects, whether by ordering armies into battle or by condemning a person to death. It can inflict torture or other means to punish and to deliberately bend the will of another. This form of power may be enforced through legislation, edicts, and other codes and commands. But because it is highly visible, sovereign power is also easy to identify in action and potentially to resist.

> Going as far back as ancient Rome, the male head of a household had power over his children and his slaves, to the point of being entitled to "dispose" of them like property (Foucault, 1978: 135). Moving to the age of feudalism and monarchies, the patriarch of the family remained the authority, and was paralleled by the king as head of empire. Pre-18th century Europe was the age of dynasties, when power passed through bloodlines and social status was based on birth, not merit (Foucault, 1978: 147). The king had authority over his subjects in two ways: he could bring about their death through his right to wage war and order his subjects to fight in his defense; and he could impose the death penalty on anyone who went against his laws (Foucault, 1978: 135). Foucault therefore argues the king's form of power was based on subtraction and suppression—taking away a portion of his subject's income, labour, blood and even life (Foucault, 1978: 136).
>
> —*Zoë Newman*

Clearly sovereign power is still exercised in contemporary Western nation states (for example, in the exercise of **juridical power** through the rule of law). However, as we have seen, power has taken on additional forms. Foucault provided his genealogies of the development of modern forms of power through his books about the history of madness, the history of the prison, and the history of sexuality, among other works. It was through his study of the history of the prison that Foucault developed his analysis of **disciplinary power**.

Disciplinary Power and Biopower

Disciplinary power was a key feature in the emergence of the modern state as a political apparatus for the government of populations. As modern forms of parliamentary government began to emerge in Western Europe, they supplanted the authority of actual monarchies.[5] These expanding systems of political authority overseeing the national territories are what are usually understood as government.

A fundamental component of the emergence of disciplinary power was the surveillance and correction of targeted populations of people and individual bodies. Consequently, this form of power is much less visible than the exercise of sovereign power, and therefore much more difficult to identify and to resist. Disciplinary power was also a more efficient exercise of power, than, for example, forms of punishment that relied on the methods used by sovereign power, such as public hanging, which risked shifting sympathy to the condemned person and away from the sovereign. While sovereign power carried highly symbolic meanings (reaffirming the supreme authority of the sovereign) and was often exercised through public spectacle that focused on the punishment of the body, disciplinary power was something very different. It was directed toward the examination and subjection of bodies through new knowledges and through new techniques for administering, in an increasingly detailed manner, to bodies and populations. Through these processes, including the **panopticon**, discussed below, even more intricate and elaborate knowledges and techniques were in turn produced.

Through disciplinary power, people were instilled in "correct training" and conduct. Foucault famously used the metaphor of the panopticon in his book *Discipline and Punish: The Birth of the Prison* (1995). The model of the panopticon (see Figure 2.4) was introduced first by Jeremy Bentham in 18th century England, just as the power of the sovereign was beginning to diminish. Bentham believed that a panopticon model of the prison would be less expensive to operate than prisons that existed at that time, because the watchmen (prison guards) could not be seen, and so would always be presumed by the inmates to be present and watching them. The inmates would then feel compelled to conduct themselves as if they were under constant surveillance. "The gaze" was not visible, but it was (or was presumed to be) everywhere. Unlike the dungeon, which enclosed people, deprived them of light, and hid them from view, the panopticon simultaneously enclosed and made the prisoner more visible to scrutiny. Visibility was ultimately more effective than darkness in altering the prisoner. Through the panopticon, external surveillance became self-surveillance and self-regulation. The panopticon thereby not only constrained prisoner's bodies but reconfigured their minds, as they were compelled to become self-disciplining subjects.

FIGURE 2.4 ■ Panopticon.

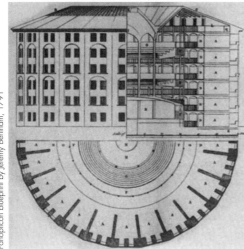

Panopticon blueprint by Jeremy Bentham, 1791

---

5   Although many Western industrialized countries still today have monarchies in place as their ultimate national authority, these monarchies in practice have little more than a ceremonial role.

Foucault identified the birth of the prison as only one example of how disciplinary power worked; he extended his analysis to factories, schools, the military, and other hierarchical institutions that were developing by the 19th century. Prisoners could be reformed, patients treated, students instructed, workers supervised, and so on, so that they would be lawful, conformist, and right-minded. Foucault believed the shaping of "docile bodies" through "the gaze" of surveillance and through normalizing judgement (a topic we will return to shortly) helped to make the development of capitalist industry possible. It produced bodies amenable to schooling, work in factories, participation in the military, and so on that would make the emerging economic system—capitalism—work. In contrast, Marxism emphasized capitalism's reliance on people being compelled to find employment as wage labourers by being deprived of other means to make a living, through being forced off of the land (for example, through a series of *Land Enclosures Acts* in 18th-century England), and through laws punishing wageless people as vagrants and vagabonds.

With the growth of capitalism, industrialization, and urbanization, the administrative apparatus of governments became increasingly detailed and pervasive in producing new techniques of power linked to disciplinary power. These were critically important developments for the emergence of the modern state. For example, state administrators began to compile data in an increasingly detailed way about political subjects. This collection of information was known as **statistics**, or the science of the state. Aggregate data was compiled on births, deaths, morbidity (patterns of illness), income, education, employment, housing, family size, and so on. This could only occur in the context of the production of new knowledges such as medicine, criminology, epidemiology, and psychology.

One important feature of this administration of populations was, by the late 19th century, the consequent classification of people into new categories, according to how they were understood within the emerging disciplines. "Mental illness," the social meanings attributed to diseases, and the naming of distinct sexual identities through a system of sexual classification are just several examples. This was disciplinary power at work. Given its growing significance and complexity, this component of disciplinary power was named **biopower** by Foucault. Biopower has two main components, the first being directed toward the administration of populations of people, and the second toward the penetration of individual bodies, so that the individual's notion of self was formulated in particular ways (for example, the 'healthy person', the 'responsible' individual, the 'sexual deviant'). The ultimate aim of biopower is to produce self-regulating subjects. Foucault believed that this was a change from earlier societies that relied on sovereign or external forms of power to enforce order and to rule. You will have a better opportunity to familiarize yourself with the dimensions of biopower in Chapter 4, where Zoë Newman introduces you to a Foucauldian approach to the study of bodies, genders, and sexualities, and again in Chapter 9, where Heidi Rimke and Deborah Brock historicize the emergence of therapeutic culture. You will find, in the words of Zoë Newman, that "the regulation of sexuality, through education, medicine, the law, and other social institutions, is the meeting place of the two forms of biopower" (Newman, unpublished manuscript, 2009).

Governmental Power

As you have seen, by the 18th century in Western Europe new forms of power were beginning to displace the predominance of sovereign power. The emergence of governments as political institutions (which is also known as "the emergence of the modern state") was certainly part of this shift, as were the profound changes to economic organization that were occurring. The modern state carried forward some of the features of sovereign power, particularly through its juridical authority, which is also known as the **rule of law**, and its policing and military authority. However, state power also became more diffuse, as it became increasingly reliant on a widening array of professional and administrative knowledges and expertise, from the psychiatric expert who judged the mental competency of the accused, to the financial analyst who advised on economic affairs, to the planners who suggested how people should be housed, schooled, and fed.

Foucault found that, in order to recognize the complexities of emerging forms of power, it was necessary to extend the concept of **government** beyond the notion of organized political institutions holding authority over a territory. Foucault introduced a broader conceptualization of government as, in effect, "the conduct of conduct" (Foucault, 1982) through organizations, through texts, between people, and even within ourselves. Foucault's expanded concept of government had three main components; first, to be governed; second, to govern others; and third, to govern the self. Governmental power is occurring when we are no longer aware of power's effects, because we have already embraced it, and reproduce it in relation to our selves and to others. This approach to power has led to the development of a new field of critical inquiry known as **governmentality**.

This indicates that contemporary power is more than a negative force that closes down possibilities. Instead, it also has a positive character in that it is productive and creative. Its circulation leads to new identities, beliefs, and practices. It is at its most effective when people experience themselves to be free; indeed, they are compelled to be free through the expectation in liberal societies that people will be largely self-regulating. These are the conditions established by liberal states, whose democratic governments are predicated on the notion of freedom, buttressed by the social sciences, which inculcate people with the notion that we must produce "our own best selves." So governmental power operates most effectively when it is expressed as a **practice of freedom**, such as the freedom to engage in self-improvement (Chapter 9), to shop (Chapter 9), to be financially responsible (Chapter 11), to travel (Chapter 14) or to embrace notions of citizenship, belonging, and nationalism (Chapter 15). Government therefore requires the use of people's capacity for action. It works most effectively not by commanding people to act in certain ways, but by supporting people's capacity to make "responsible choices" (good, normal, and moral choices). In Chapter 1, you were introduced to the concept of **normalization**, and became familiar with its significance for maintaining the centre. We now return to this concept, because it is a very useful one for making sense of Foucault's governmental approach to power.

Normalization must first be understood in relation to its opposite; the deviant designation. **Deviance** refers to any form of conduct that violates social norms, rules, or laws. To designate a person or a group as deviant is a proscriptive act; that is to say, it is to cast a negative judgement that places those who are labelled as deviant outside what is considered acceptable, right, and normal. One purpose of this designation, then, is to define and regulate differences. It also creates ideas of what is considered normal.

If you look up the definition of "normal" in a dictionary, you find it is associated with conformity, good health, or the maintenance of a natural state of being. In sociology, the concept of **norms** is widely used to indicate social expectations about attitudes, beliefs, and values. Michel Foucault provided a more critical analytic account that linked normalization to power—what Mary Louise Adams has referred to as "the trouble with normal" (Adams, 1997). Michel Foucault believed that normalization is the most effective means of social regulation in contemporary Western societies.

Foucault investigated how **normalizing power** compares, differentiates, creates a hierarchy, homogenizes, and excludes. First, it makes comparisons between people, beliefs, and practices. Second, in making these comparisons, it is also differentiating between people, beliefs, and practices. Third, once people, beliefs, and practices are compared and differentiated, a hierarchy of value is also established. Some are more important, normal, accepted, and so on, than others. Fourth, once a hierarchy of value has been established, this encourages sameness. For example, people will seek to be considered "normal," which lends itself to less variation in people, beliefs, and practices. Finally, there are repercussions for those who resist homogenization, and rank low on the hierarchy of value. They may be considered "abnormal" or deviant, and subject to exclusion (Foucault, 1979).

If we follow the logic of Foucault's analysis, normalizing power is therefore also a **dividing practice**, because it clearly involves the making of value-laden distinctions between people. We will return to a discussion of dividing practices later in Chapter 9. For now, though, you should be aware that dividing practices are invariably linked to **social inequality**. As gender theorist Judith Butler comments, "How shall I know you?" implies "How shall I treat you?" (Butler, 2004). And because dividing practices are linked to social inequality and therefore power, they can also lead to resistance.

We will conclude this section with a summary of Foucault's intriguing analysis of power in contemporary Western societies. For Foucault, there is more to power than domination, repression, and inequality. Power is not simply about the control of one individual over others or one group or class over others. Foucault is not concerned with who has power, because for him *it is not something anyone can possess and exercise over others.* Rather, it is "a multiplicity of force relations" (Foucault, 1978: 92) that does not operate through the consolidation of power as if it were an iron fist, but is produced from moment to moment, point to point. In other words, it circulates like blood, through a capillary system. As Foucault summarizes:

> Power is everywhere; not because it embraces everything, but because it comes from everywhere ... power is not an institution, and not a structure; neither is it a certain strength that we are endowed with; it is the name that one attributes to a complex strategical situation in a particular society. (Foucault, 1978: 93)

So while Marx concerned himself with the state, law, and social classes as *sources of* power, Foucault instead chose to focus on how they were actually *created through* power. The state, the law, and social classes are not sources of power, but rather "the terminal forms power takes" (92). In other words, they are produced through the operation of power. So while power is not tangible, it does have material effects. The effect might also be the making of a particular kind of **subject**, acting in particular ways. Power, therefore, is relational, rather than having a fixed character; it is always produced anew. Foucault wants to direct us away from the notion that power is intrinsically bad or good, considering it to be much more complex than that. Yet we must also be aware that power can indeed be dangerous, because techniques of power can look neutral when they are not, and the political ramifications can be invisible (Faubion, 2000: xv).

BUILDING BRIDGES

We can work with Marx and Foucault as distinct lenses through which to understand power as it pertains to a particular social issue, but in this text we also seek to build links between the work of Marx and Foucault, despite their differences. How can we do so?

For one thing, Foucault acknowledged various kinds of power, including the ongoing relevance of sovereign power, and the ways violence is produced through the exercise of such power. Sovereign power fits well with a Marxist approach.

Second, much has been made of the distinction between doing a materialist analysis (Marx) and doing one that focuses on knowledge production and discourse (Foucault). However, we can extend the definition of materialism, or the conditions of material life, to include, for example, physical bodies, and explore the relation between power and the production and disciplining of bodies. We can also insist that discourses are about much more than the production of language, as they give meaning to the material world that Marx so aptly described.

For us, the many means through which Marx's work has been taken up, adapted, and extended through feminist, anti-racist, postcolonial, and poststructural thought indicates that he is, if anything, more influential than ever upon contemporary social theory. And as we will see in the final section of this chapter, his analysis of capitalism as an economic and social system is enormously relevant for the contemporary period, and urgently needs to be engaged with.

We have indicated earlier that Foucault had an abiding interest, forged through his early Marxist training, in practices of domination. We can also see how the Italian Marxist Antonio Gramsci's conceptualization of cultural hegemony can conceivably be applied to any context in which domination occurs. That means that Gramsci's contribution of hegemony can provide a bridge to explore power and domination throughout social relations, and across approaches to power. Gramsci's work has been used to investigate practices of colonial rule, racial ordering, patriarchal authority, and so on. We will now introduce you to Stuart Hall, another important theorist who provides a multi-faceted approach to power, by building on the work of Marx, Gramsci, and Foucault.

Stuart Hall: The Politics of Representation

Stuart Hall (b. 1934) was one of the founders of **cultural studies** in England during the 1970s, an approach that blended Marx's materialism with the study of culture. Hall's work included a highly influential analysis of the rise of conservativism in England during

FIGURE 2.5 ▇ Stuart Hall.

Courtesy of Rivington Place, Angus Mill Photography

the 1970s. He laid bare the cultural and policing mechanisms through which the organization of consent was secured for Margaret Thatcher's conservative party to unseat the prevailing labour government. He referred to this organization of consent as **authoritarian populism**, because the Thatcher government was able to convince the majority of voters that their best interest lay in supporting a **New Right** agenda. As you will see in Chapters 6 and 11, the New Right combined neoliberal economics with conservative social values, in order to dismantle the **welfare state** and replace it with a more punitive, individualistic approach toward citizens and non-citizens.

Stuart Hall devoted particular attention to how racial representations were constructed, and anti-Black and anti-immigration sentiments were mobilized, as a strategy for the validation of the conservative agenda (Hall et al., 1978). Hall has continued to advance cultural studies inquiry into racial representations throughout his career. Another notable accomplishment in Hall's intellectual biography is his close analysis of the **politics of the image**, which is also known as the **politics of representation**. For Hall, representation is "the way in which meaning is being given to the things being represented" (Hall, 1997). It is here that Foucault's influence becomes more apparent, particularly through Hall's contributions to media studies. Hall urged us to engage in an interrogation of the image, in order to reveal how knowledge and power intersect.

While some media studies attempt to locate an underlying "true" meaning in visual representations of events, Hall counters that events have no true, fixed meaning. Rather, meaning depends on what people make of it, which in turn depends on how events and images are represented. Representation therefore enters into the constitution of the event. This may seem like fairly abstract analysis, so let's try to bring it back to the intersection of knowledge and power. Because meaning is always contextual, it is always open to contestation. This means that meaning is struggled over, and potentially changed. Power, however, tries to fix, or close, meaning in order to claim that one way of seeing something is true. Think about the influence of **stereotypes**, which attempt to fix the meanings attributed to certain groups. However, meaning cannot ultimately be fixed, or cemented, in place. There is an ongoing struggle over meaning.

If images produce much of our knowledge of the world, we have to open them up in order to reveal their social construction. We can, as Hall does, deconstruct them. For example, we can challenge binaries that structure representations and organize knowledge, such as white equals good and black equals evil. Otherwise, they become naturalized and taken for granted as simply true. Drawing from Hall, this raises a number of questions for our analysis, including:

- Where do images come from?

- Who produces images?

- Who is silenced?

- How is meaning closed down?

As Hall notes, much is at stake. Because representation shapes our knowledge of the world, "opening up representation allows for new kinds of knowledge to be produced, and new kinds of **subjectivity** to be explored. It makes possible new kinds of representation that have not been foreclosed by the systems of power in operation" (Hall, 1997). You will learn more about representation and discourse in Chapter 3.

Like Foucault, Stuart Hall emphasizes the importance of **discourse** for the circulation of meaning, and so for the linking of knowledge and power. Hall insists that nothing meaningful exists outside of discourse, because it is through language that meaning is communicated. This is not to deny the importance of the material world and material objects. Rather, discourse helps us to make "meaningful sense" of the world. Hall invites us to think about an object as simple as a football, a material object that only makes sense within the context of the rules of the game of football. It is discourses that provide us with the framework for understanding and interpretation. So discourses allow us to think about what it is that is to be done with that round or (in North America) blimp-shaped object. We might apply the same kind of analysis to a wedding ring, which typically represents legal union, fidelity, commitment, and so on, none of which can be discerned from the object itself. Or we might consider how a nation's flag represents rule over a territory, patriotism, and belonging. By extension, it can also symbolize who does not belong, such as non-citizens and undocumented workers (a topic of Chapter 15).

This is, however, only one side of the process. At the same time, material conditions impact the formulation of discourses, as they set the limits of what is possible for people in particular social, economic, spatial (geographic), and historical locations. For example, the flag could not represent rule over a colonized territory without conditions of control (including economic and military) being established in that territory. All of these—material conditions, discourses, and knowledge formation—are interconnected in a complex web of power relations.

FIGURE 2.6 ■ Gayatri Spivak.

Courtesy of Gayatri Chakravorty Spivak

The work of Stuart Hall reconciles some of the tensions between the approaches to power found in Marx and Foucault, because he is able to demonstrate the simultaneous importance of discourse and material conditions for shaping meaning and for delimiting possibilities for people. His work draws attention to the complexities of power in contemporary Western societies, while demonstrating how these complexities secure relations of domination and subordination that divide people from one another. Through his contributions, and those of many more theorists, including postcolonial scholars such as Gayatri Spivak, we can gain an appreciation of the range of possibilities for theoretical inquiry. We can then approach theory as a kind of a tool kit, from which we can select the best tools, or techniques, for exploring the social world. You will see in the next chapter that we can apply a similar approach to the use of methodology.

Keep in mind that not every social theorist shares this view. For example, some, indeed many, claim that the work of Marx and that of Foucault are fundamentally incompatible, largely because Marx is rooted in what became known, long after his death, as the modernist tradition, while Foucault has made a significant contribution to the development of postmodernism and poststructuralism.[6]

We have previously discussed how postmodernists and poststructuralists challenge the belief that there is an underlying reality that can be discovered and controlled. These theorists reject the belief that through scientific exploration, one could measure and understand not only the natural environment, but human behaviour. This is a key reason why they are considered to be fundamentally at odds with modernism. But does that suggest that theory should be neatly divided into opposing camps? We think not. That is why we have prepared for you a textbook that reflects our belief that thinking sociologically entails an openness to a range of approaches to intellectual inquiry, so that we might understand the world, and our everyday lives, better.

You will find that some of the authors of these chapters integrate more than one approach to power, while others are more definitively influenced by the approach to power exemplified in the work of Marx or Foucault. That said, one might argue that most sociologists who have begun to practise their craft around the time of our latest century-turn have been in some way influenced by the foundational approaches of both Marx and Foucault, as these approaches to power have challenged one another, and compelled one another to change. This is how new theoretical approaches develop. Now, one might argue, many contemporary theorists resist placing themselves in a distinct theoretical "camp" because they consider the divisions between modernism and postmodernism to be less significant than in the past.

What unifies the contributors to this textbook is the insistence that knowledge and power are indeed interconnected; that ideas are, in the words of Sut Jhally, "worth struggling over" (Jhally, 1997); and that with these ideas we can more fully become participants in processes of social change. But first, we need to know more about how power is typically conceptualized in Western capitalist countries. It is an approach to power fundamentally challenged by Marx, Foucault, Hall, and the numerous other critical theorists whose influence can be found in *Power and Everyday Practices*.

LIBERALISM, NEOLIBERALISM, AND POWER

The development of the liberal approach to power is very much tied to the rise of a particular economic system, capitalism, and the political philosophy and practice that accompanied it, democracy. It is also linked to the modernist and humanist traditions, although clearly leagues away from the approach of Karl Marx.

While Karl Marx believed that the transition from the feudal order to capitalism in the West merely replaced one system of domination with another, the liberal approach describes this shift quite differently. Liberals found that while feudalism was structured through a

---

6   This despite the fact that Foucault himself denied being either a postmodernist or poststructuralist theorist.

traditional hierarchy that allowed no possibilities for social mobility, the development of capitalism and democratic ideals opened the possibility of greater freedom for those who had been relegated by birth to the status of landless peasants (that is, the vast majority of the population). As the transition from the feudal order to capitalism occurred, the control of land and wealth that was virtually exclusively held by the aristocracy began to break down. Merchants, traders, and craftspeople were able to accumulate wealth of their own, and with this accumulation of economic resources, they began to demand political rights as well. The development of parliamentary systems in Western Europe was a direct outcome of this growing demand for a political voice among the emerging propertied class. Over the course of the next two centuries, the right to political inclusion was gradually extended to non-property-owning white men, to white women, to non-white people, and to aboriginal people. Full citizenship, political participation, and indeed formal legal equality only gradually came to be considered rights, and only as a result of the demands for inclusion by the excluded groups themselves, including women (again, first white women, and later racialized and aboriginal women), racialized peoples, and aboriginal peoples. Non-citizens continue to be excluded from full political participation, as Nandita Sharma discusses in Chapter 15, as do children, as Rebecca Raby discusses in Chapter 7.

In liberal philosophy, full citizens who reside within a nation now have the right to political participation, and to accumulate private property to the extent of one's ability to do so. While liberalism is now premised on the belief that all citizens have these rights, liberalism does not assume that everyone has (or should have) the same economic rewards. Rather, liberalism is predicated on the belief that Western, capitalist, and formally democratic nations are systems that "provide equal opportunity to compete for unequal rewards" (Forcese, 1986: 72) by providing the conditions for competitive individualism to flourish. Those who accumulate wealth, prestige, and power are thought to do so largely because of their ability to maximize the social and economic opportunities made available to them by a competitive market economy.

Liberal philosophy drew upon scientific and social scientific research from the Enlightenment period in order to naturalize capitalism's economic premises, particularly competitive individualism. Herbert Spencer (1820–1903) had been among the first to apply Charles Darwin's research on evolutionary biology to human social life (Darwin himself only studied natural selection). Spencer coined the term "survival of the fittest" in his hypothesis that economic principles were similar to evolutionary principles. His approach came to be known as **Social Darwinism**, although its links to Darwin's theory of evolution are weak and flawed. Social Darwinism was extended to model and rationalize a hierarchy among human groups as a taxonomy of human types was expanded, particularly through the creation of a (pseudo-) scientific system of racial classification. Not surprisingly, persons of their own racial classification, gender, class, and geographical location (white, male, bourgeois Europeans) were determined to be the most highly evolved of all. **Ethnocentrism**, the belief that one's own nation and culture are superior to those of others, clearly informed their scientific research, predetermining the outcome of what could be known. This exposes the myth that liberalism developed as a political system in order to promote greater social equality, and we think, lends even greater credence to the perspectives of Marx and Foucault as they worked to expose such practices of domination.

While clearly Marxism and liberalism have very different assessments of the transition from feudalism to capitalism, both would describe this transition as progress in the modernist sense. Far from merely condemning capitalism, Marx considered it an important historical stage. Through the industrial mechanisms of capitalist production, it would be possible to overcome scarcity, and to sufficiently provide for the materials needs of people that they could also develop their interests as poets, lovers, philosophers, and so on. For Marx, the trouble was that capitalism was predicated on the unequal distribution of wealth, and therefore the system would have to be replaced by a new approach to production that would distribute social resources equitably. Marx's vision is clearly still far from being realized. The neoliberalism of the present day continues to deepen and intensify economic and social inequality.

We would like you to take some time to think about the implications of neoliberalism for your everyday lives, given the profound effect that it has had on the economies of Western capitalist nations. We would also like you to think about the implications for the study of power. This model assumes that all citizens have the same formal political rights and the same economic opportunities. If social inequality exists, it is not the fault of the system, but of the individual. It assumes that power is something that can be earned and possessed by individuals, if only they seek to maximize the possibilities made available to them. While power is not shared equally, neoliberalism assumes that power is available to those who seek to achieve it, and is widely enough shared so that everyone in a democratic society can have their interests addressed. It is the role of the nation state to ensure that citizens have the same access to formal political rights and to free markets, so that they might participate in this system. This reveals a contradiction of liberal states; while they are to function as **pluralist** states (as a neutral arbitrator between competing interests), their overriding purpose is to defend this economic order.

This "trouble" with capitalism, and with liberalism as a philosophy that supports it, has intensified since the 1970s. Neoliberalism has expanded as an international economic force since it was popularized by the republican government of Ronald Reagan in the United States and the conservative party of Margaret Thatcher in Britain. It has spurred the development of **economic globalization**, and provided a political rationality for dismantling welfare states and for privatizing public resources in western capitalist nations. Advocates of neoliberalism have argued that a fully competitive economy must allow unfettered access to national and global markets (the so-called **free market**), without competition from the state in the form of public resources, such as publicly funded health and education systems and public corporations managing national resources. Nation states facilitate this process by dismantling publicly funded institutions, and by extending the same legal rights to corporations as to individual citizens. The effects of this neoliberal platform are explored in Chapter 11. We have seen the outcome of these processes; a historic near-collapse of global markets in 2008. This is in some way a fitting irony of the "survival of the fittest" philosophy that neoliberals themselves espoused, although neoliberalism has far from disappeared as a result of this crisis. Following such conditions of crisis, which have had such far-reaching effects on people's lives, how can neoliberalism be sustained?

Foucault's analysis of governmental power has provided subsequent researchers with a compelling approach for exploring the rise of the neoliberal subject. This subject is highly individualistic, and motivated by self-management, self-improvement, and achievement, and by consumption-oriented goals. In the neoliberal subject, the government of the self is most fully realized. We invite you to explore the constitution of neoliberal subjectivity, and to reflect upon how you might embody many of these same principles, as you read the chapters that follow.

CONCLUSION

You have now explored two important theoretical approaches for thinking about power and everyday practices. You will encounter these approaches, as well as some of the key concepts that you have been introduced to in Chapters 1 and 2, repeatedly throughout this textbook. In the next chapter, you will add to your tool kit, as Andrea Noack deepens your comprehension of representation, discourse, what counts as knowledge, and how we learn about the world. You will be instructed in how to become better critical consumers of information, as you unpack discourses and representations. You will then be prepared for an analytic engagement with the everyday world in the subsequent chapters, where you will discover within our everyday beliefs and practices the links to some of the key issues for our time.

STUDY QUESTIONS

1. Compare and contrast the approaches to power suggested by Karl Marx and Michel Foucault.

2. Foucault suggests that normalization is the most effective means of social regulation in contemporary Western societies. Discuss.

3. You have learned something about the distinct approaches of modernism and post-modernism. How has modernism informed your beliefs and assumptions about the social and material world? Are there ways in which postmodernism and poststructuralism challenge your existing beliefs and assumptions?

4. How has humanism's emphasis on human agency and neoliberalism's emphasis on the autonomous competitive individual influenced how you think about your own life? How does a governmentality approach either complement or challenge your beliefs and assumptions?

EXERCISES

1. Adopt a concept. Select one of the concepts highlighted in Chapters 1 and 2, and in your own words explain its meaning to other students in your study group. In the process of explaining this concept, provide your own examples of how the concept can be applied to studies of power and everyday practices. As you continue reading this textbook, look for other instances in which this concept is used, or in which you think it might be appropriately applied.

2. Keep a record of all of your activities over the course of a single day. Think about all the ways you take your everyday practices for granted, so that they are in effect normalized. Then connect these everyday practices to Marx, Foucault, and Hall's conceptualizations of power.

REFERENCES

Adams, Mary Louise. 1997. *The Trouble with Normal: Postwar Youth and the Making of Heterosexuality.* Toronto: University of Toronto Press.

Berger, Peter. 1963. *Invitation to Sociology.* Doubleday.

Bhabha, Homi K. 1994. *The Location of Culture.* London: Routledge.

Brock, Deborah, ed. 2003. *Making Normal: Social Regulation in Canada.* Toronto: Nelson.

Butler, Judith. 2004. *Precarious Life: Powers of Mourning and Violence.* London: Verso.

Faubion, James, ed. 2000. In Paul Rabinow, series ed., *Essential Works of Foucault 1954–1984. Volume 3: Power.* New York: The New Press.

Forcese, Dennis. 1986. *The Canadian Class Structure*, 3rd ed. Toronto: McGraw-Hill Ryerson.

Foucault, Michel. 1978. Right of death and power over life. *The History of Sexuality: An Introduction. Volume I.* New York: Random House. 135–159.

Foucault, Michel. 1982. The Subject and Power, Excerpt from "the Subject and Power" "Michel Foucault: Beyond Structuralism and Hermeneutics" University of Chicago, p. 208.

Foucault, Michel. 1989. *The Order of Things.* New York: Routledge.

Foucault, Michel. 1995. *Discipline and Punish: The Birth of the Prison.* New York: Vintage.

Gramsci, Antonio. 1971. *The Prison Notebooks.* New York: International Publishers.

Jhally, Sut. 1997. Introduction. In Stuart Hall, *Representation and the Media.* [Video.] London: Open University.

Hall, Stuart, et al. 1978. *Policing the Crisis: Mugging, the State, and Law and Order.* Teaneck, NJ: Holmes and Meier.

Hall, Stuart, ed. 1997. *Representation: Cultural Representations and Signifying Practices.* London: Open University.

Lee, Ruthann. 2010. The production of racialized masculinities in contemporary North American popular culture. Ph.D. dissertation. Department of Sociology, York University, Toronto.

Marx, Karl. 1969. Preface to a contribution to a critique of political economy. In K. Marx and F. Engels, *Selected Works.* Vol. 1. Moscow: Progress Publishers. 502–506.

Marx, Karl, and Friedrich Engels. 1848. *The Communist Manifesto.* (1985.) Harmondsworth, UK: Penguin.

McDowell, L., and J. Sharp. 1999. *A Feminist Glossary of Human Geography.* New York: Oxford.

Spivak, Gayatri Chakravorty. 1988. "Can the subaltern speak?" In Cary Nelson and Lawrence Grossberg, *Marxism and the Interpretation of Culture.* Illinois: University of Illinois Press.

Assembling Our Tool Kit: Interrogating Representations and Discourses

3

Andrea M. Noack *Ryerson University*

How can we study our everyday assumptions? As you learned in the introduction, it can be hard to be critical about things that are a part of our "normal" lives. Often, we don't notice that we are making assumptions because they are completely embedded in the way that we understand the world. As social researchers, though, there are methodological tools that we can use to help us step outside of our common sense understanding of the world. This chapter will introduce you to some general strategies for interrogating representations and discourses. You can use these strategies to "unpack the centre" and to identify how power operates in your everyday life.

The analytic techniques I discuss in this chapter are designed to supplement what you will learn about how to do research in an introductory social science methodology course. I begin by describing approaches to knowledge and ways of knowing, and then identify key questions that will help you to become a critical consumer of information. I then briefly discuss how we interpret signs in order to create meaning, before moving on to illustrate several strategies for analyzing representations and discourses. This chapter is theoretically informed by the work of both Michel Foucault and Stuart Hall. Following Foucault, I maintain that our senses both of ourselves and of the everyday world we live in are shaped by larger social discourses. Stuart Hall extends these ideas by arguing that the way we understand the material world reflects our participation in a shared culture. Both theorists help us to understand how the discourses and representations that circulate within a culture are connected to power relations.

I encourage you to think about the strategies I introduce in this chapter as elements of a "tool kit" that you can draw on in order to help you interpret what is happening in the world around you. You can use these tools to investigate how things are portrayed in your everyday life and in the media you encounter. You can also use these tools as part of a more formal research project in which you analyze texts or interview transcripts, or to interpret field observations. Sometimes these tools will be helpful for critiquing academic journal articles, research reports, or official policy documents. Many of these strategies can also be used to critically analyze everyday conversations. In general, learning to use these strategies and tools will help you to become a critical thinker and a savvy consumer of knowledge.

WHAT COUNTS AS KNOWLEDGE?

The chapters in this book encourage you to question how our society is organized. They prompt you to think about who is in "the centre," who is in "the margins," and what strategies are used to create a divide between "the centre" and "the margins." By identifying these dividing strategies, you can begin to see how power works on an everyday basis.

One good place to start is by questioning what types of knowledge are considered real and what types are considered fictional. The study of what constitutes knowledge and how we come to know things is part of a branch of philosophy called **epistemology**. Epistemological perspectives tell us about what counts as "evidence," what criteria need to be met in order to develop new knowledge, and how knowledge is related to morals or values.

Ideas about what counts as knowledge have changed radically in the past several hundred years. Before the mid-1600s in North America and Western Europe, most truth claims were justified by appealing to a higher power—God or a king or queen.[1] With the Enlightenment, however, scientific investigation gained prominence as the dominant way of knowing. Recall from Chapter 2 that the period of the **Enlightenment** was characterized by an emphasis on rational thought and experimentation as a means of discovering the natural laws that governed the world.

During the Enlightenment period, **positivism** became the dominant epistemological approach. This approach emphasizes the systematic collection of information using the five human senses, and then grouping those observations together to generate new knowledge. The rise of positivism was related to modernist ideas about the value of using scientific, rational, and secular techniques to systematically create a better society. In the social sciences today, positivist approaches are typically reflected in quantitative approaches to research. Quantitative researchers often use experiments or surveys to make claims about the "facts" of the social world. As you might surmise, quantitative researchers typically strive to quantify or precisely measure the phenomenon they are investigating so they can make statistical claims.

Positivists generally adopt a **realist** perspective; that is, they believe in a single reality that exists independent of society and that is governed by unchanging natural laws. Instead of appealing to "God's will," scientists provide explanations for the natural world based on systematic research, experimentation, and logical reasoning. Positivists also strive to be **objective** or value-free in their work, arguing that any person doing the same research should come to the same conclusion. However, while scientific inquiry is theoretically objective or value-free, it will come as no surprise that the practice of science is also influenced by power relations, as you'll read in Chapter 8.

You might think these debates about the source of knowledge were only contentious in the past; but even today we see echoes of the conflict between religious and scientific explanations. For example, there are debates concerning whether American students should be taught about theories of intelligent design, about theories of evolution, or both. Proponents of "intelligent design" theory argue that the complexity of the universe shows evidence of the intelligent intervention of a supreme being, and not just a process of natural selection (as evolutionists would argue). These debates about the origin of the human species are complicated by the fact that the proponents of each theory appeal to different ways of knowing as justification for their position.

---

1   It was widely believed that kings and queens were given a divine right to rule by God, and so their authority was also established through an appeal to religion (Kantorowicz, 1957; Kings are justly called Gods, 2009).

Some social scientists are critical of positivist approaches, and instead take an epistemo-logical position known as interpretivism. **Interpretivism** is based on the idea that studying people is not the same as studying elements of the natural world, because people interpret and respond to their environment in different ways, and then act on these interpretations. For interpretivists, the goal of social science research is to find out how people's varying understanding of the world affects how they behave. An interpretivist approach to reality is typically associated with qualitative approaches to research, such as ethnographic methods, in-depth interviews, or the analysis of cultural texts. Qualitative researchers seek to describe the complexities and nuances of how people understand their world by studying how people within a culture communicate, the messages they convey, and why they act in certain ways.

Interpretivists generally adopt a social constructionist perspective on reality. **Social con-structionists** believe that what we understand as reality is constructed by our culture. The idea of "culture" refers to the totality of socially transmitted ideas, behaviours, customs, and products of a group of people. There may be different cultures operating in a single place at any one time and a single person can be influenced by the many different cultures they are part of. For instance, you may be influenced by the culture of your own ethnic identity, the larger Canadian culture, and even the student culture you participate in on campus. For social contructionists, reality is understood as culturally (and thus historically) specific. That is, what we understand to be "real" depends on the ideas, behaviours, and customs of our culture. For instance, most people in North America believe that disease is the result of viruses or bacteria invading the body; in contrast, adherents of traditional Chinese Medicine believe that disease is the result of an imbalance in the system of the body.

In a social constructionist framework, every person can have his or her own unique per-ception of reality. We are able to communicate and interact with each other because our perceptions of reality overlap as a result of our shared culture. Because social constructionists believe that people have varying perceptions of reality, they are less likely to strive for objectivity in research. They argue that this standard is unachievable, because the researcher's subjectivity can never be completely eliminated. The idea of **subjectivity** refers to how a person's perspec-tives, experiences, and values shape their perception of their everyday world. Psychological experiments show that even people's basic sense perception of a situation varies based on their past experiences (Manjoo, 2008). Instead of striving for objectivity in research, many social constructionists argue that it is more useful to understand the unique perspective of the researcher, and to acknowledge how it might influence his or her investigation and conclusions. Many of the authors in this book acknowledge that research can never truly be value-free, and instead use a social constructionist perspective to examine how social structures have shaped our understanding of what is "normal" and "real." In this chapter, I use a social constructionist perspective to introduce you to strategies for critically analyzing your own knowledge.

HOW DO WE LEARN ABOUT THE WORLD?

Take a moment to think about how you personally learned about the world and the people in it. We learn about some things because we experience them ourselves. You learned how to ride a bicycle or how to swim by physically doing these activities, although you probably had someone helping you as well. You might know what it feels like to win a competition or to be discriminated against. The things we learn through our personal experiences tend to be somewhat haphazard, as they depend on the situations we have encountered in our life, which are in turn, affected by power relationships. Whether you recognize it or not, aspects of your identity such as your gender, social class, racial, or ethnic affiliation, age, religion, or sexual orientation have influenced the types of situations you have personally been in. Ever been to a mosque? A gay bar? A tourist resort? An Asian mall? Not only does your identity affect the situations you have encountered, your experience within each of these situations is framed by whether you are perceived to be a member of a dominant or powerful social group. For example, upon entering an expensive store in the mall, well-dressed adults are often warmly welcomed by salespeople, whereas teenagers wearing jeans are often treated with suspicion. These shopping experiences affect your ideas about what types of stores you like shopping in and the brands you like to buy.

Most people strongly believe in the lessons they have learned through their personal experiences, because they are meaningful to them. Yet we tend to overestimate how similar our experiences are to those of others. It's not reasonable to claim racism does not exist in Canada because you have never experienced racism. It is also not enough to find out whether your friends have had the same experiences as you, because we tend to be friends with people who are similar to us. At the same time, there *are* patterns in people's experiences, and understanding these will help you understand how society is organized. The key is to be able to determine how generalizable your own experiences are. **Generalizable** knowledge is knowledge that can be extended to understand a group of people (or population) larger than the group from whom information was collected. In order to learn how relevant your own experiences are to everyone in a society, you need more information.

Most of what we know and believe was not learned through direct personal experience. Instead, we learned it from people in positions of authority, such as teachers, parents, or religious leaders. We believe what these people say because of their credentials or because of their role in our lives. Sometimes, though, people in positions of authority make claims about things they are not experts in. For instance, if your sociology professor tells you about what brand of car is the best, you should be skeptical. It can be difficult to be critical of people in positions of authority, however, because they often hold some sort of power over us. For example, institutional roles dictate that teachers assign grades to students, and legal statutes dictate that parents make decisions for minor children. Even if people do have expertise in the area they are making claims about, you should still maintain a critical mind; in many cases "expert knowledge" is conflicting and contradictory. We often see examples of this phenomenon in health research, when different scientists report contradictory findings about the effectiveness of a treatment or procedure. It can be difficult to determine what to believe when we encounter contradictory information from experts. Some of the strategies outlined below can be useful for helping to sort out the claims experts make.

Another way we tend to learn things is through "common sense." Instead of collecting and assessing information for ourselves, we make choices and form opinions on the basis of what "everybody knows." Appeals to common sense are based on the idea that we all agree about what is "sensible," but this is clearly not the case. Even if we could all agree about what is sensible, many widely accepted commonsense beliefs have been disproved by systematic research. For instance, many parents tell their children to wait thirty minutes after eating before going swimming according to the notion that you will get cramps as your stomach competes with your muscles in order to get enough oxygen. Digestive health researchers find that your body has more than enough oxygen to go around, though, and that unless you are a competitive swimmer, there is no need to wait to go swimming after you eat (CBC, 2005). A critical approach to knowledge suggests that things widely believed do not necessarily reflect the "truth"—that, rather, these shortcuts work to maintain the dominant power structure at the expense of those with less power. For instance, racial profiling by police officers and border officials is often presented as a "common sense" shortcut for making traffic stops or security screenings more effective. In this case, common sense prompts people to systematically discriminate against certain groups of people. Many of the chapters in this book will encourage you to question commonsense ideas about the world, and will challenge the things that "everybody knows." Questioning such ideas is a first step toward "unpacking the centre" and revealing the underlying power relations.

One of the ways "everybody" in our society comes to know something is through the mass media, which include all types of communication to a "mass" audience: newspapers, books, television shows, music, art, graffiti, posters, blogs, websites, and more. Mass media provide us with quite a bit of information about our world that we could not get through personal experience. Textbooks teach us about history, news tells us what is happening on the other side of the world, and nursery rhymes teach us moral lessons. Media give us a quick and easy way to learn things, but the speed at which information spreads through media means it can be difficult to identify errors or misinformation. Media also tend to direct our attention to some events and stories, and in doing so implicitly direct our attention away from other events and stories. At times, news media create a self-reinforcing "news waves," in which reporting about a key event leads to disproportionate coverage of similar stories or events (Vasterman, 2005). Despite the potential diversity of media, most television, print, and radio news in Canada is controlled by five large corporations: CTVglobemedia, Astral Media, Quebecor, Canwest Global, and Rogers. The prominence of mass media as a source of information in our culture means that it has a substantial effect on our understanding of the world we live in. The convergence of media ownership in Canada means that these five corporations have a substantial amount of power to shape our ideas about what is important what is "normal," and what is "in the centre."

BEING A CRITICAL CONSUMER OF INFORMATION

We are often encouraged to be smart shoppers and savvy consumers. We are taught (often by our parents) to assess the quality and usefulness of something before we purchase it. Unfortunately, though, we are rarely encouraged to be critical consumers of information. In order for you to hone these skills, this chapter discusses some questions you might ask when presented with information about the world that provide a framework for you to develop your own questions as you become a more critical "information shopper."

It is easiest to start asking these questions whenever you encounter new information, but as you become more proficient, I encourage you to use these same strategies to question things that you have "known" for a long time.

What "Worldview" Does the Information Rely On?

Most information is based on an assumption about how reality is constituted. Earlier, I introduced the ideas of realism and social constructionism. Realists hold there is a single, unchanging reality, whereas social constructionists hold there are multiple realities that are the product of our cultures. A key difference between these approaches is in their ideas about the relationship between human consciousness and reality. The types of explanations for things that happen and the types of solutions proposed will vary according to the worldview that information relies on. Whenever you encounter information, try to identify the underlying approach and consider how it influences the assertions made.

What Concepts and Systems of Classification Does the Information Rely On?

All information implicitly relies on concepts and systems of classification. A **concept** is a mental representation that groups together things that are similar in some way. Concepts enable us to cognitively hold on to the idea of something by giving it a name or a symbol that we can incorporate into our thinking. They also give us a context for understanding the many people, objects, and events we encounter every day: she's another *student*, that's a *chair*, they are having an *argument*. We often use concepts to designate specific types of people in our society: *deadbeat dads*, *terrorists*, or *the mentally ill*. These designations are based on the presumption that we have a shared cultural understanding about who belongs in these groups. **Systems of classification** extend our models of the social world by placing concepts in relation to one another; they tell us what types of things are alike, and what types of things are different. For instance, in science class you might have learned about the Linnaean taxonomy, a system that groups all life into domains, kingdoms, phyla, classes, orders, families, genera, and species. We also rely on complex systems of classification in the social world, though we rarely explicitly list the elements of these classifications. For example, the idea of "race" relies on a system of classification based on many criteria, including skin colour, facial structure, hair type and colour, language, cultural background, and geographic origin. Just like taxonomies of the natural world, systems of classification for the social world are created by people and change over time. They are often sustained by "commonsense" knowledge and media portrayals. But, upon further scrutiny, many of our concepts and systems of classifications break down. The fact that these systems of classification nevertheless persist is another manifestation of power. Typically, groups with more power in a society work to maintain and reinforce categorizations that support their position. Critically analyzing these systems of classification help us to "unpack the centre" by questioning how the boundaries between the "centre" and the "margins" are created and maintained.

One of the easiest ways to begin developing critical analysis of concepts and classifications is to investigate how members of a category are designated. For example, if the information refers to a group of people (for example, *terrorists*), do you have enough information to determine who is included in the group and who excluded? Do the criteria for inclusion or exclusion make sense? If news reports announce that "people are increasingly falling into debt," ask how they have classified whether someone is in debt—missing a credit card payment? Having a student loan? Filing for bankruptcy? Whenever you assess information, an easy way to begin is to identify the concepts and classifications that the information relies on. Then, critically assess who or what is being referred to, and consider how the concepts and classifications encourage you to understand the world in a particular way. Finally, consider who benefits from each classification: Whose power is reinforced and whose diminished

What Type of Evidence Is Provided?

It is good practice for people making claims to explicitly detail what they have based their conclusions on. Whenever someone makes an assertion, ask what evidence they are using as the basis for that assertion. Are they making a claim on the basis of their personal experience? Something their friend told them? A scientific study they completed? The type of evidence provided will influence how much weight you give to a claim, or how much value you assign to the information. We tend to be more confident about evidence that comes from more people. For instance, information collected from a survey of 10,000 people is usually considered more authoritative than a survey of 10 people (see the box "Questioning Official Statistics"). You should also ask questions about how the people were selected—those who are randomly selected are generally preferred to those who are not. The number of people who make a claim is not always a good indicator of how much weight to assign a piece of information, however. As noted in the discussion of common-sense knowledge, often many people believe things that have not been established by some sort of systematic inquiry.

QUESTIONING OFFICIAL STATISTICS

The Canadian news media often report on **official statistics**. These are usually collected or compiled by a government agency in order to find out more about a national population with the goal of informing policy. In Canada, many official statistics are produced by Statistics Canada using survey research. Others are compiled from administrative data, such as birth and death records, claims for Employment Insurance, or records of healthcare expenses.

Official statistics are often presented as objective and factual representations of our society. For example, a recent news release from Statistics Canada confidently states that in July 2010, "the unemployment rate edged up 0.1 percentage points to 8.0%" (Statistics Canada, 2010). Because the information is presented in numeric form, it is easy to report, and can seem hard to question. Some people simply assume that because the information is "statistical" or "mathematical," it must be correct. Like other types of information, however, official statistics should be critically examined.

Official statistics are usually only available about topics the government considers important. The head of Statistics Canada reports to the Minister of Industry. This being the case, it is no surprise that many of the statistics they collect are about the Canadian economy and people's ability to find and keep work. It is much harder to find official statistics about people's sense of civic engagement or willingness to participate in protests. The topics captured in official statistics reflect power relationships, because they represent the issues the government wants to know about to inform policy decisions.

Most official statistics are collected in a methodologically sound way; that is, they use a random sample that can be generalized to the population. It is more important to question how each item reported on is actually measured. Even things that seem relatively easy to count can actually become quite complicated. For example, you might think it would be easy to count the number of births in Canada in a given time period, since parents are supposed to register every birth in a provincial office. But in some provinces you have up to a year to register, and some people delay even longer. You might collect hospital records of births. But some people give birth at home with the services of a midwife or doula. And what if a baby is stillborn or dies shortly after birth? Do you still count it? Statistics Canada calculates by compiling registrations of "live births" from each province. All provinces rely on parents' registrations of births, though in some provinces this is supplemented by reports from physicians or other types of birth attendants.

If something as simple as a birth is difficult to count, you can imagine the potential problems with measuring something more complicated such as being unemployed. Statistics Canada counts someone as unemployed if they meet one of the following three criteria at the time of the survey: (1) the person was temporarily laid off with an expectation of recall and was available for work, or (2) the person was without work, had actively looked for work in the past four weeks, and was available for work, or (3) the person has a new job he or she expects to start within the next four weeks and was available for work (Statistics Canada, 2008). Some of these criteria might not fit with your initial idea about what it means to be unemployed. The definition excludes workers who have become discouraged in their job hunt, and who have stopped looking for work—these people are considered out of the labour force. The 8 percent unemployment rate doesn't mean that 8 percent of all Canadians are unemployed; it means that 8 percent of the Canadians considered part of the labour force are unemployed. People who are under age 15, who live in an institution, who are in the military, or who haven't looked for work in the past month are considered out of the labour force and are excluded from these calculations.

As you develop your skills as a critical consumer of information, I encourage you to ask just as many questions about official statistics as you would about information from other sources. When you encounter official statistics, be sure to ask why the government is motivated to collect this information and what exactly is being measured by each number.

You should also be critical when documents, such as news reports, policy papers, or letters, are used as evidence. A major concern with documents as evidence is that documents from people who have power or status in a society are much more likely to be available to use as evidence, and are much more likely to be treated as authoritative. For example, in historical studies it is often much easier to locate and access the diaries and letters of people from the upper class than from the working or servant classes. This is partly because of limited literacy among the lower classes, but also because their ideas were less likely to be considered important and thus less likely to be preserved.

It is also important to be critical about how generalizable a claim is. Often, people extend their claims beyond what they can justify. For instance, a parent might assert that the characteristics of their child are representative of all children; similarly, American youth researchers often suggest that their findings are applicable to youth everywhere in the world. Get in the habit of being critical of the evidence used as the basis for the claims you encounter, and thinking carefully about whether each claim is legitimately supported.

Who Benefits If the Information Is Believed to Be True?

Information that is widely circulated becomes part of people's knowledge about the world; it becomes what "everybody knows." This knowledge fundamentally shapes how we behave, how we perceive other people, and how we understand ourselves. Often, some groups of people systematically benefit when some information is believed to be true and other information is believed to be false. The source of information can thus be part of power relations that benefit some over others. For instance, in Canada, research done by the Fraser Institute promotes free markets, less government intervention, and more personal responsibility (Fraser Institute, 2009), attributes usually aligned with conservative economic policies. In contrast, research done by the Canadian Centre for Policy Alternatives promotes a "progressive" approach to issues of social and economic justice (CCPA, 2009), an approach usually aligned with more liberal or left-of-centre policies. Both groups routinely present the results of their research in the media, make competing claims about how to understand a situation or event, and present radically different types of solutions for social problems. Whenever you encounter information in your everyday life, ask whether political motivations or power relationships might be at work. You may need to do a bit of extra research about the source of the information, but taking the time to do so will give you a much broader context in which to assess and understand competing claims.

Asking these types of questions is the first step toward becoming a critical consumer of information and starting to unpack our everyday assumptions about the world. But, as I explain below, as soon as we use language to ask a question, we are already reinforcing certain ways of being and ways of understanding the world.

ANALYZING LANGUAGE AND REPRESENTATIONS

In contemporary North American society, spoken and written language is one of the main ways we communicate with one another. Cultural theorists refer to formal language as a symbolic system. A **symbolic system** is an interconnected group of symbols that have acquired a cultural meaning that is widely understood. For example, the colour-coded threat-level ranking created by the U.S. Department of Homeland Security is a rudimentary symbolic system. The most prominent of our shared symbolic systems is language, in which a series of letters stand in for an idea or a concept. Many of our symbolic systems are visually based, but we also assign relatively complex cultural meanings to smells (such as fresh-baked cookies) or sounds (such as a gentle harp).

In semiotic terms, we refer to the symbol that represents a concept or idea as a **signifier**, which means a symbol that calls up our conceptual understanding of an object, event, experience, feeling, or action. For example, think about the Nike swoosh. The actual shape of the symbol is meaningless, but we have learned that that particular shape symbolizes the Nike brand. Often, there can be different signifiers for a single concept. For example, the words "dog" and "chien" and "Hund" all refer to the same group of domestic animals. There are even more English language variations that refer to the same thing: doggie, pooch, and so on. The concept or idea represented by a signifier is called the **signified**. In the examples above, the Nike brand and the concept of a dog are the things signified. There is also no guarantee that every person will interpret a signifier in the same way. If you ask a group of people to all imagine what a dog looks like, each person will have a slightly different conceptual image: a Labrador retriever, a poodle, a Chihuahua, a greyhound. There will be shared features between the dogs that people imagine—four legs, a barking sound, and possibly a tail—because we have a shared cultural understanding of what constitutes a dog. The less overlap there is between people's cultures, the more divergent their interpretation of signifiers will be. The signifier of the Nike swoosh represents something completely different to the North American consumer than it does to a worker who makes below-poverty-level wages manufacturing Nike products in an export processing zone. The idea of **polysemy** refers to the fact that a single sign can have more than one meaning or be interpreted in multiple ways.

Cultural researchers speak of signs having three levels of signification. A useful example that illustrates these levels of signification comes from pedestrian traffic symbols around the world (see Figure 3.1). The first level (or order) of signification refers to what is being explicitly shown by the signifier. The pedestrian symbols in the figure show the palm of a hand and people in various body positions. The symbols are also in different colours: white, green, and red. The second level (or order) of signification refers to the cultural meaning of what is being explicitly shown. These pedestrian symbols—the different-coloured illuminations of people in various body positions—convey to us when it is safe or not safe to cross the street. As children, we learned that these symbols tell us when we should "walk" or

FIGURE 3.1 ■ Pedestrian signals from Canada, Poland, Germany, Japan, and Austria (left to right) show different cultural representations of a "normal" pedestrian.

"don't walk." The third level (or order) of signification refers to how the signifier is related to larger cultural expectations. At the third level, signifiers and what they refer to are associated with a larger social consensus or understanding of the world (Deacon et al., 2007). In the pedestrian signal example, attending to the third order of signification tells us about how people envision a pedestrian in the city. There are differences in gender, body shape, body posture, types of attire, and accessories. These differences can give us insight into how people in different cultures imagine a typical pedestrian. The associations made at the third level usually give us the most insight into cultural norms and power relationships.

Signs and signifiers are the building blocks for practices of **representation**, a concept introduced in the previous chapter. The traditional way of thinking about representation is as a representation of something that has already happened (Hall, 1999). You might also think about representation as "standing in" for something. So, for example, Members of Parliament are supposed to represent or "stand in" for us in the House of Commons (Hall, 1999). In contrast to these traditional ways of thinking about representation, cultural theorists such as Stuart Hall argue that we should think about a representation as being *constitutive* of an event (1999). Hall argues that there can be multiple interpretations of events. Because there is no single correct interpretation of any event, the practice of representation is more than just a simple re-presentation of something that is already there. Instead, the representation of an event becomes part of the event itself. It is through the process of representation that an event is given meaning in the context of our shared culture. Often, we only know about an event through its representation in the mass media. If we have not experienced an event personally, the media representation of the event effectively becomes the event for us. For example, most people can describe what happens on New Year's Eve in Times Square and explain what the meaning of the event is, even if they have not personally been in New York City on December 31. For them, the representation of the event in the media has *become* the event. The ability to represent and thus shape our shared understanding of people, objects, and events is a substantial source of power.

The **circuit of culture** maps the relationships between representations, people's identities, practices of social regulation, and practices of production and consumption (see Figure 3.2; DuGay et al., 1997). As you analyze representations, it can be useful to think about how they are connected to other cultural practices. For instance, representations affect the range of identities available to us and our perceptions of the characteristics associated with those identities. Some identities are simply unavailable to us, because there is no concept or word for that group of people in our culture. For example, we have a word for the group people who collect stamps (philatelists) and some cultural stereotypes about the characteristics of those people (obsessive, nerdy). We have no word for people who collect, say, matchbooks, and no corresponding cultural notion of their general characteristics. People who claim an identity—like being a philatelist, or a mom, or a student—learn to

FIGURE 3.2 ■ The circuit of culture. The circuit of culture links practices of representation with identities, social regulation, production, and consumption.

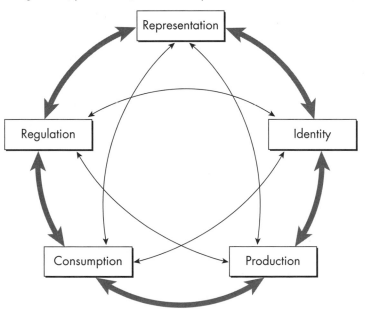

Source: Reproduced by permission of SAGE Publications, London, Los Angeles, New Delhi and Singapore, from Paul DuGay et al., *Doing Cultural Studies: The Story of the Sony Walkman,* Copyright © Open University Press, 1997.

compare themselves and are compared by others to representations of that social group. For instance, people are often surprised upon meeting mature students because they don't conform to our cultural representations of what a student is supposed to look like.

Together, representations and identities work as a form of social regulation by constraining how people are perceived and understood in our culture. They affect our own ideas about normal or acceptable behaviour for someone like us. Even if we decide not to conform to the behaviour expected, our actions are still interpreted and understood in relation to the cultural norm we are rejecting.

The circuit of culture also links representations and identities to practices of production and consumption. We can reinforce and maintain our identities by purchasing the products and brands associated with the type of person we want to be. For example, the ownership of products such as an iPad or a BlackBerry each become associated with a particular type of person. In turn, practices that are a part of production and consumption—such as advertising and branding— work to create new representations and new identities. For example, a recent ad campaign for Apple features conversations between two men: one representing an Apple computer and the other representing a PC. The Apple computer is represented by a young, thin, stylish white man, while the PC is represented by a middle-aged, overweight, balding, white man. With this campaign, the purchase (consumption) of an Apple computer is associated with being young, stylish, and hip, while the purchase of a PC is associated with the opposite of those things. Microsoft has countered this campaign with one of their own which shows people from a diverse range of ages, ethnicities, and occupations all happily proclaiming "I'm a PC." Although the computer you use has little relationship to the type of person you are, through these advertising campaigns the production and consumption of computers has become linked to personal identities.

The concept of a circuit of culture is valuable because it illustrates how meaning circulates through everyday social processes and practices (Hall, 1997). It links seemingly personal traits (such as identity) to larger social practices such as the production and consumption of consumer goods. It is particularly useful for our analysis, because it highlights the importance of representations and their relationship to practices of social regulation.

Language and representations are the building blocks of **discourses**. As you learned in Chapter 1, discourses are the interconnected systems of knowledge we use to give meaning to the material world and our social interactions in that world. Discourses rely on elements of our shared cultural knowledge in order to produce a particular version of reality. This is not to say that the material world does not exist, since it clearly does. But social constructionists argue that the material world only becomes meaningful to us through the concepts and systems of classification provided by language and discourses. As you have already read, this approach to understanding social reality is consistent with the work of theorist Michel Foucault. Foucault illustrated how discourse works to actively produce the things it claims to describe (Tonkiss, 2001). Stuart Hall extends this work by investigating how Foucault's theories can be understood in relation to more traditional Marxist ideas of power and ideology.

We are surrounded by (and embedded in) a multitude of discourses in our everyday lives—discourses about race, class, gender, economics, health, disability, immigration, religion, crime, and many more. As you might expect, because discourses are based on shared cultural knowledge, they can emerge, change, and disappear over time. Some scholars use a military metaphor to talk about how discourses are "deployed" in a society. Discourses are often deployed in mass media, but they become entrenched in our everyday social interactions. Whenever we use certain types of language or rely on specific representations to talk about the world in a particular way, we become part of the process of producing meaning through discourse. It is in this way that our everyday practices become part of the system that legitimizes and maintains the dominant system of power relations. It may surprise you to think you have unknowingly supported the exercise of power through your everyday practices. But the maintenance of power through language and discourse means we can also challenge the dominant power structure by conscientiously changing how we speak and think about the world. As more people begin to do this, new discourses emerge.

The analysis of signifiers, representations, and discourses usually reveals patterns of power and authority in a society. Even though signifiers and representations are polysemous (that is, they exhibit polysemy, as defined above), one dominant meaning often prevails. The ability to fix and limit the meanings people assign to representations reflects the dominant systems of power in a society (Hall, 1997). We also see "official" and "alternative" explanations of an event or outcome. For instance, medical practitioners argue that heart attacks are the result of individual lifestyle factors, such as smoking, inactivity, and genetic predispositions. This is the dominant discourse around heart disease and heart health in Canadian society. An alternative discourse is presented by researchers who adopt a social-determinants-of-health approach. They argue that heart attacks are the result of social factors, such as poverty, social exclusion, and income inequality (Raphael, 2002). Indeed, much of this textbook focuses on identifying dominant discourses and presenting alternative, rival explanations. The dominance of one discourse over another also reflects the dominant ideologies and systems of power in a society. In the case of heart disease, the dominant discourse reflects our culture's emphasis on individualism, personal responsibility, and capitalist competition. These characteristics are the features of **neoliberalism**, which you will learn about in Mary Beth Raddon's chapter on financial fitness (Chapter 11). The analysis of representations and discourses can be a useful strategy for understanding how reality and meaning are produced in a particular way, and for learning more about how power affects our everyday lives.

INTERROGATING REPRESENTATIONS AND DISCOURSES

In this section, I introduce a series of strategies for developing a critical analysis of representations and discourses. It might be useful to think about this process as an interrogation. The typical meaning of "interrogating" is to ask hard questions, like a police officer would ask a suspect (Hall, 1997). Interrogating representations and discourses is also about asking hard questions. Unlike in police interrogation, though, our questions are not necessarily directed to finding out what the "truth" is from a suspect. Instead, we are interested in finding out how representations and discourses constitute people, events, and objects in a particular way. We are interested in investigating how they shape our understanding of reality and maintain power relationships.

Many of the strategies I describe below rely on a cultural studies approach, though I also borrow from the practices of discourse analysis in social psychology and literary studies. As previously noted, I focus on qualitative strategies for assessing representations and discourses. Quantitative strategies for assessing cultural products—such as **content analysis**—are typically well covered in introductory research methods courses and textbooks. Quantitative content analysis is a method that relies on creating a coding scheme and then systematically counting how often some symbolic content occurs in a series of texts or images. Content analysis can provide a good starting point for interrogating representations and discourses, but I encourage you to go beyond simply noting whether a symbol is present or absent, and to also assess what the meaning of each symbol is.

You might start by using these strategies to analyze conversations, media reports, or advertisements that you encounter in your everyday life. You can also use these approaches in the context of a more structured social science research project. If you do interviews or focus groups, you can use these strategies to analyze written transcripts. If you do content analysis research, you can use these strategies to analyze any communication that relies on language or symbols. For example, researchers have used some of these techniques to analyze the discourses in Wikipedia entries (Ferriter, 2009), Beatles songs (Cook and Mercer, 2000), and presidential speeches (Collet, 2009). Whether you use these techniques in a structured research project or to assess your everyday communication, these strategies will help you to develop a critical analysis of how our society is organized. Once again, these questions below are not meant to be exhaustive; instead, think of them as a launch pad for your own critical interrogation strategies.

What Representations and Discourses Are Most Prominent?
What Types of Representations and Discourses Are Presented as "Alternatives"?

One of the easiest ways to begin analyzing the representations and discourses that you encounter is to look for patterns. To start, look for the representations and discourses that are most prominent. Ask questions about why these things are so prominent. How did they come to be that way? When did they become part of our cultural knowledge? How do they connect with your everyday practices and knowledge? How do they reflect larger power relationships in our society? You might have to do some research to come up with satisfactory answers to these questions.

Once you have identified the most prominent representations and discourses, start to look for variations, or "alternative" representations and discourses. These alternatives can give you useful insight into some of the other ways a topic or an issue might be understood. When you find competing representations and discourses, pay close attention to how different types of language and symbols are used to make one representation seem more plausible than others.

How Do Representations and Discourses Cluster?

It is also useful to look at the types of representations and discourses that tend to be grouped together. Ask questions about how this clustering affects the way we understand the thing being represented. For example, until the rise of the gay and lesbian liberation movement, representations of homosexuality were often paired with representations of pedophilia. Although the two phenomena are not related, the proximity of these representations in the media helped to reinforce the idea in popular culture that homosexuality was deviant and immoral. By looking at how representations are clustered, we can begin to understand how people, objects, and events are positioned on the "margins" or at the "centre" by association.

How Are Identities Represented? How Are Different Identities Positioned in Relation to Each Other in Discourses?

As a next step, ask how people and identities are portrayed in representations and discourses. One way to do this is to look at the identities or social roles established by a discourse. It might help to think of these identities as the characters in a story. For instance, crime stories usually identify a victim, a perpetrator, a person with legal authority, and sometimes a witness. Each of these subjects is framed differently by the discourse, and is expected to have different experiences, ways of speaking, and interpretations of the event. Discourses also tell us how people in these social roles are related to one another. Some people are seen as social actors with authority, while others are framed as victims of circumstance; some people are portrayed as being at "the centre" while others are portrayed as being on "the margins." These types of representations affect how people understand their own role in society.

Social psychologists tell us that people develop a sense of identity or subjectivity based on the interpretive repertoires they use. An **interpretive repertoire** is a cluster of terms, descriptions, metaphors, and figures of speech that people use to understand the world around them. They provide a framework that people use to locate their own position in the world relative to other people, and thus a subjectivity that they use to give meaning to their experiences. When we say things like "I'm a Capricorn" or "I'm a shopaholic" to provide an explanation for our behaviour or actions, we are drawing on complex interpretive repertoires. Representations and discourses affect how we construct identities and social roles by shaping the interpretive repertoires available to people in a society.

Another strategy for critically assessing how identities are structured by discourses is to look at how language is used to position people as insiders and outsiders. When you encounter representations and discourses, look for how words like "our," "we," and "us" are used, compared to words like "your," "they" and "them." The people who are included in the "our" and the "we" are usually people at the centre of social power. The people who are included in the "your" and the "they" are usually people at the margins of social power. For instance, a recent headline in the *Toronto Sun* proclaims "Deporting woman may cost us jobs" (Godfrey, 2009). This headline draws on the notion of a collective "us," who are implicitly positioned as naturalized, hardworking Canadians. This imagined "us" is contrasted with the position of the failed refugee who faces deportation. Using these linguistic strategies, discourses shape our sense of who we are and where we fit into the social structure relative to other people.

Who Are Presented as "Experts" and How Is Their Authority Established?

The identification of the "experts" in a discourse also provides a good indicator of power relationships in a society. It reveals whose authority is considered legitimate, and whose version of events is considered questionable. In contemporary North American society, people such as scientists, military leaders, elected officials, and police/fire officers are often framed as having expert knowledge about an object, event, or situation. Experts are often designated in discourses through the use of titles (Sergeant), honorifics (The Right Honourable), or formal positions (President and CEO). They might also be represented as experts through their attire, such as a white coat for a scientist or a formal uniform for a fire chief. Pay attention to whether people's area of expertise is a legitimate match for the event, object, or issue they are discussing. Think about what qualifications are used to justify a person's expertise, and how this reflects the larger epistemological framework of our culture.

What Rhetorical Devices Are Used by the Representation or Discourse?

The study of rhetoric focuses on how language is structured and used to persuade. **Rhetorical devices** are linguistic techniques used to promote a particular understanding of a person, object, or event. Metaphors, alliteration, and hyperbole are commonly used rhetorical devices. An easy way to start looking for rhetorical devices in a discourse is by looking at the word choices. Is the language emotive, assertive, or inflammatory? Is there evidence of hyperbole (deliberate exaggeration)? What other types of words could have been used, and how might the use of alternative words change your understanding of the topic? For instance, two headlines reporting about the same incident paint a slightly different version of events: *Al-Jazeera* had "Dozens killed in Afghan bus ambush" ("Dozens killed," 2008), while the *Globe and Mail* had "Taliban kill dozens in brazen bus hijacking" ("Taliban kill dozens," 2008). The latter headline explicitly characterizes the event as "brazen," implying that it took particular daring. Also, the idea of an "ambush" suggests that the perpetrators came out of nowhere, whereas the idea of a "hijacking" suggests that the perpetrators took control of a bus and steered it toward a new destination.

The headlines above also illustrate another common rhetorical device: the use of numbers to create a sense of authority or precision. Military officials estimate that about thirty people were killed in the incident described in the headline above; this has been portrayed as "dozens" killed. Another common practice is to report that something has "doubled" or "tripled" without reporting the original incidence, a practice that creates the impression of rapid change or an increase in severity, when it may not be warranted. This is a typical strategy in health care (and especially health scare) reporting. If a single person is infected with a rare disease, and then two more people become infected, it is common for media reports to say that the number of people with the disease has tripled. The actual number of people infected is still quite low (three), but the use of a proportion makes it appear that the severity of the situation has increased dramatically. Work to critically assess the numbers that you see by asking how the information was collected and what was actually measured.

It is also useful to assess the grammatical structure of a discourse and to ask questions about how this shapes our understanding of the world. One common practice in the news media is to omit an active subject, such as in the first headline from Al-Jazeera above, which does not identify who is doing the killing. Another common practice is to assign agency to things that cannot independently act, such as "Financial crisis threatens legal protection for the poor" (UNDP, 2009). Both these rhetorical devices work to conceal the people responsible. They may also contribute to a sense of powerlessness, whereby people come to believe no one is able to act or to create social change, since no one is assigned agency.

How Are Representations and Discourses Organized, and Why?

Asking questions about the organization of a discourse means asking about the sequence of presentation and how different elements of the discourse are situated in relation to each other. Sometimes, cause and effect relationships are implied by the sequence in which a story is told. For instance, a government report might discuss both rising unemployment in Canada and changing immigration policies. Depending on how the report is organized, you might be led to believe that either changing immigration policies has led to rising unemployment, or that rising unemployment has led the government to change its immigration policies. As you assess representations in your everyday life, consider how stories are constructed by placing events into a sequence, and ask whether your interpretation would change if the sequence of events was changed.

Discourses are also organized based on master narratives. **Master narratives** are dominant accounts of how the world operates which provide us with organizing principles for understanding events, behaviours, and beliefs. For instance, the archetypal struggle between the forces of good and evil is a prominent master narrative in North American discourses. Representations of good and evil are embedded in many our explanations about why things happen and how the world works. Because they rely on familiar aspects of our culture, the use of master narratives can make representations and discourses seem particularly powerful and salient.

What Is Absent or Missing from a Representation or Discourse? Who Is Not Represented? Whose Voice Is Not Heard?

All representations and discourses inevitably privilege one, partial version of reality to the exclusion of many others. A useful strategy for interrogating representations and discourses is to read "against the grain" in order to assess what is excluded, and why. The things that are absent from a representation signify just as much as (and sometimes more than) what is present in a representation (Hall, 1997). Take a moment to close your eyes and imagine a police officer. You likely imagined a young, white, clean-shaven man, because these are the images of police officers that are circulated in our culture. Now, look at the police officer in Figure 3.3. When we interpret this representation, we implicitly compare it to what we expected to see, which is influenced by our preexisting ideas of what a police officer looks like. When we assess what is absent in a representation or discourse, we are forced to assess our expectations, think about how they were established, and then consider how they are or are not met in that particular instance. This can be a difficult skill to learn, but once you have mastered it, it is an exceptionally useful strategy for understanding how representations and discourses shape our social reality.

FIGURE 3.3 ▧ Ottawa police officer Debbie Miller. Miller is a 17-year veteran of the Ottawa Police service. When we see this representation of a police officer, we interpret it in relation to what we expected to see in the image.

Courtesy of Debbie Miller

What Is Framed as "Normal" or "Common" in the Representation or Discourse?

The ability to frame something as "normal" in a society is a powerful tool, because it also designates that which is deviant or unusual (or not normal). Critically assessing the "commonsense" knowledge that representations and discourses rely on tells us about what is considered an uncontested element of the social order. As you encounter new representations and discourses, think about what type of background knowledge you need to have in order for them to be culturally intelligible. What types of experiences are you assumed to have? What types of things are you already expected to know? Are there phrases like "of course" or "as usual"? These signifiers illustrate what people consider to be the shared stock of knowledge in a society. It is even more common for things considered "normal" to be left unmarked in representations and discourses. For instance, it used to be common for news reports to only identify the race of a person if they were not white. The implication was that if a race was not specified, the person was white. These practices of racial identification have not disappeared completely; but they have become less common, reflecting a very slow change in some of the racial discourses in our society. At the same time, since the September 11, 2001, attacks in the United States, religious affiliations have become more common markers of identity in news reports, especially in relation to terrorism. It is rare for the news reports to identify members of the dominant religions in North America—Catholics and Protestants—but those who are Muslim or Sikh are often identified as such, linguistically setting them apart from "the centre." A critical analysis of what is framed as "normal" gives us substantial insight into power relations in our society. Representations of normality shape our expectations about how people should be and behave, and alternative representations are interpreted in relation to this established norm.

MAKING CROSS-CULTURAL AND HISTORICAL COMPARISONS

In addition to the strategies described above, making comparisons across cultures or across time can also help you to develop a critical analysis of representations and discourses. If you have travelled internationally, you likely know that it can be much easier to see what is unique about your own culture by stepping outside of it. The international pedestrian symbols shown in Figure 3.1 help to illustrate what is unique about Canadian pedestrian symbols. Comparative research investigates how representations and discourses vary in different countries, regions, places, or cultures. Comparative research can also be done across groups, organizations, or sectors. A key issue in this kind of approach is deciding what to make comparisons across. For instance, if you are going to compare several countries' discourses of nationalism, which countries will you choose? Many people start with their own country (or city or organization), and then try to make comparisons to other countries with similar histories or political situations. In the case of Canada, researchers often make comparisons with Australia because of the two countries' shared history as monarchies and their similar legal systems. At other times, researchers compare Canada with the United States because of their proximity. There is no single right way to determine what you should make comparisons with, but be aware that your choices about what to compare will affect your analyses.

Making historical comparisons has the added advantage of revealing how representations and discourses emerge and become dominant (or fade) over time. For example, Karen Dubinsky uses the history of tourism at Niagara Falls to investigate how the idea of the honeymoon became part of our discourses about heterosexual marriage in the post–World War II period (1999). By investigating how representations and discourses change over time, we can see how new forms of social organization emerge, and can theorize about how they are related to economic, political, and other social changes. A word of caution though—at any given historical moment, representations and discourses tend to be intertwined and interrelated in complex ways. This can make it difficult to separate out how specific historical representations and discourses have influenced contemporary representations and discourses.

A particular challenge when doing both historical and cross-cultural research is assessing how representations and discourses are or were understood by people in different cultures. Typically, historical researchers are concerned with the credibility of sources—that is, whether the source is an accurate representation of reality. If we think that discourses work to constitute reality, however, it is more crucial to know how a representation or discourse was regarded by people at the time or in the place it was produced. By knowing how the people in a culture perceived a representation or discourse, we can assess how much power it had to create meaning and shape reality. For instance, in a hundred years' time, both the *Globe and Mail* and the *National Enquirer* will be found in archives—but the representations in one of these publications have much more power to affect our understanding of the world and the people in it than those in the other. In our culture, representations in the *National Enquirer* are rarely treated as "facts," whereas those in the *Globe and Mail* are treated as authoritative. When you make historical and cross-cultural comparisons, you might need to do some outside research to learn more about how people perceived the representations and discourses you are interested in.

Finally, for all analyses of representations and discourses, and particularly in historical and cross-cultural analyses, it is crucial that you have enough cultural knowledge to be able to understand what is being signified. When we step outside our own culture, it requires extra work in order to understand the range of meanings that might be assigned to a representation or discourse. Even when interpreting symbols within our own culture, we must work to step outside our own worldview and be open to the multiplicity of potential meanings.

These strategies and tools provide you with a starting point for interrogating representations and discourses, whether in your everyday environment or in the context of a formal research project. By asking hard questions about how things are represented, we can start to question and critically assess our everyday assumptions about the world and how it works. Our identities, our behaviours, and our perceptions of the world around us are shaped by representations and discourses, which is one way that power influences our everyday practices. As we begin to unpack these representations and discourses, we can start to see alternative ways of being, acting, and thinking that challenge dominant assumptions and power relationships.

CONCLUSION

I have outlined an approach to understanding social organization that is informed by a social constructionist worldview. Signifiers, representations, and discourses are central to how we come to know the world around us, and as a result they help to constitute social reality. The fixing or limiting of representations or discourses can be understood as an act of power. I began the chapter by introducing ideas about how we acquire knowledge, and outlined some of the strengths and weaknesses associated with the various ways we learn about the world. Although you should undertake a systematic study if you want to make defensible generalizations about the world, I encourage you to develop the habit of interrogating representations and discourses as you encounter them in your everyday lives. The ability to critically analyze representations and discourses is a "craft" that becomes easier with practice. Learning to routinely use these strategies in your everyday life will help you to become a critical thinker and consumer of information.

STUDY QUESTIONS

1. Explain what it means to say that signifiers are *polysemous*. What implications does this have?

2. In your own words, explain what a discourse is and why discourses are useful for understanding the organization of the social world.

3. Identify two different rhetorical devices that can be used to affect the interpretation of a text. Give an example of each device.

4. Explain what it means to say that "absence" is also a signifier.

5. Describe the strengths and weaknesses associated with making historical and cross-cultural comparisons.

EXERCISES

1. Choose a cultural symbol that is prominent in North America and identify the meanings associated with it. Then investigate whether that symbol has the same meaning in other contexts: in other countries or at other time periods. Some examples of possible symbols to investigate are road signs, hand gestures, and company logos.

2. Select an article from the front page of your local newspaper or news website. Read the article carefully, and critically assess what representations and discourses are being mobilized by the writer. Think about how the story might have been written differently and speculate about how this might have changed people's understanding of the news.

REFERENCES

Canadian Broadcast Corporation (CBC). 2005, June 30. "No eating before a swim" rule holds no water. *CBC News*, Online Edition.

Canadian Centre for Policy Alternatives (CCPA). 2009. *About the Canadian Centre for Policy Alternatives*. http://www.policyalternatives.ca/index.cfm?call=03513ce0&act=main.

Collet, T. 2009. Civilization and civilized in post-9/11 US presidential speeches. *Discourse & Society* 20: 455–475.

Cook, G., and N. Mercer. 2000. From me to you: Austerity and profligacy in the language of the Beatles. In I. Inglis, ed., *The Beatles, Popular Music and Society: A Thousand Voices*. New York: Macmillan.

Deacon, D., M. Pickering, P. Goldring, and G. Murdock. 2007. *Researching Communications: A Practical Guide to Methods in Media and Cultural Analysis*, 2nd ed. London: Hodder Arnold.

Dozens killed in Afghan bus ambush. 2008, October 19. *Al-Jazeera*, Online Edition.

Dubinsky, K. 1999. *The Second Greatest Disappointment: Honeymooning and Tourism at Niagara Falls*. Toronto: Between the Lines.

DuGay, P., S. Hall, L. Janes, H. Mackay, and K. Negus. 1997. *Doing Cultural Studies: The Story of the Sony Walkman*. New York: Open University Press.

Ferriter, M. 2009. "Arguably the greatest": Sport fans and communities at work on Wikipedia. *Sociology of Sport Journal* 26(1): 127–154.

Fraser Institute. 2009. *Getting to know the Fraser Institute*. http://www.fraserinstitute.org/aboutus.

Godfrey, T. 2009, November 15. Deporting woman may cost us jobs. *Toronto Sun*, Online Edition.

Gwyn, R. 1999. "Killer bugs," "Silly buggers" and "Politically correct pals": Competing discourses in health scare reporting. *Health* 3(3): 335–345.

Hall, S. 1997. "Introduction" and "The work of representation." In S. Hall, ed., *Representation: Cultural Representation and Signifying Practices*. Thousand Oaks, CA: Sage.

Hall, S. 1999. *Representation and the media* [video]. Northampton, MA: Media Education Foundation.

Kantorowicz, E. 1957. *The King's Two Bodies: A Study in Mediaeval Political Theology.* Princeton, NJ: Princeton University Press.

Kings are justly called Gods. 2009. [Speech by King James I, March 1609]. *Essential Speeches.* EBSCO Academic Search Premier.

Manjoo, F. 2008. *True Enough: Learning to Live in a Post-Fact Society.* Hoboken, NJ: John Wiley and Sons.

Raphael, D. 2002. *Social Justice Is Good for Our Hearts: Why Societal Factors—Not Lifestyles—Are Major Causes of Heart Disease in Canada and Elsewhere.* Toronto: CSJ Foundation for Research and Education.

Statistics Canada. 2008. *Methodology of the Labour Force Survey.* Catalogue no. 71-526-X. Ottawa: Statistics Canada.

Statistics Canada. 2010. *Latest Release from the Labour Force Survey.* August 6. Retrieved September 1, 2010 from http://www.statcan.gc.ca/subjects-sujets/labour-travail/lfs-epa/lfs-epa-eng.pdf.

Taliban kill dozens in brazen bus hijacking. 2008, October 19. *Globe and Mail*, Online Edition.

Tonkiss, F. 2001. "Analyzing discourse." In C. Searle, ed., *Researching Society and Culture.* Thousand Oaks, CA: Sage. 245–260.

United Nations Development Program (UNDP). 2009. Financial crisis threatens legal protection for the poor. UNDP Newsroom: March 4.

Vasterman, P. 2005. Media-hype: Self-reinforcing news waves, journalistic standards and the construction of social problems. *European Journal of Communication* 20(4): 508–530.

PART 2

The Centre, Normalization, and Power

Deborah Brock, *York University*

INTRODUCTION

We will begin this first section of *Power and Everyday Practices* by introducing you to a theorist who has been a major influence on the practice of thinking and doing sociology. C. Wright Mills first published *The Sociological Imagination* in 1959, yet his analysis has not lost its relevance. Indeed, it might be said to be more relevant than ever. His work inspires us to take up sociology not only as an intellectual vocation (regardless of whether or not one has "Sociologist" in one's job description) but also as a political practice. Thinking sociologically will lead us to do sociology in our everyday lives, and to make connections between our everyday lives and the larger events shaping the social world.

Having read this far, you have already begun to engage your sociological imagination. You have probably reflected on your own life, and the lives of your family members and friends. In other words, you have made the connection between the personal and the social. So what is the sociological imagination? Mills described it this way:

> ... a quality of mind that will help men [sic] to use information and to develop reason in order to achieve lucid summations of what is going on in the world and what may be happening within themselves. (Mills, 1959: 5)

For Mills, the "first fruit" of the sociological imagination is that individuals can only understand themselves and their experiences by locating these within their own historical time, geographical location, and political context. They can judge their own chances in life only through awareness of the chances of people in a similar position. For Mills, "The sociological imagination enables us to grasp history and biography and the relations between the two" (Mills, 1959: 6). Far from positioning people as mere passive effects of social processes, Mills (like the other theorists that we have discussed so far) believes that people can be active participants in making history, particularly if we are cognizant of the social forces at work around us, and are able to develop, along with others, a plan of action for shaping that history. We do indeed participate in the making of the social world at the same time that the social world shapes who we are.

In this section, we begin to build upon the framework that we have established in Part I, as we deepen our engagement with the practice of unpacking the centre, identifying practices of normalization, and comprehending power. You will be introduced to four topics that can be considered as building blocks for doing sociological analysis, and that you will inevitably encounter when you engage your sociological imagination.

In Chapter 1, "Unpacking the Centre," you were introduced to the idea that normalization is a dividing practice. Now you will see how sex–gender and sexuality categories, racial marking, class relations, and age relations are significant means through which social difference is established, and social inequality organized. In Chapter 4, "Bodies, Genders, Sexualities," Zoë Newman reveals the social and historical construction of what are usually taken to be simply natural and normal ways of being. As you read this chapter, we want you to think about how scientific claims about sexed bodies are grounded in cultural beliefs about gender. We want you to consider how Western science and culture have produced a dualism of two sexed bodies (female and male), and two genders (woman and man). Similarly, we want you to then consider how the construction of a heterosexual–homosexual binary is actually a very limited means of classifying sexual desires and possibilities. Finally, we want you to challenge normative assumptions about bodies, genders, and sexualities as you address the question "How does this kind of analysis take us beyond liberal claims for tolerance and equal rights, toward a fundamental rethinking of bodies, genders, and sexualities?"

In Chapter 5, "Whiteness," Cynthia Levine-Rasky redirects our analytic lens to the study of whiteness. She demonstrates how whiteness is a social location that provides privileges and entitlements to people considered to be white, even where those people may lack privileges and entitlements in other areas of their lives. As you read through this chapter, we would like you to consider how "race" is always contingent on the social context that gives it meaning. We want you to explore the everyday experiences of racialization and racial ordering that are part of your own life. As you engage in this process, you can reflect on social institutions and contexts that are considered raceless, but in which whiteness occupies the centre.

In Chapter 6, "Class, State, and Power," Mark P. Thomas explores the social relations of capitalism and the economic interests that have propelled it (and with it, most of us) into a financially precarious time. He situates his analysis within a more general introduction to how capitalism works, the integral place of a class structure for capitalism's functioning, and the significance of state processes for the maintenance of this economic system. In this chapter, Thomas distinguishes between two classical sociological approaches to the study of class, those of Karl Marx and Max Weber, and emphasizes the difference between sociological concepts of "class" and "status." In creating these distinctions, Thomas identifies the importance of recognizing the class structure as a form of social organization that disconnects many people from the ability to control their labour and that accords social and economic power to those with wealth. The chapter suggests that, while not always visible, class remains a central social relationship—and a central aspect of social organization—in contemporary society. It asks you to consider the relation between class and power, and how class is a feature of your everyday life. It asks you to question the assumptions you make about your own class position.

In Chapter 7, "Age," Rebecca Raby challenges the widely accepted model of the life course by revealing how it has been socially and historically organized into stages, in a manner that privileges the stage of adulthood. She asks: How do we define adulthood and how are conceptualizations of childhood, adolescence, and old age pivotal to that definition? How have these age-based categories been produced historically, and how do they reflect relations of power and inequality? How do current definitions of adulthood commonly assume and normalize certain kinds of privilege? How do such definitions in turn exclude or marginalize?

These chapters reveal how a normative centre is created and reproduced. You will find that the topics of these chapters—bodies, genders, sexualities, racialization, age, and class—are very much linked and interdependent, as is national belonging and citizenship (the topic of Chapter 15), in the making of normativity. Let's take a moment to further explore how these chapters are linked through one of the main themes of *Power and Everyday Practices*, "unpacking the centre."

CLAIMING CENTRE STAGE

Each of the chapters in this Part presents students with a number of important analytic issues for thinking and doing sociology. In order to elaborate upon our theme, "unpacking the centre," and link it to normalization and power, I will now compare some of these issues: heterosexuality, adultness as an age stage, whiteness, and the middle-class location.

Heterosexuality

Our contemporary understanding of heterosexuality as an erotic identity and practice is of recent historical origin. Moreover, heterosexuality is only meaningful when understood in relation to its opposite, homosexuality. This binary notion of sexuality also recognizes a third category—bisexuality—but typically only as a provisional middle position made up of those who have not yet fully established a hetero or homo identity. This binary model therefore reduces a larger and often fluid range of sexual desires and practices to two essential choices, straight or gay. It also privileges heterosexuality as the normal and natural condition. However, as Mary Louise Adams queries, if heterosexuality is so normal and natural, why has such an enormous range of social resources (including educational, health, and legal resources) been devoted to teaching people to be proper heterosexuals throughout their lives (Adams, 1997)? Yet the social construction of heterosexuality is rarely the focus of research. After reading Chapter 4, we hope you will come to recognize that heterosexuality is much more than simply part of the natural and normal order of things.

Being an Adult

The centrality of heterosexuality has also often been tied in with assumptions of adulthood that associate it with forming a heterosexual family. Just as heterosexuality tends to occupy the unexamined centre, so does adulthood, with research and theorizing either likely to assume an unspoken adult subject or to overtly focus on (and problematize) childhood and older age. Adulthood is commonly framed as the pinnacle of development and associated with independence (for example, through attaining a job, a house, and a complete education), rationality, maturity, and a command of emotions. Consequently, childhood and old age become problematized, children for their perceived incompleteness and dependence, elders for their perceived dependence and lack of productivity. After reading this chapter, we anticipate that you will further consider the ways in which age is perceived and understood, and how it is a taken-for-granted feature of everyday life.

Whiteness

The pervasiveness of whiteness as a system of privilege is often invisible to white people themselves; they are largely unaware of the extent to which it permeates their lives. In societies dominated by people of Western European origin, white people are commonly understood as "non-raced" and simply get to be human beings (Dyer, 1997). It is then easier to identify racial ordering as something that takes place outside of their own lives, instead of recognizing how we are all implicated in this systemic organization of power. White people can therefore remain blinkered about the ways in which they might unwittingly participate in reproducing systemic racism, despite a personal abhorrence for racist beliefs and practices. This does not imply that we should not also think about the impact racism has on those who are the targets. Both considerations are important for sociology, and for social action. However, after reading this chapter, we anticipate that you will have a better sense of the need to unpack not only racism, but whiteness. You will gain an appreciation of how whiteness confers privilege on white people regardless of their gender, sexuality, age, or class, at the same time that white privilege is bolstered by the existence of other forms of social inequality.

The Middle Class

If you were to be asked what your class position is, chances are very good that you would respond that you are middle-class. Given that you have the **cultural capital** to pursue a university or college education, it may very well be that you can accurately claim this position. Indeed, most of the population of Western industrialized countries would describe themselves in this way. In economic terms, therefore, they position themselves as part of an amorphous, largely unmarked category, occupying the centre position between rich and poor. The position of middle class appears to be claimed by those who have a certain degree of material comfort, and who have relatively easy access to financial and social resources such as credit cards, electronic equipment, good health care, and good schools. If this is indeed the case, why is the middle class now shrinking? We would like you to think about what our tool kit of theory and methodology can offer in order to explain this phenomenon. After reading this chapter, we would like you not only to be more aware of the existence of class-based inequalities in North America, but also to question why class position is so rarely a topic of public discussion.

As you read Part I, we want you to interrogate the centre, normalization, and power. We would like you to turn to your sociological tool kit to enrich your comprehension of the social world, as you practise the craft of thinking and doing sociology. It is through this kind of engagement that we embrace the vision of C. Wright Mills, and enrich our sociological imagination.

BIBLIOGRAPHY

Adams, Mary Louise. 1997. *The Trouble with Normal: Postwar Youth and the Making of Heterosexuality*. Toronto: University of Toronto Press.

Dyer, Richard. 1997. *White*. London: Routledge.

Mills, C. Wright. 1959. *The Sociological Imagination*. London: Oxford.

Bodies, Genders, Sexualities: Counting Past Two

4

Zoë Newman *York University*

INTRODUCTION

If I asked you to name some common biological differences between women and men, chances are you might say that women have a vagina and men have a penis, or men and women are hormonally different. People often feel expected to be able to identify whether someone is a man or a woman—when meeting a stranger, for instance—and it is possibly something that we imagine should be easy to do. I want to put it to you that this supposedly obvious thing we are doing is actually a very complicated, tricky, and often misleading process. For example, by asking how women and men are biologically different, I have just asked you to treat **gender** categories (woman and man) as if they are the same as sex categories (female and male). If you do not think of gender and sex as different, if you are not sure how they are different, if you do not see why it matters, or if you want to figure out where our ideas about sex and gender come from, then keep reading.

Blurring sex and gender reflects a long-standing assumption in Western culture that your anatomical body is the same as your social identity, or at least that one determines the other. If you are born with female genitals, you are presumed to be a girl. Since being a "girl" or a "boy" carries all kinds of dominant cultural meanings—from how you should look and act, to what kind of job and partner you should desire someday—treating sex and gender as the same allows bodily anatomy to predetermine your interests and abilities. In other words, "biology is (or becomes) destiny," as the saying goes. For example, women are often said to be maternal because of the physical ability to bear children. This assumes that being female and being a woman follow directly from one another, and that for example the "essence" of womanhood is having a child, which does not leave a lot of room for choosing not to have children, or being infertile, or being a woman with ambiguous genitals or one who is **transsexual** or **transgendered**. The dominant way of conceptualizing the link between sex and gender is through **essentialism**: it is the assumption that your social identity is profoundly determined by your physical self, and that your identity is therefore unchanging across time and place (Vance, 2006). In dominant culture, essentialist thinking can often be seen in ideas about **race**, as well as in ideas about sex and gender. In both cases, universalism is a feature of essentialism, as in describing the experience of "women" or "Black people" as if they are all the same. Focusing only on what homogenizes women into a single category assumes that womanhood is inborn, and further makes a problem out of differences and non-conformity.

Yet many feminists and other gender theorists point out that being a woman or man does not come naturally. In the words of philosopher Simone de Beauvoir (1953), "one is not born, but rather becomes, a woman" (249). Gender theorist Michael Kimmel similarly challenges the conventional view that masculinity is natural, biological, only possessed by some people, and the same in all men. Instead, Kimmel sees masculinity as "a constantly changing collection of meanings that we construct ourselves, with each other, and with the world" (2007: 73). In his analysis, manhood comes not from some inner essence, but from the world around us. The point is that we need to step back from saying that masculinity and femininity are the result of biology and anatomy, and that they are naturally each other's opposites. Rather, we need to examine how we come to understand sex and gender the way we do, which will be one of the goals of this chapter.

Where We Are Going

The focus of this chapter is the dominant **sex–gender system**: we will look at what it means to say that there are only two sexes (female and male), and that your gender (being a woman or a man) automatically follows from your sex; we will consider some of the history of those ideas and the shape they take in everyday life; and we will look at how and why we might "do" sex and gender differently. In the next section I will introduce and investigate the idea of gender as socially constructed rather than naturally occurring. As we move through the chapter, I will offer historical examples to show where our current naturalized ideas come from, and how they have been shaped by political, economic, and social events. We will consider various ways binary categories have been enforced: through **colonial** regulation, through scientific **discourse** and the "disappearance" of different kinds of bodies, through narrow and unequal definitions of masculinity and femininity, through **sexuality**, and through what Michel Foucault called **biopower**. These examples help to answer why we need to pay attention to assumptions about sex and gender. We will end by questioning everyday ways that we participate in the dominant sex–gender system, and everyday ways that we might interact critically with it. These critical approaches may be things you already do, or wish you could put into words, such as reflecting on your own gender practices and **agency**, or being aware of gender ambiguity, flexibility, and multiplicity all around you.

At the centre of what we will be examining are two basic, interconnected dominant ways of thinking that make it seem possible and even simple to determine a person's sex or gender: **binary** opposition and biologizing. Various kinds of social divisions and hierarchies have been established and reinforced by people, and yet are difficult to challenge because they have been biologized: they have been made to seem natural and unchangeable as a result of being said to be located in the body. Yet many gender theorists suggest that our current dichotomous, scientific sex–gender system dates only as far back as the late 18th century.

Among the most significant ways difference has been located in the body or biologized are sex–gender categories and racial categories. As we will see, there are some very significant similarities between the production of sex–gender differences and the production of racial differences. While there are also many important divergences in the histories and effects of racial and sex–gender categories, they share a starting point in the late 18th century. These categories were invented in the new biological terms of the time, which claimed to know the true, deep meaning of bodies. More specifically, racial and sex–gender categories were organized through binary opposition that defined bodies as either white or non-white, male or female, sexually normal or deviant, and perhaps most troubling, superior or inferior. What we have inherited from these systems is that "differences" are signs of inferiority, some ways of being are naturally better than others, and bodies that do not conform to binary categories need to be fixed. As you learned in the introduction to this book, in naming these ideas we are "unpacking the centre." We can continue this line of critical thinking to question how a binary system of sex and gender has come to occupy such a privileged place, as if it is simply normal and natural. We will see how this binary also reinforces a privileging of heterosexuality. And as you learned in the introduction to this book, we can compare the position of privilege given to heterosexuality to that ascribed to whiteness in Western industrialized societies, a topic that we will pursue further in this chapter, and that you can then read more about in Chapter 5.

SOCIAL CONSTRUCTION ZONE

Let me first clarify separate meanings of sex and gender, and then complicate each category. "Sex" has two distinct uses. First, where sex is often used to refer to biological characteristics of being either male or female, gender tends to be constructed as the cultural codes of femininity or masculinity projected onto your body. The dominant assumption is that if you have male sexual organs, and your gender characteristics (such as the pitch of your voice, the way you sit and stand, your tastes and hobbies) are considered masculine, you must be a man. As historian Joan Wallach Scott puts it, gender is "a social category imposed on a sexed body" (2006: 19). So "gender" is not just a thing or category, it is also a process known as **gendering**.

Distinguishing between sex and gender, and saying that "feminine" is not simply something you are born as, but rather something shaped by the culture around you, reflects a **social constructionist** approach. Social constructionism points out that how gender and sex, and more broadly human bodies, are seen and understood changes in relation to other social and political shifts. Feminist theorist Rosemarie Garland-Thomson writes that the body is "made ... within social relations"; it is "a cultural text that is interpreted, inscribed with meaning" (Garland-Thomson, 1997: 22). Social constructionism is as everyday as noticing that if a white man has long hair in heavy-metal culture, it is a sign of hypermasculinity, but if a Grade 3 boy in a mainstream school grows his hair past his chin, he is often teased (see Figure 4.1). If we shift contexts yet again, to 18th-century England, we would find that any affluent, fashionable white man would have had long hair (or at least a long-haired wig). And yet today short hair as a sign of "normal" masculinity has been made to appear "natural and inevitable" to the members of this culture (Vance, 2006). By seeing how gender codes change across time and vary within a culture—by giving them context—we can start to question dominant ideas.

FIGURE 4.1 ■ How are the social meanings of white male bodies created? What does long hair signify in each of these photos?

"Gender" thus interacts with dominant systems of race, class, sexuality, and ability, and as a result, varies both within and between societies (Jackson & Scott, 2002). As we proceed, you will read more about these intersections, in the process developing skills for intersectional analysis that will be useful in "unpacking the centre."

The Histories of Sex and Gender: Connecting Past and Present

A central theme of this chapter is that human bodies exist in context. This is a reminder that we need to be specific about our subject: we are discussing late-20th- and early-21st-century Western ideas about human bodies, which we are tracing back to the late 18th century. Thinking about bodies as contextual means we need to think about how bodies have been constructed and by whom, as well as the social, political, and economic effects of Western constructions of bodies. Finally we need to consider how we might think about bodies differently. The idea behind this kind of "self-reflexivity" or critical thinking is that if we conceptualize bodies differently, we can begin to reconceptualize dominant structures.

If we go back just a little over two centuries, we arrive at a time when many of today's dominant European, Canadian, and U.S. political, economic, social, and scientific institutions were emerging. The late 18th and early 19th centuries in the West were periods of revolution and European state formation, capitalist industrialization and urbanization, and new authority for Western **science**; they were also a time of imperial conquest, mass human enslavement, and colonization by white people of indigenous peoples in African, North American, and Asian continents. Each of these major sets of events can be said to have had profound social and political effects, and each could easily have a chapter of its own (as many of them do in this book). At the risk of glossing over important details, or conversely confusing you with too many ideas, here are some key issues to keep in mind.

With revolution and state formation came the rise of individual rights and voting power. Industrialization and urbanization produced the separation of work and home and dramatically altered family and gender roles. Western science brought about new theories of the body, and claims that the body held secrets about the "true" self that only science could decode. Imperial conquest involved violent rule over people and the exploitation of their labour and land. The reason I list these major events and their corresponding effects is because they have had an impact on how we "see" the body (Martin, 2006; Rubin, 1993). In very broad terms, the results of the late 18th century have been the invention of racial, sexual, and gendered categories (Rubin, 1993). As we will examine, categorization was profound not only because bodies were gendered, sexualized and racialized, but also because bodies were then put into a hierarchy by sex, gender, sexuality, race, and class. Though it might seem to trivialize these profound world events, let me now move from the macro to the micro, to show you how our everyday, familiar experiences fit into and can shape this big picture.

SEX, GENDER, AND ... QUICHE

We began this chapter by introducing the distinction between sex and gender. We are now going to carry on with this line of inquiry, in order to unpack further the assumptions embedded in naturalized sex–gender dichotomies. We will do this by looking at some late-20th-century history of the social construction of men and women as each other's opposites; a little later in the chapter, we will see how these opposites are constructed as "naturally attracting."

In North American dominant culture, gender divisions get applied to everything from clothing and occupations, to how you describe and display yourself on Facebook, to cars and even food. For example, back in the 1970s and 1980s, quiche was thought of as food that "real men" did not eat. Other foods have been consistently associated with dominant masculinity. Each year, around the time of the Super Bowl in the United States, newspapers run menus of what to serve for watching the big game: chili, spicy chicken wings, and blue cheese dip are all deemed appropriately masculine. What is implied is that men and women should not borrow from each other's characteristics too much, and particularly that men should not be too "feminine" even in their meal choices, which raises two important effects of gendering. First, as well as teaching people to see themselves as distinct from or opposed to each other on the basis of sex and gender, the dominant Western sex–gender system also works through internal divisions, teaching us there are ways of being gendered that are "normal" and ways that are "deviant": only effeminate men eat quiche. Second, the example of some foods being categorized as wimpy tells us that gender works by assigning unequal social, political, and economic value to those categories. More specifically, in the context of a patriarchal culture like ours, femininity is devalued (for another example, see the text box here).

Consider a more recent example of devaluing femininity, from a *NOW* Magazine article back in the fall of 2008 weighing the various federal party leaders. The journalist wondered, "So what do we want in a leader anyway? ... Generally, experts say the public prefers candidates who broadcast steadfastness but stay cool. 'Usually, those who show a lot of emotion tend not to get elected,' says [Concordia marketing professor Harold] Simpkins ... 'We prefer the rational to the emotional'" (Cash, 2008: 27). Strength and rationality are both typically thought of as masculine traits, whereas being emotional is often equated with femininity. Although the article does not tell us that you have to be a man to be strong and "cool," it seems that at the very least you have to act masculine to become prime minister and perhaps to belong in the world of politics.

POWER SOURCES

Putting ideas about sex and gender into historical context ultimately is also about looking at how **power** works at different moments, and how power has been theorized. That is, when we say that gender is socially constructed, we are also saying that it is shaped by power (rather than by god or nature). Further, we can say that social categories like sex, gender, race, class, and sexuality are forces of power in another sense: they give legitimacy to stratified relations between people as groups and individuals, and they work in tandem with institutions and structures that have the capacity to grant people authority (for example, as "experts" on a subject, as teachers, as doctors) or to distribute resources (access to schools, medical care, housing). As you know, analyzing power is a main goal of this book, and each chapter's author offers you particular insights into how to think about power. To both give you some background on where current ideas about the power of sex–gender divisions come from and tell you how I think about power, let me return for a minute to quiche, or at least to the era when quiche was getting attention for being both gourmet and "too feminine."

In Canada, the late 1960s was a time of establishing the Royal Commission on the Status of Women, to investigate how women in Canada were faring, relative to men, and what the government could do to promote "equality." The final report of the Commission, released in 1970, was a rallying point for many Canadian women, and the beginning of new political institutions and grassroots activism.[1] The work of "second wave" feminists both within and outside the mainstream produced many profound legal, social, and cultural changes in Canadian life.[2] In universities, some of this feminist

---

1 Among the new political institutions that came out of the final report of the Royal Commission on the Status of Women were the National Action Committee on the Status of Women, government ministries dedicated to women's issues, and some institutional support for grassroots feminist activism around reproductive rights and violence against women (McKeen, 2004; Rankin & Vickers, 2001; Razack, 1991).

2 We can credit "second wave" feminism with influencing the following shifts: legal changes including the decriminalization of abortion; recognition of rape within marriage; adding protection from sexism to the *Canadian Charter of Rights and Freedoms*; community initiatives including rape crisis response and women's shelters; and cultural and intellectual innovations including women's bookstores, women's centres, and women's studies departments (Armstrong, 2005; CARAL, 2009; Dua, 1999; Crow & Gottell, 2009).

thinking was concerned with gender inequality, particularly in domestic labour and paid work. That era's feminist analysis showed us that in the paid labour force, women earn less than men for the same work.[3] In addition to giving us phrases such as "the glass ceiling" and "the wage gap," work on gender inequality also drew our attention to women's disproportionate burden of domestic labour and the lack of public childcare support (Friendly, 2009).[4]

This kind of gender analysis provided openings for feminists to argue for political and economic changes, but "second wave" feminism has also been criticized for what it left out. Much of the gender inequality analysis that got attention in the 1970s and into the 1980s was written by white women, many of whom were middle-class and identified as heterosexual, and they often wrote only from the point of view of their own experiences (Alexander & Mohanty, 1997; Carby, 2001; B. Smith, 1983). The result was that the issues of "womanhood" were imagined as if all women were the same as each other,[5] but more particularly, as if all women were white, heterosexual, and middle-class (Combahee, 2001; Lorde, 1984). Analysis and issues of women of colour, indigenous women, and lesbians (and frequently all three) were often omitted, treated as side issues, or as detracting from the overall message of women's common cause (Dua, 1999; Echols, 1992; Loomba, 2005; Lorde, 1984; Maracle, 1996). Yet the problem of a one-dimensional "gender inequality" analysis is that it treats all women as if they are the victims of all men (Combahee, 2001; Echols, 1992; B. Smith, 1983). In other words, this analysis of inequality can be said to construct power in one-dimensional ways: as primarily top-down, and as something that you either have or not.

A one-dimensional, universalizing analysis of gender inequality and power creates two very significant gaps. First, it means that we lose sight of how for example women in the global north can benefit from and participate in unequal power systems, while women from formerly colonized nations often experience profound forms of impoverishment and exploitation that then lead to the development of different forms of resistance. Second, we treat all men as equally dominant, when men can also be subordinated—and sometimes "feminized," as we will see—on the basis of race, sexuality, ability, and class. While women in the global north may generally have less power than men in the global north, many of them still have more power than women in the global south, and some women in the

---

3 According to the Canadian Labour Congress, overall there has been some improvement in income discrimination since the 1970s, when women on average earned only 2/3 of what men did. In 2005, women working full time for the full year earned on average 70.5 percent as much as men, or $39,200 per year to men's average salary of $55,700. But the picture gets complicated—and worse—when we add in more factors. On average, university-educated women experience a higher income gap, on average earning only 68 percent of what men do, and women of colour earn only 64 percent as much as men. For further details, see www.canadianlabour.ca/action-center/womens-economic-equality/fact-sheets.

4 We also learned that in paid work, women are "horizontally" segregated in jobs like nursing and teaching that are supposedly linked to their natural capacities for caring, and women are "vertically" segregated in lower-level jobs within a given sector—being, for example, more often found in clerical positions than managerial ones in white-collar jobs (Armstrong, 2005).

5 *Sisterhood Is Global*, the title of a well-known feminist text published in 1984 by Robin Morgan, summarizes this kind of homogenizing view of all women as sharing common experiences.

global north even have more power than some men in the global north, if they are seen to embody **whiteness**, wealth, and heteronormativity. This example suggests three important characteristics of how I think of power: power is relative and complex; power produces not just inequality, but also privilege; and power is created and exchanged in social interactions, that in turn shape individuals, social relations, and social structures. These are the forms of power that influence and work through the sex–gender system. Colonial rule in Canada is one of the places where we can see complex power operating through gendered and racialized social relations, representations, and categories.

COLONIZING BODIES: STEREOTYPES, COLONIAL RULE, AND THE SEX–GENDER SYSTEM

We can think about "gendering" as a set of power relations by replacing it with the word **stereotyping**. Much like Stuart Hall's work on **representation** discussed in Chapter 3, stereotyping draws on complex interpretive repertoires to create deceptively simple labels. Stereotyping is a process of slotting people into dichotomous or opposite groups by ignoring subtleties, and concentrating only on the characteristics that emphasize difference. Drawing on the work of Sander Gilman (1985), Ania Loomba, a postcolonial theorist, says

> Stereotyping involves a reduction of images and ideas to a simple and manageable form; rather than simple ignorance or lack of "real" knowledge, it is a method of processing information. The function of stereotypes is to perpetuate an artificial sense of differences between "self" and "other." (Loomba, 2005: 55, paraphrasing Gilman, 1985)

Note Loomba's choice of words: stereotyping is "a method of processing information"—not "a method of distilling the truth," but a way of picking and choosing some details to emphasize while disregarding other qualities. This little phrase is an important way into thinking about dominant forms of knowledge, whether they are presented as "scientific truths" or "commonsense fact" as Aryn Martin discusses in Chapter 8. The other significant point that Loomba makes above is that stereotyping is about creating differences, or as Stuart Hall says, "*stereotyping reduces, essentializes, naturalizes and fixes 'difference'*" (1997: 258, emphasis in original). The "artificial sense of differences" that Loomba refers to was part of **colonialism**: from the 15th century onward, colonial power both directly and indirectly worked through the structure and social relations of the sex–gender system, often imposing patriarchal rule on egalitarian communities, as we will see below.

Colonialism profoundly reshaped social relations and structures not only through force, but also through categorizing. European explorers positioned themselves as different from and superior to non-Europeans by constructing binary categories of civilized and savage, and representing unfamiliar cultures as the latter. **Civilization** was often defined on the basis of how differently from one another men and women in a culture looked or behaved; in imperial Britain, waist-cinching fashions to display a lady's delicate "nature" were one aspect of a social division that assigned women to the home, child-rearing, and entertaining, and men to the world of government, war, and finance. Through writing and images—travel accounts, visual representations, and then early anthropology, advertising, and newspaper articles about the absence of such "civilization" among non-Europeans— European explorers justified their often violent actions and authority in the new world (Loomba, 2005; McClintock, 1995; Stoler, 2002). In addition to using repression and coercion to create harshly unequal power structures, colonial elites similarly achieved domination through **hegemony**, a term introduced in Chapter 2. Like Stuart Hall, the larger point Loomba is making about stereotyping is that it is a *cultural* form of domination. Through hegemony, dominant culture sufficiently incorporates and transforms the beliefs and practices of the dominated that the dominated are persuaded to see themselves reflected in the dominant culture and through the lens of the dominant culture, and then become willing to participate in it—to a point. When we tell ourselves that colonial gendered divisions are "common sense," and we organize our lives according to narrow definitions of what men and women can and cannot do, we participate in reproducing colonial social structures. We can however also "unpack the centre" of colonial gender relations by looking at how gender was constructed in and through colonialism, how colonialism and gendered divisions propped each other up, and how this continues in present-day ideas about gender and race differences.

To continue with an examination of hegemony, in addition to social and physical risks associated with gender nonconformity (from teasing and social exclusion to gay bashing), there are also rewards for shaping ourselves in the image of the dominant culture. In aspiring to "match" our gender to our sex, and wanting to be like the (gender-appropriate) Hollywood celebrity of the moment, say, we are "consenting" to a system that may be as much invested in our subordination as our participation. For some theorists of **cultural hegemony**, this makes us victims or dupes, because we are participating in our own domination. But theorists like Loomba and Hall point out that consent is only ever partially and temporarily secured. Our identities are always shifting, and binary categories can get messy pretty easily in our lived experiences of gender (Hall, 1997; Loomba, 2005). We can also challenge assumptions, by looking critically at colonial gender divisions and racial hierarchies that frame white settler violence as part of processes of "civilization," and European cultures and their gender relations as innately superior. Finally, as well as being implicated in dominant constructions of sex, gender, and race, people also have agency, making strategic choices about when and how to conform, often for survival. People also exercise agency by resisting colonial definitions and divisive structures, and instead unearthing, circulating, and embracing alternative discourses that celebrate "difference," or acknowledge experiences of complex, multiple identities.

Binary ideas about race and gender have been imposed and reproduced through hegemonic means, with exclusionary effects. For instance, colonial scientific theories have been used to justify blocking white women and people of colour from participating in public sphere institutions like education, government, and business. For much of the 19th century and the beginning of the 20th century in Canada and the United States, exclusion from the public sphere because of "biological difference" further meant that white women and people of colour were largely disqualified from challenging scientific ideas about sex, gender, and race differences (Gordon, 2006; Gould, 2006; Loomba, 2005; Rowbotham, 2006). The bitter irony should be obvious: because white women and people of colour were defined by science as inherently incapable of rational thought, they were prevented—though not always successfully—from producing knowledge that could demonstrate their range of capabilities (Loomba, 2005). In other words, we need to pay attention to which information gets processed, how, and by whom, as Chapter 8 demonstrates in relation to the history of Western science. In sum, stereotyping and the production of sex and gender differences are historical, social processes that can profoundly shape and limit our lives and our sense of ourselves; they can also be questioned and challenged, as this chapter does.

HEGEMONY AND NORMATIVITY: WHAT "REAL" MEN ARE AND ARE NOT

Binary sex and gender categories suggest that women and men are very dissimilar, *and* in particular ways. Social theorists analyze and name the "particular ways" as normative: they carry messages that there are right and wrong, normal and abnormal, ways to be, with risks and benefits for conforming. Patricia Hill Collins, a sociologist, talks about what happens when the culture of the most privileged members of society is made the standard for all people. Throughout this text book, you will find dominant culture centring and normalizing whiteness, heterosexuality, European belief systems, middle-class practices, and even what constitutes the healthy, able body. This dominant culture is currently pervasive in Western industrialized nations, and is "the centre" we seek to unpack here. When dominant culture defines gender "norms," the result is what we can call hegemonic masculinity and femininity. As we have just seen above, hegemonic categories and stereotypes filter our lives back to us in selective ways to secure our participation.

In dominant culture, hegemonic masculinity is often preoccupied with domination—from control over women and other men, to control over emotions, money, leadership, and violence (Collins, 2005). These are standards of masculinity that Michael Kimmel points out are actually "unrealizable" for men (2007: 75). He writes that because hegemonic masculinity is premised on being superior to and different from all women and many men, it requires constant **gender policing** or monitoring of self and others. What I would add is that dominant representations of masculinity, or how men are supposed to act, are also about refuting the very possibility of gender complexity and blurred boundaries.

By contrast, dominant femininity is not defined as being about amassing money, pursuing a sexual partner, or being physically strong. Instead, the dominant construction obliges women to "wait passively, depend on physical maturation, and hope that the adult female bodies they receive will meet social approval" (Collins, 2005: 194). Yet there is a hidden contradiction in this idea of femininity, since there are countless everyday ways in which being "naturally" feminine requires women to *actively* work on their bodies and appearances, by shopping, exercising, dieting, shaving, plucking, putting on makeup, monitoring how we sit, walk, stand, and so on. However, in dominant culture, women are by definition supposed to be unlike men, who are active, so being physically passive and submissive to men have become markers of femininity, even as passive femininity requires action

(Collins, 2005: 196). For sociologist Dorothy E. Smith, this way of thinking about femininity offers the possibility of an alternative gender discourse: even as "being feminine" requires that you take an objectifying stance toward your body's "problems," acting and looking feminine is a creative process of skilled, technical work (D. E. Smith, 1993: 141–3).

Certainly, dominant representations do not tell us how all men or all women act, and on their own, they do not have the power to determine what is "masculine" or "feminine." Many people would argue that there is room for choice and critical engagement in how we read mainstream media, what we do with the stories they tell, whether we take their messages literally or questioningly. But what many theorists of mass media talk about are the cumulative, normative effects of these images: what happens when they are piled one on top of the other every day, in magazines, on billboards, on television, at school, with friends, and so on (Dines, 1998; Katz, 2003). And what is further powerful about these images is the way they interact with other social systems and norms, so that what they are saying begins to take on the appearance of "truth" and "fact" (Ghosh, 2003; Hall, 1997). This again is where denaturalizing and contextualizing, processes described in the previous chapter, become important, and even offer a form of resistance.

We can begin to unsettle naturalized gender divisions by saying that hegemonic masculinity is relative rather than absolute. Hegemonic masculinity gathers its power through the simplistic binary structures that we previously saw in colonial racial categories. In the words of Kimmel, "we come to know what it means to be a man in our culture by setting our definitions in opposition to a set of 'others'—racial minorities, sexual minorities, and, above all, women" (2007: 73). For example, filmmaker and critical theorist Richard Fung points out that Asian men in dominant imagery are either "the egghead/wimp" or "the kung fu master/ninja/samurai": "sometimes dangerous, sometimes friendly, but almost always ... desexualized" (Fung, 1991: 148). For a recent instance of the "egghead/wimp," think of the Eric Yorkie character in the *Twilight* movies: played by Korean-American actor Justin Chon, Eric is somewhat effeminate in the movie, and on the Internet is described as a "the overly-helpful, geeky, chess club type."[6] The other stereotype of Asian men in dominant imagery can be seen in the latest remake of *The Karate Kid*, in which Jackie Chan plays the mysterious and asexual kung fu master Mr. Han. Only white heteromasculinity is repeatedly represented as active and desirable, which Fung says reflects a colonial version of whiteness (150). Hegemonic masculinity then is a set of standards that is as much (or even more) about proving what you are *not*—feminine—as proving how masculine you are.

Another way hegemonic gender is relative rather than absolute is that it is inseparable from dominant ideologies of class, sexuality, and race. As social theorist Beverley Skeggs says, "being, becoming, practicing and doing femininity are very different things for women of different classes, races, ages and nations" (Skeggs, 2002: 311). As much as we talk about gender operating to position men above women, we also need to understand that there are internal hierarchies within gender categories. Analyzing gender then means we have to think about multiple social categories, because the unstated requirements of "femininity," for example, are that it is embodied by someone white, middle-class, and

6 *Twilight* Wiki site, http://twilightsaga.wikia.com/wiki/Eric_Yorkie.

able-bodied, as well as female and **heteronormative**. Collins observes therefore that gender has also operated to strengthen the **ideology** of whiteness: if being properly gendered is a path to social acceptance, and being properly gendered is defined in terms of white culture, then social mobility requires assimilation to whiteness (2005). The flip side can mean that Black women who are not gendered in white terms get defined negatively in dominant culture (Collins, 2005). We can continue this exercise of unpacking hegemonic masculinity and femininity by thinking about gender as *performed* rather than innate.

Performing Gender: A Social Construction Approach

At the beginning of this chapter, you were introduced to the concept of social construction. For some people, thinking about gender as socially constructed means saying it is **performative**. This term is often associated with Judith Butler, who wrote about gender as something acquired or brought into existence through repetition (Butler, 1990). Repeated acts create an illusion of our core selves as gendered—"I *am* a woman"—and as having always been that way. Talking about gender as performative can therefore help us to understand that dominant masculinity and femininity are not stable or universal or biologically based. Russell Shuttleworth, a medical anthropologist, builds on Butler's theory by adding that gender performativity usually involves the body and how it looks and moves (2004). For example, dominant masculinity is in part about having a voice that is seen to match the gender you identify with, or a body that appears a certain way. Shuttleworth interviewed 14 men with cerebral palsy, to talk about their experiences with intimate and sexual relationships. The men Shuttleworth spoke with described struggling with how to "properly embody masculinity in relationships" (169). They identified this as an issue because masculinity is defined through behaviours like initiating dating and sex, being strong, or being able to "take care of" a woman (170). The effect of this dominant version of masculinity is that if you cannot perform in physically typical ways then you are not a "real" man.

Saying that social difference is constructed, however, does not mean it is not real for the people living it. We need to hold onto two competing ideas at once. First, a social constructionist approach points out that sex and gender have fluidity and ambiguity and are certainly much more flexible than hegemonic culture suggests. If we consider all the ways in which gender is socially constructed and changing, we allow for the possibility of individual choice and agency. This means that we have to consider how we contribute to the construction of divisive, hierarchical categories. But we can also disrupt, question, and resist these structures, personally and collectively.

The second idea, which competes with the one above, is that though they may not be natural, gender binaries are sustained by systemic and structural forces. Thus we cannot just redefine here what "masculinity" means and expect social constructions everywhere to crumble. Even though thinking about the ways social identity is constructed can cause us to question "essential truths" about who we think we are, or who others say we must be, and even though we can make choices including changing our given sex or gender, social construction is not something that just happens at the individual level (Butler, 1993; Vance, 2006). Gender norms are deeply embedded in dominant culture, shaping what kinds of individual decisions seem possible. People are rewarded or punished for how closely they resemble the dominant gender or racial construction. For example, Beverley Skeggs writes about the experience of working class women in the United Kingdom who talk about trying to "pass" as feminine through their clothing and mannerisms. For these women, in a class-stratified society, "failing" to perform middle-class femininity can result in being categorized as "sexual, vulgar, tarty, pathological and without value" (Skeggs, 2002: 322). So perhaps even when gender performance is literally about what we put on in the morning, performing dominant femininity does not really involve a simple choice between two things of equal worth. When the cost of nonconformity is rejection or worse, perhaps gender is also something we "choose" in order to avoid social exclusion. Whether we are talking about clothing, grooming, or dating, sex and gender divisions are everyday personal and social practices; but they are also structural and systemic forms of inequality in Canadian life.

The dominant representation of female masculinity is another place where we can see the narrow path from sex to gender being made to seem natural; it is also a place where we can make space for alternatives by questioning the meanings assigned to nonconforming bodies. Gender theorist Judith Halberstam does this by looking at how female masculinity is depicted in late-20th-century Hollywood movies. Female masculinities, which are sometimes but certainly not always lesbian, are often absent from or invisible in mainstream films. When butch or other gender-nonconforming women do appear on-screen, they are usually shown as ugly, laughable, or predatory. Film theorist Barbara Creed has a similar analysis of some Western cultural representations of lesbians. In stories that have a cautionary tone, feminine sexuality and girlhood are depicted at the brink of crisis, often endangered by lesbians, but ultimately rescued or "guided" toward a proper heteronormative life (Creed, 1999). The "dangerous lesbian" is often represented as masculinized: she is a woman whose behaviour, clothing, and actions suggest that she is a man "trapped" in a woman's body (Creed, 1999: 113). Although Creed is writing about lesbians, these same narratives have obvious implications for people who are transgendered or transsexual—for people whose gender expression is different from their assigned sex, or people who alter their sex. The message seems to be a holdover from biological essentialism, whereby the gender you present must "match" your body.

Creed suggests that "the tomboy" or the "masculinized" female body is threatening because "her image undermines patriarchal gender boundaries that separate the sexes" (118). In dominant culture, one way to deal with that threat is by circulating dominant culture representations of female masculinity as freakish and predatory, and often literally or figuratively eliminated.[7] "True" masculinity—in the form of white male-bodied heterosexual men—then triumphs in some way, usually by "winning the girl" (Halberstam, 2002: 350).

---

7 In mainstream movies, the butch woman is usually "feminized" (for example by donning stereotypically feminine clothing, often to win the affections of a man), criminalized, or meets with tragedy and violence, usually connected to her gender identity. Some recent films in which masculine female characters are feminized in the course of the movie's plot development include *Bend It Like Beckham*, 2002; *Girlfight*, 2000; and *Lara Croft: Tomb Raider*, 2001. Recent films in which masculine female characters are or become criminal and mentally unstable include *Foxfire*, 1996; *Heavenly Creatures*, 1994; *High Tension*, 2003; *Lost and Delirious*, 2001; *Matilda*, 1996; *Monster*, 2003; *My Summer of Love*, 2004; and *Thelma and Louise*, 1991. In all of the films listed in the second category, masculine female characters are victims of violence or suicide.

Heterosexual male masculinity is left as the only authentic, desirable masculinity, and anything that challenges it is represented as false—or worse. We have already seen how the construction of dominant masculinity excludes effeminate men, and here dominant masculinity is limited to something that can only belong to male bodies. In these ways, the binary between male-bodied, forceful masculinity, and female-bodied, delicate femininity is naturalized, and the experience of people whose embodied sex and presented gender do not follow dominant lines is denied.

In summary, sex and gender categorization are processes of making meaning, ordering and dividing the world. When we start to take the approach that the "difference" between men and women is located in human interactions, social structures, and power relations, we are denaturalizing the link between sex and gender. That means we are moving away from the assumption that if you are born male-bodied, you will inevitably be masculine and identify as a man, and you will "naturally" be attracted to someone of the opposite sex (and gender). A social constructionist approach to gender also disrupts the idea that masculinity is inherently superior to femininity—and even that we can be sure what "masculinity" really means. The point is to get us to reflect on cultural rules that govern masculinities and femininities, and to think about how masculinities and femininities are both shaped by power relations and changeable in relation to politics and culture.

Complicating the Two-Sex Model: Counting Past ... One?

We have seen that in a social constructionist approach "male and female" are often used to refer to "sex," functioning as terms to describe biology, whereas "masculine and feminine" are often used to refer to cultural practices such as gendered behaviour and appearance. As is illustrated above, critical theorists have long argued that there are differences between sex and gender, and that your biology cannot simply be equated with your social identity. However, those arguments have been concerned with the "gender" side of the problem, often leaving unexamined the assumption that "sex" binaries dividing all humans into either female or male are natural. Gayle Rubin, a cultural anthropologist, calls this **sexual essentialism**, or "the idea that sex is a natural force that exists prior to social life" (1993: 9). And yet, as I mentioned early in this chapter, and as we will see shortly, it is only since the late 18th century that Western science has categorized human bodies into two dichotomous, separate sexes.

According to biologist and feminist Anne Fausto-Sterling, "European and American culture is deeply devoted to the idea that there are only two sexes" (2000: 30). We can see this denial of any other reality in language. While writing a piece on 17th-century legal cases in the United States and Western Europe involving people who at the time were labelled as **hermaphrodites** (see Glossary), Fausto-Sterling describes having to "invent" terms, opting to alternate between using "he" and "she" when discussing people defined as hermaphrodites. Fausto-Sterling observes that gendered pronouns reflect the significant relationship between language and the invention of categories—from who comes up with terms and what kinds of cultural meanings they assign, to what becomes unimaginable and "unnatural" because it does not fit neatly into a category or does not have a name.

Another example of the power relations of naming is that "hermaphrodite" is a term that was not invented or adopted by the people whose bodies were being described. Judith Halberstam points out that "hermaphroditism" was used by medical practitioners as a kind of catchall category (2002). The term would have included both what we call **intersex** today, and something much broader, such as females whose gendered appearance and behaviours made them seem incompatible with the category of woman. "Intersex" by contrast is a self-chosen name for many people.[8]

Scientific binary classifications of sex are not just a matter of defining and labelling, however. Since the mid-20th century, surgical techniques have been used to assign babies to one sex or the other immediately following birth. Case studies of genital surgery in the United States from the mid-1950s onward reveal that the sex assigned to babies by doctors depends on highly cultural and changing criteria, mostly having to do with doctors' ideas about the minimum acceptable size of a penis (Fausto-Sterling, 2000). To go back to Fausto-Sterling's attempt to bring language into line with the range of human experience, though the Intersex Society of North America currently recommends that babies and children with ambiguous genitalia be identified as either a boy or a girl (but without early surgical intervention), transgendered and transsexual communities have proposed terms that offer a disruption of categories, using "hir" rather than his or her, and "ze" rather than she or he. In "disappearing" people Fausto-Sterling calls "mixed sex," whether through naming them as either male or female or through surgically remaking their bodies into one sex or the other, it has been made "natural" that most bodies are only one of two possible, dichotomous sexes. These effects tell us about the power relations of naming, and the importance of the two-sex system for dominant structures.

The "two-sex system" has been strictly enforced and maintained since the late 18th century, with the emergence of Western biology. The new field of science gave primary importance to gonads, organs that secrete hormones and produce gametes. In scientific discourse, gonads are divided into two categories: ovaries, which produce eggs, or testes, which produce sperm. This "dualistic sexual division" of the world in the late 18th century was a new approach to **classifying** and treating bodies (Fausto-Sterling, 2000: 32). Earlier practitioners of medicine, such as Galen, the highly influential 2nd-century Greek physician and philosopher, did not conceptualize sex in binary terms. He devised a continuum of sex and gender rather than an unchanging and absolute line between male and female (Fausto-Sterling, 2000). Male and female genitals were seen and understood as being the same: the female was described as simply an "outside in" version of the male with comparable anatomy. No separate term for "ovaries" existed until the 17th century, because they were considered the same as testes. There was, in other words, said to be only one sex, though male bodies were supposedly more perfect (Laqueur, 1997). These "one-sex" ideas prevailed

---

8   We can see a comparable history with sexual designations—**homosexual** is a term that comes from medicine, and is part of a larger process of treating same-sex desire as pathological; "dyke" and "fag" were insults for a long time, until they were reclaimed as forms of resistance. There are also similar patterns with racial designations—there's a big difference between the meaning and effect of "coloured people" and "people of colour," and there's a history to how the terms came about. For some of that history, see www.naacp.org.

in Renaissance Europe, where from approximately the 14th through the 17th century, scientific and medical theories were unable to pinpoint bodily gender differences (Fausto-Sterling, 2000). What followed in the 18th century was therefore a "radical" redefinition of human sexuality, particularly of women's bodies. But as historian Thomas Laqueur argues, if you look more closely at the events of the time, it was not bodies that changed, so much as the meaning of their parts that was "reinterpreted" (1997).[9]

For Laqueur, the tremendous anatomical shift in the late 18th century cannot be explained on the basis of scientific breakthroughs. Instead, we need to understand the rise of biology and its apparent discovery of fundamental dissimilarities between female and male bodies in the context of the European **Enlightenment**. In France after the revolution of 1796, rights and freedoms were to be distributed equally, rather than only or primarily to the nobility. Condorcet, an 18th-century French philosopher, proclaimed that "rights of men result simply from the fact that they are sentient beings, capable of acquiring moral ideas and of reasoning concerning these ideas." The potent idea that followed was that "women, having these same qualities, must necessarily possess equal rights" (Condorcet in Laqueur, 1997: 219). Yet the outcome of European revolutions and reforms was not universal rights for all humans. Instead, it was argued by some that because their physical "nature" was different from men's, women should not engage in politics and government (Laqueur, 1997).

The logic about binary sex went that if female and male anatomies were different, then men and women must be different from each other. It therefore became possible to simultaneously argue for universality, equality, and democracy, while categorically excluding whole segments of the human population on the basis of "difference." As I will discuss further shortly, among the greatest obstacles faced by Western women arguing for political and educational rights was the dominant culture's absolute insistence on only two, drastically dissimilar and unequal sexes.

Having explored the history of the two-sex model, and the politics behind its introduction during the European Enlightenment, we now turn to how Foucault explained the new forms of power shaping what we know about human bodies.

Biopower: Regulating Gender, Sexuality, and Race

You are by now aware that the theories of Michel Foucault have profoundly contributed to theorizing how power works in liberal democracies. To explain contradictions such as egalitarian democracies being based on raced and sexed exclusions of some people, Foucault traces changes in the social order. As outlined in Chapter 2 and the previous section, by the 18th century new mechanisms of power had emerged in Western Europe, with the move away from monarchies and rule based on bloodline (Foucault, 1978). With the rise of democratic society came **biopower**, as Foucault refers to it. At the level of the individual, physical body, the focus of biopower is to shape the human body, to harness its maximum physical potential, and to ensure its obedience through discipline in places such as schools,

---

9   Note that people who study the development of human embryos have long reported structural similarities among humans, supporting the one-sex model (Oudshoorn, 2006).

the family, and the army (Foucault, 1978). At the level of humans as a species, biopower is about monitoring and regulating entire societies, collecting demographics on populations from birth, through life expectancy, to mortality. For example, in Canada, the government takes an official census every five years. Among other things, the Statistics Canada General Social Survey "monitors the changes in the structure of families with respect to marriages, common-law unions, children and fertility intentions" (www.statcan.gc.ca). This statement reflects Foucault's argument that in the 19th century, disciplining people's individual bodies and overseeing the population as a whole merged in what he calls "the deployment of sexuality" (140).

Sexuality became the focus of power because it "happens" in the individual body, and heterosexual intercourse can lead to the reproduction of the species. Regulating sexuality is therefore a way to have influence over both forms of the body, which is why Foucault says sexuality crops up as a theme in everything from morality tales, to government policies and nationalist campaigns, to childhood psychology, social movements, and self-definition. Regulating bodies through sex–gender binaries, and through their naturalized forms of sexuality, has been a longstanding preoccupation of Canadian governments. The following example from Canadian history returns us to colonial relations to demonstrate how ideas about biological difference have been produced, embedding racial and sexual inequalities in state structures.

During the fur trade, in what would become known as Western Canada, sexual and social interactions between British men and Aboriginal women were encouraged by white colonial governors (Mawani, 2002). This was apparently a practical necessity in the eyes of the British: there were few white women in the colony in the 17th and 18th centuries (Stevenson, 1999). "Mixed race heterosexuality" was therefore often encouraged as an alternative to "sodomy" (other sexual acts then considered unnatural, particularly sexual acts between men) (Perry, 2001), and was not defined as a problem until after the mid-19th century, when the British colonial project changed from fur trade to white settlement and the reservation system. The British became invested in colonial sexual regulation at the same time as they were legally defining the category "Indian," and positioning themselves as the natural governors of the territory. These classifications, which would be used by the colonial government to determine entitlement to land and rights, entrenched dichotomous and hierarchical definitions of men and women, and biological definitions of race (Mawani, 2002; Perry, 2001).

The new official definition of "Indian-ness" was ultimately decided on the basis of "blood purity" and Eurocentric patrilineal descent. Accordingly, children were "Indian" if their father had "Indian blood," and Section 12(1)b of the *Indian Act* dictated that "Indian" women would lose status through marriage to a non-Indian man. Loss of status under Section 12(1)b became a powerful mechanism to discourage intermarriage between First Nations women and white men, given that it would mean losing their official identity, band membership and voting powers, your right to live on and be buried on reserve property, and your claim on inheritance, educational funding, services, and treaty money (Lawrence, 2004).

Cree scholar Winona Stevenson says that Section 12(1)b "embodied and imposed the principle that Indian women and their children, like European women and their children, would be subject to their fathers and husbands" (Stevenson, 1999: 68). For example, under the *Indian Act*, men became sole owners of the house where a married couple lived.

First Nations communities that had often been egalitarian and matrilineal were legally displaced by a system that saw men as fundamentally different from and superior to women (Lawrence, 2004). The British colonial government was simultaneously imposing a British gender hierarchy, while constructing white and "Indian" bodies as biologically different.

In the context of this colonial social order, interracial heterosexual sex became a "problem." If conception resulted from British–First Nations sex, the offspring would be mixed-race people, who could "confuse" racial hierarchies (Mawani, 2002; Perry, 2001). As a result, mixed-race people themselves were classified as "illicit," subjected to intensified government regulation, and pitted against people in their communities who were officially recognized as "Indian" (Mawani, 2002).

As we have seen, European and Canadian institutions were deeply committed to binary constructions of sex, gender, and race. Belonging to one sex or the other and one race or the other became the basis of your social status, the rights you could expect to enjoy or that you could be denied, and was foundational to the social order as a whole. Fausto-Sterling therefore advances the possibility that if we reconceptualize or complicate the neat binary divisions of "sex," we call into question "cherished aspects of European and American organization" (Fausto-Sterling, 2000: 376). If we challenge the notion of clear divisions between categories, we unsettle the argument that people have inherently different (and unequal) abilities, and begin to discredit justifications for the inequitable distribution of rights.

Heterosexual by Nature?

As we have seen, "gendering" is a process of categorizing human behaviours into discrete, seemingly opposite camps, so that we become not only "gendered," but as I will suggest, we also become **heterogendered**. As sociologist Chrys Ingraham says, in effect "to become gendered is to learn the proper way to be a woman in relation to a man" (2002: 83), or as Patricia Hill Collins suggests, gender binaries construct women and men as "complementing one another and as incomplete and imperfect without the other" (2005: 182). In this sense, sexual "orientation" becomes a literal directing of women and men in each other's direction. As useful as it is to talk about gender as socially constructed, we also need to analyze the sexualization of sex and gender binaries. If we do not, we miss how learning to be a girl, boy, woman, or man is also a process of learning to be heterosexual.

This is where the second usage of **sex** comes in, having to do with erotic practices and desires, who you want to have sex with, or what you want to do with them. Much like gender being equated with your identity, "sex" is treated as more than just a feeling or an act, but is dominantly extended to sexuality, and has become associated with who you are: for example, some people say, "I *am* heterosexual." As with the apparently simple categorizing of people as men or women, there is a lot packed into this statement of sexuality as identity. We will see that the dominant version of saying you are heterosexual (rather than that you *are attracted to* person A or B or C) often assumes that there is a natural line from your sex, to your gender, to your sexuality (see the text box). Gender theorist Judith Butler refers to this hegemonic set of ideas as "the heterosexual matrix": when bodies, genders, and desires are naturalized as binary, oppositional, and hierarchical, heterosexuality becomes compulsory rather than natural or a choice (Butler, 1990: 151).

Here is one everyday example of how the binary sex–gender system is heteronormative. If in the summer of 2009 you found yourself watching the auditions for the second season of *So You Think You Can Dance Canada* (SYTYCDC), you would have been witness to a variety of dominant practices playing themselves out. In addition to non-Western styles of dance being referred to as "cultural," and bodies that are not skinny being commented on negatively, there was a remarkable enforcement of the sex–gender system when it came to auditions by relatively feminine dancers who were apparently male. At least two dancers who seemed to be male-bodied and were very graceful and balletic in their choreography were told by the judges that they needed to be "stronger," that their dance was better suited to someone female, that they should "man it up," and in one case, that they needed to wear their balls in the front!

Embedded in the SYTYCDC judges' comments, as in much of the prevailing Western sex–gender system, is the dominant assumption that "normal" gender is packaged up with "normal" sexual desire and practices. If you do not embody and express your assigned gender role, there is something "queer" about you. That is, it is likely presumed that the femininity of some male dancers on SYTYCDC is evidence they are gay, whereas a hegemonically masculine male-bodied person or dancer is assumed to be sexually attracted to a "feminine" woman, and to be better able to lead them on the dance floor. It is through assumptions such as this that "masculinity" becomes "heteromasculinity."

The version of heterosexuality that is naturalized and dominant today is relatively new, or, to be more accurate, it is relatively new for the label to exist at all. In late-19th-century medical literature in Canada and the United States, heterosexuality was first discussed as a perversion—because it was defined as sexuality not directed toward procreation (Kinsman, 1996). The colonial sexual standard going back to the 17th century had been that sexual activities were sanctioned only within marriage between a man and a woman, and sex was only for the purposes of procreation (Stokes, 2001). Anything else, whether "sodomy," "heterosexual fornication," or prostitution, was lumped together and frowned upon (D'Emilio, 1997; Kinsman, 1996). In that precapitalist time, white settler families were patriarchal yet interdependent: the whole family worked land owned by the male head, and labour was gender-segregated, but the survival of family members was only possible if everyone participated (D'Emilio, 1997). Within that context, encouraging white people to form family units and produce enough children to work the land was part of the larger racial project of white survival and settlement. That colonial ideology, of sex acts as part of marriage and procreation—not sex for pleasure, or sex as part of your personal identity and "lifestyle"—held sway for over two centuries.

In the late 19th century in the United States, however, dominant social attitudes toward sexuality changed significantly. The meaning of sexuality broadened from a focus on reproduction, to allow for what Mason Stokes calls "a pleasure-driven heterosexuality"—though still only within marriage (15). Again, the new definition of socially acceptable sexuality was shaped by economic and political events. With increases in mechanized mass production, and the accompanying urbanization, the family was no longer the basic, essential unit for survival. With wage labour, fewer bodies were required for work. Men and women left the household to enter the capitalist workplace; the family ceased to be the unit of work and production, making it possible for sexuality to be something other than an imperative, and become instead a source of intimacy and pleasure (D'Emilio, 1997). In that period of increased industrialization and urbanization, medical science redefined marital heterosexuality from a perversion, to a way to correct other forms of sexual **deviance** (Stokes, 2001). So although "heterosexuality" is currently naturalized as the sexual "norm" in Western culture, Stokes reminds us to think of it as socially constructed. And, as a T-shirt slogan proclaims, "Heterosexuality is not natural; just common."

The social and medical shift from an emphasis on marital heterosexual sex for procreation only, to marital heterosexual sex for pleasure, signalled a major departure from the prevailing economic model. Interdependent farming-based household economies were being replaced by capitalist industrialization and liberal separations between public and private. What did not change is that sexuality remained tied to the racial project of white purity and dominance, and that heterosexuality remained the norm. Racialized difference hinges on physical characteristics, which for the most part can be reproduced or passed on through heterosexual sex. So heterosexuality is central to literally maintaining "the white race" (Stokes, 16). But—and this is a big but—racial purists were concerned that heterosexual desire could also "endanger" whiteness, through interracial sex, as we saw in the example of British regulation of Aboriginal–white interactions (Dyer, 1997). Foucault might remind us here that sexuality is at the intersection of the two forms of biopower—and that the control of populations to enforce an essentialist, hierarchical idea of race took hold through shaping the sexual and gender normativity of individual bodies.

CONCLUSION: LOSING COUNT

We are surrounded by claims that there is a straightforward biologically based link from sex to gender to sexuality, which means there are only two possible results—male-born, heterosexual men, and female-born, heterosexual women. We are encouraged to believe that those "natural" conclusions are applicable everywhere and at all times. This is the centre that this chapter has focused on "unpacking."

In this chapter, we took those common assumptions about sex and gender being the same as each other, being universal, and being natural, and we teased them apart so that we could think about their many layers. We did this by giving historical background to the scientific shift from the one-sex model, and putting it into political context. Examples such as representations of female masculinity and surgical "disappearance" of intersex people gave us further evidence of how a strict sex–gender binary has been enforced, positioning white male-bodied masculinity as superior. By looking at Canadian colonial practices of sexual regulation, late-19th-century medical definitions, and some current popular culture images of women and men, we saw how ideas about binary sex and gender also contain within them heteronormativity and essentialist racial ideas. We have also seen that there is actually very little certainty or universality about sex–gender differences, and the scientific explanations offered to us contain their own culturally-specific, historically shifting beliefs about gender.

We might be better served by drawing on our critical "tool kit" to think about sex, gender, and sexuality in much more complex terms than the models we have been offered. We can also seek out the alternative models that already exist, ones that do not reproduce gender inequality, that do not degrade difference (such as female masculinity), and that do not implicitly assert white supremacy. For example, in addition to hearing about struggles with dominant masculinity and dominantly gendered romantic conventions, Shuttleworth also found a different story being told by some men with disabilities. The men in his study talked about negotiating romantic expectations by being more communicative and sexually innovative, or behaving in ways that are not seen as typically masculine—letting women make the first move sexually, or being more concerned with emotional intimacy. Shuttleworth describes these men as shifting more flexibly between "different self-identities," rather than rigidly mirroring hegemonic masculinity (174–5). Author and transgender activist Leslie Feinberg (1996) quotes a person who thought up 49 different gender identifications, in just one go, reflecting a wide range of masculinities, femininities, and other gender positions. An email I received recently refers to "past, present or future women—identified or bodied." In other words, even though dominant representations and language are often inadequate and invisibilizing, gender fluidity and complexity are all around us.

Individually and collectively, in our everyday lives as students, workers, activists, consumers, we need to consider the wider context for how differences between men and women are defined, and the meaning given to supposedly inherent differences. Further, we need to question and "denaturalize" the contents of biologized categories such as sex and race, and make visible the ways constructions of sex, gender, sexuality, and race are intertwined. We need to do this in our personal relationships, to the movies we watch, the books we read, as part of social movements; we need to do this to address **social inequality**, to seek change and new possibilities.

Perhaps the most crucial idea to end on is that we need to notice how hegemonic gender operates as a form of subordination, and think critically about gender positionings that work by marking some bodies as inferior, deviant, or dangerous. In questioning those divisive assumptions, we are denaturalizing larger hierarchical structures.

STUDY QUESTIONS

1. What does it mean to say that gender is socially constructed? What does it mean to say that gender is performative?

2. What is the significance of the shift from the one-sex model to the two-sex model? How does this shift remind us that we need to complicate sex binaries as well as gender binaries?

3. In this chapter, how have we seen that the social constructions of binary gender and heterosexuality are intertwined? How have we seen that the social constructions of binary gender, heterosexuality, and whiteness are intertwined?

EXERCISES

1. Look for images in dominant culture of gender ambiguity or fluidity. What meanings are conveyed by the images, what points are they used to make? If you can't find any images, why do you think they're so scarce?

2. Think about some ways that you produce your gender. What do you imagine or have you experienced are the risks of not doing gender according to the dominant rules? What do you imagine are the rewards or reasons for doing gender "right'?

3. Pay attention to how you hear boys and girls being discussed in the mainstream media, for example in debates about boys-only education. How are "sex" and "gender" used, is there recognition that "sex" or "gender" is socially constructed, or are all boys/girls assumed to be the same as each other? What might be some effects of thinking about sex and gender each way?

REFERENCES

Alexander, M. Jacqui, and Chandra Mohanty. 1997. Introduction: Genealogies, legacies, movements. In M. Jacqui Alexander and Chandra Mohanty, eds., *Feminist Genealogies, Colonial Legacies, Democratic Futures*. New York: Routledge. xiii–xlii.

Armstrong, Pat. 2005. Restructuring public and private: Women's paid and unpaid work. In Barbara Crow and Lise Gottell, eds., *Open Boundaries: A Canadian Women's Studies Reader*. Toronto: Pearson. 154–163.

Beauvoir, Simone de. 1953. *The Second Sex*. New York: Knopf.

Butler, Judith. 1990. *Gender Trouble: Feminism and the Subversion of Identity*. New York: Routledge.

Butler, Judith. 1993. *Bodies That Matter: On the Discursive Limits of "Sex."* New York: Routledge.

CARAL. 2009. A special report to celebrate the 15th anniversary of the decriminalization of abortion: Protecting abortion rights in Canada. In Barbara A. Crow and Lise Gottell, eds., *Open Boundaries: A Canadian Women's Studies Reader*, 3rd ed. Toronto: Pearson Prentice Hall. 226–228.

Carby, Hazel. 2001. The politics of difference. In Barbara Ryan, ed., *Identity Politics in the Women's Movement*. New York: NYU Press. 19–22.

Cash, Andrew. 2008. Media for the masses: We don't care if our leaders are strong—We only want them to look it. *NOW* Magazine, October 9–15. 27.

Collins, Patricia Hill. 2005. Prisons for our bodies, closets for our minds: Racism, heterosexism, and Black sexuality. *Black Sexual Politics: African Americans, Gender, and the New Racism*. New York: Routledge. 87–116.

Combahee River Collective. 2001. A Black feminist statement. In Barbara Ryan, ed., *Identity Politics in the Women's Movement*. New York: NYU Press. 59–66.

Creed, Barbara. 1999. Lesbian bodies: Tribades, tomboys and tarts. In Janet Price and Margrit Shildrick, eds., *Feminist Theory and the Body: A Reader*. New York: Routledge. 111–124.

Crow, Barbara A., and Lise Gottell. 2009. What is women's studies? In Barbara A. Crow and Lise Gottell, eds., *Open Boundaries: A Canadian Women's Studies Reader*, 3rd ed. Toronto: Pearson Prentice Hall. 1–9.

D'Emilio, John. 1997. Capitalism and Gay Identity. In Roger N. Lancaster and Micaela di Leonardo, eds., *The Gender/Sexuality Reader: Culture, History, Political Economy*. New York: London. 169–178.

Dines, Gail. 1998. King Kong and the white woman: *Hustler* magazine and the demonization of Black masculinity. *Violence Against Women* 4(3): 291–307.

Dua, Ena. 1999. Canadian anti-racist feminist thought: Scratching the surface of racism. In Enakshi Dua and Angela Robertson, eds., *Scratching the Surface: Canadian Anti-Racist Feminist Thought*. Toronto: Women's Press. 7–31.

Dyer, Richard. 1997. *White*. New York: Routledge.

Echols, Alice. 1992. The taming of the id: Feminist sexual politics, 1968–83. In Carole S. Vance, ed., *Pleasure and Danger: Exploring Female Sexuality*. London: Pandora Press. 50–72.

Fausto-Sterling, Anne. 2000. *Sexing the Body: Gender Politics and the Construction of Sexuality*. New York: Basic Books.

Feinberg, Leslie. 1996. *Transgender Warriors: Making History from Joan of Arc to Dennis Rodman*. Boston: Beacon Press.

Foucault, Michel. 1978. Right of death and power over life. *The History of Sexuality: An Introduction. Volume I*. New York: Random House. 135–159.

Friendly, Martha. 2009. Why women still ain't satisfied: Politics and activism in Canadian childcare. In Barbara A. Crow and Lise Gottell, eds., *Open Boundaries: A Canadian Women's Studies Reader*. 3rd ed. Toronto: Pearson Prentice Hall. 1–9.

Fung, Richard. 1991. Looking for my penis: The eroticized Asian in gay video porn. In Bad Object-Choices, ed., *How Do I Look?: Queer Film and Video*. Seattle: Bay Press. 145–160.

Garland-Thomson, Rosemarie. 1997. Theorizing disability: Feminist theory, the body, and the disabled figure. *Extraordinary Bodies: Figuring Physical Disability in American Culture and Literature*. New York: Columbia University Press. 19–51.

Ghosh, Sanjukta. 2003. "Con-fusing" exotica: Producing India in U.S. advertising. In Gail Dines and Jean M. Humez, eds., *Gender, Race, and Class in Media: A Text-Reader*, 2nd ed. Thousand Oaks, CA: Sage Publications. 274–282.

Gilman, Sander. 1985. *Difference and Pathology: Stereotypes of Sexuality, Race, and Madness*. Ithaca, NY: Cornell University Press.

Gordon, Linda. 2006. Malthusianism. In Inderpal Grewal and Caren Kaplan, eds., *An Introduction to Women's Studies: Gender in a Transnational World Second Edition*. Toronto: McGraw-Hill. 57–60.

Gould, Stephen Jay. 2006. Women's brains. In Inderpal Grewal and Caren Kaplan, eds., *An Introduction to Women's Studies: Gender in a Transnational World Second Edition*. Toronto: McGraw-Hill. 43–46.

Halberstam, Judith. 2002. The good, the bad, and the ugly: Men, women, and masculinity. In Judith Kegan Gardiner, ed., *Masculinity Studies & Feminist Theory: New Directions*. New York: Columbia University Press. 344–367.

Hall, Stuart, ed. 1997. *Representation: Cultural Representations and Signifying Practice.* Thousand Oaks, CA: Sage Publications. 15–64.

Ingraham, Chrys. 2002. The heterosexual imaginary. In Stevi Jackson and Sue Scott, ed., *Gender: A Sociological Reader.* New York: Routledge. 79–84.

Jackson, Stevi, and Sue Scott. 2002. Introduction: The gendering of sociology. In Stevi Jackson and Sue Scott, eds., *Gender: A Sociological Reader.* New York: Routledge. 1–26.

Katz, Jackson. 2003. Advertising and the construction of violent white masculinity: From Eminem to Clinique for Men. In Gail Dines and Jean M. Humez, eds., *Gender, Race, and Class in Media: A Text-Reader,* 2nd ed. Thousand Oaks, CA: Sage Publications. 349–358.

Kimmel, Michael S. 2007. Masculinity as homophobia: Fear, shame and silence in the construction of gender identity. In Nancy Cook, ed., *Gender Relations in Global Perspective: Essential Readings.* Toronto: Canadian Scholars' Press Inc. 73–82.

Kinsman, Gary. 1996. "These things may lead to the tragedy of our species": The emergence of homosexuality, lesbianism, and heterosexuality in Canada. *The Regulation of Desire: Homo and Hetero Sexualities,* 2nd ed. Montreal: Black Rose Books. 107–147.

Laqueur, Thomas. 1997. Orgasm, generation, and the politics of reproductive biology. In Roger N. Lancaster and Micaela di Leonardo, eds., *The Gender/Sexuality Reader: Culture, History, Political Economy.* New York: Routledge. 219–243.

Lawrence, Bonita. 2004. Regulating native identity by gender. *"Real" Indians and Others: Mixed-Blood Urban Native Peoples and Indigenous Nationhood.* Toronto: UBC Press. 45–63.

Loomba, Ania. 2005. *Colonialism/Postcolonialism.* New York: Routledge.

Lorde, Audre. 1984. *Sister Outsider: Essays & Speeches.* Freedom, CA: The Crossing Press.

Maracle, Lee. 1996. *I Am Woman: A Native Perspective on Sociology and Feminism.* Vancouver: Press Gang.

Martin, Emily. 2006. The egg and the sperm. In Inderpal Grewal and Caren Kaplan, eds., *An Introduction to Women's Studies: Gender in a Transnational World Second Edition.* Toronto: McGraw-Hill. 10–15.

Mawani, Renisa. 2002. In between and out of place: Mixed-race identity, liquor, and the law in British Columbia, 1850–1913. In Sherene Razack, ed., *Race, Space, and the Law: Unmapping a White Settler Society.* Toronto: Between the Lines. 47–69.

McClintock, Anne. 1995. *Imperial Leather: Race, Gender and Sexuality in the Colonial Contest.* New York: Routledge.

McKeen, Wendy. 2004. *Money in Their Own Name: The Feminist Voice in Poverty Debate in Canada, 1970–1995.* Toronto: University of Toronto Press.

Oudshoorn, Nelly. 2006. Sex and the body. In Inderpal Grewal and Caren Kaplan, eds., *An Introduction to Women's Studies: Gender in a Transnational World Second Edition.* Toronto: McGraw-Hill. 6–9.

Perry, Adele. 2001. *On the Edge of Empire: Gender, Race, and the Making of British Columbia, 1849–1871.* Toronto: University of Toronto Press.

Rankin, L. Pauline, and Jill Vickers. 2001. *Women's Movements and State Feminism: Integrating Diversity into Public Policy.* Ottawa: Status of Women Canada.

Razack, Sherene. 1991. *Canadian Feminism and the Law: The Women's Legal Education and Action Fund and the Pursuit of Equality.* Toronto: Second Story Press.

Rowbotham, Sheila. 2006. Feminist approaches to technology. In Inderpal Grewal and Caren Kaplan, eds., *An Introduction to Women's Studies: Gender in a Transnational World Second Edition.* Toronto: McGraw-Hill. 35–40.

Rubin, Gayle S. 1993. Thinking sex: Notes for a radical theory of the politics of sexuality. In Henry Abelove, Michele Aina Barale, and David M. Halperin, eds., *The Lesbian and Gay Studies Reader.* New York: Routledge. 3–44.

Scott, Joan Wallach. 2006. Gender and the politics of history. In Inderpal Grewal and Caren Kaplan, eds., *An Introduction to Women's Studies: Gender in a Transnational World Second Edition.* Toronto: McGraw-Hill. 19.

Shuttleworth, Russell P. 2004. Disabled masculinity: Expanding the masculine repertoire. In Bonnie G. Smith and Beth Hutchison, eds., *Gendering Disability.* New Brunswick, NJ: Rutgers University Press. 166–178.

Skeggs, Beverley. 2002. Ambivalent femininities. In Stevi Jackson and Sue Scott, eds., *Gender: A Sociological Reader.* New York: Routledge. 311–325.

Smith, Barbara. 1983. Introduction. In Barbara Smith, ed., *Home Girls: A Black Feminist Anthology.* Latham, NY: Kitchen Table Press. xix–lvi.

Smith, Dorothy E. 1993. *Texts, Facts, and Femininity: Exploring the Relations of Ruling.* New York: Routledge.

Stevenson, Winona. 1999. Colonialism and First Nations women in Canada. In Enakshi Dua and Angela Robertson, eds., *Scratching the Surface: Canadian Anti-Racist Feminist Thought.* Toronto: Women's Press. 49–80.

Stokes, Mason. 2001. *The Color of Sex: Whiteness, Heterosexuality, and the Fictions of White Supremacy.* Durham, NC: Duke University Press.

Stoler, Ann Laura. 2002. *Carnal Knowledge and Imperial Power: Race and the Intimate in Colonial Rule.* Los Angeles: University of California Press.

Vance, Carole S. 2006. Social construction theory. In Inderpal Grewal and Caren Kaplan, *An Introduction to Women's Studies: Gender in a Transnational World*, 2nd ed. Toronto: McGraw-Hill. 29–32.

5

Whiteness: Normalization and the Everyday Practice of Power

Cynthia Levine-Rasky *Queen's University*

INTRODUCTION

The term **whiteness** means different things for different readers. It might be interpreted literally: whiteness signals a skin colour. It might intimate "racism" or "White supremacy," or simply "dominant group." It might signify "power"; it might mean something to be feared, pitied, desired, or avoided. And for some, it might communicate nothing at all.

At the very least, most would link whiteness to a White racial identity, itself implying European ethnic heritage. Should this claim be accepted as common sense? Contemporary thought on race and ethnicity has taught us to be cautious of defining our identity in terms of fixed, singular traits. Identity is no longer regarded as an attribute "attached" to an individual like age or nationality. Nor is it best understood "objectively" in the sense that identity exists outside the historical and political contexts that created meanings of "White," "Asian," "Aboriginal," "Black," and so on. These categories are problematic, because they imply that the formation of identities somehow transcends conditions that gave rise to them, and that such conditions are benign. The study of whiteness, therefore, like the study of any racial or ethnic category, is best understood not as a character trait, skin colour, or adherence to a particular (for example, German, English, Polish) or general (for example, European, Canadian) ethnic consciousness. "Whiteness" is a term whose meaning turns out to be more complicated than that which is understood when it is taken at face value.

Consistent with critical perspectives in sociology, whiteness should be regarded as a social location whose meaning and status stands in strict relation to others. That is, even though whiteness refers to a position of structural advantage and social dominance facilitating the practice of power over subdominant groups, white **racefulness** (the quality of whiteness as a racial identity and social location) alone does not sufficiently explain whiteness (Levine-Rasky, 2002). Whiteness is characterized by differences in power. It is modified by its intersections with social class, gender, ethnicity, sexuality, ability, religion, age, and other dimensions of social identity. For example, Wray and Newitz (1997) state that poverty and working-classness among Whites challenge the generalization that whiteness is power. Frye (1992) argues that it is a mistake to regard White women as absolutely privileged when sexism, objectification, violence, and dependency continue to affect White women. Ethnicity provokes another set of questions about whiteness. Jewish whiteness, for example, is mitigated by the collective memory of the Holocaust as the ultimate moment in defining racial difference among a people now taken for granted as

White (despite the fact that not all Jews are racialized as White). Much attention has been given to the complex whiteness of other European groups (Roediger, 2005; Jacobson, 1999) including Irish (Ignatiev, 1995; Kenny, 2006), Italians (Guglielmo, 2003; Richards, 1999), and Romany (Mayall, 2004), and non-European groups like Latinos and Asians (Yancey, 2003). What can be concluded from this literature is that class, gender, and ethnicity sometimes reinforce and sometimes contradict whiteness (Anthias, 2005). In other words, the social domination enabled by the practice of whiteness can be fortified or mitigated for particular groups of White people, including the working class, women, and members of ethnic groups, as well as for others occupying positions of social difference marked by sexuality, age, religion, and ability. Despite the fact that these social dimensions produce real effects for White people, such differences within whiteness do not remove the imperative to study its broad effects. On this point, Garner explains, "the invocation of White identities may suspend other social divisions and link people who share whiteness to dominant social locations, even though the actors are themselves in positions of relative powerlessness" (2007: 3). For Garner, the structural advantage and social dominance conferred upon White people overrides any discrimination they may experience associated with their gender, class, ethnic, ability, and so on. Whiteness is practised despite the inequalities deriving from these other positions that can produce marginality.

In relation to social groups, whiteness functions not in the abstract or theoretical sense, but as a set of everyday practices that confer inclusion and exclusion among different groups. It affects the access subdominant groups have to power, resources, rewards, and choices. Canadian history is rife with examples. For decades, Canadian aboriginal peoples were constructed as "wards of the state," a concept that appears in the introduction of the 1876 *Indian Act* by the Minister of the Interior (its implication of dependency survives in the current term "fiduciary relationship"). The use of beaches, parks, movie theatres, clubs, and hotels by Jewish- and African-Canadians was controlled through restrictive signage, and de facto segregation continued even after antidiscrimination acts were passed in most of the provinces by 1964. During World War II, Japanese people (the majority of whom were Canadian-born) were constructed as national security risks, were interned in rural settlements, and had their property expropriated. Over a period of years in the 1960s, the neighbourhood of Africville in Halifax, Nova Scotia, was destroyed to "clear the slums" created by the city's neglect to provide public services to the community. A contemporary example is the heightened surveillance of Muslims through legislation such as the *Anti-Terrorism Act* of 2001 and the *Immigration and Refugee Protection Act* of 2002. Each of these examples shows not only the meaning of racial difference, but also how the meaning of whiteness is constructed in direct relation to that difference. Through such examples, racialized difference was identified as the object of social control, while whiteness was affirmed as generic, natural, and normal, and for which social control was irrelevant.

The social construction of difference and sameness, of racialized categories and of whiteness, are not dispassionate social processes. They are embroiled in power relations. To say that whiteness involves the practice of power implies a responsibility to critically examine it in relation to race, racism, and racialization, and to question how and why it ought to be studied at all. As a set of practices, such examination involves the "ways of whiteness," that is, how whiteness works in everyday life in addition to its economic and social effects. This chapter contributes to "unpacking the centre" by identifying whiteness as a vital component in that project. It shows how whiteness emerged historically, and its structural effect on producing material inequalities among groups. It then describes four "ways of whiteness," how whiteness actually works and how it accrues its power. Finally, it discusses what is entailed in challenging whiteness. Throughout, it takes a Foucaultian view of power—one in which power not only represses what is possible, but also, and more importantly for our purposes, creates possibilities. This chapter shows how whiteness-as-power enables identities, freedoms, and innocence, but at the expense of **racialized Others**.

The rationale for unpacking the centre occupied by whiteness is based on a few related principles:

1. Social justice and anti-racism must always inform the critical examination of whiteness. Social justice is a commitment to respecting legal structures that protect the human rights of all persons equally. However, "where social group differences exist and some groups are privileged while others are oppressed, social justice requires explicitly acknowledging and attending to those group differences in order to undermine oppression" (Young, 1990: 3). In other words, social justice entails the redistribution of opportunities in society to more fairly respond to the structural disadvantages of some groups. Anti-racism places the problem of racism at the centre of analysis, examining "how those asymmetrical power relations serve to position different bodies and their experiences in the larger web of systemic and institutionalized networks" (Dei, 2008: 51).

2. Critical studies of whiteness are impelled by the need to understand the impact of racism not on those groups who are always regarded as its victims, but on whiteness itself and on those groups racialized as white. This entails what Toni Morrison calls a "serious intellectual effort to see what racial ideology does to the mind, imagination, and behavior of masters" (Morrison, 1992: 11–12).

3. Whiteness is thoroughly relational, that is, it produces disadvantage and exclusion for racialized groups and affirmation, advantage, and inclusion for White groups.

4. An analysis of the social relations of power replaces individualistic explanations of racism. Racial and social inequities are structured in society in such a way that they affect the quality of engagement between groups of people.

5. Whites can never entirely know the scope and experience of racism just as the economically privileged can never entirely know the scope and experience of poverty. Since White peoples' standpoint excludes a full knowledge of racism, it is critical to turn to the standpoint of racialized Others whose everyday experience of racism confers **epistemic privilege** upon them. Whiteness studies "must remain open to those non-white voices that continue to reveal the extent to which they actually suffer and feel terrorized by whiteness" (Yancy, 2004: 17). Dyson explains the basis of the epistemic privilege of Black peoples and why the knowledge of whiteness that they and other racialized Others have is credible:

> … white folk placed us behind them, in what they deemed an inferior position. As a result, we were able to learn white folk [*sic*]—their beliefs, sentiments, contradictions, cultures, styles, behaviors, virtues, and vices. Black survival depended on black folk knowing the ways and souls of white folk. It's only fitting now that we turn to African American and Latino, Asian, and Native American scholars, workers, intellectuals, artists, and everyday folk to understand whiteness. (Dyson, quoted by Chennault, 1998: 325; annotation mine)

It is incumbent upon those who support these principles to listen to and act upon the epistemically privileged knowledge of racism possessed by racialized peoples.[1] In a final section, this chapter discusses how whiteness may be challenged. First, however, some terms must be defined.

POWER

Power is one of the driving concepts in sociological inquiry. As you have read in previous chapters, French philosopher Michel Foucault (1926–1984) introduced a unique way of conceptualizing power that has been enormously influential. While Foucault's writings on power are extensive and diffuse, this chapter focuses on one of his approaches to the problem of power that parallels an analysis of whiteness. Foucault (1980: 57–8) suggests that "nothing is more material, physical, corporal than the exercise of power," but power does not work in one direction from the top down as from leaders to subjects. Nor do modern forms of power work through direct coercion or physical violence. Foucault explains that power should not be regarded in the negative sense as in "power over" something. In his words, it "is more than that which limits, obstructs, or refuses." Instead, Foucault urges that power is productive, constructing new capacities and modes of activity. "What makes power hold good, what makes it accepted, is simply the fact that it doesn't only weigh on us as a force that says no, but that it traverses and produces things, it induces pleasure, forms of knowledge, produces discourse" (1980: 119). Power is not an abstract force, but a practice. It proceeds in and through and amid social groups and individuals. The kind of "pleasure" it produces involves personal identity, personal capacities, and a desire for change. Power can repress the possible but it can also create new conditions of the possible.

Theorists of critical whiteness may find a radical parallel in Foucault's approach to power in the way it provides an alternative to the language of critique. Writing on whiteness usually refers to White racism and its denial, its resistance to dialogue, its ignorance

---

1   This is not to suggest that all racialized individuals share identical knowledge of racism or that all such knowledge is of identical value (Narayan, 1988). This assumption is common in anti-racism workshops in which racialized participants, seen as representatives of their group, are burdened with alleviating racism by disclosing their experiences of it. The problem is that avoidance of talk about whiteness and racism protects the innocence of the White participants (Srivastava, 2007). Instead of attributing "truth" to a speaker by virtue of her identification as racialized, it's preferable to concede to the "critically conscious knower" (Wylie, 2003: 34). This kind of speaker has a specifically critical perspective and insight into power relations.

of injustices, its defensiveness. It analyzes how whiteness oppresses and how it excludes. Focusing exclusively on this language obscures a crucial feature of whiteness: its negative effects are also productive for whiteness. The practice of whiteness creates even as it oppresses. That is, denial, ignorance, and distance accomplish something positive for whiteness: they support its demands for **normalization**. In this sense, whiteness operates like Foucault's concept of power. If as Foucault contends, power does not descend but circulates, if it is "exercised upon the dominant as well as on the dominated" (Dreyfus & Rabinow, 1983: 186), it follows that power is productive as it shapes a positive whiteness in relation to the racialization of difference (Layder, 1997). Power exercised through whiteness accomplishes its relative "superiority," a legitimacy in its distance from the difficult, an immunity from its complicity in racism, a confirmation of its merits and entitlements, a reproduction of its power, a pleasure in itself, and so on. Cast in terms of the productive, we may learn a great deal about what whiteness does rather than simply acknowledging its negative effects on non-White groups (Levine-Rasky, 2000).

Three related terms remain to be defined: race, racism, and racialization. **Race** is an arbitrary and socially constructed classification of persons on the basis of real or imagined physical characteristics. Race has no scientific meaning; there is only a singularity known as the human race. *Race is not a natural occurrence, but a consequence of power relations.* The persistence of the term can be explained by its emphatically social significance. Used to define and reinforce the unequal relations between dominant and subordinate groups, race came into being and continues to be deployed for purposes of social control. Its meaning is elastic, engaging social, cultural, and national differences wider than the physical distinctions the term commonly signals. This elasticity enables powerful agencies to put it to use to justify their domination over racialized groups, whether that domination takes the form of genocide, segregation, colonization, assimilation, or merely keeping people "in their place."

Racism involves the discrimination of a group of people differentiated and evaluated on the basis of their alleged or real physical or social qualities. Often attributed to institutional procedures, systemic inequities, or structural practices, racism is evident in its effects as it affirms power relations and structural advantage and disadvantage. Racism needn't involve hate, nor even intentionality (Goldberg, 1993: 100), as evident in one manifestation of racism: the exclusion of racialized people from equal competition in the labour market, housing, and schools. Decisions and policies (such as limiting access to schools located in privileged neighbourhoods, or restrictive immigration policies) are unlikely to make any reference to hate, but they assert racism nonetheless by controlling or preventing access to goods and services, opportunities and privileges, on the basis of racialized difference. Racism is not only manifest at the level of social structures and institutions; it also involves exclusion at the level of everyday interactions. It is "manifest not only in extreme epithets but in insinuations and suggestions, in reasoning and representations, in short, in the microexpressions of daily life" (Goldberg, 1997: 20).

Racialization is a process in which "race" is attributed to a population of people, facilitating the practice of racism against them. Such groups are regarded as fundamentally different from the dominant group. Their ostensible differences are seen as essential to the nature of that group and as determining its capacities. As such, they form a basis on which to evaluate members of the group relative to the dominant group (Miles & Brown, 2003). Historically, racialization arose during the time of subjugation of non-Western civilizations through colonial control, physical and cultural domination, and economic superiority. A scientific catalogue of racial otherness generated "a classificatory order of racial grouping—subspecies of Homo sapiens" as well as categories for these groupings such as "exotic," "oriental," "Negro," "Indian," and so on (Goldberg, 1993: 29–30). This classification of racial difference included the racialization of whiteness. "[T]he European, or Euro-American, nations fiercely competing for the world's colonial spoils recognized an identity … which they baptized 'White'" (Balibar, 1990: 286).

THE EMERGENCE OF WHITENESS

The first mention of "White" to denote a social group reflects the undeniable relationality of whiteness to racialized difference; its articulation was entirely contingent on the presence of Blackness. According to Taylor (2005) this event was unrelated to England's involvement in the slave trade or its colonization of Ireland. It arose instead in London's popular culture. In a play written by Thomas Middleton in 1613, it is a Black character, a "king of the Moors," who first uses the descriptor "White" for the London masses in attendance at this popular cultural event (Taylor, 2005: 126). Europeans learned they were "White" only through their recognition as such by other groups with whom they came in contact whether they were "Roanokes in 1584, Mohawks in western New England in the early 1630s, [or] Africans in Barbados in 1666" (Taylor, 2005: 188).

Whiteness and Englishness became conflated in London popular culture as well as in elite discourse of religion, politics, science, and philosophy. English whiteness—and its attachment to moral superiority—grew with the Reformation of 1517 when Catholics were concentrated in southern Europe and Protestants in the north creating the "distinction between the 'The Southern man, a Black deformed elf' and the 'Northern White, like unto God himself'" (Peyton, 1620, cited in Taylor, 2005: 229). The putative superiority of whiteness gleaned from economic expansion was deployed to justify England's involvement in the very slave trade that produced its economic wealth. From the 15th to the 17th centuries, morality, intelligence, and status were linked irretrievably to whiteness (Babb, 1998). You will learn more about these processes in Part IV of this text book, "Thinking Global."

In the British colonies, White supremacy received support from policy and legislation created by London's Council for Foreign Plantations. In a 1661 document in which the first generic use of the term "White" was made, the Council refers to the desirability of White to Black slaves. The former were free "after certain years," while the latter were "perpetual servants" and a "treacherous and unsteady people" (Taylor, 2005: 263, 264). The document aided in institutionalizing this hierarchy that had been established in the American and Caribbean colonies decades earlier. Poor and unpropertied Englishmen could obtain land in the colonies if they agreed to become indentured workers for a number of years in either agriculture or a trade. Their treatment was as harsh as that of

Black slaves. By 1619, English tobacco planters in Virginia were trading in "English men and boys," whose conditions were so bad there and elsewhere that a group of English servants staged an armed insurrection in Barbados in 1634. To control the limits of such conflicts in which English workers demanded property rights, authorities began to use the term "White" to distinguish between forms of servitude. By the 1670s, Blacks were slaves, Whites were servants.

It took some time before American labour organizations were to exploit this distinction. Prior to the American Revolution of 1775–1781, Black and White groups in the south interacted in labour and in social life. During this period, wage labour was sometimes called "wage slavery" regardless of the race of the workers, but northern Whites appreciated that the conditions for enslaved Blacks were worse than even for the poorest Whites (Roediger, 1991). The Black population was the antithesis of a free and independent workforce. To this end, White workers were encouraged by abolitionists (those who advocated an end to slavery) to abandon the phrase "wage slavery" in the interest of forming a distinct and cohesive labour force. Yet this campaign was challenged by organized White labour movements concerned with maintaining White supremacy in the workplace. Thus, the new republic of the United States engaged the slogan of freedom but sustained a dependency on the enslaved Black against which it generated itself. In this way, fundamental difference between White and Black workers was a fabrication deliberated through legal, economic, and ideological means to buttress the interests of an emerging White middle class.

"White" was demarcated from "Black" and from "Native" in order to maintain White privilege through the political and legal boundaries of marriage, property rights, and economic and physical mobility.[2] All that came to matter was whiteness, an expansive process that elided real differences among European settlers. These settlers included those of Scottish, Welsh, Irish, and English origin, and eventually others (Dutch, German, etc.), who became monolithically White regardless of significant differences in class, occupation, and ethnicity. As diverse and often inhospitable these groups were to each other, they were collectively unambiguous in relation to aboriginals and African slaves. Their collectivity expedited the emergence of whiteness as a constructed social category enabling the formation of a myth of commonality resilient enough to withstand challenges by diverse religious, migrant, and racial groups.

THE EFFECTS OF WHITENESS

The effects of whiteness can be observed in social life and institutions. Its structural impacts are overwhelming in scope and sobering in their human cost. The effects of whiteness are made concrete in people's lives through the quality of their participation in society, which is often measured by differences in income, wealth, occupation, and opportunity that empowers Whites as it disempowers non-Whites (Galabuzi, 2006;

---

2   Avid dedication to maintaining those boundaries eventually led to the notorious 1857 "one drop" rule governing ineligibility for such privileges due to the presence of the smallest proportion of non-White heritage.

Li, 1988, 1998; Pendakur & Pendakur, 1996; Gee & Prus, 2000; Galarneau & Morissette, 2008). The totality of such effects is not restricted to economic benefits. They also touch people in subtle ways encountered every day. Young observes that the injustices that some groups suffer are conveyed by the "often unconscious assumptions and reactions of well-meaning people in ordinary interactions, media and cultural stereotypes, and structural features of bureaucratic behavior and market mechanisms—in short, the normal processes of everyday life" (1990: 41).

THE WAYS OF WHITENESS

Given that whiteness confers structural advantage and privilege, that it operates like a conceptual standpoint, and that it intersects with other notions of social identity, including gender, class, sexuality, and age (all of which are explored in this textbook) (Frankenberg, 1993; 2001), what can be said about how it works? Four answers to that question are elaborated in this section: (1) Whiteness works through processes of normalization by silently imposing itself as the standard by which social difference is known; (2) Whiteness is assumed to arise from no particular social context and imply no particular bias in its knowledge about the world; we may identify this problem as one of **White solipsism**, a concept discussed below; (3) Whiteness controls the terms through which it engages racialized difference; this involves the classification and differentiation of racialized people and assignment of degrees of significance and agency to them; and (4) Whiteness is sustained and rationalized through ideological commitments to colour-blindness and **democratic racism**, an ideology characterized by a simultaneous commitment to both liberal democratic values of fairness, justice, and equality *and* attitudes and behaviours consistent with racism. While overlapping in the practice of everyday life, each of these points is discussed separately. Each involves whiteness as structural advantage and as a set of practices, and each of them is made complex by the way individuals understand their intersecting social identities. Finally, each of them is informed by the principles outlined above: social justice/ anti-racism; relationality; a critical perspective on the social relations of power; and the epistemic privilege embodied in the knowledge of **racialized persons** who share that perspective. Examples gleaned from research and personal narrative are integrated to convey the quality of everyday experience.

Normalization

Whiteness works through processes of normalization by silently imposing itself as the standard by which social difference is to be known.

As you read in Chapter 2, **normalization** is a term developed by French philosopher Michel Foucault to denote the way in which a particular version of things comes to be seen as standard, true, or "normal." It is used to differentiate, hierarchize, homogenize, and exclude, in social institutions that include education, social welfare organizations, and the justice system (Foucault, 1977: 183). In this way, the knowledge that emerges forms a **regime of truth**, and creates the conditions for what is considered possible.

FIGURE 5.1 ▨ Detail of the San Giusto Polyptych by Paolo Veneziano. This work represents Christ, angels, and human figures, all of whom have darkly pigmented skin. Early Christian art includes many examples of Jesus, Mary, saints, and other figures who appear in various shades of brown consistent with their Mediterranean origin. The figure was "whitened" beginning in the late 15th century during the Italian Renaissance (Taylor, 2005), becoming increasingly white over time (Dyer, 1997). Today, Christ is normalized as a white European, "with flowing wavey, fair hair and a light complexion … indubitable exemplars of white as moral symbol" (Dyer, 1997: 68).

© Elio Ciol/CORBIS

Sanctioned knowledge such as that authorized by whiteness cannot be constant, unified, or true in any form distinct from its particular context. Whiteness emerges from the approved knowledge of a period sanctioning some relationships and censoring others. Processes of differentiation and normalization, of discrimination and affirmation, are coextensive such that white individuals constitute themselves as raced, classed, and gendered subjects through the exclusion of Others as raced, classed, gendered subjects. In explaining the implications of this, Stubblefield makes a statement generalizable to the relations between whiteness and all forms of racialized difference: "… white supremacist belief need not involve conscious dislike for what is symbolic of or associated with blackness, but rather exists so long as a person takes what is symbolic of or associated with whiteness as normative" (2005: 74).

Normalization has become a popular theoretical tool for identifying the arbitrariness of assigning "normal" status to many things most of us take for granted, and many of which are discussed in this textbook: heterosexuality, capitalism, the nuclear family, poverty, individuality, conspicuous consumption, romantic love. It is a powerful concept for uprooting certainty about foundational categories of thought and forces us to account for the way in which a particular meaning has become hegemonic. Whiteness is normalized by functioning in Western and non-Western societies as the standard against which "difference" is contrasted. It is unremarkable, featureless, and common. An example: How often does a White person think about the proportion of White professionals with whom they deal? More rarely: How often does a White person think about White privilege as a factor in obtaining access to property, university, or a good job? Indeed, the most common response to such a question is vehement resistance, even hostility. The normalization of whiteness is strictly guarded, since a characteristic of normalization and what gives it such power is its ability to not know itself. "Power is tolerable only on condition that it mask a substantial part of itself. Its success is proportional to its ability to hide its own mechanisms" (Foucault, 1979: 86), in effect concealing its own invention through institutional practices (Foucault, 1972).

Dyer (1997) provides an insightful exploration of the normalization of whiteness. He states, "The wide application of White as symbol, in non-racially specific contexts makes it appear neutral: White as good is a universal abstraction, it just happens that it coincides with people whose skin is deemed White. The uncertainties of whiteness as a hue, a colour and yet not a colour, make it possible to see the bearers of White skin as non-specific, ordinary and mere.... To name and to sense White people as White ... has provided a breathtakingly effective means of maintaining our non-particular, particular power" (1997: 70). In many contexts, whiteness functions as a symbol for "neutral" and "good." It appears to have no relation to the racialization of White people. Instead, the whiteness of White people is purely accidental, nonspecific, and ordinary. It passes without comment and is detached from considerations of race and racism, much less from considerations of structural advantage, standpoint, or the practice of power. Whiteness transcends the particulars of race (and racism) because it symbolizes the universal, the human race. "It is everything and nothing, literally overwhelmingly present and yet apparently absent, both alive and dead" (Dyer, 1997: 39). This position is paradoxical, for how can whiteness be everything and yet nothing at the same time? Yet this instability is precisely how whiteness is normalized, through the ability to conceal itself. We often hear, for example, that race doesn't matter because everyone shares the same essential qualities in "just being human." However, for white peoples, this asserts a kind of arrogance in dismissing the experiences of racialized groups. It centres whiteness as the universal standard for "being human," yet it also makes it disappear by presuming that race is irrelevant. Whiteness is at once everything and nothing.

As in the **ideology** of colour-blindness, whiteness makes it taboo to talk of the body. In this situation, normalization functions by placing the body at the centre of discourse, where the body assumes central meaning but is unacknowledged. We can think of this as the creation of a particular **body politic** that comes to "incorporate a vision of power" through the way it includes and excludes members and non-members (Goldberg, 1993: 54). This power arises from how the body is "read" since "visible inscriptions" on the body are "correlated with rational capacity, epistemic reliability, moral condition, and, of course, aesthetic status" (Alcoff, 1999: 23). Race is therefore a repository of power and a symbol for social relations, despite the ways of whiteness that render this knowledge less visible.

Solipsism

Whiteness assumes social and epistemological independence, a problem we may identify as "White solipsism." This involves the achievement of a psychic distance from its interdependence with racialized Others as well as an abdication of responsibility for its effects.

Solipsism—the idea that only the self can be known—is evident in the everyday practices of whiteness. Most Whites can go about their lives giving race no thought whatsoever except as it may intrude upon the accepted privileges of their lives. Even in cases of relationships with friends and coworkers, race is articulated at the risk of offending social propriety. Most White, middle-class people can live, shop, travel, raise families, attend school, marry, work, and die without meaningful interactions with racialized people. The adage that "some of my best friends are Black" is often false; available research indicates that only 9.4 percent of Whites can name one good Black friend (Jackman & Crane, cited in Bonilla-Silva, 2001: 98). Feagin and O'Brien (2003: 61) observe that White American college students' friendships with racialized peers are usually limited in nature and superficial in quality. This is characteristic of life in the "White bubble," note the authors. Are things better in Canada? When measured by attitudes toward intermarriage, immigration, and integrated neighbourhoods, "social distance" between groups has diminished in Canada and the United States, but especially in Canada (Reitz & Breton, 1998). However, people in the two countries typically share the belief that minorities are responsible for their own inequality, and they are "extremely reluctant" to support equity policies. These findings suggest White solipsism in which there is social distance of a kind that permits detachment from the experiences of racialized groups.

There is tremendous resistance to self-reflection around the social taboo of racism. White solipsism ensures an abdication of responsibility for the problem by dismissing the relevance of economic and cultural inequalities organized on the basis of race. The ways of whiteness are consistent with theories that explain racial inequality in a publicly acceptable way. Success is attributed to individual exceptionality in the case of the socially marginalized, and failure is attributed to personal inadequacy (Frankenberg, 1993; Stanfield, 1991). Alternatively, Whites minimize the significance of racism by defining the social issues associated with it as "non-problems" easily identified with personal or group characteristics (Kluegel & Smith, 1986). White solipsism may generate outright denial of racism construed as a humanitarian gesture of equality. However, as Sullivan points out, "White people's naïve ignorance of race and racism has become the gift they offer non-White people in place of their recognition of non-White gifts to the world. Its wistfulness is composed not only of the regretful apology that White people are (allegedly) unable to notice race, but also of a yearning desire that non-White people accept the gift and thereby absolve White people of any responsibility to learn to see race and racial injustice" (2006: 128). Conversely, when sympathy for racialized groups arises, Whites may express the view that all people are alike regardless of colour, or that "they" are ultimately like "us." The implication is that Whites are benevolent in extending a common humanity from White people to Others. The problem with this position should be evident.

Sullivan (2006: 17) argues that White solipsism produces an "ethical solipsism" in which only White values, interests, and needs are considered important and worthy of attention. This problem goes beyond the lack of meaningful relationships with racialized people or the denial of racism. It means the creation of a psychic distance between a population identified as "us," and another identified as "them." Ultimately, it expresses a lack of emotional investment—of care—in regarding this social arrangement as problematic as a

FIGURE 5.2 ■ Arab stereotypes. Racial stereotyping is a common feature of popular culture. How do these representations, found in graphic novels, provide insights into their impact from the perspective of their racialized authors? How does this challenge readers' white solipsism?

Source: Toufic El Rassi, 2007. *Arab in America,* p. 76 and 77. San Francisco: Last Gasp. Reprinted by permission of the publisher.

social injustice meted out to racialized groups. Mills writes that Whites cultivate "patterns of affect and empathy that are only weakly, if at all, influenced by nonwhite suffering" (1997: 95). Goldberg (2006: 347) is poignant in his remarks on this point: "Why are the experiences of some alive to us while others fail to be recognized…. Why do we recognize the death or disappearance of some, of those we deem 'our own' individually and collectively, more so, more readily than others? We deem some closer, more recognizable, more like or connected to us physically, temporally, culturally, and consequently we more readily commemorate their contributions to our social lives. What brings them closer, elevates them, sanctifies them?"

If "we" rarely think about "them" much less take responsibility for distancing "ourselves" from "them," surely this weighs heavily against the potential for building relationships of true engagement.

Control

Whiteness controls the terms through which it engages racialized difference. This involves the differentiation of racialized people and assignment of degrees of significance and agency to them.

Various forms of control over racialized Others are exercised in the everyday practice of whiteness. One is the invention of knowledge about the Other. For example, knowledge on colonized populations, which was deemed integral to the functioning of colonial administration, was collected all over the world (Neu & Therrien, 2003). This official information acquired the status of objective fact, while the subjective knowledge of colonized peoples evident in their own stories and histories was silenced. As a result, self-determination was impaired. A related practice is the conferral of a collective identity upon the racialized Other as an undifferentiated mass. In contrast, whiteness is regarded as supremely individualistic

One strategy deployed by the mass media is exemplified in the reporting on the new Africentric schools in the Toronto school board. Rejected by a majority of readers of the national newspaper, the issue was often reduced to one of African-Canadians' desire for "segregation," a concept in conflict with Canadian values of multiculturalism. This word choice ignores the meaning of segregation in the history of African-Canadians, whose segregation in schools and elsewhere in society was legal up to the 1950s. With overrepresentation of African-Canadian students in special education programs, and their disproportionate subjection to disciplinary measures, de facto segregation in schools continues in many jurisdictions. The discourse favoured by the mainstream media (and its readers) in its coverage of this issue demonstrated what van Dijk calls "speech acts" involving accusations to derogate "them" and defences to legitimate "us" and "our" dismissal of "them." In this case, the language used by the mainstream media confirmed the legitimacy of the dominant ahistorical interpretation of "segregation." It disqualified its meaning for the group who were fighting for a public education that would mitigate their inequality that has been produced by segregation. Media coverage of discrimination and racism in society is "at most about popular resentment (very seldom or never about elite racism), about individual cases of discrimination, for example, on the job, or about extremist racist parties. In other words, discrimination and racism, when discussed at all in elite discourse, are always elsewhere" (van Dijk, 2002: 153). The orientation of public discourse in the mainstream media and in organizations reflects selective meanings, beliefs, and concerns about racialized groups. The most powerful messages are those endorsed by leaders in society who enjoy privileged access to dominant institutions and hence control the means of engaging racialized difference.

FIGURE 5.3 ■ Multicultural festivals are a popular form of controlling the terms on which racial difference is engaged. Not only is difference reduced to historical artifact whose meaning has long dissipated for the groups it is intended to represent, but the personal experience of difference is made irrelevant. Instead, such events render racial difference as apolitical and thus highly appropriate for family entertainment.

(Garner, 2007). The process of racialization creates negative meanings for entire social groups that have been racialized. Hurtado calls this "degrouping" and explains its consequences for racialized groups: "In effect, the nonwhite ethnic/racial group is (de)grouped and cannot serve the usual positive functions that groups serve—providing a basis for positive social identity, group solidarity, a sense of belonging and empowerment. At the same time, whiteness does serve those functions for its possessors" (Hurtado, 1996: 156). The boat carrying Tamil people, which was escorted to a military port on the British Columbia coast in August, 2010, serves as an example. Described as victims of human smuggling rings and housed in prisons while being processed, the refugees were constructed as symbols of lax Canadian immigration policy despite the existing *Immigrant and Refugee Protection Act* that penalizes offenders with $1 million and life in prison (and employers of such refugees a maximum of $50,000). Virtually no attention was given to the reasons why the refugees needed to flee their country of origin. As a result, they are regarded as a pathetic mass, a people without their own identity or power. The Canadian state appears as benevolent (or foolhardy according to its critics) to have accepted the refugees as its burden.

An example of the ways in which whiteness controls the terms on which it engages racial difference can be found in research on White parents' responses to the presence of non-White students enrolled at the neighbourhood elementary school (Levine-Rasky, 2007). Parent interviews reveal the construction of such children as ignorant of Western education, disruptive in behaviour, neglected at home, and traumatized by the refugee experience. Two excerpts follow.

> So, the teacher was dealing with not just children from a different culture—like, if you came from France of something—she was dealing with someone who has never even been exposed to books before. And so, they're light years behind children that have been to kindergarten and junior kindergarten and all that kind of stuff. And that's very hard for a teacher. I mean, they, you know, she's dealing with kids at that level and there's several behavioural problems.

> I mean, I don't want my kid to associate with kids whose parents don't care whether their kids do well at school, who don't care about whether [she] is, you know, filthy dirty ... so, if a lot of those kids are coming from homes where the parents have maybe been so traumatized because of escaping from wherever they were that they don't have—they're so busy trying to make a living here that their kids are kind of neglected in some way or whatever—that's not a common, a common, that's not a common thing for my kids to—that's not a common experience.

The first speaker, Fern, believes that the immigrant children with whom her sons shared a classroom were markedly behind, even backward, in their adaptation to life at the school. Their cumulative deficits would be detrimental for children like Fern's, who have more than adequate preparation for the demands of elementary school. Fern is leading to a conclusion that such classrooms are inappropriate for her children since, among other things, the teachers can't cope with the diverse range of needs. The second speaker, Barb, differentiates the immigrant children and their families on the basis of their alleged neglect and trauma. She hesitates, but despite her recognition of the impact of the refugee experience, Barb will conclude that this degree of difference is simply too much for her children to endure.

Research such as this demonstrates how whiteness works through differentiating racialized people and using such differentiation to justify personhood in terms of relative merit and agency. Despite his use of the Black/White binary, Yancy's remarks have a broader meaning: "The problem is that one's whiteness, a center from which one has always already cut up the social world, makes sense of things, evaluates and judges, remains invisible while the discursive field of White power/knowledge continues to open up a social space of intelligibility in terms of which the Black/White body appears" (Yancy, 2004: 9–10). Ultimately, whiteness effects an idea of personhood. Conferred upon Whites who take it for granted, personhood is mitigated for non-Whites through the ways in which whiteness operates.

Ideology

Whiteness is sustained and rationalized through ideological commitments to colour-blindness and **democratic racism***.*

Complex networks of ideas play a role in maintaining the everyday practice of whiteness. This is the function of ideology. While ideology generally functions as broad prescriptive frameworks for making sense of the world, such frameworks do not draw from a neutral repertoire of beliefs or ideas, but from "relations of domination" (Bonilla-Silva, 2001: 63). Ideology is best understood as an unconscious system of beliefs representing the interests of a particular group and edging out alternative systems. As you read in Chapter 2, even though it is enforced through dominant structures such as the state, ideology typically operates peacefully through cultural means, reflected in the distribution of popular knowledge. In this way, the ruling ideas of a society operate hegemonically through forging a "common sense" shared even by those groups for whom it is not in their interest to do so. The convergence of political and moral beliefs affects groups differently. With regard to hegemonic values affecting racism and racialization, ideology shapes "the conscious and unconscious sum of ideas, prejudices, and myths that crystallize the victories and defeats of the races …" (Bonilla-Silva, 2001: 64). Commonsense knowledge about racialized difference reflects the "ways of whiteness," since people do not mechanistically follow ideology, but rather "participate in the construction, development, and transformation of racial ideology as, after all, it is in their racial interest to maintain White supremacy" (Bonilla-Silva, 2001: 64).

One of the most common ideological instruments deployed by whiteness is colour-blindness. Colour-blindness allows the avoidance of racist terminology and provides a variety of "rhetorical shields" against the allegation of racism (Bonilla-Silva, 2001: 69). Although colour-blindness sounds progressive, it is ironically used to explain and justify racial inequality. In supporting equality, fairness, and meritocracy as abstract principles, it denies the existence of systemic discrimination. As a result, colour-blindness furnishes acceptable ways to reject race-sensitive equity policies and to do so while sounding principled. This is because widely respected terms like "equality," "fairness," and "individuality" are "motherhood" concepts; it's virtually impossible to mount an argument against them. However, their actual meanings are wide and vague enough that they can be strategically deployed as justification for discrimination, even racism. Predictably, colour-blindness reveals inconsistencies in its position. The excerpt below summarizes Canadian survey research on opinions about multiculturalism that reflects the contradictions intrinsic to the position of colour-blindness.

> There is now substantial evidence to show that normative inconsistencies regarding democratic principles and the signification of "race" comfortably coexist in the ideas of Canadians…. Several opinions polls gathered in 2002 and 2003 confirmed that Canadians overwhelmingly considered multiculturalism to be important to Canadian identity. They also agreed that the preservation and enhancement of Canada's multicultural heritage promotes the sharing of common values and enhances Canadian citizenship (Jedwab and Baker 2003; Jedwab 2002a cited in Li 2005). Yet, in another poll conducted in 2002, 43 per cent of respondents thought there were too many immigrants from Arab countries; 40 per cent thought there were too many from Asian countries; and 24 per cent thought there were too many from African countries (Jedwab, 2002b cited in Li 2005). Meanwhile, 39 per cent of the respondents said the number of immigrants coming each year was right, and another 14 per cent said the number was too few (Jedwab 2002b; *Ottawa Citizen* 2002 cited in Li 2005). In short, it would appear that many Canadians have little trouble accepting the democratic values of multiculturalism and diversity on the one hand while supporting policy choices premised upon colour or origin on the other. (Li, 2005: 4, 7)

These "normative inconsistencies" in which people support beliefs both in multicul-turalism and in limiting multiculturalism indicate what Henry and Tator (2000; 2006) call "democratic racism." **Democratic racism** functions to reconcile a deep contradiction in North American society. On the one hand, there is knowledge of pervasive racism as evidenced by patterns of social, economic, and cultural exclusion. On the other hand, there is popular commitment to liberal democracy whose tenets include equality, justice, and individual rights and freedoms. Whiteness is concurrent with faith in the latter at the expense of acknowledging the former. This is accomplished through support for those policies that uphold these abstract principles like equality but work against other policies designed to respond to social factors that hold people back from taking advantage of equal opportunity. We often hear remarks like this one uttered by a white middle-class man who adopts a form of colour-blindness in reaction against affirmative action policies:

> I would be more inclined to … view myself with others who have done or are going to do or would like to do the sorts of things that I have done with my life, whether they were black, pink, or purple. I don't think there's much difference…. I think that people ought to be judged on the merits of what they do or have done or plan to do. (Cited in Feagin & O'Brien, 2003: 73)

Reducing the effects of racism to a fiction on par with pink or purple skin colour, Whites like this individual deploy the ideology of colour-blindness to maintain their power.

CHALLENGING WHITENESS

In this chapter, whiteness is defined as a position of structural advantage and social dom-inance facilitating the practice of power over the inclusion and exclusion among different groups. This set of practices involves differential access to resources, rewards, and futures and more subtle inequities experienced in the everyday quality of life. In challenging whiteness, thought and action should be informed by the principles of social justice and anti-racism. Participants must commit themselves to struggling against whiteness in terms of the structural advantages it confers, the standpoint it provides, and the practices that spin off from it. If power is productive in the Foucaultian sense as suggested in this chapter, its exercise confers legitimacy upon the ways of whiteness. It enables a peaceful-ness with itself and with its disengagement from questions of race. Whiteness must be challenged in a relational way such that positive white identities, freedoms, and discourse are understood to exist in direct relation to their effects on racialized Others. Because we live within social relations, there is no absolute disjuncture between whiteness and Other. At some level, White people are aware of their interdependency with Others. Yet the powerful ways of whiteness inhibit full knowledge of how this relationship is shaped by normalization, solipsism, control, and ideology. What is required is a refusal to accept ignorance of this relationship as the final position on whiteness. Ignorance may feel like innocence. It extends advantages such as an ease with the effects of the everyday practice of whiteness, a feeling that one's conduct is appropriate. The challenge, however, is to reject a self-shielding and social shielding from racial realities; to reject what Mills refers to as

epistemology of ignorance (1997: 45, 93), a term that stresses how whiteness is sustained. Mills argues that White peoples not only passively derive advantages through normalization, solipsism, control, and ideology; they also are actively invested in unknowing racism. Ignorance accords a moral benefit to whiteness involving "an agreement to *mis*interpret the world … validated by white epistemic authority" (Mills, 1997: 18). Ignorance makes sense for whiteness. It facilitates positive things like confidence, achievement, justification, pleasure, and the effects of power that circulate through the social body.

The way forward is not easy. It requires emotional work. How so? For White people, recognition that one is participating and deriving benefits from whiteness can be traumatic. It risks making a profound offence against the internalized acceptance that social arrangements basically make sense and that one's position in life is entirely legitimate, rational, and justified. The admission of the wide context in which not fairness, but structural unfairness exists, upsets the whole house of cards in which whiteness precariously lives.

At the very least, it is necessary to refuse participation in all forms of exclusion of racialized Others, including gross structural injustices as well as subtle everyday practices. However, more is required. On this, Goldberg asserts that "those occupying any position of power be open to the deep and abiding influences of those deemed Other, of 'the Other's' values and commitments. It requires that the society not just acknowledge 'incidents' or 'events,' but that it engage in dialogic exchanges, taking seriously—and being moved by— the positions and ideas of those who have been marginalized; that those in positions of relative power be open, in theory and practice, policy and social structure, to the transformative implications of those over whom they exercise power" (Goldberg, 1997: 24). This means granting epistemic privilege to the knowledge of racialized Others; this requires "methodological humility" and "methodological caution" (Narayan, 1988: 37, 38).

Challenging whiteness entails really listening to and hearing remarks like this one, expressed by a participant in a study on the effects of racial profiling of Canadian Muslims after 9/11.

> It's very difficult to describe to someone who hasn't gone through these experiences about how painful and how humiliating it [racial profiling of Canadian Muslims] is … it's really a horrible feeling…. I learned the hard way just to live with it. So, do I want to continue living with it? No, it's horrible it's very stressful doing something to his or her own humanity. You are ripping someone apart not because they're a bad person but because of the colour of their skin or where they were born and raised…. (Participant RPAI-45, cited in Gova & Rahat 2008)

Learning from this knowledge requires Whites to abandon the impulse to assume their own knowledge of racism. Instead, Whites must reverse this tendency and strive to "unknow epistemic authority, unknow innocence, and unknow exaggerated white agency" (Howard, 2009: 264) in a spirit of humility and faith. The process will feel uncomfortable for many. The key is to neither expect a reconciliation of one's feelings nor to accept reconciliation as a goal of such learning. Filemyr's insights are valuable in this regard:

> I would have to say that all White people are naïve about the persistence of the color line. We prefer naïveté—in fact we insist on it. If we as White people actually faced the entrenched injustice of our socioeconomic system and our cultural arrogance, we might suffer tears, we might suffer the enormous weight of history, we might face the iceberg of guilt which is the underside of privilege. We might begin to glimpse our losses, our estrangement from others, our intense fear as the result of a social system that places us in the precious position of the top. (Filemyr, 1995: 174)

What is required is a thorough examination of the ways of whiteness with the goal of dismantling its effects. The endeavour need not be individualized. Indeed, when the ways of whiteness are reduced to individual acts of racism, the everyday and unknowable dimensions of racism are rendered invisible. Assuming the broader social view of whiteness as structural advantage and everyday practice rather than the narrower view of personal culpability will facilitate the process of taking responsibility for the emotional work ahead.

STUDY QUESTIONS

1. Reflect on the number and kind of relationships you have with individuals who are different from yourself with respect to their "race." Is "psychic distance" in evidence in these relationships? To what extent is the epistemic privilege of racialized persons heard, understood, and used as a guide for action in these relationships?

2. Formulate a rationale for colour-blindness. Then formulate a criticism of that position. Can you link colour-blindness with the official position or policy of any social institution—for example, public education, government, religious organizations, business? How would the official position be defended in the face of criticism generated by the principles of social justice and anti-racism?

3. What is your personal response to the suggestion that "For White people, recognition that one is participating and deriving benefits from whiteness can be traumatic"? In reflecting on what is required to challenge whiteness, how might you elaborate on this claim in such a way that the ways of whiteness are rendered personally meaningful?

EXERCISES

1. Locate empirical research studies on racial and ethnic inequality in Canada. How does the data support the analysis that has been developed in this chapter? Three useful research reports are:

   Canadian Council on Social Development. 2007. *Populations vulnerable to poverty: Urban poverty in Canada, 2000.* Ottawa: Canadian Council on Social Development. http://www.ccsd.ca/pubs/2007/upp. Accessed August 9, 2009.

Colour of Poverty. 2007. *Understanding the racialization of poverty in Ontario*. Fact Sheets #110. http://www.colourofpoverty.ca.

Reitz, Jeffrey G., and Rupa Banerji. 2007. *Racial inequality, social cohesion and policy issues in Canada*. Montreal: Institute for Research on Public Policy. http://www.irpp.org/indexe.htm. Accessed February 7, 2007.

2. Select three people who identify as White and ask them to elaborate on their ethnicity, social class, gender, and any other dimensions of their social position they experience as salient. To what extent do the intersections "sometimes reinforce and sometimes contradict" whiteness as discussed in the "Introduction" section of this chapter?

3. In the section titled "Challenging Whiteness," readers are advised, "At the very least, it is necessary to refuse participation in all forms of exclusion of racialized Others, including gross structural injustices as well as subtle everyday practices." In small groups, develop some ideas for how you (or White people you know) may intervene so as to challenge whiteness. Consider barriers to progress, especially the "intense fear" many White people have when broaching the problem of racism, as noted by Filemyr. How may White people acquire the "methodological humility" and "methodological caution" described by Narayan?

REFERENCES

Alcoff, Linda M. 1999. Towards a phenomenology of racial embodiment. *Radical Philosophy* 95: 15–26.

Anthias, Floya. 2005. Social stratification and social inequality: Models of intersectionality and identity. In F. Devine, M. Savage, J. Scott, and R. Crompton, eds., *Rethinking Class: Culture, Identities and Lifestyle.* Houndmills, UK, and New York: Palgrave MacMillan.

Babb, Valerie. 1998. *Whiteness Visible: The Meaning of Whiteness in American Literature and Culture.* New York: New York University Press.

Balibar, Etienne. 1990. Paradoxes of universality. In David Theo Goldberg, ed., *Anatomy of Racism.* Minneapolis: University of Minnesota Press. 283–294.

Bonilla-Silva, Eduardo. 2001. *White Supremacy and Racism in the Post–Civil Rights Era.* Boulder, CO: Lynne Rienner Publishers.

Canadian Council on Social Development. 2007. *Populations Vulnerable to Poverty: Urban Poverty in Canada*, 2000. Ottawa: Canadian Council on Social Development. http://www.ccsd.ca/pubs/2007/upp. Accessed August 9, 2009.

Chennault, Ronald E. 1998. Giving whiteness a black eye: An interview with Michael Eric Dyson. In J. L. Kincheloe, eds., S. R. Steinberg, N. M. Rodriguez, and R. E. Chennault, *White Reign: Deploying Whiteness in America.* New York: St. Martin's Press. 299–328.

Colour of Poverty. 2007. Understanding the racialization of poverty in Ontario. Fact Sheets #110. http://www.colourofpoverty.ca.

Dei, George Sefa. 2008. Theorizing anti-racism. In C. Levine-Rasky, ed., *Canadian Perspectives on the Sociology of Education.* Don Mills, ON: Oxford University Press. 51–68.

Dreyfus, H. L., and P. Rabinow, 1983. *Beyond Structuralism and Hermeneutics*, 2nd ed. Chicago: University of Chicago Press.

Dyer, Richard. 1997. *White.* London: Routledge.

Feagin, Joe, and Eileen O'Brien. 2003. *White Men on Race: Power, Privilege, and the Shaping of Cultural Consciousness.* Boston: Beacon Press.

Filemyr, Ann. 1995. Loving across the boundary. In M. Golden and S. R. Shreve, eds., *Skin Deep: Black Women and White Women Write About Race.* New York: Anchor Books. 162–188.

Foucault, Michel. 1972. *The Archaeology of Knowledge and the Discourse on Language* [1969]. Translated by A. M. Sheridan Smith. New York: Pantheon.

Foucault, Michel. 1977. *Discipline and Punish: The Birth of the Prison* [1975]. A. Sheridan, trans. New York: Vintage.

Foucault, Michel. 1980. *Power/Knowledge: Selected Interviews and Other Writings, 1972–1977.* C. Gordon, ed.; C. Gordon, L. Marshall, J. Mepham, and K. Soper, trans. New York: Pantheon.

Frankenberg, Ruth. 1993. *White Women, Race Matters.* Minneapolis: University of Minnesota Press.

Frankenberg, Ruth. 2001. The mirage of an unmarked whiteness. In B. B. Rasmussen, E. Klinenberg, I. J. Nexica, and M. Wray, eds., *The Making and Unmaking of Whiteness.* Durham: Duke University Press. 72–96.

Frye, Marilyn. 1992. *Willful Virgin: Essays in Feminism, 1976–1992.* Freedom, CA: The Crossing Press.

Galabuzi, Grace-Edward, 2006. *Canada's Economic Apartheid.* Toronto: Canadian Scholars Press.

Galarneau, D., and R. Morissette. 2008. "Immigrants' education and required job skills." December. Catalogue No. 75-001-X. Ottawa: Statistics Canada.

Garner, Steve. 2007. *Whiteness: An Introduction.* London: Routledge.

Gee, Ellen, and Steven Prus. 2000. Income inequality in Canada: A "racial divide." In M. A. Kalbach and W. E. Kalbach, eds., *Perspectives on Ethnicity in Canada: A Reader*, Toronto: Harcourt Canada.

Goldberg, David Theo. 1993. *Racist Culture: Philosophy and the Politics of Meaning.* Oxford: Blackwell.

Goldberg, David Theo. 1997. *Racial Subjects: Writing on Race in America.* New York: Routledge.

Goldberg, David Theo. 2006. Racial Europeanization. *Ethnic and Racial Studies* 29(2): 331–364.

Gova, Alnoor, and Kurd Rahat. 2008. The impact of security based racial profiling of Muslims. Metropolis British Columbia Working Paper Series, No. 08-14.

Guglielmo, Thomas A. 2003. *White on Arrival: Italians, Race, Color, and Power in Chicago, 1890–1945.* New York: Oxford University Press.

Henry, Frances, and Carol Tator. 2000. The theory and practice of democratic racism in Canada. In M. A. Kalbach and W. E. Kalbach, eds., *Perspectives on Ethnicity in Canada: A Reader.* Toronto: Harcourt Canada. 285–302.

Henry, Frances, and Carol Tator. 2006. *The Colour of Democracy: Racism in Canadian Society*, 3rd ed. Toronto: Nelson.

Howard, Philip. 2009. The double-edged sword: A critical race Africology of collaborations between blacks and whites in racial equity work. Unpublished Ph.D. dissertation. Ontario Institute for Studies in Education/University of Toronto, April 14.

Hurtado, Aida. 1996. *The Color of Privilege: Three Blasphemies on Race and Feminism*. Ann Arbor: University of Michigan Press.

Ignatiev, N. 1995. *How the Irish Became White*. New York: Routledge.

Jacobson, Matthew Frye. 1999. *Whiteness of a Different Color: European Immigrants and the Alchemy of Race*. Cambridge, MA: Harvard University Press.

Kenny, Kevin. 2006. Race, violence, and anti-Irish sentiment in the nineteenth century. In J. J. Lee and M. R. Casey, eds., *Making the Irish American: History and Heritage of the Irish in the United States*. New York: New York University Press. 364–378.

Kluegel, J. R., and E. R. Smith. 1986. *Beliefs About Inequality: Americans' Views of What Is and What Ought to Be*. New York: Aldine de Gruyter.

Layder, D. 1997. *Modern Social Theory*. London: UCL Press.

Levine-Rasky, Cynthia. 2000. The practice of whiteness among teacher candidates. *International Studies in Sociology of Education* 10(3): 263–284.

Levine-Rasky, Cynthia. 2002. Introduction. In Cynthia Levine-Rasky, ed., *Working Through Whiteness: International Perspectives*. Albany, NY: SUNY Press. 1–22.

Levine-Rasky, Cynthia. 2007. School choice and the analytics of power. *Review of Education, Pedagogy and Cultural Studies*, 29(5): 397–422.

Li, Peter S. 1988. *Ethnic Inequality in a Class Society*. Toronto: Thompson Educational Publishing, Inc.

Li, Peter S. 1998. The market value and social value of race. In V. Satzewich, ed., *Racism and Social Inequality in Canada*. Toronto: Thompson Educational Publishing, Inc. 115–130.

Li, Peter S. 2005. Contradictions of "racial" discourse. Presidential address at the Canadian Sociology and Anthropology Association meeting, University of Western Ontario, June.

Mayall, David. 2004. *Gypsy Identities, 1500–2000: From Egipcyans and Moon-Men to the Ethnic Romany*. London: Routledge.

Miles, Robert, and Robert Brown. 2003. *Racism*, 2nd ed. London: Routledge.

Mills, Charles W. 1997. *The Racial Contract*. Ithaca: Cornell University Press.

Morrison, Toni. 1992. *Playing in the Dark: Whiteness and the Literary Imagination*. New York: Vintage Books.

Narayan, Uma. 1988. Working together across difference: Some considerations on emotions and political practice. *Hypatia* 3(2): 31–47.

Neu, Dean, and Richard Therrien. 2003. *Accounting for Genocide: Canada's Bureaucratic Assault on Aboriginal People*. Blackpoint, NS: Fernwood Publishing.

Pendakur, Krishna, and Ravi Pendakur. 1996. The colour of money: Earnings differentials among ethnic groups in Canada. Research on Immigration and Integration in the Metropolis (RIIM), Working Paper Series No. 96-03. Burnaby, BC: Simon Fraser University.

Reitz, Jeffrey G., and Rupa Banerji. 2007. *Racial Inequality, Social Cohesion and Policy Issues in Canada.* Montreal: Institute for Research on Public Policy. http://www.irpp. org/indexe.htm. Accessed February 7, 2007.

Reitz, Jeffrey G., and Raymond Breton. 1998. Prejudice and discrimination in Canada and the United States: A comparison. In V. Satzewich, ed., *Racism and Social Inequality in Canada: Concepts, Controversies and Strategies of Resistance.* Toronto: Thompson Educational Publishing, Inc. 47–68.

Richards, David A. J. 1999. *Italian American: The Racializing of an Ethnic Identity.* New York: New York University Press.

Roediger, David R. 1991. *The Wages of Whiteness: Race and Making of the American Working Class.* London: Verso.

Roediger, David R. 2005. *Working Toward Whiteness: How America's Immigrants Became White.* New York: Basic Books.

Srivastava, Sarita. 2007. Troubles with "anti-racist multiculturalism": The challenges of anti-racist and feminist activism. In S. P. Hier and B. Singh Bolaria, eds., *Race and Racism in 21st Century Canada: Continuity, Complexity, and Change.* Peterborough, ON: Broadview Press. 291–311.

Stanfield, J. H. 1991. Racism in America and in other race-centered nation-states: Synchronic considerations. *International Journal of Comparative Sociology* 32(3/4): 243–260.

Stubblefield, Anna. 2005. Meditations on postsupremacist philosophy. In G. Yancy, ed., *White on White/Black on Black.* Lanham, MD: Rowman & Littlefield Publishers, Inc. 71–82.

Sullivan, Shannon. 2006. *Revealing Whiteness: The Unconscious Habits of Racial Privilege.* Bloomington: Indiana University Press.

Taylor, Gary. 2005. *Buying Whiteness.* New York: Palgrave Macmillan.

van Dijk, Teun A. 2002. Discourse and racism. In D. T. Goldberg and J. Solomos, eds., *A Companion to Racial and Ethnic Studies.* Oxford: Blackwell Publishers Ltd. 145–159.

Wray, M., and A. Newitz, eds. 1997. *White Trash: Race and Class in America.* New York: Routledge.

Wylie, Alison. 2003. Why standpoint matters. In R. Figueroa and S. Harding, eds., *Science and Other Cultures.* New York: Routledge. 26–48.

Yancey, George. 2003. *Who Is White? Latinos, Asians and the New Black/Nonblack Divide.* Boulder, CO: Lynn Rienner Publishers.

Yancy, George. 2004. Fragments of a social ontology of whiteness. In G. Yancy, ed., *What White Looks Like: African-American Philosophers on the Whiteness Question.* New York: Routledge. 1–24.

Young, Iris M. 1990. *Justice and the Politics of Difference.* Princeton, NJ: Princeton University Press.

6

CLASS, STATE, AND POWER: UNPACKING SOCIAL RELATIONS IN CONTEMPORARY CAPITALISM

Mark P. Thomas *York University*

In the fall of 2008, newspaper headlines around the world carried stories of the biggest economic crisis since the Great Depression of the 1930s. Stock values plunged. Financial institutions failed. Unemployment at levels not seen in decades was looming, as were personal bankruptcies and mortgage failures. And amidst all of the reports, predictions began to emerge that the principles of free-market capitalism that had for so long shaped the world economy were about to face a serious challenge (Brown, 2009).

It was not just those on the left of the political spectrum who were questioning the logic of capitalism as an economic system. In the months leading up to the economic crisis, Joseph Stiglitz (2008), former Senior Vice-President and Chief Economist of the World Bank, warned that the ideology of **neoliberalism**, which had guided economic policy around the global economy for three decades, "was never supported by an economic theory" nor "historical experience." In fact, in outlining his concerns about neoliberalism and free market capitalism, Stiglitz went so far as to claim that "Neoliberal market fundamentalism was always *a political doctrine serving certain interests*" (emphasis added). While some analyses of the crisis deflected attention from its systemic character, pointing out the bad investment practices of a small number of financial institutions, or the questionable ethics of a small number of elite executives, Stiglitz's words indicated something more. Without saying it explicitly, his warning about the impending economic crisis (which would hit the global economy only a couple of months later) pointed attention to the social relations of **capitalism** and the economic interests that drive those social relations.

The period of economic crisis that began in 2008 raises many profound questions not only about the specifics of the crisis, but about the world we live in and the social relationships that shape our lives. What is it about capitalism that creates such opportunity for some and such insecurity for many? What are the social relations that simultaneously produce such wealth and such profound inequality? What are the "interests" that benefit from the doctrine of free market capitalism and in what ways have governments contributed to this situation? It was no accident that the language of Karl Marx began to appear in some of these commentaries, as the effects of the crisis rippled through the world economy (Brown, 2009). Marx wrote of capitalism as a system that is inherently prone to inequality, conflict, and crisis. One hundred and fifty years later, his writing on the class relations of capitalism continue to provide a compelling account of the social organization of class power.

This chapter provides an introduction to the sociological concept of **class** and illustrates how class—as a social relation—may have profound connections to many aspects of our daily lives. Of course, Marx was not the only sociologist who wrote about class relations.

This chapter first reviews the work of another prominent sociologist—Max Weber—who has also been very influential in shaping the study of class within sociology. The chapter distinguishes between the concept of class as it has been developed in both the Weberian and the Marxist traditions of sociology and then focuses on Marx's writing in greater detail, suggesting that Marx's work provides great insight into the profound ways in which class relations are fundamentally connected to the social organization of power (Lukes, 1986). As an example of class power, the chapter also explores connections between capitalist power and the role of the state, building from another Marxist theorist Antonio Gramsci. The chapter concludes by raising a discussion of *neoliberal hegemony*, setting the stage for the chapter by Mary Beth Raddon, "Financial Fitness."

While the primary focus of the chapter is on the development of class analysis, the chapter aims to develop an approach to power through the lens of class in a way that can be integrated with the other approaches and examples developed through this book. As I discuss the class system in Marx's terms, I also point up how we can connect this class analysis to other chapters in this text (for example, the chapters "The Imaginary Indian," "Coffee and Commodity Fetishism," "Going Shopping," and "Financial Fitness") in order to begin to think about the ways a wide range of social relationships, practices, and everyday experiences may have class dimensions. Overall, the chapter aims to contribute to our understanding of the broader framework of "relations of ruling" (see **ruling apparatus**) constructed by Dorothy Smith (1987, 1999) by indicating how class relations are a central part of the wide array of institutions, processes, and discourses that shape our everyday world.

BEGINNING WITH THE END (OF CLASS ANALYSIS)

The "return to class" implied in the introduction to this chapter actually runs against some currents of sociological thinking that have developed over the past several decades. Patrick Joyce (1995: 3) notes that the profound economic, political, and social change of the latter half of the 20th century led to the belief that class may be "unequal to the task of explaining our present reality." For example, in writing about the economic growth and "postindustrial" transformation of industrialized economies in the decades following World War II, a prominent social theorist Daniel Bell (1973) suggested that the exploitation of industrial factory work would give way to the more favourable work environments of white-collar offices, and that new technologies would give people greater leisure time. This "postindustrial" society would lead to a reduction of class-based inequalities and conflicts.

Taking a related, though somewhat different approach, in *Return of the Actor* Alain Touraine (1988) suggested that as "postindustrial" society emerged, the class experiences and conflict of the industrial era would disappear and the traditional institutions that represented working class interests—specifically trade unions—would fade. Without the class inequality of industrial capitalism, working class movements would be replaced by a wide range of "identity-based" social movements. According to Touraine, while working class movements were predominant in the early and mid-20th century, other kinds of social movements were more likely to reflect the conditions of inequality and social conflicts of the late 20th century, as class relations faded.

Similarly, in *The Death of Class*, Jan Pakulski and Malcolm Waters (1996) argue that economic and social transformation of the late 20th century created the need to fundamentally decentre class as a sociological concept. More specifically, they state that class divisions are eroding in the industrialized economies of the capitalist West to the point where these societies are "no longer class societies" (4). Similarly, class identities and ideologies are dissolving as a basis for political movements. They do not suggest that these societies are becoming egalitarian or free from social conflict, but rather that class should no longer be considered a basis for inequality or conflict.

Certainly, these authors draw attention to the need to understand how capitalist societies may have changed in the late 20th century, as compared to the early years of industrial capitalism. And certainly, they point up the need to understand the wide array of social relationships that shape patterns of social organization and inequality. But as capitalist societies have changed over time, is it fair to say that the class relations of industrial capitalism have disappeared? Given the devastating impacts of the most recent economic crisis, should we not ask if and how class relations may have changed and what form they may take in the present day?

CLASS, STATUS, AND STRATIFICATION

When asked "What is your class identity?" many students will answer "middle class." This reflects a common understanding of class as a position within a socioeconomic hierarchy. Seen this way, one's class position is generally taken to refer loosely to one's income level, with people often identifying upper (wealthy), middle, and lower (poor) class as the range of "class positions." All those who are neither extremely poor nor extremely wealthy are placed somewhere in the "middle." This approach to class has been widely accepted and developed within sociology, and has been very influential in studies of socioeconomic inequality.

Understanding class as a system of stratification has its roots in the work of German sociologist Max Weber (1864–1920). In *Economy and Society: An Outline of Interpretive Sociology*, Weber (1978) developed a complex and multidimensional system of "class situations" to describe the social organization of 19th-century capitalism. This term, "class situation" refers to the likelihood of "(i) procuring goods; (ii) gaining a position in life; and (iii) finding inner satisfactions" (302). He considered the likelihood of achieving a particular "class situation" to be determined "from the relative control over goods and skills and from their income-producing uses within a given economic order" (302). What this means is that people who may have similar levels of ownership and control over things like property (land) or a business, or who had similar levels of skill and/or education, would have a similar "class situation."

He then used the term "class" to describe those who held a set of shared interests that emerge through their class situation. One's class, for Weber, was determined through a wide range of situations defined by ownership of property, individual assets, occupation, and skills. For example, property owners were a class, as were commercial investors, as were skilled artisans, as were industrial factory workers. But Weber did not see class as a singular experience, as an individual could experience different "class situations" through their lives. This could include upward mobility between different class situations (Breen, 2005). While one's class was rooted in a set of shared interests with others of the same class, because of the wide variety of class situations and potential for class mobility, his understanding of social class was that there was little potential for broad-based uniformity and unity in class situations.

While class situations were quite variable, Weber (1978) nonetheless identified four major social class groupings: (1) the working class; (2) the petty bourgeoisie (small business owners); (3) propertyless intelligentsia and specialists (white-collar employees, civil servants, etc.); and (4) classes "privileged through property and education." But consistent with his view of the complexity of class, he saw great potential for differentiation within these groupings. For example, different skills could create differentiation among the working class and different levels of education could create variation in class situation among white-collar workers. For those with property, there might be differentiation based on whether wealth was hereditary or built up through business ownership. So, overall, while he identified four major social classes, he saw a great deal of diversity within these major groups.

Making this picture of social hierarchies even more complex, Weber also introduced the concept of **status**, which he used to denote a form of "social esteem" (305). Status was not simply associated with income, but could come through formal education or training, or from more traditional means like family background. Status may be connected to class, but for Weber was not directly determined by class. Owning property may not necessarily produce high status in and of itself, though it might if it enabled access to higher education. One might belong to a very privileged class (due to wealth and property for example), but as an individual have very low status if one held an occupation that was of low esteem or if one did not pursue higher education. Thus, the idea of status further complicates the levels of differentiation that may exist between individuals and social groups, according to Weber.

This approach to understanding class and status became quite influential in 20th-century sociology as a way to understand patterns of stratification. Because this perspective draws attention to different levels of class and status markers, it is sometimes also referred to as a "gradational" approach to class (Edgell, 1993). Stratification theorists built on Weberian concepts to study the ways in which income, education, and occupation become connected to patterns of socioeconomic inequality (Crompton, 2008). Sociologists working from this perspective have made many attempts to break these categories down into detailed class schemes that reflect different class positions including primary groups of upper, middle, and lower class, as well as subgroups within these, such as upper middle class and lower middle class. These class groupings are defined by income level, and by status indicators such as education credentials, occupational categories, and formal measurements of skill (Edgell, 1993). Within this approach to studying class, the category of "middle class" is often taken as the norm, as it is meant to capture those who are neither extremely wealthy nor poor. Thus, when asked about our class position or class identity, so many of us automatically respond with "middle class."

From this "gradational" approach, we are able to see levels of inequality that may exist between different class groupings. However, because of its emphasis on class as a position within a grid or hierarchy, this approach tells us very little about the social relationships that may exist *between* these classes. More specifically, and in relation to our interests in this textbook, seeing class in a system of stratification tells us very little about the power relations that produce and reproduce class, and the social conflict that may result from those relations (Aronowitz, 2003).

TOWARD A "RELATIONAL" CONCEPT OF CLASS

❚   The history of all hitherto existing societies is the history of class struggle.

—*Marx and Engels (2002: 219)*

What does it mean to say class is a social relation and not simply a position in an income hierarchy? And why might this be an important distinction? If we see class as a social relation, we can begin to understand how classes are produced in relation to one another, rather than existing independently of one another. And more importantly, given the aim of this text to explore the social organization of power, we can see how the production of power in an economic form emerges through *class relations*. It is through critically examining these class relations that we can begin to see how the privilege experienced by some is directly related to the marginalization of others.

To understand class as a social relation, we first look to the writing of the German political economist Karl Marx (1818–1883), who, along with his collaborator, Friedrich Engels, argued that "classes," as social groups, are formed through relationships with other social groups. In the highly noted statement from *The Communist Manifesto* above, we see that, for Marx, class is a fundamental social relationship, and that social conflict is a primary aspect of the social relations that exist between classes. David Stark (1980: 97) explains:

> a class … is not a collection or aggregation of individuals. Classes, like the social relations from which they arise, exist in an antagonistic and dependent relation to each other. Classes are constituted by these mutually antagonistic relations. In this sense … *the object of study is not the elements themselves but the relations between them.* (Emphasis added)

Framing class analysis in this way moves beyond simply examining levels of difference (inequality, stratification) between different classes or between individuals within class groupings.

The Method of Analysis: Historical Materialism

To understand class as a social relation, we can look to the method Marx developed in his studies of capitalism: **historical materialism** (Fine & Saad-Filho, 2004). There are two essential elements to this methodology. First, it emphasizes that social structures, social relationships, and social change can only be understood in *historical context*. While Marx saw class struggle as a definitive aspect of all human history, the specific social relations that shape class struggle will vary considerably in different historical periods. Second, it places focus on the *material conditions* under which individuals live: specifically, the activities they undertake to produce their existence (Marx & Engels, 1969). In other words, understanding class as a social relation begins with looking at how people produce and reproduce themselves in their daily lives. Canadian sociologist Dorothy Smith (1987: 123) explains:

> [Marx and Engels] insist we start in the same world as the one we live in, among real individuals, their activities, and the material conditions of their activities. What is there to be investigated are the ongoing actual activities of real people.

According to Smith, when we look at how people produce and reproduce themselves and the world through everyday activities, we can begin to understand a wide array of "ruling relations" that shape our lives.

Class Relations in Capitalism

> The modern bourgeois society that has sprouted from the ruins of feudal society has not done away with class antagonisms. It has but established new classes, new conditions of oppression, new forms of struggle in place of old ones.
>
> —*Marx and Engels (2002: 220)*

Using the method of historical materialism, Marx suggested that human history is divided into identifiable periods, each of which is characterized by a particular **mode of production**. The mode of production refers to the economic organization of a society, the ways in which people produce, distribute, and consume goods. Capitalism, for example, is a mode of production. Within capitalism, the social relations of production, exchange, and consumption are very different from those in other modes of production, such as feudalism. Keith Faulks (2005: 29) identifies *four primary features of capitalism*:

i. the **means of production** are owned and controlled by relatively few people (capitalists);
ii. the "primary objective of capitalists is to maximize profit by producing and selling goods and services for as little cost as possible, and selling them on to consumers for as much profit as possible";
iii. "[p]rofits are achieved largely through the exploitation of wage labour"; and
iv. goods and services (commodities) are exchanged on a "free" market, "where they are bought and sold according to the laws of supply and demand, and for a value determined not by their intrinsic worth but by their market value."

To better understand capitalism Marx first looked at **feudalism**, the predominant mode of production that existed in Western Europe before capitalism (Naiman, 2008). Feudalism was an agricultural system in which land was held by feudal lords and worked by serfs, who produced for the feudal lord. In exchange for this production, they were allowed a small portion of land on which to produce for themselves. In Western Europe by the 1500s, these peasants were increasingly being expelled from feudal lands so an emerging landed aristocracy could use the lands for new and profitable purposes like growing sheep for wool manufacture. In other words, a new class—capitalists—was emerging in this context and was seizing control over land to put it to use for profit making. The creation of a landless class of people resulted from cutting the ties peasants had to the land—their means of production. This transition was aided by both legislation that legalized the expropriation of land and severe violence against those who resisted.

Marx termed this process **primitive accumulation**: the expropriation and enclosure (privatization) of land. Two key interrelated developments resulted from the process of primitive accumulation: (1) the establishment of private control over land so that it could be used for capital accumulation; and (2) the creation of landless masses of people. This mass of people had no means to support or reproduce themselves, since their access to land and livelihood had been eliminated. As capitalism developed, this process of expropriating land spread to other parts of the world, in particular through European colonization. Colonial expansion— whether in Asia, Africa, or the Americas—was a means by which European powers secured additional wealth to finance the development of capitalism in Western Europe. So the birth of capitalism is rooted in both violent expropriation of land and resources *and* exploitation of labour in many parts of the world. In Marx's (1976: 925–6) words, "capital comes [into the world] dripping from head to toe, from every pore, with blood and dirt."

These processes were central to the formation of Canada as a nation state, through the colonialism of the British and French, as they settled in North America and established control over land that First Nations peoples had lived on for centuries (Satzewich & Wotherspoon, 2000). In British North America (as Canada was known in the early years of colonization), a process of land appropriation (primitive accumulation) followed the arrival of settlers. Through treaty arrangements, large amounts of land were exchanged for very small amounts of money. Moreover, white settlement continued to expand even in areas where there were no treaty agreements. This process of land appropriation secured large amounts of land at little cost for the growing European settlement and the expansion of a capitalist economy. It also produced conflicts over land, natural resources, and political sovereignty that continue to this day.

In her chapter "The Imaginary Indian," Margot Francis explores some of the cultural legacies of this process as they are manifested in contemporary Canada, by looking at the ways in which the colonization of First Nations peoples also produced the racist stereotypes and myths associated with the "imaginary Indian." In contemporary times, we can see this discourse present in many realms of popular culture, whether in movies, television shows, or logos for major-league sports teams. When we critically examine the everyday cultural practices that Francis raises, we can see that they are a part of longstanding historical processes that are also shaped by struggles to control land and resources.

While in Marx's writing primitive accumulation was something that happened a long time ago, we can still see many ongoing examples of this process today. According to the economic geographer David Harvey (2005), who uses the term **accumulation by dispossession** to refer to the introduction of market forces into spaces that were previously non-capitalist, we can see the results of "primitive accumulation" in a wide range of settings. This includes the dispossession of peoples of their land in the search for resources (for example, oil in Africa) or the development of factories (such as export-processing zones in Indonesia). This may also include the privatization of public services—for example, in health care or education—through neoliberalism, which is discussed in the chapter "Financial Fitness" by Mary Beth Raddon.

The Social Relations of Production

Primitive accumulation created the basis for the emergence of private ownership over land, labour and capital, and thereby the class relations of capitalism. According to Marx, this process produced two fundamental classes: the bourgeoisie, or **capitalist class**, and the proletariat, or **working class**. Rather than simply looking at unequal incomes, Marx argued that these classes are defined through their relationship to the means of production—the materials, infrastructure, and natural resources needed to produce goods and provide services (including factories, technology, tools, etc.). Specifically, the capitalist class are those who own and control the means of production. The working class are those who do not own means of production, and therefore must sell their **labour power**—their *capacity* to labour—in order to earn wages and ensure their subsistence. It is through the sale and

FIGURE 6.1 ■ The capitalist class of 21st-century capitalism: Bob Greifeld (L), CEO of NASDAQ, Paul Calello (C), CEO of Credit Suisse, and Bob Diamond (R), President of Barclays, listen to a speech by U.S. President Barack Obama about reforming Wall Street and the financial reform bill, April 22, 2010.

SAUL LOEB/AFP/Getty Image

purchase of labour power that these two classes are brought into relation to one another. While Marx saw the working class and capitalist class as primary within this system of class relations, he also recognized intermediate classes, such as the petite bourgeoisie—small business owners, independent farmers and craftspeople, and self-employed professionals. However, the relationship between capitalist class and working class constitutes the central driving force within capitalist societies (Marx & Engels, 2002).

Here is where we begin to see connections between Marx's analysis and the social organization of everyday practices. Marx wanted to understand one of the most normalized and taken-for-granted everyday practices many people experience in capitalism—wage labour. On the surface, wage labour may appear as an equal and fair exchange: being paid a wage for the number of hours you work at a job. But what underlies this exchange?

Recall that the first step in the emergence of the working class was the process of land expropriation. This created the condition of landlessness needed to produce the industrial workforce of early capitalism. Thus, primitive accumulation created masses of **free wage labour**: those who are (1) freed (separated) from the means of production and who must sell their labour power to survive and (2) freed any from legal constraints that would *prevent* them from selling their labour power (for example, slavery) (Lebowitz, 2003). These conditions of "freedom" ensure that working classes within capitalism have no other ability to reproduce themselves other than through wage labour. This is the essence of the class relations of capitalism: the working class sells their labour power in order to survive; and capitalists buy this labour power to produce goods (or provide services).

As mentioned above, this system may appear as a fair exchange between two parties where each party—worker and capitalist—gets something out of the exchange. The worker gets their wage and the capitalist gets the labour power of that worker to produce something. It is assumed to be mutually beneficial and is generally defined in the everyday term *employment*. Marx rejected the view of this as a fair exchange, however. Instead, he saw it as profoundly unequal. More specifically, he considered it to be *exploitative*, and aimed to make visible the unseen power dynamics that underpin this social relation.

The Commodity

Underlying this analysis of class relations is Marx's concept of the **commodity** (Albo, 2010; Fine & Saad-Filho, 2004). Marx argued that capitalism is ultimately a system of commodity production, in which commodities are "use values produced by labour for exchange" (Fine & Saad-Filho, 2004: 19). **Use values** are goods like food, clothing, and houses, and services like education, and health care. These are all things that we use (or want) as we reproduce ourselves. A commodity also has an **exchange value**, which is "an equivalence relationship between objects" (Fine & Saad-Filho, 2004: 17). The exchange value is a quantitative measure that can be used in the process of commodity exchange. In a capitalist market, the exchange value of a commodity is represented through money. So commodities in capitalism have both use values (based on an ability to meet a human need or want) and exchange values (a representation of its value in the form of money).

How does this help us understand the class relations of capitalism? Looking at the organization of wage labour, we can see that the labour power of the working class is itself treated like a commodity. Its use value is its ability to create products or provide services and its exchange value is represented in a wage. This is really just a very abstract way to describe the *everyday experience of going to work*. Think of these terms by looking at a job you may have had, such as working at a coffee shop or in a clothing store at a shopping mall. Your use value is your capacity to pour cups of coffee or sell a pair of jeans. Your exchange value is the hourly wage you are paid to do these things. By recognizing the ways in which our own labour power is treated as a commodity, we are able to begin to unpack the power relations that shape the social organization of the workplace.

On its surface, employment appears in our everyday experiences as a fair exchange. Wage labour becomes normalized in the sense that we do not question the power relations that underlie this exchange. According to Marx, when we work for a wage, we create **surplus value**—profit—for our employer based on the fact that wages paid are less than the value of the commodities produced or the services provided. So wage labour is inherently a system of **exploitation** based on the commodification of people's labour power that occurs unseen at the "point of production" in the capitalist workplace (Burawoy, 1979). This emphasis on class relations as being defined through exploitation is a fundamental point of distinction between Marx's approach to class relations and stratification approaches developed through the Weberian tradition (Wright, 2005).

Exploitation and Alienation

What are the consequences of these kinds of class relations? Certainly levels of economic inequality between two major classes are a primary result. But Marx, and others who have been influenced by his ideas about class relations, have argued that these social relations produce profound conditions of **alienation** within capitalist society (Braverman, 1974). Because working for a wage entails giving up control over the ability to decide what kind of work one will do, and how it will be done, Marx suggested we lose much of our creative capacity through engaging in wage labour. When we look at the class relations of wage labour, we can see people becoming alienated in multiple ways: from the products of labour (what is created); from the tasks of work (how they are determined and carried out); from creative capacities for expression through work; and from one another (without having the collective capacity to control work) (Rinehart, 2006).

We can see examples of alienation—to varying degrees—in a wide range of jobs. The easiest examples that come to mind are of course factory assembly lines. But what about other kinds of workplaces? Fast-food workplaces, for example, are also characterized by high degrees of management control over workers, with the labour process deskilled much as in a factory (Barndt, 2008; Royle, 2000). Working in fast-food production typically includes: the general routinization of jobs (preparing food, taking orders, serving food); a high degree of repetition of simplified tasks; little opportunity for decision making; and the use of technology to minimize worker knowledge (for example, cash registers to organize orders and prompt order takers with phrases). What this means is that in addition to low

FIGURE 6.2 ■ The working class of 21st-century capitalism. A factory manufactures McDonald's toys in Dongguan, Guangdong, China.

wages and little job security, workers are easily replaced and have little autonomy. What we can see from this example is that the experiences of alienation that may be common on a manufacturing assembly line may also be present in a wide range of service economy workplaces.[1]

Interaction between customers and workers in the service economy introduces another dimension to how alienation may occur, creating more subjective and less obvious forms of labour control (Leidner, 1996; Ritzer, 2008). Specifically, in the context of the service economy, a new dimension of alienation occurs through control over **emotional labour**: "the conscious manipulation of the workers' self-presentation either to display feeling states and/or to create feeling states in others" (Leidner, 1996: 30). Customer interaction alters the relations of the labour process in service work, in which the customer becomes an important factor in a system of labour control. The personal interaction with customers required by service work makes demands upon the emotional labour of service workers, in which "[i]nstead of being held accountable only for their physical exertions, workers' moods, facial expressions, and words are subject to supervision" (30). Customers become part of this process by expecting smiling, cheerful service, and play a key role in establishing

---

1 Harry Braverman (1974), for example, looked at the social organization of office work and found the same kinds of conditions of alienation present among white-collar workers. Similarly, studies of jobs in "high technology" sectors—for example, web designers and software developers—have found that these jobs are often characterized by low control, long hours, and job insecurity (Ó Riain, 2000; Ross, 2001). Ursula Huws (2003) coined the term "cybertariat" to describe the proletarianization of work experienced by many in the so-called "new economy" of high-technology industries.

control over service work through channels for customer input and assessments of service provision. "Service with a smile" becomes not only part of the skill set of service work, but also a form of self-governance (see **governmentality**) for service-sector workers.

This is not to say that all forms of work are equally alienating, or that the conditions of alienation experienced by people today are exactly the same as during the time when Marx was writing (over 150 years ago). But we can use these ideas that were developed a long time ago to begin to better understand the so-called "fair exchange" of our labour power for a wage in many kinds of workplaces in today's economy.

We can also use these ideas as a beginning to understand dimensions of class conflict that play out in the workplace and beyond, in terms of both collective and individual responses to alienation and exploitation. For Marx, the dynamics of working class resistance to exploitation are a central driving force in capitalist society. As the polarization between classes increased, according to Marx, so too would mass movements against capitalist power (Marx & Engels, 2002). We can see the emergence of trade unions as one example of a collective response to exploitation. Trade unions formed as a way to provide working class people with a collective voice in determining wages and working conditions, acting to counter the absolute power of employers in the workplace (Rinehart, 2006). At the individual level, we can see many kinds of "everyday" acts of resistance to alienated labour that include absenteeism, developing one's own way to perform standardized work tasks, and adding personal touches to company uniforms. More broadly, we can see the emergence of mass "antiglobalization" movements as a response to capitalist class power at the international scale. While exploitation and alienation are key dynamics of the class relations of capitalism, resistance to these social relations is undoubtedly present in many individual and collective forms.

FIGURE 6.3 ■ Activists march along the streets of downtown Toronto while participating in a protest ahead of the G20 summit on June 25, 2010, in Toronto, Canada.

THE FICTION—COMMODITY FETISHISM

If capitalism is producing these conditions of exploitation and alienation, why do they remain hidden? Marx developed the concept **commodity fetishism** to explain the process whereby the value of any commodity comes to be reflected in its price, making the social relations of its production invisible. What this means is that the value of a commodity becomes seen as separate from the actual labour that went into its production, and separate from the relationships that exist between capitalists and workers. As Leah Hagar Cohen (1997: 11) states, commodity fetishism refers to "the habit of perceiving an object's price as something intrinsic to and fixed within that object … rather than as the end result of a history of people and their labour."

In Chapter 13, Gavin Fridell outlines how this practice is present in the cup of coffee. When we buy a cup of coffee, we see a hot, caffeinated beverage. Yet this drink is the product of an exploitative process created through a global division of labour that is connected to patterns of inequality between the Global North and Global South (James, 2000). The labour that is behind the cup of coffee—growing, harvesting, roasting, and transporting the beans—remains invisible because of the process of commodity fetishism. All we see is the final product in front of us, which we consume as if it exists independently of those who produced it. Using the concept commodity fetishism, we see that the everyday experience of buying a cup of coffee is very much a part of the class system and power relations of capitalism.

Class as an Intersectional Social Relation

So far, we can see that the class relations of capitalism are defined through how the labour power of the working class is treated as a commodity through the system of wage labour and how the capitalist class holds the capacity to extract surplus value through this system. Marx's relational approach to understanding class provides the means to understand class, not simply as an indicator of social inequality, but also as a social relationship fundamentally connected to the social organization of power in capitalist societies.

While we focus on class relations in this chapter, we must recognize that class cannot be separated from other social, cultural, and political relations examined in this textbook. In order to understand the everyday dimensions of class relations, we have to study the intersection of class with other social relationships, including race, gender, sexuality, and citizenship (Bannerji, 1995; Brenner, 2000; Creese, 2007; Sharma, 2006; Smith, 1999). This method of analysis does not mean simply "adding on" other social relations; rather, it involves recognizing differences in social experience (different class experiences depending on gender, for example), and building a recognition of these differences into sociological research (Clement & Miles, 1994). To treat class separately from other social relations would be to detach it from its material, historical, and social context (Acker, 2006; Adib & Guerrier, 2003; Bannerji, 2006; Hawkesworth, 2006). So while the work of Marx emphasized the organization of wage labour as central to the class system of capitalism, taking an *intersectional* approach means we cannot understand wage labour unless we seek to uncover its gendered and racialized dimensions. It means we cannot consider *the* working class or *the* capitalist class to be large, homogenous groups defined solely through relationships to the means of production. We must also pay equal attention to social differentiation based on race, gender, disability, citizenship status, and sexuality, for example.

We can see examples of this through both racialized and gendered divisions of labour in contemporary capitalism. **Racialization** is deeply embedded in the social organization of paid and unpaid work and is central in shaping patterns of labour market inequality in capitalist economies. A prime example of this is through immigration policies that limit the participation of racialized workers in a labour market, such as the temporary foreign worker programs that create a system of "unfree" migrant labour, as discussed in depth by Nandita Sharma in this textbook. We can see discourses of "desirable" and "undesirable" work forming in racialized terms and contributing to class dimensions of whiteness as a relation of privilege. For example, in the Seasonal Agricultural Workers' Program that brings foreign workers to Canada for seasonal harvesting work, Mexican and Caribbean men are considered physically well suited for agricultural harvesting, work that most Canadians are unwilling to do because it is very physically demanding, with long hours and low pay. But because of racist conceptions of Canadian citizenship, these same men are socially constructed as "undesirable" future citizens, thereby justifying the policy that requires them to leave the country once the harvesting season is complete (Satzewich, 1991). Thus, class and race are profoundly intertwined through these policies and practices.

By taking an intersectional approach, we can also see connections between class and gender, specifically through the organization of **social reproduction**—"the activities required to ensure day-to-day and generational survival of the population" (Luxton & Corman, 2001: 29). Discourses and practices of masculinity and femininity become part of the class relations of capitalism through gendered norms about women's responsibilities in the home and men's role as "breadwinners," which produce feminized and masculinized norms of employment and gendered occupational structures (Creese, 1999; Steedman, 1997; Vosko, 2000). Similarly, racialized ideologies have contributed to the construction of domestic work as a key site of employment for women of colour, where discourses about the "natural" abilities of women from racialized groups have legitimized further racialized divisions of reproductive labour (cooking, cleaning, caring) (Acker, 2006; Arat-Koç, 2006; Brand, 1999; Glenn, 2001). In private households, women from racialized groups have long been employed as servants to assist upper- and upper-middle-class white women in the completion of household work, thereby absolving white women and men of the most onerous aspects of this work. As reproductive labour has been increasingly commodified during the economic expansion of the service sector, women from racialized groups have been employed in a variety of "lower-level" forms of reproductive labour, such as nurses' aides, kitchen workers, maids in hotels, and cleaners in offices, while white women are more likely to be employed as supervisors, professionals, administrative support staff.

These examples illustrate how racialized and gendered norms interact with and through class relations to produce the normative "centre" that includes hidden but highly exploitative and alienating labour practices.

We can better understand intersections between gender and class relations when we look at the gendered dimensions of contemporary labour markets (Clement, 2007). For example, gendered divisions of labour within the home have limited women's access to full-time paid employment, as it is women who are primarily held responsible for the unpaid domestic labour (Armstrong & Armstrong, 2010; Eichler et al., 2010). Moreover, gendered assumptions about women's responsibilities in the home have shaped the types of occupations available to women workers, with dominant social norms of femininity defining the types of jobs that are considered "women's work," most often those kinds of jobs that involve elements of caregiving, nurturing, and personal service.

In Canada, we can see that while women's participation in the labour force increased dramatically from the 1950s to the 1990s, increases in participation were not accompanied by increases in diversity of employment opportunities. For example, between 1941 and 1991 women's participation in paid employment increased from 20 to 60 percent (Armstrong & Armstrong, 2010). By 2006, over 70 percent of women were working outside the home. However, women continue to be more likely to be employed in the service sector, in public service occupations such as nursing and elementary teaching, and private-sector service occupations such as retail salespersons, secretaries, and cashiers (Jackson, 2009; Krahn et al., 2006). Further, women are much more likely to be employed in lower-tier (retail and consumer) services than men. In 2004, 87 percent of women in the labour market were employed in the service sector, with one-quarter of these employed in the "lower-tier" services.

These gendered divisions of labour have a dramatic impact on patterns of economic inequality. The five most common jobs for women are retail salespersons, secretaries, cashiers, general office clerks, and registered nurses, jobs often undervalued in terms of pay due to patriarchal norms that identify them as "women's work" (Krahn et al., 2006). Moreover, 31 percent of women, as against 20 percent of men, are employed in some form of low-paid (under $12/hour) job. Employment in jobs that are undervalued due to gender norms produces a persistent wage gap whereby women in full-time, year-round employment earn on average 70 percent of the earnings received by similarly employed men. Gender and class intersect in the production of flexible labour forces as well, with women overrepresented in nonstandard and "flexible" jobs, those that are part-time and temporary. By 2006, 26 percent of women, in contrast to 10 percent of men, held some form of part-time employment, a division most frequently explained through women's responsibility for caregiving in the home (Jackson, 2009). Overall, from these patterns we see that gender and class relations intersect to produce highly gendered divisions of labour, and in particular gendered forms of "flexible labour," which both reflect responsibilities for unpaid household labour and reproduce norms regarding "women's work."

THE GROWING GAP IN CANADIAN SOCIETY

While the middle class grew through the course of the 20th century in many industrialized countries, including Canada, in recent times there is much evidence of growing economic polarization that is contributing to an erosion of the middle class. In Canada, this pattern of polarization can be traced back through the past 30 years (Naiman, 2008; Yalnizyan, 1998). For example, in the 1970s, the wealthiest 10 percent of the population received 23 percent of total market income. This increased to 28 percent by the 1980s and 37 percent by the 1990s. By 1999, the wealthiest 10 percent of families held 53 percent of the wealth in the country. Furthermore, between 1970 and 1999, their average wealth increased by 122 percent, while the poorest 10 percent saw their debts increase by 28 percent. The city of Toronto provides a snapshot of how these trends have continued in recent years. Since 2001, fifteen of Toronto's middle-income neighbourhoods have vanished. The majority became low-income areas, where individual earnings are 20 to 40 percent below the city average. In 1970, 86 percent of the suburban neighbourhoods around the city (the "905" area) were middle-class. By 2005, this had decreased to 61 percent. From 2000 to 2005, the number of city neighbourhoods with very low earnings—those with more than 40 percent below the Toronto-area average—grew by almost 50 percent (Winsa, 2009).

This growing gap has been compounded though the growth in low-wage and insecure employment that has occurred during this same time period (Cranford et al., 2003; Thomas, 2009). When we see the predominance of low-wage jobs in the service sector, we must remind ourselves again of the labour that goes into the cup of coffee or the selling of designer jeans. The people brewing and pouring our "everyday" cup of coffee at places like Tim Hortons, Timothy's, Starbucks, and Second Cup, or stocking shelves at The Gap, Loblaws, and Walmart, are very much a part of this growing low-wage workforce. The experiences of low-wage work are thus a key part of the everyday practices of buying a cup of coffee or going shopping.

Moreover, these employment patterns reflect the highly racialized composition of the working class in Canada (Creese, 2007; Galabuzi, 2006; Thomas, 2010). While making up approximately 13 percent of the Canadian population, racialized groups are disproportionately represented in low-income occupations such as those in the sewing, textile, and fabric industries (40 percent), taxi and limo drivers (36 percent), and electronics assemblers (42 percent). This racialized segmentation is reflected in a persistent double-digit earnings differential, in which the average earnings of workers of colour are approximately 85 percent of that of the average earnings of all Canadians. Racialized groups constitute 21.6 percent of the urban population, but 33 percent of the urban poor. Further, racialized families are two to four times more likely to fall below low-income cutoff measures, creating a broader condition of racialized poverty in Canada.[2] Conversely, at

---

2 "Understanding the Racialization of Poverty in Ontario," Fact Sheet. #110, http://www.colourofpoverty.ca.

the other end of the class system, racialized groups are vastly underrepresented in senior positions, making up only 3 percent of top executives and 1.7 percent of directors on organizational boards. Overall, when we look at this "growing gap," we see that there is growing polarization in Canadian society characterized by high levels of racialized inequality.

CLASS, POWER, AND THE STATE

So far we have looked at class and power in terms of wage labour, and the normalization of conditions of exploitation and alienation through the everyday experience of going to work. In this last section of the chapter, we look at ways in which Marx's approach to class analysis may help us to understand connections between class, power, and **the state**—the set of political institutions that encompass governments and their agencies (the police, military, courts, legislature, public service) (Godard, 2005; Miliband, 1969).

Returning to Marx, he saw the state as a source of political power for the dominant class in a society, suggesting that political institutions such as government and the courts protect the interests of the capitalist class: "[t]he executive of the modern State is but a committee for managing the common affairs of the whole bourgeoisie" (Marx & Engels, 2002: 221). The dominant class uses state institutions, whether it be laws, the courts, or the police, to establish the political and legal conditions necessary for capitalist production and to repress working class resistance.

Marx (1976) saw examples of this as capitalism emerged in Western Europe. This included legislation that was used to criminalize the poor and unemployed, requiring them to be whipped, branded, and starved if they did not work. These brutal methods were used to establish a new work ethic as people were dispossessed of their land through the process of primitive accumulation. In addition to legitimating the use of violence against the poor to condition them to wage labour, early laws in capitalist society included legislation to regulate wages by keeping them down, and to lengthen the working day. But Marx never fully developed his theory of the state and class power. Thus, his brief statements about the state left many questions and prompted many further debates about the nature of the state in capitalist societies.[3]

How do connections between class power and political institutions become normalized? How do political institutions that protect class interests gain legitimacy in the eyes of the masses? To understand this phenomenon, Antonio Gramsci's theory of **hegemony** is useful. For Gramsci (1971: 57, 161), hegemony is "intellectual and moral leadership" that takes into account the interests of subordinate groups through compromises that may benefit many but do not ultimately threaten the rule of the dominant group. Hegemony acts to secure the consent of the masses and operates, in part, through the state, which is the source of political power for the ruling class in capitalist society. Gramsci argued

---

3 For discussions of key debates, in particular those about the **relative autonomy** of the capitalist state, see Miliband (1969), Poulantzas (1978), and Jessop (1990).

that the capitalist class maintains its rule through complex systems of political, cultural, intellectual, and moral leadership across civil society, constituting dominant class interests as those of an entire society. In other words, political institutions forge consent across society by producing kinds of "common sense" that act to normalize class relations in capitalism.

Neoliberalism, a phenomenon discussed in detail by Mary Beth Raddon in Chapter 11, is the latest example of capitalist hegemony. As economic theory, neoliberalism is based on the assertion that economic prosperity can be achieved through reduced government intervention in the market. At the level of the individual, neoliberalism promotes economic "well-being" by normalizing entrepreneurialism throughout our everyday practices, as we are expected to increasingly embrace the individualization of economic risks. As governments have brought neoliberal principles into public policy, we see an increasing benefit to private capital, legitimated through the popular discourse of mutual prosperity through individualized competitiveness, much in the way described by Gramsci's general notion of hegemony. When we look closely at neoliberalism, as Raddon does in her chapter, we can see that while in principle it calls for a reduction of state intervention in the economy, neoliberal policies are in fact about reorienting the way governments operate by developing policies increasingly favourable to the interests of capitalists (Connell, 2010; Harvey, 2006). This may involve eliminating policies and programs that provide social and economic security (e.g. unemployment insurance), increasing the user costs of public services (e.g. university tuition), and intensifying how people's labour power is treated as a commodity by lowering standards that regulate working conditions. As we read of the everyday practices of financial fitness alongside this discussion of class and state power, we see that these practices are very much part of a broad process of social transformation driven by neoliberal hegemony, shaped by the ways in which governments interact with and support business interests.

CONCLUSION

In this chapter, we developed a discussion of class that began with Marx's analysis of the class system of capitalism, a perspective that has received a renewed interest due to the financial crisis of recent times. The fact that there has not yet been a sustained and revolutionary working class movement that has fundamentally transformed capitalism has led many to reject Marx's ideas. In this chapter, however, we have identified ways in which we can use his analysis of class relations to understand a central aspect of power that has profound connections to our everyday lives.

While focusing primarily on class analysis, in this chapter I have also pointed out ways we can begin to understand patterns of intersectionality with other social relationships— for example through the racialization of the "growing gap"—in the formation and reproduction of class relations. I have also pointed out ways we can connect this chapter to other chapters in this text ("The Imaginary Indian," "Coffee and Commodity Fetishism," "Going Shopping," "Financial Fitness") in order to begin to think about how a wide range of social relationships, practices, and everyday experiences may have class dimensions.

As class relations remain central to our lives in many ways, we can build on the analysis presented in this chapter to see its connections to the organization of multiple forms of power operating throughout our everyday world.

STUDY QUESTIONS

1. Why does Marxist theory conceptualize power as domination? How does this approach to power remain relevant and important?

2. What are some other examples of ways in which class analysis could be developed through an intersectional framework of power?

3. How can the materialist analysis of class relations be integrated into the Foucauldian analysis of power relations?

EXERCISES

1. Take notes on the social organization of your workplace. Who has control and decision-making power? Map out your own labour process. How much control do you have? Over what aspects of your work? Use this exercise as a way to evaluate Marx's theory of alienation and the labour process.

2. Think about the last major purchase you made. What is its use value and exchange value? Where did it come from? Deconstruct this commodity by mapping out the stages of its development from production to consumption. Use this exercise as a way to explore Marx's concept "commodity fetishism."

3. One of the main principles of neoliberalism is that public institutions should be run like businesses. List all of the ways in which your university runs like a business. How does this shape your everyday experience of going to school?

REFERENCES

Acker, Joan. 2006. *Class Questions, Feminist Answers*. Toronto: Rowman and Littlefield Publishers.

Adib, Amel, and Yvonne Guerrier. 2003. The interlocking of gender with nationality, race, ethnicity and class: The narratives of women in hotel work. *Gender, Work and Organization* 10(4): 413–32.

Albo, Greg. 2010. The "new economy" and capitalism today. In N. Pupo and M. Thomas, eds., *Interrogating the New Economy: Restructuring Work in the 21st Century*. Toronto: University of Toronto Press.

Arat-Koç, Sedef. 2006. Whose social reproduction? Transnational motherhood and challenges to feminist political economy. In K. Bezanson and M. Luxton, eds., *Social Reproduction: Feminist Political Economy Challenges Neo-Liberalism*. Montreal & Kingston: McGill-Queen's University Press. 75–92.

Armstrong, Pat, and Hugh Armstrong. 2010. *The Double Ghetto: Canadian Women and Their Segregated Work*, 3rd ed. Don Mills: Oxford University Press.

Aronowitz, Stanley. 2003. *How Class Works: Power and Social Movement*. New Haven: Yale University Press.

Bannerji, Himani. 1995. *Thinking Through: Essays on Feminism, Marxism, and Anti-Racism*. Toronto: Women's Press.

Bannerji, Himani. 2006. Reflections on class and race: Building on Marx. *Social Justice* 32(4), 144–60.

Barndt, Deborah. 2008. *Tangled Routes: Women, Work and Globalization on the Tomato Trail*. Lanham: Rowman & Littlefield.

Bell, Daniel. 1973. *The Coming of Post-Industrial Society: A Venture in Social Forecasting*. New York: Basic Books.

Brand, Dionne. 1999. Black women and work: The impact of racially constructed gender roles on the sexual division of labour. In E. Dua and A. Robertson, eds., *Scratching the Surface: Canadian Anti-Racist Feminist Thought*. Toronto: Women's Press. 83–96.

Braverman, Harry. 1974. *Labour and Monopoly Capital: The Degradation of Work in the Twentieth Century*. New York: Monthly Review Press.

Breen, Richard. 2005. Foundations of a neo-Weberian class analysis. In E. O. Wright, ed., *Approaches to Class Analysis*. Cambridge: Cambridge University Press. 31–50.

Brenner, Johanna. 2000. *Women and the Politics of Class*. New York: Monthly Review Press.

Brown, Ian. 2009. The 18th Brumaire of Barack Obama. *The Globe and Mail*, June 13.

Burawoy, Michael. 1979. *Manufacturing Consent: Changes in the Labor Process Under Monopoly Capitalism*. Chicago: University of Chicago Press.

Clement, Wallace. 2007. Methodological considerations: Thinking about researching work. In V. Shalla and W. Clement, eds., *Work in Tumultuous Times: Critical Perspectives*. Kingston & Montreal: McGill-Queens University Press. 30–51.

Clement, Wallace, and John Myles. 1994. *Relations of Ruling: Class and Gender in Postindustrial Societies*. Montreal & Kingston: McGill-Queen's University Press.

Cohen, Leah Hager. 1997. *Glass, Paper, Beans: Revelations on the Nature and Value of Ordinary Things*. New York: Doubleday.

Connell, Raewyn. 2010. Understanding neoliberalism. In S. Braedley and M. Luxton, eds., *Neoliberalism and Everyday Life*. Montreal & Kingston: McGill-Queen's University Press. 22–36.

Cranford, Cynthia J., Leah F. Vosko, and Nancy Zukewich. 2003. Precarious employment in the Canadian labour market: A statistical portrait. *Just Labour* 3: 6–22.

Creese, Gillian. 1999. *Contracting Masculinity: Gender, Class, and Race in a White-Collar Union, 1944–1994*. Toronto: Oxford.

Creese, Gillian. 2007. Racializing work/reproducing white privilege. In V. Shalla and W. Clement, eds., *Work in Tumultuous Times: Critical Perspectives*. Montreal & Kingston: McGill-Queen's Press. 192–226.

Crompton, Rosemary. 2008. *Class and Stratification*. 3rd ed. Cambridge: Polity.

Edgell, Stephen. 1993. *Class*. London and New York: Routledge.

Eichler, Margrit, Patrizia Albanese, Susan Ferguson, Nicky Hyndman, Lichun Willa Liu, and Ann Matthews. 2010. *More Than It Seems: Household Work and Lifelong Learning*. Toronto: Women's Press.

Faulks, Keith. 2005. Capitalism. In G. Blakeley and V. Bryson, eds., *Marx and Other Four-Letter Words*. London: Pluto. 28–45.

Fine, Ben, and Alfredo Saad-Filho. 2004. *Marx's Capital*. 4th ed. London: Pluto Press.

Galabuzi, Grace Edward. 2006. *Canada's Economic Apartheid: The Social Exclusion of Racialized Groups in the New Century*. Toronto: Canadian Scholars' Press.

Glenn, Evelyn Nakano. 2001. Gender, race, and the organization of reproductive labor. In R. Baldoz, C. Kroeber and P. Kraft, eds., *The Critical Study of Work: Labor, Technology, and Global Production*. Philadelphia: Temple University Press. 71–82.

Godard, John. 2005. *Industrial Relations, the Economy and Society*. 3rd ed. Concord: Captus Press.

Gramsci, Antonio. 1971. *Selections from the Prison Notebooks*, trans. Q. Hoare and G. N. Smith. New York: International Publishers.

Harvey, David. 2005. *The New Imperialism*. London & New York: Verso.

Harvey, David. 2006. *The Limits to Capital*. London & New York: Verso.

Hawkesworth, Mary. 2006. *Feminist Inquiry: From Political Conviction to Methodological Innovation*. New Brunswick, NJ: Rutgers University Press.

Huws, Ursula. 2003. *The Making of a Cybertariat: Virtual Work in a Real World*. New York: Monthly Review Press.

Jackson, Andrew. 2009. *Work and Labour in Canada: Critical Issues*. 2nd ed. Toronto: Canadian Scholars Press.

James, Deborah. 2000. Justice and Java: Coffee in a Fair Trade Market. *NACLA Report* XXXIV: 2 (September/October): 11–14.

Jessop, Bob. 1990. *State Theory: Putting the Capitalist State in its Place*. University Park, PA: Pennsylvania State University Press.

Joyce, Patrick, ed. 1995. *Class*. Oxford & New York: Oxford University Press. Krahn, Harvey, Graham Lowe, and Karen Hughes. 2007. *Work, Industry, and Canadian Society*. 5th ed. Toronto: Thomson Nelson.

Lebowitz, Michael A. 2003. *Beyond Capital: Marx's Political Economy of the Working Class*, 2nd ed. New York: Palgrave.

Leidner, Robin. 1996. Rethinking questions of control: Lessons from McDonald's. In C. L. Macdonald and C. Sirianni, eds., *Working in the Service Society*. Philadelphia: Temple University Press. 29–46.

Lukes, Steven. 1986. *Power*. New York: New York University Press.

Luxton, Meg, and June Corman. 2001. *Getting By in Hard Times: Gendered Labour at Home and on the Job*. Toronto: University of Toronto Press.

Marx, Karl. 1969. Preface to a contribution to a critique of political economy. In K. Marx and F. Engels, *Selected Works. Vol. 1*. Moscow: Progress Publishers. 502–506.

Marx, Karl. 1976. *Capital: A Critique of Political Economy, Volume One*, trans. Ben Fowkes. Harmondsworth: Penguin.

Marx, Karl, and Friedrich Engels. 1969. *The German Ideology*. In K. Marx and F. Engels, *Selected Works. Vol. 1*. Moscow: Progress Publishers. 16–80.

Marx, Karl, and Friedrich Engels. 2002. *The Communist Manifesto*. London: Penguin.

Miliband, Ralph. 1969. *The State in Capitalist Society*. New York: Basic Books.

Naiman, Joanne. 2008. *How Societies Work: Class, Power and Change in a Canadian Context*, 4th ed. Black Point NS: Fernwood.

Ó Riain, S. 2000. Net-working for a living: Irish software developers in the global workplace. In M. Burawoy, J. A. Blum, S. George, Z. Gille, T. Gowan, L. Haney, M. Klawiter, S. H. Lopez, S. Ó Riain, and M. Thayer, eds., *Global Ethnography: Forces, Connections, and Imaginations in a Postmodern World*. Berkeley: University of California Press. 175–202.

Pakulski, Jan, and Malcolm Waters. 1996. *The Death of Class*. London: SAGE.

Poulantzas, Nicos. 1978. *Political Power and Social Classes*. London: Verso.

Rinehart, James. 2006. *The Tyranny of Work: Alienation and the Labour Process*, 5th ed. Toronto: Harcourt Canada.

Ritzer, George. 2008. *The McDonaldization of Society*. Los Angeles: Pine Forge Press.

Ross, Andrew. 2001. No-collar labour in America's "new economy." In *Socialist Register, Volume 37: Working Classes, Global Realities*. London: Merlin Press, 77–87.

Royle, Tony. 2000. *Working for McDonald's in Europe: The Unequal Struggle?* London & New York: Routledge. 58–70.

Satzewich, Vic. 1991. *Racism and the Incorporation of Foreign Labour: Farm Labour Migration to Canada Since 1945*. London & New York: Routledge.

Satzewich, Vic, and Terry Wotherspoon. 2000. The state and the contradictions of Indian administration. In *First Nations: Race, Class and Gender Relations*. Regina: Canadian Plains Research Center. 15–41.

Sharma, Nandita. 2006. *Home Economics: Nationalism and the Making of "Migrant Workers" in Canada*. Toronto: University of Toronto Press.

Smith, Dorothy. 1987. *The Everyday World as Problematic: A Feminist Sociology*. Toronto: University of Toronto Press.

Smith, Dorothy. 1999. *Writing the Social: Critique, Theory, and Investigations*. Toronto: University of Toronto Press.

Stark, David. 1980. Class struggle and the labour process. *Theory and Society* 9(1): 89–130.

Steedman, Mercedes. 1997. *Angels of the Workplace: Women and the Construction of Gender Relations in the Canadian Clothing Industry, 1890–1940*. Toronto: Oxford University Press.

Stiglitz, Joseph. 2008. A global lesson in market failure. *Globe and Mail*, July 7. A17.

Thomas, Mark. 2009. *Regulating Flexibility: The Political Economy of Employment Standards*. Montreal & Kingston: McGill-Queen's University Press.

Thomas, Mark. 2010. Neoliberalism, racialization, and the regulation of employment standards. In S. Braedley and M. Luxton, eds., *Neoliberalism and Everyday Life*. Montreal & Kingston: McGill-Queen's University Press. 68–89.

Touraine, Alain. 1988. *Return of the Actor: Social Theory in Postindustrial Society*. Minneapolis: University of Minnesota Press.

Vosko, Leah F. 2000. *Temporary Work: The Gendered Rise of a Precarious Employment Relationship*. Toronto: University of Toronto Press.

Weber, Max. 1978. *Economy and Society: An Outline of Interpretive Sociology. Volume 1*. Berkeley: University of California Press.

Winsa, Patty. 2009. Poor neighbourhoods growing across Toronto. *Toronto Star*, February 8.

Wright, Erik Olin. 2005. Foundations of a neo-Marxist class analysis. In E. O. Wright, ed., *Approaches to Class Analysis*. Cambridge: Cambridge University Press. 4–30.

Yalnizyan, Armine. 1998. *The Growing Gap: A Report on Growing Inequality Between the Rich and Poor in Canada*. Toronto: Centre for Social Justice.

AGE: DECENTRING ADULTHOOD

Rebecca Raby *Brock University*

7

INTRODUCTION

"Why are so many people in their 20s taking so long to grow up?" asks a 2010 New York Times article (Henig, 2010). Over the past decade, many articles, both popular and scholarly, have alternatively lamented that childhood ends too soon, that teenagers grow up too fast, and that young adults, or "kidults," are refusing to grow up (Blatterer, 2007; Danesi, 2003). Which raises the question: How do we even know when we are adults? Are there certain key markers in Western society indicating that someone is now a "grownup"?

While age is generally understood to be natural, such age-based categories are social, reflecting a specific time and place, namely mid-20th-century, Western society. And like other normative categories, they reflect relations of power. In this chapter, I "unpack" such age-based categories. How does a certain understanding of adulthood as rational, independent, and productive come to occupy the centre, for example? How are growing up and growing old positioned in relationship to such an understanding of adulthood?

This chapter draws primarily on a Foucaultian analysis of power to deconstruct and decentre adulthood in relation to understandings of childhood, adolescence, youth, and old age. I consider what beliefs and social contexts underpin our definitions of these stages of life. These beliefs are not benign, but steeped in relations of power—both disciplinary power and the perpetuation of gender, class, and cultural hierarchies articulated by feminist and Marxist scholars outlined in previous chapters. In this chapter I introduce and evaluate some key sociological concepts related to the study of age, and then discuss specific life "stages" as situated in particular historical, economic, and political contexts. I then consider some dimensions through which the normative life course may be disrupted: intersections between age and other social identities, production and consumption, dependency, and finally advocacy.

THE LIFE COURSE: NORMS, STAGES, AND TRANSITIONS

In the study of growing up and growing old, sociologists have developed key concepts that are both useful and problematic. The **life course** refers to our lives, from infancy to death, and includes consideration of "the way in which social institutions shape and institutionalize individual lives" (Settersten & Mayer, 1997: 234). Sociologists have tended to prefer the term life course over "life cycle," as the latter implies a repetition of the same pattern and/or a return at the end of life to an organism's beginnings, much as we see in the *Ages of Man* woodcut shown here, leaving little room for change or diversity (Settersten, 2003).

FIGURE 7.1 ■ *Ages of Man*, a popular woodcut from early-19th-century France, provides a historical representation of the life course. This image makes intuitive sense to many of us as the body goes through initial growth, midlife, and then eventual waning, with very old age represented as a return to the dependency of infancy. Yet our aging bodies, while relevant, are not the whole story, for they are always interpreted through the lens of culture. Thus, midlife is shown in this woodcut at the peak of the arc, described as "maturity" and "discretion," while both infancy and old age are associated with being bedridden and *enfance*, the oldest phase being quite negatively represented through terms such as decline, decadence, and decrepitude. The images are also clearly gendered and show affluent, heterosexual couples.

© The Art Archive/Alamy

Many discuss the life course in terms of stages, transitions, and norms. Our lives are frequently thought to unfold through concrete **stages**, each of which is assumed to come with certain features and/or crises. Social psychologist Erik Erikson's well-known life stages (1968) is based on having to complete specific tasks of **identity** development.

ERIKSON'S STAGES

Infancy. Basic trust is acquired.
Early childhood. Autonomous will develops.
Childhood. Anticipation of roles, display of initiative, and gradual influence of gender, guilt, and morality.

School age. Task identification, development of a sense of industry.
Adolescence. Gradual aquisition of independent identity.
Adulthood. Crisis of intimacy.
Old age. Development of integrity.

Stage approaches are common in developmental psychology, focusing on how we proceed through sequential stages of morality, emotion, physicality, cognition, and so forth, especially in childhood and adolescence. From this perspective, failure to appropriately move through a particular stage can have lifelong repercussions, and often adulthood is assumed to be the pinnacle of accomplishment. For instance, Erikson is particularly interested in how we develop into having a "healthy" personality in adulthood, based on active mastery of our environment, unity in personality, and a correct perception of oneself and the wider world (1968). Stages are similarly defined and framed by **transitions**, or pivotal points of change from one stage to another. Neugarten, Moore, and Lowe's classic "social clock theory" suggests major life transitions are expected at certain ages, with adverse consequences for those who are "off track" (1965). Transitions to adulthood, through graduation, work, marriage, and parenthood have been of particular interest to sociologists, because they are assumed to be central to becoming a mature, independent adult.

Finally, stages and transitions are considered the scaffolding for **age norms**, shared ideas and expectations about what is typical behaviour at certain ages (Lawrence, 1996). Much of the early sociological research in this area was influenced by the theoretical framework of **structural functionalism**. As you may have learned in courses covering classical sociological theory, this approach argues that social structures and shared values foster consensus in society. Structural functionalists consider shared age norms as valuable to the functioning of society, and necessarily enforced through social control (Settersten & Mayer, 1997).

Concepts such as stages, transitions, and age norms have usefully informed a wide body of research into the life course. They have also been important for identifying needs for support when people are "off time." If a young person is not meeting expected stages of educational progress, for example, educators can be alerted to their need for help. However, work with these concepts has also been problematized for neglecting links to diversity, power, and inequality. A more critical perspective suggests that age norms are used by more dominant social groups to maintain power and to attempt the **moral regulation** of others, establishing, and reinforcing narrow ideas of what is correct or ideal behaviour. What assumptions are embedded in certain described stages, for instance? Or when we focus on certain transitions rather than others? If we look back at Erikson's broad stages, we can see that they favour independence, initiative, and industry, all traits we know are particularly valued within Western capitalist society.

Dannefer (1984) is concerned that a focus on such predefined stages and transitions ignores the broader social context, including diversity across groups of people. When individual and group patterns do not fit normative models of stages or transitions, they are often problematically defined by the dominant group as deviant, whereas in fact they are frequently logical, patterned variations arising as people from diverse backgrounds engage with their environments across their lives. Normative stages and transitions are thus complicated by poverty, gender diversity, racialization, geographical displacement, minority cultural traditions, single parenthood, and so forth (Settersten & Mayer, 1997). To illustrate, Dannefer describes American "homeboys," or gang members, who have distinct internal age gradations linked to proving themselves in a context in which few expect to live into adulthood. Dannefer links these gang members' life courses to their marginalization within larger society (2003) rather than individual deviance. In another example, Geronimus (2003) presents the provocative argument that campaigns against teenage childbearing tacitly privilege middle-class, European-Americans for whom late childbearing brings rewards. While it is commonly assumed that teenage childbearing is a burden on teenagers, on their families, and on broader social supports, Geronimus argues that for African-Americans in high-poverty, urban areas, early childbearing may be a logical choice as poverty and racial inequality can lead to a shortened healthy life expectancy. For this community, teen pregnancies, alongside grandparents' childcare involvement, can have better social outcomes than later pregnancies. Geronimus contends that in this context, the resources invested in negative categorization of early childbearing reflects how European Americans educate their own youth for success in ways that may marginalize others (see also Burton, 1990).

We thus need to consider how our assumptions about specific times of the life course contribute to the *creation* of dominant stages, transitions, and age norms. What interests are served by these dominant views, and how do they justify the evaluation and regulation of certain groups of people? Consider the everyday practice of asking someone's age, and how the answer contributes to how we categorize and evaluate them. We are deeply invested in locating others and ourselves within age-based markers and expectations, providing solidarity, pleasure, security, self-understanding, and a base from which to act. But they can also bring pressure, self-regulation, judgement, discrimination, and exclusion.

Through disciplinary power, we are all participants in the normative regulation of age, even though it can marginalize those people whose lives do not fit comfortably into dominant age-based expectations and exclusions. Age may thus trigger self-critique, marginalization, and challenge. Joanna Gregson's (2009) ethnographic study into the lives of American teenage mothers provides an illustration. Because of their youth, the moms in her study found their mothering to be under constant critical scrutiny and comment from healthcare professionals and the public. While these comments were marginalizing and sometimes fostered self-doubt, the girls often responded with what Gregson calls "competitive parenting," trying to show how they were better parents than both their peers and the older women who may have had their babies "on time." Thus these young mothers both internalized normative critique and sought to combat it.

ADULTHOOD

Central to the formation of dominant age norms is the western, twentieth-century understanding of "modern adulthood," a concept premised on several key features.

- Adulthood has been commonly framed as the stable endpoint of growing up, associated with attaining stability, completeness, self-knowledge, and self-possession (Blatterer, 2007; Lesko, 1996a).

- Adulthood is associated with rationality, maturity, and a command of emotions, as contrasted to the irrationality and emotionality of other age groups (Lesko, 1996a; Walkerdine, 1993).

- Adulthood is often assumed to rest on middle-class benchmarks such as completed education, a career, marriage, parenthood, and property ownership (Blatterer, 2007).

- Finally, adulthood is defined through independence, in contrast to the frailty, dependence, and potential confusion often associated with old age (Hockey & James, 1993).

All these benchmarks seem to reflect common sense; yet they begin to unravel in the face of personal histories, shifting economic conditions, diverse life experiences, and the contrasting categories of childhood, youth, and old age.

The concept of **recapitulation** provides an example of how the development of our current beliefs about childhood, adolescence, and adulthood are not benign. Recapitulation, popular in the late 19th and early 20th centuries, posited that the development of human beings from children to adults mirrors the evolution of "the race," "a term that variously meant the human race or the white or civilized race" (Adams, 1997: 44). From this perspective, children were equated with "savage" or "primitive" peoples, and both were also variously equated with criminality, womanhood, and even old age (Gould, 1977). This presupposition problematically positioned "normal" white, European men as the pinnacle of development, while non-whites were considered less evolved, less able to be fully mature, and "arrested" at earlier stages of both evolutionary and human development, implying that only certain (white, male) young people could develop into full adulthood (Adams, 1997).

The notion of rationality has similarly been used to distinguish those deserving of adult status. Historically, the attribute of rationality was used to contrast the white, bourgeois man from the **other**, categories of exclusion and assumed inferiority, including women, children, lower classes, and the "savage" (Alsop, Fitzsimons & Lennon, 2002). Those defined outside of rationality have also included criminals and adults with physical and mental disabilities. The centrality of rationality to adulthood continues to hold sway, with the implication that emotionality—whether of women, children, people from non-Western cultures, or certain racialized categories—undermines access to the status of adulthood. Through such marginalizing definitions of adulthood, Lesko suggests that "we are specifying a normal developmental outcome that is [actually] gender, race, and class specific" (Lesko, 1996a: 142)—we see this pattern repeated in discussions of dependency at the end of this chapter.

The modern notion of adulthood has also rested on certain economic and political structures of the mid-20th century, including the availability of stable careers and the support of the welfare state, especially through pension provisions (Kohli, 2007; Lee, 2001). However, with the current erosion of possibilities for solid, long-term careers, support networks and provisions of the welfare state including pensions (see Chapter 11), some argue that this modern understanding of adulthood has shifted (Lee, 2001). It is argued that these changes are making social roles, including those linked to age, more flexible. Blatterer contends that within this context, adulthood is no longer about learning to fulfill preset social roles but about individual self-reflexivity and self-control—a psychological rather than material adulthood (2007). These unbounded possibilities might seem exciting, but they are also uncertain and risky, masking structural inequalities that impede people and putting blame for failure on the individual (Blatterer, 2007; Cartmel & Furlong, 1997).

However, others oppose the idea that age norms defining adulthood are weakening. Kohli (2007) argues that 20th-century life course norms persist, particularly in countries that have retained strong welfare systems. For example, most Western (male) adults retain stable, long-term jobs and then retire; and most people develop lifelong relationships. Also, alongside the erosion of certain normative life course markers, new ones have taken their place, as we see in upward shifts in expected ages for childbearing (Roberts, Clifton & Ferguson, 2005), and Blatterer's assertion that material markers of adulthood are being replaced by psychological ones. Furthermore, new age-based identity categories such as "tween" and "Third Ager" (see below) have been created, legal stipulations related to age continue to flourish, and age-based identities continue to be intersected by powerful structures of inequality, especially class and gender. As Blatterer argues, the 20th-century norm of a stable, structured conception of adulthood certainly continues to hold *ideological* sway when people are judged "successfully" adult on the basis of having a stable career, home, and family, and this is why we see such hand-wringing and worry about "prolonged adolescence" today.

CHILDHOOD AND ADOLESCENCE

How we think about childhood and adolescence is determined by how we define adulthood, particularly in relation to adult rationality. Childhood (including adolescence and youth) is framed as undeveloped, irrational, peer-focused, closer to nature, and incomplete, while adulthood takes the dominant half of each of these pairs: developed, rational, independent, socialized, and complete (Castaneda, 2002; Davies, 2002; Lesko, 1996b).

Childhood

The modern, Western conceptualization of childhood emphasizes innocence, dependence, and development. These should be fairly familiar to most readers of this chapter, and for many it is considered so natural that children exposed to sexual exploitation, war, or labour are often defined as having "lost" childhood itself. Yet while childhood innocence and dependency have been important for championing children's rights and well-being, they can also remarginalize children. For example, this definition of childhood can, ironically, be deployed to avoid protection of certain young people because they are no longer considered children due to sexual experiences (Kitzinger, 1988), or to suggest that the protection they seek is inappropriate, for example in the case of young people seeking contraceptives adults do not wish them to have (Pilcher, 1997).

Current definitions of childhood are also historically and contextually specific. As James and Prout (1990) and many others have contended, the concept of childhood is not universal and timeless; it shifts across history, location, gender, class, and so on. The classic yet controversial text on the history of childhood in Western society is Phillipe Ariès' *Centuries of Childhood* (1962), in which the author argues that the modern conception of childhood as a separate stage of life emerged in Europe between the 15th and 18th centuries, together with bourgeois notions of family, home, privacy, and individuality. Ariès asserts that prior to this time, childhood as a unique category requiring special provisions did not exist, with individuals from across the life course sharing in games and work. Young people were fully integrated participants in society and were afforded no special protection (Qvortrup, 2005). Ariès contends that only in the 1700s did artistic and literary representations begin to mark childhood as a unique domain set apart from the everyday life of adult society.

FIGURE 7.2 ■ *Madonna* and *Child*, Duccio di Buoninsegna, about 1284–1286. Historian Phillipe Ariès noted that until the 12th century, medieval art tended to portray children with adult-like features. An example can be seen in this image.

Crevole Madonna, c.1284 (The Virgin and Child with Angels), Duccio di Buoninsegna, (c.1278-1318)/Museo dell'Opera del Duomo, Siena, Italy/The Bridgeman Art Library

This viewpoint has not gone unchallenged. Albanese (2009) cites various authors who contend that in other, non-Western societies a concept of childhood predated medieval Europe's "invention" of it. Karen Calvert and others have also criticized Ariès' methodology, including the way he generalized from limited, bourgeois sources such as paintings. Calvert nonetheless argues that Ariès' work illustrates that the form childhood takes, and whether age differences are prioritized, changes over time. Albanese agrees that the notion of childhood has taken on different significance at different times.

Indeed, our modern conceptualizations of the child can be seen to have emerged primarily through social, economic, and political changes in the 19th century, when gradual separation of the private home from the public workplace resulted from the shifts from rural farming to urban industry (Piekoff & Brickey, 1991). Bourgeois beliefs arose valuing innocent childhood and domestic motherhood (Chunn, 2003) and social reformers allied with this vision of childhood sought to protect young people who were gradually removed from the workforce through both law and compulsory education (Valverde, 1991). These reform projects promoted Anglo-Saxon, middle-class understandings of childhood among working classes, native peoples, and new immigrants, including ideas about children as protected, innocent, wayward, and subordinate (Chunn, 2003), distinctions that came to be supported through law and eventually embraced by all.

As discussed in Chapter 8, it was also at the end of the 19th century that the social sciences, especially psychology and sociology, took hold—disciplines intent on measuring, scrutinizing, evaluating, and regulating large populations (Foucault, 1978). Population surveys became a new mechanism of governing to measure and manage large groups of people. The social sciences, while seeking the truth about populations, constructed knowledge about them (Walkerdine, 1993), including ideas of normalcy and deviancy. The growth of developmentalism was part of this process.

Developmentalism

As suggested at the opening of this chapter, the dominant template of the life course comes from developmental psychology, which focuses primarily on the early years but also extends to frame adulthood and old age (Dannefer, 1989). Normative and non-normative paths of development are identified, largely to facilitate intervention when there are abnormalities or problems (Rose, 1990). For many, such interventions have been important and valuable, in identifying and addressing learning disabilities for instance. Such a developmental framework has also granted young people an important degree of leeway in their behaviours, as it is believed that their immature emotional and thinking processes are undergoing growth and change. That is why young people tend to be treated differently than adults in courts of law, why they have come to be organized into age-graded classrooms, and why there is a United Nations Convention specifically addressing children's protection rights.

Developmentalism is frequently presented as a fact-based, neutral, scientific system, uncovering what already exists. But Walkerdine (1993) and others have countered that developmentalism *produces* a particular understanding of what is there. Development is thus a discourse "produced in particular circumstances, for particular reasons, and perhaps in the interests of particular persons or groups" (Morss, 1996: 48). Thus developmentalism both reflects and contributes to the historically specific understandings of both adulthood and childhood shaping how we think about each child, and childhood in general, including what children are capable of, how they should be raised, and what to do when they fail to meet normative expectations.

An example of how this works is illustrated when we look at children's play. Within the developmental approach to childhood, play is currently categorized as a vital, primary way in which children learn, and parent–child play is therefore encouraged to maximize childhood development (Lancy, 2007). Yet Lancy draws on anthropological work to counter this advice, arguing that this position reflects a privileged Western, middle-class conceptualization of childhood and parenting. He argues that in a large number of societies, parents do not play with their children and play is in fact discouraged. These contrasting orientations arise from cultural beliefs that resonate with necessity, where parents, especially mothers, do not have the time to play and children must make early contributions through work. Lancy suggests that by exporting an ideal of mother–child play based on Western privilege and ideals, parenting (and poverty) are problematized across a number of other cultural settings.

Shifting from play to "inherent" childhood curiosity, Walkerdine (1993) challenges a developmental framework through the lens of class. In her example, a girl in a wealthy family shows "natural" (developmental) four-year-old puzzlement in trying to figure out how it is that someone is paid to wash her windows, while a working class girl is considered to have a deficit when she fails to "puzzle" over a question of money. But for this second girl, questions of money are far more fraught, emotional, and meaningful than the term "puzzlement" can capture. So when puzzlement is universalized in this instance as a four-year-old trait, class and inequality can be ignored and reproduced. Developmental frameworks now take on the disciplinary power of scrutiny, evaluation, and self-regulation, Walkerdine claims: "This ... child has every action calibrated so as to assure that development will be normal and natural,... because abnormal and pathological development has to be noted, classified, corrected" (455).

Finally, a focus on developmental stages in childhood and adolescence is of concern to sociologists of childhood who contend that by focusing on what young people will become in the future there is little regard for who or what they are in the present (James & Prout, 1990; Lesko, 1996b). Lesko argues that this abstraction of young people as *always becoming* keeps them from knowing and therefore representing themselves, with presumably fully developed and rational adults always knowing them better (1996b).

Adolescence

While we commonly hear concerns about "natural" teenage risk-taking, rebelliousness, and emerging sexuality, the ideas of adolescence and teenagehood as unique stages of life are similarly historically and culturally specific. While primarily male, upper-class youth had formed recognizable groups that were subject to public worries prior to this time (Kett, 2003), the term **adolescence** as a broad category emerged in the late 19th century, fostered through industrialization and the gradual removal of young people from the workplace and into age-graded schooling. Pivotal to popularizing the concept was Stanley G. Hall's book *Adolescence*, published in 1904. While previously, advice to young people "urged the early cultivation of adult responsibility" (Kett, 2003: 357), Hall drew on recapitulation theory, arguing that adolescents were in an instinctual, "primitive state" of "storm and stress," and that their development required careful management for a successful transition to adulthood (Adams, 1997). Hall's concerns sought to address broader worries about emasculated adulthood and the needs of the American nation, so his advice was primarily directed toward boys and the appropriate development of their masculinity through organizations such as the YMCA and Boy Scouts (Kett, 2003).

Concerns linking this time of life to the state of the nation were again prominent across North America in the mid-20th century when the new concept of **teenager** became popularized largely as a new consumer group (Adams, 1997). Uncertainty permeated the North American psyche after World War II, particularly with the rise of the Cold War with the Soviet Union, and teenagers, embodying the future of the nation, were of specific concern. Anxiety grew that young people had not been supervised enough during the war and now were being drawn into a growing teen consumer culture that was increasingly considered a social problem. Solutions sought to foster the ideal nuclear family, e.g. with a stay-at-home mom, and channel young people's developing sexuality through moral hygiene films such as *Dating Do's and Don'ts* (1949) and *Molly Grows Up* (1953).

So we see adolescence and teenagehood as primarily 20th-century categories, developed through the social sciences, marketing, and political concerns. Over the course of the 20th century, these categories became more rigorously linked to high school peer cultures, dating, consumerism, and fears of delinquency. While there was criticism of Hall's approach when it was first introduced, it still influences how we think about adolescence today, for example in the notion that adolescence is a time of explosive, dangerous sexuality (Adams, 1997), and in need of special investigation and guidance by "experts" (Kett, 2003).

An example of how these ideas are cultural is Amy Schalet's (2004) comparison of parental attitudes toward teenage sexuality in the United States and in the Netherlands. Schalet found that American parents assumed teenagers to be irrationally and irresponsibly driven by hormones and therefore unable to fall in love. They also assumed that young men simply want sex, leaving young women vulnerable to heartbreak and pregnancy. In contrast, Dutch parents felt that "teenagers are self-regulating sexual agents who pace their sexual development and use contraceptives when they deem themselves ready" (11). Sexuality is considered to be ordinary and gradual, developing for both boys and girls through courtship and love. Perhaps unsurprisingly, rates of teenage pregnancies and abortion are much higher in the United States than in the Netherlands, because young people in the Netherlands have had far more opportunities to talk to their parents about sex and to learn about contraceptives.

IS YOUTH THE NEW CENTRE?

In this chapter, I position adulthood as the commonly unproblematized **centre** of the life course, suggesting that it is the dominant position against which other age categories are defined; yet youthfulness is idealized in marketing, media, consumption practices, and popular commentary (Danesi, 2003). Could it be youth who are really in the dominant life course position? With rampant marketing of youthfulness and preferences for flexibility, adaptability, and changing technologies, youth may indeed be the new "centre." It is young people that we see on television and who are described as bringing new energy and ideas to workplaces. And yet while many people may want to look and feel young, young people themselves remain marginalized and hold very little power in society generally. As students, they are marginalized socially by being subjected to a wide range of disciplinary tactics that significantly limit their autonomy. Economically they are marginalized from relations of production due to extended schooling and short-term, part-time, low-wage work (Côté & Allahar, 2006). And discursively they are marginalized because they are understood as irrational, unstable, and incomplete compared to adults.

Of course, these emphases on turbulent, sexualized young people again imply that adulthood is, in contrast, stable, rational and sexually restrained (Adams, 1997; Lesko, 1996a; Raby, 2002). When adolescence is distinguished from adulthood, it is frequently in ways that marginalize young people. For example, by framing teenagers as inherently peer-focused, they can be homogenized and dismissed as dangerous others, without regard for how peer culture has developed through intense school segregation (Lesko, 1996a). For racialized teenagers these othering processes are even more marked (Ferguson, 2000; Morris, 2005). Another example is found in recent "teen brain" research in neuroscience. Monica Payne (2009) contends that popularized "teen brain" literature argues that young people lack a fully mature brain and therefore the ability to think rationally, manage their emotions, be empathetic, and multitask, suggesting that they require surveillance and supervision well into their twenties. Payne is concerned with how this research has been embraced while defining young people as inferior, citing similar historical accounts of scientific research used to discriminate against groups of people, including Jews and women, through suggesting that they have inferior brains (Payne, 2009).

The 20th-century removal of young people from the workforce and into long-term, age-segregated schooling also reinforced adolescence as a category of incompleteness and preparation for adulthood. Marxist theorists have focused on how these processes have bolstered capitalist hierarchies as schools "sort and select" them into future workers (Bourdieu & Passeron, 1977; Oakes, 1985) and as age is used to legitimize their inferior wages (Tyyska, 2009).

In this section I have illustrated that while adolescence and teenagehood arose as social categories only within the past century and a half, they are frequently defined through naturalizing discourses and institutionalized inequalities. These processes in turn lead to the regulation, surveillance, and marginalization of teenagers, while reinforcing the idea of a stable, rational, and independent adulthood.

WHAT IS A TEENAGER IN KATHMANDU, NEPAL?

Mark Liechty (1995) suggests that state emphasis on progress and modernization alongside globalized consumer culture created a new concept in Kathmandu in the late 20th century: the teenager. Commercial interests, such as a new magazine called *Teen*, channelled young people's interests toward consumerism and image. To Nepali adults, teenagers were young people deeply invested in modern consumption and image (as represented in *Teen*) and/or young men who used pornography and drugs. In any case, the identity of the teenager was unique to a small group of young people and linked to corrupting, modern, Westernized consumerism. Yet for most young people, this notion of teenagehood was difficult to attain due to their unemployment and poverty, a conflict alienating many youth.

POST-ADULTHOOD? THE "THIRD" AND "FOURTH" AGES

Just as conceptualizations of childhood have emerged and changed across time and place, so have conceptualizations of old age. Stephen Katz (1996) argues that in Western, premodern thought, aging was considered spiritual and physical. Age was considered a decline but not a disease, and there was optimism about overcoming old age. In contrast, early modern **gerontology** (the study of aging) tended to focus on the uncovering of innate characteristics of aging, separating the aged body from other parts of life, and framing age in terms of disorder, disability and eventual death. Miraculous possibility was replaced by biological certainty as "modernity's forms of calculation, division, and hierarchy separated it as a distinct, developmental stage" (Katz, 2005: 32). Conventional gerontology arose, making an ordinary part of life subject to expert understanding and intervention, to evaluate and treat apparent pathology. As such, conventional gerontology is an example of expertise as productive and disciplinary, a topic we return to in the Part III of this textbook. In contrast, **social gerontology** "focuses on what it means to age in society" (Markson, 2003: 12). This perspective encompasses a wide range of approaches that share a focus on social rather than biological factors. Social gerontologists tend to recognize how aging is affected by context, personal experiences, and social structures. Social gerontology includes **critical gerontology**, which focuses on power and inequality in age relations, noting that naturalization of the life course can legitimize a social order (Baars, Dannefer, Phillipson & Walker, 2006).

Katz documents modern governmental and disciplinary processes that have constructed the elderly as a homogeneous group. For example, the introduction of pension plans in the 20th century were important, positive attempts by the labour movement and governments to protect and support workers in their old age. Yet pension plans that were based retirement on age, not incapacity, served to contribute to a single view of the life course that "hardened the boundaries around the constitution of the elderly population" (Katz, 1996: 63) and created a new identity: the retired. As a result, old age also became a new **subject position**, or social category, through which to define oneself and be defined by others as distinct from the middle-aged.

This subject position is vulnerable to negative stereotyping about old age, which can contribute to elder abuse (Chappell, McDonald & Stones, 2008). Importantly, however, it can also be used to make demands, including demands for services unique to an older population. Similarly, through diversity in experiences, contexts, and redefinition, Katz suggests that old age can "undiscipline," or disrupt, generalizations about aging. Thus the variability of old age challenges any attempt to scientifically "capture" what it is.

This new subject position is not only discursive but material, as it is grounded in the separation of elderly people from productive work. While retirement may be something to look forward to, political economists of aging argue that its 20th-century institutional-ization in fact ensured the dependency of older people (Chappell, McDonald & Stones, 2008). The loss of a productive role is often linked to negative attitudes toward aging, for "In the processes of modernization and technological development, the skills [of] older persons have lost their value" (Spector-Mersel, 2006: 74). A political economy of aging thus considers the relationship between capitalist modes of production, the allocation of resources, status, and age stratification.

When we discussed adulthood, it was defined as the dominant, independent centre, in contrast to dependent old age. Within the 20th century, normative conceptualizations of old age have reproduced this discourse of dependency, which I return to in the following section. Katz and others, however, have now observed a more recent shift toward "positive aging," focusing on the importance of activity in older age. It is argued that this focus on positive aging, alongside a longer lifespan in the West, and an increase in post-retirement wealth among some middle classes, has produced a new age category, the "Third Age." This period is considered a time of choice, "active leisure," or "creative fulfillment" (Bury, 1995: 22) before a "Fourth Age" of very old age, decline and dependence (Laslett, 1989). This shift has been profoundly empowering for some older people as it reflects "western accounts of agency, autonomy and empowerment" (Wray, 2003: para. 2.4) through activity and independence. But this Third Age is also troubles some critical gerontologists, who argue that it is really a bourgeois position that problematizes older, poorer, and less active bodies, consequently reproducing the centrality of market-oriented, independent adult-hood. Indeed, Katz and Laliberte-Rudman suggest that this new formulation of aging is strategic to the **neoliberal** rationality of declining state support "that maximizes individual responsibility in the service of meeting political goals of minimizing dependency and uni-versal entitlements" (2004: 146).

The concept of a Third Age does suggest that, like other parts of the life course, conceptualizations of old age are not rigid and natural, but reflect certain conditions linked to history, culture, economy, health, and people's political demands. These con-ceptualizations are directly related to understandings of adulthood, drawing on current dichotomies of independence and dependence, bodily health and frailty, and productivity and retirement.

WHAT ABOUT THE BABY BOOMERS?

From quite another perspective, it is not adulthood that has occupied the centre but a specific group of adults, the Baby Boomers, who are now moving into their Third Age. This group was born just after World War II and reaped the benefits of state and career supports over the second half of the 20th century. Commentators have argued that their sheer numbers, their electoral power, and their economic security have significantly shaped social policy in their favour, in turn shifting resources away from other generations. Such a generational analysis notes that specific **cohorts**, or groups of people of the same age, can significantly influence how resources are distributed, and consequently how age is understood and experienced. We can thus explore how our conceptualizations of adulthood and older age are shifting not only through the advance of neoliberalism and the decline of the welfare state but as the Baby Boomers move more deeply into their Third and Fourth Ages.

DISRUPTING THE CENTRE STAGE

I have argued that over the course of the 20th century, certain life course stages and their associated traits became normalized, with modern adulthood as the stable, untroubled centre. Despite commonly held assumptions about childhood, adolescence, youth, adulthood, and old age, we have seen that this life course organization has arisen within a certain context, and carries many consequences. It has provided people with clear, familiar expectations for growing up and growing old, and a mechanism for intervention when things go wrong; but normative expectations have also produced ideas regarding who should be valued and who should have authority, while devaluing what is non-normative. In this next section, I focus on points that problematize all clear life stages and very specifically the "adult centre."

Intersections

An emphasis on homogeneity in life course stages downplays their internal diversity; yet normative stages are complicated by experiences, particularly those structured around the multiple intersections of gender, class, culture, race, sexuality, and disability, and so forth (Rattanski & Phoenix, 2005). For example, an adult centre premised on labour force productivity is complicated by the many adults outside the labour force because they are unemployed, raising children, or disabled, and by children who work in the labour force. Similarly, those who do not marry and/or are not heterosexual complicate the historical centrality of heterosexual marriage; and linking adulthood to the traditional nuclear family is complicated by teenage childbearing, extended families, and infertility.

Intersections can also have profound ripple effects across our lives due to the interdependence of earlier and later life (O'Rand, 1990), particularly in terms of class. For example, men who marry before finishing school tend to have a lower socioeconomic status later in life (O'Rand, 1990). And as populations age they become more heterogeneous, which some attribute to strengthening individuality, but which Dannefer (1987) considers a feature of the **Matthew Effect**, or the accumulated consequences of inequalities across the life course. Patterns of education and employment differentiate people over time, increasing differences between them in terms of health as well as economic and **cultural capital**, the values, beliefs, habits, attitudes, and skills deemed valuable by the dominant members of society. Consequently as a cohort ages, income inequality within it increases, often exacerbated by issues of race and gender.

For example, the standard model of the modern life course has been premised on the trajectory of a male breadwinner. Yet as Mandell, Wilson, and Duffy (2008) discuss, Canadian women at midlife are particularly susceptible to the Matthew Effect. Women's economic inequality increases with age due to their propensity to be in lower-paying and/or part-time jobs, and to have spent a portion of time outside of the labour market for child-rearing. While the Canadian poverty rate of elderly women has dropped over the past few decades, still 20 percent of elderly women are living alone in poverty (Evans, 2010). As Evans explains, these women tend to be separated or divorced, and therefore have less access to spousal retirement benefits and often lack adequate benefit packages due to having been out of the workforce when raising children. Women of visible minorities who have experienced discrimination in the workplace face an even greater likelihood of poverty in old age (Calasanti, 2008; Evans, 2010). Finally, gendered beauty standards make women particularly susceptible to ageism, which negatively affects their employment prospects and outcomes. As one woman puts it, "You disappear off the map once you hit 45 or 48…. You can go and apply for a million jobs and you might as well be invisible because … they're going to take the young woman" (Hurd Clarke & Griffin, 2008).

These examples of class and gender are just some of the intersections that complicate and denaturalize normative age and transitions. Yet when we generalize about categories such as old age, lauding the freedom and consumption of the Third Age, for instance, these divisions are obfuscated.

Production and Consumption

Clear distinctions across the life course have also been complicated by late-20th-century shifts in production and consumption of goods. Recall that the modern conceptualization of adulthood was linked to entry into a stable career, with retirement signalling a transition into a new life stage (Lee, 2001). This conceptualization neglected to address work inside the home, largely undertaken by women. It is also now under threat due to the decline of lifelong careers, which are being replaced by so called "flexible" employment arrangements marked by periods of labour skills retraining. These shifts potentially unmoor an adult centre and disrupt clear transitions between youth and adulthood, and between midlife and old age (Lee, 2001). For both young people and adults, extended education and movement back and forth into the labour market create both choice and uncertainty. For older people, unease is intensified as the assurance of some form of state financial support in old age becomes less certain. Settersten and Trauten are concerned about the consequent mental health and quality of life of older people, particularly those with limited resources (2008).

Shifts in emphasis from production to consumption have created opportunities for the more affluent young and old. For instance, Western children's disposable income has increased substantially, and children increasingly influence their families' spending choices, challenging earlier assumptions that children are sheltered from the world of commerce (Schor, 2004; Pugh, 2009). Similarly, the rise of Third Agers has also been largely based on consumerism extending well beyond retirement (Katz, 2005). Yet ironically, while consumption practices de-centre adulthood, consumption and marketing strategies often reinforce age categories and construct new, ever more graded ones. New terms and consequent identities that have been developed include toddlers, pretweens, tweens, preteens, teens, young adults, the boomers, empty-nesters, and Third Agers, all of which Katz defines as segmented consumer subgroups. Similarly, the late-20th-century movement to redefine aging has led to a powerful marketing culture based on anti-aging products (Katz, 2005). This sale of youthfulness problematizes age by promising to stretch middle age forever, reminding us of premodern hopes for miraculous longevity (Katz, 2005). On the one hand, age stages are blurred through marketing and consumption that promote youthfulness. On the other hand, age stages are created and exploited. Both suggest the social nature of these categories and the political and economic investments in them.

Dependency

Another key Western distinction between childhood, adulthood, and old age has been based on the assumption of adult independence, through participation in the labour force, personal autonomy, and able-bodiedness. Once again, these features distinguish adulthood from the physical and financial dependence of both childhood and old age. British scholars Hockey and James (1993) point out that, sadly, this focus on independence often results in the infantalization of the old, especially in retirement facilities. And while links between dependency and marginality in childhood are considered acceptable because they are transitory and even idealized, this is not so for the elderly. Hockey and James argue that, for this reason, the tendency to treat older people as if they were children might be more comfortable for caregivers, as it may allow adults to shore up the "ideological dominance of adulthood" (37) and to distance themselves from their own potential dependency. While infantalization may help middle-aged adults maintain life course boundaries, however, it is experienced by many elderly and those with disabilities as insulting and marginalizing, as they are not taken seriously or included in decision-making (Hockey & James, 1993).

Hockey and James also challenge the notion of independent adulthood in and of itself. First, they argue that dependence is framed through a Western history of personhood that invests value in independence, individualism, and productivity. They find that these conceptualizations define productivity and personhood through labour force participation, which again marginalizes children, many women, those with disabilities, and the elderly. We see this theme also in Spector-Mersel's (2006) research, where she demonstrates that aging can challenge men's sense of self because they have to negotiate the difficult disjuncture between Western masculinity's focus on male power and control alongside their own reduced social power as older men.

Yet associations between adulthood and independence, and between childhood, old age, and dependence can be complicated in various ways, particularly through the concept of **agency**, or people's ability to make and act on choices about the world around them. Childhood researchers such as James and Prout have emphasized how children are active agents in creating their social worlds in the present (1990), a position supported through a breadth of studies, including Cosaro's (1997) observations of children's play in Italian and American nurseries, Renold's (2005) research into British primary school children's negotiation of gender and sexuality, and Laws and Davies' (2000) observations of students' negotiation of being disciplined in elementary school. These examples challenge the idea that children are entirely dependent and passive by indicating that they are interdependent beings.

Sharon Wray (2003) provides cross-cultural examples to uncouple the Western conflation of old age, dependency, and powerlessness. She argues that "it is possible ... to remain a powerful agent despite the threat or presence of potentially debilitating illness, a change in appearance or a loss of physical functionality" (para. 2.9). She supports her position by citing interviews with Pakistani and Bangladeshi immigrant women in England who said that it was in old age that they felt most in control of their lives, supported through interdependence with family, friends, and, for one, deferment to God. These experiences counter Western conflations of agency, control, and autonomy. Further, the women saw good health, including health of interrelationships and surrounding community, as key to agency and empowerment. Hockey and James similarly cite various non-Western contexts in which social interconnection and cohesion are actively created through interdependence, disrupting the Western obsession with independence (1993).

Finally, Nick Lee (2001) similarly counters the position that independence and maturity are central to agency. He echoes Hockey and James (1993) in suggesting that all people rely on social supports, language, technology, and so forth, in order to accomplish our goals, so all people are socially embedded and dependent.

Advocacy for Young and Old

Finally, the above discussion of agency is directly linked to the question of advocacy. Advocates for children's participation, recognition, and rights have challenged children's discursive construction as incomplete, immature, and irrational. They counter that children are to be valued for what they are in the present, as different from adults but not inferior to them. Advocates in the **sociology of childhood**, for example, prioritize children's agency and insight in research about themselves. They study children's culture through techniques such as ethnography, and through children's participatory involvement, in family, school, and legal decision making (James & Prout, 1990). Acharya (2009) documents a compelling example from Orissa in India, where children reported on the conditions of their villages to top decision makers. In another example, Denton (2003) describes the ongoing Jefferson Committee, an American high school committee with student representatives from all classes, that drafted school rules and now regularly reviews them.

FIGURE 7.3 ■ The Raging Grannies, who first emerged in Victoria, B.C., in the 1980s, play with stereotypes of old age to educate and rally for peace and social justice.

Another advocacy tool has been the *United Nations Convention on the Rights of the Child* (1989), signed by most nations, which emphasizes children's rights not only to health, family, education, and safety but also to participation in decisions that will affect them. Yet the Convention has also been criticized for reinforcing and globalizing a specifically Western definition of childhood, one based on dependency and protection, and for failing to address underlying root causes of inequality in children's lives (for example, see Fernando, 2001).

For the elderly too, various movements have sought to create positive images and experiences. While Katz (2005) and Settersten and Trauten (2008) are concerned that these movements may remarginalize those who are dependent or frail, they also recognize that these forms of activism, often initiated by older adults, can politicize and redefine their collective identities (Katz & Laliberte-Rudman, 2004). Katz and Laliberte-Rudman cite, for example, the Universities of the Third Age in the United Kingdom, a mutual-education movement of "lifelong learning cooperatives of older people" (www.u3a.org.uk). Another example is the Raging Grannies, started in Canada in 1987, a nonviolent protest group that is part of the women's movement. As their website states, one of their strategies involves embracing popular stereotypes of older age through "dressing like innocent little old ladies so we can get close to our 'target'" (http://raginggrannies.org/philosophy).

Advocacy has also involved denaturalizing life course stages and their features, just as this chapter has done. Such disruptions involve recognizing diversity, deconstructing life course categories or stages, and recognizing moments of disruption and resistance. Lesko, for example, disrupts divisions created between teen, adult, and old by recognizing that each life stage simultaneously embodies "mature and immature, old and young, traditional and innovative" (2001: 196).

Such projects raise crucial questions for how we understand growing up and growing old. What might be gained or lost, for example, in denaturalizing our assumptions about childhood? While those in the sociology of childhood advocate a focus on young people as beings in the present to recognize their voices as worthy, others are concerned that it is only by considering young people as incomplete "becomings" that they are deemed worthy of important social investment (Giroux, 2003). Can we accept that young people are distinct from adults in some ways while at the same time dismantling processes of normalization and marginalization? And what of those in older age? Can young people and those in old age have a legitimate, equal voice to that of able-bodied, "independent" adults? And how can practitioners properly account for diversity across age categories? Finally, we need to more deeply consider the role of the body itself. We must account for the growing and weakening body, as it too plays a culturally mediated but also active role in how we understand, represent, and experience the life course (Castaneda, 2002).

CONCLUSION

Historical examinations of childhood and old age have suggested that there was a pre-modern integration of young and old into everyday life, with little importance given to differences between people occupying various ages. Arguably, this lack of clear categorization prevented modern discrimination based on age differences, but also prevented age-based protections (Qvortrup, 2005). With the ascent of modern institutions such as the factory, the school, and the nuclear family, alongside the categorizing and normalizing embedded in disciplines such as psychology and sociology, the modern life course emerged, divided into specific ages and stages. This process created new identities based on age, identities that have allowed for the protection of the young and old, but that have also marginalized them in relationship to the dominant adult centre, and marginalized those not fitting the normative unfolding of stages and transitions.

As I examined earlier when discussing adulthood, many believe that these modern categories have begun to erode in response to the rise of global neoliberalism, displaced stable careers, changing family forms, and the rise of lifelong consumerism. The modern life course's centre of stable adulthood has thus been problematized and potentially de-centred through changing material conditions. At the same time, old and new age norms continue to be asserted. Martin Kohli suggests that what is really at the centre is a life course *regime*, with the modern Western life course remaining an evaluative benchmark, despite its narrow reflection of Western, middle-class, 20th-century ideals (Katz, 2005). While adulthood may be losing some of its material privilege in this new regime, I have contended that it remains at the centre and continues to marginalize children and youth—who are key players as consumers but controlled and diminished through discourses of immaturity and irrationality. This new regime also continues to marginalize the frailty and dependence of age, though it has pushed this old age stereotype later into the life course. Finally, as these processes are embedded within a capitalist system that favours production and consumption, and therefore marginalizes those outside of these processes due to disability, poverty, and/or age, even the adult centre is not truly a unified position of dominance, but is fractured by inequalities.

STUDY QUESTIONS

1. With the erosion of many standard markers of adulthood and the deepening embrace of youthfulness, is youth displacing adulthood as the dominant "centre" of the life course? Why or why not? What are the implications of your choice?

2. Identify three potential areas of distinction between childhood and adulthood or between midlife and old age. Can you also identify concrete examples that disrupt these distinctions?

3. Identify several examples of behaviour that you feel challenge age norms. Do these norm-breakers face sanctions? What kind? What resources might some people have at their disposal to facilitate their breaking of age norms?

EXERCISES

1. *Freaky Friday, 17 Again, Big,* or *The Curious Case of Benjamin Button* all play with disruptions to temporal aging. How do movies such as these normalize certain beliefs about age-appropriate behaviour? Do they also challenge them?

2. Write a personal reflection on your own life course position in relation to adulthood. Do you consider yourself an adult? Why or why not? What assumptions are you making about adulthood in your assessment? How might your self-location be influenced by institutions such as the school or the family and structural categories such as class or gender?

REFERENCES

Acharya, Lalatendu. 2009. Child reporters as agents of change. In Barry Percy-Smith and Nigel Thomas, eds., *A Handbook of Children and Young People's Participation: Perspectives from Theory and Practice.* London: Routledge. 204–214.

Adams, Mary Louise. 1997. *The Trouble with Normal: Postwar Youth and the Making of Heterosexuality.* Toronto: University of Toronto Press.

Albanese, Patrizia. 2009. *Children in Canada Today.* Don Mills: Oxford University Press.

Alsop, Rachel, Annette Fitzsimons, and Kathleen Lennon. 2002. *Theorizing Gender.* Malden, MA: Blackwell Publishers Inc.

Ariès, Phillipe. 1962. *Centuries of Childhood: A Social History of Family Life.* New York: Knopf.

Baars, Jan, Dale Dannefer, Chris Phillipson, and Alan Walker. 2006. Introduction: Critical perspectives in social gerontology. In Jan Baars, Dale Dannefer, Chris Phillipson, and Alan Walker, eds. *Aging, Globalization and Inequality: The New Critical Gerontology.* Amityville, NY: Baywood Publishing Co. Inc. 1–14.

Blatterer, Harry. 2007. *Coming of Age in Times of Uncertainty.* New York: Berghahn Books.

Bourdieu, Pierre, and Jean-Claude Passeron. 1977. *Reproduction in Education, Society and Culture.* London: Sage Publications.

Burton, Linda. 1990. Teenage childbearing as an alternative life course strategy in multi-generational black families. *Human Nature* 1: 123–143.

Bury, M. (1995), Ageing, gender and sociological theory. In S. Arber and J. Ginn, eds., *Connecting Gender and Ageing: A Sociological Approach.* Buckingham, PA: Open University Press. 12–25.

Calasanti, Toni. 2008. Theorizing feminist gerontology, sexuality and beyond: An intersectional approach. In V. Bengston, M. Silverstein, N. Putney, and D. Gans, eds., *Handbook of Theories of Aging.* New York: Springer Publishing Company. 471–485.

Cartmel, Fred, and Andy Furlong. 1997. *Young People and Social Change: Individualization and Risk in Late Modernity.* Buckingham, UK: Open University Press.

Castaneda, Claudia. 2002. *Figurations: Child, Bodies, Worlds.* Durham, NC: Duke University Press.

Chappell, Neena, Lynn McDonald, and Michael Stones. 2008. *Aging in Contemporary Canada,* 2nd ed. Toronto: Pearson Education Canada.

Chunn, Dorothy E. 2003. Boys will be men, girls will be mothers: The legal regulation of childhood in Toronto and Vancouver. In N. Janovicek and J. Parr, eds., *Histories of Canadian Children and Youth*. Don Mills: Oxford University Press. 188–206.

Cosaro, William. 1997. *The Sociology of Childhood*. Thousand Oaks, CA: Pine Forge Press.

Côté, James E., and Anton L. Allahar. 2006. *Critical Youth Studies: A Canadian Focus*. Toronto: Pearson Prentice Hall.

Danesi, Marcel. 2003. *Forever Young: The "Teen-Aging" of Modern Culture*. Toronto: University of Toronto Press.

Dannefer, D. 1987. Aging as intracohort differentiation: Accentuation, the Matthew effect and the life course. *Sociological Forum* 2: 211–236.

Dannefer, Dale. 1984. Adult development and social theory: A paradigmatic reappraisal. *American Sociological Review* 49: 100–116.

Dannefer, Dale. 1989. Human action and its place in theories of aging. *Journal of Aging Studies* 3 (1): 1–20.

Dannefer, Dale. 2003. Whose life course is it, anyway? Diversity and "linked lives" in global perspective. In R. A. Settersten, ed., *Invitation to the Life Course*. Amityville, NY: Baywood Publishing Company, Inc.

Davies, Bronwyn. 2002. *Shards of Glass: Children Reading and Writing Beyond Gendered Identities*. New Jersey: Hampton Press.

Denton, Paula. 2003. Shared rule-making in practice: The Jefferson Committee At Kingston High School. *American Secondary Education* 31 (3): 66–96.

Erikson, Erik. 1968. *Identity: Youth and Crisis*. New York: W. W. Norton.

Evans, Patricia. 2010. "Women's poverty in Canada: Cross-currents in an ebbing tide." In Gertrude Schaffner Goldberg, ed., *Poor Women in Rich Countries: The Feminization of Poverty over the Life Course*. Oxford: Oxford University Press. 151–173.

Ferguson, A. 2000. *Bad Boys: Public Schools in the Making of Black Masculinity*. Ann Arbor: University of Michigan Press.

Fernando, Jude. L. 2001. "Children's right: Beyond the impasse." *Annals of the American Academy of Political and Social Science* 575: 8–24.

Foucault, Michel. 1978. Governmentality. In G. Burchell, C. Gordon, and P. Miller, eds., *The Foucault Effect: Studies in Governmentality*. Chicago: University of Chicago Press.

Geronimus, Arlene T. 2003. Damned if you do: Culture, identity, privilege, and teenage childbearing in the United States. *Social Science and Medicine* 57: 881–893.

Giroux, Henry A. 2003. Racial injustice and disposable youth in the age of zero tolerance. *Qualitative Studies in Education* 16(4): 553–565.

Gould, Stephen Jay. 1977. *Ontogeny and Phylogeny*. Cambridge, MA: The Belknap Press of Harvard University Press.

Gregson, Joanna. 2009. *The Culture of Teenage Mothers*. Albany: SUNY Press.

Henig, Robin Marantz. 2010. "Why are there so many people in their 20s taking so long to grow up?" *The New York Times*. http://www.ndtv.com/article/world/why-are-so-many-people-in-their-20s-taking-so-long-to-grow-up-46414?trendingnow. Accessed August 23, 2010.

Hockey, Jenny, and Allison James. 1993. *Growing Up and Growing Old: Ageing and Dependency in the Life Course*. London: Sage Publications.

Hurd Clarke, Laura, and Meredith Griffin. 2008. "Visible and invisible ageing: Beauty work as a response to ageism." *Ageing and Society* 28: 653–674.

James, Allison, and Alan Prout. 1990. *Constructing and Reconstructing Childhood: Contemporary Issues in the Sociological Study of Childhood*. Basingstoke, UK: Falmer Press.

Katz, Stephen. 1996. *Disciplining Old Age*. Charlottesville: University Press of Virginia.

Katz, Stephen. 2005. *Cultural Aging: Life Course, Lifestyle, and Senior Worlds*. Toronto: Broadview.

Katz, Stephen, and Debbie Laliberte-Rudman. 2004. Exemplars of retirement: Identity and agency between lifestyle and social movement. In S. Katz, ed., *Cultural Aging: Life Course, Life Style and Senior Worlds*. Toronto: Broadview. 140–160.

Kett, Joseph F. 2003. Reflections on the history of adolescence in America. *History of the Family* 8: 355–373.

Kitzinger, Jenny. 1988. Defending innocence: Ideologies of childhood. *Feminist Review* 28: 77–87.

Kohli, Martin. 2007. The institutionalization of the life course: Looking back to look ahead. *Research in Human Development* 4(3/4): 253–271.

Lancy, David. 2007. Accounting for variability in mother–child play. *American Anthropologist* 109(2): 273–284.

Laslett, Peter (1989). *A Fresh Map of Life: The Emergence of the Third Age*. London: Weidenfeld and Nicolson.

Lawrence, Barbara. 1996. Organizational age norms: Why is it so hard to know one when you see one? *The Gerontologist* 36(2): 209–220.

Laws, Cath, and Bronwyn Davies. 2000. Poststructuralist theory in practice: Working with "behaviourally disturbed" children. *Qualitative Studies in Education* 13(3): 205–221.

Lee, Nick. 2001. *Childhood and Society: Growing Up in an Age of Uncertainty*. Maidenhead, UK: Open University Press.

Lesko, Nancy. 1996a. Denaturalizing adolescence: The politics of contemporary representations. *Youth and Society* 28(2): 139–161.

Lesko, Nancy. 1996b. Past, present and future conceptions of adolescence. *Educational Theory* 46(4): 453–472.

Lesko, Nancy. 2001. *Act Your Age! A Cultural Construction of Adolescence*. New York: Routledge.

Liechty, Mark. 1995. Media, markets and modernization: Youth identities and the experience of modernity in Kathmandu, Nepal. In V. Amit-Talai and H. Wulff, eds., *Youth Culture: A Cross-Cultural Perspective*. London: Routledge. 166–201.

Mandell, Nancy, Susannah Wilson, and Ann Duffy. 2008. *Connection, Compromise, and Control: Canadian Women Discuss Midlife*. Don Mills: Oxford University Press.

Markson, Elizabeth W. 2003. *Social Gerontology Today: An Introduction*. Los Angeles: Roxbury Publishing Co.

Morris, Edward. "Tuck in that shirt!" Race, class, gender and discipline in an urban school. *Sociological Perspectives* 48(1): 25–48.

Morss, John R. 1996. *Growing Critical: Alternatives to Developmental Psychology*. London: Routledge.

Neugarten, Bernice, Joan W. Moore, and John C. Lowe. 1965. Age norms, age constraints and adult socialization. *The American Journal of Sociology* 70: 710–717.

O'Rand, Angela M. 1990. Stratification and the life course. In R. H. Binstock and L. K. George, eds., *Handbook of Aging and the Social Sciences*. San Diego: Academic Press, Inc.

Oakes, Jeannie. 1985. *Keeping Track: How Schools Structure Inequality*. New Haven: Yale University Press.

Payne, Monica A. 2009. Teen brain science and the contemporary storying of psychological (im)maturity. In H. Blatterer and J. Glahn, eds., *Times of Our Lives: Making Sense of Growing Up and Growing Old* [e-book]. Oxford: Interdisciplinary Press.

Piekoff, Tannis, and Stephen Brickey. 1991. Creating precious children and glorified mothers: A theoretical assessment of the transformation of childhood. In *Dimensions of Childhood: Essays on the History of Children and Youth in Canada*. Winnipeg: Legal Research Institute of the University of Manitoba.

Pilcher, Jane. 1997. Contrary to *Gillick*: British children and sexual rights since 1985. *International Journal of Children's Rights* 5: 299–317.

Pugh, Allison J. 2009. *Longing and Belonging: Parents, Children and Consumer Culture*. Berkeley: University of California Press.

Qvortrup, Jens. 2005. Varieties of childhood. In *Studies in Modern Childhood: Society, Agency, Culture*. Houndsmills: Palgrave Macmillan. 1–20.

Raby, Rebecca. 2002. A tangle of discourses: Girls negotiating adolescence. *Journal of Youth Studies* 5(4): 425–450.

Rattanski, Ali, and Ann Phoenix. 2005. Rethinking youth identities: modernist and postmodernist frameworks. *Identity: An International Journal of Theory and Research* 5(2): 97–123.

Renold, Emma. 2005. *Girls, Boys and Junior Sexualities: Exploring Children's Gender and Sexual Relations in the Primary School*. London: Routledge Falmer.

Roberts, Lance W., Rodney A. Clifton, and Barry Ferguson, eds. 2005. *Recent Social Trends in Canada, 1960–2000*. Montreal: McGill-Queens University Press.

Rose, Nikolas. 1990. *Governing the Soul: The Shaping of the Private Self*. London: Routledge.

Schalet, Amy. 2004. Must We Fear Adolescent Sexuality? *Medscape General Medicine* 6(4): 1–23.

Schor, Juliet. 2004. *Born to Buy*. New York: Scribner.

Settersten, Richard A., Jr. 2003. Propositions and controversies in life-course scholarship. In R. A. Settersten, Jr., ed., *Invitation to the Life Course*. Amityville, NY: Baywood Publishing Company, Inc. 15–45.

Settersten, Richard A., and Karl Ulrich Mayer. 1997. The measurement of age, age structuring, and the life course. *Annual Review of Sociology* 23: 233–261.

Settersten, Richard A., Jr., and Molly E. Trauten. 2008. The new terrain of old age: Hallmarks, freedoms, and risks. In V. Bengston, M. Silverstein, N. Putney, and D. Gans, eds., *Handbook of Theories of Aging*. New York: Springer Publishing Company.

Spector-Mersel, Gabriela. 2006. Never-aging stories: Western hegemonic masculinity scripts. *Journal of Gender Studies* 15(1): 67–82.

Tyyska, Vappu. 2009. *Youth and Society: The Long and Winding Road*, 2nd ed. Toronto: Canadian Scholars Press Inc.

United Nations. 1989. *Convention on the Rights of the Child* [treaty]. Geneva: Office of the United Nations High Commissioner for Human Rights. http://www2.ohchr.org/english/law/crc.htm. Accessed January 21, 2011.

Valverde, Mariana. 1991. *The Age of Light, Soap and Water*. Toronto: McClelland and Stewart.

Walkerdine, Valerie. 1993. Beyond Developmentalism? *Theory and Psychology* 3(4): 451–469.

Wray, Sharon. 2003. Connecting ethnicity, agency and ageing. *Sociological Research Online* 8 (4).

PART 3

EVERYDAY IMAGES AND PRACTICES

Rebecca Raby, *Brock University*

INTRODUCTION

In our everyday lives we regularly make decisions and take certain actions in the face of day-to-day demands, personal goals, and personal problems. We engage in regular routines and habits, but we also face many moments when we have to choose the best course of action, even in such basic areas as what to buy for dinner, how to spend our money, or how to talk to a loved one about a difficult issue. In Part II, we illustrated how our everyday practices are embedded within broader structural categories and patterns of inequality. In this Part we focus on how power permeates such everyday choices and practices: through what we do, the conversations we have with each other, the guidance we seek, and the common "truths" that guide us.

Recall that when C. W. Mills pointed out that "Neither the life of an individual nor the history of a society can be understood without understanding both" (1959: 3), he was recognizing that by placing our thoughts, feelings, and desires within the context of the social, political, historical, cultural, legal, and religious milieus, we can see how personal experience is socially produced and understood. Foucault, Marx, and many other theorists investigating the workings of power also see personal biographies as embedded within broader historical and structural forces. Mills argued that the task of sociology is to provide the tools for us to see these otherwise blurred or hidden connections. Some of the conceptual tools that can be used to identify these hidden connections have been laid out in the preceding sections. Through such tools we can investigate that what is often seen and represented as individual, personal, natural, normal, private, and so forth is instead embedded in historical and cultural relations of power. As such, in this section we specifically locate what often feel like personal, everyday decisions and practices in a broader context. As neo-Foucauldian Nicolas Rose suggests, "we can question our present certainties—about what we know, who we are, and how we should act—by confronting them with their histories" (Rose, 1999: x).

Karl Marx argued that structural forces of power and inequality are masked in our everyday lives through **ideology**, belief systems that reflect relations of domination. By attributing inequalities or personal hardships to individual choices or to nature, for instance, the deep inequalities embedded within capitalism are hidden from view. To Marx, ideology hides the truth of exploitation. Rather than hiding the truth, however, Foucault understood **discourse** as knowledge, and through this, "truth" and "fact." As we saw in Chapter 2, knowledge is always linked to power. The concept of discourse thus suggests that belief systems embedded in expert knowledges can influence how we think about our personal lives, currently in ways that emphasize personal responsibility over larger patterns of inequality.

The influence of trained others is frequently with us in our everyday practices. Sometimes these influences are invisible to us, in the way a supermarket has been designed by marketers, for instance, or in the background scientific truths that we simply take for granted. At other times, we actively seek out the advice of experts, when we pick up a self-help book, for example, or we consult a financial advisor. Often we may feel that forces beyond our understanding or control are responsible for shaping social life and so we desire the guidance of experts to make sense of this world for us. In turn, we frequently take up what they say and embed their views in our everyday decisions, conversations, and other practices. Those drawing on a Marxist approach would suggest that such advice is not always in our interests, however, as it frequently supports dominant capitalist relations. Foucauldians would similarly point out that such expert truths are not neutral but arising from certain contexts and producing specific kinds of ways of thinking about ourselves and the world around us. By introducing such concepts as power, ideology, discourse, and inequality, it becomes clear that our personal lives are really quite deeply connected to broader historical and cultural knowledges and inequalities. In turn our personal decisions and practices produce and reproduce expert ideas of what is "true," ideal, and normal, regulating ourselves and others in the process.

While we frequently seek out the guidance of experts, we also live in an era of growing skepticism about expertise—as authorities clash with each other over what is considered true, as we are exposed to a wide range of possible types of advice through the Internet and a plethora of advice books, and as authorities are shown to be fallible. As Raddon discusses in her chapter on finance, for example, the financial crisis of 2008 undermined much of the presumed truth about investments and the markets. Postmodernism itself is defined by skepticism in grand narratives and declarations of truth, as Brock discussed in Chapter 2. The chapters in this Part provide us with resources to guide and ground such skepticism through sociological analysis. It provides four chapters which contextualize the language of experts in terms of historical and cultural processes. Such expertise, in turn, permeates our everyday practices, contributing to the reproduction of inequalities through revealing the workings of power. These chapters also explore critiques of, and challenges to, these dominant truths.

Aryn Martin's chapter on science examines how it pervades our lives. Martin asks how the social might shape the naming of scientific "truths" and how this then suggests the need to turn a critical eye to contemporary scientific truth-making. We often consider science to be outside of culture, as it is assumed to convey a biological or natural truth. For this reason, the authority of science is embedded in relations of power. Martin's chapter challenges this position by arguing that science is embedded in the social and that science is "craftwork" involving human, and therefore socially embedded, labour. Martin draws on several current and historical examples to describe how scientists are humans, with human limits of observation and preconceptions. She also describes how scientific findings are produced within a scientific community, a cultural entity with norms and expectations that shape what is considered a valid finding and what is not. Often such protocols as blind peer review of others' work are considered essential to ensuring objective findings, yet peers commonly share each others' worldviews, raising questions regarding what forms of science come to be neglected or marginalized. Further, often very tentative, carefully worded findings are picked up in the popular media and quickly transformed into assumed truths that in turn shape people's everyday practices. The very words and images scientists draw on in order to understand and communicate their findings are also grounded in familiar language and worldviews. Finally, like the rest of us, scientists are humans who occupy certain identity locations based in gender, class, age, race, ethnicity, religion, politics, and so forth. Martin's view is not that all of these influences bias science, because such a position suggests that a fundamental truth is knowable. Rather, Martin's poststructural position is that the cultural embeddedness of science is part of science itself.

In their chapter on therapy, Heidi Rimke and Deborah Brock examine how specifically psychological expertise has permeated our lives. Through the culture of therapy and its resonance with **neoliberal** individualism, people's problems are increasingly located within the individual and the individual is increasingly pathologized. Drawing largely on the work of Foucault, Rimke and Brock outline the historical rise of such individualizing, psychocentrist expertise and critique its inclination to categorize, individualize, normalize, and therefore judge a wide range of behaviours—processes that ultimately exclude certain people. They similarly illustrate how these processes have reflected unequal gender and race relations. Rimke and Brock conclude their chapter by bringing us back to our own self-examination with a focus on the culture of therapy as reproduced through self-help books. While such books can provide useful advice and a soothing balm in the face of everyday (and also more overwhelming) challenges, through such books we participate in turning psychocentrism onto ourselves. Rimke and Brock situate such self-help books in the rise of neoliberal individualism and a decline in social services. They also argue that reading self-help books is a means of governing the self. Rimke and Brock end their chapter with some examples of challenges that have been launched at psychocentrism, such as those within the anti-psychiatry movement.

Dennis Soron examines shopping, an activity most of us undertake at least every week that has been celebrated as the bedrock of national economic stability. Shopping is often presented to us in terms of a wide range of options and choices, choices framed as integral to our democracy and democratic involvement. Yet often we draw on certain kinds of experts here, too—from magazine writers to store clerks—in making these choices. Soron thus explores how these "free choices" are really practices of governing, as our choices are constrained and guided by marketing experts, often without our even realizing it. Here we see an illustration of the productive nature of power identified by Foucault, as desires and practices are produced, with consumers enlisted as eager participants. Yet consumer choice as democracy also rings hollow for people who identify the influence of marketers, seek to address social inequality, and seek more genuine democratic citizenship. As such, Soron draws on **political economy** to explore the underlying workings of capitalism that require such constant consumption, despite troubling social and environmental consequences.

Finally, Mary Beth Raddon's examination of finance looks at financial expertise, developing on some of the economic history and deeply unequal economic practices that were discussed by Mark P. Thomas in Chapter 6, which deals with class and the state. Raddon first discusses finance through the lens of political economy, examining the historical rise of **financialization**, which means the increasing influence of financial institutions and experts around the world and over our everyday lives. In doing so, Raddon illustrates how this influence has significantly bene-fited certain people and groups over others, resulting in the reproduction of deep inequalities. Raddon also explains how current financialization arose through an important 20th-century shift from Keynsianism to neoliberal economics. The latter part of Raddon's chapter looks closer to home, through the lens of cultural economy, a lens that focuses more on how finance and current financial values are lived and performed "on the ground" in financial institutions and in people's everyday lives. One way financialization has penetrated our lives is through certain strategies for responsible financial fitness that have become normalized and perpetuated through advice and decision making regarding people's personal finances and estimations of people's financial health. Raddon's chapter thus leads us to ask how our practices of financial fitness locate us inside power, and specifically neoliberal forms of power. She concludes by discussing some alternative financial movements, specifically slow money and local currencies.

Together, the chapters in this Part III aptly illustrate that through such everyday practices as reading about scientific findings in the newspaper and then incorporating this information into our everyday lives, thumbing through self-help books to deal with a personal trouble, going on a shopping spree at the mall, and worrying about whether we are budgeting or investing appro-priately, we are embedded in a wide range of unequal power relations and we participate in their reproduction. Neoliberal individualism suggests that we increasingly make decisions on our own, outside of hierarchies of inequality and domination. And yet these chapters illustrate how a wide range of professional expertise influences our everyday practices, often in ways that are not immediately transparent. Nor are they neutral, but reflect power relations and reproduce exclu-sions and inequalities. This section therefore illustrates that power is not simply exercised "out there," as an abstract, structural, and coercive force, but also reflected in our personal practices.

REFERENCES

Mills, C. Wright. 1959. *The Sociological Imagination*. New York: Oxford University Press.

Rose, Nicholas. 1999. *Governing the Soul: The Shaping of the Private Self*. London: Free Associations Books.

SCIENCE AS CULTURE

Aryn Martin *York University*

8

INTRODUCTION

Science is often considered to be outside of, and separate from, society and culture. Some might even argue that this is what defines it: the scientific is that which is independent of politics, culture, and individual human bias. In this chapter, you will read about a perspective that rejects the view that science and society are separate spheres and sees science as *part of* culture, and inseparable from it. Because science comes from inside of culture, and, in turn, shapes culture through its unique access to authority, expertise, and truth claims, it is deeply interconnected with power. This makes it a fascinating and important topic to study from a sociological perspective.

Whether we are aware of it or not, science and technology pervade our everyday activities, experiences, choices, and possibilities. We sometimes hear about scholars, activists, or policy makers who study the *effects* of science *on* society. This is certainly important work, especially when areas such as genetics, medical research, climate science, and computers are changing so rapidly. However, when we pose the question this way—what *effects* are science and technology having *on* human lives and communities?—we mistakenly perpetuate the idea that science and technology (or *technoscience*) operate in a sphere separate from society. Moreover, this mysterious world of technoscience seems to act autonomously, and the facts and things it produces seem inevitable and beyond our control. It acts on its own, and we can simply lap up its rewards or brace ourselves for irreversible changes in our ways of living.

An alternative view, which sees science and society as inextricably wound together, has developed in the last several decades through careful study by sociologists, anthropologists, philosophers, historians, and activists. Their studies include, for example, descriptions of how scientists in laboratories build consensus through talk, movement, and persuasive rhetorical practices (such as writing, arguing, and drawing). They include careful histories of how particular human knowers were embedded in, and influenced by, their religious, political, or gendered convictions, about how what they could know depended on the people around them, the time and place, their class, and their own identities and interests.

Importantly, exploring science as a social practice is not the same as saying it is bad, misguided or morally wrong (though particular bits of knowledge or technologies may be so). *Because it is done by humans it cannot <u>not</u> be social.* We will see that the social is a source of contingency in what becomes scientific knowledge and what does not. **Contingency** is an important concept throughout this chapter. In this context, it means that a specific scientific discovery or invention is dependent on the (social) chain of events that preceded it. If the historical sequence leading up to the scientific event were different, the science would be different too. However the social—human scientists at work together—is also where innovation and dogged perseverance come from. So the social is not such a bad thing for science, even if it requires us to shift our expectations of whether pure objective knowledge is possible or desirable.

One possibility for adjusting our views of science is to imagine scientists as highly skilled and knowledgeable craftspeople or artisans, who build tangible things (called "facts" or "artifacts") that are often useful, but sometimes worrisome. This view is easier to imagine in the context of engineering: people make bridges, just as they make plumbing systems or woven fabrics. The results can be sturdy or weak, pretty or ugly, but they aren't true or false. Couldn't the same be said of a DNA molecule? An equation? This idea of science as craftwork is explored in this chapter. But first let's look at why we might even want to think about science, and participate in it, differently.

SCIENCE AND POWER

Think for a moment about words we associate with science. Chances are, you came up with examples like "objective," "unbiased," "truth," "facts," and "rationality." When we invoke a scientific fact during an argument—about healthy foods for example—we are attempting to resolve the argument in our favour with a foolproof piece of evidence. What's more solid than a fact? We can have *opinions* about religion, laws, families, but what can be said to counter a fact? Science wields a great deal of authority in most contemporary cultures. Science often sits at the top of the hierarchy of kinds of knowledge, and even within science, certain disciplines are perceived as more solid or "hard"—math and physics for example—than others such as biology and psychology. While other ways of knowing about the world—religious belief, intuition, and personal experience for example—command authority in many local settings, and coexist with science and biomedicine in many people's lives, formal institutions of governance in modern liberal democracies privilege scientific knowledge.

Building on theories of power you encountered in Chapters 1 and 2, you will recognize both Marxist and Foucauldian themes in this chapter. Because science emanates from elite, mostly Western, institutions closely allied with capital, a Marxist conception of power is sometimes invoked. More central, though, is Foucault's influence. Science is implicated in how institutions govern individuals and populations. Genetics, for example, is increasingly playing a role in how people are defined and administered by medical and legal institutions. Moreover, science is a dominant discourse at work in the minutest aspects of our *self-conduct*: what we eat, how we control our sexual and reproductive lives, our hygienic practices, how we think about and treat pain and disease, how we care about the environment (or don't), when we judge other people's behaviours as "unnatural," and on and on. One key insight in the work of Michel Foucault is that whatever is taken to be "truth" in a given time or place has an important relationship to power. We know that what people consider to be true has changed over time and varies somewhat in different places according to local ways of making sense of the world. Foucault writes:

> Each society has its régime of truth, its "general politics" of truth: that is, the types of discourses which it accepts and makes function as true; the mechanisms and instances which enable one to distinguish true and false statements; the means by which each is sanctioned; the techniques and procedures accorded value in the acquisition of truth; the status of those who are charged with saying what counts as true. (1980: 131)

In our time and place, truth comes in "the form of *scientific discourse and the institutions which produce it*" (131). Those who say what counts as true, then, are often scientists or medical doctors. In keeping with the themes of this text, scientific knowledge is marked by the priorities and sensibilities of the *centre*.

We are examining the forces and hierarchies that organize our social and material world in ways that are often hidden from our everyday consciousness. This chapter argues that science is a thoroughly social institution whose power in relation to other kinds of knowledge is often invisible precisely because it is understood as extra-social, inevitable, and unchanging. Yet facts are pieced together through ingenious, meticulous, collaborative *human labour*, and if we look closely we can see the marks of their social context. Scientists do not just make things up; their work is constrained by the nonhuman nature that participates in most kinds of science, and some descriptions and some tools may be more useful than others. But scientific facts are contingent: while they couldn't be just any old way, they could perhaps be different than they are. How they are is not arbitrary, however; it is linked to relations of power.

Three centuries of experience has shown us that the scientific method produces enormously useful facts and artifacts, but bracketing their inevitability and authority allows us to ask questions like: Useful for whom? Who does science, who is excluded, and why does it matter? Which occupations and activities become understood as "scientific" and which are denied this label and the resources it confers? How do economic and global considerations play into what questions are asked of science, and what answers offered? How do classifications and expectations that get called "natural" shape our everyday behaviours and possibilities and reproduce patterns of inequality? What are the sources of inevitable ambiguity that get in the way of scientific or medical facts becoming solid or certain, and how are these resolved?

In what follows, we will explore the social dynamics of science by attending to aspects of scientific practice that we normally do not see. Instead of taking scientific facts for granted when they are already solidified, we will look at the human labour and decision making that goes into their solidification (we'll call this process "science-in-the-making"). First, and at the most basic level, scientists are humans. Certain human-specific (**anthropocentric**) features make their way into what people can and do know about the world. Foregrounding *observation*—a cornerstone of the scientific method—we will look at what sociologists and philosophers have noted about human perceptions of nature. Next, we explore how scientists exist always and only in communities. They inevitably work as part of a team, but in addition, their work is enabled and constrained by the necessity of persuading the larger official collective—the institution(s) of science—of the reliability and usefulness of their knowledge claims. Finally, scientists belong to the same larger society that we all do, with multiple identities and allegiances (gendered, raced, religious, political) that find their way into fact-making. We will see how theorists have proposed that this "social" is not a force that contaminates so-called "biased" science (often considered false or bad science), rather it's an unavoidable resource that shapes what *makes sense* in any given time and place, whether that knowledge is later judged to be "true" or "false." Finally, we ask the question: how does scientific knowledge (as culture) travel not just in "ideas" but in everyday socio-material[1] representations (such as language, maps, and classifications) and in objects (such as technologies and nonhuman nature around us). In each of these sections, we will encounter numerous specific examples of science-in-the-making.

SCIENTISTS ARE HUMANS

It is useful to begin a consideration of the humanness of scientists with a brief account of the history of science. It is generally considered that science as we now understand it (a method for acquiring knowledge about nature's regularities, certified by a community of experts) began during the **Scientific Revolution**, stretching from the mid-16th century to the end of the 17th century, in Europe. Observations and theories that we now consider "scientific"—about planetary motion and the workings of the human body for example— long predated this period and come, most notably, from Ancient Greece and later the Islamic world. During the Scientific Revolution, however, the scientific method was self-consciously consolidated by early practitioners and promoted as a way of obtaining certain knowledge about nature.

Observation is critical to the scientific method. The earliest proponents of this method urged their fellow investigators to build careful accounts of phenomena in nature by collecting observations yielded by their own senses. These senses alone were to be trusted, rather than appealing to superstition or religion, to explain the natural world. This prominence accorded to human observation in the foundations and practice of science implies two important assumptions:

1. Scientific descriptions and laws have a built-in reference to a human perceiver; they are anthropocentric.
2. Because the laws of science are meant to be universal, any two human perceivers ought to make the same observations given the same sensory stimulus.

While scientists no doubt rely on touch and smell at times, and feeling and hearing perhaps more, *vision* is paramount to most science. We will elaborate on the two points above by looking closely at the example of seeing in science.

While it may seem obvious to say that scientists make observations that are specifically human, it's also easy to forget. There are limits on our observations that are peculiar to being creatures about our size who stand upright and see from the front of our heads. Much instrumentation in science—telescopes and microscopes for example—is used to translate very large objects (like planets) and very small objects (like cells) into sizes that

---

1   The phrase "socio-material" draws attention to the fact that these items are symbolic parts of cultural communication (socio-) and *at the same time* they have substance (material).

are appropriate for human observation and manipulation. While these instruments extend or augment our senses, they appeal to specifically human sense and cognition, and as such, anthropocentric constraints are embedded in them.

To understand this point more fully, let us look at what a frog sees:

> Consider a frog's visual cortex. Studies indicate that objects at rest elicit little or no neural response in a frog's brain. Maximum response is elicited by small objects in rapid, erratic motion—say, a fly buzzing by. Large objects evoke a qualitatively different response than small ones. This arrangement makes sense from a frog's perspective, because it allows the frog to identify prey from non-prey, and prey from predators that want to eat it. Now imagine that a frog is presented with Newton's laws of motion. The first law, you recall, says that an object at rest remains so unless acted upon by a force. Encoded into the formulation is the assumption that the object stays the same; the new element is the force. This presupposition, so obvious from a human point of view, would be almost unthinkable from a frog's perspective, since for the frog moving objects are processed in an entirely different way than stationary ones. (Hayles, 1991:76)

The lesson to take from this comparison, Katharine Hayles tells us, is not that humans know things that frogs can't even imagine, but that the things that we humans observe are permeated by the ways in which our bodies and brains organize the information we receive from our environment. Rather than giving us "nature," science gives us, at best, regularities and approximations observable by humans (which might be all we want or need). This constrains not just what scientists can see and know, but how they communicate that to each other: they use language and visual representations that are specific not just to human potentialities, but also to the times and places in which they are produced. This is something we will return to.

The second assumption built into linking the primacy of observation and objectivity is that any two human viewers will see the same thing if they are looking at the same thing. Does this assumption hold up? What do you see in Figure 8.1?

Such simple optical illusions illustrate that a single viewer can see two completely different "things" in the same image. Sometimes we can switch back and forth, while sometimes we are frustratingly unable to do so. Often we identify one object in a picture immediately, stairs seen from the bottom for example, and others see something quite different, stairs seen from the top, immediately. This example is perhaps

FIGURE 8.1 ▨ "Schroeder Stairs," an illustration of interpretive flexibility.

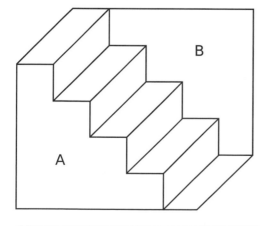

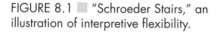

Source: Wikimedia Commons

too contrived to compare to less ambiguous objects, but it does illustrate that even when exactly the same visual content hits our retina at the same time as someone else's, we may make sense of it differently. The content of these differences is dependent on our own prior experiences, culture, and language. When Figure 8.1 is shown to members of an African community whose representational practices do not include rendering 3D objects in 2D space, let alone staircases, they do not see a staircase at all (Chalmers, 1999: 6). They simply see a geometric design. (See if you can make the image look flat, not like stairs at all.) The concept that different people see different things despite the same visual information is called **interpretive flexibility**.

Some examples from the history of science demonstrate that this visual ambiguity, or flexibility, is not isolated to deliberate optical illusions. N. R. Hanson writes about a difference in observation between Kepler and Brahe, two 16th-century astronomers:

> Let us consider Johannes Kepler: imagine him on a hill watching the dawn. With him is Tycho Brahe. Kepler regarded the sun as fixed: it was the earth that moved. But Tycho followed Ptolemy and Aristotle in this much at least: the earth was fixed and all other celestial bodies moved around it. *Do Kepler and Tycho see the same thing in the east at dawn?* (1958: 5)

In considering the answer "no," Hanson argues that seeing is an experience, while a retinal reaction is only a physical state. He says: "People, not their eyes, see" (6).

Another example comes from the history of anatomy. Until the early 18th century, it was uncommon to see a female skeleton in an anatomical atlas; the male form represented the generic human, and women were thought to be less perfect specimens (Schiebinger, 1986). Anatomist Marie Thiroux D'Arconville (a rare woman practising the art) produced one of the first paired illustrations. Compared both to the male skeleton and to present-day measurements, D'Arconville's female skeleton had an unusually small skull and rib cage, yet an unusually large pelvis. Presumably D'Arconville drew what she saw; what she saw depended on prevailing cultural expectations about womanhood that included emphasis on reproduction and lack of emphasis on intellect (Schiebinger, 1986). When scientists draw on preexisting theories about what the world ought to be like to make sense of their sensory information, this is called **theory-laden observation**. The theory preceded the observation, and it is embedded in the seeing.

Often the expectations that viewers bring to their observations come from theories and observations that already exist in their research domain. When Newton said, "If I have seen a little further it is by standing on the shoulders of Giants," he was acknowledging that science is a deeply cumulative and social endeavour; no one can start from scratch and trust only his or her own senses, or science would get stuck in rudimentary and repetitive insights. However, this means that at any given time in any given specialty, certain norms, expectations, and theories prevail. These norms (be they cultural, like male superiority or racism, or more properly understood as "scientific," like **heliocentrism**, the idea that the sun goes around the earth) shape what humans are able to see and know.

In this section we have seen that differing experiences and interpretations of sensory observations can coexist legitimately. These differences open up spaces of ambiguity and uncertainty in science and its applications. How these are resolved has a relationship to power, a theme that will be elaborated upon below.

AN ASIDE: SYMMETRY

But, you might say, aren't these just mistakes? Aren't they rare examples of bias in science that were correctly overturned with the passage of time, technological progress, and the pursuit of truth? Isn't it the case that Tycho Brahe and D'Arconville were just wrong? This is the standard account of these incidents, but making use of our new tenet that "science is culture" requires us to put a slightly different spin on these occasions.

Imagine the time in any controversy where it is equally plausible that either party will win the day and be determined to be right. At that moment (sometimes very short, sometimes dragging on for years), the evidence seems to equally support both parties, or they have each generated their own persuasive evidence through plausible experimentation, convincing graphs, and sound theory. To judge them by any later moment is to be influenced by present knowledge, and to assume that it was inevitable that things would turn out the way they did. In that moment of open possibility, we ask: Why do they each believe what they believe? It just doesn't make sense to imagine that those scientists later judged by their communities to be "right" were guided by the facts, while those later judged to be "wrong" were subject to bias and social contamination. The *kinds* of reasons for believing—intuition, prior commitments, persuasion by others, the elegance of one explanation over another, loyalty to funders—must be the same *kinds* of reasons on either side of the controversy. For neither side is the argument "because it's true" a valid cause of a belief, because at that moment, it is impossible to know what is true.

Our assessments of how science works, early sociologists of science said, must look at different kinds of knowledge claims **symmetrically** (the same from both sides), whether they are generally believed to be right or wrong (Bloor, 1976). Our guiding sociological question is not what is true, but why people believe what they do, and the answers to this question are deeply social in all cases, not just those later found to be wrong. The social isn't contamination or bias (which presumes such a thing as unbiased), it's just there because scientists are humans. Social institutions do not wreck what we know, but produce what we know. Looking at it this way, we see how knowledge can be both scientific and social at the same time; this is neither a contradiction nor a condemnation of the usefulness of that knowledge.

SCIENTISTS ARE HUMANS WORKING IN COMMUNITIES

So far we've covered that individual scientists are humans who bring distinctively human senses and embodiment to what they perceive. Furthermore, prior expectations, some linked to their cultural context, shape their acts of observation, measurement, and experiment. Remember, the argument is not that scientists are *more* susceptible to culture, economics, and politics than other types of knowers, only that they may not be less so. Now we consider scientists as members of institutions and communities—as social beings—whose work is collaborative, and relies on building consensus about what is true.

Think for a moment of traits you might list when asked to describe a scientist. Chances are, you thought of "intellectual," "brainy," "genius" or "nerdy." Other traits that might fit the bill are "skeptical," "rational," "analytic," "technical." Maybe even "antisocial." Maybe you pictured a bespectacled man with crazy hair, wearing a white coat and working in his basement lab. If I said "Name a specific scientist," what would you say? Einstein probably comes to mind most readily. Perhaps Isaac Newton or, if you are thinking of the present, Stephen Hawking. My point is that there is a scientific persona in our shared cultural imaginary in the West (though those in other parts of the world, or people who know scientists well, might answer differently). This image of the lone, socially awkward, white male genius is cultivated in media and in early schooling.

When sociologists and anthropologists began to pay more attention to scientists at work, they learned that these stereotypes do not hold up. Of course there is wide diversity among people who do science. Their intellect, rationality, and social prowess (if these things were easily measurable) would fall everywhere on the continuum. While women and some visible minorities are dramatically underrepresented in science, they do exist in nontrivial numbers. But most importantly, for our consideration, is the insight that no successful scientist works alone. Laboratories and field sites are intensely social places. University scientists are far more likely to work in close-knit groups with a discernable hierarchy (lab director, post-docs, graduate students, and undergraduates) than are scholars in the social sciences or humanities. The webs of interaction—in which training, labour, ideas, and friendship flow freely—are represented by the fact that most scientific publications have multiple authors. Moreover, many workers who are involved in scientific labour don't get official credit as authors, or even as scientists. These include spouses, other family members, and "invisible technicians" (Shapin, 1989).

Hence, we see a great deal of collaboration in science, in which workers are communicating in the same physical space, negotiating about what questions to ask, differing interpretations of evidence, and production of texts. Beyond face-to-face collaboration, scientific institutions (such as peer review, described below) ensure that scientific knowledge must be certified by a wider community of colleagues in order to exist at all. In more simple terms, you cannot make a fact or a discovery alone in your basement laboratory. This is especially true if you fail to communicate it to other members of the scientific community, and/or they don't believe you. No matter how convinced you are of your own groundbreaking discovery, without community approval the fact will not exist as knowledge in the world. Hence, a great deal of scientists' time is spent communicating—in writing, at conferences, and through teaching—in order to persuade their peers of the correctness and significance of their claims. Bruno Latour and Steve Woolgar call this recording and writing **inscriptions**. They observe that scientists spend much of their time producing inscriptions and moving them along from the most preliminary forms (scribbles in a laboratory notebook, counts, readouts from a machine) to text that is tentative, and combined with many texts that have come before (reference manuals, calculations, others' published articles), to more certain statements of fact that are polished and ready to submit for publication (1986). As statements move from tentative to certain, specific transformations in language occur. "It is possible that the substance we found is X" becomes "X was found." The fact statement gradually loses any marks of the scientist(s) who first championed it: eventually something becomes so taken for granted that a citation to the source of the claim drops out of the picture. The ultimate form of "fact" appears in textbooks without any indications of its tentative beginnings.

There is an irony at the heart of this. More than any other genre of writing, scientific writing removes the observer/persuader from view. By relying on the passive voice ("the experiment was done …," "results were observed …") the impression is created that the humans who did the work and made the observations are irrelevant. It seems that anyone (or no one) would have come up with the same ideas, experiments, and observations; they were just there in Nature waiting to be decoded. Donna Haraway calls this "the view from nowhere" (1991). Historians Steven Shapin and Simon Schaffer trace the history of this "modest" way of writing to Robert Boyle, a prominent early experimental philosopher in the 17th century (1985). The deliberate erasure of the writer from the text is meant to be a persuasive rhetorical style—Shapin and Schaffer call it a **literary technology**—that makes the writer seem more trustworthy and the evidence more objective. In other words, when it comes to communicating science, the less you seem to be trying to be persuasive, the more persuasive you are. Allies are meant to be convinced that they are not being convinced (Latour, 1987).

Facts acquire greater power as they are moved along the chain from tentative observations to conjectures to facticity; whether they successfully make this translation depends on social and institutional processes including peer review, sometimes replication by other laboratories, conference presentations, and prestigious speeches, and informal modes of communication, such as teaching, emails, and conversations in hallways. At any of these stages, a fact-in-the-making might be believed, but it might also be contested or ignored. The closer one is to the centre—in this case elite scientific institutions and universities (Harvard, Cambridge, etc.)—the greater likelihood one has of being heard and believed. People on the margins—those without university accreditation, activists, farmers, patients, non-Westerners, etc.—have a far lesser likelihood of producing scientific facts that are accepted by the centre. Although there are exceptions, this is so even when the relevant group of lay people actually have a great deal of lived expertise about the questions at issue.

Peer Review: Social Certification of Knowledge

The practice of science has evolved formal institutions for making sure that the bits of knowledge or fact that find their way into textbooks and (sometimes) popular knowledge are validated by other members of the community of scientists. One of the earliest of these institutions, founded by experimental philosophers (the precursors to scientists) in the 1660s, was called The Royal Society. This group of learned gentlemen from the upper classes, including Robert Boyle, met weekly to show each other experiments. Demonstration was an extremely persuasive tactic, but of course the size and geographic spread of the community of experimental philosophers grew with its success, and other methods for reaching out to colleagues were established. Journal articles became the most common first step of communicating research results beyond the laboratory in which they were made.

Peer review is an important cornerstone in the process of certifying knowledge. When scientific articles are submitted to a journal, or grant applications submitted to a funding body, they will be sent out by the editor or funder to credentialled experts in the same field who are asked to "referee" the article for its veracity, originality, and significance. While it doesn't always work, this process is also meant to weed out fraudulent claims or bogus evidence. In most cases, the process will be "double-blind," meaning that the referees don't know who the authors are and vice versa. Scientists are very skeptical of any findings or facts that do not undergo peer review. When scientific discoveries appear first in the media, in advertising, or on a (non-journal) website, they will likely be dismissed or at least called into question. This all sounds sensible as a form of quality control, but when we look at peer review through the lens of "unpacking the centre," the editors of journals and their circle of trusted referees wield significant power in determining what gets funded and what becomes knowledge.

If we consider the perspective of marginalized people or unpopular claims, we see that peer review operates as a *gatekeeping* mechanism whereby editors and reviewers have the ultimate say in accepting or rejecting articles, and therefore policing what becomes known in the broader scientific community.[2] Most referees and readers have a tendency to support likeminded authors, and to be leery of ideas or experiments that seem radical, unpopular, or contrary to accepted views and theories. Hence, reviewers reinforce prevailing **paradigms** and exclude outliers, even when they are not aware they are doing it. While making the process blinded lends it an air of objectivity, clues to cultural capital and elite training—like language and grammar for example—operate against researchers who are writing in an unfamiliar language, or who have not been taught community-specific genres of academic writing.

An "Old Boys' Club"?

Examining peer review closely, as we have done here, shows one way science may operate like an "old boys' club." Many other forces are at work to privilege some groups of people over others. Women are underrepresented in science and math classes, university majors, and employment positions at every level from high school to retirement, and the gap grows larger as you move from undergraduate education to graduate school to junior faculty to senior positions such as dean and college president. Reasons for this "leaky pipeline" are many and complicated. They include teacher attention that favours boys in science classes, a drop in adolescent girls' self-confidence, differential mentorship in university, and more-vocal participation by men in university classrooms with subsequent encouragement by their professors (Pell, 1996).

A disincentive to following a scientific or technological path for girls and women, and an incentive for boys and men has to do with the co-production of what is widely considered to be the scientific persona (discussed above) and masculinity. If what is considered to be "feminine" excludes computers and telescopes, and some sorts of positive masculinity include

---

2   Incidentally, this gatekeeping process plays a significant role in most scholarly fields, including sociology, not just science.

them, it makes sense that (1) boys might be more likely to choose science and technology and (2) the cultural associations between masculinity and science/technology will strengthen. While these pushes and pulls on identity formation are not absolute, the subtle costs to not being considered appropriately feminine may play into young women's choices.

When women make it far enough along the pipeline to finish graduate school and acquire faculty positions, they are often excluded from the informal communication of departmental culture that happens in collegial spaces such as the lunchroom or the pub. Loneliness is more likely to be experienced by women and other minorities, who may have trouble "fitting in" to these informal social exchanges (or may prefer not to). Expectations and pressures regarding publishing productivity make combining career and family difficult for women, who therefore leak from the pipe at the child-rearing stage and have trouble getting back in later on (Pell, 1996). Rather than a single obstacle, therefore, women (and other marginalized people, including visible minorities and disabled people) face a relentless series of often subtle discouragements from pursuing scientific careers, even when no formal barriers exist.

Exclusion of certain members of society because of their identity or group membership unfairly curtails people's possibilities for success in meaningful and lucrative professions are unfairly curtailed, and those who do take the sometimes lonely path may face unnecessary structural and social difficulties. However, there is another cost that spreads beyond the people involved or excluded. This cost is **epistemological**—it has to do with the *content* of scientific knowledge, and our methods for gaining knowledge. If there are constraints on who becomes a scientist, we end up with an unrepresentative population of scientists in terms of gender, class, race, ability, and global location and the truth is inevitably somewhat weighted in ways that are consistent with their set of experiences and training. *Thus, while scientific knowledge purports to operate equally everywhere, free from politics, it usually emanates from the centre.*

Boundary Work and Professionalization

So far in this chapter I have been writing as though it is possible and even easy to know what is and what is not science, and who is and who is not a scientist. Yet even the very process of determining what is scientific and what isn't, and who does science and who does not, is deeply political, social and economic. **Boundary work** is a concept for understanding the labour that goes into rendering certain kinds of knowledge projects as legitimately science (Gieryn, 1983). The stakes are very high in this constant negotiation. That which is understood as science inherently assumes certain valued attributes: authority, objectivity, universality, and truth. In practical terms, that which is understood as science commands economic and political resources. On the other hand, those enterprises cast outside of the realm of legitimate scientific activity ("pseudoscience" or "alternative medicine," for example) are less able to access cultural and economic capital. What is inside and what is outside this boundary often maps onto the centre and the margins, as discussed throughout this textbook.

In a prenatal advice book, for example, a woman might read that epidurals (injections of drugs into the spine by an anaesthetist) block the experience of pain during childbirth. In a small section at the end of the chapter on pain management, "alternative" or "complementary" approaches are mentioned, and she reads that practitioners of acupuncture *believe* that needles applied in meridians alleviate the pain from contractions. Why do doctors "know" what works while acupuncturists simply "believe" in their technique? This tiny word—believe—is an example of boundary work that keeps the practice of acupuncture outside the legitimate sphere of science and reinforces this dichotomy to a popular audience. On the other hand, that acupuncture is even included in such a book—something less likely a few decades ago—speaks to the movement of acupuncture toward legitimacy. Professionalization occurs when an occupation moves into the realm of legitimate authoritative knowledge. Boundaries are inherently flexible and respond to boundary work in the form of lobbying, marketing, experiments, attacks, and other political and social wrangling. In other words, sociologists argue, there are no absolute and timeless criteria that demarcate "science" from "non-science."

KNOWLEDGE IS SOCIAL AND MATERIAL

Thus far this chapter's focus has been on who scientists are and how they go about their jobs. In this section, we will look at the product of their work: knowledge. What do we mean, specifically, when we talk about scientific knowledge? We often think of knowledge as something that resides in people's brains: I *know* the alphabet, I *know* the formula to calculate the circumference of a circle. But in order to do anything with our knowledge, we must give it material form: to articulate it outside of our brains and bodies in the form of language, symbols (such as numbers), and images (such as graphs and maps). Power/ knowledge can also become material and travel in tools for administering people and populations, such as actuarial tables, disease classifications, and numerical standards. These tools are vital to Foucauldian governmentality (see Chapter 2) whereby institutions (including, but not limited to, governments) produce certain kinds of citizens amenable to control. Finally, power becomes hardened through science into things (such as technologies; see below), which continue to act upon us, even when their human creators are long separated from them. Each of these types of material power—language, images, and things—are fundamental to scientific practice, and are its effects. Because of their physicality, they are sturdier than beliefs and more difficult to change. We will examine each category in turn with examples from technoscience.

1. *Language*

While scientific language may seem dry and technical, it is remarkably rich in **metaphors** and figurative expressions. How would you describe DNA (deoxyribonucleic acid)? Chances are, even with a rudimentary education in biology you can come up with some descriptions like "the blueprint for building a body" or "a hereditary code." Both "blueprint" and "code" are metaphors that evoke a whole set of associations from everyday objects to better understand abstract concepts. Some of these descriptions are especially prevalent when scientists talk to nonscientists or to students, but many are deeply embedded in the technical language of science itself. Scientists draw on the analogy between DNA and information when they write about genetic code, messages, transcription, and copying. This particular set of representations has worked very well to bring molecular biology to the forefront of the sciences in the late 20th century, and much use has come from them. However, it is because of a historical collision in the late 1950s and 1960s of early molecular biology and a thriving interdisciplinary field of study called *cybernetics* (the study of regulatory systems) that information theory found its way into biology, and has stayed there (Kay, 2000). Had different people been involved, with different influences, DNA might have been described and understood through very different metaphors, which might have led to different uses and theories. In other words, the overlap of molecular biology and cybernetics was historically contingent; it could have been otherwise.

A very well known example of the contingent and culture-bound nature of scientific language is the tale of fertilization. Emily Martin, an anthropologist of science, observed that when biological textbooks described the activity of the egg and the sperm leading up to, and at the moment of, fertilization, their language drew heavily on "fairy-tale" stereotypes of gendered behaviour (1991). For example, Martin found the phrases in quotations below in scientific textbooks and journal articles:

> It is remarkable how "femininely" the egg behaves and how "masculinely" the sperm. The egg is seen as large and passive. It does not move or journey, but passively "is transported," "is swept," or even "drifts" along the fallopian tube. In utter contrast, sperm are small, "streamlined," and invariably active. They "deliver" their genes to the egg, "activate the developmental program of the egg," and have a "velocity" that is often remarked upon. Their tails are "strong" and efficiently powered. Together with the forces of ejaculation, they can "propel the semen into the deepest recesses of the vagina." For this they need "energy," "fuel," so that with a "whiplashlike motion and strong lurches" they can "burrow through the egg coat" and "penetrate" it. (1991: 489)

The millions of sperm, moving en masse toward the egg, are often also described in very competitive and even militaristic terms. The sperm are depicted as being on a "quest," a "perilous journey," at the end of which the victor might expect to find a damsel in distress. While this imagery seems to make sense at first, because we are so accustomed to it, it is telling to step back from our expectations and remember that neither sperm nor eggs have a *gender*. We ought not to expect them to behave in any way "masculine" or "feminine" not only because they are non-cognizant cells, but also because what kind of behaviours deemed masculine or feminine are socially constructed and have changed radically over time, and presumably the mechanics of fertilization haven't.

Martin argues that the *contingency* of this particular way of describing and seeing fertilization is becoming apparent as some alternative investigators describe a very different sort of encounter. According to these scientists, the egg is very active indeed. It uses a biochemical lasso to "capture" the sperm it chooses. Arguably, this aggressive egg plays on a different set of gendered tropes (the *femme fatale*), but the point is that evidence may be available for a variety of different cultural images. Because we are never outside of culture, it may be impossible to sort out what the egg and sperm are "really" up to. Metaphors are inescapable, because communication of observations and ideas requires human language. It may not even be desirable to escape metaphors altogether, for they can generate novel research directions. However, the specifics of language do matter, because descriptions of what is "natural," rendered in the authoritative voice of science, structure uneven and hierarchical patterns of human relationships. Gender is not only imposed from culture onto descriptions of fertilization; in a circular manner, the biological is invoked to prescribe how gender is supposed to operate. Gendered hierarchy is thus *naturalized*.

2. Images and Inscriptions

Images are extremely persuasive tools for convincing people of your viewpoint and gathering allies. As such, they are important places to look in trying to understand how some people gain power over others, and how some facts become established as knowledge and some fall away from view. Maps are a good example of how important drawings are to the success of technoscience. Imagine an early explorer who stops on land in the Pacific with the purpose of bringing back to Paris a better map (Latour, 1990). He encounters a Chinese inhabitant of the island, who knows the geography of the land well. The Chinese man picks up a stick and draws a very good map of his island, to scale and with important identifying details, in the sand. Seeing that the tide is rising, the explorer quickly makes a copy of the map with a pencil in his notebook. This simple difference—something that is an object of communication with a brief existence (the map in the sand) has far less power than something solid, mobile, and reproducible back in Paris (the map on paper)—makes all the difference to the subsequent relations of colonization on this island. Latour, who tells this story, writes:

> Commercial interests, capitalist spirit, imperialism, thirst for knowledge, are empty terms as long as one does not take into account Mercator's projection, marine clocks and their makers, copper engraving of maps, rutters, the keeping of "log books," and the many printed editions of [previous voyages] that [the explorer] carries with him. (1990: 25)

These inscriptions aren't simply powerful on their own, but they acquire power in particular contexts where they are used to "muster, align, and win over new and unexpected allies … they bear on certain controversies and force dissenters into believing new facts and behaving in new ways" (25).

Anthropologist of science Joseph Dumit (2003) provides a contemporary example of the power of images to compel certain meanings and relations and eclipse others. Brain scans of "normal" and "disordered" brains are increasingly objects of medical and popular scrutiny.

As an example, Dumit describes a set of images published in the magazine *Vogue* in which "three similar, oval-like blobs filled with dissimilar patterns of bright colors" are accompanied by three labels: NORMAL, SCHIZO, DEPRESSED (36). The juxtaposition

FIGURE 8.2 ■ Brain scan image. A PET brainscan simplifying human difference.

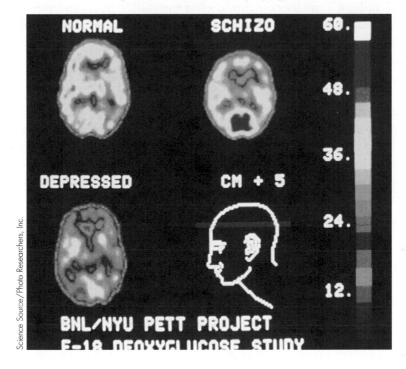

of image and text implies three different kinds of brains from three different kinds of people; their illness (or normality) results from an essential brain difference that can be seen thanks to modern medicine. In this one simple graphic, uncertainty, ambiguity, and the complexities of mental illness are resolved into the "fact" of brain difference. Regardless of which of the three images we identify with, we are invited to see ourselves somewhere in this graphic. Moreover, medical images such as these can become arbiters of how we are governed ("Do I qualify for disability?") and how we govern ourselves ("Should I ingest psychoactive drugs?"). Understanding behaviours and emotions as biologically determined (and the same in all people diagnosed) rather than products of experience (such as inequality) have—for better or worse—different political and very personal implications. Critics of such a simple snapshot, as Dumit is, would argue that the reality is much more complicated.

Classifications such as diagnoses are special kinds of inscription in science that figure prominently in how we understand natural and social worlds (or, as this chapter insists, nature-culture). Classification is a means by which to carve up the world into non-overlapping categories, to bring order to what might otherwise seem like unmanageable chaos (Bowker & Star, 1999). Examples of prominent classification tools in science and medicine are **phylo-genetic** trees (showing species and evolutionary origins), the periodic table in chemistry, and disease classification systems such as the DSM (*Diagnostic and Statistical Manual of Mental*

Disorders), which will be discussed in Chapter 9. Perhaps the most pervasive "biological" classification, and one that shapes each and every human life to some degree, is sex: male and female are widely understood to be natural, mutually exclusive categories into which all human animals (and most others) can be unproblematically sorted. Zoë Newman challenged this premise in Chapter 4, showing both that the two-sex system has a contingent history and that many peoples' anatomical makeup defies the notion of a biological binary.

Rather than being simply found in nature, classification systems represent collective human decision making through processes of negotiation and codification. They have histories, and often change over time. Despite lacking inevitability, classifications have "material force" (Bowker & Star, 1999: 3). Whether they begin arbitrarily or purposely, whether they have political underpinnings (such as race classification in apartheid South Africa) or are politically benign in their origins, they act in and on the world and the people and things in it. They form identities and physical space (think of everyday spaces such as sex-specific bathrooms, for example). Their consequences, intentional or not, are long-lasting and difficult to change.

3. *Things*

A final modality through which power becomes material goes by a number of words: technology, artifacts, objects, things. This is the "hardware" portion of technoscience, and it has been integral to scientific work since its inception. Instruments were, in the foundations of the scientific method, seen to both extend and to correct the human senses, and to accomplish things beyond the limits of our senses. Early examples are the air pump and the telescope, while today we hear more about superconducting supercolliders or DNA sequencing machines. Instruments simulate conditions of the unwieldy natural world in the laboratory under circumstances carefully controlled by humans. Outside of the lab, phenomena are often too large (an ecosystem), too small (bacteria), too far away (the planets), too dangerous (an atomic reaction), or just too complex (depression) for easy observation. We have been tracking sources of ambiguity or uncertainty in scientific knowledge-making, and when specific areas of research are studied closely, one finds many disputes about whether the laboratory test or "field site" is close enough to the "real world" to count as viable or useful knowledge. For example, a particular industrial pollutant is tested in isolation in the laboratory and declared to be safe. In the real world, however, one only ever finds this pollutant in combination with others in industrial parks (often in low-income and racialized neighbourhoods) where the cumulative toxicity is hazardous, but the producer of the single pollutant cannot be held accountable. **Reductionism** is the name often given to this problem inherent in scientific and technical knowledge, where the messy world (in which nature is never separated from culture "out there") is studied in tiny, isolated parts. While reductionism sometimes presents problems for translating findings back into appropriate applications in the world, it may also be why science works so well at some kinds of things.

It is an important insight that technologies are fundamental to almost all kinds of science, because when we mistakenly assume that science is cognitive ("ideas") or even statements of facts, we forget the tremendous human and the machine labour that goes into stabilizing those facts and making them believable to relevant communities. In a sense, the machines, like the people, disappear from view and the fact stands alone. We place enormous trust in these machines and in their lack of bias. Historians of science Lorraine Daston and Peter Galison call this **mechanical objectivity**, and locate it historically:

> "Let nature speak for itself" became the watchword of a new brand of scientific objectivity that emerged in the latter half of the nineteenth century. At issue was not only accuracy but morality as well: the all-too-human scientists must, as a matter of duty, restrain themselves from imposing their hopes, expectations, generalizations, aesthetics, even ordinary language on the image of nature. Where human self discipline flagged, the machine would take over. (1992: 81)

While mechanization has assumed the burden of removing human bias, it is not a guarantor of objectivity. Instruments are crafted by humans, and particular theories are built into their possibilities. Moreover, their output (a photograph from a camera, for example) is always a selection from among alternatives, and requires human interpretation. The ways social values and ideologies become "built in" has been studied thoroughly by sociologists and historians of technology, and we'll look at a few examples.

Instruments are not just used in science to make facts, they are also often the products or outputs of science and engineering. These products—modes of transportation, computers and information technology, consumer goods, pharmaceuticals, and medical technologies—are important actors in our everyday lives and social organization, especially in the 21st century. New technologies are often equated with progress, and have no doubt favourably changed how we live. However, "technological development has not been an unqualified blessing. Technologies frequently have negative social and environmental side effects; can enable a (desirable or undesirable) shift of power from one group or another; or can be 'misused' and have destructive consequences" (Johnson & Wetmore, 2009: xi).

One way objects can become social actors is by embodying discriminatory assumptions of their designers. While this is sometimes a deliberate strategy to maintain certain alignments of power, it is often a result of the blindness associated with being in the centre and not seeing how technologies and knowledge affect those on the margins. In his renowned article "Do Artifacts Have Politics?" Langdon Winner describes a classic case of the first kind. Robert Moses was a city bureaucrat and public works giant in the mid-20th-century New York. Moses built overpasses and highways with specifications that would discourage buses from using them.

> [T]he reasons reflect Moses' social class bias and racial prejudice. Automobile-owning whites of "upper" and "comfortable middle" classes, as he called them, would be free to use the parkways for recreation and commuting. Poor people and blacks, who normally use public transit, were kept off the roads because the twelve-foot-tall buses could not handle the overpasses. (Winner in Johnson & Wetmore, 2009: 212)

One deliberate outcome of this plan was to limit access of minorities and low-income groups to Moses' great outdoor park on the ocean, Jones Beach.

Winner's story is somewhat of a parable about technological discrimination, of which there are unfortunately many examples. One of the main lessons of these stories has to do with the longevity of hardware: sociotechnical apparatuses keep producing their effects long after they have become divorced from the humans and institutions who made them, and responsibility is hard to locate. While Moses is long since deceased, "many of his monumental structures of concrete and steel embody a systematic social inequality, a way of engineering relationships among people that, after a time, became just another part of the landscape" (Johnson & Wetmore, 2009: 212).

A final example ties together the critiques of mechanical objectivity introduced above, and how social hierarchies get embedded in technologies. Richard Dyer makes the case that photographic media and therefore movie lighting "privilege and construct whiteness" in that "photographing non-white people is typically construed as a problem" (Dyer in Johnson & Wetmore, 2009: 258). A number of technical factors (the reflective properties of light, the chemistry of photographic paper or celluloid, the length of development and use of artificial light) are interconnected with social factors (the assumption that white faces constitute the norm and touchstone of photography and film). "It may be—certainly was—true that photo and film apparatuses have seemed to work better with light-skinned peoples, but that is because they were made that way, not because they could be no other way" (259). The decisions that went into building the technology are erased by time, and we are left with the impression that it is somehow a "natural" property of white skin that enables easier representation in these media. Dyer points out that it's not even a matter of accuracy of the image—the "white" that white people appear in images and movies was (is?) an engineered product that conforms to expectations guiding what hue "white people wanted white people to be" (259). So much for mechanical objectivity.

Dyer's example points up the flipside of embedding politics and society in particular artifacts and technologies. It is worth giving some thought to the power structures evident in what things *aren't* in the world—such as the male contraceptive pill (Oudshoorn, 2003)—and what facts or knowledge *don't exist*. Every experiment not done or design path not taken is also a result of social, economic, and political pressures (in addition to feasibility) that act in conjunction with "nature" to constrain what we know of the world, and what exists in it.

CONCLUSION

This chapter complicated the picture of science as a sacred space outside of time and culture that simply holds up a mirror to allow Nature to speak for itself. Instead we have seen that the very perceptual activities at the heart of the empirical methods used in science are subject to individual and cultural contingency. Second, we have looked at how science is a social institution much like the other institutions that have long undergone sociological scrutiny. As in other social milieus, we find elitist gatekeeping mechanisms, rhetorical and political strategies for persuading colleagues, economic considerations, and informal exclusion of certain gendered, raced, or class bodies from full participation. This may not be surprising, especially to scientists, but it does contrast with a prominent popular picture of science as the one and only source of certain truth. Finally, we explored the materiality of scientific knowledge. Paying attention to language, images, charts, and objects complicates the notion that science is composed of ideas and theories, and happens in geniuses' brains. It also allows us to see how products of science exert regulatory power in the social world.

Because this chapter has aimed to problematize received notions of scientific facticity, my examples are weighted toward rather flagrant uses and abuses of science and technology in the interests of upholding or justifying privilege. Many examples we could have explored are much more subtle and many may be free of the markers that we often think of as "social context" such as gender, race, class, and global location. However, all the products of technoscience are social accomplishments to some degree, and the methods that have evolved in the past 300 years—as much literary and representational as experimental—work to obscure the contingent origins of facts and things. The result is a perceived certainty and stability that is invoked and remade through institutions of governance and social order. It is also privileged over other ways of knowing and being. The erasure of contingency implied by the scientific worldview in large part fortifies its cultural privilege.

What do we gain by opening up the "black boxes" of facts and technologies? Sometimes a more shaky and uncertain worldview that isn't entirely reassuring. In the end, we have to live inside the existing world that, at the moment, is deeply scientific and technological. No matter how critical we are, most of us live with medical diagnoses, we get on airplanes, we use email, and we trust that our tap water is safe. Usually we are glad of all these things. We want better science to make personal and societal decisions in the face of uncertainty, and to alleviate human and nonhuman suffering. Science is often a useful instrument for social movements aiming to challenge inequalities, as it has been in demystifying dated and dangerous ideas about biological race (see Chapter 5). But science is one social resource among many. The insights of this chapter suggest that we can live better in critical relation to technoscience if we draw on the kinds of tools outlined in Chapter 3 to replace the view that facts are inviolable and ask where they come from, to become skeptical when people invoke "nature" to justify or prohibit certain social relations, and to view science, technology, and medicine as permeable social spaces that we all can and do participate in.

STUDY QUESTIONS

1. Explain, in your own words, what Donna Haraway means when she calls science "the view from nowhere."

2. Think of a classification system you encounter in your own life (for example, computer files, university departments). Are the categories fixed or arbitrary? How could they be organized otherwise? What are the effects of the ways in which they are organized?

3. Using the story about Robert Moses' bridges as an example, come up with another case in which discriminatory politics become built into technologies.

EXERCISES

1. Watch the film *A Beautiful Mind* (2001). How is this portrayal of John Nash consistent with the stereotypical scientific persona described in this chapter? What aspects of the story challenge the idea that scientists work in social isolation?

2. Find a newspaper article that reports on a new scientific finding. Examine the "literary technology" adopted in this article: Is it written in the first person or the third? Are there any graphs or images, and what are these meant to do? Can you locate any incidences of reductionism?

REFERENCES

Bloor, David. 1976. *Knowledge and Social Imagery*. New York: Routledge.

Bowker, Geoffrey, and Susan Leigh Star. 1999. *Sorting Things Out: Classification and Its Consequences*. Cambridge, MA: M.I.T. Press.

Chalmers, A. F. 1999. *What Is This Thing Called Science?* Indianapolis: Hackett Pub. Co.

Daston, L., and P. Galison. 1992. The image of objectivity. *Representations* 40: 81–128.

Dumit, Joseph. 2003. Is it me or my brain? Depression and neuroscientific facts. *Journal of Medical Humanities* 24(1/2): 35–47.

Foucault, Michel, and Colin Gordon. 1980. *Power/Knowledge: Selected Interviews and Other Writings, 1972–1977*. New York: Pantheon Books.

Gieryn, Thomas F. 1983. "Boundary-work and the demarcation of science from non-science: strains and interests in professional ideologies of scientists," *American Sociological Review* 48: 781–795.

Hanson, Norwood Russell. 1958. *Patterns of Discovery: An Inquiry into the Conceptual Foundations of Science*. Cambridge: University Press.

Haraway, Donna Jeanne. 1991. *Simians, Cyborgs, and Women: The Reinvention of Nature*. New York, NY: Routledge.

Hayles, N. K. 1991. Constrained constructivism, locating scientific inquiry in the theater of representation. *New Orleans Review* 18 (1): 76–85.

Johnson, Deborah G., and Jameson M. Wetmore. 2009. Technology and society: Building our sociotechnical future. *Inside Technology*. Cambridge, MA: The MIT Press.

Kay, Lily E. 2000. Who wrote the book of life? A history of the genetic code. *Writing Science*. Stanford, CA: Stanford University Press.

Laqueur, Thomas Walter. 1990. *Making Sex: Body and Gender from the Greeks to Freud*. Cambridge, MA: Harvard University Press.

Latour, Bruno. 1987. *Science in Action: How to Follow Scientists and Engineers Through Society*. Cambridge: Harvard University Press.

Latour, Bruno. 1990. Drawing things together. In Michael Lynch and Steve Woolgar, eds., *Representation in Scientific Practice*. Cambridge, MA: MIT Press. 19–68.

Latour, Bruno, and Steve Woolgar. 1986. *Laboratory life: The Construction of Scientific Facts*. Princeton, NJ: Princeton University Press.

Martin, E. 1991. The egg and the sperm—How science has constructed a romance based on stereotypical male–female roles. *Signs* 16(3): 485–501.

Oudshoorn, Nelly. 2003. *The male pill: A Biography of a Technology in the Making.* Durham NC: Duke University Press.

Pell, A. N. 1996. Fixing the leaky pipeline: Women scientists in academia. *Journal of Animal Science* 74(11): 2843–8.

Schiebinger, L. 1986. Skeletons-in-the-closet—The 1st illustrations of the female skeleton in 18th-century anatomy. *Representations* 14): 42–82.

Shapin, S. 1989. The invisible technician. *American Scientist* 77(6) (November/December): 554–63.

Shapin, Steven, and Simon Schaffer. 1985. *Leviathan and the Air-Pump: Hobbes, Boyle, and the Experimental Life.* Princeton, NJ: Princeton University Press.

9

The Culture of Therapy: Psychocentrism in Everyday Life

Heidi Rimke *University of Winnipeg*

Deborah Brock *York University*

> Has life got you down? Do you have trouble getting out of bed in the morning? Have you stopped eating? Or perhaps, you are unable to stop eating? Do you have trouble falling asleep at night or staying asleep? Have others expressed concern about your mental or emotional state? Have you wondered whether your sexual desires are normal? Do you experience feelings of helplessness, meaninglessness, worthlessness, or powerlessness? Are you worried about having an addiction to something, such as television, video or computer games, the Internet, sex, food, alcohol, shopping, a relationship, texting, pornography, sports, or anything else?

You have probably encountered questionnaires with questions similar to these while reading a magazine, watching television, or surfing the Internet. Perhaps a psychiatric association, pharmaceutical company, or government agency has posted them. The questions act as a set of identifiable warning signs for the reader's self-reflection. These might then create a crisis in the reader's sense of "normalcy," suggesting to the reader that s/he may be suffering from a treatable mental or emotional disorder, requiring professional help. However, far from referring to exceptional conditions, such lists include common feelings and practices, some of which all of us may experience at some points in our lives. Indeed, as this chapter will discuss, virtually every form of human behaviour has been classified within the normal/abnormal dichotomy—and there appears to be no end in sight to the growing index of human dysfunctions, disorders, and diseases. The growth of human scientific discourses is the most significant driving force behind what can be understood as "the shrinking spectrum of normalcy" in contemporary Western societies.

The idea that some people are psychologically sick or disordered reflects the growth of the **pathological approach**, a distinctly Western and recent historical phenomenon, in which it is assumed that personal problems are individual and caused by biological and/or psychological factors. Everyday terms such as "psycho," "messed up," "crazy," and "nuts" reflect the current popularity of the therapeutic ethos of our time and place. We come to think of ourselves as not smart enough, attractive enough, rich enough, skinny enough, fulfilled enough, sexy enough, successful enough, or healthy enough; that we must smarten up, straighten out, grow up—so that we can "measure up." Our cultural beliefs and practices about what it means to be a human being in the early 21st century hinge on the idea that there is this objective thing called "normal" that we should all strive for.

However, the notion of "normal" has a history. It has not always been a part of everyday life. Nor are Western or North American ideas and discourses about what is normal found in other societies, as Kleinman's (1991, 2006) cross-cultural research on mental illness demonstrates. As you have learned in previous chapters, the emergence of the idea of normal is key in understanding the establishment of modern systems of discipline. Discourses of normalcy and abnormality have been inserted into the very **subjectivities** of people through techniques of domination and self-regulation derived in large part from the human sciences. Therefore, the "psy" discourses (psychology, psychiatry, psychotherapy, etc.) wield enormous influence in shaping our everyday lives and practices in the early 21st century.

The general popularity of psy discourses, which attempt to explain human problems by identifying their psychological or psychiatric origin, is particularly evident in the growing consumption of self-help material and prescription drugs for mental and emotional reasons. The now-pervasive presence of "psy" in our everyday lives and practices as Westerners can be seen in the widespread acceptance of a particular psychotherapeutic ethos that shapes social practices, which has become known as **the culture of therapy**. As modern subjects, we have at our disposal an immense medicalized vocabulary for speaking about our inner selves. Modern individuals speak with ease and confidence about their thoughts, memories, beliefs, emotions, and the like through psy discourses. Convinced that we should understand our selves in psychological terms of adjustment, empowerment, fulfillment, good relationships, personal growth, and so forth, we actively seek the wisdom of experts and cling to their promises to assist us in the quest for self-change that we "freely" undertake (Rose, 1998). The popularity of psy discourses reflects a deeply held belief that psychology in one way or another can make one happy, and that at the root of our difficulties are psy problems that can be treated with professional therapy, self-help, and/or prescription drug use.

In this chapter, we will explore how the modern subject has been shaped through the cultural authority of the **psy complex**—which itself is derived from the reigning culture of science, as you have just explored in Chapter 8. We will employ Foucault's conceptual and historical approach to present the social and historical construction of psy knowledge. We will then provide some important examples of how the development of the psy disciplines' system of classification has had particular ramifications for the production of gender, race, sexual orientation, and class. Later we will turn to an analysis of contemporary therapeutic culture, and an explanation of what Heidi Rimke (2000, 2010a, 2010b) refers to as **psychocentrism**: the outlook that all human problems are innate pathologies of the individual mind and/or body, with the individual held responsible for health and illness, success and failure. Through this analysis, we want to continue our task of interrogating the centre by demonstrating *how* power–knowledge relations permeate our every day, taken-for-granted world. We want you to think about *how* particular knowledges acquire the status of truth, and *how* people or subjects are "made up" (Hacking, 1986) or **constituted** through the **expert knowledge** of psy and medical professionals, including psychiatrists, teachers, social hygiene reformers, psychologists, health workers, sexologists, and social workers. The rise of these experts reflects the development of professional knowledges relying upon a scientific rationality to understand, explain, and control human conduct.

Our aim is to overthrow the "naturalness" of dominant ways of thinking about individual pathology by studying the historical relationship between forms of knowledge, the exercise of power, and the creation of subjects. For example, researchers have demonstrated the multiple and shifting ways subjects have been constituted or created by expert discourses seen in critical social studies on anxiety (Tone, 2008), multiple personality disorder (Hacking, 1995a), suicide (Marsh, 2010), antisocial personality disorders (Rimke, 2003), self-esteem (Ward, 1996), shyness (Lane, 2008), stuttering (Petrunik & Shearing, 2002), depression (Horwitz & Wakefield, 2007), ADD/ADHD (Conrad & Schneider, 1980) and hysteria (Didi-Huberman, 2004).

While this chapter draws primarily on the work of Foucault, we can also consider the significance of the work of Karl Marx when studying the culture of therapy. In order to understand the economic conditions and financial motivation which are significant factors in the growth of the culture of therapy, we ask you to think back to your study of Karl Marx in Chapter 6. Marx's work is significant for our study in many ways. Therapeutic culture has created an enormously profitable economic sector, from the dozens of self-help books and videos released annually to the dramatic growth of pharmaceutical companies (now referred to as "big pharma"), to the proliferation of wellness retreats and wellness practices. Further, by asking who gains from the development and growth of a psy-oriented industry, we can question who has the ability to define reality. While it is too simplistic to claim that the dominant class simply controls the oppressed class, it is fair to say that historically the medical explanations for mental illness shifted according to the patient's class position. For example, while the mental illness of the poor was often attributed to factors as coming from "bad stock" or personal failures, the economically privileged were rarely blamed or held accountable for a psychiatric diagnosis. Instead, it was attributed to the climate, a fever, or a "blow to the head." That said, the "psy effect" should not be identified with a particular "cause" or a singular powerful social group, but rather by its *effects* in everyday life and how it weaves throughout our lives, connecting and dividing as well as producing and constraining our movement. Thus while class is certainly significant in the politics of mental health and illness, it is a Foucauldian analysis of the politics of truth and science that most guides this chapter.

When we engage in this kind of analysis, it is not intended to deny that many people do have, either chronically or periodically, mental or emotional issues that significantly affect their ability to get along in the world, to meet their own emotional needs, to develop good relationships with others, and so forth. Similarly, it is not our intent to pass a final judgement on psy discourses by claiming that they are necessarily good or bad, or by declaring them merely ideological. Clearly they can be enormously beneficial for many people, just as they can be destructive for others (for example, by imposing social stigma and discrimination). More often, our engagement with psy discourses and practices can be mixed, with positive, negative, or ambivalent implications. The point is that they do shape us in various ways.

The issues and debates surrounding mental illness or psychological problems are complex, contradictory, and conflicting as the growing literature in the sociology of medicine and psychiatry demonstrates. Just as we do not intend to evaluate the rightness or wrongness of psy discourses, we do not seek to provide answers and resolutions to this broad domain of contested expert claims and varied human experience. Our objective is a more modest one: to discuss the social and historical development of psy discourses, institutions, and practices, with particular attention to largely taken-for-granted popular and expert discourses about normalcy and abnormality.

NORMALIZATION AND CLASSIFICATION

Critical scholarship about historical and contemporary psy discourses, institutions, and practices owe much to the guidance of Michel Foucault, whose scholarship includes two books on the history of madness and on the emergence of treatment regimes: *Madness and Civilization* (1961) and *The Birth of the Clinic* (1963). Foucault's governmentality approach and his attention to practices of regulation and **normalization** have been particularly important for studying the culture of therapy. As you learned in Chapter 2, distinguishing between the normal and the abnormal is an expression of **normalizing power** (Foucault, 1979). Specifically, normalizing power compares, differentiates mental states, establishes a hierarchy of value between them, homogenizes by presenting a particular notion of "normal," and excludes those who are in some way considered abnormal. From this explanation, we can see that normalizing power is simultaneously a **dividing practice**. People, beliefs, and practices are distinguished and divided from one another. By encouraging certain ways of life over others, discourses of normalization offer implicit conceptions of whom and what constitutes a good self or normal person.

For example, the hypothetical questionnaire at the beginning of this chapter is a starting point for not only diagnosing people, but for **classifying** them according to "signs" or "symptoms." The psy disciplines, like other human sciences, have developed an ever-expanding system of classifying people, making distinctions between and among them. These evaluations and distinctions are not neutral. As Turner and Edgley (1983) have demonstrated, the very core of psychiatric categories and diagnosis is based upon subjective social and moral values. They critique the assumption that "chemical imbalances" are at the root of "deviance" because it is not possible to distinguish, medically or chemically, behaviours that are socially defined as acceptable or unacceptable. The seemingly "neutral" language of psychiatry masks value judgements about good and bad, or right from wrong. In the previous chapter, you read that no scientific test can determine morals and morality; such determinations are always already cultural.

Another example of how systems of classification work is found through an account of the ever-expanding *Diagnostic and Statistical Manual of Mental Disorders* (DSM). The DSM was first published in 1952 by the American Psychiatric Association (APA). It was intended to be a comprehensive account of mental illness in American society, and today acts as the "psychiatric bible" by defining the criteria for an ever-increasing number of mental illnesses and disorders (Kutchins & Kirk, 1998). Once an official DSM classification of mental illness is declared, the category begins a life of its own, which can result in unanticipated consequences. As Hacking (1995b, 1999) shows, what develops is an interaction or **looping effect** between a classification and those people who are classified.

Humans inevitably respond to being classified or classifying others, which in turn alters their conduct, which then has an effect on the classification, and so on. As Hacking (1999) explains, "All our acts are under descriptions, and the acts that are open to us depend … on the descriptions available to us. Moreover, classifications do not exist only in the empty space of language but in institutions, practices, material interactions with things and other people." Expert classifications thus operate at the level of the everyday culture, shaping our views of ourselves and of others.

While we are on the topic of the DSM, it is worth noting that the original DSM, the DSM-I (1952) was 130 pages long, listing 106 disorders. By its fourth edition, published in 1994, the DSM-IV was 886 pages long and listed 297 disorders, thus nearly triple the volume (Grob, 1991). The controversial DSM-V has an expected publication date of May 2012. It is expected that the new version will expand the basis for psychiatric diagnosis and classification by including "new" disorders such as personality and relational disorders, night eating syndrome, sensory processing disorder, cannabis withdrawal, obesity, anxious depression, childhood disintegrative disorder, parental alienation, compulsive buying, and Internet addiction (American Psychiatric Association, 2009; Block, 2008; Kaplan, 2009).[1]

A Foucauldian approach interrogates the assumptions and certainties embedded in our cultural attitudes, beliefs, desires, and practices concerning the normal and the pathological. We can thus attend to the power–knowledge relations that inform our everyday beliefs and practices about mental health and illness, including the dominant assumptions about whom or what forms of conduct are socially defined as normal or abnormal. Yet scholarly critiques of beliefs and practices about mental illness by no means began with, or are limited to, Foucault and those whom he has influenced. For example, Rosenhan's (1973) classic sociological study, "On Being Sane in Insane Places," also demonstrates the subjective nature of psychiatric medicine. Rosenhan had eight "pseudopatients" relying on scripts present themselves as mentally ill patients in a psychiatric institution. The actors did not display any form of symptomatic behaviour yet were nevertheless diagnosed and treated as if they were indeed mentally ill. The study demonstrated that even psy professionals cannot always distinguish the sane from the insane because of the subjective nature of judging human conduct.

---

1   Critics argue that the addition of new disorders to the DSM-V is another ploy in an endless series of scientific rationalizations for prescribing profitable drugs for one of the fastest-growing industries in North America. For example, in 2002, the combined profits of the ten largest pharmaceutical companies in the Fortune 500 totalled $35.9 billion amounting to more than the combined profits ($33.7 billion) of the remaining 490 companies together (Angell, 2004). Big pharma has become a profit-oriented industry to advertise and sell drugs of questionable benefit. In 2007, the *British Medical Journal* published a study analyzing approximately 2,500 common medical treatments and found that 13 percent were found to be beneficial, 23 percent were likely to be beneficial, 8 percent were as likely to be harmful as beneficial, 6 percent were unlikely to be beneficial, 4 percent were likely to be harmful or ineffective, and 46 percent were unknown in terms of helpful or harmful effects (Clinical evidence, 2007). The economic power of the pharmaceutical industry has resulted in the co-optation of every institution that might get in its way, including government, health, and drug regulatory bodies, academic medical centres, and the medical profession itself (Levi, 2006).

THE HISTORY OF THE PRESENT

As Nikolas Rose comments, "We can question our present certainties—about what we know, who we are, and how we should act—by confronting them with their histories" (Rose, 1999: x). As you learned in Chapter 2, Foucault referred to his historical approach as the **history of the present**. Rather than understanding historical developments as inevitable, or as determined by universal laws, he viewed history as **contingent**, because for any event, other directions and outcomes were also possible. So while the contemporary interpreter of historical events might assume that the development of psychiatry and institutions to house the insane were practical, humane, unavoidable, or even evolutionary, Foucault provides us with a way of thinking about how this outcome was the result of power–knowledge relations. Foucault's methodology is a **counter-history** because it is written against the taken-for-granted or dominant histories, as our examples below will show. Foucault eventually began to refer to this critical approach as his **genealogical method**. Genealogy starts with the present, not to affirm or deny it, but to ask how the present has come to be constituted as it is. The aim is to overthrow the "naturalness" of dominant ways of thinking by studying the historical relationship between forms of knowledge and the exercise of power.

Foucault explored the multiple, contradictory, and shifting discourses that were emerging from the **Enlightenment** onwards, particularly those with a profound effect on how people were understood. Before the human sciences began to develop in the 19th century, ideas about human nature and human conduct were derived from a religious framework determined by Church authorities. Humans were understood in religious terms of evil or virtue, rather than medically and scientifically. With the Enlightenment, scientific theories began to claim that human nature was the result of biological, physiological, and/or psychological factors. Thus by the end of the 18th century, Western theories shifted toward scientific rather than theological explanations. **Positivists** insisted that through systematic observation, human behaviour could be explained in the same objective manner as the hard sciences explained the natural world. The "discovery" that madness was not the result of demonic possession or a punishment from God, but a disease entity that required medical attention, was a catalyst for the formation of a medical model of mental pathology. The scientific search for endogenous (internal) causes rooted in the person thus became a hallmark of **modernity**.

By the mid-to-late-19th century, the human sciences developed numerous new branches of study, such as comparative psychology, phrenology, anthropology, neurology, criminology, experimental psychology, physiognomy, craniology, necrology, and psychological medicine. Psychiatry as a distinct specialization only expanded in the mid-20th century. These areas of study often competed with one another, so the human scientific project of studying the normal/abnormal divide did not develop as a single and unified discipline (Rimke, 2008; Rimke & Hunt, 2002).

Modern society thus rested upon the new ideals of science and progress. Human differences or problems were increasingly viewed as scientific problems that could be studied, known, categorized, regulated, and treated or cured. The modern claim that deviance or madness was a scientific, rather than religious, matter drastically altered how we interpret and perceive the self and others in the everyday. Human scientists began insisting that the cause of deviance was rooted in the body itself and that religious ideas were outdated by modern, scientific ideals and standards.

While the medical model's view of the diseased individual has gradually replaced the religious model's view of the evil sinner as a means of understanding and explaining human conduct, the historical effects of religious practices and discourses still exist and affect current ideas. Rather than explain the historical shift in linear terms, where religious authority was simply displaced by the scientific, Foucauldian research has demonstrated that a hybrid discourse of Christian theology and Western science together medicalized immorality as an objective fact (Rimke & Hunt, 2002). So, for example, while religious discourses held that the sodomite (today, the "gay male") was a sinner who engaged in immoral sexual practices with other men, the invention of the category of the homosexual by the human sciences, as Foucault has shown, relied on a notion of "perversion" derived from this earlier notion of sin. The importance of this example is that it demonstrates the influence wielded by two dominant discourses—religion and science—in the making of the idea of the homosexual. We will return to this example shortly. We will now present you with some brief historical accounts, or fragments, concerning the history of institutionalization, diagnosis, and treatment, which disrupt and trouble the **grand narrative** of medical and scientific progress. They illustrate that so-called "progressive" historical measures carried with them certain assumptions about class, race, gender, and sexuality. They compel us to think further about the myriad ways knowledge and power intersect, and the impact upon populations and the daily lives of people.

Confinement: The Emergence of the Asylum

Seventeenth-century Europe witnessed an unprecedented programme of building institutions designed specifically for disciplining and regulating certain populations of people, in asylums, prisons, workhouses, and so on. Foucault referred to this as the **great confinement**. He was intrigued by the emergence of new strategies to administer to and discipline the population, which included both those who found themselves confined, and those who feared that they could one day be (the poor, and women of all classes). These **spaces of exclusion** were both a cause and an effect of the growth of the **disciplinary society**. People considered mad were initially confined in the same institutions as the poor, the criminal, the unemployed, and the idle. As the psy disciplines expanded, institutions specifically designed for the diagnosis, retention, and treatment of the mad were created. A diagnosis of madness became a **dividing practice**, through which those labelled were separated from their communities, both conceptually, and often physically. The process of diagnosing and locking up the mad in houses of confinement allowed for the observation of significant numbers of people under controlled conditions, making them objects of scientific study and knowledge. Moreover, this administration and control of the mad within public institutions came to increasingly

FIGURE 9.1 ■ The tranquilizing chair. Benjamin Rush (1745–1813), considered the father of American psychiatry, wrote the first American psychiatric textbook and invented the "tranquilizing chair" in 1811 to immobilize the patient using the "treatment" of restraint and sensory deprivation.

Source: Engraved by Benjamin Tanner after John James Barralet. © Bettmann/CORBIS

depend on the classification and separation of different types of madness. Diagnostic classifications, in turn, fostered their own forms of treatment. In addition to confinement, the mad were subjected to practices that included the frontal or icepick lobotomy, the clitorectomy, physical restraints, involuntary drugging, and electroconvulsive shock therapy (Valentin, 1986). Some of these practices have been ended, while others continue, although not without controversy.

Drapetomania

The psy disciplines have also participated in processes of racialization where, as you read in Chapter 5, scientific method was used to construct distinct racial types, each with its own morphology and character. A stark historical example is the classification of **Drapetomania**, introduced by a Dr. Cartwright in 1851, which was defined as the pathological desire of African-American slaves to escape captivity from their natural and God-given masters (Szasz, 1971b). We find here another example of how both religious and medical discourses have been simultaneously exercised to make claims that buttress social inequalities. Contemporary readers should have no difficulty identifying the absurdity of this diagnosis. However, it should remind us to consider more closely how, in our own time, racialized people are **pathologized** as an explanation for the "social problems" of their communities. For example, the claim that there is an "epidemic" of single mothers and absent fathers among African-Americans not only identifies the single-parent family as non-normative, but alleges that male irresponsibility and family instability are integral features of Black communities.

DRAPETOMANIA, OR THE DISEASE CAUSING NEGROES TO RUN AWAY

It is unknown to our medical authorities, although its diagnostic symptom, the absconding from service, is well known to our planters and overseers....

In noticing a disease not heretofore classed among the long list of maladies that man is subject to, it was necessary to have a new term to express it. The cause in the most of cases, that induces the negro to run away from service, is as much a disease of the mind as any other species of mental alienation, and much more curable, as a general rule. With the advantages of proper medical advice, strictly followed, this troublesome practice that many negroes have of running away, can be almost entirely prevented, although the slaves be located on the borders of a free state, within a stone's throw of the abolitionists.

If the white man attempts to oppose the Deity's will, by trying to make the negro anything else than "the submissive knee-bender," (which the Almighty declared he should be,) by trying to raise him to a level with himself, or by putting himself on an equality with the negro; or if he abuses the power which God has given him over his fellow-man, by being cruel to him, or punishing him in anger, or by neglecting to protect him from the wanton abuses of his fellow-servants and all others, or by denying him the usual comforts and necessaries of life, the negro will run away; but if he keeps him in the position that we learn from the Scriptures he was intended to occupy, that is, the position of submission; and if his master or overseer be kind and gracious in his hearing towards him, without condescension, and at the same time ministers to his physical wants, and protects him from abuses, the negro is spellbound, and cannot run away.

Source: "Diseases and Peculiarities of the Negro Race," by Dr. Cartwright (in *DeBow's Review,* 1851)

Moral Insanity and Psychopathic Disorder

Dr. James Prichard created the diagnosis of **moral insanity** in 1833. The invention of this diagnosis reflected the growing medical fixation on immoral or disrespectable conduct, particularly in response to what was perceived as increasing vices arising from industrialization and the growth of cities. Social danger increasingly came to be seen in violations of the norms of respectable society. Moral insanity would later be codified by the psy disciplines as "defects of character," and eventually as "personality disorders" and other "mental and emotional disturbances." As psy expertise distinguished itself from the wider category of medicine, it simultaneously generated a knowledge base about what it meant to be a normal individual through the study of the abnormal individual. By the turn of the 20th century, the list of **psychopathic disorders** grew to include: kleptomania, erotomania, pyromania, and dipsomania, masturbation, obscene language, gender transgressions, nymphomania (in females) and satyriasis (in males), vagrancy, gambling, poor personal hygiene, laziness, prostitution, general lawlessness, and the destruction or squandering of property or money. Modern human sciences thus sought to target and regulate "bad" social subjects, those who in some way resisted the normative expectations of civility and propriety (Rimke, 2003; Rimke & Hunt, 2002).

Homosexuality

From its initial publication, it was accepted wisdom that homosexuality be included in the DSM as a recognized form of mental illness, and that every attempt should be made by psychiatric and medical professionals to cure the afflicted of this "sexual malady." Foucault describes how in the 19th century sexuality in the West became an object of scientific analysis and regulation through the pathologizing of sexual difference. Experimental methods for the "cure" of homosexuality included electroshock therapy and the frontal lobotomy, although no evidence of a successful cure was ever derived from these methods. By the early 1960s a homophile (soon to be known as "lesbian and gay') liberation movement was beginning to emerge in North America and Western Europe. Together with sympathetic psychiatrists such as Dr. Evelyn Hooker, they produced counter-narratives and political protest to successfully challenge the methodology and facticity of such scientific claims (see *Changing Our Minds*, 1991). Homosexuality was removed from the DSM II in 1973. However, various other sexuality- and gender-related diagnoses remained in place, or were subsequently added, such as the designation *sexual orientation disturbance*.

Female Depression

As you learned in Chapter 2, Foucault uses the concept of the "gaze" to highlight and explain the process of surveillance and the growing influence of expert knowledges. The gaze of the expert attempts to define who people are, without direct input from those under observation. It thus reflects relations of power in which those at the centre can define and categorize those on the margins. Feminist scholars have identified many of the ways in which this gaze has been deployed to inculcate "proper" standards of behaviour in women. For example, in the late 19th and early 20th centuries, women who displayed masculine traits such as independence, assertiveness, and sexual self-confidence might find themselves classified as "morally insane," because such conduct contradicted cultural conceptions of females as essentially weak, chaste, and passive.

More recently, women subject to the psychiatric gaze have unsurprisingly also been the target of pharmaceutical companies. For example, introduced in 1963, Valium quickly became a widely prescribed tranquilizer, which was intended to relieve symptoms of boredom, anxiety, and depression and to increase relaxation—and it was targeted at house-wives (Tone, 2008). Unfortunately, it was also highly addictive, especially with long-term use, and could produce numerous side-effects. Prescribing Valium and other sedatives to post–World War II white middle-class women was such a widely recognized practice that it formed the subject matter of a well-known song by the Rolling Stones, "Mother's Little Helper."

The **medicalization** of white middle- and upper-class women's disaffection with their lives was soon challenged by the development of a feminist analysis. In 1963 Betty Friedan published the landmark book *The Feminine Mystique*, in which she presented "the problem with no name":

> The problem lay buried, unspoken, for many years in the minds of American women. It was a strange stirring, a sense of dissatisfaction, a yearning that women suffered in the middle of the twentieth century in the United States. Each suburban wife struggled with it alone. As she made the beds, shopped for groceries, matched slipcover material, ate peanut butter sandwiches with her children, chauffeured Cub Scouts and Brownies, lay beside her husband at night—she was afraid to ask even of herself the silent question—"Is this all?" (Friedan, 1963: 13).

Feminists began to explicitly critique the role of psychiatry in pathologizing women, claiming that women's mental health issues would be better addressed by trying to change women's social, political, and economic conditions rather than attempting to change the women themselves by coercing them to conform to traditional roles and expectations. As Dorothy Smith and Sara David entitled their 1975 collection of papers challenging psychiatry, "I'm Not Mad, I'm Angry" (Smith & David, 1975). Anger in this context refers to the collective emotional response of women and girls to the socially created limitations they encounter throughout their lives. Women's collective frustration surrounding unequal wages, lack of access to birth control, abortion, and child care, lack of opportunities for advancement in the paid labour force and limited educational opportunities was seen as having nothing to do with women's mental health, and everything to do with a gendered organization of social relations that benefited males to the disadvantage of females. We will return to the growth of the anti-psychiatry movement toward the conclusion of this chapter.

Lest you think this is now all history, with no bearing on the lives of contemporary Western women, we need look no further than advertisements used by pharmaceutical giant Eli Lilly to introduce and promote the antidepressant Prozac to physicians. One particular ad, placed in *The British Journal of Psychiatry*, displayed images of a dirty, disordered kitchen, inset with a picture of a clean, tidy kitchen. Such a visual representation links women's mental health to her attention to household chores. As we explored in Chapter 8, this is an example of how scientific and medical discourses can carry with them some highly gendered assumptions, which are grounded in presumptuous social practices rather than objective, scientific "fact." The persecution of women alleged to be witches, and the invention of hysteria, moral insanity, and now "female" personality disorders—borderline, dependent, and histrionic—demonstrate an ongoing pattern of gendered regulation. Each respective era has proclaimed an official category for females who in one way or another defied socially prescribed behaviour according to gender rules (Rimke, 2003; Szasz, 1974; Wirth-Cauchon, 2001; Ussher, 1991). Szasz asserted in 1974 that the contemporary phenomenon of diagnosing women as "mentally ill" continues to define acceptable female conduct and punish transgression, now often in the form of medical "treatment" (1974). We want you to think about how his assertion continues to have relevance, despite the successes of feminism.

Psychoanalysis

Finally, in the early 20th century the creation of psychoanalysis occurred through the work of Sigmund Freud and Carl Jung. **Psychoanalytic theory** claims that individuals are motivated by strong and dynamic unconscious drives and conflicts arising in early childhood rather than biological functions of the brain and central nervous system. Psychoanalysis thus provided a non-biological theory of emotional and mental life alongside the dominating neurological, behaviourist, evolutionary, or hereditarian paradigms (Rimke, 2008). "Talk therapy" was introduced as an alternative form of diagnosis and treatment. While more humane than some of our earlier examples, talk therapy was also to become a means of expanding the scope of diagnosis and treatment to well beyond the confines of the asylum, as you will learn more about when we turn our attention to therapeutic culture.

In summary, this section has challenged the official histories of medicine and psychiatry. These histories typically glorify the "great men of science" as benevolent, humanitarian reformers who freed the mad from brutal and inhumane institutional treatment. However, our brief examples suggest an entirely different phenomenon: the "Age of Reason" produced new regimes of discipline. Rather, than a new respect for humanity, the success of the human sciences involved the establishment of more finely tuned mechanisms of surveillance that resulted in a more effective web of power infiltrating everyday life and practices (Foucault, 1979). The psy experts thus established their expertise on the basis of the general argument that society required remedies for its mental ills and only certain human experts possessed the scientific knowledge to achieve such ends.

By the mid-20th century, the psy disciplines had accomplished a level of respectability in the West that conferred upon them significant authority in public and political affairs. In particular, the physician and the psychiatrist (who, unlike the psychologist, are required to hold a medical degree to legally prescribe drugs) experienced growing social recognition and authority. Psy experts increasingly were called upon to analyze and intervene in a growing array of social, scientific, and legal developments. This included activities from forensic psychology and legal psychiatry (linking certain criminal acts to psychiatric illness), to education and welfare reform, to shaping domestic and foreign policy to commenting on public TV watching habits. By the postwar period, psychiatric and medical discourses were therefore shaping state policies and practices on an increasing range of public matters. This is one example of how expert knowledges have come to exert their influence on the contemporary state, expanding governmental power. But there is another facet to the rise of psy knowledge, and its increasingly detailed classification and specification of the human subject. This knowledge has now been popularized and packaged in particular forms, so that it pervades contemporary Western popular culture, to the point where it has indeed become what some have referred to as a **culture of therapy**. It is to this popularization that we now turn.

Self-Help and Therapeutic Culture

The therapist's office, the self-help group, and the blog are all examples of what Foucault referred to as the **modern confessional** (Valverde, 1985). Foucault claims that the modern person has become a "confessing animal." Rather than turning to the priest to confess and absolve our sins, modern individuals rely on psy analyses for guidance, comfort, and direction. Today people may go to their therapists' offices or their support group to confess—but the important point for Foucault is that it is in the process of confessing that the self is *created* rather than *revealed*. One of the main tenets of therapeutic discourses is the assumption that there is an inner core or "truth" about ourselves, which therapeutic techniques can help us to reveal to ourselves. Foucauldians, however, invert the common or traditional assumption that expert discourses reveal a "hidden truth," and instead argue that the expert discourses themselves shape the individual's interpretation and perception of self.

The self-help genre forms an important part of the modern culture of therapy in **neoliberal** societies. A massive and growing industry, self-help culture provides a dizzying array of groups, books, experts, shows, podcasts, and so forth to guide us in our exploration of our inner selves and our relations with others. Self-help literature comes in numerous different forms of advice: spirituality, how-to manuals, personal change, dealing with loss, relationship advice, and more. We are incited to seek self-enlightenment by excavating and exposing our "true" selves to the therapeutic gaze in multiple forms, such as our MSN friends, online diagnostic questionnaires, Facebook applications, or fashion magazine quizzes. We may search for our "inner child," reveal our "codependency," insist on "tough love," recover our "true" or "real" selves, or experiment with Eastern, aboriginal, or otherwise "alternative" healing practices. As such, we are part of a **culture of recovery**.

The culture of recovery now clearly has a very public character. Far from the privacy of the psychiatrist's office, self-revelation takes place through the gamut of public media. Self-help discourses circulate and proliferate on television, the internet (websites and webcasts), in autobiographical books, in celebrity interviews, in magazines and newspapers, radio shows, psy-related books and texts, movies, and documentaries. Often, now, self-help can also be considered a form of popular entertainment, seen especially on shows like *Dr. Phil*, *The Dr. Oz Show*, or *The Oprah Winfrey Show*. Increasingly, this psy network contributes more in terms of entertainment than enlightenment, and treatment programs rather than cures. Moreover, "reality" TV shows such as *Intervention*, *Hoarders*, or *Celebrity Rehab* centre on the pathologies of people in multiple guises, rarely examining the relations and cultural expectations in which the suffering individual is embedded.

In our culture of therapy, most, if not all, of us engage in activities designed to keep ourselves emotionally healthy, regardless of whether we ever go to the therapist's office. We commonly use what Foucault referred to as **techniques of the self** to "diagnose" and classify ourselves and others. When we employ these techniques of the self, we are being governed, we govern ourselves, and this also leads us to govern others.

Let's focus now on a very popular technique of the self: reading self-help books. A trip to your local bookstore will make obvious the popularity of this genre. Shelves are now filled with books dedicated to self-improvement; to helping us to remake ourselves into "better people" living more "successful" lives. We can see evidence of how virtually every human experience is reframed in **psychocentric** terms. Do you have difficulty with managing your weight? Do you drink too much? Do you choose partners who are bad for you? Do your kids rule your life? Are you a shopaholic? Could your soul benefit from some chicken soup? Do you "sweat the small stuff"?

Why are self-help books so popular? First, they promise to improve us not only mentally, but also spiritually, physically, and even financially, if this is what we seek. Second, they make "normalcy" or mental health accessible to everyone, regardless of income or access to a therapist, and in the privacy of our own homes, if that is our preference. Third, they really can help. They may actually provide some useful or practical advice on how to get along better with one another, or how to feel better about ourselves. Maybe we will learn to be more understanding and forgiving of other people, as we learn to do the same toward ourselves.

Perhaps we *will* become "better" people, but according to whose definition and evaluation?

Much self-help advice appears to be simply "common sense," although certain phrases (such as the *Don't Sweat the Small Stuff* reminder that soon the world will be completely populated by new people) can have a lasting impression for many readers. Part of the commonsense quality derives from the "homey" character of advice one might get from a wise elder such as a grandparent. Another part also derives from the everyday popularity of psychocentrism. The notion of "the self" as knowable, and as a work in progress, is now as familiar to us, and as taken for granted, as brushing our teeth.

The first book of the popular self-help series *Don't Sweat the Small Stuff … And It's All Small Stuff* was published in 1997. The author, Richard Carlson, was a psychotherapist who had already published a number of books on stress management, one of which lead to an appearance on *Oprah*, guaranteeing instant success. The first volume begins with a quote from William James (1842–1910), an American pragmatist philosopher and psychologist, whose prolific writings contributed significantly to the development of psy discourse. Relying on a psychocentric logic, he argued that "the greatest discovery of my generation is that a human being can alter his life by altering his attitude" (Carlson, 1997: 1). The first *Don't Sweat* book remained on the *New York Times* bestseller list for over two years. Its success led to the publication of more *Don't Sweat* books, which taught how not to sweat the small stuff at work, in love (co-written with his wife, Kris Carlson), for women (authored by his wife), for men, with your family, for teens, for parents, for moms, and for graduates. The series was successful because of its simplicity; it provided short bits of practical, commonsense advice for achieving a better life, ones that a person could apply immediately: Focus on the things that go right, rather than the things that go wrong. Find time for yourself every day. Write things down that you feel good about. Be compassionate toward other people. Accept your imperfections. Pick up litter. Don't argue with your partner about inconsequential matters. When you die, your in-basket will not be empty. In one hundred years, all new people will be here.

By defining human normality, and thus by extension, abnormality, self-help experts profess to offer strategies and truths to achieve the good life, and indeed the good self. Consequently, popular self-help projects have attempted to affect all areas of social life: how to live, how to work, how to parent, how to love, and how to behave in various spatial and temporal settings. In self-help books, subjects are cast as damaged and injured commodities, as potential consumers of unique and presumably preferable selves, but also as redeemable from within. As a result our culture has witnessed "the transformation of ordinary behaviours of ordinary persons into the extraordinary awe-inspiring symptoms of mental diseases" (Szasz, 1978: 194).

Some of the impetus for a focus on individual well-being emerged from the social movements of the 1960s and 1970s, as people sought personal and social liberation through collective social action and resistance. For example, throughout the 1970s and 1980s, a feminist therapy movement emerged to treat and heal women who had been victimized by physical, emotional, and sexual abuse in a patriarchal world. However, in the 1990s, feminist and *Ms. Magazine* founder Gloria Steinem began emphasizing women's need to focus on "the revolution within" after years of feminist activism aimed at challenging socially and historically structured gender inequality. Self-help technologies resonated in Steinem's book. The once-popular slogan of the 1960s women's and civil rights movement that declared "The personal is political" was inverted by Steinem's advice to focus on one's self to achieve an "inner" revolution. Over time, the focus on self-transformation, joined with competitive individualism, has increasingly undermined social movements' emphasis on collective resistance to achieve social justice and equality. As a result, prescriptions for revolutionary action or social change are being replaced by psychocentricity, thus propping up neoliberal ideals and practices glorifying the individual at the expense of social and political change and analysis. Furthermore, the increasing focus on individual responsibility and accountability has been occurring simultaneously with the dismantling of public services, including health care, forcing individuals to absorb structural deterioration—one partial explanation for the rise of self-help. You have already learned that neoliberalism is predicated on the valorization of free markets (that is, the unfettered movement of capital), on limiting state powers for the regulation of capital, and on competitive individualism. From the 1970s onward, the rise of both neoliberalism and the culture of therapy had a common theme: a focus on the "I" over the "we."

Nikolas Rose commented while giving a public lecture in Toronto in the mid-1990s that he had recently seen at a political demonstration by the unemployed, a picket sign demanding "Jobs, not Prozac." This slogan neatly encapsulates the sociological insistence that the personal is also social and public. For example, the unemployed person is often not without work because s/he lacks skills or initiative, but rather because local and national economic arrangements have increased joblessness. While some economists claim that a certain unemployment rate is "healthy for the economy" because it drives competition, what of that percentage of the population that suffer the harsh realities of unemployment? Are they to feel individually responsible or proud for contributing to the health of the economy? Should they feel personally inadequate or otherwise psychologically inferior to those who are in advantageous social and economic positions? The fact is there are more people than there are jobs. Prozac may chemically help some individuals cope with the negative personal impact of unemployment, but it is the creation of new jobs that will resolve personal crises resulting from depression, stress, and anxiety, resulting from job loss.

From this example, you can see how Marx's analysis of capitalism and its class structure, as well as Foucault's approach to government, both contribute to our understanding of how people (neoliberal subjects) are constituted through a therapeutic culture that serves to secure relations of domination as much as it portends to liberate the self. The growth of neoliberalism has resulted in the increasing de-responsibilization of social authorities. Moreover, psychocentrism ensures that social and political authorities are exonerated while individuals are held responsible and accountable for situations they did not necessarily create.

CONCLUSION: CHALLENGING PSYCHOCENTRISM

To summarize our recent analysis, struggling with the self has become a key cultural theme in modern life. There seems to be a persistent impulse among North Americans to worry about whether they are what they should be, and whether they have the sort of personal traits, skills, social manners, or inner strengths they should have. Experts translate all aspects of human life into myriad dysfunctions, addictions, disorders, pathologies, or destructive behaviours that require expert attention and self-treatment. Indeed, the diversity of the psy complex is what makes it so effective: no one is ever really good enough. We are incited, directed, and instructed to be self- and other-critical. In the early 21st century, the psy complex has become the most influential field in determining the best or proper way of being human, thus wielding tremendous social influence. Consistent with the political rationalities of neoliberalism, psychocentrism dominates a cultural landscape, masking how broad and unequal political and social structures, discourses, and practices impact individual lives physically, emotionally, and mentally.

The psy sciences provide a corpus of knowledge that categorizes social problems as individual deficiencies or pathologies without seriously examining the social contexts and conditions that define or produce those experiences and differences. While human differences certainly exist, the psy complex classifies and hierarchalizes those differences into binary categories of good/bad, healthy/sick, normal/abnormal, moral/immoral, and so forth. "Wellness" has become conflated or synonymous with culturally prescribed notions and practices of "normalcy." Productive subjects have to be healthy, upstanding, obedient, and efficient—in one word, self-governing—in order to sustain neoliberalism in the face of a weakening and quickly shifting global economy, as you will read more about in Chapter 11. We live in a society in which our search for meaning has shifted away from the public sphere toward the privatized self. Yet, whatever self the self is pursuing, we must remember that we are always within the boundaries of cultural meanings. We learn how to appraise and judge ourselves, and how to behave in different contexts: one must not look, act, or talk like the marginalized or abnormal, and if one does, one is socially expected to fulfill the obligations of the "sick role" (Parsons, 1951), which includes following doctors' orders and prescriptions.

The growing mental, physical, and emotional tensions, strains, and struggles of contemporary culture are indeed expressed in multiple forms. Loneliness, isolation, violence, anxiety, anger, apathy, repulsion, depression, suicide, and so forth, while individually experienced, must be placed within the context of social patterns and inequalities outlined in other chapters of this textbook. These include increasing economic deterioration, social conflicts based on axes of age, sexual orientation, class, gender, physical appearance, familial ties, educational attainment, religious status, ethnicity, and so forth. Consider also how cultural prescriptions are contradictory, unrealistic, and naïve in the face of many people's daily lives and social insecurities, such as the lack of affordable housing, growing unemployment, the erosion of pensions, rising food and energy prices, increasing environmental disasters, and the credit crisis. Yet the resounding messages provided by the psy complex imply that people's struggles are personal and internally produced, as though our experiences in the world were somehow separate and distinct from the social conditions that shape, produce, and order those experiences. Psychiatric discourses have been—and continue to be—contentious and problematic for many reasons: classifications can be ambiguous, they often lack sufficient evidence or are based upon conflicting data, and they are premised on highly subjective notions such as normal and abnormal. The long, political, and controversial use of psy discourse renders the moral and intellectual status of the psy complex scientifically and socially problematic.

As we have already seen in our examples from the early women's and lesbian and gay liberation movements, the rise of psychiatry has not gone unchallenged. The anti-psychiatry movement emerged in the 1960s as part of the larger anti-establishment movement, which included the collective struggles aimed at achieving women's liberation and civil rights. Leading anti-psychiatrists include Michel Foucault, R. D. Laing and David Cooper, Felix Guatarri, and Thomas Szasz, all of whom received formal training in medicine and psychiatry. Hostile to the fundamental assumptions and practices of the discipline, anti-psychiatry arguments influenced the Western deinstitutionalization movement of the 1970s, which resulted in the dismantling of many state-run psychiatric institutions in favour of community-based treatment. Anti-psychiatry advocates have challenged the modern assumption that confinement in a hospital or other institutional setting for the majority of those diagnosed as mentally ill was necessary.

Today anti-psychiatry advocates also challenge the growth of "chemical restraints" (drugs) for those targeted as at risk, dangerous, disorderly, disruptive, and so forth, which has become commonplace in the West. Patients and ex-patients have challenged and resisted traditional assumptions and labels by embracing and celebrating their differences as strengths rather than weaknesses—as witness, the growing "psychiatric survivor" and "mad pride" social movements (Crossley & Crossley, 2001; Curtis et al., 2000; Shaughnessy, 2001).

We can also contribute to resistance strategies through our engagement with history and theory. The Foucauldian approach critically interrogates the psychocentricity of the human sciences. This perspective allows something new to be thought, and as Foucault announced, "to learn to what extent the effort to think one's own history can free thought from what it silently thinks, and so enable it to think differently" (1986: 9). After all, the purpose and promise of the sociological imagination is to produce theories and research methods, as well as new forms of knowledge, useful for understanding the link between private troubles and public issues. Understanding the practices and discourses of therapeutic culture thus necessarily entails critiquing the psychiatrization of everyday life that produces and masks the social and historical bases of human struggles.

STUDY QUESTIONS

1. What does it mean to say morality has been medicalized? What is a current example of this that was not addressed in this chapter?

2. In what ways has the treatment of those classified as mentally ill changed over the past 100 years? How does a Foucauldian approach explain these shifts?

3. How does the distinction between normality and abnormality contribute to social regulation? Provide examples.

4. How have counter-discourses challenged psychocentrism? What alternatives to psychocentrism have been proposed? Try also to think of some examples that are not discussed in this chapter.

EXERCISES

1. Go to a bookstore to investigate the titles in the self-help genre. Check sections such as health and wellness, business, travel, biography, spirituality, new age, women, lesbian and gay, and sociology. What themes emerge from your investigation?

2. Research a criminal legal case in which a psychiatric diagnosis has been an important component of the evidence and sentencing. How have psy discourses been deployed in the construction of legal evidence?

3. Take note of how many times in a given day you encounter or make use of psy discourse. How does this exercise contribute to your comprehension of Foucault's notion of government?

REFERENCES

American Psychiatric Association. 2009. *DSM-V: The Future Manual.* http://www.psych.org/MainMenu/Research/DSMIV/DSMV.aspx, accessed February 11, 2009.

Angell, M. 2004. *The Truth About Drug Companies.* New York: Random House.

Block, J. 2008. Issues for DSM-V: Internet addiction. *American Journal of Psychiatry* 165(3): 306–307.

Carlson, Richard. 1997. *Don't Sweat the Small Stuff … And It's All Small Stuff.* New York: Hyperion.

Cartwright, Dr. Samuel. 1851. Diseases and peculiarities of the Negro race. *De Bow's Review, Southern and Western States* (New Orleans) XI. New York: AMS Press, Inc., 1967. Africans in America, Resource Bank, Public Broadcasting System site, http://www.pbs.org/wgbh/aia/part4/4h3106.html, accessed January 24, 2011.

Changing Our Minds: The Story of Dr. Evelyn Hooker [video recording]. 1991. Richard Schmiechen, Director. Katy, TX: Intrepid Productions.

Clinical evidence: How much do we know? 2007. *British Medical Journal.* http://clinical-evidence.bmj.com/ceweb/about/knowledge.jsp, accessed February 2, 2010.

Conrad, P., and J. Schneider. 1980. *Deviance and Medicalization: From Badness to Sickness.* St. Louis: The C. V. Mosby Company.

Crossley, Michele L., and Nick Crossley. 2001. "Patient" voices, social movements and the habitus: How psychiatric survivors "speak out." *Social Science & Medicine* 52(10): 1477–1489.

Curtis, T. R., R. Dellar, E. Leslie, and B. Watson. 2000. *Mad Pride: A Celebration of Mad Culture.* London: Spare Change Books.

Didi-Huberman, G. 2004. *Invention of Hysteria: Charcot and the Photographic Iconography of the Salpetriere.* Massachusetts: The MIT Press.

Foucault, Michel. 1961. *Madness and Civilization* [1988]. New York: Vintage, 1961.

Foucault, Michel. 1963. *The Birth of the Clinic* [1994]. New York: Vintage, 1963.

Foucault, Michel. 1979. *Discipline and Punish: The Birth of the Prison.* New York: Vintage Books.

Foucault, Michel. 1986. *The Use of Pleasure: The History of Sexuality, Volume Two*. Penguin: Harmondsworth.

Friedan, Betty. 1963. *The Feminine Mystique*. New York: Norton.

Grob, G. 1991. Origins of DSM-I: A study in appearance and reality. *American Journal of Psychiatry* 148(4): 421–31.

Hacking, Ian. 1986. Making up people. In T. Heller, M. Sosna, and D. Wellbery, eds., *Reconstructing Individualism*. Stanford: Stanford University Press. 222–36.

Hacking, Ian. 1995a. *Rewriting the Soul: Multiple Personality and the Science of Memory*. Princeton, NJ: Princeton University Press.

Hacking, Ian. 1995b. The looping effect of human kinds. In D. Sperber et al., eds., *Causal Cognition: An Interdisciplinary Approach*. Oxford: University Press. 351–383.

Hacking, Ian. 1999. Madness: Biological or constructed? In *The Social Construction of What?* Cambridge: Harvard University Press. 100–124.

Horwitz, A. V., and J. C. Wakefield. 2007. *The Loss of Sadness: How Psychiatry Transformed Normal Sorrow into Depressive Disorder*. Oxford: University Press.

Kaplan, Arline. 2009. DSM-V controversies. *Psychiatric Times* 26(1) (January 1): 1–5.

Lane, Christopher. 2008. *Shyness: How Normal Behavior Became a Sickness*. New Haven: Yale University Press.

Levi, R. 2006. Science is for sale. *Skeptical Inquirer* 30(4) (July/August): 44–46.

Kleinman, Arthur. 1991. *Rethinking Psychiatry: From Cultural Category to Personal Experience*. New York: The Free Press.

Kleinman, Arthur. 2006. *Writing at the Margin: Discourse Between Anthropology and Medicine*. Berkeley: University of California Press.

Kutchins, Herb, and Stuart Kirk. 1998. *Making Us Crazy: DSM: The Psychiatric Bible and the Creation of Mental Disorders*. New York: Free Press.

Marsh, Ian. 2010. *Suicide: Foucault, History and Truth*. Cambridge: University Press.

Parsons, Talcott. 1951. *The Social System*. London: Routledge.

Petrunik, M., and C. Shearing. 2002. Stutterers' practices. In E. Rubington and M. Weinberg, eds., *Deviance: The Interactionist Perspective*, 8th ed. Toronto: Allyn and Bacon. 384–396.

Rimke, Heidi. 2000. Governing citizens through self-help literature. *Cultural Studies* 14(1): 61–78.

Rimke, Heidi. 2003. Constituting transgressive interiorities: C19th psychiatric readings of morally mad bodies. In Arturo Aldama, ed., *Violence and the Body: Race, Gender and the State*. Indiana: University Press. 403–28.

Rimke, Heidi. 2008. The developing science of the mind. In Russell Lawson, ed., *Research and Discovery: Landmarks and Pioneers in American Science*. New York: M. E. Sharpe. 526–529.

Rimke, Heidi. 2010a. Consuming fears: Neoliberal in/securities, cannibalization, and psychopolitics. In J. Shantz, ed., *Racism and Borders: Representation, Repression, Resistance*. New York: Algora Publishing.

Rimke, Heidi. 2010b. The pathological approach to crime: Individually based theories. In Kirsten Kramar, ed., *Criminology: Critical Canadian Perspectives*. Toronto: Pearson. 79–92.

Rimke, Heidi, and Alan Hunt. 2002. From sinners to degenerates: The medicalization of morality in the C19th. *History of the Human Sciences* 15(1): 59–88.

Rose, Nikolas. 1990. *Governing the Soul: The Shaping of the Private Self.* London: Routledge.

Rose, Nikolas. 1999. *Inventing Ourselves: Psychology, Power, and Personhood.* Cambridge: University Press.

Rosenhan, D. L. 1973. On being sane in insane places. *Science* 179(4070) (January 19): 250–258.

Shaughnessy, P. 2001. July 9th: Day of action. Mad pride view. *Asylum: The Magazine for Democratic Psychiatry* 13: 7–8.

Smith, Dorothy, and Sara David. 1975. *Women Look at Psychiatry: I'm Not Mad, I'm Angry.* Vancouver: Press Gang.

Sothernô, Matthew. 2007. You could truly be yourself if you just weren't you: Sexuality, disabled body space, and the (neo)liberal politics of self-help. *Environment and Planning D: Society and Space* 25(1): 144–159.

Szasz, Thomas. 1971b. The sane slave. *American Journal of Psychotherapy* 25: 228–239.

Szasz, Thomas. 1974. *The Myth of Mental Illness.* New York: Harper Collins.

Szasz, Thomas. 1978. *The Myth of Psychotherapy.* New York: Syracuse University Press.

Tone, Andrea. 2008. *The Age of Anxiety.* New York: Basic Books.

Turner, Ronny E., and Charles Edgley. 1983. From witchcraft to drugcraft: Biochemistry as mythology. *Social Science Journal* 20(4): 1–12.

Ussher, J. 1991. *Women's Madness: Misogyny or Mental Illness?* Amherst: University of Massachusetts Press.

Valentin, Elliot S. 1986. *Great and Desperate Cures: The Rise and Decline of Psychosurgery and Other Radical Treatments for Mental Illness.* New York: Basic Books.

Valverde, Mariana. 1985. *Sex, Power and Pleasure.* Toronto: Women's Press.

Ward, S. 1996. Filling the world with self-esteem: A social history of truth-making. *Canadian Journal of Sociology* 21: 1–23.

Wirth-Cauchon, J. 2001. *Women and Borderline Personality Disorder: Symptoms and Stories.* New Brunswick, NJ: Rutgers University Press.

Going Shopping: The Politics of Everyday Consumption

Dennis Soron *Brock University*

In the aftermath of the September 11 attacks in 2001, a number of prominent U.S. politicians—including New York City mayor Rudolph Giuliani and then-president George W. Bush—made appeals to the American people to do their bit for the national recovery effort by going out and shopping more. Indeed, as Miami-Dade County Mayor Alex Penelas pronounced shortly after the attacks, "it has never been more patriotic to go shopping" (in Vardy, 2001). In material terms, such appeals for consumers to dutifully shop for the greater good were intended to ramp up economic growth and prevent the flagging U.S. economy from toppling into recession. In psychological or cultural terms, such appeals also served as a kind of collective coping mechanism, encouraging people to defiantly return to their familiar consumer rituals in the face of traumatic events that had disrupted their sense of security and stripped their everyday social reality of its aura of innocent normality.

In Canada, similar appeals from government leaders have not typically been accompanied by the jingoistic patriotism seen in the United States, but they have been underpinned by the same assumption that consumer spending is the means by which citizens can help their country stave off crisis and ensure that the collective good prevails. In the fall of 2008, for instance, at the outset of an international financial crisis triggered by the bursting of the U.S. housing bubble, Prime Minister Steven Harper urged Canadian consumers to avoid falling into "panic" because of tightening credit and rising unemployment, and to resolutely "keep spending" so that Canada could remain sheltered from the effects of a global economic slowdown (MacCharles, 2008; CTV, 2008). To the extent that Canadian consumer spending was, according to Harper, "a rock that has sustained the economy" (CTV, 2008), his primary objective was to ensure that such spending continued apace in economically insecure times—by cutting sales taxes such as the GST, for instance, and rejecting proposals then being made by the Liberal party for punitive carbon taxes on environmentally unfriendly forms of consumption.

Such examples offer a particularly vivid illustration of the often contradictory ways in which consumer activity is now regarded in the United States, Canada, and other affluent regions of the world. Today, shopping and consuming serve as powerful symbols of individual agency, marketplace democracy, and the "Western" way of life that is supposedly threatened by terrorists and a variety of other looming threats and crises. In this way, they can be considered part of "the centre" we need to "unpack." At the same time, they also figure in our everyday lives as cultural and economic imperatives, as activities in which we are in various ways constantly cajoled and compelled to participate. In different instances,

NEL

203

increasing levels of private consumption are regarded both as the undisputed solution to problems such as economic stagnation and as the source of other vexing problems like environmental destruction and escalating rates of private debt and bankruptcy. In equally confused and confusing ways, we are also entreated to take up our responsibilities as citizens in and through our daily consumer choices, and yet such choices strike many as an inadequate substitute for genuine democratic power, one that is largely inconsequential in comparison to the scale and variety of pressing crises in the contemporary world. While corporate marketing and the mass media continue to glamorize the endless acquisition of commodities as the gateway to fulfillment, this vision of the good life has increasingly run up against a growing countercurrent of dissatisfaction with the negative and often unjust social, political, economic, cultural, and environmental effects of affluent, consumption-intensive lifestyles. To this extent, as consumption has become more morally and politically contested, it has also become an important site for the expression of popular resistance and opposition.

Picking up the threads of this latent sense of popular disenchantment with "consumer society," this chapter aims to challenge some dominant, taken-for-granted assumptions about the nature of everyday consumer behaviour. In contrast to the commonsense view that this site of practice is largely innocent, apolitical, and driven primarily by the autonomous needs and preferences of individuals, it emphasizes how that consumer behaviour is socially embedded, institutionally organized, and enmeshed in complicated ways with prevailing structures and relations of power. Adopting a hybrid theoretical perspective that selectively draws upon insights from both Foucauldian and Marxist theory, this chapter aims to highlight some of the key ways power operates in and through consumer behaviour. After challenging dominant commonsense understandings of everyday consumption that are overly rationalistic and individualized, it proceeds to lay the groundwork for a more socially embedded model of consumer behaviour, highlighting the complex web of social, cultural, economic, and political influences upon such behaviour, and pointing briefly to the various ways anti-consumerist impulses have become an important spur for the expression and development of different forms of contemporary resistance.

THE IDEAL OF "CONSUMER SOVEREIGNTY"

It has become commonplace in much popular and academic debate to claim that consumption has become uniquely central to the operation of contemporary Western societies. Indeed, it is for this reason that otherwise diverse nations are often grouped together under the broad banner of **consumer society**. In a quantitative sense, this widely used term points us to the historically unprecedented volume of material consumption in such societies, and to the expansive range of consumer goods, brands, advertisements, and commercialized environments that have become an omnipresent feature of our everyday life. In a more qualitative sense, this term highlights the unparalleled degree to which consumption practices in affluent nations have become a crucial site for broader processes of social integration, **social reproduction**, and identity formation. While the

FIGURE 10.1   In the affluent world today, our prevailing notions of freedom, personal identity, and agency are all closely entwined with shopping and consuming.

term "consumer society" is often used to describe a broad set of historical changes that have given a new prominence to consumption within modern social life as a whole, it typically retains a critical charge, implying there is something fundamentally problematic about a way of life in which materialistic values predominate as a life-focus, and in which individuals derive their primary sense of meaning, satisfaction, and selfhood from the purchase and use of **commodities**.

Ironically, while the widely invoked notion of "consumer society" by its very nature implies that the everyday consumption practices of individuals reflect and embody a larger social logic, conventional ways of conceptualizing consumer behaviour often bracket off and isolate such practices from their social context. Prevailing common-sense ideas about consumer freedom typically hold that everyday decisions over what, where, and when to buy are not and should not be regulated or determined by social influences external to the individual. Indeed, as sociologists such as Zygmunt Bauman (1988, 2007) in particular have emphasized, the ideal of unconstrained consumer choice has become an almost sacred value in contemporary capitalist society, one that has come to provide the template for our cultural understanding of freedom itself. This is one of the reasons socialism—capitalism's "other"—is so often portrayed in the popular media as a system of grey conformity in which consumer goods beyond the most immediate necessities are highly scarce, choice of personal lifestyle is minimal, desire is kept in check, and centralized state institutions determine from on high what people's essential needs should be. In contrast, the capitalist marketplace is typically celebrated not only for its teeming cornucopia of enticing consumer goods, but for its seeming absence of top-down authority, its ostensible willingness to grant people the unimpeded freedom to choose what to buy, where and how to live and work, and—consequently—who to be.

This idealized conception of individual freedom is reflected in an explicit way in the concept of **consumer sovereignty**, which has gradually established itself as a key part of the vocabulary of mainstream economic theory and of **neoliberal** political discourse. The basic import of this concept is that consumers are "sovereign" insofar as their self-defined needs and wants ultimately determine the shape and direction of economic life as a whole. To the extent that consumers have the power to rationally determine which goods and services match best with their own preferences, this formulation holds, consumer demand is ultimately the force that determines an economy's production priorities, regulates its allocation of resources, and decides what is and isn't brought to the market for sale. In this scenario, the only real power that exists is the power of consumers to take stock of available alternatives and independently decide what they will purchase. Accordingly, markets are seen as highly responsive mechanisms for communicating consumer demand to producers, who themselves simply exist to provide people with the goods and services they desire. In this version of marketplace democracy, the power and success enjoyed by giant corporations like Walmart, McDonald's, IBM, Microsoft, Time-Warner, and Exxon Mobil only derives from their heightened capacity to understand and serve consumer desire. Similarly, products such as fast food, SUVs, celebrity gossip magazines, cell phones, designer clothing, formulaic blockbuster movies, bottled water, and so on, only exist in such abundance because they accurately reflect what people really want. This familiar equation of the market with democracy and the popular will—which American social critic Thomas Frank (2000) calls **market populism**—is what fuels claims by neoliberal ideologues that efforts to regulate and direct private economic activity in the name of collective principles such as equality, social justice, and environmental sustainability is inherently elitist, paternalistic, and/or latently authoritarian.

While the ideal of consumer sovereignty is often used to legitimize political programs designed to cut back social services and other non-market public goods and to keep powerful economic actors free of government regulations and collective obligations, it does possess a certain popular resonance and appeal. Historically speaking, consumers in affluent regions of the world today do have access to an unparalleled range of choices, even though the content of these choices—between Coke and Pepsi, for instance, or between single-ply, double-ply, quilted, perfumed, coloured, patterned, embossed, aloe-coated, bleached, and unbleached toilet paper—may often not be especially momentous or life-enriching. Indeed, in some ways the undue importance ascribed to often trivial and insubstantial consumer choices in contemporary society has a rather desperate and compensatory ring to it. Ordinary people may not have much freedom and control in their workplaces and other everyday institutional settings, exert much influence over large-scale events like wars, hurricanes, financial meltdowns, and oil spills, or have much say over the major economic and political decisions that affect their futures, but they do typically exert some measure of control over what to eat, drink, wear, and so on. In this sense, the heightened value now accorded to the sphere of consumer choice is, at least to some extent, indicative of the desire many people feel for greater autonomy and control in other spheres of their social lives.

RE-SOCIALIZING CONSUMPTION

Whatever political and cultural meanings and aspirations it may embody, the notion of consumer sovereignty presents us with a highly dubious model of consumer behaviour, one in which—as sociologist Juliet Schor argues—"consumption is largely stripped of its social dimensions, becoming reduced to the question of goods and the functionality they provide to the individual" (in Soron, 2004). This view of the rational, utility-driven consumer seriously downplays the extent to which everyday consumption decisions are invariably enmeshed in a wide variety of non-instrumental, irrational, and often semiconscious psychological and cultural motivations and desires. Similarly, it fails to consider how income, class, gender, ethnicity, age, and other key determinants of sociocultural identity can all differentially influence consumer behaviour and pattern or cluster our choices in particular ways. Most crucially, by putting such exaggerated emphasis on the individual consumer's supposed power to freely and self-consciously choose their own autonomous course of action, it neglects to consider the fact that consumption practices are always socially and institutionally embedded, and are shaped, driven, and constrained by a wide variety of social forces that the individual does not immediately control or even fully comprehend.

Such insights carry us into the broad terrain of what has come to be known as the **sociology of consumption**, a field of critical inquiry whose primary concern is with the social dynamics that drive and constrain consumer behaviour, and the complicated ways in which such behaviour interacts with prevailing structures and relations of power. Attempting to analyze everyday consumption practices in such explicitly "social" terms can often quickly lead to the charge that one is being overly deterministic and ignoring the vital role of consumer agency. It is true that some early sociological critiques of "mass society" were overly deterministic and patronizing in their effort to portray modern consumers as hopelessly duped into a range of false and superfluous needs by the commercial media and thereby rendered subservient to the dictates of the capitalist economy. While such rigid, over-totalizing, and condescending accounts of the gullible consumer masses have been rightly subjected to rigorous critique, this should not simply steer us back into an embrace of market populism and the individualistic assumptions of the "consumer sovereignty" model. Indeed, as Don Slater has argued, much recent work within the sociology of consumption has attempted to approach the everyday consumption of ordinary people with sympathy and respect for the varied meanings and aims they invest in it, while at the same time seeing their consumption as "a valid starting point from which to map the networks of power in which they are enmeshed" (2005: 175).

To "map" the diverse forces shaping consumer behaviour in this manner, we need to first develop a working conception of "power" that goes beyond the theoretical limitations of the consumer sovereignty model. In line with the long tradition of economic liberalism, this model is oriented primarily toward curbing the state's arbitrary power to interfere with the autonomous choices of individual economic actors in a market setting. In this sense, it is vulnerable to Foucault's critique of the broader intellectual tendency to simply equate power with intentional, overt repression and coercion by state institutions and other dominant social actors. Clearly, contemporary consumer behaviour is not overwhelmingly subject to "power" in this narrow sense—that is, our routine purchasing choices are not rigidly subjected to top-down regulation and control. State functionaries do not typically follow us to Tim Hortons, for instance, to ensure that we choose a particular type of donut and beverage, nor do they throw us in jail for ordering french fries instead of salad as a side dish. That said, it would be wrong to infer from this that people's ongoing choices over what and how to consume are somehow independent of power and the complex web of social relations, practices, and institutions in which it manifests itself.

Historically speaking, consumption practices (around food selection and preparation, dress and self-adornment, the intake of alcohol, tobacco, and other substances, and so on) have always been subject to some degree of state regulation, religious control, and communal sanction; but such overt prohibitions and taboos have waned to an unprecedented degree in contemporary consumer society. To this extent, we need a more subtle understanding of power itself in order to understand the ways it shapes and influences contemporary consumer behaviour. Resources drawn from both Foucauldian and Marxist theory can help us in this regard. As outlined in Chapters 1 and 2, for Foucault, power is not a finite substance simply "possessed" by the powerful few and applied externally onto the powerless many; it is something dispersed widely and embedded into the impersonal operations of a variety of institutions, social relations, and everyday life settings. Instead of just functioning in a "repressive" manner by explicitly prohibiting and punishing certain types of unapproved consumer behaviour in which we want to engage power acts in a "productive" manner, helping to engender and discipline our very consumer desires, motives, and **subjectivities**. As the following section emphasizes, our understanding of the ways in which everyday consumer behaviour is shaped by power can also be deepened by engaging with Marxist ideas about the variety of subtle, impersonal, and seemingly nonpolitical ways economic power and the dynamics of class inequality operate in capitalist society.

THE PRODUCTION OF CONSUMPTION

In contrast to the consumer sovereignty model, which assumes that consumers rationally seek to maximize their own welfare by choosing the goods and services that best fulfill their self-defined needs, much work in the sociology of consumption has highlighted how prevailing consumption patterns are socially produced. While work in this field has undoubtedly been extremely diverse, much of it has attempted to "re-socialize" consumption by underlining that consumer goods such as food, clothing, cars, furniture, and so on are not valued by individuals simply for their material attributes, but also for how they embody cultural meanings and act as means of social communication. Across a range of recent sociological studies of everyday consumption practices, Sylvia Reif writes, the "common ground is that goods are not simply consumed for their function or use value, but for their symbolic and communicative qualities that help express and mediate social relations, structures, and divisions" (2008: 562). Within sociology, one longstanding focus of this **communicative model** of consumer behaviour has been how material goods can act as markers of status and help to symbolically map out the relative social positions of those who own and use them. The earliest and perhaps most famous example of this critical tradition can be found in Thorstein Veblen's (1934) analysis of **conspicuous consumption**—that is, the ostentatious acquisition and display of rare, expensive, and often frivolous goods by the wealthy in order to symbolically communicate their superior status and to arouse the envy and admiration of those below them on the socioeconomic hierarchy.

While some aspects of Veblen's analysis of the quasi-aristocratic "leisure class" of 19th-century America might strike the contemporary reader as a bit dated, its basic insights about the symbolically competitive and comparative nature of consumer behaviour are still highly relevant. Indeed, consumption practices continue to be key sites in which a wide range of people in today's supposedly "classless" world struggle to buttress and elevate their social status. If anything, as Juliet Schor has emphasized in works such as *The Overspent American* (1999), such competitive pressures have only intensified over the past few decades as personal identity has been increasingly drawn into the vortex of consumer culture, as daily social life has become ever more saturated with advertising imagery and brand symbolism, and as socioeconomic inequalities have continued to widen. In the past, Schor claims, ordinary working-class and middle-class consumers tended to emulate and try to "keep up with" the material standards of friends and neighbours ("the Joneses") who were at best moderately better off. Today, with the rise of suburbanization, the decline of face-to-face community interaction, and the growing influence of mass media and its glamorized depictions of wealth and celebrity, consumers of even relatively humble means tend to be drawn into the process of **upscale emulation**, deriving their material aspirations by looking to the extravagant lifestyles and consumption patterns of the "rich and famous." In trying to keep up with these escalating consumption norms, they often end up taking on enormous debt loads, overworking themselves, depriving themselves of stress-relieving free time and meaningful social contact, and ultimately undermining the non-material bases of their happiness and personal well-being.

Such accounts of competitive consumption address, in part, how consumer capitalism continually fosters new types of want and desire, encouraging impulsive or excessive purchasing choices that are economically profitable for producers but ultimately undermine consumers' own subjective and material well-being. To this extent, they both highlight the complex social and cultural dynamics underlying everyday consumer behaviour and open up onto a broader critical reconsideration of the real forces driving economic life in capitalist society. From Adam Smith onward, a basic assumption of liberal economics has been that consumption is the guiding purpose of all economic activity, and hence that production's chief role is to enhance the well-being of consumers by materially furnishing them with what they desire. From the perspective of Marxist theory, this picture of economic life is effectively upside down. Indeed, to the extent that capitalism is an economic system driven by the pursuit of private profit and not by the satisfaction of human needs and the enhancement of collective welfare, its prevailing consumption patterns tend to be systematically shaped in ways that serve the ends of producers first and foremost. In spite of what the proponents of **market populism** might have us believe, capitalist markets are not democratic, nor are they responsive to what people in general need. Because the only "votes" that count in the marketplace are those backed with money, resources and labour in capitalist society tend to get allocated toward forms of production that yield the greatest profit for producers, even when this leaves the basic needs of many people unsatisfied, compromises the health and happiness of workers and consumers in various ways, and generates a troubling array of externalized social and ecological costs.

Understanding this process requires us to grapple with the subtle ways economic power operates in capitalist society. As discussed in Chapter 6, in contrast to previous socioeconomic systems in which political and economic power were unified in the hands of an overt ruling class (a hereditary aristocracy, for example), capitalism has tended to decouple economic and political power, such that the economy becomes a private, contractual sphere relatively free of direct political control, and those who own the means of production have no formal, legal authority over those who do not. It is precisely because capital cannot formally command or prescribe our product-related activities, Dawson argues, that it has had to develop indirect forms of control that are effective but "subtle enough to avoid recognition and resistance" (2003: 54). While Dawson himself is inspired chiefly by Marxist theory, his analysis clearly intersects in some ways with Foucault's conception of power. Indeed, to the extent that contemporary consumers are largely free of overt commands and restrictions on their daily behaviour, power operates in a more subtle manner by generating the contexts and conditions in which we come to govern ourselves and express our will in socially approved, system-supportive ways that do not require the continual application of external coercion. Over the past several decades in particular, as Erik Assadourian (2010) has suggested, business interests in the advanced capitalist world have been engaged in a constant struggle to find novel ways to "coax more consumption out of people"—for instance, by liberalizing consumer credit, designing products for quick physical and stylistic obsolescence, channelling productivity gains into wage increases rather than reduced work time, lowering costs by seeking out cheap sources of labour and resources, undermining the state provision of collective goods (such as public transportation) that cut into the demand for private commodities (such as cars), harnessing the authority of science and technical expertise to reshape consumer needs and develop new standards of normality and acceptability, so on.

The prevailing tendency to downplay the abiding influence of economic power in capitalist society is, as Michael Dawson (2003) has insightfully argued, embedded in the very notion of "consumer" itself. By making consumption our primary source of identity and the definitive category for almost all of our off-the-job activities, this notion represents a highly reductive understanding of our complex everyday motives, aspirations, and self-understandings, implying that we are simply "money-spending garbage disposals" (4) driven by an innate desire to acquire and use up commodities. While ordinary people do not have any innate desire to "consume" (in the literal sense of using up or destroying the objects they acquire), and would be amenable to alternative means of meeting their needs were they practically available, capital itself has a clear interest in maximizing consumption. The patronizing image of the insatiable, appetite-driven "consumer," Dawson holds, basically transfers responsibility for the wasteful and irrational nature of capitalist growth onto the backs of ordinary individuals, distracting us from the various ways powerful business interests continually struggle to increase profit by inducing us to consume more.

ADVERTISING: "A CONSTANT BACKGROUND HUM"

One key sphere of contemporary social life in which the effort of producers to induce and shape consumer desire and behaviour for their own ends is particularly evident is that of corporate advertising and marketing. Global marketing is now a massive, multibillion-dollar industry that saturates commercial media and other everyday domains, drawing upon huge stores of demographic and psychological research to develop intricate strategies for shaping our mental or informational environment in ways that "coax" more consumption out of us.

Advertising, as Annie Leonard has argued recently in *The Story of Stuff* (2010), has become such a massive and influential industry today that it has effectively become "a constant background hum in our lives." Some statistics cited by Leonard drive this point home. Global advertising expenditures have grown more than nine-fold in the past sixty years, with over $276 billion spent on ads in 2005 in the United States alone (164). Advertising has saturated not only the commercial media, but increasingly insinuates itself into other noncommercial public spaces and institutions such as schools and hospitals. As a consequence of this blanketing of everyday life with commercial messages, the average North American now spends roughly an entire year of his or her life encountering advertisements (163).

In his film *Advertising and the End of the World* (1998), media critic Sut Jhally has provided an illuminating account of the unique cultural role of advertising in contemporary capitalist society. From a historical vantage point, as he argues, capitalism is the most dynamic and productive economic system ever known, harnessing and exploiting human labour and nature on a massive scale to produce what Marx famously referred to as "an immense accumulation of commodities." To this extent, Jhally believes, the abiding problem faced by capitalism has not been its productive capacities, but its ability to ensure that this immense output is purchased and consumed so that profit can be realized and the cycle of capital accumulation can continue.

To this extent, as American economist Victor Lebow (1955) frankly and famously put it several decades ago:

> Our enormously productive economy demands that we make consumption our way of life, that we convert the buying and use of goods into rituals, that we seek our spiritual satisfactions, our ego satisfactions, in consumption. We need things consumed, burned up, worn out, replaced, and discarded at an ever increasing pace.

As Lebow's comments suggest, advertising in capitalist society has gradually assumed the important institutional function of maintaining and expanding aggregate consumer demand by investing goods with heightened social and cultural meaning and significance, and by constantly inducing fresh new needs and desires in the general population.

Ironically, as Jhally acknowledges, even though advertising is a now a massive, global, multibillion dollar industry whose nonstop blandishments to consume have colonized extensive domains of our culture and everyday lives, most people feel personally immune to its messages. While this contrast between the absolute centrality of advertising to contemporary culture and our common tendency to dismiss it as something trivial and inconsequential may indicate that many people are simply unaware or in denial about what really motivates them, it also forces us to discern between what Jhally calls the **marketing role** and the **cultural role** of advertising. The marketing role of advertising pertains to the ability of particular promotional campaigns to measurably increase consumption of specific products or services. In contrast, the cultural role of advertising relates to the consistent "story" and set of basic values that cut across all advertisements—even those that appear on the surface to have failed.

As our culture's primary storyteller, Jhally insists, advertising relentlessly inculcates us with the idea that happiness and well-being come from the individual acquisition and consumption of marketplace commodities. It does so primarily not by communicating detailed information about consumer goods and their physical characteristics, but by symbolically linking them to valued human qualities—acceptance, love, empowerment, belonging, freedom, connection to nature, sensuality, eroticism, and so on—that many people in today's society feel that their lives lack. Consequently, advertising's ongoing "propaganda for commodities" inflates consumer demand by leading us into a futile quest to individually satisfy such social and interpersonal needs through the market, rather than collectively renegotiating and transforming the broader social, economic, and political conditions that thwart their fulfillment.

Jhally and other cultural analysts have drawn critical attention to how advertising, far from providing us with a gateway to a promised land of happiness and abundance, ramps up consumer spending largely by aggravating people's sense of dissatisfaction with their existing lives and sharpening their feelings of insecurity about their identities, bodies, status, desirability, and worth. This insight has been particularly well developed by feminist critics such as Jean Kilbourne (2000), who have grappled with the ways commercial advertising can perpetuate dominant gender ideologies and deepen the oppression of women in society more generally. Highly idealized, airbrushed, and eroticized images of women's bodies and faces are pervasive in contemporary advertising, Kilbourne notes. One effect of this has been the growing entrenchment of a narrow cultural definition of femininity premised upon women's appearance alone, and oriented to the unending pursuit of largely unattainable standards of thinness, beauty, and physical perfection.

While this fruitless pursuit has been accompanied by a variety of painful physical, emotional, and mental costs for many women themselves, it has also proven to be extremely profitable for a variety of industries (from cosmetics to dieting to plastic surgery) that feed off of women's underlying sense of not measuring up to the culture's approved standards of femininity. Indeed, across a wide range of ads targeted at women, Kilbourne provocatively asserts, the message is clear: "You're ugly; you're disgusting; buy something." Beyond directly promoting certain forms of gendered consumer behaviour, advertising also indirectly contributes to the perpetuation of broader gender norms and inequalities. By presenting us with a narrow range of images of hypersexualized vixens and vapid Swiffer-loving housewives, it often helps to perpetuate archaic gender stereotypes and to rigidify traditional gender roles at a time when many women and men have begun to chafe against the constraints they impose. By continually objectifying women and presenting them as inert "things" that are interchangeable with commodities, advertising also contributes to wider problems such as rape and domestic violence. While advertisements cannot be held directly or solely responsible for such problems, Kilbourne argues, they make a vital contribution to perpetuating a wider cultural mindset that encourages violence and contempt toward women by dehumanizing them, transforming them from subjects of their own experience into simple objects of men's desire and will.

CONSUMPTION IN CONTEXT

As advertising has woven its way ever more intimately into our desires and identities, it has also expanded outward, colonizing, and occupying ever more spheres of our daily social life. No longer confined to the discrete, bounded frames of television and print advertisements proper, commercial messages now saturate the everyday life world of advanced capitalist societies: the billboards and signs that dominate its streetscapes; the ubiquitous product placements worked into the storylines of popular films, television shows, and news programs; the walls and playing surfaces of sports facilities and the attire of the athletes that use them; the conspicuous logos emblazoned on clothing, shoes, hats, handbags, watches, cars, and other everyday personal items; not to mention the endless entreatments to consume that have sprung up in previously noncommercialized spheres such as schools, hospitals, public restrooms, and even—thanks to the efforts of **stealth marketing**— personal discussion and casual social interaction in public places. In a very real sense, Dawson argues, people in such societies go about their everyday routines in "personal milieux" that abound with "scores of effective reinforcers and boosters of commodified, corporation-prescribed ways of living" (2003: 140).

As Dawson and others have argued, however, marketing/advertising is merely one of the many institutional factors that have rendered the imperative to spend and consume an essential feature of people's everyday social and material environments. Understanding the social organization of consumption today, as prominent social theorist and sociologist of consumption George Ritzer has argued, requires us to first confront "the almost dizzying proliferation of settings that allow, encourage, and even compel us to consume so many … goods and services" (2005: 2). The paradigmatic environment for the contemporary shopper is not the bustling, face-to-face setting of the open-air market or the varied attractions of the neighbourhood main street, but huge, enclosed, homogenized corporate-controlled milieux such as shopping malls, which bring together an enormous array of goods, brands, services, and public attractions in a single location in an attempt to create an ideal environment for encouraging consumption.

In today's world, Ritzer argues, not only shopping malls, but theme parks, hotels, cruise ships, casinos, sports facilities, airports, and other hypercommercialized settings have effectively become **cathedrals of consumption** that provide 'magical' and 'enchanting' settings for people to experience the plenitude of their desires and participate in the rituals of acquisition. Chapter 14 discusses such patterns in the context of tourism. In spite of their seemingly 'enchanted' character, Ritzer suggests, such environments are actually highly rationalized and carefully engineered to entice us to consume; indeed, "these places do more than simply permit us to consume things; they are structured to lead and even coerce us into consumption" (2005: x). In equal measure, even though they often attempt to resemble traditional public spaces and town centres by incorporating things such as gardens, fountains, plazas, old-fashioned benches, and historical building facades, they are also carefully designed and regulated in order to dissuade unprofitable activities (such as political leafleting, loitering, shoplifting, and panhandling). Whereas traditional public spaces such as parks and town squares are inclusive and typically allow for a wide range of both commercial and noncommercial social activity, such commodified and privately controlled versions of public space aim explicitly to exclude 'undesirables' (through tight surveillance and policing) and to orient all forms of personal and social activity toward the primary goal of promoting private consumption.

Such analyses of commodified public spaces such as malls indicate the degree to which our individual consumer behaviour is subtly shaped by the everyday environments that encircle us. Beyond the behavioural influences exerted by the immediate retail settings in which people shop, a much wider variety of environmental or contextual factors underpin and reproduce prevailing consumption patterns in contemporary capitalist society. Consumers do not define and pursue their preferences in a vacuum; indeed, their individual aspirations and actions are always heavily influenced by the institutions, relationships, material settings, and patterns of power in which they are embedded. Such factors can often quietly but powerfully steer us into particular types of routine behaviour, and propel us into consumption habits that are to some degree involuntary or "locked in", rather than freely chosen.

The range of contextual influences on our daily transportation choices provides an apt illustration of what the Organisation for Economic Co-operation and Development (OECD, 2002) has labelled the **infrastructure of consumption**—that is, the whole contextual matrix of social, material, political, and economic constraints and pressures that effectively compel ordinary people into adopting particular patterns of consumption. To this extent, the OECD and others have suggested, we cannot really understand the "software" of everyday individual consumer behaviour without giving proper consideration to the infrastructural "hardware" in which it operates.

AUTOMOBILE DEPENDENCY AND CONSUMER "LOCK-IN"

The issue of transportation provides a particularly compelling illustration of the "locked in" quality of many forms of contemporary consumption. While environmentalists and urban planners may decry our current overreliance on inefficient modes of transportation such as the private automobile, for instance, they often fail to recognize that the roots of this problem go deeper than the commuter's personal values and preferences. Indeed, they grow out of a whole range of contextual social influences—urban zoning laws, commercial land use patterns, incentives for low-density suburban housing, state subsidies for the petroleum and auto industries, underfunded or nonexistent public transit systems, growing distances between nodes of daily activity, the growth in exurban employment, inflexible work routines, inadequate childcare arrangements, and so on—that make energy-intensive car use the most practical option for many people as they navigate their way through their complicated daily work and household responsibilities. In turn, such transportation patterns help to engender complementary modes of consumption—drive-through services, fast-food strips, sprawling suburbs, peripheral big box stores rimmed by oceans of free parking, and so on—which reinforce automobile-dependent lifestyles, while further marginalizing and excluding those who do not or cannot drive.

For instance, a great deal of media attention in Canada and the United States in recent years has been paid to the growth of diet-related health disorders (such as diabetes and obesity) among poor and socially disadvantaged groups. While it may be tempting to simply dismiss such problems as a "software" defect related to the impulsive, self-destructive, or uneducated choices of poor individuals themselves, the "hardware" dimension of this issue often remains unexplored. Quite often, poor and marginalized people live in urban areas that are effectively "food deserts," lacking neighbourhood grocery stores (which have mostly fled to suburban locations), and containing high concentrations of unhealthy food sources such as fast-food outlets and variety stores. Beyond the issue of geographical availability is the fact that, under our current food production and distribution system, healthy items such as fresh produce tend to be more expensive—and hence less financially accessible—than unhealthy, highly processed, and nutritionally empty items. Like all of us, poor citizens live in a mental environment where our knowledge about food is heavily influenced by corporate marketing and industry-sponsored junk science, but they may lack equal access to alternative information sources and educational opportunities that could help them reframe their understanding of food and its effects. So, while public health officials and others may bemoan the unhealthy food choices some poor people make, in practice such choices are quite constrained and shaped by circumstances beyond their immediate control.

FIGURE 10.2 ◼ Food deserts such as these, which contain dense clusters of fast-food establishments and few if any sources of healthy food, have a strong influence on the food choices of residents.

David McNew/Getty Images News/Getty Images

As the cases of shopping malls, automobile-dependent urban landscapes, and inner-city "food deserts" all suggest, the contextual influences that subtly and impersonally condition our consumption choices have an important spatial dimension. That said, we should not forget that such influences also include a crucial temporal dimension. Indeed, time distribution and routine daily schedules are also contextual factors that dynamically contribute to the creation and reproduction of particular consumer behaviours. Although we tend to associate opportunities for private consumption with "free time" or leisure, certain prevailing consumption patterns in the advanced capitalist world are actually engendered by stressful daily schedules in which many people experience a chronic sense of "time poverty." The looming sense of time scarcity makes speed and convenience cardinal virtues, predisposing consumers toward labour- and time-saving goods and services. Even where relatively good public transit or active transportation amenities are in place, for instance, commuting by car is still typically faster, and easier to coordinate with other daily routines such as shopping, picking up children, paying bills, and so on. To the tired person coming home from a long day at work, picking up a bag of fast food at a drive-through window may be more appealing than making a multi-course family meal from scratch, even though he or she might ultimately prefer eating the latter rather than the former.

In this sense, time pressures often compel people to adopt forms of everyday consumption that they would not have chosen in different, less harried circumstances. While they may bear down on all of us to one degree or another, such pressures have increasingly acquired a strongly gendered dimension. In the past few decades, as feminist thinkers such as Susan Strasser and others have argued, the accelerating entry of women into the full-time work force has sapped the domestic sphere of its traditional source of labour power, intensifying the commodification of household goods and services traditionally provided by the unpaid efforts of women. While shopping (largely due to its strong cultural association with the supposedly trivial leisure pursuits of women) has tended to be disparaged as a superficial pastime, it is in many cases inseparable from vital forms of domestic caregiving. Feeding and clothing one's family, furnishing one's home, purchasing toiletries and medical supplies, finding appropriate gifts for friends and relatives, and so on are all forms of domestic labour that make notable time demands on those (primarily women) who take responsibility for them. Beyond the domestic sphere, the time constraints associated with labour in the paid workforce also have an important influence on how and what we consume. By apportioning the lion's share of our daytime efforts toward paid work for employers and fragmenting the time we have for self-initiated activities (such as growing food, making clothes, learning how to build or repair the daily items we use, engaging in the political process, working collaboratively on community projects, learning how to cook or play a musical instrument, and so on), wage labour in capitalist society tends to ultimately deplete our productive capacities and deskill us, making us increasingly dependent upon the consumer marketplace for our varied social, psychological, and material needs.

THE POLITICS OF CONSUMPTION

Shifting our critical attention from the seemingly autonomous choices that consumers make to the encircling conditions that shape and constrain such choices helps us to generate new understandings of why people today consume the way they do, and why certain problematic, unjust, and/or unsustainable consumption patterns are so slow to change. It also returns us squarely to the notion that everyday consumption practices are invariably underpinned by and enmeshed with prevailing structures and relations of power. As we considered above, conventional conceptualizations of consumer sovereignty assume that consumers, within the limits of their buying power or "effective demand," are innately free to choose what goods and services they please, as long as they are not unduly encumbered by external regulations and prohibitions imposed by the state, religious institutions, and so on. In a Foucauldian vein, this "repressive" conception of power fails to adequately address the "productive" nature of power—that is, how it engenders the contexts and conditions in which we form our identities and come to spontaneously govern ourselves in ways that are compatible with dominant social, cultural, economic, and political prerogatives. In this broad sense, the infrastructure of consumption is a key part of the underlying disciplinary architecture of everyday life, crystallizing many different power-laden processes operating at multiple scales—from the unequal structures of the global capitalist economy, to state and municipal policy, financing and consumer credit, marketing strategy, retailing practices, urban planning, the intricate dynamics of family life, and beyond.

Consumer behaviour today can be said to be "political" not simply because it is passively shaped by external structures and relations of power, but also because it is actively involved in the maintenance and reproduction of social and ecological conditions that are highly problematic and contested. While sociologists are particularly well positioned to engage with the political underpinnings and ramifications of consumer behaviour, the sociology of consumption itself over the past couple of decades has often shied away from this type of engagement. Indeed, by seeking to defend ordinary consumers from harshly elitist or moralistic judgements, influential figures in the field such as Daniel Miller have often fallen into a rather uncritical celebration of the creative and transgressive aspects of everyday consumer behaviour that echoes the precepts of consumer sovereignty and market populism. In so doing, they have failed to consider that the sociological critique of consumer behaviour need not simply be oriented around judging and dismissing the supposedly vulgar tastes of the masses—who prefer Kraft Singles to Brie, or Lady Gaga to Beethoven. In a more productive vein, by highlighting the contingent origins and drivers of consumer behaviours, the sociological critique of everyday consumption can engage respectfully with popular tastes and practices even while challenging people to resituate their understanding of such practices within a much wider horizon of social and environmental concern.

One of the chief problems with the knee-jerk populist defence of conventional consumer behaviour is that it positions ordinary First World consumers as passive victims of elitist judgement by haughty intellectuals, failing to consider the ways their supposedly innocent everyday consumption practices involve an array of troubling extra-individual effects, and are themselves implicated in actively reproducing unjust and destructive social arrangements. This textbook revisits such practices in Chapter 13, which examines coffee, and in Chapter 14, on tourism. The default populist position, with its aversion to normative thinking about what types of consumption are excessive, damaging, or exploitative, is one of the reasons that much work in the sociology of consumption has been so reluctant to directly engage with the environmental impacts of overconsumption in the affluent world. Particularly since the Rio Earth Summit in 1992, environmental activists have advanced a powerful critique of the devastating impact of consumption patterns in the affluent world. Worldwide, per capita material consumption has skyrocketed over the past several decades, putting tremendous strain

FIGURE 10.3 ■ Global consumption, 2004 (in billions of U.S. dollars). This chart dramatically illustrates the degree to which consumption of world resources is overwhelmingly skewed toward the minority of the globe's population living in high-income countries.

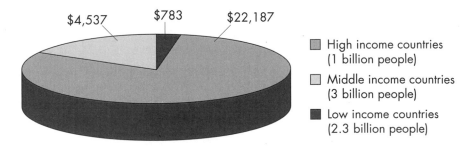

Source: Courtesy of World Resources Institute

upon both renewable and nonrenewable resources, generating tremendous amounts of waste, fraying local ecosystems, and helping to dangerously accelerate problems such as global warming, deforestation, drought, desertification, and toxic air and water pollution.

While such problems are often attributed to the wayward habits of humanity as a whole, they are largely the specific responsibility of the world's wealthiest countries, which have enjoyed the overwhelming share of the historical consumption boom. Ironically, it is quite often the poorest regions of the world that bear the brunt of the environmental effects of First World overconsumption, and that supply the stores of cheap labour and resources that keep the supermarket shelves of affluent nations flush with wave upon wave of affordable new consumer goods. In the context of ecologically constrained conditions, achieving a decent standard of living for all global citizens will require a substantial reduction in the material intensity of consumption patterns in affluent nations, alongside concurrent consumption increases in poor regions now suffering from vast shortfalls in basic needs such as food, water, housing, clothing, education, and medical care.

In recent years, a growing popular recognition of the need to reckon with the heavy environmental and human toll of consumer society has been evident in the mounting popularity of anti-consumerist discourses, of ethical and "green" consumption practices, of fair-trade and "no sweat" consumer products, and so on. While the effectiveness of such responses to the social and environmental repercussions of overconsumption in the affluent world is ultimately in doubt, such developments do represent at least a partial challenge to what Marx famously referred to as **commodity fetishism**. The commodities we interact with on a daily basis are fetishized to the extent that their economic value and everyday cultural meanings are largely detached from any critical awareness of the exploitative conditions in which they were produced. We have little sense of the horrible animal suffering that lay behind our cutely packaged and marketed burgers and chicken nuggets, for instance, nor are we aware of the forests razed for our desks and pencils, or of the life conditions of the sweatshop workers who made the trendy athletic shoes we wear with such pride at the gym. Ethical and green consumerism, at least in part, represents a provisional effort to bridge the psychological and geographical distance that now typically divides the point of production and the point of consumption, and to ensure that the human and ecological costs of production—and not simply price—are decisively factored into our understanding of a product's ultimate value and worth.

Looking forward, perhaps the most valuable lesson that sociological critiques of consumer behaviour can offer us relates to the limits of individualized responses to the crises engendered by contemporary consumer society. To the extent that prevailing consumption patterns are not simply a reflection of individual preference, but are entwined with a variety of social and institutional forces, they can only be significantly transformed through a broad renegotiation of cultural values and collective action aimed at structural economic and political change. Such insights about the value of solidarity, community-building, and

FIGURE 10.4 ■ As this image from the magazine *Adbusters* suggests, we are often only dimly aware of the devastating effect current consumption patterns are having on planetary ecology.

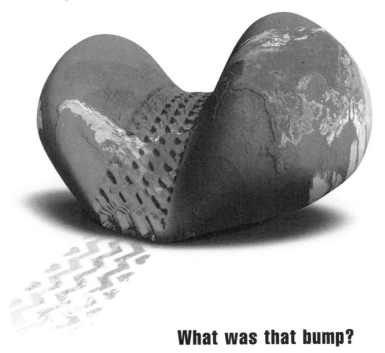

What was that bump?

Source: Courtesy of adbusters.org

collective action are an implicit part of a range of contemporary anti-consumerist social movements oriented around issues as diverse as **culture jamming**, fair trade, voluntary simplicity, downshifting, **freeganism**, slow food, media literacy, community barter systems, and beyond.

As Michael Maniates (2002) and others have argued, "individualizing responsibility" for the social and ecological fallout of consumer society (by asking us to recycle more, or drive less, or buy ethically sourced goods, and so on) might offer a practical and immediate way of putting our values into action; but it ultimately steers clear of any confrontation with the powerful institutions and vested interests that underpin current ways of life in advanced capitalist society. In this sense, steering consumption practices in the direction of social justice and environmental sustainability will necessarily require us to transcend our very subjectivity as individuated consumers in the pseudodemocratic marketplace. Indeed, it will require us to embrace a new understanding of ourselves as active democratic subjects working together to transform the broader economic, political, and cultural conditions that sustain our consumer behaviour, restricting the fullest development of our capacities, perpetuating human and nonhuman exploitation, and offering us only a pale, commodified substitute for what freedom can ultimately be.

STUDY QUESTIONS

1. After reviewing the notion of "consumer sovereignty," and the critique advanced of it in this chapter, analyze some of the ways aspects of your own daily consumer behaviour are socially shaped and constrained.

2. After reviewing this chapter's discussion of the role and influence of advertising in contemporary capitalist society, develop your own analysis of a current television advertising campaign that has recently caught your attention.

3. Explain and provide examples for the assertion that consumer behaviour is unavoidably "political" in nature.

EXERCISES

1. Take a 3–4 day "fast" from a familiar consumer good in your everyday life (computer, cell phone, car, fast food, cosmetics, etc.), and reflect carefully on your experience of going without it. Did this experience give you a better "sociological" understanding of the variety of influences that condition your typical use of and relationship to this good?

2. Using the "**communicative model of consumption**" as a starting point, analyze your relationship to one particular consumer good that has traditionally carried a lot of symbolic meaning and importance for you. How and why has this good acquired the importance it has for you?

3. In your view, does transcending the problems of consumer society simply mean relinquishing all pleasure and enjoyment in life? Develop a list of qualities that define what you consider to be a satisfying, fun, and meaningful life, then try to imagine the ways in which consumer society actually impedes this kind of life. How could a post-consumerist social order actually improve our quality of life?

REFERENCES

Assadourian, Erik. 2010. The rise and fall of consumer cultures. In *State of the World 2010: Transforming Cultures*. New York: W. W. Norton & Company. 3–20.

Bauman, Zygmunt. 1988. *Freedom*. Milton Keynes, Buckinghamshire, UK: Open University Press.

Bauman, Zygmunt. 2007. *Consuming Life*. Cambridge: Polity Press.

CTV News. 2008. Harper to Canadians: "Keep spending." CTV.ca, September 19. http://www.ctv.ca/servlet/ArticleNews/story/CTVNews/20080919/harperbanks_080919?s_name=&no_ads=, accessed January 28, 2011.

Dawson, Michael. 2003. *The Consumer Trap: Big Business Marketing in American Life.* Chicago: University of Illinois Press.

Frank, Thomas. 2000. *One Market Under God: Extreme Capitalism, Market Populism, and the End of Economic Democracy.* New York: Doubleday.

Jhally, Sut [writer, producer, editor]. 1998. *Advertising and the End of the World* [film]. Northampton, MA: Media Education Foundation.

Kilbourne, Jean [creator]. 2000. *Killing Us Softly 3: Advertising's Image of Women* [film]. Northampton, MA: Media Education Foundation.

Lebow, Victor. 1955. Price competition in 1955. *Journal of Retailing* 31(1): 5–10, 42, 44.

Leonard, Annie. 2010. *The Story of Stuff.* Toronto: Free Press.

MacCharles, Tonda. 2008. PM urges Canadians to keep spending. *The Toronto Star*, September 19. http://www.thestar.com/FederalElection/article/502221, accessed January 28, 2011.

Maniates, Michael. 2002. Individualization: Plant a tree, buy a bike, save the world? In Thomas Princen, Michael Maniates, and Ken Conca, eds., *Confronting Consumption.* Cambridge: MIT Press. 43–66.

OECD. 2002. *Towards Sustainable Consumption: An Economic Conceptual Framework.* Paris: Organisation for Economic Co-operation and Development.

Reif, Sylvia. 2008. Outlines of a critical sociology of consumption: Beyond moralism and celebration. *Sociology Compass* 2(2): 560–576.

Ritzer, George. 2005. *Enchanting a Disenchanted World: Revolutionizing the Means of Consumption*, 2nd Edition. Thousand Oaks, CA: Pine Forge Press.

Schor, Juliet. 1999. *The Overspent American: Why We Want What We Don't Need.* New York: HarperPerennial.

Slater, Don. 2005. The sociology of consumption and lifestyle. In Craig J. Calhoun, Chris Rojek, and Bryan S. Turner, eds., *The Sage Handbook of Sociology.* London: Sage Publications. 174–187.

Soron, Dennis. 2004. The politics of consumption: An interview with Juliet Schor. *Aurora: Interviews with Leading Thinkers and Writers.* http://aurora.icaap.org/index.php/aurora/article/view/13/24, accessed January 28, 2011.

Vardy, Jill. 2001. Shopping is patriotic, leaders say. *National Post*, September 28. A1.

Veblen, Thorstein. 1934. *The Theory of the Leisure Class: An Economic Study of Institutions.* New York: Modern Library.

Financial Fitness: The Political and Cultural Economy of Finance

Mary Beth Raddon *Brock University*

INTRODUCTION: A GLOBAL FINANCIAL CRISIS

Financial news from the United States topped the headlines beginning in the late summer of 2007 when the collapse of an inflated U.S. housing market triggered an unprecedented chain of events: the failure of giant U.S. financial institutions resulting in the largest bankruptcies and takeovers in history and multibillion-dollar government bailouts. It did not take long for news analysts to identify what was happening as a global financial crisis of major proportions. The financial turmoil also exposed cases of fraudulent investment and shady lending on a massive scale. Just as riveting in the news was the daily stock market volatility, especially the record drops in the value of indexes such as the Dow Jones Industrial Average, which peaked in October 2007 and then fell by more than 40 percent in just over a year. As a result, approximately US$30 trillion in the value of stocks world-wide evaporated by the end of 2008. The value of real estate and oil, likewise, plunged by trillions (Hanieh, 2009).

Central banks in all the advanced capitalist countries responded to the financial crisis by coordinating a drop in interest rates and infusing trillions of dollars into the global financial system, while governments committed tens of billions to stimulate their national economies. Talk of economic recession followed in the news, as grim readings on indicators such as job loss, personal bankruptcy, foreclosures, housing sales, consumer spending, and manufacturing output were reported. In Western media coverage, the typical human face of the calamity was the formerly well-to-do investor whose stock portfolio had plunged in value. As the effects of the crisis spiralled through the global economy, however, it became clear that those most severely hit would be the most economically vulnerable in every country. Economic conditions would worsen, especially, in the global South, where three billion people, half of the world's population, already in 2008 subsisted on less than US$2.50 a day (Hanieh, 2009).

Despite the severity of the financial crisis, which is undisputedly the most catastrophic in the postwar period and likely to be as historically pivotal as the Great Depression (Gonick, 2009), there has been no consistent explanation of how it came about. The two figures that oversaw the emergence of the crisis from the highest positions of authority in the U.S. economy were two-term President George W. Bush (January 2001 to January 2009) and Alan Greenspan, the Chair of the U.S. Federal Reserve Board (1987 to 2006). Both leaders dodged responsibility for what happened during their tenure by suggesting that events were beyond anyone's control. President Bush commented offhandedly at a

July 18, 2008 luncheon, "There is no doubt about it. Wall Street got drunk. ... It got drunk and now it's got a hangover. The question is how long will it sober up and try not to do all these fancy financial instruments?" A few months later, on October 23, Alan Greenspan was required to testify at the U.S. House of Representatives Committee Hearing on the Financial Crisis and the Role of Federal Regulators in Washington, D.C. This committee wanted to probe Greenspan's responsibility for scrapping financial regulations, such as rules that would have limited the sale of faulty mortgage-backed securities in which the failed banks had so heavily invested (Hudson, 2009). In his opening comments, however, Greenspan sidestepped this issue of deregulation and instead summed up the financial crisis as a "once-in-a-century credit tsunami" (Testimony of Dr. Alan Greenspan, 2008).

Such statements, likening the institutional failure of major banks around the world to an episode of binge drinking or equating the global financial crisis to a natural disaster, deny that economic and financial policy were relevant to what transpired. Both remarks frame the financial crisis as an ordinary though rare event that strikes at random. Such descriptions may encourage sympathy with the victims but do not invite questions about its causes. In short, Bush and Greenspan's comments are instances of attempts to naturalize finance and thereby avoid naming the dominant power relations that produced the present-day financial system. The two leaders acknowledged that some parts of the financial system failed, but upheld the legitimacy of the financial system as a whole in its present organization.

In this chapter, I present a more complex way of framing the global financial crisis according to historical and cultural processes of financialization. The term **financialization** refers to the increasing power of financial institutions, financial markets, and discourses of finance to shape and govern everyday reality. Accordingly, a major goal of the chapter is to examine how financial power works. A related goal is to show how a dominant financial rationality occupies the centre of our thinking about money and pushes alternatives to the margins. In the context of the financial crisis, the overt exercise of power is most clearly evident in the attempts of financial and political elites to restore the functioning of global financial markets by pouring enormous sums of public money into rescuing insolvent institutions (Loxley, 2009). Less obvious as a process of power is the shaping of a consensus that a rescue of the global financial system should be prioritized over other types of responses. More subtle still is the normalization and de-politicization of (supposed) financial imperatives in everyday life, such as the apparent need to practice **financial fitness** in order to secure a healthy future for ourselves as individuals, as members of families, and as contributors to national and global financial markets.

The sociological literature offers two distinct lenses for examining the workings of financial power: the longstanding tradition of political economy and the more recent literature on cultural economy. I examine each in turn and then conclude the chapter by discussing two practical movements, **slow money** and local currencies, that might represent alternatives to conventional practices of financial fitness. In bringing into view financialization as a political process, I hope to challenge our dependence on financial markets for economic security. **Financialization** has created dramatic inequalities over the past 30 years (McNally, 2009). Few people have become more economically secure during this period, and so many have lost homes, jobs, savings, social services, and chances for education. Most troubling has been the shrinking of political space for alternatives and the loss of confidence that other kinds of economic politics are possible (Gibson-Graham, 2006). The critical political and cultural analysis of financialization reopens space for new ways of thinking about and creating economic security.

THE POLITICAL ECONOMY OF FINANCIALIZATION

The scholarly tradition known as **political economy** dates back to the late 1600s, almost two centuries before economics, sociology and political science emerged as separate and distinct fields of study. Enduring as an interdisciplinary program of study, through its classical and Marxian versions, political economy takes as a fundamental premise that the domain of the economic does not follow natural laws, but is shaped by competitive struggles of groups whose class power or state authority largely derives from their economic position (Foster & Magdoff, 2009). Political economists analyze the mutual influence of politics and economics in many ways, but generally they attempt to combine analysis of state policy and social relations of imperialism, exploitation, and gendered and racialized forms of dominance among states, geopolitical blocs, transnational organizations, and social classes.

In addition to conceiving of the economy in political terms, the tradition of political economy carries forward Marx's method of social analysis, which emphasizes historical contingency and asks how current structures emerged from specific social relations in the past. By this way of thinking, economic formations, such as currencies and markets, are not to be taken as timeless or universal. Even when formations seem to be stable or permanent, political economists investigate the processes and interrelationships that sustain them. Political economy, then, is concerned with the long-term history of, and prospects for, social change and especially the potential of emancipation from unjust and exploitative social relations under **capitalism**.

From a political economy perspective, the financialization of the economy is just such a structural trend that must be understood historically and systemically. Interest in financialization goes back to Marx's analysis of the workings of capitalism. Marx observed that typically the process of capitalist accumulation occurs when capital—which is all forms of wealth that are used to create new value—is invested in the production and sale of commodities. Those profits are then reinvested, and so on, on an ever-expanding scale. However, opportunities may arise for capital to expand through financial investment independently of commodity production and exchange. Under certain economic conditions, in Marx's words, "barren money ... [acquires] the power of breeding and thus turns ... into capital, without the necessity of its exposing itself to the troubles and risks inseparable from its employment in industry" (Marx, 1967 [1887]: 706). To the extent that those conditions for money to breed money become available, financial activity will overtake productive enterprise as the dominant form of capital accumulation. In other words, under some conditions more new wealth will be created through financial machinations than through investment in the production of material goods and services. As this happens, the economy will have entered a phase of financialization.

Lately capitalists have indeed been seizing opportunities to grow their wealth without having to employ people in mines and factories, on cargo ships, and so on. The first task of a political economic analysis of late-20th- and early-21st-century financialization, then, is to bring this phenomenon into view as a coordinated change in the structure of the economy and not something inherent in capitalism. Observing the growth of financial markets on a global scale is one way to notice how making money from money has only recently become central to the "normal" function of economies. For instance, Kapoor (2009) tells us that the rate of money changing hands in currency markets annually has increased exponentially from $4 trillion in the 1970s to $40 trillion in the 1980s to over $500 trillion in the 2000s. Global bond markets, equity markets and markets for new financial products known as derivatives, futures, and hedge funds have similarly seen turn-over rise manyfold in recent decades.

Beyond evidence of the volume and growth of financial activity, financialization is evident when compared with the productive economy. According to Hutchinson, Mellor, and Olsen (2002), less than 5 percent of the value of all transactions on global markets pertains to trade in real commodities, whereas over 95 percent is purely financial. To make this comparison more concrete, Foster and Magdoff (2009) point out that *every day*, the dollar value traded in global currency markets alone is equivalent to the combined annual gross domestic product (market value of goods and services) of every domestic economy *in the world* (56).

Financialization pervades domestic as well as global markets. For Krippner (2005), the key indicator of domestic financialization is the relative share of corporate profits of financial and non-financial sectors. She compares corporate profits of the manufacturing sector, the service sector and the sector comprising finance, insurance, and real estate (FIRE) in the U.S. economy over the period 1950 to 2001, taking into account changes in corporate structure such as outsourcing and subsidiary formation, as well as the relocation of manufacturing bases outside of the U.S. In this analysis, the financial industry is clearly ascendant. The profitability of manufacturing corporations, which through the 1950s and 1960s enjoyed between forty and fifty percent of the share of profits among U.S. industries, has declined relative to the other sectors. The service sector, although it is the largest sector for employment in the U.S., has only slightly increased its share of profits. Most significantly, the profitability of the sector representing finance, insurance and real estate has grown since the mid-1980s to overtake manufacturing and services starting in the mid-1990s.

The evidence for financialization is even more striking when we look beyond the towering headquarters of banks and investment companies at the financial activities of non-financial firms. As many political economists have pointed out, the profitability of non-financial corporations in the U.S. began to stagnate or decline in the 1970s (Brenner, 2002). In response to this crisis of profitability, non-financial corporations diverted capital from productive enterprise toward financial ventures where the returns were higher (Evans, 2009; Krippner, 2005). In other words, non-financial firms have relied increasingly on revenues from their financial portfolios to subsidize their productive activities. For example, even though in 2003 General Motors was the largest auto manufacturer in the world,

FIGURE 11.1 ■ Krippner—Relative Industry Shares of Corporate Profits in US economy, 1950–2001

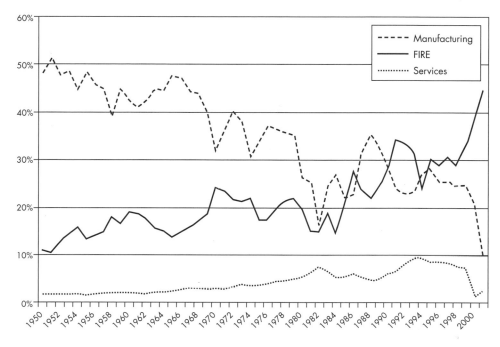

Source: Krippner, G. R. "The financialization of the American economy," *Socio-Economic Review,* 2005, Volume 3, Issue 2, pp. 173–208, by permission of Oxford University Press and the Society for the Advancement of Socio-Economics.

Forbes Magazine called it "a bank that happens to build automobiles" (Muller, 2003). Its financial subsidiary, GMAC, sold auto insurance and provided financing for car buyers and dealerships, but it also was one of the largest home mortgage sellers in the U.S. At the time, the financial proceeds of GMAC accounted for ninety percent of GM's profits. Prior to the 2008 financial crisis, another iconic North American manufacturer, General Electric, likewise, earned more from its financial division, GE Capital, than it did from its manufacturing divisions. This pattern is typical of many other large industrial and retail corporations (Foster & Magdoff, 2009).

Historical Perspectives on Financialization

Having established that a shift toward a finance-led economy has been occurring, the next task when working in the political economy tradition is to interpret its historical significance. From the standpoint of the "centre," people often read present day capitalism as an outcome of human progress. The financialized economy from this perspective represents the high point of capitalist development or at least a more mature stage of capitalism. This impression of continuous positive development is reinforced by the growing sophistication of new digital technologies that allow for instantaneous trading, constant tracking of data and the massive volume of transactions (Preda, 2009). To "unpack the centre" we need to ask what benefits and costs the technologies of finance are bringing to people everywhere, and what alternatives are being closed off.

Current events, particularly, contradict the faith that a financialized economy can provide security and prosperity for most people. Repeatedly, we have been witnessing that financialized economies are volatile. For example, a decade before the subprime market melt-down of 2007–2008, many North Americans were optimistic that investment in Internet start-up companies and the sale of bandwidth and digital technologies would provide high and sustained returns on investment (Henwood, 2003). The financial euphoria about the so-called "new economy" was short-lived, however, as the inflated dot.com market behaved like a classic financial bubble which burst in the early 2000s (Galbraith, 1993).

In other examples worldwide, we have seen a series of financial crises affecting entire national states and their regional trading partners, such as the crisis in Mexico in 1994, Russia in 1998, Japan and East Asia in 1997–1998 and Argentina 1999–2002. The colossal market failures in these cases, in addition to the cases of scandalous fraudulent specula-tion that resulted in the collapse of large banks and corporations, such as Barings in 1995, Enron in 2001 and WorldCom in 2002, have wiped out the savings and destroyed the jobs of a great many people.

Lest such cases be taken as merely a series of unfortunate events, another problem endemic to financialization should raise doubts about its link to progress. That problem is the concentration of economic power and the growth of wealth disparities between and within nation states. Financialization allows a very small fraction of the population to own or control very large assets and gives the super-wealthy inordinate political and economic influence. These few have participated in the structuring of an economy that rewards the ruthless pursuit of short-term profit and punishes the prioritization of worker well being or eco-system viability, even though these considerations are vital to long term economic sustainability (Hutchinson et al., 2002).

This problem of inequality is best illustrated by the gap between promise and out-comes of financialization for developing countries. Advocates of loosening restrictions on the movement of money had postulated that as global financial flows increased, developing countries would attract foreign portfolio investment that could, in turn, support trade and productive investment. Unfortunately, this has not happened. As Kiely (2005) explains, foreign financial investment has mainly bypassed the poorest countries. Meanwhile, those that have succeeded in attracting financial investment have found it destabilizing because it is easily reversed and also because the high interest rate policies necessary to secure it discourage productive investment of the kind that creates jobs and infrastructure.

If financialization cannot be taken as signifying progress in the long sweep of history, what more can a political economy perspective tell us about how it came about and what it means for the workings of economic power? Perhaps the most important insight of a long-term his-torical analysis is that, even though financialization is occurring on an unprecedented scale, the phenomenon is not unique to our time. Giovanni Arrighi makes this argument in *The Long Twentieth Century* (1994). Arrighi describes how, in its 600-year history, the capitalist world economy has seen a sequence of long cycles (*longue durées*) of capitalist expansion and restructuring. In each cycle, "particular communities and blocs of governmental and business agencies" have used the geopolitical, military, commercial or financial power base of a territorial state to organize a regime, or ruling system, of capitalist accumulation (9). As competition among states and capitalists intensifies, each hegemonic (dominant) regime— Genoa in the 15th century, Holland in the 17th, Britain in the 19th, and the United States in the 20th—has undergone a period of financialization, characterized also by tolerance of debt and social inequality. The recurrent pattern seems to show that financialization fore-shadows decline and prefigures the formation of a new hegemonic regime by a different set of governmental and business elites based in a different territorial state.

Arrighi emphasizes that the financialization phase that marks the long periods of transformation from one regime to the next in these world-systemic cycles does not come about automatically, but is driven by particular elite groups and individuals who happened to be "uniquely well placed to turn to their own advantage the unintended consequences of the actions of other agencies" (9). Large financiers (bankers, brokers, investors), for example, represent a fraction of the capitalist class that can profit when the collapse of certain capitalist industries leads to generalized insecurity. Such a political economic analysis, which sees a role for historic actors, can be illustrated by a closer examination of the implementation of policies and events that have accelerated financialization in the late 20th and early 21st century.

From Keynesianism to Finance-Led Neoliberalism

From a political economy perspective, current financialization is a major outcome of an elite-led struggle to establish a new social order known as **neoliberalism** and to dis-mantle the previous arrangement known as Keynesianism. **Keynesianism** got its name from the British economist John Maynard Keynes (1883–1946), who was concerned with the widespread unemployment of the 1920s and 1930s. Keynesian theory holds that full employment is possible if governments act to stimulate economic demand through social spending during times of recession. Following World War II, the advanced capitalist states were spurred to adopt models of Keynesianism, partly under pressure from working class movements for economic justice, and partly due to competition with the Soviet Union, which represented an alternative economic model. These governments' common objective was achieving economic growth by actively managing the economy and providing stable conditions for industry and employment within a capitalist framework. Central to the Keynesian endeavour were principles such as social equality, social integration, and social rights through citizenship that guided economic and social policy.

Keynesian policies did achieve steady economic growth and enable rising standards of living for the general population from 1945 to the early 1970s. These policies were designed to foster high wages, decent working conditions, stable employment, predictable pensions, and a social safety net of unemployment insurance, welfare, and disability benefits. In Canada, it was during this period that labour-friendly legislation was passed and many of our major social programs, such as state-provided universal health insurance, were introduced.

As mentioned, Keynesian fiscal policy encouraged governments to go into deficit during times of recession when people lacked money or were reluctant to spend. In such times, governments would spend public money on projects and programs that were considered of broad social benefit. This injection of new money would encourage consumer spending, which would create demand for goods and services, stimulating production. As growth ensued, governments would reduce spending and pay off debt, thus withdrawing money from the economy in order to avoid inflation. As critics of Keynesianism have pointed out, however, there was always a risk of inflation if governments continued social spending through growth periods. They might be tempted to do so to sustain the large public sector bureaucracy that had been created to deliver standardized services, or to maintain popularity in the polls. In the early 1970s, Keynesian economies did encounter a wave of inflation to which they could not easily respond, especially after the world price of oil spiked in 1973 and again in 1978.

The economic downturn of the 1970s opened the way for pro-business activists, working through well-funded policy think tanks and other channels of influence, to aggressively challenge the Keynesian model with neoliberalism (Carroll & Shaw, 2001). Neoliberal political philosophy had been around for a long time, but was not considered a serious threat to Keynesianism until 1979 when the U.K. Conservative party under Prime Minister Margaret Thatcher came to office, followed by the election of Republican President Ronald Reagan in the United States in 1980. Neoliberal governments came to power elsewhere too, including in Canada under Prime Minister Brian Mulroney in 1984, with the goal of radically transforming the Keynesian welfare state. However, neoliberalism should not be understood as political project of only conservative governments. The neoliberal model has become so dominant and pervasive that even social democratic governments have come to espouse neoliberal principles and implement neoliberal policy.

Some critics of neoliberalism liken it to a religion whose main article of faith is that markets provide the best mechanism for allocating wealth and, by extension, government should not have an active role in the economy. Looking beyond this explanation of neoliberalism as "market fundamentalism" (Giroux, 2004), other critics consider it a project of restoring economic power to the wealthiest capitalist class (Dumenil & Levy, 2005; Harvey, 2005). The highest stratum in the class hierarchy includes those who control financial institutions and whose wealth consists largely in financial securities. The ambitions of this group were hampered by the redistributive tax policies and regulations protective of workers, the environment, and national economic stability set in place in the Keynesian period. The neoliberal challengers were eager to institute new rules of capitalism that would favour the financial sector and their own interests in class dominance (Dumenil & Levy, 2005).

As important as financial elites have been to neoliberal financialization, it was a confluence of historical circumstances and not their agency alone that set it in motion. Again, understanding the context of the Keynesian period is important to understanding the course of financialization. In 1944, nearing the end of World War II, a large group of planners and state officials gathered at Bretton Woods, New Hampshire, to negotiate a new set of rules for the international monetary system. The overarching goal of the Bretton Woods Agreement was for stable, managed trade between countries. However, the United States exercised its dominance in these arrangements through disproportionate control of international monetary institutions and its insistence, contrary to other proposals, that the U.S. dollar act as the world currency. It was established that the value of the U.S. dollar would be fixed relative to the value of gold. Specifically, the dollar was convertible to gold at $35 an ounce and other currencies were fixed in value relative to the U.S. dollar. Convertibility of European currencies came about gradually through the 1950s, establishing a multilateral trading system with the U.S. positioned to set the rules (Block, 1977). By 1971, pressured by severe monetary disequilibrium (a chronic balance-of-payments deficit connected to the cost of the Korean and Vietnam Wars) that threatened its domestic economy and imperialist ambitions, the U.S. government unilaterally overturned the rules of the international monetary system. The United States removed the convertibility of the dollar to gold and subsequently abandoned the system of fixed exchange rates. Following the shift to a system of floating exchange rates, currencies now find their value in international markets.

These changes in the rules of the international monetary system opened the way for speculative trade in the fluctuating currencies. Currency speculation, coupled with removal of restrictions on the global movement of money under neoliberalism, has resulted, as we have seen, in an international monetary system that is prone to crisis and capable of destabilizing national economies, but beneficial to transnational financial elites who have the flexibility to convert capital to different financial forms and move it to wherever gains are highest.

Interestingly, the response of governments to the recession of 2008–2009 shows neoliberalism to be more of a pragmatic than a utopian movement. In response to the recession, governments everywhere, no matter their stated adherence to the neoliberal tenet of nonintervention in the economy, temporarily introduced economic stimulus programs, much as Keynesianism prescribes. This move prompted many to wonder if neoliberalism has ended (Fernandez, 2009). However, as Harvey (2005) argues, neoliberalism has never been a coherent ideology: "There are … enough contradictions in the neoliberal position to render evolving neoliberal practices (vis-à-vis issues such as monopoly power and market failures) unrecognizable in relation to the seeming purity of neoliberal doctrine" (21). It makes sense then, to see neoliberal ideology as a shifting strategy for legitimizing a more encompassing project to reestablish the class power of economic elites, to reverse the postwar gains that working classes had achieved under Keynesianism, and to counter working class claims to a share in the national wealth (19).

The Keynesian-like response to the global financial crisis has prompted rethinking of the meaning of neoliberalism for another reason. Since the 1990s, neoliberal policy has made it easier for individuals to qualify for credit cards, personal lines of credit, bank loans, and home mortgages. In the face of stagnated or falling real wages, low- and middle-income households maintained their standard of living only by going into debt, but in doing so their consumer spending also combated recession.

Crouch (2008) defines the neoliberal model as a system of "privatized Keynesianism" because personal debt replaced government debt in maintaining consumer demand and smoothing out market instability. In other words, rather than governments taking on debt

PRIVATIZED KEYNESIANISM

What are the costs or disadvantages to Canadians of creating economic stimulus through consumer spending, stimulus which was formerly provided by Keynesian governments through deficit financing?

Canadians' debt-to-income ratio has grown steadily since the early 1980s, and more sharply since 2001. Two thousand two was the first year that Canadians' total personal debt exceeded disposable income. By 2005, the average Canadian owed $1.16 for every dollar of disposable income (Statistics Canada, 2007). Following the recession of 2008, Canadians took on even more debt. According to Bank of Canada data, between April 2008 and April 2009, personal lines of credit increased 20.4 percent, personal loans from banks went up 8.1 percent, and the amounts owing to banks on credit cards jumped by 8.9 percent (CBC News, 2009).

to stimulate the economy, the state and financial industry have encouraged individuals to do the borrowing. Risks associated with non-repayment of debt have been transferred from the state onto individuals and households.

To summarize, financialization is a historical process resulting in economic instability and inequality. Though not inevitable; it has been a recurring feature of capitalism. Present-day financialization accelerated when elites seized the opportunity of a breakdown of international monetary arrangements in the 1970s to discredit and dismantle Keynesianism and replace it with a neoliberal social order that furthered financial interests at the expense of the productive economy.

This analysis raises an interesting question, however. If we conceive of neoliberal financialization as benefiting financial elites, how do we make sense of the mass participation in neoliberal practices, such as the consumer spending that makes privatized Keynesianism possible? The political economy tradition has no easy answers to this question; but the more recent tradition of cultural economy may help, especially in the way it draws attention to everyday practices.

CULTURAL ECONOMY OF FINANCIALIZATION

A more recent literature on financialization both complicates and supplements the political economic analysis of financial crisis. Just as the tradition of political economy opposes the conceptual distinction between the political and the economic, the newer field of cultural economy attempts to break down binary divisions between the cultural and the economic (Allan, 2002). Cultural studies emerged as a discipline partly in reaction to orthodox Marxist versions of political economy. Cultural studies scholars were critical of tendencies to explain oppression and exploitation as deriving, above all else, from unequal class relations under capitalism, as well as tendencies to read historical change as moving in a linear direction toward an inevitable end point. Until recent decades, this reaction against economic determinism and teleological thinking within orthodox strands of political economy turned many cultural studies scholars away from researching economic life altogether (Martin, 2009). As a result, political economists who also struggle against oversimplified economic analysis have only recently begun to engage with the insights that cultural studies brings to the new field of cultural economy (du Gay & Pryke, 2002).

The field of cultural economy has been well attuned to the growing centrality of finance to economic life (Pryke & du Gay, 2007). Its approach to financialization overlaps to some degree with that of political economy in that both rely on historical analysis of transformations in financial activity in order to problematize that which often appears as a natural reality. Beyond this similarity, cultural economy contributes new ways of thinking about how power operates through financialization and neoliberalism.

Political economists' analyses of financialization tend to present a rather top-down conception of power. Power is perceived either as a commodity that is wielded by financial elites or as an abstract force that emanates from financial districts such as Wall Street. While recognizing the hierarchies, disparities, and exclusions that financialization produces, cultural economy scholars look more closely at the everyday workings of power that make this possible.

In order to preserve, theoretically, the widest scope for human agency, cultural economists avoid theorizing people as victims who are oppressed by a monolithic, external financial system. In thinking about historical change, they place as much emphasis on changes in economic subjectivity as on structural conditions. Their historical method is to identify significant moments when meanings and moralities are fluid and contested because in such times the significance of human action to the shape of change is more perceptible. In contrast, an over-simple reading of Arrighi's work, for example, conjures the image of world-systemic cycles of financialization following a predetermined capitalist logic making it difficult to imagine people's historical agency or to consider how everyday resistance could meaningfully make a difference (Martin, 2009). In order to avoid this pitfall, cultural economy shifts our thinking from finance as a system that acts upon us from "out there" to finance as a discursive domain threaded through everyday life (de Goede, 2005). As Langley puts it, "financial power is not a force that operates 'from the outside' on everyday saving and borrowing, but is necessarily present 'on the inside' of everyday networks" (Langley, 2008: 31).

Cultural economy researchers recognize the cultural in the financial through a variety of topics and research strategies (Pryke & du Gay, 2007). For example, ethnographic studies of the trading floors and boardrooms of large firms in major financial centres such as London demonstrate how global financial markets are embedded within culturally specific social networks, routines, and ways of thinking (Thrift, 1994). Media analysis of popular money shows and financial news programs on radio and television reveal how financial discourses have proliferated in everyday life and how they, in conjunction with neoliberalism, translate into new forms of governance (Greenfield & Williams, 2007). Fundamentally, cultural economists study how the power of modern finance operates through the calculative, scientific, technical, and rational financial discourses that infuse the daily deliberations of a wide range of people, whether financial advisors, bank owners, home buyers, day traders, or Wal-mart shoppers.

A key theoretical premise of the cultural economy perspective is that we cannot easily distinguish an underlying financial reality from the practices undertaken to represent that reality, practices such as devising and compiling statistics, accounting, pricing financial products, calculating risk, rating bonds, creating and applying regulations, and making moral and legal determinations of what is and is not legitimate financial activity. We commonly imagine that financial reality consists in abstract flows or that it is produced through the activities of mostly white, male managers, specialists, and technicians working in financial hubs. A cultural economy perspective, in contrast, sees finance as "performed, lived and given meaning" through a wide array of routine and everyday practices in various settings (Langley, 2008). Pryke and du Gay (2007) argue, for example, that seemingly technical financial theories do not merely describe or analyze financial activities and markets, but transform them. This insight applies to other ways in which discursive practices—shared ways of thinking and speaking about, naming, categorizing, and defining the boundaries of finance—produce a financial domain with particular features, which we then take as objective financial reality (Pryke & du Gay, 2007).

Marieke de Goede (2005) offers several ways to illustrate this understanding, "of financial discourse as performatively constructing the reality it is supposed to measure and analyze" (179–80). She traces the history of financial morality over two centuries in Europe and the United States to understand how modern finance gained its current reputation as an economically necessary, scientifically respectable natural reality. In the 19th century, the principled way of gaining wealth was through industry, whereas financial investment was considered immoral. Dissociating finance from the vices of fraud and gambling occurred through a slow process of rewriting anti-gambling laws, conceiving of risk as calculable, and establishing professional legitimacy for financial speculators. This moral and political

CAN FINANCIAL REPORTING CREATE FINANCIAL REALITY AS A SELF-FULFILLING PROPHECY?

In economic news reports, gains in stock market indexes are often presented as more significant measures of national economic health than increases in employment or wage levels. As Martin (2009) observes, "Fox and CNN 24-seven news broadcasts run a visual ticker-tape of stock prices at the bottom of their broadcast screens as if the modulations of equity prices were an EKG to the global body" (118). Stock market performance is less tangible or immediate to the majority of people compared to rates of joblessness, housing costs, or food bank use. Yet when analysts report on financial market upticks, many take this as a positive and meaningful signal to spend, borrow and invest (Krippner, 2005).

struggle to create a domain of normal finance is necessarily ongoing, because there exists no absolute distinction between gambling and finance, as we see in the common reference to "casino capitalism" by critics of global finance (Hutchinson et al., 2002; Milani, 2000).

Similarly, Langley (2008) analyzes another ongoing cultural shift that began in the 1980s in the United States and the United Kingdom. Prior to that time, depositing one's money in savings accounts and purchasing insurance, were seen to demonstrate the Puritan virtues of hard work, thrift, and prudence. With neoliberalism, financial products for the everyday investor have proliferated and a new financial ethos has emerged in which investment, not saving, appears as the most rational way to provide for future needs. At the same time, consumer credit became available to groups with higher risk of default, including members of low-income households, those with precarious employment, seniors, and students. The use of credit cards required another break with Puritan morality, severing the connections between earning and spending (Manning, 2000). Langley argues that the growth of global financial markets, as well as the trading of financial instruments derived from the default risk of mortgages and credit card debt, which brought on the 2008 global financial crisis, has been **contingent** on such new forms of financial morality of individuals and households. Financialization has required that people think like investors in their everyday identities, while acting to boost their personal credit and "financial fitness."

Langley's analysis significantly overturns the impression we often have of global finance as a force that penetrates into everyday life. Instead we glimpse how cultural interpretations of everyday borrowing and investing are integral to the workings of financial markets. The financial system, in other words, cannot operate without discourses about finance.

Neoliberal Governance Through Financial Fitness

We can apply Langley's analysis of financialization in everyday life to Canada. More Canadians than ever before are participating in financial markets through share owner-ship, mutual funds, occupational pension plan contributions, and retirement and educa-tional savings funds. As a result of this drive for investment portfolios, more people have a direct stake in the performance of global financial markets and conceive of their economic security as dependent on their rates of return. Avoiding or failing to invest is considered financially negligent. Financial advisors also recommend taking on and repaying consumer debt to acquire a good credit rating.

These practices and expectations did not come about automatically but emerged through a political process of making investment seem rational and trustworthy. An explicit goal of neoliberalism is the creation of citizens who are heavily invested in financial mar-kets. As Wilby (2009) explains, neoliberal policy assumes that "everyone would become, in their private if not in their working life, a member of the bourgeoisie, owning a house, acquiring debt to improve themselves, trading in shares and bonds" (30).

An example of a culturally directed neoliberal policy initiative is the launch in June 2009 of a task force for a national strategy for **financial literacy**. Headed by executives of large investment and insurance companies, the 13-member task force will make recommendations to the Minister of Finance of ways to enhance financial literacy in Canada. This may involve improving the resources and coordination of agencies such as schools and budget counselling offices that are currently providing financial training. The official website of the Task Force on Financial Literacy (Task Force on Financial Literacy, 2009) alludes to the financial crisis as an impetus for the initiative. Given the complexity of the financial crisis, financial education that might help people understand events in historical context and analyze policy alternatives would be immensely valuable (Magdoff & Yates, 2009). Far from being educational in this way, the financial literacy initiative appears more like a mode of neoliberal governance through which people will learn to be smart investors.

The money columnist for the *Toronto Star* who reported on the launch of the Task Force wrote that financial literacy is "much like physical fitness" (Roseman, 2009). The analogy to fitness has become so commonplace that financial literacy can be termed "financial fitness." Financial fitness is a pervasive neoliberal discourse about financial truth combined with a particular social morality about responsibility, calculation and self-care.

We can see three interrelated themes of financial fitness in the Task Force's mandate. First, financial fitness is about people supporting the economy rather than the other way around. When announcing the Task Force, the Minister of Finance expressed this view:

> "Our economy is built on millions of everyday financial decisions by Canadians," said Minister Flaherty. "Recent events have shown us that there are major risks and that financial literacy is an important life skill. Whether it is a question of saving for retirement, financing a new home or balancing the family chequebook, improving the financial literacy of Canadians *will add to the stability of our financial system and make our economy stronger.* (Office of the Minister of Finance and Department of Finance, 2009, emphasis added)

From this perspective, national economic health depends on individual financial fitness. Du Gay (2000) points out that in contemporary economic discourse we see an inversion of previous understandings of the economy as a resource that serves the well-being of the national state and society. In a sense, then, financial fitness refers not only to personal finances, but also to the financial health of collectivities: government, universities, firms, local and national economies, and so on. Just as individuals must make a concerted effort toward improving financial fitness, so are members implored to serve the financial fitness of the institutions to which they belong. Moreover, Canadians must achieve economic fitness in a competitive global arena. *Toronto Star* columnist Roseman (2009) emphasized this aspect of neoliberal market competition when she ended her column on the importance of financial literacy with the warning that "many countries are way ahead of us."

The second theme of the new Task Force is that encouraging financial fitness through teaching people about financial services and products puts responsibility on individuals for their financial status. In fact, a message of personal responsibility is the foremost statement on the site:

> **Financial literacy** is the ability to understand personal and broader financial matters, apply that knowledge and *assume responsibility for one's financial decisions*. Financial literacy is the foundation for budgeting, saving, and the responsible use of credit. Financial literacy allows people to act to achieve their personal and financial goals. (Emphasis added)

Responsibilization, a form of neoliberal governance, is the process of affirming and constructing people as responsible, self-managing moral agents (Shamir, 2008). Financial fitness is a case in point. People are to watch their financial health in the same way they are told to use exercise and diet to maintain their physical health. If "debt is the new fat," we are morally charged to do everything possible to exercise self-control in using credit while simultaneously maximizing our investments (Atwood, 2008). "Control is the key to a fit life," explains Martin. "All this self-management requires ongoing learning and constant vigil to eliminate the flab of ignorance that will lead one to fall out of the fit middle class. ... a steady diet of the right information will build a self-regulated body" (Martin, 2002: 92).

Governance by responsibilization comes about not through the top-down exercise of power, such as the enforcement of legal or bureaucratic rules, but through self-regulation. Responsibilized people act as though whatever befalls them is a consequence of their own action that they should willingly bear. Financial literacy responsibilizes when it teaches that individuals must be responsible to pay their credit card balance in full each month, grow a nest egg for retirement, and avoid relying on state income supports. Failing to be responsible in these ways reflects personal weakness rather than income shortfalls, the cost of education, gaps in employment, household needs, the lack of social supports in dealing with crises, and so on.

The third, related theme of financial fitness that appears in the launch of the Task Force is the repeated description of financial literacy as an "essential life skill." The desire to improve such skills through the practice of financial fitness requires and activates an ethic of constant self-improvement. Thus, financial fitness produces the image of its practitioners as "**entrepreneurs of the self**" (du Gay, 2000). Du Gay explains that fulfilling this image means acting toward oneself as though one's life is a business enterprise and oneself is the owner and manager: "Once a human life is conceived of primarily in entrepreneurial terms, the 'owner' of that life becomes individually responsible for their own self-advancement and care; within the ideals of enterprise, individuals are charged with managing the conduct of the business of their own lives" (du Gay, 2000: 120).

It is clear how the responsibility to produce maximal "fitness" by developing one's financial skills feeds back into the first theme because financially self-managing people sustain and enlarge the financial economy. This is an explicit goal of the financial literacy Task Force: "Effective financial information and increased financial literacy can result in better consumer choices, *a larger and more dynamic market for financial sector services, and greater participation in capital markets*" (Office of the Minister of Finance and Department of Finance, 2009, emphasis added). A cultural economy analysis of the Task Force on Financial Literacy thus highlights how the discourse of financial fitness has come to permeate everyday life and maintain finance at "the centre" of neoliberal capitalism. Unpacking the discourse, we can see how financial fitness produces financialization by creating responsible, entrepreneurial subjects, people who are expected to serve the economy rather than the reverse, who personally shoulder social risk and who conceive of their own lives in terms of return on investment.

CONCLUSION: ALTERNATIVES TO FINANCIALIZATION

Financial fitness is a pervasive discourse and we do not always know that we are inside of it. According to de Goede (2005), "current financial discourses have taken shape instead of and at the expense of alternative financial possibilities and representations" (xxvi). She argues that by looking historically at possibilities that were closed down and moments when alternatives could have been implemented, we can begin to imagine alternative economic futures. But another way to break with financial fitness is to begin to relate to monetary life and economic security in the present from positions other than that of the entrepreneurial investor.

One example of a departure from financial fitness is a movement called **slow money**, which is an outgrowth of the "slow food" movement (Tasch, 2008). Slow money investors want to know where money goes when it is invested, so they put their funds into diversified, sustainable local food systems. They reject the dictate of financial fitness that high rates of return should be the primary criteria for financial decisions. Rather, they believe that their long-term financial interests cannot be separated from their interest in food security and ecological health. Since global capital markets undermine these interests, slow money investors instead support small food enterprises, organic farms, farmers' markets, and restaurants that carry local food.

Such shifts are what Hazel Henderson (2009) has in mind when she writes about "democratizing finance." She means something quite different than financial literacy. Like slow money investors, she too advocates that the best way to respond to the financial (and ecological) crisis is for people to bypass the global financial economy. People are doing so in many ways, and their success demonstrates that wealth is not synonymous with money. Henderson's goal in pointing out alternative ways to achieve collective security and quality of life is to reveal that the financial crisis is partly a crisis of perception.

From a different theoretical perspective, de Goede says something similar when she asserts that finance is best understood as ongoing "interpretive and *textual* practice" (5) rather than an autonomous global force or a stable system, because money, credit, and accounting, as forms of writing, all bring into being what they name. Both Henderson and de Goede are interested in alternative currencies, Henderson as a prospect of creating sustainable economies, and de Goede as a kind of performance art that can reveal the creativity of discourse.

For Henderson money is most properly used as a means of exchange, that is, a form of information. To assign the additional role of storing value (and bearing interest) to money leads us to forget that wealth is only generated by people whose social and labour practices and relationship to land and environment is healthy and sustainable. Local currencies help create more ecologically and socially sustainable economies, because they facilitate local exchange and allow people to rely less on scarce national currency, which flows to where it may be invested for the highest return (North, 2007, 2008).

A rudimentary form of local exchange is an organized gift-giving arrangement. Swap meets where people are invited to come with goods to give away are one example. The gift exchange website Freecycle is another. Mutual credit currencies are a more highly organized and money-like **local currency**. Organizations such as LETS (Local Employment and Trading System), also known as "barter exchanges," rely on a newsletter, bulletin board, or online message board to let members know what others are offering. Members exchange

FIGURE 11.2 ■ Community currencies that circulate in Calgary.

goods and services with one another using a (virtual) accounting currency, whose unit is sometimes called the "greendollar" but might go by any name. Computer software keeps track of the balance of greendollars in each member's account.

Local paper currencies are yet another model, and some examples in Canada include the Calgary Dollar, Toronto Dollar, and Salt Spring Island Dollar. Like LETS, their purpose is to improve quality of life by keeping money circulating, while creating high quality, face-to-face exchange that involves conversation along with commerce. They also address the scarcity of the national currency and social exclusion stemming from lack of money. Unlike LETS, paper currency users do not have to be members. Anyone who holds a paper note may spend it where it is accepted. Each paper currency model differs according to how the money is issued, its rules of valuation, and its convertibility to the Canadian dollar (Raddon, 2003).

Independent small businesses often agree to accept local currency because it increases business loyalty and connects the business with a pool of potential employees and local services. Local currency is also exchanged for personal services such as dog walking, driving lessons, gardening, cooking, tutoring, party organizing, and snow-shovelling. The significance of local currencies is that they provide a different perspective on money and financial security, as well as a buffer against financial hardship. For many people financial security through investment is unavailable. Local currencies increase the financial self-sufficiency and economic agency of the people that create and circulate them.

In summary, I have discussed the financial crisis in terms of political economy and financial fitness in terms of cultural economy in order to reveal the multiple dimensions of economic power that are part of "the centre" of contemporary capitalism. Cultural economy, although it is the more recent tradition, does not replace political economy, because, as Martin (2009) argues, each approach expands the field of the political and "each perspective might make better use of the other" (116). In this chapter, the complementary focus of political economy on large structures and cultural economy on everyday life has helped bring into view different aspects of financialization. To review one example, political economy has shown how the growing rate of personal debt among Canadians is a structural feature of the economy that has partially replaced government debt-stimulus programs in the transition from Keynesianism to neoliberalism. This shift in the debt burden, referred to as "privatized Keynesianism," would not have been possible, however, without a change in our everyday morality of spending and borrowing, and our commitment to financial fitness, which cultural economy helps us see. Both perspectives reveal that financialization is not a stable or complete process, for political economy because of the recurrent crises that arise, and for cultural economy because of the dependence of financial authority on tenuous discursive practices that can be broken down and resisted. Both approaches are also interested in alternatives to financialization, such as slow money and local currencies. For political economy, slow money and local currencies can be social structures that really help people get what they need. They can also provide a fallback for people and a means to sustain meaningful livelihoods during crisis. For cultural economy, slow money and local currencies can be seen as a form of resistance, because they enact an economy outside of financial fitness and destabilize the dominant discourse of financial security that sustains financialization.

STUDY QUESTIONS

1. Comedian Woody Allen (1975) wrote, "Money is better than poverty, if only for financial reasons." Interpret the humour of this line. Is it merely a tautology (a statement that, instead of explaining a concept, simply repeats it in different words)? How does the line also critique Western financial culture?

2. What attitudes and orientations toward education, work, social relationships, and the purpose of life does financial fitness promote? See the 18th-century aphorisms of Benjamin Franklin for an illustration of Puritan morality at (www.poorrichards.net/benjamin-franklin). How does the social morality of financial fitness diverge from the Puritan virtues of frugality, thrift, prudence, and hard work? How would you describe the relationship between these shifting cultural conceptions of economic virtue and transformations in global financial markets?

3. How have strategies for financial fitness come to be normalized and come to have such a positive and prominent social value? As we practice financial fitness, how are we inside of power?

EXERCISES

1. Visit two or three financial literacy websites such as the following:

   http://www.financialfitnesschallenge.ca

   http://themoneybelt.ca

   http://www.financialfitness.ca

   http://www.investorED.ca

   http://www.balancepro.net

   How do these sites represent people as responsible, self-disciplined consumers of financial services and as "entrepreneurs of the self"? What is missing in these approaches to financial education? How would you imagine financial education differently?

2. Visit two or three activist websites that critically analyze reasons for the escalation in consumer debt or student debt:

   http://www.stopthesqueeze.org

   http://www.cfs-fcee.ca/studentdebt

   http://www.studentloanfairness.ca

   http://www.affil.org

   How do these activist sites represent people simultaneously as engaged citizens and as victims of a financial system that exerts top-down power? What additional images of political agency might be introduced to these critiques? For instance, you might think about ways that people resist practising financial fitness in everyday life. How is such resistance a potential resource in movements for financial justice? You might also explore contradictions within financial fitness. How are such contradictions relevant to activism for financial fairness?

3. In a group of ten to twenty people, make a list of group members' resources and skills. Next make a second list of resources and services that members may want or need. If the items on the first list were "offers" and those the second list "wishes," how many matches might be made? Can you think of a method to keep score of the value of exchanges in your group so that fairness in giving and receiving does not require the unlikely scenario of equal two-way barter? In other words, invent some form of currency so that the possibility of exchange does not depend on two people offering each other items of equal value and each wanting what the other has. Read about a local currency project such as LETS (mutual credit exchange systems), Time Dollars (service credits), or HOURS. How did your exchange system compare to one of these models? How do such projects invite us to reimagine money? If a fraction of our transactions, both for things we want and contributions we can make to others, were done with local currencies, what would you imagine to be some effects?

REFERENCES

Allan, J. 2002. Symbolic economies: The "culturalization" of economic knowledge. In P. du Gay and M. Pryke, eds., *Cultural Economy: Cultural Analysis and Commercial Life.* London: Sage. 39–58.

Allen, W. 1975. *The Early Essays Without Feathers.* New York: Ballantine Books.

Arrighi, G. 1994. *The Long Twentieth Century: Money, Power and the Origins of Our Times.* New York: Verso.

Atwood, M. 2008. *Payback: Debt and the Shadow Side of Wealth.* Toronto: House of Anansi Press.

Block, F. L. 1977. *The Origins of International Economic Disorder: A Study of United States International Monetary Policy from World War II to the Present.* Berkeley, LA; London: University of California Press.

Brenner, R. 2002. *The Boom and the Bubble: The U.S. in the World Economy.* London and New York: Verso.

Carroll, W. K., and Shaw, M. 2001. Consolidating a neoliberal policy bloc in Canada, 1976 to 1996. *Canadian Public Policy* 27(2): 195–217.

CBC News, 2009. Canadian household debt swells to $1.3 trillion. May 26. Consumer Life. CBC.ca. http://www.cbc.ca/consumer/story/2009/05/26/canada-household-debt854.html, accessed January 28, 2011.

Crouch, C. 2008. What will follow the demise of privatised Keynesianism? *The Political Quarterly* 79(4): 476–487.

De Goede, M. 2005. *Virtue, Fortune and Faith: A Genealogy of Finance.* Minnesota: University of Minnesota Press.

Du Gay, P. 2000. Representing "globalization": Notes on the discursive orderings of economic life. In P. Gilroy, ed., *Without Guarantees: In Honour of Stuart Hall.* London: Verso. 113–125.

Du Gay, P., and Pryke, M., eds. 2002. *Cultural Economy: Cultural Analyses and Commercial Life.* London; Thousand Oaks; New Delhi: Sage Publications.

Dumenil, G., and Levy, D. 2005. The neoliberal (counter-)revolution. In A. Saad-Filho and D. Johnston, eds., *Neoliberalism: A Critical Reader.* London; Ann Arbor: Pluto Press. 9–19.

Evans, T. 2009. The 2002–2007 U.S. economic expansion and the limits of finance-led capitalism. *Studies in Political Economy* 83(Spring): 33–59.

Fernandez, L. 2009. We're all Keynesians—again. In J. Guard and W. Antony, eds., *Bankruptcies & Bailouts.* Halifax; Winnipeg: Fernwood. 107–122.

Foster, J. B., and Magdoff, F. 2009. *The Great Financial Crisis: Causes and Consequences.* New York: Monthly Review Press.

Galbraith, J. K. 1993. *A Short History of Financial Euphoria.* New York: Whittle Books in association with Viking.

Gibson-Graham, J. K. 2006. *A Postcapitalist Politics.* Minneapolis: University of Minnesota Press.

Giroux, H. A. 2004. *The Terror of Neoliberalism: Authoritarianism and the Eclipse of Democracy.* Boulder: Paradigm.

Gonick, C. 2009. A great leap forward? In J. Guard and W. Antony, eds., *Bankruptcies & Bailouts.* Halifax; Winnipeg: Fernwood Publishing. 8–17.

Greenfield, C., and Williams, P. 2007. Financialization, finance rationality and the role of the media in Australia. *Media, Culture and Society* 29(3): 415–433.

Hanieh, A. 2009. Hierarchies of a global market: The South and the economic crisis. *Studies in Political Economy* 83(Spring): 61–84.

Harvey, D. 2005. *A Brief History of Neoliberalism.* Oxford: Oxford University Press.

Henderson, H. 2009. Democratizing finance. Editorial. http://www.hazelhenderson.com/editorials/democratizing_finance.html.

Henwood, D. 2003. *After the New Economy.* New York; London: The New Press.

Hudson, I. 2009. From deregulation to crisis. In J. Guard and W. Antony, eds., *Bankruptcies & Bailouts.* Halifax; Winnipeg: Fernwood. 46–61.

Hutchinson, F., Mellor, M., and Olsen, W. 2002. *The Politics of Money: Towards Sustainability and Economic Democracy.* London: Pluto Press.

Kapoor, S. 2009. Financial transaction taxes: Burden sharing to finance the costs of the bailouts—a conceptual note. *Re-Define: Rethinking Development, Finance & Environment.* http://www.re-define.org/publications.

Kiely, R. 2005. *Empire in the Age of Globalisation: U.S. Hegemony and Neoliberal Disorder.* London; Ann Arbor: Pluto Press.

Krippner, G. R. 2005. The financialization of the American economy. *Socio-Economic Review* 3(2): 173–208.

Langley, P. 2008. *The Everyday Life of Global Finance: Saving and Borrowing in Anglo-America.* Oxford: Oxford University Press.

Loxley, J. 2009. Financial dimensions: origins and state responses. In J. Guard and W. Antony, eds., *Bankruptcies & Bailouts*. Halifax; Winnipeg: Fernwood Publishing. 62–76.

Magdoff, F., and Yates, M. D. 2009. *The ABCs of the Economic Crisis: What Working People Need to Know*. New York: Monthly Review Press.

Manning, R. D. 2000. *Credit Card Nation: The Consequences of America's Addiction to Credit*. New York: Basic Books.

Martin, R. 2002. *Financialization of Daily Life*. Philadelphia: Temple University Press.

Martin, R. 2009. The twin towers of financialization: Entanglements of political and cultural economies. *The Global South* 3(1): 108–125.

Marx, K. 1967. *Capital: A Critique of Political Economy. Volume 1: The Process of Capitalist Production* [1887]. S. Moore and E. Aveling, trans. New York: International Publishers.

McNally, D. 2009. Inequality, the profit system and global crisis. In J. Guard and W. Antony, eds., *Bankruptcies & Bailouts*. Halifax; Winnipeg: Fernwood Publishing. 32–45.

Milani, B. 2000. *Designing the Green Economy: The Postindustrial Alternative to Corporate Globalization*. Lanham, MD: Rowman & Littlefield Publishers.

Muller, J. 2003. The house that GM built. Forbes.com. http://www.forbes.com/2003/07/17/cz_jm_0717gm.html.

North, P. 2007. *Money and Liberation: The Micropolitics of Alternative Currency Movements*. Minneapolis; London: University of Minnesota Press.

North, P. 2008. Voices from the trueque: Barter networks and resistance to neoliberalism in Argentina. In A. Smith, A. Stenning and K. Willis, eds., *Social Justice and Neoliberalism: Global Perspectives*. London; New York: Zed Books. 16–38.

Office of the Minister of Finance and Department of Finance. 2009. Minister of Finance Launches Task Force on Financial Literacy. June 26, 2009. http://www.financialliteracyincanada.com/eng/media/press-releases/2009-06-26.001.php.

Preda, A. 2009. *Framing Finance: The Boundaries of Markets and Modern Capitalism*. Chicago; London: University of Chicago Press.

Pryke, M., and du Gay, P. 2007. Take an issue: Cultural economy and finance. *Economy and Society* 36(3): 339–354.

Raddon, MB. 2003. *Community and Money: Men and Women Making Change*. Montreal: Black Rose Books.

Roseman, E. 2009. Financial literacy a must-have. *Toronto Star*, July 5. A15.

Shamir, R. 2008. The age of responsibilization: On market-embedded morality. *Economy and Society* 37(1): 1–19.

Statistics Canada. 2007. Personal debt. *Perspectives on Labour and Income*, Catalogue No. 75-001-XIE). 28–34. http://www.statcan.gc.ca/pub/75-001-x/commun/4235072-eng.pdf.

Tasch, Woody. 2008. *Inquiries into the Nature of Slow Money: Investing as If Food, Farms, and Fertility Mattered*. White River Jct., VT: Chelsea Green.

Task Force on Financial Literacy. 2009. http://www.financialliteracyincanada.com.

Testimony of Dr. Alan Greenspan. 2008. Committee on Government Oversight and Reform. http://oversight.house.gov/documents/20081023100438.pdf.

Thrift, N. 1994. On the social and cultural determinants of international financial centres: The case of the City of London. In S. Corbridge, R. Martin, and N. J. Thrift, eds., *Money, Space and Power.* Oxford: Blackwell. 327–355.

Wilby, P. 2009. Just as the Industrial Revolution transformed lifestyles, family relations and the very rhythm of existence, so has the financial revolution. All of us now live by the logic of finance. *New Statesman*, February 9. 28–33.

PART 4

Thinking Global: "The West and the Rest"

Mark P. Thomas, *York University*

INTRODUCTION

One of the starting points of this book was C. W. Mills' idea of the **sociological imagination**, which enables us to situate our everyday, individual experiences within wider social contexts. In commenting on the centrality of this concept to critical social science research, geographer David Harvey (2005) suggests we also need to integrate a "spatial consciousness" into the socio-logical imagination, in order to capture the significance of geography in shaping social relations. This is particularly pressing in today's global economy, as

> Globalization (however it is construed) has forced all sorts of adjustments into how the sociological imagination … can now work. It cannot, for example, afford to ignore the basics of political economy, nor can it proceed as if issues of national and local differ-ences, space relations, geography and environment are of no consequence.

What this means is that as part of a sociological imagination, we must also develop a "geographical imagination," which "enables the individual to recognize the role of space and place in his own biography" (Harvey, 1973, quoted in Harvey, 2005: 212). In other words, when analyzing social organization we must "think global" by situating our everyday experi-ences within a geographic context that highlights the interconnections between place, space and power. The chapters of Part IV take up this approach by studying the organization of power in ways that highlight the centrality of relations of colonialism, imperialism, and globalization to the shaping of many everyday practices.

This final Part also aims to weave together two of the primary approaches we have developed to understand the social organization of power. Throughout the book, we have seen examples of the organization of power as understood through frameworks connected to the work of both Michel Foucault and Karl Marx, and we have seen examples of how these approaches may be used in conjunction with one another. We now build on these approaches and continue to move toward an integrated and multidimensional approach to the analysis of power. First we look at the social theorist Stuart Hall and his work on *"the West and the Rest."* Under this theme, we study how discourse, political economy, the politics of representation, and processes of normalization connect with one another in organizing taken-for-granted assumptions and everyday practices. And by developing not only a sociological imagination but also a geographical imagination, we analyze these social relations in ways that account for both past and present global dynamics in shaping power and everyday practices.

THE WEST AND THE REST

As discussed in the introductory chapter to this text, while some of Stuart Hall's early work was influenced by the Marxist approach to understanding class relations within capitalism, he was very interested in the politics of race, systems of representation, and how social relations of race and class intersected. He ultimately found a traditional Marxist analysis inadequate to understand these phenomena. Like Foucault, Hall believed that discourses produce and transmit knowledge, and that the production of knowledge always occurs in relation to the production of power. A discourse produces "meaningful knowledge" about a subject, thereby limiting "other ways in which the topic can be constructed" (Hall, 1996: 201). Moreover, he suggested it is not useful to focus on the distinction between true and false, because a discourse that becomes dominant, whether "true" or not, can have real effects: "people act on them believing that they are true, and so their actions have real consequences" (203). The knowledge produced by discourse "influences social practices, and so has real consequences and effects" (205). Again, this is what he meant by stating that discourses are *effective*.

But, for Hall, the effects of discourse are not disconnected from political economy, or social relationships connected to control over economic resources and political institutions. If we look at Hall's (1996) work on "the West and the Rest," we see the importance of constructing an analysis of power that includes both political economy (class relations) and the politics of representation. Hall (1996) illustrates this approach in looking at the expansion of the West, which as a geographic category was originally associated with Western Europe. But according to Hall, the West is not simply a place/geographical area that you can point to on a map. As he states, "'the West' is as much an idea as a fact of geography" (249). What he means by this is that "the West" is part of a discourse—a system of representation—about the world as well. Specifically, he suggests that "the West" refers to industrialized, developed, urban, capitalist, and secularized societies. It represents progress. The idea of "the West" originated with European colonizers through the process of colonization that began in the 15th century. It provided these Europeans with a way of interpreting the world and with a justification for the entire project of colonization.

As a discourse, this idea of "the West" organizes a way of classifying societies into different categories. As a system of representation, it characterizes and classifies. It does this by working with other words that have linked meanings. For example, urbanism equals progress, while agrarian equals underdeveloped. As a discourse, it sets out the criteria for ranking societies in relation to one another. "The West" is equated with developed, good, and desirable, while "the Rest" are underdeveloped, bad, undesirable. As Hall states, this discourse of "the West and the Rest" "produces a certain kind of knowledge about a subject and certain attitudes towards it" (249).

Returning to David Harvey (2005), we can see a more contemporary illustration of the interconnection between these kinds of systems of representation and the capacities for political and economic domination:

> Stereotypes about geographical "others" abound and prejudicial commentary can be heard daily in casual conversations even in elite circles. It then becomes all too easy for the US to portray itself as the bearer of universal principles of justice, democracy and goodness while in practice operating in an intensely discriminatory way. The easy way in which various spaces in the global economy can be "demonized" in public opinion (Cuba, China, Libya, Iran, Iraq …) illustrates all too well how geographical knowledge of a certain sort is mobilized for political purposes while sustaining a belief in the US as the bearer of a global ethic…. If the rest of the world fails to conform to US standards of behavior … then it deserves to be persuaded, cajoled, sanctioned or bombed into conformity.

In other words, discourses of "the West and the Rest" are both *produced and productive* (Hall, 1996). They have real effects by enabling people to know or speak of certain things in certain ways (produced knowledge). And they cannot be abstracted (separated) from economic and political institutions in the production of systems of power. Historically, these discourses were produced through the process of European colonization, which involved the appropriation of resources (land) and the exploitation of labour as Europeans colonized many parts of the world beginning in the 15th century. We can see many examples of these kinds of discourses in contemporary times as well, for example in the proliferation of negative images of Islam in parts of the Western world, which, as Harvey (2005) points out, may enable contemporary practices of discrimination, exclusion, and domination.

Thus, in understanding "the West and the Rest," we need to understand the idea of "the West" in the context of colonialism and European expansion. According to Hall, discourses of superiority, difference, otherness, etc., justified economic and political domination. They produced a representation (an understanding) of "the West" in relation to the places that were being colonized. In these ways we can see how Hall brings Marx and Foucault together in his analysis of both the discourse of "the West and the Rest" and its connection to systems of economic power. While Hall developed his discussion of "the West and the Rest" through the study of the history of European colonialism, using Harvey's idea of the "geographical imagination," we can see a number of contemporary examples of these processes in the chapters that follow.

THE CHAPTERS

We begin first with Margot Francis' chapter, "The Imaginary Indian," which takes stereotypes of Indigenous peoples in Canada as a starting point. The chapter builds upon the theme of "thinking global" by situating the production of these stereotypes in relation to the colonization of North America by the British and the French. Francis' chapter raises the following questions. *What are some common representations of Indigenous peoples in Canadian culture? How are Indigenous peoples part of "the Rest" in "the West"? How are images, ideas, and forms of representation of Aboriginal peoples connected to the political economy of land, politics, and colonialism in Canada?* The chapter examines how popular discourses about Indigenous peoples shape stereotypes, in which the term "Imaginary Indian" is used in recognition that the term "Indian" is itself a creation of colonialism. The use of "Indian play" in non-indigenous settings such as Ontario summer camps is a particularly central representation of Indigenous people examined in this chapter. Francis aims to understand how the "Imaginary Indian," as constructed through stereotypes, comes to represent Aboriginal peoples in Canada, and the profound implications of this system of representation in Canadian society. This chapter also examines how Indigenous people "speak back" to such representations through political art.

Building from Marx's analysis of commodity fetishism, Gavin Fridell asks, "What power relations are embedded in a cup of coffee?" How do our consumption practices contribute to these power relations? Can "fair trade" practices challenge these power relations? In this chapter, Fridell explores the sociology of coffee by: (1) turning our attention to the highly unequal social relations of production that form of the base for the entire coffee industry; (2) analyzing the social rituals, symbolic identities, and labour relations associated with coffee-drinking in the North; and (3) discussing various "coffee battles" to re-adjust global inequality in the coffee chain through fair trade coffee, for instance. In presenting the cup of coffee as a commodity, Fridell demonstrates how coffee is embedded within a complex set of global economic and political relationships: it is produced through global commodity chains characterized by often highly exploitative labour practices; and it has a history deeply connected to European colonization of regions of the global south. In recognizing that coffee is connected to these various social relationships and practices, the chapter demonstrates that when we consume a cup of coffee, we are ourselves part of the global economy that produces these social relationships.

Next, taking a sociological approach to the practice of tourism, Rebecca Raby and Joan Phillips ask "How do some people become tourists?" *How has tourism developed as a consumer practice of citizens of the West? How have some parts of the world become constituted as tourist sites, and how has this shaped the relations between tourists and the local people who serve them? How are we coached into knowing how to be a tourist?* Raby and Philips demonstrate how tourism as a practice refers to travel for business and for pleasure, and how tourism is a massive global industry. Again, this chapter builds upon the framework of the "West and the Rest" to explore how certain places in the global economy have become popular, cheap, and "exotic" tourist destinations for those in advanced capitalist societies where travel to these places becomes normalized and taken for granted. Raby and Philips complicate these practices by illustrating that tourism is profoundly classed, racialized, and gendered. Along with the global political economy of tourism, this chapter examines the "Disneyfication" of tourism to illustrate how a Foucauldian analysis also reveals power relations that shape the tourist experience. They also weigh the transformative potential of eco and voluntary tourism.

Finally, in her chapter "Nation States, Borders, Citizenship, and the Making of 'National' Difference," Nandita Sharma unpacks the idea of national identity. In what ways does one's national identity get reproduced in everyday life? What is the contradiction between ever-more-global operations of power and the reinforcement of anti-immigrant politics? National borders, far from being natural, have been organized through a set of institutionalized relationships based on the law, the global capitalist market, and social relations of "race," class, and gender, all of which act to shape who can and cannot be a member of the nation. The policing of national borders and identities becomes connected to creating insiders and outsiders in terms of who has access to the national community. It also becomes a way of creating social differentiation within national communities, as "foreigners" and "outsiders" are nonetheless present, though as non-citizens they experience unequal access to economic and political rights. In unpacking the complexities of the categories of nation and citizenship in this way, Sharma illustrates another example of how "the Rest" are very much present within "the West," though on a very unequal footing.

While these chapters cover a wide range of practices, processes, and social relations, they all "think global" to develop integrative frameworks for understanding the global dynamics of the social organization of power in everyday practices.

REFERENCES

Hall, Stuart. 1996. The West and the rest: Discourse and power. In S. Hall et al., eds., *Modernity: An Introduction to Modern Societies*. Oxford: Blackwell. 184–228.

Harvey, David. 1973. *Social Justice and the City*. Baltimore: Johns Hopkins University Press.

Harvey, David. 2005. The sociological and geographical imaginations. *International Journal of Politics, Culture & Society* 18: 211–255.

12

The Imaginary Indian: Unpacking the Romance of Domination

Margot Francis *Brock University*

It's the spring of 2009, and I'm up in the community of Garden River First Nation (GRFN) just outside Sault Ste. Marie, in northern Ontario. I am here to write about a new play called *Treaty Daze* by Alanis King, the former artistic director of the Saskatchewan Native Theatre Company, with a team of **Indigenous**, mixed-race, and Euro-Canadian youth actors. The focus of the play will be on the history of "treaties" or land agreements between Euro-Canadian settlers and **Anishinaabec** people in this region. The team has mapped out the main characters and is now looking for a "hook" for an opening scene to grab the attention of the audience and signal that we "know" how this history plays out in the taken-for-granted interactions between contemporary youth in schools.

One of the actors, Teddy Syrette, starts to talk about his own very recent experiences. Like roughly 70 percent of Indigenous youth on reserves, he dropped out of secondary school—but his reasons had nothing to do with apathy. For the past three years, Teddy has been the lead actor in this local theatre company, and he's someone we've all come to know as bright, funny, and uber-responsible. So he talks about his secondary-school experience: about being on the receiving end of nasty comments about "Indians getting special privileges"; about social events where white people were getting drunk, and being told they were acting "just like Indians"; and about not knowing how to respond when white friends said that "Indians get things for free."[1]

I'm using the term "Indian" because I want to signal that it refers to the ideas that many non-Indigenous Canadians—such as Teddy's high school friends—have taken up as the "truth" about Indigenous people. This chapter will explore how these stereotypical ideas developed in the context of Canadian colonialism. This link to the colonial origins of language is important, because the term Indian actually originates from the confused navigation skills of European explorers: they thought they had found India when they came upon North America. But these explorers were not simply curious to investigate new territory. Funded by commercial and national interests in Europe, they wanted to find natural resources and new land. The process of **colonization**, then, involved the takeover of territory that originally belonged to a wide range of Indigenous nations. This movement proceeded differently in the United States and in Canada, but the results have been similar, with European settlers using their economic and military power to gain access to land and resources to enrich their own people.

---

1 Teddy Syrette, interview with the author, April 2009.

Consequently the ideas that Teddy Syrette faced in secondary school originated through colonialism. In this chapter, beginning with an historical overview, I unpack how ideas normalized through colonization continue to pervade our everyday practices. In Canada, 1876 marked the passage of the *Indian Act*, legislation that provided a coercive and patriarchal set of "cradle to grave" directives governing Indigenous culture and education, while also setting arbitrary standards for who was, and was not, a "status Indian." Until 1985, Indigenous women who married Euro-Canadian men lost their "status" as Indigenous, and government regulations continue to regulate who is considered a "real Indian." The *Act* has also profoundly undermined local self-governance and has marginalized women's spheres of authority within communities (Lawrence, 2004). Further, Indigenous people were the last group to be included in the federal franchise, only gaining access to the vote in 1960 (Miller, 2004). The use of legal and military force to negotiate land agreements, the seizure of huge tracts of non-treaty land, and the relocation of Indigenous communities to isolated reserves deprived most of a sustainable economic and political base. On the cultural front, the state outlawed Indigenous religions, cultural practices, and languages, and distorted the integrity of familial and community structures by removing several generations of children to residential schools. As a result of the profound impacts of residential schools, in 2008 Prime Minister Stephen Harper made a formal apology for the actions of the Canadian government, which he acknowledged constituted a **cultural genocide**—the effects of which continue today (Milloy, 1999; Miller, 1996). As Stasiulis and Jhappan conclude:

> … taken together, these and other measures denied Indigenous people access to legal or political forums and betrayed a clear and plain intent to destroy their cultures and economies and indigenous forms of female autonomy, as well as to abrogate their citizenship and democratic rights. (Stasiulis & Jhappan, 1995: 115–116)

As a result of this history, the United Nations Department of Economic and Social Affairs noted in 2006 that the situation of Indigenous peoples remains "the most pressing human rights issue facing Canadians" in the new millennium (United Nations, 2006). Despite Prime Minister Harper's widely praised apology for the residential schools, and Canada's recent decision to sign the *United Nations Declaration on the Rights of Indigenous Peoples*, the Harper Government has cancelled the Kelowna Accord, a $5 billion plan to improve the lives of Indigenous, Métis, and Inuit peoples. In this context, perhaps it should also not be surprising that a recent survey by the Coalition for the Advancement of Indigenous Studies done in collaboration with the Canadian Race Relations Foundation (2000–2001) found that 80 percent of first-year university and college students had gained little exposure to Indigenous issues, while those in elementary and secondary school felt unprepared to address contemporary conflicts between Indigenous and non-Indigenous peoples (Coalition for the Advancement of Indigenous Studies, 2008).

How might one explore the **politics of representation** in relation to Indigenous people in this context? And how influential are the prejudicial ideas about "Indians" that Teddy faced in secondary school and the broader stereotypes found in popular culture?

As many scholars have argued, thanks to the seductive influence of Hollywood westerns, and of consumer and sports icons, imaginary ideas about Indians have been dispersed on a global scale (Francis, 1992; Deloria, 1998). An everyday example can be found in the summer rituals of many North American families that include backyard games of "cowboys and Indians," complete with homemade or commercial teepees. Indeed, the latest trend in childhood teepees can be found on the popular Posh Tots website, which markets the dream of returning to nature through domesticated fabric teepees that can be set up inside a child's bedroom or in the wilderness of the backyard. (http://www.poshtots.com)

While these childhood games have been a taken-for-granted aspect of many Euro-Canadian childhoods, Indigenous scholars have often challenged the assumptions about their "harmless" appeal. Indeed, Carol Lee Sanchez asks: "Would you allow your children to play Nazis and Jews? Blacks and the Klu Klux Klan? Complete with costume?" (quoted in Tremblay, 1993: 10) Yet the assumption that "playing Indian" is a completely innocuous form of childhood entertainment has global appeal. For example, the Indo-Canadian film-maker Ali Kazimi opens his award-winning film *Shooting Indians* (1997) with an image from his family's home movies in Delhi, where his parents are receiving visitors from England. Their gifts for the children include plastic cowboys (who were good) and red Indians (who were bad).

FIGURE 12.1 ■ Fabric teepee.

© Photolibrary/Alamy

In a reverse set of representations that also have global currency, films like the Disney blockbuster *Pocahontas* (1995) portray Indians as "Noble Savages" living in harmony with nature, while a plucky Pocahontas (who looks like an Indigenous Barbie) stars as the Indian princess in the main role. Thus, in places that range from Delhi to Toronto to Sault Ste. Marie, and in a wide range of everyday contexts, from children's toys to Hollywood films to the daily banter of friends, an imaginary set of ideas portrays Indians as lazy, savage, drunk freeloaders, or as noble and spiritual figures who are closer to nature. These contradictory ideas, however, are like two sides of the same coin, and demonstrate that Indigenous people, like other people of colour, are rarely racialized as "just people," who are entitled to the full complexity of human behaviour and emotions. Instead, as the Tuscarora artist Jolene Rickard asserts, they must always speak back to the "white man's Indian" (quoted in Smith, P. C., 1995: 6).

So how exactly do we explore the politics of representation implicit in these contemporary images of "Indianness"? One recent example of Indigenous people taking centre stage is the unprecedented inclusion offered Indigenous nations who signed on as co-hosts to the 2010 Vancouver Olympics. From the Inukshuk-inspired logo to the ceremonial opening, it was clear that Indigenous people were key to how Canada wished to position itself on the global stage. In order to explore the politics of representation implicit in the Canadian Olympics, it is important to take up a series of uncomfortable questions. Toban Black has highlighted these through queries such as: What did the superficially "indigenous" rhetoric and imagery have to do with the rest of the Olympics? Were Indigenous people, in fact, benefiting from the Olympics in a way that might justify the appropriation of Inuit imagery? Further, what proportion of the profits from Olympics sales and tourism did Indigenous groups actually receive? How many Indigenous athletes did Canada support to compete at an Olympic level? And to what extent did Indigenous groups actively participate in Olympics organizing?[2]

As some of the questions highlighted above suggest, this chapter will inquire into the connection between images of Indigenous people and the economic benefits that accrue (or not) to Indigenous communities. Insofar as I am interested in exploring how everyday practices are rooted in an exploitation of labour, I draw on a Marxist analysis of power. However, Marxist ideas are not sufficient to understand the politics of representation in relation to "Indians." For example, at the 2010 Olympics, Canada projected the idea that Indigenous people are respected, empowered, and well integrated in Canada. Yet Indigenous people are the only group in Canada who continue to live in "Third World" conditions in a country that consistently rates among the top ten in the United Nations Human Development Index.[3] (See the box here.) Here Foucault's ideas of **normalization** can provide a conceptual framework to help understand this contradiction. Both the

---

2 Toban Black, "An Indigenous Olympics," *Racialicious*, February 24, 2010, available http://www. racialicious.com/2010/02/24/an-indigenous-olympics; originally published at Contexts.org.

3 "The Reality of First Nations," Fact Sheet, Assembly of First Nations website, http://www.afn.ca/article. asp?id=764. For further information on the racialization of Indigenous experience, see National Anti-Racism Council of Canada website, http://action.web.ca/home/narcc/issues.

THE REALITY OF INDIGENOUS COMMUNITIES IN CANADA TODAY

Live in Third World conditions:

1. Indigenous living conditions or quality of life ranks 63rd, or amongst Third World conditions. [1]
2. Indigenous' infant mortality rate is 1.5 times higher than the Canadian infant mortality rate. [2]

Die earlier than other Canadians:

- An Indigenous man will die 7.4 years earlier than a non-Indigenous Canadian. An Indigenous woman will die 5.2 years earlier than her non-Indigenous counterpart (life expectancy for Indigenous citizens is estimated at 68.9 years for males and 76.6 years for females). [3]

Face increased rates of suicide, diabetes, tuberculosis and HIV/AIDS:

- The Indigenous suicide rate is more than twice the Canadian rate. Suicide is now among the leading causes of death among Indigenous youth between the ages of 10 and 24, with the rate estimated to be five to six times higher than that of non-Indigenous youth. [4]

- Tuberculosis rates for Indigenous people on-reserve are 8 to 10 times higher than those for the Canadian population. [6]

- Indigenous peoples make up only 5% of the total population in Canada but represent 16% of new HIV infections. Of these, 45% are women and 40% are under 30 years old. [7]

Face a crisis in housing and living conditions:

1. Health Canada states that as of May 2003, 12% of Indigenous communities had to boil their drinking water and approximately ¼ of water treatment systems on-reserve pose a high risk to human health.
2. 5,486 of the 88,485 houses on-reserve are without sewage service.
3. Almost half of Indigenous people residing off-reserve live in poor quality housing that is below standard. and most Indigenous homes off-reserve are crowded.

Are not attaining education levels equal to other Canadians:

- About 70% of Indigenous student's on-reserve will never complete high school. [14]

- 10,000 Indigenous students who are eligible and looking to attend post-secondary education are on waiting lists because of under-funding.

- About 27% of Indigenous people between 15 and 44 years of age hold a post-secondary certificate, diploma, or degree, compared with 46% of the Canadian population within the same age group. [15]

Lack jobs and economic opportunities:

- Unemployment rates for all Indigenous groups continue to be at least double the rate of the non-Indigenous peoples. [16]

- Registered Indigenous people have the lowest labour force participation rate of any Indigenous group, with a rate of 54%. [17]

Yet Indigenous peoples receive less from all levels of government than non-Indigenous Canadians:

- The average Canadian gets services from governments at an amount that is almost two-and-a-half times greater than that received by Indigenous citizens.

- In 1996, the federal government capped funding increases for Indian Affairs' core programs at 2% a year, which does not keep pace with inflation or the growing Indigenous population. A recent Indian Affairs study found that the gap in "quality of life" between Indigenous and Canadians stopped narrowing in 1996.

[1] Indian and Northern Affairs Canada (INAC), 1998. The Human Development Index examines per capita income, education levels and life expectancy to compare the world's countries.
[2] Statistics Canada; Health Canada, *Healthy Canadians, A Federal Report on Comparable Health Indicators*, 2002.
[3] INAC, 2002.
[4] Health Canada, *Health Sectoral Session Background Paper*, October 2004.
[5] Health Canada, *Diabetes Among Aboriginal People in Canada: The Evidence*, March 2000.
[6] Health Canada, *A Statistical Profile on the Health of First Nations in Canada*, March 2003.
[7] Health Canada, *FNIHB Community Programs Annual Review 1999–2000*, August 2000.
[8] Indian and Northern Affairs Canada.
[9] First Nations Centre, National Aboriginal Health Organization, *Preliminary Findings of the First Nations Regional Longitudinal Health Survey 2002–2003*, November 2004.
[10] *2003 Report of the Auditor General of Canada*.
[11] National Aboriginal Health Organization, *Regional Longitudinal Health Survey*.
[12] Health Canada.

[13] *2004 Report of the Auditor General of Canada.*
[14] INAC, *Nominal Roll 1994–2000.*
[15] *2004 Report of the Auditor General of Canada.*
[16] Statistics Canada, *DIAND Core Census Tabulations*, 1996, T-11.
[17] Ibid.

Source: Adapted from "The Reality for First Nations in Canada," Fact Sheet, Assembly of First Nations, http://www.afn.ca/article.asp?id=764. Used by permission.

everyday stereotypes about Indians as "savage" or "noble" and the spectacular displays of Indianness at the Olympics help to *normalize* Canada's continuing colonial relationship with Indigenous people. In so doing, they obscure contemporary inequalities, thus allowing the "centre"—or the existing relations of power—to survive unquestioned and intact.

However, as Foucault notes, power is not only a negative, repressive force that operates through the mechanisms of law and censorship (Foucault, 1978: 82). Indeed, "there are no relations of power without resistances; the latter are all the more real and effective because they are formed right at the point where relations of power are exercised" (Foucault, 1980: 142). Thus, I join my assessment of the imaginary "Indian" with an exploration of the forms of resistance that Indigenous artists are themselves mobilizing against precisely this image. Consequently, the second section of this chapter will highlight the photographic work of Jeff Thomas, a contemporary Iroquoian photographer, who is challenging and reconfiguring the "white man's Indian." Thomas employs **mimicry**, irony, and visual **spectacle** to portray Indians who play against type, *intensifying* specifically erotic representations in ways that ask viewers to consider how Euro-Canadian amnesia and desire in relation to the Indian continues into the present moment.

I begin with a brief analysis of an early photograph found in the Canadian National Archives and shown as part of an exhibit by Jeff Thomas at Gallery 44 in Toronto during the 2004 Contact Festival of Photography.

This image, reproduced in Figure 12.2, shows Hayter Reed, the Deputy Superintendent General of Indian Affairs from 1893 to1897, at the Governor-General's Historical Fancy Dress Ball in Ottawa in 1896. The event was sponsored by the Governor-General's wife, Lady Aberdeen. As a theme for the evening, participants were asked to appear in the costume of a historic Canadian figure or group. Reed dressed as the Iroquoian Chief Donnacona, the man who first greeted Jacques Cartier on his voyage down the St. Lawrence in 1534, and whose village Kanata gave rise to the word "Canada." The image shows Reed sporting a plains-style headdress and a variety of buckskin and feather regalia, collected while working on the western plains, but which bore little resemblance to the traditional garments of the Iroquoian leader he was supposed to be imitating. Nevertheless, Reed led an entourage of similarly attired partygoers, and their parade was said to be the highlight of the ball (Titley, 1993).

FIGURE 12.2 ■ Hayter Reed, Deputy Superintendent General of Indian Affairs, and his stepson, Jack Lowery, dressed in Indian costumes for a historical ball on Parliament Hill, Ottawa, February 1896.

William James Topley/Library and Archives Canada/PA-139841

How might we understand this photograph when we assess it in the light of Hayter Reed's career, from his first term as an Indian Agent in Saskatchewan through to his appointment to the top post of the Indian department in 1893? Historian Brian Titley highlights that, in the late 1800s, the Canadian government was consolidating its claims to the West and was determined that Indigenous people have no recognized political or economic role in this important new frontier. Reed was responsible for enforcing the many restrictive features of the *Indian Act*. Titley tells us he proved a competent, if ruthless, administrator (see also Andrews, 1975). However, during his period as Deputy Superintendent, he made his mark by lobbying for at least two crucial amendments to the *Act*. In 1894, the *Act* was changed to ensure that all Indigenous children were compelled to attend school, usually residential schools. This meant that parents would be sent to jail or fined if they refused to allow their children to be sent away to boarding schools. The schools operated through an **imperial ideology** that forbade children to speak their language and taught them that their own culture and spirituality were sinful and "primitive." The schools were so poorly run and underfunded that many became incubators for disease: in fact, the Indian Department itself admitted that between 25 and 50 percent of children who went through these schools in the 1920s died there. This mortality rate was higher than if these children had been sent to war (Milloy, 1999). In 1895, Reed lobbied for another amendment to the *Indian Act* making spiritual and cultural practices of the potlatch and prairie dancing indictable offences (Titley, 1993).

How should we understand Reed's own demonstration of "Indianness" at the Governor-General's Ball in Ottawa in 1896, when we know of his determined attempt to separate Indigenous people from their own children and culture through residential schooling and the criminalization of their religious and ceremonial practices? And how, in Canada, did these seemingly contradictory positions—*of celebrating "Indianness" while criminalizing actual Indigenous people*—come to be so normalized? And finally, how, for the past 150 years, has it become a widely accepted practice to "play" with imaginary variations on "Indianness," in sites that have varied from Hollywood films to backyard teepees to New-Age vision quests, while Indigenous peoples themselves were often prohibited from claiming the culture and spirituality that inspired these very practices? I explore these questions within one particular site that served to normalize the "imaginary Indian": children's summer camps.

PLAYING INDIAN

It was the Canadian naturalist Ernest Thompson Seton whose ideas about Indians profoundly influenced the development of children's summer camps. Seton was an artist, a naturalist, a storyteller; he was also founder of the Woodcraft Indians (1902), a movement that was the forerunner of the Boy Scouts and a major influence on the Girl Guides, Cub Scouts, YM/YWCA, and Canadian and American Camping Associations. The Woodcraft movement had two distinct themes: a focus on Indians as idealized role models and the study of nature as a key strategy for human rejuvenation (Keller, 1984). One of Seton's first booklets was *How to Play Indian* (1903), and a central feature was the symbolic importance of "Indian" costumes and rituals and the awarding of "Indian" feathers for competitive games.

Like the summer camping movement as a whole, Seton's "Indian" philosophy reflected the Euro-Canadian middle-class unease with the rapidly urbanizing, increasingly secular, and fast-paced world of the early 20th century. However, as Sharon Wall argues, this experience of "going Native" had little to do with honouring Indigenous traditions. Instead, it provided a balm for the non-Indigenous experience of **modernity** (Wall, 2005). While Seton was one of the best-known figures to popularize "Indianness" as a form of **mimetic play**, we can see from the earlier analysis of Hayter Reed's performance as Chief Donnacona that Seton built on a practice that was already a recurring theme in North American culture. His innovation was to systematize existing activities into a set of skills and games that were promoted to various organizations, with a profound impact on a host of turn-of-the-century youth groups.

While we might think of this phenomenon of "playing Indian" as a relic of the distant past, recent investigations into youth wilderness programs in Ontario and Quebec provide an intriguing glimpse into the *continued* influence of "Indian play" in contemporary camping.

In interviews undertaken in 2001 with five camp directors, three of whom continue to use traditional "Indian" programming, and with programs serving 3750 children, Ty Hamilton found that aspects of the mythology associated with the "imaginary Indian" are still a significant component of programming at several prestigious Ontario camps. The most significant Indian event in these camps is the "Council Ring," a ceremony first initiated by Seton in his manual *The Birch Bark Roll of Woodcraft* (1902). This weekly event is essentially a campfire with Indian-themed activities including storytelling, passing the "peace pipe," reciting the "Omaha Tribal Prayer," and performance, dancing, and singing.

One of the organizations included in Hamilton's research is the Taylor Statten Camps located in Algonquin Park and established in 1921. Taylor Statten was a pivotal figure in the early history of camping in Ontario, and the Statten program has been influential in the development of a host of other summer camps throughout the 20th century. Statten was a great admirer of Ernest Thompson Seton, and invited him to begin the Indian-themed programming at his camp in 1922. Thus it was Seton himself who initiated the first Native Council Ring in the first Canadian boys' camp in Algonquin Park. He showed the earliest campers how to perform dances, construct sweat lodges, and make Indian crafts (Lundell, 2000). Indeed, in Hamilton's research, one camp director suggested that the only difference between the contemporary Council Ring and the original ceremony initiated in the 1920s is that the Indian characters no longer speak in broken English and female campers now have roles in the event (Hamilton, 2001). While this comment acknowledges the implicitly racialized and gendered meanings associated with the Council Ring, camps continue to reference this legacy through decorations from a hodgepodge of divergent Indigenous groups.

As Hamilton suggests, these generic representations of Indianness obscure the distinctive histories, languages, and cultures of different Indigenous nations at the same time as they present an **ethnographic** vision of people stuck in the vanishing past. Further, many camps also rely on the idea that Indians have a "natural" affinity for the spirituality and spectacle of nature. In keeping with these assumptions, a counsellor's manual at Taylor Statten camps (1968) and a volume about the Kilcoo Camp (1999) both stress the importance of constructing the surroundings for the Council Ring in a way that "lend[s] enchantment" to the occasion so that "nothing interfere[s] with the magic of the Council Fire" (Hamilton, 2001: 34–35; see also Eastaugh, 1968, and Latimer, 1999). Indeed, at the Taylor Statten this wizardry is exemplified by the "Magic Fire" which the "Chief," using various behind-the-scenes chemical manipulations, miraculously calls up to enhance the magical atmosphere of the evening (Hamilton, 2001).

Stereotypic references to Indianness and "nature" also pervade non-Native aspects of the Council Ring; an example is the Ranger Reports, in which campers, often referred to as "braves," report wildlife sightings and other points of interest from the day, and which are opened by the "Chief" commenting on the model of "the redman" and his superior "ability to observe detail" (quoted in Hamilton, 2001: 36; Latimer, 1999). Finally the gendered nature of the stories and performances acted out in the Council Ring are also worthy of note. As Hamilton tells us, "in the story of Hiawatha, the young 'braves' must walk on burning embers to determine who will replace the departed chief. The boy who is mentally tough enough to successfully complete this ordeal then goes into the woods for an all-night vigil to further prove his bravery" (Hamilton, 2001: 39). In the Iroquois tradition from which the historical figure of Hiawatha is taken, it was usually the women of the clan who chose the new chief; and they also had the power to remove him if necessary (Hamilton, 2001; Richter, 1992). However, in the camp version of the story the masculinist fervour of imaginary braves proving their character through a "primitive" ceremony of dancing on hot coals has clearly won out over any pretence of referencing actual Indigenous people or practices, living or dead (Hamilton, 2001).

Why might these rituals have been appealing when Seton first introduced them in the 1920s, and why do aspects of these practices remain popular today? Gail Bederman provides an important analysis of the civilizational ideals that were the framework for the early development of these representations. At the turn of the 20th century, ideas about **primitivism** and **civilization** were implicitly racial concepts which referred to precise stages in human racial evolution. While "primitive" people were assumed to live in a state of "savagery," the "civilized" marked the high point on the evolutionary scale. As Bederman notes, human races

> were assumed to evolve from simple savagery and violent barbarism, to advanced and valuable civilization. But only white races had, as yet, evolved to the civilized stage. In fact, some people spoke of civilization as if it were itself a racial trait, inherited by all Anglo-Saxons and other "advanced" white races. (Bederman, 1995: 25)

Indeed, most commentators assumed that if Indigenous people "failed" to survive the onslaught of European settlement, this could simply be attributed to their lack of civilization. As David Theo Goldberg notes, if "primitive" societies were theorized in binary distinction from a civilized order, these **discourses** were also utilized for more directly political purposes: for if "primitive" peoples were "childlike ... and spontaneous," it was only "natural" that they would need the "iron fist of European governance and paternalistic guidance to control inherent physical violence and sexual drives" (Goldberg, 1993: 156).

In this context, powerful discourses about the need to civilize the primitive races were instrumental in changing ideas about masculinity. During this period manliness was not thought to be something intrinsic to all men, but rather an ideal concept. "Just as manliness was the highest form of manhood, so civilization was the highest form of humanity. Manliness was the achievement of the perfect man, just as civilization was the achievement of a perfect race" (Bederman, 1995: 27). At the same time as this **ideology** was gaining dominance in the popular imagination, economic changes meant that many men were forsaking manual labour for white-collar work. As many men lost the context for proving their manliness through skilled physical labour, "manliness" became an enormous preoccupation, generating waves of anxiety particularly in the middle and upper classes. In this context, ideas about manliness and civilization also generated considerable ambivalence: including the notion that *too much* civilization was "unhealthy." "Over-civilized" or "sissified" men had lost touch with their savage core. The repression of this innate "savagery" could lead to illness and various other social infirmities. Consequently, it became increasingly popular for middle- and upper-class men to try and prove their manliness through increasingly popular forays into "savage" pursuits such as the acquisition of the virile skills of primitive man through camping and hunting (Bederman, 1995).

In the 21st century, with the shift into the knowledge economy, this material separation between men's everyday worlds and the forms of physical competence traditionally associated with masculinity has ensured that anxieties about "being a real man" continue. Further, the contemporary era has also been witness to a more intensive regulation of childhood. Thus, the continued popularity of Indian programming at summer camps could also be linked to the ways these activities allow a physical and metaphoric release from the emotional confines of modern childhood (Wall, 2005). In this context, the continued draw to playing the "primitive" is that it allows an outlet for primarily white middle- and upper-class progeny to safely play out a primitivist fantasy, through indulging their "innately savage" core. Thus summer camps mediate that ambivalent space between civilized and savage manliness through mimetic forms of play in which predominately white children imitate the most natural of all men, the Indian. As Deloria argues, the distinctiveness of "Indian play," particularly in boys' camps, is that it has allowed participants to hold together a particularly North American contradiction: the possibility of living out a primitivist fantasy while at the same time preparing for a very modern world through learning obedience, competition, and hierarchy-building (Deloria, 1998: 117). Thus, the continued emphasis on the tradition of Indian play at Ontario summer camps means that children are allowed a temporary opening into savage and wilderness spaces precisely in order to enable them to return to the ordered, respectable, and "civilized" pursuits expected of them throughout the rest of the year (Deloria, 1998: 120).

The history of Ontario summer camps, then, has been marked by the incorporation of imaginary ideas about Indians into camp programs, *but rarely any actual Indigenous people*. Indeed, while many camping organizations have made the appeal to "tradition" a key selling point in their literature, extolling their continued use, for example, of wood and canvas canoes, Indigenous-styled tumplines, and wannigans (food barrels) in their canoeing trips,[4] this loyalty has rarely been extended to the Indigenous guides, who have on occasion been employed by these same organizations. For example, in *The Keewaydin Way: A Portrait 1893–1983*, Brian Back describes Indigenous involvement in the three eras of guides who served at the camp, detailing "the Indians and Métis of 1902–15; the Mattawans of 1916–60; and the Preppies from the '60s onward" (Back, 1983: 142). This history highlights that from 1902 to 1915 (with a few Métis guides continuing until

---

4   A tumpline is a 6-metre-long leather strap wrapped around wannigans or packs so that its centre point forms a headband to carry the heavy loads across portages. Wannigans are wooden boxes used to transport food.

1959), some camp guides were Indigenous men who had the skills in canoe maintenance and trip navigation crucially important for a camp that specialized in canoe excursions on the largely uncharted waterways of the Canadian north (Back, 1983). However, in 1959 when the guides staged an impromptu strike for higher wages, the "Chief" (the camp director) immediately fired them, and brought in camp assistants ("chore boys and kitchen boys") to take their place (Back, 1983: 147). By this time the northern canoe routes had been mapped, and so the need for guides who could speak Anishinaabemowin to the local people was no longer a priority. Thus Back concludes that the "loss of the Métis guides had little effect on the quality of the trips" (Back, 1983: 148). Ironically, since the Indigenous and Métis people had only ever been employed as guides, and not as "staffmen," it is unlikely they had ever actively participated in the Indian components of the camp program in any case: namely, the Council Ring festivities that in 2001 were still a central feature of Keewaydin's activities.

These tensions—on the one hand promoting generic images of "Indianness" at Ontario camps, on the other hand excluding Indigenous *people* from camping organizations—are also evident in broader wilderness discourse, for example in a recent issue of *Paddler Magazine* (Reimers, 2003). Here Frederick Reimers provides a veritable hymn of praise to the maintenance of "tradition" at Camp Keewaydin, which suggests that his dedication to the camp customs is rooted both in the character-building lessons in self-reliance offered by extended canoe trips and in the organization's history of employing "real" First Nations people (Reimers, 2003). Reimers' article, titled *The Keewaydin Way* (2003), notes that "Unlike the pretend Indian rituals in place at so many summer camps, the Indians at Keewaydin were real" (Reimers, 2003). However, as we have already noted, most Indigenous guides at Keewaydin were edged out of their jobs by 1915 (with a few Métis continuing until 1959), while the "Indian rituals" in place at Keewaydin, as in most other camps, are based on the legacy of Seton, along with the Euro-American poet Henry Longfellow. Nevertheless, Reimers continues,

> Keewaydin's staff take pride in the fact that the traditions they're using were handed down directly from the Native American guides who led the camp's trips.... In fact one of the camp's most notorious alumni was nearly Native American. In the main lodge ... are plaques listing every camp member. On the 1911 and 1912 plaques is the name: Archie Belaney, only a young Englishman then, but later internationally famous as the Indian author Grey Owl. Brian Back, author of Keewaydin's history, *The Keewaydin Way*, theorizes that the camp is where Grey Owl really learned his renowned canoe-tripping skills. (Reimers, 2003)

Here, the Euro-Canadian who became famous through pretending to be an Indigenous person, Grey Owl, is the trump card in Reimers' narrative. Indeed, Archie Belaney's spectacular legacy as a "nearly Native American" guide deflects attention from the fate of the Indigenous and Métis guides, most of whom have not been working at the camp since the early 20th century, and whose traditions are not reflected in the generic representations of "Indianness" suggested by the Council Ring. Thus the legacy of the white man who became a celebrity through imitating Indianness is much more important than the legacy of the actual Indigenous people who did, at one time, work at Keewaydin.

The distinction between using the imaginary Indian to structure camp programming while exhibiting few ties of loyalty to actual Indigenous and Métis people can also be seen in camps' response to Indigenous *campers'* perceptions of their programs. For example, at the prestigious Taylor Statten camps, it was a Mississauga Ojibwa youth who articulated an early critique of the Council Ring. "In the early 1970s this counselor-in-training, also the daughter of the chief of the Ontarian Curve Lake band, complained to the camp administration: 'I was so shocked to go to Council Ring last night … having to watch you people make fun of my people'" (quoted in Wall, 2005: 541). While the camp administration initially responded by attempting to pacify the youth through "removing the 'dress-up' element from the ceremony," this prompted other campers and staff to complain that "something was lost" and so the ritual was reinstated in its original form (Wall, 2005: 542). Interestingly, the Taylor Statten Camps were one of the five camping organizations researched by Hamilton in 2001, and thirty years after this critique by a Mississauga Ojibwa camper they were still using the Council Ring in their summer programs.

As these examples of the relationship between elite camps and their Indigenous guides and campers suggest, children's camps have seen little conflict in using racialized games and rituals based on the imaginary Indian to build an implicitly white Canadian "community spirit" while ignoring the actual struggles of Indigenous people in the communities where these camps were located. To take just one example from many, for most of the 20th century the Temagami First Nation on Bear Island have had an outstanding land claim with the federal government and have not formally been assigned reserve land. They have survived, despite increasing white encroachment, and without clear rights to hunt and fish. Throughout this period white hunters depleted access to local game putting the fur supply into serious decline while Temagami First Nation members dealt with continual harassment by local game wardens (McNab, 2009). This systematic undermining of the Indigenous Temagami community's possibilities for economic development contributed to various forms of familial and community disintegration, and to systemic poverty. However, the influential recreation-based community of Temagami did little to stand in solidarity with the Bear Island community in their fight to gain legal rights to the land they had lived on for centuries.[5] Instead, most focused on preserving the area as a wilderness escape or tourist mecca, while white cottagers and resort owners complained about Indigenous "behavior problems" and called for increased medical and police surveillance.

---

5 Wall (541, n. 85) notes that one exception to this was the camp historian (and former camper) for Keewaydin, Brian Back, who did serve as the director for the Temagami Wilderness Society (precursor to Earthroots), which fought for environmental protection and a just settlement for the Temagami peoples. In 1989 the society's 84-day blockade of the Red Squirrel Road in Temagami brought national attention to the region. See articles in Matt Bray and Ashley Thomson, ed., *Temagami: A Debate on Wilderness* (Toronto; Oxford: Dundurn Press, 1990).

Thus the romantic invocation used in several northern Ontario camps which reminds children that they "walk on Indian land" seems to carry little weight when Indigenous communities themselves lobby to resolve endlessly postponed claims to that same territory (Wall, 2005). Indeed, the imaginary Indian of camp ritual presents a generic, noble Indian vanishing into a premodern past; a discourse that continues to trivialize the contemporary struggles of Indigenous people. Just as importantly, this discourse also provides a vehicle for campers to learn to think of themselves as "real" Canadians with an intimate connection to the wilderness landscape. Thus the imaginary Indian offers a metaphoric vehicle for primarily white Canadians to imaginatively "indigenize" their own relationship to the land, at the same time as these token representations work to invisibilize the actual struggles of Indigenous *people* on that same territory.

Just as authors like Toni Morrison have examined how **whiteness** required particular kinds of cultural imaginings in relation to "Blackness" in the United States (see Morrison, 1993), so has Canadian national identity required the figure of the Indian in constituting a claim to what the national anthem describes as "our home and native land." Indeed, Rosaldo Renato argues that the idea of the "Noble Savage" is a form of "imperialist nostalgia" (1989: 68) entirely characteristic of colonial relations—in which people mourn the passing of what they themselves have destroyed or transformed. It was precisely this kind of discourse that naturalized the "Indian play" in summer camps. The mourning or loss associated with the (regrettable but "natural") passing of a traditional society and imperialist nostalgia cannot be neatly separated. Here, as Renato asserts, "romance is at play with domination, and works through selective attention to draw attention away from fundamental relations of inequality" (Renato, 1989: 87).

In this context, representations of the "Noble Savage" are **metaphors**. The logic of the metaphor is that it can provide an image through which people distance themselves from those things which are closest to them (White, 1978: 84–85). By the late 19th century, the Canadian and American governments had for generations engaged in an "Indian policy" that would today be described as "ethnic cleansing." Not surprisingly, the idolization of these same "savages" as "noble" could only occur after this long conflict had been decided, and actual "Indians" were no longer a real threat to white settlement. For the most part, this discourse troublingly represents the idealization of the "safely dead Indian" (Berkhofer, 1978: 90).

We can see that Ernest Thompson Seton's early, more historical work also evidences an ambivalent relationship to the "safely dead Indian." His example of perfect manhood was the Shawnee Chief Tecumseh. However, Seton characterized Tecumseh in terms that had less to do with the legacy of this important historical figure and more to do with his own interests in providing "role models" that would assist in producing robust, manly, and well-behaved youth. Thus he described Tecumseh as "a great athlete, a great hunter, a great leader" but at the same time "silent and friendly," and even as the most "Christlike character presented on the pages of American history" (quoted in Rosenthal, 1986: 65). Yet the most significant of Tecumseh's features seems also to be that which Seton and many other commentators have found most difficult to reconcile:

namely that his life work and vision were fundamentally in *opposition* to American and Canadian colonialism and nation-building (Sugden, 1998). Indeed, in his principled resistance to Indigenous assimilation, his sustained pride in Indigenous cultures, and his work for a federation that could mount a military offensive to challenge colonial settlement and regain Indigenous land, Tecumseh's vision could more plausibly be compared to that of the early Malcolm X, whose development of the ideals of Black power, self-determination, and armed self-defense echo elements of the earlier leader's philosophy. Thus representations of the imaginary Indian have drawn symbolic power from nostalgic visions of "Indianness" in order to bolster a white vision of national identity at the same time as they eviscerate the deeply oppositional contributions of Indigenous peoples—a contradiction epitomized both in the generic Indian representations in the Council Ring and in the impoverished presentation of visionary leaders such as Chief Tecumseh.

To conclude, Ontario summer camps employ cultural fantasies about "Indianness" to construct deeply idealized visions of Native difference. These practices provide a captivating impression of benign involvement with Indigenous traditions even while avoiding the difficult work of engaging with the historic and present-day claims of Indigenous peoples. While the past thirty years have seen a resurgence in Indigenous resistance, the use of "Indianness" among white North Americans has continued apace. More broadly, "Indian play" has emerged in a host of different social movements from Robert Bly's men's groups that attempt to reinvigorate the "wild man" through drumming circles in the forest, to environmental campaigns that have reimagined the speeches of iconic leaders such as Chief Seattle to suit their own purposes (Bly, 1992; Swann and Krupat, 1987). Indeed, the symbolic legacy of "Indianness" has usually elided the historic and contemporary interventions by Indigenous people themselves that are often an indictment of Euro-Canadian and American colonialism, a message not nearly as attractive as the peaceable kingdom evoked by the Council Ring.

RESPONDING TO THE WHITE MAN'S "INDIAN"

If discourses about the "imaginary Indian" have most often worked to dismiss Indigenous lives and experiences, ignored histories of inequality and colonization, and delegitimized their demands for redress, how are Indigenous artists challenging these representations? In this second section of the chapter, I focus on the work of Iroquoian artist Jeff Thomas (www.scoutingforindians.com/biography.html), whose photographs have been shown throughout Europe and North America and whose practice also includes major projects of archival research and curation for the Canadian National Archives and the Museum of Civilization. Thomas' work has drawn attention to the "monumental landscape," and through reconfiguring these images he challenges the representations of "Indianness" found in national statuary and commercial buildings throughout North America. The focal point of my analysis is an installation titled *What's the Point?* which reimagines the statue of the Indian "Scout" originally located at the feet of the Champlain Monument in Ottawa. (See Figure 12.3.)

FIGURE 12.3 ▦ The Indian "Scout" in its original location at the Champlain Monument.

Photo by Jeff Thomas

In 1996 the Scout was the focus of a protest by the Assembly of First Nations (AFN), who objected to the statue's subservient position in relation to Champlain. After extended public debate, the Indian monument was moved to a garden of Indigenous flowers in Major's Hill Park across from Parliament Hill. However, despite the AFN's hopes that the Scout's new location could rehabilitate the statue, this new site represents an equally problematic view of the "Native" as a "natural" representation of the *human* life of the continent. Most importantly, the National Capital Commission declined to put any marker at the new site that might trace the historic relationship of the Scout to the Champlain monument. This failure to acknowledge the Scout's history erases the colonial legacy shaping representations of Indianness—which is exactly the problem the AFN highlighted in the first place.

Thomas' exhibit was also a response to the visual problematics signified by the Scout. However, Thomas suggested a mode of viewing public art that did not require the Scout to be censored or relocated. His images attempt to reconfigure, rather than censor or relocate, monuments that echo historical inequities. In *What's the Point?* Thomas presents the Scout in five photographs that provide a 360-degree view of his chiselled shoulders, bulging biceps, rippling chest muscles, and revealing loincloth. The sculpture's well-muscled form is consistent with historic images of the "Noble Savage," an impression reinforced through

Thomas' juxtaposition of these images with contemporary Harlequin romance novels. Figure 12.4 suggests how each image was juxtaposed with a Harlequin book cover.[6] The last component of the diorama is the addition of text taken from the Harlequin novels, which accentuates the erotics both in the novels and in the photographic images.

FIGURE 12.4 ■ My Brave Indian: a Harlequin romance cover alongside the Indian "Scout" in Ottawa, ON.

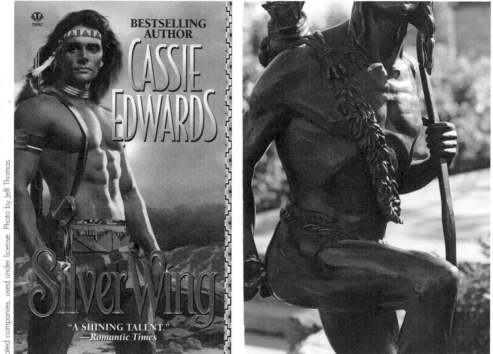

In this threefold composition, Thomas highlights how both historic statues and popular culture representations of the Indian present a *primitivized* masculinity. In both Thomas' photographs and in the novel's pictures and text, it is the eroticized elements of "Indianness" that are particularly available for the viewer's attention. For instance, under an image of the Scout's magnificent chest we read: "Her eyes focused on each portion of his copper body that shone back at her in the moonlight. His bare bronze chest swollen with pride." In another text we are informed that "... his breechcloth lifted from his long muscled legs in the gentle breeze." And the series continues: "He was a man of thick muscle, broad shoulders, and a chiseled face of nobility and intelligence," and "it was his

6   All these novels were available from the Chapters bookstore in Ottawa in the spring of 2000.

eyes that mesmerized her most. They were dark and deep like midnight, inviting yet dangerous. Seeing how enchanted she was by his difference made Bold Wolf's chest swell with pride."[7] The visual meanings suggested by these novels imply that for the imagined white, female reader the well-muscled Indigenous male signifies a twin set of dangers and desires: namely the fear of a raw and potentially violent sexual primitivism together with the lure of erotic pleasure. No doubt the narrative tension generated by these images generates precisely the kind of unstable excitement that fuels the popularity of these novels in the first place. Thus the Indigenous protagonist stands in for a naturalness that seems to come before the "artifice" of "civilization." Just as in Ernest Thompson Seton's Council Ring, the Disney film *Pocahontas*, and the recent blockbuster *Avatar*, these novels present Indians who are valorized as closer to a "free" existence in nature.

However, in this most popular of modern incarnations, the Harlequin novels accentuate the Indians' primitive power precisely in order to construct the visual field through which white female protagonists can attain a fantasy of unfettered sexual fulfillment and psychic escape. But what of the method Thomas uses to draw viewers into exploring these images? *What's the Point?* implies a critique of the primitivization of Indigenous men—but it also *intensifies* the specifically erotic aspects of this representation in ways that ask us to consider how our obsession with the body of the Indigenous **other** continues into the present moment. Here Thomas' juxtaposition of the statue's well-muscled physique with the contemporary Harlequin novels plays white imaginings of "Indianness" back against themselves. Indeed, the artist's humorous approach pokes fun at the earnest sobriety and anxious guilt that has often characterized Canadian responses to this colonial legacy (Ryan, 1999). Consequently, Thomas' photographs do not simply reveal public statues as an embarrassing relic of an imperial past. Instead, his images invite us to see once again, and to see differently, how ideas about race, the body, and the nation are reproduced in myriad everyday places from pulp novels to public art.

The juxtaposition of national statues with contemporary images from popular culture suggests that in portraits of Indigenous men it is usually the racial balance of power that remains stuck in colonial patterns. Indeed, most representations of Indigenous people present bodies that seem perpetually tamed, whether they are subdued at the feet of Champlain, tokenized as the generic Indian in summer camps, or acting as a spectacularized fantasy in Harlequin novels. Thomas' juxtaposition of these images invites viewers to consider how the sexualized Indian body has rarely been represented in ways that assume its own subjective or erotic autonomy. Of course, some might observe that in Hollywood westerns, Indians were seen to operate through an erotics of violence that resulted in constant threats to white women. But these seemingly contradictory images (of tame and savage Indians) are mutually reinforcing poles of the same binary. Whether Indians were portrayed as "bloodthirsty" *or* "noble" they were always primitivized, and have rarely been depicted in ways that portray them exercising a sense of legitimate agency for their own ends.

---

7   Ernest Thompson Seton's "Indian" name within the Woodcraft movement was Black Wolf.

If Thomas' photographic juxtapositions highlight the forms of Indian play implicit in everything from national statuary to popular fiction, they do so in ways that make explicit the sexual undercurrents in all of these representations. Similarly, while the versions of Indian play enacted at traditional Ontario summer camps have always kept overt references to sex at a discreet distance, camp participants nevertheless used "Indianness" to construct a "wild" and unfettered connection to their own "savage" core. And as contemporary Harlequin novels make clear, many women also rely on these stereotypes for the sexual and romantic fantasies that fuel their psychic escape. In Thomas' installation the threefold juxtapositions of the Scout statue, Harlequin romance novels, and text invite viewers to consider the continuing salience of Indian play. Indeed, the exhibit reappropriates these images not in order to censor them, but rather to make them available for comment. Thus Thomas asks: *What is the point?*

"THE REST" IN THE "WEST"

Ideas about the imaginary Indian popularized in sites that range from Hollywood films to Ontario summer camps to Harlequin romance novels are what Stuart Hall would call **regimes of truth** through which Western society has imagined Indigenous people and itself anew. In this context Indigenous people are "the rest" *within* Western nation states: those who are imagined as "primitive others" and against whom Euro-Canadians have measured themselves as being among the most "civilized" nations on Earth. What is important to remember, however, is that Canada and the United States are not "postcolonial" nations. For in many parts of North America, Indigenous people continue to dispute the conditions under which Europeans settled the land and these debates highlight deep and ongoing inequalities.

Throughout this chapter I have explored how a variety of engagements with "Indian play" challenge ideas about the benign nature of Canadian identity. As Philip Deloria has commented, many "Indian performance options" have been notable for the ways they contribute to the profoundly creative process through which American and, I argue, Canadian, citizens imagine *themselves* and their country anew. Yet the shifting terrain of meanings associated with these images suggests that it is never possible to assume they are received in the ways intended. Freud suggests that the ability to mimic is tied to power, and that people use this form of play to deal with powerful and overwhelming situations. Thus mimicry allows them to "abrogate the strength of the impression and … make themselves master of the situation" (quoted in Hill, 2000: 25). In the context of Canadians' largely unacknowledged imperial history, the continuing draw to mimetic forms of "Indian play" has most often worked to assure white citizens of their own sense of authentic belonging while in the same moment providing an uncanny reminder of the colonial legacy. Yet the workings of mimicry are still more complex than this. For Indigenous people have also engaged this legacy, though from the perspective of very different histories and for their own distinct purposes. The work of Jeff Thomas provides an example of the way artists can reappropriate the legacies of "Indianness" and create new interpretations in just the places we would least expect (Hill, 2000).

This chapter has focused on reassessing "taken-for-granted" images of Indianness, ones that easily allow most Canadians to imagine that our national legacy in relation to Indigenous people is relatively benign. Yet there are also moments when the stakes involved in this colonial relationship appear in stark relief. I was back in Garden River First Nation in the spring of 2010, this time to write about a new play called *Reservations* developed by a mixed team of Indigenous and non-Indigenous youth in collaboration with Debajehmujig Theatre Group on Manitoulin Island (*Debajehmujig* means "storytellers" in the Cree and Ojibwa languages). This year the production highlighted the conflict sparked by the new Harmonized Goods and Services Tax (HST). Local tensions between Indigenous and non-Indigenous Canadians were highlighted in May 2010 when the GRFN band council erected a sign on the side of the Trans-Canada Highway just outside the reserve notifying travellers they would be charged a poll tax for crossing Anishinaabec land if the HST was levied against status Indigenous people—an action they argue contravenes treaty rights. Within 24 hours vandals had retaliated by spraypainting the sign with their own message: on one side "White Power" and on the other "This mean war" (Figure 12.5). During this same period local Indigenous children in elementary school reported being harassed by white boys, who were also responding to conflict regarding the HST. Their taunts: "Why don't we just kill all the Indians?"[8]

FIGURE 12.5 ■ "WHITE POWER" and "THIS MEANS WAR": Graffiti on a sign erected by Garden River First Nation just outside the reserve in 2010.

Photo by Margot Francis

Photo by Margot Francis

---

8 Teddy Syrette, interview with the author, August 2010.

These actions highlight the stakes implicit in the colonial relationship, for racist graffiti and school bullying are not simply the result of random acts by individuals with no relationship to the larger structure of Canadian society. Instead, actions like these make explicit the ideological stakes in Canada's imperial history. In this context it is particularly crucial, as Lawrence and Dua argue, "to acknowledge that we all share the same land base and yet to question the differential terms on which it is occupied." Indeed, it is only our contemporary negation of this differential history that allows many of us not to see the "colonial project that is taking place around us" (Lawrence & Dua, 2005: 124). This chapter has brought together a fusion of art and analysis to highlight the stakes involved in discourses about the imaginary Indian. I hope this critique will contribute to new forms of solidarity to challenge these same discourses.

STUDY QUESTIONS

1. What are the connections and differences between the ways the concept of the "Noble Savage" is understood in Seton's writings and the ways Jeff Thomas takes up the same concept in his artwork?

2. What aspects of Jeff Thomas' artwork are most striking for you? How would you answer the question articulated in the title for this piece, *What's the Point*?

3. Are there connections between the kinds of "Indian play" covered in this chapter and contemporary films such as *Avatar*? How are the representation of Euro–North American peoples and Indigenous peoples similar, and how might they differ?

4. How do the practices of "Indian play" highlighted in this chapter relate to Indigenous peoples within a context of contemporary colonialism?

5. What stereotypes of "Indianness" have been part of your experience? Was "Indian play" ever a part of your childhood? Has reading this chapter changed any of your perceptions?

EXERCISES

1. Survey friends, relatives, and acquaintances of varying ages about their summer camp experiences. Did they experience any of the "Indian play" activities listed in the chapter? Or, if they travelled to provincial or national parks, were images of "Indianness" a taken-for-granted aspect of the park architecture? Alternatively, when they were travelling outside Canada, were these images part of how Canada represents itself in airport gift shops? How do images of the "imaginary Indian" affect all our perceptions of Indigenous people? Have representations of Indigenous people changed over time? Do the discussions from this survey confirm or change your perception of the ideas in this chapter?

2. Choose one area from the following list to explore how Indigenous people are being portrayed or discussed: Hollywood film; television; magazines; newspapers; advertising; comic books, graphic, and mass-market novels; public art; outdoor/nature organizations; and educational materials and textbooks.

3. Are references to Indigenous people hard to find? Are current issues such as land treaty negotiations, health and poverty, and the rights of Indigenous peoples referred to or discussed? What stereotypes appear? Are there representations of the "Noble Savage" (or the Bloodthirsty Savage), the Primitive who is closer to Nature, the Lazy Drunk Freeloader, or a primitivized sexuality? Who created the images and what version of history is being presented? Which are references to Imaginary Indians and which represent genuine Indigenous realities? How do you tell the difference? Do the images feel different to you than they would have before reading the chapter?

REFERENCES

Andrews, Isabel. 1975. Indian protest against starvation: The Yellow Calf incident of 1884. *Saskatchewan History* XXVIII(2) (Spring 1975): 41–51.

Back, Brian. 1983. *The Keewaydin Way: A Portrait 1893–1983.* Temagami, ON: Keewaydin Camp, Ltd.

Bederman, Gail. 1995. *Manliness and Civilization: A Cultural History of Gender and Race in the United States, 1880–1917.* Chicago: University of Chicago Press.

Berkhofer, Robert F. Jr. 1978. *The White Man's Indian: Images of the American Indian from Columbus to the Present.* New York: Alfred A. Knopf.

Bly, Robert. 1992. *Iron John: A Book About Men.* New York: Vintage.

Coalition for the Advancement of Indigenous Studies. 2008. *Learning About Walking in Beauty: Placing Indigenous Perspectives in Canadian Classrooms.* http://www.crr.ca/index2.php?option=com_content&do_pdf=1&id=252, accessed January 29, 2011.

Deloria, Philip. 1998. *Playing Indian.* New Haven; London: Yale University Press.

Eastaugh, W. J. 1968. *Indian Council Ring.* Toronto: Taylor Statten Camps. 23–2.

Foucault, M. 1978. *The History of Sexuality.* R. Hurley, trans. Penguin Books.

Foucault, M. 1980. Body/power *and* Truth and power. In C. Gordon, ed., *Michel Foucault: Power/Knowledge.* UK: Harvester.

Francis, Daniel. 1992. *The Imaginary Indian: The Image of the Indian in Canadian Culture.* Vancouver, BC: Arsenal Pulp Press.

Goldberg, David Theo. 1993. *Racist Culture: Philosophy and the Politics of Meaning.* Oxford UK; Cambridge, MA: Blackwell.

Hamilton, Ty. 2001. The representation and appropriation of indigenous cultures at Ontario summer camps. Unpublished undergraduate thesis, McMaster University, submitted April 13th, 2001. Used with permission of the author.

Hill, Richard William. 2000. Drag racing: Dressing up (and messing up) white in contemporary First Nations art. *Fuse Magazine* 23(4): 18–27.

Keller, Betty. 1984. *Black Wolf: The Life of Ernest Thompson Seton.* Vancouver; Toronto: Douglas & McIntyre.

Latimer, John. 1999. *Maker of Men: The Kilcoo Story.* Saint-Laurent, QC: Transcontinental Printing.

Lawrence, Bonita. 2004. *Real Indians and Others: Mixed-Blood Urban Native Peoples and Indigenous Nationhood.* Vancouver: UBC Press. See esp. 25–104.

Lawrence, Bonita, and Ena Dua. 2005. Decolonizing antiracism. *Social Justice* 32(4): 120–143.

Lundell, Liz, ed. 2000. *Fires of Friendship: Eighty Years of the Taylor Statten Camps.* Compiled from contributions from the Alumni. Toronto: Taylor Statten Books. 23.

McNab, David T. 2009. *No Place for Fairness: Indigenous Land Rights and Policy in the Bear Island Case and Beyond.* Kingston: McGill-Queen's University Press.

Miller, J. R. 1996. *Shingwauk's Vision: A History of Indigenous Residential Schools.* Toronto: University Press.

Miller, J. R. 2004. *Reflections on Native–Newcomer Relations: Selected Essays.* Toronto: University Press. See esp. 107–170.

Milloy, John. 1999. *A National Crime: The Canadian Government and the Residential School System—1879 to 1986.* Winnipeg: University of Manitoba Press. See esp. Chapter 5.

Morrison, Toni. 1993. *Playing in the Dark: Whiteness and the Literary Imagination.* New York: Vintage Books.

Reimers, Frederick. 2003. The Keewaydin way: At 110 years old Keewaydin shows that canoe camps are still at the heart of paddling culture. *Paddler Magazine* 28(3) (May/June).

Renato, Rosaldo. 1989. *Culture and Truth: The Re-making of Social Analysis.* Boston: Beacon Press. 68–87.

Richter, Daniel K. 1992. *The Ordeal of the Longhouse: The Peoples of the Iroquois League in the Era of European Colonization.* Chapel Hill, NC: University of North Carolina Press. 42–44.

Rosenthal, Michael. 1986. *The Character Factory: Baden-Powell and the Origins of the Boy Scout Movement.* New York: Pantheon Books. 65.

Ryan, Allan J. 1999. *The Trickster Shift: Humour and Irony in Contemporary Native Art.* Vancouver: UBC Press; Seattle: University of Washington Press. 3–12.

Seton, Ernest Thompson. 1902. *The Birch Bark Roll of Woodcraft.* New York: Brieger Press, Inc. 7–10.

Seton, Ernest Thompson. 1903. *How to Play Indian.* Philadelphia: Curtis Publishing Company.

Smith, P. C. 1995. Ghost in the machine. *Aperture* 139 (Summer): 6–9.

Stasiulis, Daiva, and Radha Jhappan. 1995. The fractious politics of a settler society: Canada. In Daiva Stasiulis and Nira Yuval-Davis, eds., *Unsettling Settler Societies: Articulations of Gender, Race, Ethnicity and Class.* London: Sage Publications. 95–131.

Sugden, John. 1998. *Tecumseh: A Life.* New York: Henry Holt & Co.

Swann, Brian, and Arnold Krupat, eds. 1987. *Recovering the Word: Essays on Native American Literature*. Berkeley: University of California Press.

Titley, Brian. 1993. Hayter Reed and Indian administration in the West. In R. C. Macleod, ed., *Swords and Ploughshares: War and Agriculture in Western Canada*. Edmonton: The University of Alberta Press. 109–148.

Tremblay, Gail. 1993. Constructing images, constructing reality: American Indian photography and representation. *Views*, Winter. 8–13.

United Nations, Department of Economic and Social Affairs, Division for Social Policy and Development, Secretariat of the Permanent Forum on Indigenous Issues. 2006. International Expert Group meeting on the Millennium Development Goals, Indigenous Participation and Good Governance, New York, January 11–13. http://www.un.org/esa/socdev/unpfii/documents/workshop_MDG_chartrand.doc, accessed January 1, 2008.

Wall, Sharon. 2005. Totem poles, teepees, and token traditions: "Playing Indian" at Ontario summer camps, 1920–1955. *The Canadian Historical Review* 86(3) (September 2005): 513–544.

White, Hayden. 1978. *Tropics of Discourse: Essays in Cultural Criticism*. Baltimore; London: Johns Hopkins University Press.

COFFEE AND COMMODITY FETISHISM

13

Gavin Fridell *Trent University*

Every day, millions of consumers throughout the world drink hundreds of millions of cups of coffee. The vast majority of these consumers live in North America and Europe, where coffee has become a core component of daily diets and social rituals. In Canada, 81 percent of Canadian adults drink an average of 2.6 cups per day, making coffee the most popular adult beverage in the country (aside from tap water) (Coffee Association of Canada, 2003). Yet, despite its immense popularity, not a single coffee bean is or can be grown in the temperate climate of Canada or any other Northern Hemisphere country. All coffee beans are produced in the tropical regions of Latin America, Africa, and Asia areas that consume the least amount of the world's coffee. Just as millions of Northern consumers wake up every day and grab a cup of coffee on their way to work, so do millions of small farmers and rural labourers in the Southern Hemisphere wake up and go to work with the task of growing, harvesting, and processing the world's coffee beans. Coffee is the second most valuable legally exported commodity by the South, after oil, and provides a livelihood for around 25 million coffee-producing families. Over 70 percent of the world's coffee comes from small farms of less than 10 hectares (Fridell, 2007; Oxfam International, 2002). It is the quintessential global **commodity**, linking the daily routine of millions of Northern consumers and Southern producers who live thousands of kilometres apart through a complex web of social, economic, cultural, and political relations.

It is not merely geographic distance or a vast array of linguistic and cultural traditions that separate coffee consumers from producers, but highly unequal disparities in wealth and power. While there are major differences between coffee-producing countries in the South, coffee tends to be produced in poorer countries among the poor and more marginalized rural communities by small-scale farmers or highly exploited, low-paid workers. This contrasts sharply with the typical middle-class coffee consumer in rich Northern countries. While the life expectancy for the average Canadian in 2006 was 80 years, in coffee-dependent Guatemala it was 70 years and in Burundi it was 49 years. Similarly, while the GDP per capita (in purchasing power parity) was $36,687 in Canada, it was only $4,311 in Guatemala and $333 in Burundi (UNDP, 2008). Thus, the production and consumption ends of the global coffee industry are composed of highly unequal participants, a situation reproduced through the operations of the global coffee market itself. For example, Oxfam International (2002) has calculated that the average Southern coffee farmer at the start of the millennium was receiving around $0.14 per kilogram for green coffee beans that were then transported, roasted, and sold by companies in the North for

FIGURE 13.1 ▨ Coffee and commodity fetishism. Even though you can't see it, every cup of coffee has the labour of the grower within it.

Source: oku/Shutterstock (coffee cup); haak78/Shutterstock (grower's hand in coffee beans)

upwards of $26.40 per kilogram, representing a price inflation of more than 7,000 percent; most of the wealth created by the global coffee industry would appear to go firmly into the hands of Northern companies.

The typical coffee consumer might be forgiven for being unaware of these wealth disparities and how they are reproduced by the everyday operations of the global coffee market. After all, Northern-based coffee corporations hardly put the poor working and living conditions of coffee farmers and workers at the heart of their marketing strategies. Instead, they spend tens of millions of dollars a year on massive advertising campaigns designed to skirt these issues in favour of winning consumer loyalties by promoting upbeat, sexy images of the coffee-drinking lifestyle (Oxfam International, 2002). Moreover, the very nature of the global market serves to mask the relationship between producers and consumers and prevent flows of feedback and accountability between them. When consumers survey various coffee options at a supermarket chain store, the products stacked on the shelves appear as independent, abstract commodities without connection to the workers who actually produced them. Similarly, thousands of kilometres away, coffee producers work hard each day to harvest a coffee crop that will ultimately be consumed by people they will never meet. On both ends of the coffee chain, people's knowledge of the lives of those who consume what others produce and those who produce what others consume remains obscure and mediated by the market. In the 19th century, Karl Marx famously coined the term **commodity fetishism** to refer to this condition of modern capitalism: the commodity itself becomes fetishized as an independent object with its own intrinsic value—a "$10 bag of coffee"—rather than being the end result of the work of other people (Bernstein & Campling, 2006a, 2006b; Hudson & Hudson, 2003; Princen, Maniates, & Conca, 2002; Marx, 1978).

Intertwined with the market relationships that underpin commodity fetishism are multiple taken-for-granted, everyday practices which, in a Foucauldian sense, embed the seemingly simple and direct act of drinking a "cup of joe" in complex power relations around common discourses and images (such as nationalism, gender, and domesticity) and the normalization of particular practices that sustain and reproduce material conditions of inequality. What the everyday "cup of joe" has served to obscure, academics, social justice activists, and development workers involved in the coffee industry have long worked to reveal by uncovering and challenging the accepted "normal" social organization that reproduces coffee consumption and production daily.

Coffee is a complex commodity produced through the operations of an international social division of labour that has a long and often painful history, interwoven with the histories of slavery and **colonialism**, from the late 15th century to the 20th, during which time Western European nations forcibly colonized much of what are today independent nation states in the global South. These social and historical processes are the focus of this chapter, which examines coffee as a commodity through an assessment of both the production and consumption ends of the global coffee chain. Taking a Marxian lens, we see power relations embedded in the exercise of economic and political power from the dominant classes. The global coffee elite, who own the transnational coffee companies or the giant plantations in the South, possess significant power over all other participants in the coffee chain through their control of coffee income, massive marketing budgets, and overall economic might. This notion of power is intertwined with a Foucauldian approach, focused on the power of dominant discourses and representations, and a post-colonial approach, which highlights the historical power of the West to define the norms, values, and assumptions around the coffee industry in a way which serves to obscure the inequalities in the industry, making them look like the outcome of a natural global hierarchy, rather than historical conflict.

This chapter seeks to make visible these power relations which are central to our everyday social world. Section 1 discusses coffee production in the South and examines the highly unequal social relations of production that form of the base for the entire coffee industry. Section 2 analyzes coffee consumption in the North, the social rituals and symbolic identities associated with coffee drinking, and the labour relations on the Northern side of the coffee chain. Finally, Section 3 assesses various "coffee battles" to readjust global inequality in the coffee chain.

1. COFFEE PRODUCTION AND POWER

Coffee beans have not always been global commodities with literally billions of kilograms produced and exported each year. Coffee only emerged as a significant world trade commodity alongside the development of the world system, which first took root in the late 15th and early 16th century on the heels of European colonial expansion. Prior to this, coffee was predominately used in Abyssinia (now Ethiopia), the birthplace of coffee, where it was cultivated for a variety of purposes and was integral to Abyssinian culture. It was also traded by Arab merchants on a relatively minor scale for ceremonial or medicinal use and, beginning in the 15th century, it gained increasing popularity among intellectuals and merchants in the Islamic world as an alternative stimulant to alcohol, which was prohibited by Islamic law (Dicum & Luttinger, 1999; Pendergrast, 1999; Topik, 1998).

It was European colonial expansion that set in motion the process by which coffee, as well as other tropical crops like sugar, tea, bananas, and cocoa, would become major global commodities. Finding themselves squeezed between limited agricultural productivity, the high costs of constant warfare, and the rising tide of peasant resistance and rebellion, Western Europe's feudal elite sought to resolve the crisis by expanding beyond European frontiers and seizing new resources: agricultural land, gold, silver, and slaves. In the process, highly concentrated states based on coalitions between political elites and the merchant classes were formed which would come to dominate the evolving world system. The Spanish and Portuguese Empires originally took the lead in this process in the 15th and 16th centuries, during which time they colonized most of Latin America, followed by the rise of the Dutch in the 17th century and the British and French Empires in the 18th and 19th centuries (Wolf, 1997).

As the Spanish and Portuguese were primarily concerned with gold, silver, and sugar, it was not until the second half of the 17th century that coffee began to emerge as a significant traded commodity when the Dutch initiated coffee growing in the colonies of Ceylon, Java, Sumatra, Celebes, Timor, Bali, and other islands of the East Indies. To find labour to produce the coffee beans, the Dutch brutally enslaved the native populations of the conquered territories. The intense exploitation of slave labour allowed the Dutch to sell the coffee beans cheaply on European markets, which sparked increasing demand, thereby leading to expanded production and the growing use of slaves. In the 18th century, the rising demand for coffee attracted the interest of other colonial powers and provided further impetus to the Atlantic slave trade, which had originally been initiated by the Portuguese for the production of sugar in the Caribbean. From 1701 to 1810, the colonial powers of Europe, led by the British and the French, forcibly exported over six million slaves from Africa, over three-and-a-half times the number exported during the previous two-and-a-half centuries. In 1771, the tiny French colony of Saint Domingue (today Haiti) supplied half the world's coffee and had nearly 500,000 slaves (Dicum & Luttinger, 1999; Pendergrast, 1999; Topik, 1998; Wolf, 1997; Mintz, 1985).

In the 19th century, the nature of the world coffee trade changed fundamentally. In Europe, the growth and expansion of industrial capitalism gave way to an unprecedented increase in demand for coffee and other tropical crops to meet the consumption needs of the growing working class. Coffee regions became increasingly integrated into the international capitalist economy and previous forms of agricultural production, which frequently involved largely self-sufficient economic units, big or small, were replaced by monoculture plantations dependent on the production of goods for sale on the international market (Fridell, 2007; Wolf, 1997). During this same time, many major coffee-producing regions gained political independence from the colonial powers—much of Latin America, which emerged as the world's lead coffee-producing region in the 19th century, gained formal independence from Spain and Portugal in the 1820s. Neither the expansion of capitalism nor the emergence of national independence, however, altered the brutal working and living conditions of coffee workers. In Brazil, the growth of coffee production on giant plantations gave way to a historically unprecedented increase in slave imports from 1800 to 1850, by which time Brazil produced nearly half of the world's coffee supply and had a slave population of over two million people (Pendergrast, 1999; Dicum & Luttinger, 1999; Topik, 1998). In Central America, where many indigenous populations were self-sufficient and did not need or desire waged labour on coffee plantations, the political and economic elite frequently compelled them into debt peonage or onerous tenant relations, stripped them of their communal lands, and forced them to work on coffee plantations under the barrel of a gun (McCreery, 2003; Topik, 1998; Weeks, 1985).

While forced labour was encouraged by the spread of the coffee economy in Latin America, smallholder cultivation also emerged as a major source of coffee production. The widespread existence of communities with claims to the land prior to the coffee boom gave way to a mixture of smallholder farms and large-scale plantations, with the former often providing a major source of forced and waged labour for the latter (Samper, 1994). Throughout the 20th century, the pendulum swung in favour of waged labour, although under extremely exploitative conditions. The gross inequalities in most coffee regions between the wealthy coffee elite and the mass of poor smallholders and rural workers frequently gave way to resistance, rebellion, or calls for reform, which the political and economic elite often met with brutal suppression. Perhaps one of the most famous examples of this was Guatemala's radical reformist project from 1944 to 1954, the "Ten Years of Spring." When democratically elected President Jacobo Arbenz attempted a land redistribution to address the country's grossly unequal land ownership—72 percent of the country's agricultural land was controlled by slightly more than 2 percent of the farms—he was overthrown by a CIA-backed coup in 1954 and replaced by an authoritarian regime that rolled back the redistribution and set the country down a path of decades of brutal dictatorship, underdevelopment, and civil war (Handy, 1994; Weeks, 1985).

Today, despite a changing political landscape in several major coffee countries, coffee workers continue to toil at the very bottom of a highly unequal global class hierarchy. Workers must compete in highly saturated labour markets for seasonal jobs that pay near-starvation wages under generally deplorable conditions, especially women and indigenous people. In Guatemala, for example, the government considers the minimum wage to cover only 40 percent of basic needs. Yet even this low wage is considered too high by the coffee elite: a survey of plantations in Guatemala in 2000 found that none of them paid the country's minimum wage and a majority did not even pay half the minimum wage. Small-scale farmers are not much better off and must struggle in highly competitive and volatile markets in which they can barely make enough to survive. In many cases, they are forced into bankruptcy or seasonal migration in search of work (Dicum & Luttinger, 1999; Oxfam International, 2002; UNCTAD & IISD, 2003; World Bank, 2003). Journalist David Ransom accurately captures the life of indigenous coffee farmers along the Tambopata river valley in Peru:

> ... if your coffee harvest brings you in less than it costs you, if you have labored for a year without reward, then you will have nothing to pay for treatment for you or your children when sickness strikes, as it invariably does in

places such as this…. The prevailing certainty becomes that if you get sick you die—it's as simple as that. Whether or not you will be able to keep your children in school is doubtful. So there are not enough schools. The cumulative effect of all this continuing year after year, and of having to submit your life entirely to the whims of world coffee prices, is what powerless really means. (Ransom, 2001: 46)

Moving up the social hierarchy from poor farmers and workers are local middlemen, who generally monopolize local transportation and credit and make their profits by buying beans low from small-scale farmers and selling at higher prices to coffee processors. The top of the chain in the South consists of powerful plantation owners, who generally own extensive transportation and processing infrastructure, employ a variety of low-paid workers, have considerable political influence over the state, and possess significant economies of scale allowing them to make profits even under price conditions that can be highly destructive for the livelihoods of smallholders (Fridell, 2007; Talbot, 2004).

Unequal relations of wealth and power do not stop in the South, but rather work their way up to the North through a complex network of **global value chains**: "labour and production process whose end result is a finished commodity" (Bernstein & Campling, 2006a, 2006b; Gereffi & Korzeniewicz, 1994; Gibbon & Ponte, 2005; Talbot, 2004). Along the chain are a series of nodes where the original commodity is transformed, value is added, profits are generated, and states, corporations, and households battle for their share of the wealth. At the global level, the coffee value chain is dominated by transnational trading companies and roaster/distributors, some of whose history goes back over 100 years. These giant corporations exercise a loose and indirect form of governance over the coffee chain through their control of the supply of massive volumes of coffee beans and the "value-added" processes of distribution, packaging, marketing, and retailing. They use their oligopoly control of access to Northern markets to exercise significant power over the entire chain, artificially increasing the gap between the relatively low price for unprocessed green beans paid to Southern farmers and the higher prices paid for roasted coffee beans by consumers on retail markets in the North (Talbot, 2004). The ultimate effect is a vastly unequal process whereby the wealth created through the commodification of the coffee bean is transferred out of the hands of the Southern farmers and workers who first produce the coffee beans and into the hands of powerful transnational traders and roaster/distributors.

2. COFFEE CONSUMPTION AND COMMODIFICATION

Like the production side of coffee, the consumption end has emerged out of a long historical process characterized by unequal wealth and social power. Although it might come as a surprise to the average Northern coffee drinker today, coffee has not always been central, or even minor to the Northern diet. It was not until the 17th century that coffee was introduced into European markets on a significant scale, and not until the 18th century that coffee consumption really began to take off among the masses. Driving this consumption was the emergence of a new industrial working class, initially in England where industrial capitalism first developed. The working class became the basis for a new mass consumer market in cheap everyday goods, such as clothing and food, and coffee was particularly well suited for the new factory setting. Under the new factory system, men, women, and children were employed outside the home for long hours and had little time to prepare and eat meals. Coffee could be prepared quickly, would not spoil easily, provided calories, and could serve as a replacement for alcohol, something welcomed by capitalists concerned about a sober, controllable labour force. As a result, coffee consumption in Europe grew tenfold from 1739 to 1789 (Mintz, 1985; Pendergrast, 1999; Topik, 1998).

Coffee consumption continued to grow in the 19th century and spread throughout Western Europe and North America, spurred on by increasingly lower coffee bean prices. As production ramped up, the international coffee market became swamped with coffee beans, which in turn dragged prices down. Workers in the North responded to these lower prices by increasing their consumption, especially in the United States, which by the end of the century had emerged as the world's largest coffee-consuming country with per capita consumption more than doubling between 1830 and 1860 (Pendergrast, 1999).

Once established as a major commodity, coffee sales continued to expand throughout the 20th century. This process took place amidst the general triumph of a mass consumer society as social life became increasingly dominated by the consumption of mass-produced commodities that were standardized and sold at chain stores part of vast international distribution networks targeting a mass consumer base with increasingly generic tastes. Coffee was well suited to the faced-paced, sometimes chaotic lifestyle of modern capitalism, and could be purchased and drank quickly and easily while on the go. It became one of many mass commodities of "petty consumption," such as the donut, which was cheap and easy to handle, and convenient and affordable to people from a wide range of social classes (Penfold, 2008).

To a significant degree, coffee's place at the heart of the Northern diet was driven by the efforts of large coffee companies that dominated Northern markets and used their economic power to expand coffee consumption by ensuring a steady supply of increasingly cheaper coffee beans and through the use of expensive marketing campaigns designed to persuade people to drink more and more coffee. The use of massive marketing campaigns to engineer consumer tastes toward increased consumption gained growing importance among Northern corporations, especially those in the United States, throughout the 20th century (Dawson, 2003). The coffee industry was no exception. In 1949 General Foods spent a previously-unheard-of $2.5 million advertising Maxwell House coffee. Competitors responded with their own massive marketing campaigns, setting in motion a process which has culminated today with major coffee transnationals spending tens of millions of dollars every year on increasingly larger and larger marketing efforts (Pendergrast, 1999).

Central to the power of Northern coffee companies has been their oligopolistic control over Northern markets. This has given them the power to manipulate prices on the global coffee market and has given them significant advantages over domestic competitors due to their economies of scale, massive marketing budgets, and "brand power," and access to new technologies and innovations (Oxfam International, 2002). During the colonial period, the coffee trade was dominated by large colonial companies which were granted official trade monopolies by their imperialist home states in Europe. Beginning in the 19th century, these companies were broken up and replaced by private corporations who gained more and more control over the import, processing, and distribution of coffee. Today, the five largest roasters in the global coffee industry are responsible for purchasing nearly half of the world's supply of green coffee beans, with Kraft General Foods buying just over 13 percent of the total, followed by Nestlé (13 percent), Sara Lee (10 percent), Procter & Gamble (4 percent), and Tchibo (4 percent) (see text box here) (Dicum & Luttinger, 1999; Oxfam International, 2002; Pendergrast, 1999; Talbot, 2004).

CORPORATE CONCENTRATION IN THE COFFEE INDUSTRY

The tendency toward oligopoly in the coffee industry is perhaps best exemplified by the historical development of the major coffee roaster/distributors within the United States in the 20th century. In 1915, there were over 3,500 roasters in the United States. As these companies grew, competition between them for market shares heated up, and they adopted increasingly expensive national advertising strategies or cost-cutting measures to enhance their competitiveness. Such pressures sparked a series of mergers, bankruptcies, and acquisitions. By 1945, the number of roasters in the United States had dropped to only 1,500. By the late 1950s, it had declined to 850, and the five biggest roasters—General Foods, Standard Brands, Folger's, Hills Brothers, and A&P—accounted for well over 40 percent of the U.S. coffee market. In 1965, there remained only 240 roasters in the United States, and of them the top eight accounted for 75 percent of all coffee sales (Dicum & Luttinger, 1999; Pendergrast, 1999).

These patterns have persisted until the present day, as major coffee roasters have become increasingly transnational. During the 1980s, the Swiss giant Nestlé made a bold move to increase its market share in North America, buying up several U.S. coffee companies, along with the major Canadian roaster, Goodhost. In 1985, the giant tobacco transnational corporation Philip Morris, seeking to diversify into the agro-food industry, bought General Foods for $5.8 billion, which it later merged with Kraft Foods in 1988. Not to be outdone, in 1999 the Dutch corporation Sara Lee bought Chock Full o' Nuts, the fourth-largest coffee company in the United States, as well as several other U.S. coffee companies. By the start of the new millennium, just a handful of roasters dominated the global coffee industry, with the four largest—Kraft General Foods, Nestlé, Sara Lee, and Procter & Gamble—each having coffee brands worth $1 billion or more in annual sales.

Sources: Dicum and Luttinger, 1999; Oxfam International, 2002; Pendergrast, 1999: 345–366; Talbot, 2004: 103–104.

Given their enormous size, these coffee giants possess significant political, economic, and cultural power which they have used to make coffee the common drink that it is today. At the same time, there are intrinsic qualities to the coffee bean which makes it, in its own right, very desirable to consumers. The greatest of these qualities is the fact that coffee is a drug. Coffee contains caffeine, a stimulant that acts on the brain and temporarily provides energy and, most famously, helps to keep people awake. Consequently, coffee has generally been accorded a more positive place in society than other stimulants, such as alcohol, which can trigger aggressive, idle, or antisocial behaviour. Yet coffee consumption has several undesirable effects: caffeine can make people irritable, upset their digestive systems, and cause dehydration; withdrawal from regular consumption can come with headaches, lack of awareness, and short-temperedness (Dicum & Luttinger, 1999; Pendergrast, 1999). Moreover, coffee contains almost no nutritional value, a fact galling not only to health experts, but to environmentalists given the massive resources expended on the growing, processing, and transport of coffee beans on a daily basis.

Coffee is a socially acceptable and legal drug, and the people who consume it on a regular basis are not considered drug addicts. This is in part owing to the fact that coffee's effects are generally milder than many harder drugs, but it is also due to the efforts of coffee promoters to normalize caffeine addiction and coffee rituals and integrate them into our everyday practices. There are many socially acceptable everyday behaviours associated with coffee consumption, perhaps the most famous being the "coffee break," first introduced and promoted by the Pan American Coffee Bureau in 1952 (Pendergrast, 1999). The widespread acceptability of coffee compared to other stimulants is apparent if one tries to imagine colleagues taking a fifteen-minute "beer break" in the middle of the working day. Yet this acceptability cannot be assumed as "natural." Despite coffee's addictive qualities, the coffee industry has had to expend considerable resources waging marketing battles to ensure coffee's preeminence as the ultimate tropical crop. These battles were not always won. In the 1960s, the Pan American Coffee Bureau launched another campaign, this time to win over the youth market in North America, targeting adolescent "Mugmates" and asking them to decorate their coffee mugs. The campaign failed, defeated by more expensive and sophisticated advertising campaigns from the rising stars of the caffeinated beverage industry, Coke and Pepsi, who together in 1965 spent twice as much money on advertising as the coffee industry did. Since that time, it has generally been accepted as the norm in North America for youth and children to drink soft drinks and for adults to drink coffee, though both contain significant quantities of caffeine (Pendergrast, 1999).

While perhaps missing the boat with the 1960s youth campaign, the major players in the coffee industry have more often than not known the right buttons to push to appeal to consumers' beliefs, values, and insecurities. Consumer loyalties and brand identities have been constructed around powerful symbols of gender, class, and nationalism, often reflecting the complex nature of the **politics of representation**. The rapid growth of coffee consumption in the 20th century in North America, for example, occurred in part due to massive advertising campaigns that contained highly gendered messages about the "good wife" who knew how to serve a "good cup of coffee." One particularly telling and cruel cartoon strip advertisement for Chase & Sanborn coffee in 1934 is described vividly by journalist Mark Pendergrast:

> "Here's your coffee, dear," a wife says to her scowling businessman husband over the breakfast table. "I thought we were too old to play mud pies," he growls. Flinging the hot coffee at her, he yells, "What did you put in it this time? Bricks or gunpowder? See how you like it!" She cries, "Oh, you brute! I'm all black and blue." In the final two frames she wears a catcher's mask and holds a shield while offering him a cup of Chase & Sanborn…. Of course the husband loves it. "Take off the mask, darling…. This is too fresh and good to waste a drop" (Pendergrast, 1999: 202).

Aside from the broader story that this ad tells about violence and unequal gender relations in the 1930s, to the housewife at the time it conveyed the message that if you failed at providing a good cup of coffee, you failed at being a good wife and were a deficient woman; quite a bit of social power to bring to bear on the average housewife to compel her to buy a particular brand of coffee!

Class identities have also been drawn into the marketing fray by the coffee industry. Large, mainstream coffee companies, like Tim Hortons, Coffee Time, and Dunkin' Donuts have over time developed their brand images as signifiers of blue-collar, working class, and suburban identity. To blue-collar workers, coffee chain shops have emerged as places where people from all social classes can meet and enjoy the act of consumption, serving as a cheap form of social levelling. In Canada, regular customers often express their devotion to the larger chain stores through what historian Steve Penfold (2008) has termed "donut populism," whereby the coffee shop is imagined as a place for simple, hard-working people, as opposed to more "highbrow" establishments for upper-class snobs. Suburbanites, in contrast, frequently from middle- or upper-class backgrounds, have often expressed their devotion to mainstream chain stores in opposition to the culture of big urban centres and demonstrated "a sense of ironic pride in the lack of cultural alternatives relative to other cities" (Penfold, 2008: 171). In both instances, the major coffee chains have been quick to incorporate these powerful signifiers into their marketing strategies and build on them.

Speciality coffee roasters, whether small or large, have tended to promote their brand images around white-collar, upwardly mobile, urban identities (see McLaren, 2001). To a degree, this is a direct reflection of socioeconomic status: middle- and upper-class consumers tend to be targeted because they have the income required to pay for more expensive coffee. In 2001, the wealthiest 16.2 percent of Canadian households spent 56 percent more money on coffee per person and were 46 percent more likely to shop at food specialty stores than the poorest 43.2 percent of Canadian households (Statistics Canada, 2003). Having more money, of course, does not in itself explain why people in higher-income groups would be willing to spend more on specialty coffee. Writing at the turn of the 20th century, sociologist Thorstein Veblen effectively argued that modern consumption patterns stem from complex social customs that have developed alongside the emergence

FIGURE 13.2 ■ Cartoon strip, Chase & Sanborn coffee, 1934. Coffee companies have often used highly gendered, and in some cases violent, advertisements to sell their coffee beans.

Source: Image courtesy of The Advertising Archives

of industrial society. These customs have increasingly assigned the possession of private property as the single greatest symbol of honour and success. Under these conditions, argued Veblen, the easiest way for one to demonstrate their "pecuniary strength" in relation to others is through **conspicuous consumption**—explicitly wasteful and indulgent consumption. While people from all classes generally struggle to demonstrate some level of conspicuous consumption to stave off feelings of inadequacy, ultimately those who have the greatest wealth are in the best situation to do so (Veblen, 1953: 36–40, 60–80).[1]

---

1   While Thorstein Veblen's concept of "conspicuous consumption" is evoked in this passage to assess the consumer culture of the masses, Michael Dawson has convincingly argued that many have emphasized this perspective to the neglect of Veblen's analysis of class coercion. Of greater concern to Veblen than the "delusions of the masses" was how consumer habits were engineered by corporate marketing projects in the interests of the capitalist class (Dawson, 2003: 11–15).

Thus, when middle- or upper-class consumers purchase specialty coffee in greater quantities than poorer consumers, they are not doing so merely as a result of taste preferences, but as a demonstration of their "pecuniary ability" and class identity.

Nationalism is frequently interwoven with gender and class identity in promoting coffee consumption. The ultimate symbol of this in Canada is Tim Hortons, long a popular signifier of patriotic nationalism. The mythology around the corporation is built into its very name, taken from its founder, Tim Horton, a legendary, all-star professional hockey player born in Northern Ontario, portrayed as being a large, physical player *and* a "gentleman." Homey, manly, folksy, nostalgic notions around hockey in Canada have been appropriated by Tim Hortons and combined with the donut. Through expensive marketing campaigns, Tim Hortons has successfully nurtured and promoted these images, appealing to Canadian nationalism and to a sense of community and tradition in a country that typically has experienced what cultural sociologist Patricia Cormack (2008) characterizes as an awkward and empty "state-sanctioned culture and identity."

The current popularity of Tim Hortons as a symbol of Canadian nationalism might give the impression that this has long been the case. However, donut chain stores did not emerge in Canada until the 1960s, and did not begin to attain popular currency as a cornerstone of Canadian identity until the 1980s, when the media began to make reference to donut shops as the Canadian equivalent of the English pub (Penfold, 2008). Even then, the generic donut shop was taken as a symbol of Canadian identity, not exclusively Tim Hortons. The growing popularity of the donut in the 1980s and 1990s took place during a time when the Canadian national identity was highly fragmented after a series of constitutional conflicts and regional disputes. Due to the lack of a unified Canadian identity, the ubiquitous donut and its mass production and distribution emerged as an "ironic" symbol of a "Canadian mass culture experience" that was imagined as distinct from America. Eventually recognizing this process of nationalist identification, in the late 1990s Tim Hortons moved to take full advantage of it with a massive advertising campaign costing tens of millions of dollars, one which successfully moved the corporation to pride of place among the major symbols of Canadian nationalism (Penfold, 2008).

So successful have the Tim Hortons commercials been over the years that the average Canadian can be forgiven for not knowing that this "Canadian institution" is a massive fast-food chain with more than 3,000 coffee shops (even more than McDonald's in Canada), has revenues of over $2 billion per year, and has been owned by the U.S. corporation Wendy's since 1995 (Cormack, 2008; Glor, 2009). This, combined with the fact that Tim Hortons' cheaper coffee beans have been exported from faraway places where they are grown by low-paid coffee workers and small farmers, has not been enough, states Penfold (2008), to "put a dent in the home-grown donut rhetoric." One might also forget that, despite the company's friendly corporate image, the vast majority of Tim Hortons workers in the North are low-paid and non-unionized, which is common throughout the industry (Dagg, interview with author, Toronto, November 7, 2006).

Northern companies have long relied on low-paid, urban workers to process, roast, package, distribute, and sell coffee as a final product. In the South, coffee-processing facilities owned by Northern-based transnational companies have employed urban workers to clean, de-shell, and classify green beans prior to export. These workers, both historically and today, have generally worked under deplorable conditions for very low wages. In the North, coffee workers have been employed to "add value" to the final product through the roasting, packaging, marketing, and distribution processes. Historically, coffee companies have utilized a variety of methods to keep wages low, such as drawing extensively on piecework and seasonal employment. Women have particularly been targeted by coffee companies, as patriarchal norms have made women especially vulnerable to exploitation. For example, at the turn of the 20th century, women coffee workers employed at a Hills Brothers factory in the United States were paid less than half of their male counterparts' wages, worked ten hours a day six days a week, and were given only one week of vacation per year (Fowler-Salamini, 2002; Pendergrast, 1999). These exploitative working conditions were common throughout the coffee industry at the time.

In the North, general working conditions have improved considerably since the early 20th century. Nevertheless, the coffee industry today continues to compete among those sectors with the lowest wages and least worker benefits. The industry draws much of its labour force from growing "flexible" labour markets, which are based on "precarious" jobs that are low-paying with limited health and pension benefits. These jobs tend to be primarily concentrated among youth and "high risk" groups (such as single mothers, recent immigrants, Aboriginal Canadians, persons with disabilities, and adults with limited education). They also tend to have a significant risk of unemployment—the average annual employee turnover rate for the coffee service sector is around 200 percent, one of the highest of any sector of the economy (Jackson, 2003; Pendergrast, 2002). Major coffee companies have not just taken advantage of these labour market conditions; they have actively worked to create them, by lobbying Northern governments to lower real minimum wages, employment and welfare benefits, and corporate taxes, and aggressively fighting against unionization and workers' rights to collective bargaining.[2] This would generally be the case for most of the major players in the global coffee industry; giant coffee companies spend tens of millions of dollars per year to promote the coffee lifestyle while obscuring the labour conditions under which coffee beans are produced, traded, processed, and sold.

3. COFFEE BATTLES

Just as the global coffee industry has been built around a complex web of unequal social relationships that are reproduced on a daily basis through the actions of millions of participants, so too has resistance to the dominant power relations within the coffee industry formed a central part of the global coffee chain's history and everyday reproduction.

---

2 Philip Morris (owner of Kraft General Foods, the largest coffee company in the world) has the dubious distinction of having been on *Multinational Monitor*'s "Ten Worst Corporations" list in 1988, 1994, 1997, and 2001. See www.multinationalmonitor.org. For an assessment of the poor ethical and labour records of Procter & Gamble and Nestlé, see the Corporate Watch website (www.corporatewatch.org.uk), and for Sara Lee see the Responsible Shopper website (www.responsibleshopper.org/basic.cfm?cusip=803111). For a discussion of Starbucks and its anti-unionization efforts, see Fridell (2007: 225–275)

Battles against inequality and injustice within the coffee industry have taken many forms and have been driven by a variety of actors, including Southern governments, Northern-based nongovernmental organizations, and an array of civil society groups. This section summarizes three examples of resistance: the International Coffee Agreement (ICA); the **fair trade** network; and the Ethiopian trademarking initiative.

The ICA was developed in the postwar era by Southern coffee-producing and Northern coffee-consuming countries in the attempt to combat the **commodity problem** of low, volatile and unpredictable prices for coffee beans (Green, 2005; Lines, 2008). Most major tropical commodities have been vulnerable to the commodity problem, and the coffee market has been particularly susceptible due to the specific nature of coffee cultivation. Unlike many temporal crops, such as wheat and corn, coffee beans are grown on perennial plants that take several years to mature and require significant amounts of fixed capital. The result has been exaggerated boom and bust cycles that have plagued the industry. During a boom, prices are high, and coffee farmers respond by planting more trees. As it takes several years for the new trees to mature and have an impact on the international market, farmers often over-plant. When supply outstrips demand, the bust comes and farmers are left with too many coffee trees. Moreover, they are unable to easily switch to other commodities due to the relatively large amounts of fixed capital they have invested in coffee (Talbot, 2004).

The boom and bust cycle reached crisis proportions in the second half of the 19th century as coffee farmers moved increasingly toward monocrop production and greater dependency on the international market. In 1881, the New York Coffee Exchange was incorporated in an attempt to provide some assurance against risky and unpredictable price swings. On the exchange, a buyer contracts with a seller to purchase a certain amount of coffee at a certain time in the future at a guaranteed price. The Exchange arbitrates disputes and polices trade abuses. It was argued that "real coffee men" would use the contracts as *hedges* against price changes, while speculators would provide *liquidity*. However, rather than providing a degree of price stability, the Exchange has merely escalated the instability of the coffee market as speculators have sought to profit by predicting or manipulating prices (Talbot, 2004; Pendergrast, 1999).

Price instability continued to plague the global coffee industry throughout the first half of the 20th century and, despite pleas from major coffee-producing countries, Northern countries refused to participate in international agreements to address the problem. It was not until 1963 that the ICA was agreed to after Southern countries brought significant pressure to bear on their Northern counterparts. Southern governments feared declining coffee bean prices that led to waning tariff revenues and sparked despair and discontent among millions of small-scale farmers. In the North, particularly the United States, the decision to ratify the ICA was driven by Cold War fears that plummeting prices would drive Southern states into the communist camp (Talbot, 2004). Amid these pressures, the ICA was renewed several times until 1989 when a group of participants, led by the United States, withdrew their support as part of the movement toward **free trade** reforms, which included reducing or eliminating trade barriers and financial controls and devaluing local currencies to make exports more competitive.

The ICA was a quota system signed by all major coffee-producing and consuming countries designed to stabilize and increase coffee prices by holding a certain amount of coffee beans off the global market to avoid oversupply. Export quotas were assigned to all coffee-producing countries on the basis of their historical output, with all beans produced in excess of the quotas held in storage until they could be released into the market without sparking oversupply. Talbot (2004) has calculated that the ICA resulted in higher coffee bean prices, which translated into a significantly greater retention of coffee income in the South. At the same time, the agreement was plagued by many difficulties, including the inability to deal with the structural causes of oversupply, the failure to do little more than dampen the unpredictable swings of the coffee cycle, and the persistent conflict among signatory nations over the quota system. Moreover, the ICA proved to have a minimal effect on how the extra wealth retained in the South was distributed. Countries that pursued social reformist projects that distributed greater resources to small farmers and workers, such as Costa Rica, attained significantly better development gains than countries with highly unequal distributions of land and resources, such as El Salvador, Guatemala, and Brazil (Dicum & Luttinger, 1999; Fridell, 2007). Yet, as Talbot has noted, overall ICA-supported prices provided varying degrees of "trickle-down" improvements to the living standards of broad sectors in the South. In contrast, the two decades since the end of the ICA have been characterized by a widely documented crisis in the Southern coffee industry, entailing extremely low prices, mass layoffs, bankruptcy, migration, and hunger for tens of thousands of poor coffee farmers and workers (Fridell, 2007; Jaffee, 2007; Oxfam International, 2002; Talbot, 2004). In terms of meeting the basic needs of coffee producers, the ICA would appear to have been a more successful model than the unregulated, free trade coffee market that has dominated since.

As the ICA was on the decline in the late 1980s, new, market-driven alternatives emerged that have sought to use consumer power to improve the conditions of workers and farmers in global markets. One such movement has been the fair trade network, which connects small farmers, workers, and craftspeople in the South with organizations and consumers in the North through a system of "fair trade" rules and principles: democratic organization (of cooperatives or unions), no exploitation of child labour, environmental sustainability, a minimum guaranteed price, and social premiums paid to producer communities to build community infrastructure.

Recent research suggests that fair trade has been able to provide important social and economic benefits to certified producers, although with important qualifications (Hudson & Hudson, 2003; Jaffee, 2007; Raynolds, Murray & Wilkinson, 2007). This can been seen in the case of the Union of Indigenous Communities of the Isthmus Region (UCIRI) of Oaxaca, Mexico, one of the most successful fair trade coffee cooperatives in the world (Fridell, 2007). UCIRI members have attained higher incomes and significantly better access to social services through cooperative projects in health care, education, and training. UCIRI has also constructed its own economic infrastructure, such as coffee-processing and transportation facilities, and provided its members with enhanced access to credit, technology, and marketing skills. But its developmental project has not been without its limitations. In one instance, an attempt to diversify UCIRI's efforts into producing clothing for local markets met with bankruptcy due in part to the high costs of providing "fair" social security provisions to employees and tough competition from low-wage textile factories in China. Moreover, despite the cooperative's success in combating extreme misery, UCIRI members still report the persistence of general poverty. Fair trade prices are inadequately low, as they must remain somewhat competitive with lower conventional coffee bean prices dragged down by a saturated global market (Fridell, 2007).

In broader developmental terms, some critics have expressed concern that fair trade promotes continued dependence on tropical commodities and vulnerability to the commodity problem. In response, defendants argue that most small producers in the South do not have viable alternatives to tropical commodity production and those that do still require the support of fair trade standards to assist them in their transition to other economic activities (LeClair, 2002). Other critics have pointed out the limited reach of fair trade due to its dependence on small niche markets. For example, during the peak years of the ICA, its quota system provided higher coffee bean prices (frequently higher than what today is considered the "fair trade" price) to all of the world's 25 million coffee farmer families. In contrast, the fair trade network currently reaches over 670,000 coffee producers, which is an impressive number in its own right, but represents only 3 percent of the world's total coffee families (Fridell, 2006, 2007).

In recent years, concerns have also been raised that much of the growth of fair trade sales is increasingly being driven by multinational corporations and international institutions. Critics charge that these new partners, unlike the founding fair trade organizations, are using token support for fair trade to mask their broader devotion to a **free trade** agenda (Fridell, 2004; Fridell, 2007; Fridell, Hudson & Hudson, 2008; Jaffee, 2007; Raynolds, Murray & Wilkinson, 2007; Reed, 2008). Thus, the World Bank has given increasing support to fair trade while continuing to push ahead in international affairs with the very same free trade agenda that the fair trade network was originally created to

FIGURE 13.3 ▨ Tadesse Meskele, General Manager of Oromia Coffee Farmers Co-operative Union, Ethiopia, visits Planet Bean coffee cooperative in the spring of 2009. "I prefer to sell my product to small roasters like Planet Bean....The price they give is ... far higher than the multinationals."

Courtesy of Bill Barrett

counteract. Similarly, a corporation like Starbucks can gain positive publicity for selling 6 percent of its coffee beans fair trade certified, even while 94 percent of its Southern suppliers remain without fair trade standards and the vast majority of its Northern workers are non-unionized and relatively low-paid. This is in sharp contrast to more traditional fair trade organizations, such as Planet Bean in Guelph, Ontario. Planet Bean is a worker-owned cooperative coffee roaster that sells 100 percent of its beans certified fair trade, pays its suppliers above the fair trade minimum, and is explicitly devoted to promoting fair labour rights and educating consumers about the inequalities in the global coffee industry (Fridell, 2007). Yet organizations like Planet Bean are increasingly crowded out by conventional corporations. Fair trade author and activist Daniel Jaffee (2007) has expressed his concern that growing corporate involvement could ultimately limit the vision and impact of fair trade, making it "irrelevant in the face of the larger effects of corporate-led economic globalization."

In recent years, a new initiative that may hold much promise has emerged to counter the inequalities in the global coffee industry. In 2005, the Ethiopian government began a campaign to trademark its most renowned coffee beans, Sidamo, Harar, and Yirgacheffe. As one of the birthplaces of coffee, the government claimed that Ethiopia and its farmers should have intellectual property rights over the use of the specialty coffee brands and applied for the trademark registrations in the United States and other major coffee nations. Along with these formal legal efforts, the Ethiopian government also sought negotiations with major coffee companies to sign agreements acknowledging the right of Ethiopians to control these brands. Ethiopia is one of the poorest countries in the world, and with coffee farmers making up almost one-fifth of the total population it is highly dependent on coffee income. Despite accounting for only 2 percent of world coffee exports, Ethiopia depends on coffee income for two-thirds of its total export earnings. An Ethiopian coffee worker earns as little as 50 cents for a full day of work, producing beans that are then processed, transported, and sold for upwards of $26 per kilogram on markets in the North (Foek, 2007; Fridell, 2007; Oxfam Australia, 2007).

The trademarking campaign immediately met with fierce resistance in the United States, the world's largest national coffee market. The U.S. National Coffee Association (NCA) brought significant lobbying pressure to bear on the Patent and Trademark Office to reject or delay approval of the patent. Many industry critics pointed the finger at Starbucks, which was particularly threatened by the patent initiative due to its reliance on higher quality specialty coffee beans. Starbucks also rejected initial attempts by Ethiopian officials to begin direct negotiations with the company for an acceptable agreement and launched a media counteroffensive criticizing the patent project. Seeing the Ethiopian government's efforts being stymied, Oxfam began an international campaign in 2006 to pressure Starbucks and other coffee companies to engage with Ethiopia directly and to support the trademarking initiative. After Oxfam was able to mobilize over 96,000 people to contact Starbucks through emails, faxes, phone calls, postcards, and in-store visits, the corporation, fearing damage to its highly coveted brand image, gave in and in 2007 signed an agreement that brought an end to the trademark dispute. Since then, the government has successfully registered its trademarks in the United States, Canada, the European Union, and Japan.

Experts estimate that these trademarks will result a greater share of the retail price and an extra $88 million a year for Ethiopian farmers. These gains in the South, despite the fierce resistance of major coffee corporations, will have relatively little impact on coffee prices in the North: coffee historian Antony Wild estimates that even if Ethiopian farmers were to receive 1,000 percent more for their coffee beans, the price in Northern coffee shop would only rise 5 percent (Foek, 2007; Oxfam Australia, 2007).

The Ethiopian trademarking initiative reveals the importance of the symbolic value of coffee. In trademarking its coffee beans, Ethiopia is not just defending its right to control a part of its cultural heritage, but it is also readjusting power relations within the global coffee industry. Along the coffee value chain, power is distributed not solely on the basis of market share and oligopolistic dominance of roasting and distributing; but it is also distributed on the basis of the ability to define the coffee identity, norms, reference values, and quality standards—"the total coffee drinking experience."[3] In the case of the trademarking campaign, the battle over controlling the **symbolic attributes** (non-material, subjective elements embedded in a commodity's reputation) of Ethiopian beans took the form of a struggle over quality and geographical indicators and who had the right to the extra value that these attributes can garner on Northern markets. Victory in this battle over symbolic rights brings with it very material outcomes, to the tune of millions of dollars a year for Ethiopian coffee farmers. Sociologists Benoit Daviron and Stefano Ponte (2005) believe that future struggles to capture more of the symbolic, non-material attributes of coffee are essential to promoting development in the South, asserting "[a]s long as coffee farmers and their organizations do not control at least parts of this 'immaterial' production, they will be confined to the 'commodity problem.'"

CONCLUSION: COFFEE BUSINESS AS USUAL?

The forms of resistance in the coffee industry discussed above have made significant impacts on the exercise of power and domination along the global value chain. However, many argue that the same overarching power structures, while readjusted, have remained largely intact. Coffee's long and painful history of slavery, **colonialism**, imperialism, and capitalist expansion has embedded the commodity in a complex set of relationships not easily altered. Central to this is an international division of labour in which, in its most basic sense, poor farmers and workers in the South produce the coffee; relatively privileged Northerners consume it; and powerful coffee executives and plantation owners grab most of the wealth. At the bottom of the coffee chain, the life expectancy at birth for the average Ethiopian is a mere 53 years, as against 80 years at the top of the chain in a rich country like Canada. In 2003, the total pay of Starbucks CEO Orin Smith was over $38 million dollars, equivalent to the *combined* annual income of well over 36,000 Ethiopian workers.[4]

---

3   Stefano Ponte, quoted in Foek, 2007. See also Daviron and Ponte, 2005.

4   The total pay, including bonus and exercised stock options, of Starbucks' CEO Orin Smith in 2003 was $38,772,712 (Fridell, 2007: 253). The GDP per capita (PPP US$) in Ethiopia in 2005 was $1,055. That same year, the estimated earned income for females in Ethiopia (in PPP US$) was $796, and for males it was $1,316 (UNDP, 2008).

These inequalities are reproduced on a constant basis through the everyday consumption and production practices of the global coffee industry, a fact that remains largely obscured to the average coffee drinker behind the veil of commodity fetishism. The processes through which coffee became a commodity are clouded by an array of taken-for-granted assumptions about the coffee lifestyle, its various social rituals, and the common Northern presumption that global economic and social inequalities are the outcome of a natural hierarchy. This hierarchy, however, is not "natural"; it is reproduced by people, and therefore can ultimately be changed by people. To do this, however, the basic individual and collective assumptions and behaviours around coffee so central to many people's everyday lives must be interrogated. The power relations embedded in a cup of coffee must be unpacked so that citizens in both the North and the South can make informed decisions about their seemingly innocent coffee practices. This is admittedly a lot to swallow over a morning cup of joe. But, until knowledge about the uneven power relations in the coffee industry become commonplace, business as usual continues.

STUDY QUESTIONS

1. What does the term "commodity fetishism" mean? How can it be applied to coffee?

2. What were some of the dominant trends in the history of coffee in the South? What relevance does this history have to understanding the lives of coffee producers today?

3. In what ways have consumer loyalties and brand identities in the coffee industry been constructed around symbols of gender, class, and nationalism? Was coffee's rise to becoming one of the world's most popular drinks inevitable?

4. If you were having a cup of coffee with Marx or Foucault, what would you talk about when you talk about coffee?

EXERCISES

1. Ask your family and friends where coffee comes from and how it is produced. Do they know what regions of the world are the major coffee-producing ones and how many of the world's farmers are devoted to coffee? Do they know how much they get paid? Ask them why they think coffee farmers are so poor compared to coffee consumers. Do any of their opinions confirm or call into question the ideas laid out in this chapter?

2. Search for the fair trade coffee at a nearby supermarket chain and look for the fair trade coffee brands they have in stock. Look specifically for coffee products that are marked with the "TransFair" symbol. How many of the coffee brands on the shelf are fair trade? How many are corporate products and how many are distributed by small businesses, not-for-profit organizations, or cooperatives? Where are the fair trade products located: with the conventional coffee or in a special organic or fair trade section? On the middle shelves, or the bottom and top ones? (Did you know that corporations pay money to supermarket chains to attain premium shelf space in their stores)?

3. Visit different cafés in your area that have different forms of ownership or business visions, such as a locally owned café, a corporate chain store targeting upscale and urban clientele (Starbucks, Second Cup), and a corporate chain store targeting blue-collar and suburban clientele (Tim Hortons, Dunkin' Donuts, Coffee Time). What sort of imagery and symbolism exist in the different stores? Does the "feel" of the store match your expectations after having read this chapter?

REFERENCES

Bernstein, Henry, and Liam Campling. 2006a. Commodity studies and commodity fetishism I: Trading down. *Journal of Agrarian Change* 6(2): 239–264.

Bernstein, Henry, and Liam Campling. 2006b. Commodity studies and commodity fetishism II: "Profits with principles"? *Journal of Agrarian Change* 6(3): 414–447.

Coffee Association of Canada. 2003. Coffee in Canada: Highlights: 2003 Canadian Coffee Drinking Survey. http://www.coffeeassoc.com/coffeeincanada.htm, accessed June 16, 2009.

Cormack, Patricia. 2008. "True stories" of Canada: Tim Hortons and the branding of national identity. *Cultural Sociology* 2(3): 369–384.

Daviron, Benoit, and Stefano Ponte. 2005. *The Coffee Paradox: Global Markets, Commodity Trade and the Elusive Promise of Development.* London: Zed Books.

Dawson, Michael. 2003. *The Consumer Trap: Big Business Marketing in American Life.* Urbana: University of Illinois Press.

Dicum, Gregory, and Nina Luttinger. 1999. *The Coffee Book: Anatomy of an Industry from Crop to the Last Drop.* New York: The New Press.

Foek, Anton. 2007. Trademarking coffee: Starbucks cuts Ethiopia deal. *CorpWatch*, May 8.

Fowler-Salamini, Heather. 2002. Women coffee sorters confront the mill owners and the Veracruz revolutionary state, 1915–1918. *Journal of Women's History* 14(1): 34–65.

Fridell, Gavin. 2004. The fair trade network in historical perspective. *Canadian Journal of Development Studies* 25(3): 411–428.

Fridell, Gavin. 2006. Fair trade and neoliberalism: Assessing emerging perspectives. *Latin American Perspectives* 33(6): 8–28.

Fridell, Gavin. 2007. *Fair Trade Coffee: The Prospects and Pitfalls of Market-Driven Social Justice.* Toronto: University of Toronto Press.

Fridell, Mara, Ian Hudson, and Mark Hudson. 2008. With friends like these: The corporate response to fair trade coffee. *Review of Radical Political Economics* 40(1): 8–34.

Gereffi, Gary, and Miguel Korzeniewicz, eds. 1994. *Commodity Chains and Global Capitalism.* Westport, CT: Praeger.

Gibbon, P., and S. Ponte. 2005. *Trading Down: Africa, Value Chains, and the Global Economy.* Philadelphia: Temple University Press.

Glor, Jeff. 2009. Donuts to dollars: Our friendly neighbors in Canada are about to wage an international food fight over your morning coffee. *CBS News Sunday Morning*, June 7.

Green, D. 2005. Conspiracy of silence: Old and new directions on commodities. Paper read at Strategic Dialogue on Commodities, Trade, Poverty and Sustainable Development Conference, Faculty of Law, Barcelona, June 13–15.

Handy, Jim. 1994. *Revolution in the Countryside: Rural Conflict and Agrarian Reform in Guatemala, 1944–1954*. Chapel Hill, NC: University of North Carolina Press.

Hudson, Ian, and Mark Hudson. 2003. Removing the veil? Commodity fetishism, fair trade, and the environment. *Organization & Environment* 16(10): 413–430.

Jackson, Andrew. 2003. "Good jobs in good workplaces": Reflections on medium-term labour market challenges. Research Paper #21, Canadian Labour Congress.

Jaffee, Daniel. 2007. *Brewing Justice: Fair Trade Coffee, Sustainability, and Survival*. Berkeley: University of California Press.

LeClair, Mark S. 2002. Fighting the tide: Alternative trade organizations in the era of global free trade. *World Development* 30(6): 949–958.

Lines, Thomas. 2008. *Making Poverty: A History*. London: Zed Books.

Marx, Karl. 1978. *Capital, Volume One*. In R. C. Tucker, ed., *The Marx-Engels Reader*. New York: W. W. Norton & Company. 294–438.

McCreery, David. 2003. Coffee and indigenous labor in Guatemala, 1871–1980. In W. G. Clarence Smith and S. C. Topik, eds., *The Global Coffee Economy in Africa, Asia, and Latin America, 1500–1989*. Cambridge: University Press. 191–208.

McLaren, Leah. 2001. Bland, boring Tim Hortons doesn't belong in my neighbourhood. *Globe and Mail*, July 7.

Mintz, Sidney W. 1985. *Sweetness and Power: The Place of Sugar in Modern History*. New York: Penguin Books.

Oxfam Australia. 2007. Oxfam celebrates win-win outcome for Ethiopian coffee farmers and Starbucks. http://www.oxfam.org.au/media/article.php?id=361, accessed August 14, 2009.

Oxfam International. 2002. *Mugged: Poverty in Your Coffee Cup*. Cowley, Oxford, UK: Oxfam International.

Pendergrast, Mark. 1999. *Uncommon Grounds: The History of Coffee and How It Transformed Our World*. New York: Basic Books.

Pendergrast, Mark. 2002. The Starbucks experience going global. *Tea & Coffee Trade Online* 176(2). http://www.teaandcoffee.net/0202/coffee.htm, accessed January 31, 2011.

Penfold, Steve. 2008. *The Donut: A Canadian History*. Toronto: University of Toronto Press.

Princen, Thomas, Michael Maniates, and Ken Conca, eds. 2002. *Confronting Consumption*. Boston: MIT Press.

Ransom, David. 2001. *The No-Nonsense Guide to Fair Trade*. Toronto: New Internationalist and Between the Lines.

Raynolds, Laura, Douglas Murray, and John Wilkinson. 2007. *Fair Trade: The Challenges of Transforming Globalization*. London: Routledge.

Reed, Darryl. 2008. What do corporations have to do with fair trade? Positive and normative analysis from a value chain perspective. *Journal of Business Ethics* 86, Supplement 1: 3–26.

Samper, Mario K. 1994. Café, trabajo y sociedad en Centroamérica (1870–1930): Una historia común y divergente. In V. H. Acuña Ortega, ed., *Las Repúblicas agroexportadoras: Tomo IV: História General de Centroamérica*. Costa Rica: FLACSO—Programa Costa Rica.

Statistics Canada. 2003. *Food Expenditure in Canada 2001*. Ottawa: Minister of Industry.

Talbot, John M. 2004. *Grounds for Agreement: The Political Economy of the Coffee Commodity Chain*. Oxford: Rowman & Littlefield.

Topik, Steven C. 1998. Coffee. In S. C. Topik and A. Wells, eds., *The Second Conquest of Latin America: Coffee, Henequen, and Oil During the Export Boom*. Austin, TX: University of Texas Press. 37–84.

UNCTAD and IISD (United Nations Conference on Trade and Development & International Institute for Sustainable Development). 2003. Sustainability in the coffee sector: Exploring opportunities for international cooperation. http://www.iisd.org/pdf/2003/sci_coffee_background.pdf, accessed January 31, 2011.

UNDP. 2008. Human development indices: A statistical update. http://hdr.undp.org/en/statistics, accessed June 16, 2009.

Veblen, Thorstein. 1953. *The Theory of the Leisure Class*. New York: Mentor Books.

Weeks, John. 1985. *The Economies of Central America*. New York: Holmes & Meier.

Wolf, Eric R. 1997. *Europe and the People Without History*. Berkeley: University of California Press.

World Bank. 2003. *Poverty in Guatemala*. New York: World Bank.

Tourism: Globalization and the Commodification of Culture

14

Rebecca Raby *Brock University*

Joan Philips *Policy Studies Institute, U.K.*

> Come savour the easy pleasures of our Island life. Relax on an expanse of sparkling white sand, and immerse yourself in our translucent waters. Wrap yourself in warm tropical breezes while partaking of our exotic beverages, before breathtaking orange-red sunsets. Banquets of authentic island food await you. And at night, luxuriate in the best of accommodations. Paradise awaits.

Many Canadian newspapers and vacation websites open the winter season with these kinds of luring words, intent on drawing people to hot, sunny, tourist destinations. Advertisements frequently pose a young, white, lithe woman in a bathing suit reclining on the beach or playing with her family in the water. Such advertisements conjure up images of simplicity and escape that seemingly everyone can experience. In this chapter we take a closer look at the apparently normal, "everyday" practices of tourism and how they tie in to processes of **globalization**, **normalization**, and **commodification**. In so doing, we also focus on the ways in which global inequalities in income, gender, race, and labour, make such a practice possible.

In examining tourism as a practice, we need to consider a number of critical questions: How have certain places become constituted as tourist sites, and with what consequences? How do certain understandings of tourists and their destinations shape the relations between tourists and the local people who serve them? How are global and local relations of power relevant to tourism, including discourses and practices that Other-ize non-Western people? How, in turn, do these power relations create Western tourists as the centre? These questions remind us that tourism is not just about the practices of tourists or even the places tourists visit. It is also a **discourse** that shapes people's relation to other people and places—indeed, it shapes how people locate themselves and others in the world.

FIGURE 14.1 ■ A familiar scene used to promote a beachside vacation.

Photos.com

We first consider various definitions, forms, and goals of tourism and tourists. We then discuss consumption and **commodification**, with a particular concentration on two examples: **Disneyfication** and the tourist city. This consumption is then linked to unequal, global relations of production. The final section of this chapter moves from this more political-economic lens toward a Foucauldian analysis in which we discuss both the **tourist gaze** (see below) and how tourism mobilizes **disciplinary** and **governmental power** relations through surveillance and regulation. Finally we briefly address alternative, or **sustainable tourism**, with a primary focus on volunteer tourism.

WHAT IS TOURISM?

Tourism is often viewed as a recent phenomenon; but a raft of literature exists that shows that historically people travelled to remote places both out of pleasure and out of curiosity about other societies (Casson, 1994; Moscardo et al., 2001). For example, both ancient Greek and Roman citizens travelled to sporting events, festivals, and sites of archaeological interests (Moscardo et al., 2001). By the Roman era, tourism was well established in such areas as the Bay of Naples, which was well known for its beauty and climate (Casson, 1994). Similarly, Chinese and Japanese peoples have been travelling for pleasure and leisure for at least 2000 years (Pearce et al., 1988).

Turning to the growth and development of tourism in Europe, we can see a series of stages beginning with the Middle Ages (13th–15th centuries), which saw the reemergence of travel after the decline of the Roman Empire, with popular religious pilgrimages to Jerusalem and Rome (Moscardo et al., 2004). Following this, the Grand Tour, which typically involved young, aristocratic males travelling throughout Europe for several years to acquire an education in arts and culture, emerged from the 17th to early 19th century (Hibbert, 1969). In the later 19th and early 20th century, the Industrial Revolution and the concomitant growth of transportation and middle classes led to a significant increase in tourism, with recreational travel increasingly seen as a necessary leisure activity to escape from the mundane and to recoup health. New transport links facilitated day tours to the British seaside for the working classes. It is also in this era that entrepreneurial tour organizers such as Thomas Cook emerged, running day tours beginning in 1841.

By the early 20th century, expansion in transportation infrastructure and paid holidays solidified the growth of **mass** (large-scale) **tourism**. Today, however, tourist practices are shifting toward niche and individualized tourist experiences (Moscardo et al., 2001).

Definitions

This brief history illustrates that people travel for a variety of reasons. But what makes them tourists? Is someone a tourist when they go home for the weekend? What about suburbanites when they visit their city's downtown core on a Saturday night? Are Anglos who live in "ethnic neighbourhoods" tourists? What about the business traveller who only sees the insides of hotel and meeting rooms? In fact, there are a number of different defi-nitions of both tourists and tourism, based on length of stay and purpose of travel (see Wall & Mathieson, 2006).

One industry-based definition proposes that "tourist" can describe people who travel to, and stay, somewhere that is not their usual environment, for less than a year (Eurostat et al., 2001). This is quite a "technical" definition based on isolating tourist travel from other forms of travel for statistical purposes (Cooper et al., 2008).[1] Yet it has been useful for legitimizing the role of tourism in economic development, ensuring the publication of economic data, and providing a clear self-identity for those involved in the tourist industry (Wall & Mathieson, 2006). A similar definition is from the World Tourism Organization: "any person who stays away from home overnight for a limited time" (Fainstein & Judd, 1999: 3). Enloe suggests that "to be a tourist means to have someone else make your bed" (2000: 33), a definition that better recognizes the labour of providing for tourists, although it might also apply to someone who is a regular commuter, or who has a maid, or even another family member who makes their bed.

In this chapter, we adopt a more holistic approach to tourism than the above, more technical definitions. We focus on how tourism expands well beyond the activities and motivations of tourists and we look beyond tourism as an industry. We see tourism as a *phenomenon* (Wall & Mathieson, 2006), encompassing the expectations and adjustments made by host residents; the employment of a very large number of people; the involvement of numerous tourism-related agencies and institutions; the production of particular ways of seeing and understanding the world; and the associated inequalities embedded in all of these dimensions.

Tourism has now become "everyday" for most of us in the West; it is no longer a luxury activity for the select few, but an accepted lifestyle both domestically and internationally (Wall & Mathieson, 2006). Billions of people travel everyday. Some go to far-flung "exotic" tropical destinations such as Fiji or the Caribbean, while others simply hop on a bus and go to another city. Such mundane activities as going to the beach or taking a trip to visit friends and family can be considered examples of touristic activities. Tourism is also big business. Statistics show that in 2008 international tourism grew by 2 percent to 924 mil-lion and generated US$944 billion. It is forecasted to generate 1.6 billion in tourist arrivals worldwide by 2020 (UNWTO, 2009). In fact, tourism has become one of the world's most important economic sectors over past half-century, with the economies of many countries dependent on it.

Does everyone have an equal chance to travel, though? And does the tourist industry benefit all? We will return to these questions shortly.

---

1   It is also somewhat ambiguous in terms of whether it covers "day trippers," or out-of-towners who travel somewhere, such as to a monument or to the city, for the day, although Wall and Mathieson (2006) suggest that day trippers should be considered "excursionists" rather than tourists.

One of our most everyday activities is surfing the Internet. Some argue that this is, in itself, a new form of travel, in which we physically do not have to leave our homes and instead travel through the realm of cyberspace (Page, 2009). What this example suggests is that people experience some form of "tourism" every day, without thinking that it is "tourism." As Fainstein and Judd state, "At the end of the 20th century, travel to distant places has become an ordinary experience, taken for granted as a routine part of life. In this way, tourism has shrunk the globe as much as the revolutions in telecommunications and computers" (1999: 1). Indeed, the Internet has also made us think about the way we perceive tourism and how we acquire information about destinations (Page, 2009). For example, if you were thinking about physically going to the Maldives, you would only have to go on the Internet for access to information about the best hotels and attractions, information about getting there, and the worst and the best of the particular experiences, thanks to such sites as Trip Advisor, Hotels.com, The Lonely Planet, and Facebook.

Why Do People Travel?

For a comprehensive understanding of tourism, we have to unpack the goals and understandings that people bring with them when they become tourists. People travel for distraction from everyday life, and to immerse themselves in different, foreign places. They also travel to see their friends and family, to work, to make religious or spiritual pilgrimages, to study abroad, and to heal their bodies. Understanding why people travel is as complex as trying to come up with a simple definition for tourism. Tourists have different characteristics, preferences, and experiences, and the places they visit are similarly heterogeneous (Cooper et al., 2008; Wall & Mathieson, 2006). Overall, however, most tourists travel for pleasure: romance, escape, relaxation, freedom, adventure, self-improvement, to experience other cultures, and to move beyond the boundaries of their own worlds (Enloe, 2000).

Some tourism researchers have attempted to more formally classify the reasons why people travel. For example, at the rise of mass tourism, and in an attempt to bridge characterizations of tourists as interested in seeking either authenticity or superficiality, Cohen (cited in Wall & Mathieson, 2006) classified tourist types based on the relationship between the familiar and the unfamiliar:

- *Organized mass tourists* are typical of the package tourists who seek safety and familiarity. Guided itineraries ensure that familiarity is at a maximum and novelty at a minimum.

- *Individual mass tourists* have more control over their itineraries than organized, mass tourists but remain drawn to a familiar, home-like "environmental bubble" separate from the host community.

- *Explorers* are independent trip planners who avoid developed tourist attractions although they are still interested in retaining some protections and comforts of their "environmental bubble."

- *Drifters* are on their own, avoiding developed tourists attractions and immersed within the host society.

Source: Erik Cohen, "Toward a Sociology of International Tourism,"
Social Research, 39(1), 1972, 164–182.

Cohen's typology of different orientations to tourism draws on the useful notion of the **environmental bubble**, or a "home away from home" atmosphere—a goal encapsulated in a Holiday Inn claim that their "guests will have no surprises" (Wall & Mathieson, 2006). This concept points up a key tension embedded within the goals of many tourists: to experience something both familiar *and* extraordinary.

Many tourists also want to see into other people's real lives. This is difficult and intrusive, so the tourist industry, along with local peoples, create **staged authenticity** or "the creation of contrived attractions or experiences" (Wall & Mathieson, 2006: 272). Through this process, the tourist industry generates the **tourist gaze**: it creates what is considered authentic and teaches people how and what to observe and consume as a tourist (Urry, 1990). This packaging of the inauthentic contributes to the commodification of culture whereby local cultures are presented and sold in ways that tourists expect, through local

FIGURE 14.2 ▢ Staged authenticity on a large scale!

"The town has no history, Signore. It was built from scratch three years ago, entirely for the tourist trade."

Source: © James Stevenson/The New Yorker Collection/www.cartoonbank.com

BUSINESS TOURISM

Business travel often interweaves tourism and work through meetings, conferences, missions, and incentives (Cooper et al., 2008) that also include local dining and sightseeing. Tourism, commerce, and business have long been linked, since early "business" trips included those of historical traders (Marco Polo) and pillagers (Christopher Columbus). More recently, business travel has included the development of "branch plants" in the early 20th century, in which manufacturing was done at a distance from retail trade, and in the late 20th century the deep expansion of such decentralization on a global scale (Fainstein & Judd, 1999). Because corporate offices are concentrated in major urban centres, business travel contributes an important component to urban tourism. In turn, cities have developed their convention sites and promoted various activities and experiences (including sex tourism) for the business traveller. Destinations compete with other places by offering a mixture of business and pleasure.

costumes, rituals, and souvenirs (Wall & Mathieson, 2006). Many tourists will actively seek out the *unreal*, such as the artificial "Bourbon Street" at the West Edmonton Mall, as part of their travel experience, to safely escape from the mundane (Urry, 1990).

Recent observations of tourism have also suggested that there has been a shift away from mass tourism toward a **postmodern** form of tourism in which people mix tourism with other activities, such as business, and with an illusion of individualized choice through niche market tourism (Butz, personal communication, 2009; Wall & Mathieson, 2006; Meethan, 2001).[2] Niche marketing caters to specific subgroups of people, allowing them to choose their prepackaged tourist experience according to their interests, identities, and incomes (Wall & Mathieson, 2006); but it also *produces* niches by constituting certain subgroups (Butz, personal communication, 2009). For example, a fairly new tourist demographic is retirees with disposable income who have in part become a group through being positioned as potential tourists. Another area of niche tourism has developed expressly for gay and lesbian tourists. Certain places are being identified (and created) as gay spaces such as Blackpool, Brighton, and London in the United Kingdom, as well as Amsterdam in the Netherlands, and San Francisco (Meethan, 2001). Entire cruise ships and resorts are dedicated to specific niche markets.

Such categorizing of tourists must be contextualized. The growth of tourism and its related pleasures and opportunities has overwhelmingly been available primarily to citizens of advanced capitalist societies (the West), for in relation to the rest of the world, those of us in the West are affluent and most able to be tourists. This does not mean that people in the global South do not travel, for many do, particularly among local elites. Further, Western

---

2   Urry (1990) also discusses the "post-tourist," who is aware of being embedded within a tourist game of staged authenticity and rather enjoys it.

tourism encompasses a variety of incomes and tastes: tourist experiences vary by what you can afford, from the backpacker, to the package vacation, to the first-class traveller. Tourist experience is inseparable from social class, for it is fundamentally a consumption activity in which people consume places, cultures, services, and products away from home. Tourist activity is also linked to status (Urry, 1990). For example, the winter tan is a status symbol for those of who are white, Western, and relatively wealthy, because it symbolizes the ability to travel to a sunny destination (Chapkis, 1986). Tourism is also embedded in both local and global relations of class inequality, consumption, and production.

CONSUMPTION AND COMMODIFICATION

Consumption and **commodification** are central to tourism (Fainstein & Judd, 1999; Meethan, 2001) as tourism encompasses a vast array of consumption practices, including the purchase of goods and services, from souvenirs to rental cars, entertainment, and accommodations. Tourists also consume images, advertising, and understandings of what it means to be a tourist. Consumption is integral to current, globalized tourism, as most tourist experiences are mass-marketed attempts to provide what feels like an individual and personal travel experience. To be successful in the industry, many, many people must be convinced to have the same experiences—and so we have a wide range of prepackaged choices, making choice simultaneously a reality and an illusion. People also need to be convinced that sightseeing on its own is insufficient (Fainstein & Judd, 1999); a place that is visited must be transformed into objects or experiences to be consumed (T-shirts, coffee mugs, postcards, key chains, tours, and museums). Like virtually all social relations in advanced capitalism, leisure time has been absorbed into the market. Culture is also manufactured, producing very specific, created experiences, including "wholly manufactured tourism venues" (Fainstein & Judd, 1999: 2). Madame Tussaud's Wax Museum, opening in 1835, was a pioneer such developments, although Disneyland is perhaps the most iconic instance of packaged culture.

Standardization and Disneyfication

Disneyland provides commodified, standardized niche tourism, in which you can purchase a full experience of rides, Disney characters, photos, and souvenirs. Even though the souvenirs at Disneyland or Disney World are no different than those available in local malls, tourists will pay a premium price for them at a Disney site, as they validate the tourist experience and its associated status: a signifier that one has actually been there, as "the remembered fact of acquisition at the hallowed site invests the purchase with singularity despite its commonplace character" (Fainstein & Judd, 1999: 15). In this way, purchases and advertising also come full circle as the products promote the place, and the place promotes the products.

Standardization is key to the construction and commodification of tourism, with many diverse places becoming more and more alike as a way to handle large numbers of people efficiently and uniformly (Fainstein & Judd, 1999). Disney is so prominent in presenting such standardization that sociologists have created the terms **Disneyfication**, or **Disneyization** (the latter following from George Ritzer's coining of the concept of

McDonaldization), to refer to the extension of Disney-style theme parks (Disneyland, Disney World, etc.) to other areas of tourism. Disney allows the tourist family to embrace a standardized yet individualized experience, including vacation packages that provide tourists with choices of specialized meals and activities to meet their own family's interests. Further, as many readers may well know from experience, when you make a trip to Disney theme parks, you find that they are: (1) efficient, with lots of signage and every action calculated for direction, timing, and effect; (2) predictable and orderly; (3) clean and tidy, with helpful staff; and (4) familiar because the characters you encounter such as Donald and Mickey are the same as those on television, clothing, and in children's books. There is much similarity here with how McDonald's restaurants are organized.[3] In both instances, standardization is about delivering a predictable, familiar product. It is Disney, however, that expanded these patterns into the tourist industry.

Disney is also an example of how mass tourism commodifies a sense of familiarity, with the roles of tourists and hosts predefined (Wall & Mathieson, 2006). The familiarity of the Disney holiday brings with it a feeling of safety: your children are assumed to be safe; people can speak to you in your own language; you know how much things will cost; and you are guided by planned itineraries. A very similar appeal to comfort and predictability is found in cruise packages, casinos, amusement parks, and resorts. Standardization allows tourists to feel they are experiencing something unique even when it is not—a novelty experience different from home but sufficiently familiar to feel safe (Ritzer & Liska, 1997). Yet the ongoing desire for an authentic experience remains, a desire that is partially resolved through the process of having an "authentic" experience in commodity form, which brings us back to our purchases. For example, as Fainstein and Judd argue (1999), while on tour in Australia, tourists might visit a replica of an "authentic" aborigine village, or in Canada visit an exhibit of Aboriginal art. Tourists can then purchase authentic souvenirs such as jewellery or leather goods. In this way "the sum of [the tourist's] interaction with aboriginal culture is the act of purchase ..." and a purchase attempts to "make the fleeting experiences of tourism real and material" (16).

Cities as Commodified Tourist Sites

So far, much of our discussion of tourism has focused on resort or theme park tourism; but cities have also become important tourist destinations (Law, 1996). Deindustrialization of cities in Europe and North America in the 1980s led to high levels of unemployment in resource and manufacturing industries (Roche, 2000). Factories moved from the industrial centres in the global North to free trade zones in the global South. Cities have increasingly constituted and marketed themselves as sites of entertainment, leisure, and tourism:

---

3   Disneyization can be compared to "McDonaldization," an approach which emphasizes efficiency, calculation, predictability, and domination (Ritzer & Liska, 1997).

> Hamilton's galleries, museums and activities are surprisingly varied and abundant, with something that will intrigue every visitor and something for every member of the family. (http://www.tourismhamilton.com/pagedetail .cfm?id=40)
>
> Share the excitement as Vancouver, one of the world's most spectacular cities, buffs up for its shining moment as the site of the Vancouver 2010 Olympic and Paralympic Winter Games. (http://www.hellobc.com/en-CA/ RegionsCities/Vancouver.htm)

Cities vie over hosting the Olympic games to literally put themselves on the tourist map (see Figure 14.3).

Cities market museums, theatres, sports, and business activities in the hopes of regeneration and economic development in the face of industrial decline (Law, 1996); and all these have now become important sites of tourist consumption, competing with a wide range of other global destinations. Controversially, such projects also often come with political strategies to get tough on crime, crack down on homelessness, and eliminate signs of urban decay in order to create a sense of tourist safety.

There is a great diversity of cities involved in such processes and each develops distinct strategies based on their scale, amenities, and history (Law, 1996). Large cities such as Paris, New York, and Toronto have major administrative and/or business roles that invariably attract visitors. They also attract tourists through their national

FIGURE 14.3 ■ A great example of a city repackaging itself for the Olympics is London, England. For the games in 2012, London is being "reimaged" from a city steeped in history and culture to a modern sports city. The "run-down," impoverished east end of the city has been transformed—seemingly overnight—as stadiums and other sports venues have appeared on the skyline. A new London is being created.

Padmayogini/Shutterstock

museums and historic monuments and buildings. In contrast, industrial cities such as Baltimore and Manchester must try to counteract their industrial character (Law, 1996). Another kind of city is the high-amenity city, such as Munich or San Francisco, which offers services and attractions that attract business and leisure tourists. Finally, there are cities specifically oriented toward leisure tourism by being either historic sites in and of themselves (Venice) or specifically resort-type cities (Miami). Integral to city tourism is the fact that people may visit for more than one reason, combining leisure, business, and personal visiting.

These different kinds of cities are all "sold just like any other consumer product" (Fainstein & Judd, 1999: 4), frequently marketed as unique, wonderful, and significant places to visit. Think of Las Vegas in the United States. What comes to mind with its slogan "What happens in Vegas stays in Vegas"? Vegas is a city where people come to gamble, drink, party, and marry on a whim. Another good example is Dubai's ambitious plan to become a global tourism city (Page, 2009). The building and development of Dubailand, which is made up of 45 different tourist attractions and leisure activities, is intended to put Dubai squarely on the tourist map.

However, it is not usually the whole city that is shaped and marketed as a commodified tourist experience, but specific **tourist bubbles**. These are areas within a city that are preserved and remade, with famous historic and architectural sites integrated into new tourist facilities such as pedestrian malls and markets. Some examples are Picadilly Circus in London, the Trocadero in Paris, Times Square in New York, and Yaletown in Vancouver. While there is often overlap between tourist spaces and downtown working spaces (Judd, 1999), tourist bubbles effectively maintain a split between the tourist experience and the broader reality of everyday life in the city (Judd, 1999). Tourist bubbles are often assumed to be the "safer" areas of a city as they are made familiar and accessible to tourists while separated from most local people. Often these spaces reflect race and class inequalities so that tourists rarely see urban poverty. Think of the city of Washington, where thousands of people flock to see the national state monuments such as the White House, but are typically unaware of the nearby highrise projects that house the impoverished Black communities. Similarly, tourists who visit Patpong market in Bangkok, Thailand, rarely see the "hidden" poverty of the neighbourhoods just behind this well-known market.

Tourist resorts similarly divide the tourist from local living, local people, and evidence of social inequality, as we see in hotels and beaches in Cuba, Mexico, and other "sun" vacation spots. Tourist bubbles can thus have a negative effect as they are "more likely to contribute to racial, ethnic and class tensions than to an impulse toward local community" (Judd, 1999: 53). Tourist bubbles fit well with the standardization of mass tourism and tend to shift municipal money toward centralized tourist initiatives that are not always as successful for the local economy and people as hoped (Judd, 1999). Such bubbles are not impenetrable, however. For example, through Western women's attraction for romantic relationships with local Black men in Barbados, both they and the local men have become "boundary straddlers" between what is commonly presented to tourists and the local society

(Phillips, 2008). The appearance of white Western women in Black neighbourhoods in Barbados is both novel and telling, due to the fact that these relationships have now moved from the realm of the beach and hotel rooms of the "tourist bubble" into real lives of local Barbadians. Such "boundary straddling" inherently challenges the "tourist bubble."

In this section we have focused on how tourism and tourist sites are commodified, from niche resort venues to historical and declining industrial cities. While not all tourist experiences are equally "cleansed," in each of these settings individual travel goals become standardized and "adventure" becomes contained. As a result, these strategies succeed in hiding the underlying power relations that surround and support the tourist industry.

Production and Globalization

> Every native of every place is a potential tourist, and every tourist is a native of somewhere … every native would like a rest, every native would like a tour. But some natives—most natives in the world—cannot go anywhere. (Kincaid, 1989: 18–19)

As illustrated above, tourism is about both consumption and production. The social organization of tourism involves extensive labour in travel agencies, airlines, banks, marketing, resorts, souvenir production, hotels, construction, car rentals, bars, clubs, restaurants, international chains, local businesses, and so on. Producing the tourist experience is an enormous economic undertaking, providing livelihoods for many, but also reflecting and creating inequalities. Furthermore, the production of tourism is embedded in the historically unequal processes of colonialism and neo-colonialism that we discuss in other chapters in this textbook. Certain places become organized as tourist destinations more than others, and while geography may play a role in creating a desirable destination, this is certainly not the only factor: "Tourism is not just about [some people] escaping work and drizzle; it is about power, increasingly internationalized power" (Enloe, 1989: 40). Enloe is drawing on what we have called a Marxist approach to power because tourism is organized in a way that builds on and produces benefits for some, and subservience and debt for others.

Tourism's history is deeply intertwined with **colonialism**. Newly industrialized European nations expanded their global empires between the 17th and 19th centuries, often engaging in pillaging, slavery, and/or colonization. All of these practices involved attempts to extract wealth and labour from other regions and people; they also involved the representation of other peoples as exotic and, often, barbaric (Said, 1978; Tucker & Akama, 2009). These practices have contributed significantly to the ongoing global inequalities we see today, as well as their perpetuation through **neo-colonialism**, or newer, indirect colonial rule (Tucker & Akama, 2009). Neo-colonialism is embedded in much current tourism, through the domination of the West in much of the tourist industry, consequent corporate influence over developing nations, and the domination and ongoing representations of "the West and the rest." Colonial representations of the **Other** prevail and are often used in travel advertising, constructing southern cultures, places, and people as exotic, simple, primitive escapes from the humdrum living of (post)industrial, bureaucratic life in the centre, representations which construct Western life as superior (Echtner & Prasad, 2003; Said, 1978).

For example, much of the Kenyan tourist industry has depended on multinational tourism to develop capital intense tourist facilities, often providing these corporations with lucrative tax concessions (Tucker & Akama, 2009). Now over 50 percent of Kenya's industry is foreign-owned. Further, Kenya is marketed with a focus on wild animals, beaches, and the Maasai people, constructing a certain idea of Kenya that fails to acknowledge the diversity of Kenyan life:

> Images of wild and darkest Africa, complete with roaring lions, trumpeting elephants, semi-naked and bare-breasted natives, are frequently used as catch phrases to lure Westerners keen for exoticism and adventure.... [These images] define and fix both the tourist and the toured "other" in a relationship with each other which stems from colonialism and is always inherently colonial in nature. (Tucker & Akama, 2009: 510)

The global tourist industry plays a key role in Othering and neo-colonizing predominantly people in the Global South (Leiper, 1995). Lauded as the economic saviour of developing countries, tourism has been thought to bring the global South out of high debt and underdevelopment through an influx of foreign investment, tourist dollars, and employment opportunities. Today many countries continue to endeavour to develop their tourism industries in hopes of diversifying local economies, advancing social and economic development more generally (through tourism dollars), and bringing regions international attention and prestige:

> Tourism is being touted as an alternative to the one-commodity dependency inherited from colonial rule. Foreign sun seekers replace bananas. Hiltons replace sugar mills. Multinational corporations such as Gulf and Western or Castle and Cook convert their large landholdings into resorts or sell them off to developers. (Enloe, 1989: 31)

Such a focus on tourism as the economic solution is evident even among socialist countries such as Cuba. While tourism dollars may be needed, however, tourism creates a new and precarious form of dependency and inequality for poor countries whereby those in the South continue to perform menial labour for rich, visiting Westerners. Similarly, global institutions such as the **International Monetary Fund** and their associated processes such as **Structural Adjustment Programs** encourage investment in tourism at the expense of other initiatives such as social services. Such structural adjustment initiatives have produced a dependency on tourism as a strategy for economic survival—which can be precarious, for the tourists do not always come and tourist revenues do not always benefit local people.

In fact, tourism has not delivered in terms of its economic promises. While tourism has become a significant, if not the main, foreign exchange earner for many countries, global and national inequalities persist (Harrison, 1992; Mbaiwa & Stronza, 2009). Transnational companies have overtaken the more profitable elements of the tourism market, enjoy tax havens, and generally keep the high-paying, specialized jobs in the hands of outsiders. Further, head offices for multinationals tend to be located in Western nations; yet they have the economic power and investment resources to significantly influence decision making in developing nations. We can see this in the growth of hotel chains. Accor operates 25,000 hotels in 70 countries, while Holiday Inn operates 1571 hotels with a total of 2.3 million rooms (Meethan, 2001). Only smaller and less profitable pursuits are left to local entrepreneurs. Consequently, many argue that tourism maintains developing nations' dependent, neo-colonial position in relation to advanced capitalist societies (Mbaiwa & Stronza, 2009; Meethan, 2001). Some have even framed tourism as a new form of the plantation (Turner & Ash, 1975).

The division of labour in tourism reproduces a colonial history in which mostly non-white employees serve their mostly white clientele (Harrison, 1992) and women carry out many of the lower-status jobs (Enloe, 1989), including cleaning, washing, cooking, and serving. Part of the tourist experience is to have one's needs met and to forget about the labour that goes on behind the scenes. But we need to think about those workers, including those making the souvenirs and apparel: the conditions of their work; the pay they receive; and whether they ever get to go on vacations. For example, if you observe the racial organization of those employed in hotels in the Caribbean, you will appreciate how tourism has continued to reproduce the colonial status quo. In the hotels, the managers are usually white, and those employed in the lesser skilled jobs are Black, including the bartenders, bell-boys, receptionists, and maids. Like in the days of slavery, Black serves white, in the tropical heat, to the pleasing melody of steel pan music. It is not surprising that locals have used the entrepreneurial opportunities in the informal tourism sector as a means to get ahead. Take the case of beach boys who can be found along many of the tourist beaches, and ask yourself why they get involved with female tourists? Is it simply a question of romance, or something more? Phillips (2002) has pointed out that sex tourism is more about economic opportunity than romance. Sex tourism gives young Black men an economic opportunity in tourism that would have otherwise been denied to them by the virtue of their race.

While often welcomed for their contribution to local economies, tourists themselves can also exacerbate local feelings of discontent. While tourists may be middle-class at home, in the poorer communities they visit they may seem extraordinarily wealthy, raising local prices as well as feelings of relative deprivation. Further, tourists may bring social values that clash with those of a community. Tourists can also have a negative impact on the physical environment, not only through the atmospheric pollution of expanded air travel by CO_2 emissions (Page, 2010), but also through trampling over precious landmarks. The tourist traffic at such famous heritage sites as Stone Henge in the U.K. or Machu Picchu in Peru has been of concern to those wanting to preserve these sites. This has been a significant problem in such sensitive natural habitats as the Galapagos Islands, or in the threat to coral reefs through the development of tourist facilities (Holden, 2009).

Overall tourism has done little to alleviate inequality and poverty in destination countries (Harrison, 1992; Mbaiwa & Stronza, 2009). Indeed the social organization of tourism is a reflection and a function of the structural forces within the global political economy in which places, people, culture, and economies are commodified and consumed on an unequal global stage, with tourism shaped by many inequalities based on the interweavings of gender, race, and class. We need to be careful how we portray these relations of inequality, however; for just as they can perpetuate deep, ongoing patterns that exacerbate global, economic differences, some tourists and tourist providers, local governments, tourism workers, and others also resist these relations. People seek alternative forms of tourism, challenge tourist developments that will be destructive to local communities, unionize in the face of negative labour conditions, and respond to tourists on their own terms, as we will examine shortly.

The "Tourist Gaze"

In the preceding two sections we focused on consumption and production as integral to tourism, with a particular focus on the global, capitalist relations embedded within these practices. We can also think about consumption and production in relation to ideas and images. To understand this approach we will focus the concept of the **tourist gaze** (Urry, 1990). Earlier we discussed the role of "staged authenticity" in attempting to meet the desires of tourists to see other people's everyday lives. Through the process of creating this authenticity, the tourism industry and tourist discourses create the tourist gaze: teaching people what is an important site to examine, how to look at these places as a tourist, and how to interpret what we see as tourists (1990). The tourist gaze requires distinguishing a place, thing, or experience from the tourist's everyday life, and such distinctions are guided for us. Even if an individual does not physically travel, they may still understand the world through the tourist gaze as they surf the Net, watch TV, and fantasize about other people and places. Such fantasies, in turn, create an insatiable desire for an ideal tourist experience.

Tourism is a process that is both produced (as experiences are created for tourists) and productive (creating expectations of what tourists are supposed to do, understandings of places and people, and ideas of local authenticity). This draws us toward a more Foucauldian approach to power, with power embedded in the **discourses** of tourism. Through the tourist gaze we are taught how to look at places and interpret what we see through familiar signs and signifiers (a historical marker, an indicator of cultural difference, a postcard) and a certain set of expectations (a reception from "hosts"). We learn heritage, architecture, and folklore, and then we look for these to be presented to us in a certain kind of format at our destinations. These processes are guided through books on tourist destinations, travel shows, and more broadly through media representations of other places and people, textbooks, and friends' and families' vacation stories. How to be a tourist is therefore something produced within a broad web of intersecting discourses of adventure, safety, romance, gender, race, and neo-colonialism (Cheong & Miller, 2000).

This gaze is most commonly produced through images and stories "which privilege the gaze of the 'master-subject' over others" (Pritchard & Morgan, 2000: 889), or a gaze embedded in the privileged view of the West. This is why we do not hear about the tourism practices of migrant workers or domestic servants (Galani-Moutafi, 2000). Similarly, there is little room in this gaze for moments that violate preconceived images of people and places, such as deep poverty. In this context, there is the notion of the universal "Other" who is "fixed" and often sanitized by the gaze of the "Western" tourist. In other words, the tourist gaze often only sees the stereotype of the Other, for example in the idea of the happy native who smiles for the camera.

For those of us located in advanced capitalist societies (where most tourists originate), the tourism discourse puts us at the centre of the world, with other places existing primarily as sites for the production of the cheap goods that we want, or the vacations that we wish to experience. This understanding of the world has become normalized and taken for granted. Yet these processes are also the outcome of the kind of historical developments that we have examined above. Within this context, the tourist gaze constitutes tourists through a position of privilege, training tourists how to see and interpret the unfamiliar and the different, the Other, reproducing an "us versus them" dichotomy based on power and privilege. The tourist gaze is a standpoint from which we (the West) view the rest of the world as a physical, conceptual, and cultural environment. As such, like whiteness, it is rooted in a position of structural advantage and refers to a set of invisible cultural practices (see Chapter 5). It constructs a position of entitlement and superiority, based on our ability to be consumers—the world is out there for the taking, by ordinary citizens of the West. As a result, to be a tourist is often to occupy "the centre." Indeed it is through the act of becoming a tourist that the gaze from the position of the centre is strengthened and reaffirmed.

Clearly, this gaze is highly racialized, gendered, and economically structured in terms of who we consider tourists to be, who they predominantly are, and who serves them/ us. For example, despite the economic emergence of new types of tourists, and a raft of academic work critically exploring sex, gender, and society, "the signs, symbols, myths and fantasies privileged within tourism marketing [remain] male-oriented and heterosexual" (Pritchard & Morgan, 2000: 890). Thus women and sexual imagery are frequently used to portray and sell the "exotic" nature of a destination. Since these sites, attractions, and bodies are to be consumed by the white heterosexual male, women, like culture and leisure, are partly commodified through the tourist gaze.

An excellent example of the gendered landscape of leisure and tourism is sex tourism (Enloe, 1989; O'Connell Davidson, 1995). The development of sex tourism has led to an extensive industry catering to the sexual and other needs of (primarily white) male tourists in restaurants, bars, and accommodations in such areas as Southeast Asia and the Caribbean (see also Hall, 1991). This packaging and commodification of the desires of male tourists has become a massive industry. A similar, though smaller-scale, set of processes has taken place to meet the needs of the female sex tourists in such places as the Caribbean, Africa, and the Greek islands. For example, as we have touched on above, Phillips (2008) writes about sex tourism in Barbados in which a subgroup of "black men … have commodified their sexuality, with all the incumbent sexual stereotypes that go with it, in exchange for the tourist dollar" (209). This last example also underscores the racialized dynamics often embedded in sex tourism.

Complicating the Gaze

While tourism is frequently a symbol of class status, and local economies often rely on tourist spending, and while the tourist gaze suggests that it is the tourist industry and tourists themselves that create and reproduce a lens through which to see the rest of the world, others can and do "look back." Thus, while the tourist gaze is a very useful concept for recognizing the power of Western tourist discourses to construct the other, the tourist gaze too has come under some criticism. For example, the idea of the Western gaze has become decentred through globalization and the consequent emergence of non-Western tourists (Meethan, 2001). While the predominance of the white, male gaze still exists in tourism, we cannot lose sight of emerging discourse that looks at how race and class and gender are newly intersecting within the tourist gaze (see Phillips, 2001; Padilla, 2007). For example, Western women are also increasingly consumers and "gazers" of tourist sites, places, and bodies, like their male counterparts.

We can challenge the assumption that the Western gaze is one that holds exclusive power and authority by introducing the idea that there is power and agency in the local gaze, which "is based on a more complex, two-sided picture, where both the tourist and local gazes exist, affecting and feeding each other, resulting in what is termed 'the mutual gaze'" (Maoz, 2006: 222). Thus, we see the ways hosts and guests "view, grasp, conceptualize, understand, imagine, and construct each other" (222) and challenge both the common focus on an exploitative tourist gaze and binaries such as everyday/extraordinary and visitor/local (Franklin, 2009). This perspective focuses on how the tourist's body also travels to tourist destinations, engaging with other tourists and local people. While choreographed through the tourist gaze and disciplinary structures, from this perspective the tourist's bodily performance is never entirely fixed but always engaging with its environment. This approach focuses more on dialogue between people than on contrasts between hosts and locals, suggesting a dismantling of the hierarchical, neo-colonial relationship.

Overall this new wave of tourism studies attempts to focus more on performance and the flow and mixing of people in which tourism is transforming places, the people who live in them, and the people who travel to them (Franklin, 2009). It is important for reminding us of the complexities of micro-interactions between visitors and hosts, as structural power relations can become more textured as people interact in the everyday. However, readers might well question how much such local interactions can disrupt the wider, deeper structural inequalities that this chapter has been examining.

Surveillance and Discipline

The idea of the tourist gaze foregrounds various features of a Foucauldian approach to power. The gaze is understood to be both produced by and productive of certain understandings about tourists, tourism, and the places and people tourists encounter. We can see examples of this in "expert" knowledges about travel that are produced through travel writing, travel advising, and trip planning that we've discussed in terms of the gaze. One of the first things we often do when we are going to plan a trip somewhere is look for a travel guide like the ones in the *Lonely Planet* series. These guides produce particular understandings of the places and people tourists visit, as well as particular ways for tourists to understand themselves.

Foucauldian power is also relevant to the topic of tourism in quite a different sense that, like the local gaze, acts upon tourists themselves. This power is the lens of surveillance and discipline. Such a lens shifts away from the idea of tourists always having power and exploiting others toward seeing how tourists come to be regulated, as well as regulating others and themselves (Cheong & Miller, 2000). For example, when we visit tourist sites, there is an ongoing process of surveillance and regulation governing how we conduct ourselves. We can look again at Disney for an excellent example of this. The Disney empire attempts to combine nostalgia for a comfortable and simple past with a vision of a technologically advanced and better future, an illusion partly accomplished through modern, private policing. When you are at Disneyland, you are under constant surveillance, although this is a largely invisible process until you try going in the "out" door and a Disney staff person quickly appears. In this way power is invisible and diffuse, with tourists at times unknowingly managed and constrained (Cheong & Miller, 2000). Such surveillance can also be linked to the **Panopticon effect**, as discussed in Chapter 2, in which a setting is arranged in such a way that while people know they may be watched, they do not know when someone is specifically watching them. Thus, they manage their own behaviour as if they are being watched, consequently participating in their own self surveillance. In these ways, Disney constructs a form of "instrumental discipline" in which "control is embedded, preventative, subtle, co-operative and apparently non-coercive and consensual" (Shearing & Stenning, 1987: 322).[4] This form of discipline in turn facilitates the efficient mass consumption of Disney.

Even seemingly uncontrolled, individual, and hedonistic forms of tourism contain elements of control. A study on package tours in the Spanish resorts of Palmanova and Magaluf showed how tourist behaviour and consumption was highly managed, whereby seemingly individual activities such as bar crawling and drinking games were all organized by company representatives to provide tourists with "a state of child-like dependence" and freedom from responsibility, all carried out within a controlled and structured environment (Andrews, 1999, cited in Meethan, 2001). Similarly, even the more independent traveller is subject to subtle guidance through consultation and advice, from guidebooks and other "brokers," such as restaurant employees, park rangers, website developers, and government officials (Cheong & Miller, 2000). Even the organization of museum spaces involves surveillance and guidance of tourists. The local gaze also participates in guiding tourists, as locals "can lead tourists to quickly understand where they might go and what they might do" (Cheong & Miller, 2000: 385). The tourist experience is thus organized through constant management and direction of people's self-interest.

For Foucault, these invisible and subtle means of disciplining people's actions are more insidious and troubling than overt measures of social control, because people are not aware of how their actions are being governed, nor how much they come to govern their own actions in response. Through such organization, control becomes consensual: people are

---

4 Disney is also organized in a way that controls what kinds of images are collected by tourist photographers through careful manipulation of photography sites for picture-taking and "posed" moments (for example with Mickey or Donald).

the source of their own control, which is the essence of **governmentality**. Even though we are being governed, we experience ourselves as free, which is one of the reasons why this form of power is so effective. Recall from Chapter 2 that, through a Foucauldian analysis, power is not equivalent to domination and authority, although this may be an end result of power; rather, power is everywhere, in everything, producing how we know the world, our experiences, and ourselves. As such, it is even embedded in what we experience as practices of freedom, when we feel that we are making autonomous choices, including the choice to go on holiday to a resort or to Disneyland and to make certain kinds of purchases while we're at it. In this way we can see how Foucauldian power permeates not only how we know the world but how we know ourselves as well.

Tourism Alternatives?

In this chapter we have focused primarily on mass tourism as a powerful force in the processes of standardization, commodification, and globalization of tourism. It is particularly through mass tourism that the tourist gaze, the tourist identity, and tourist behaviour are produced, reproduced, and governed. Yet just as fair trade coffee production has arisen in response to an unjust coffee industry (see Chapter 13), forms of sustainable, or alternative, tourism attempt to disrupt such unequal processes. **Sustainable tourism** aims to alter tourism practices by seeking equity through an improvement of life for people in host areas, including their participation in decision making; sustainability, through protecting natural resources; and meaningful visitor enjoyment and connection with others (Mbaiwa & Stronza, 2009). In the academic literature, such forms of tourism are frequently presented as transformative for both host communities and visitors (Zavitz & Butz, 2009). Forms of tourism that attempt to address such aims include ecotourism and volunteer tourism. While it is very challenging to counter the processes of commodification, dependency, and inequality outlined earlier in this chapter, sustainable tourism is presented as an important goal as it tries to provide "a form of tourism that rebukes mass tourism and the consumptive mindset it engenders and instead [offer] alternative, more discriminating, socially and environmentally sustaining tourist experiences" (Lyons & Wearing, 2008: 3).

The environmental impacts of tourism are many, although tourism can sometimes help to promote environmental protections for endangered wildlife and national parks, for example (Holden, 2009). **Ecotourism** focuses on minimizing the environmental impact of tourism; but it is also concerned with addressing inequality. Through ecotourism, it is hoped that biodiversity will be preserved as people are educated in conservation, a goal that has been supported through various processes of environmental certification of tourist businesses (Mbaiwa & Stronza, 2009). This protection is precarious, however, as it only protects those species and places that are attractive to tourists; furthermore, very popular sites for nature-based tourism can become degraded due to overuse.

Volunteer tourism (or voluntourism) involves people going on holidays but also doing volunteer work while they are away. The growing area of volunteer tourism might be a counterweight to commodified tourism, but "deep" forms of volunteer tourism are favoured over "shallow" (Wearing & Ponting, 2009). Shallow volunteer tourism tends to be more centred on the tourist's desires to sightsee. Deep volunteer tourism instead focuses on community consultation, local ownership, the acceptance of difference, and an emphasis on interaction. Ideally, such practices might create a "Third Space of hybrid selves" (Wearing & Ponting, 2009: 257) for both volunteers and hosts, with the hope that communication will transform "'they' or the 'other' … into 'you' and 'I'" (263) to create a shared experience through which both visitors and hosts change. In these ways, deep volunteer tourism is hoped to "represent a glimmer of resistance" (256) to commodified, neoliberal forms of tourism. One example of such tourism is Holidays with Purpose, located in Indonesia, in which volunteers both surf and participate in activities such as rebuilding communities after natural disasters and planting community gardens.

For volunteer tourism to really succeed in creating a shared, decommodified experience, it must be coordinated through nongovernmental organizations (NGOs) rather than private enterprise. NGOs are more likely to have community support, to involve the community, and to be better positioned "for ensuring that the needs of host communities are placed before the bottom line of transnational corporations who have vested interest in commercializing volunteer tourism products" (Lyons & Wearing, 2008: 6). That said, NGOs sometimes contract out to private businesses and do not always involve the whole community (6).

Forms of sustainable tourism such as volunteer tourism seem like a good idea. But they also raise concerns and doubts for they remain embedded in ongoing neo-colonial relations, maintaining assumptions regarding "the West and the Rest" that locate the West at the centre as volunteers are conceptualized as helping (despite a frequent lack of skills) and undergoing self-transformation that can trump local people's needs (Zavitz & Butz, 2009). Further, many short-term volunteer ventures remain enmeshed in the for-profit tourism industry. In this way, volunteer tourism can be seen as little different from mainstream forms of tourism as it "reproduces a differentiation between Northern volunteers and Southern hosts/beneficiaries in which the former are privileged as active subjects and the latter are subordinated as passive objects of volunteers' agency and imagination" (Zavitz & Butz, 2009: 13).

CONCLUSION

Through this chapter we have looked at tourism as a form of social organization, exploring how it both reflects and produces social, political, and economic structures in the global arena. The question of power is central, both as relations of domination and authority and forms of representation and governmentality. In looking at tourism as a form of social organization, we have examined tourism as commodified and as embedded in global relations of production. This discussion drew on political economy to illustrate how tourism is both a reflection, and a function of, inequality and power both locally and internationally. We have also examined some of the ways tourism is constituted as a way of knowing and interpreting the world, using the metaphor of the tourist gaze. Further, tourism is linked to processes of surveillance and discipline, ultimately shaping what we experience as our independent choices and how we govern ourselves as tourists. Finally, we have briefly looked at sustainable tourism. This final discussion in turn prompts many more questions: is all tourism inevitably commodified? Can tourism ever be free of a problematic, tourist gaze? Is it possible to be a critical tourist while engaging in mass tourism? Through this chapter we have illustrated how power is embedded in many facets of tourism, and clearly there are no easy answers to such questions.

STUDY QUESTIONS

1. Having read this chapter, how would you define tourism? Why might it be so difficult to come up with a clear definition?

2. How do you think the Internet has changed the way that we view and experience tourism?

3. In this chapter we have argued that the tourist gaze is a privileged one. Can you think of any examples that might challenge this assumption?

4. What are some of the promises and pitfalls of sustainable tourism, such as ecotourism or volunteer tourism?

EXERCISES

1. Have you ever been a "tourist"? Where did you go and why? How have you determined that this experience should be defined as tourism? Has your understanding of your tourist experience shifted through having read this chapter? If so, how?

2. Think of a city or large town nearest you. In what ways does it attempt to construct itself as a tourist destination? What kinds of activities are marketed as tourist activities? Can you identify any examples of "staged authenticity"?

3. On page 309, we presented a quotation from Jamaica Kincaid's *A Small Place* (Kincaid, 1989). Drawing on this chapter and your own experiences and reflections, discuss what Kincaid means by this statement.

REFERENCES

Andrews, H. 1999. Landscapes of consumption: The examples of Palmanova and Magaluf. Unpublished conference paper presented at the 1st International Conference on Consumption and Representation, University of Plymouth, September.

Casson, L. 1974. *Travel in the Ancient World.* London, UK: Allen & Unwin.

Chapkis, W. 1986. *Beauty Secrets: Women and the Politics of Appearance.* Brooklyn, NY: South End Press.

Cheong, S., and M. Miller. 2000. Power and tourism: A Foucauldian observation. *Annals of Tourism Research* 27(2): 371–390.

Cooper, C., J. Fletcher, A. Fyall, D. Gilbert, and S. Wanhill. 2008. *Tourism: Principles and Practice.* Essex, UK: Pearson Education.

Echtner, C., and P. Prasad. 2003. The context of Third World tourism marketing. *Annals of Tourism Research* 30(3): 660–682.

Enloe, C. 2000. *Bananas, Beaches and Bases: Making Feminist Sense of International Politics.* London, UK: Pandora Press, Harper/Collins.

Eurostat, OECD, WTO, and UN Statistics Division. 2001. *Tourism Satellite Account: Recommended Methodological Framework.* Luxembourg; Eurostat.

Fainstein, Susan, and Dennis Judd, eds. 1999. *The Tourist City.* New Haven, CT: Yale University Press.

Franklin, Adrian. 2009. *The Sociology of Tourism in The Sage Handbook of Tourism Studies.* Tazim Jamal and Mike Robinson, eds. Los Angeles: Sage. 65–81.

Galani-Moutafi, V. 2000. The self and the other: Traveler, ethnographer, tourist. *Annals of Tourism Research* 27(1): 203–224.

Hall, D. 1991. Introduction. In D. Hall, ed., *Tourism and Economic Development in Eastern Europe and the Soviet Union.* London, UK: Belhaven Press.

Harrison, D. 1992. Tourism to less developed countries: The social consequences. In D. Harrison, ed., *Tourism and Less Developed Countries.* Chichester, UK: John Wiley & Sons.

Hibbert, C. 1969. *The Grand Tour.* London: Weidenfeld & Nicolson.

Holden, Andrew. 2009. Tourism and natural resources. In Tazim Jamal and Mike Robinson, eds., *The Sage Handbook of Tourism Studies.* Los Angeles: Sage. 203–214.

Judd, Dennis. 1999. Constructing the tourist bubble. In Susan Fainstein and Dennis Judd, eds., *The Tourist City.* New Haven, CT: Yale University Press. 35–53.

Kincaid, Jamaica. 1989. *A Small Place.* New York: Plume.

Law, C. 1996. Introduction. In C. Law, ed., *Tourism in Major Cities.* London, UK: Routledge. 1–22,

Leiper, N. 1995. *Tourism Management.* Collingwood, VIC, Australia: TAFE Publications.

Lyons, K. D., and S. Wearing. 2008. Volunteer tourism as alternative tourism: Journeys beyond otherness in journeys of discovery. In Kevin D. Lyons and Stephen Wearing, eds., *Volunteer Tourism: International Case Study Perspectives.* Wallingford, Oxfordshire, UK: CABI. 3–11.

Maoz, D. 2006. The mutual gaze. In *Annals of Tourism Research* 33(1): 221–239.

Mbaiwa, Joseph E., and Amanda L. Stronza. 2009. The challenges and prospects for sustainable tourism and ecotourism in developing countries. In Tazim Jamal and Mike Robinson, eds., *The Sage Handbook of Tourism Studies.* Los Angeles: Sage. 333–353.

Meethan, Kevin. 2001. *Tourism in Global Society: Place, Culture and Consumption.* Houndmills, Basingstoke, UK: Palgrave.

Moscardo, G., B. Faulkner, and E. Laws. 2001. Introduction: Moving ahead and looking back. In B. Faulkner, G. Moscardo, and E. Laws, eds., *Tourism in the 21st Century: Lessons from Experience.* London, UK: Continuum. xvi–xviii.

O'Connell Davidson, J. 1995. British sex tourists in Thailand. In M. Maynard and J. Purvis, eds., *(Hetero)Sexual Politics.* London, UK: Taylor and Francis.

Padilla, M. 2007. *Caribbean Pleasure Industry: Tourism, Sexuality, and AIDS in the Dominican Republic.* Chicago: University Press.

Page, S. 2009. *Tourism Management: Managing for Change.* Burlington, MA: Elsevier Limited.

Pearce, W., E. B. Barbier, and A. Markandya. 1988. *Sustainable Development and Cost– Benefit Analysis.* LEEC paper, IIED/UCL London Environmental Economics Centre. 88–03.

Phillips, J. 2002. The beach boys of Barbados: Post-colonial entrepreneurs. In S. Thorbek and B. Pattanaik, eds., *Transnational Prostitution: Changing Global Patterns.* London: Zed Books.

Phillips, J. 2008. Female sex tourism: A post-colonial perspective. *The Brown Journal of World Affairs* 14(2): 1–12.

Pritchard, A., and N. Morgan. 2000. Privileging the male gaze: Gendered tourism landscapes. *Annals of Tourism Research* 27(3): 884–905.

Ritzer, G., and A. Liska. 1997. "McDisneyization" and "post-tourism." In C. Rojek and J. Urry, eds., *Touring Cultures: Transformation of Travel and Theory.* London, UK: Routledge.

Roche, M. 2000. *Mega-Events and Modernity: Olympics and Expos in the Growth of Global Culture.* London, UK: Routledge.

Said, E. 1978. Orientalism: Western concepts of the Orient in "From Orientalism." In Patrick Williams and Laura Chrisman, eds., *Colonial Discourse and Post-Colonial Theory.* Hemel Hempstead, Hertfordshire, UK: Harvester Wheatsheaf, 1993. 132–149.

Shearing, C. D., and P. Stenning. 1987. "Say 'Cheese': The Disney order that is not so Mickey Mouse." In C. D. Shearing and P. Stenning, eds., *Private Policing.* Newbury Park, CA: Sage Publications, Ltd. 317–323.

Tucker, H., and J. Akama. 2009. Tourism as postcolonialism. In Tazim Jamal and Mike Robinson, eds., *The Sage Handbook of Tourism Studies.* Los Angeles: Sage. 504–520.

Turner, L., and J. Ash, eds. 1975. *The Pleasure Hordes, International Tourism and the Pleasure Periphery.* London, UK: Constable.

UNWTO. 2009. *World Tourism Organisation, Facts and Figures.* http://unwto.org/en.

Urry, J. 1995. *Consuming Places.* London, UK: Routledge.

Wall, G., and A. Mathieson. 2006. *Tourism: Changes, Impacts and Opportunities,* 2nd ed. Essex: Pearson Education.

Wearing, Stephen, and Jess Ponting. 2009. Breaking down the system: How volunteer tourism contributes to new ways of viewing commodified tourism. In Tazim Jamal and Mike Robinson, eds., *The Sage Handbook of Tourism Studies.* Los Angeles: Sage. 254–260.

Zavitz, K. J., and D. Butz. 2009. Volunteer tourism—An unreliable panacea. Unpublished paper.

Nation States, Borders, Citizenship, and the Making of "National" Difference

Nandita Sharma

University of Hawaii, Manoa

> The overweening, defining event of the modern world is the mass movement of raced populations, beginning with the largest forced transfer of people in the history of the world: slavery. The consequences of which transfer have determined all the wars following it as well as the current ones being waged on every continent. The contemporary world's work has become policing, halting, forming policy regarding and trying to administer the movement of people. Nationhood—the very definition of citizenship—is constantly being demarcated and redemarcated in response to exiles, refugees, *Gastarbeiter*, immigrants, migrations, the displaced, the felling, and the besieged. The anxiety of belonging is entombed within the central metaphors in the discourse on globalism, transnationalism, nationalism, the break-up of federations, the rescheduling of alliances, and the fictions of sovereignty. Yet these figurations of nationhood and identity are frequently as raced themselves as the originating racial house that defined them. When they are not raced, they are … imaginary landscape, never inscape; Utopia, never home.
>
> —*Toni Morrison*[1]

INTRODUCTION

Making and then maintaining national borders is an important part of the everyday practices of power. National borders are a set of institutional relationships shaped by the law, the market, and social relations within and across spaces claimed by nation states. These borders shape how people can move across spaces marked as national territory. The policies of individual nation states determine who can move with relative ease and who is forbidden from entering national space. Even once people have moved within the borders of a particular nation state, the ability of states to allocate different levels of status (for example, permanent, legal resident or "illegal") profoundly shapes people's lives.

---

1 Morrison, Toni, "Home," in *The House That Race Built: Original Essays by Toni Morrison, Angela Y. Davis, Cornel West, and Others on Black Americans and Politics in America Today*, Wahneema Lubiano (ed.). Vintage Books, 1998.

National borders are far from fixed. They constantly shift according to changes in global and national politics and new nation states are continuously being created. Since the 1990s, numerous nation states have ceased to exist while new ones have been recognized through international law. Moreover, the territorial reach of existing states is often in flux. In short, there is a constant reorganization of nation states, their borders, and the makeup of the "national community" that they purport to represent.

However, within the global system of nation states, borders do not affect everyone similarly. For a small select group they are a mere formality. Business elites, state officials, armed forces, people working for both international and national organizations, for instance, traverse them with very little thought. Furthermore, carrying a passport from a First World country makes border crossings much easier than one issued by a "Third World" one.

Conversely, borders constantly shadow some people's lives. For people assigned categories such as **migrant worker** or **illegal migrant**, borders follow them to school, to work, indeed in every aspect of their lives. In our globalized world, the simultaneous existence of national borders and borderless worlds confronts even those who stay put.

The topic of this chapter is national borders, in particular how they make some people feel *at home* while rendering others *homeless* in the very places where they live. I discuss the relationship between the construction of a sense of homeyness in the "Canadian nation" for some, while others are relegated to being perpetual "foreigners." Elsewhere, I have argued that a type of home economics is at play in this process of stratifying groups of people in differential state categories of belonging and non-belonging ranging from "citizen" to "illegal" (Sharma, 2006).

FIGURE 15.1 ▓ An African migrant at the CETI, Short Stay Immigrant Center, in the Spanish Enclave of Melilla, Spain.

Marco Di Lauro/Stringer/Getty Images News/Getty Images

Here I argue that there is a **materiality** to these differences between "citizens" and "(im)migrants," one based in the relationship between **ideologies of nationalism** and their interaction with those of racism, gender, and class. These ideologies act as a *material force*: they profoundly affect everything from the types of jobs one is able to secure, wage levels, ability to access services (education, health care, welfare) to whether one can feel secure without the threat of deportation. This is a **relational** process in that the nation state relies on the complicity of those who make themselves at home in the nation in order to legitimize the highly differential treatment accorded those classified as non-citizens, particularly those categorized as "migrant worker" or "illegal," who are legally constructed as "foreign." The result is not necessarily the exclusion of all those who are seen as being "foreign," but rather their subordination *in* Canada. National borders and the social organization of belonging through citizenship not only organizes intense competition between workers globally but also *within* nationalized spaces. Thus, when analyzing the hierarchical categories of belonging/not-belonging, it is useful to utilize both a Marxist understanding of power to understand the processes by which people's labour power is made available for exploitation and a Foucauldian understanding of power that sees it as productive of an entire way of life, in this case the normalization of highly differential treatment of "citizens" and "foreigners."

Ideologies of nationalism shape not only our ideas of "belonging" but also our consciousness about the nature of human society itself. Within nation state forms of **ruling**, "society" is conflated with the nation state. First, it is assumed that all those living within the state are made up of its citizenry. Second, the state is represented as the mere vehicle through which the demands of its "citizenry" are realized. What these two ideas do is provide a sense of identification with nation states for those identified as its national subjects. These subjects come to believe that the state rules *for* them. And since there has never existed a single nation state that did not also contain non-citizens, the state is also viewed as ruling *against* its "foreign" Others. The potential or actual violence of the state against non-citizens and the symbolic violence of excluding non-citizens from society itself comes to be seen as largely legitimate and the present ruling order is reproduced.

NATIONALIZING HOMELANDS

Nationalist ideas of "home" organize people's ideas of themselves, family, culture, and community. They are among the most naturalized and, consequently, most dangerous ideas of our time. This is because an everyday sense of who belongs within any given nationalized space helps to normalize the highly unequal treatment of people who live within the same nation state but who are assigned different national statuses. Differences between people constituted as indigenous, as citizens, as immigrants, as refugees, as foreign workers, and as illegal aliens, are organized through ideas of Canada being the home of some but not **Others**. With the overlaying of the idea of home onto nation, some people are easily understood as belonging in Canada, while others are rendered as foreigners even though they live and work there.

Home acts as a conceptual bridge between modern notions of family and nation—so much so that the nation is understood to be a "magnified version of the family and the circle of close friends" (Johansen, 1997: 171). This is well captured by former British Prime Minister Margaret Thatcher (1989) who proclaimed, "the family and its maintenance really is the most important thing, not only in your personal life, but in the life of any community, because this is the unit on which the whole nation is built." While society, as Eric Hobsbawm (1991: 67–8) notes, "cannot belong to us as individuals," we are encouraged to imagine that it can still belong to those of Us imagined as a "nation".

Moreover, dominant ideas of family and home today are inseparable from **patriarchal** social relations that elevate the status of the men and allow them to feel entitled to women's unpaid homemaking practices (Irigaray, 1993). As the father has authority over the patriarchal family unit, the state is seen as the political and geographical expression of the authority of the nation. Thus, with the modern family's emphasis on biological connection, **hegemonic** conceptions of home are based on the idea that there exist communities of similarity. In this, "the National family [becomes] a symbolic home" (Morley, 2000: 104). Thus, "[a] house identified with the self is called a home, a country identified with the self is called a 'homeland'" (Tabor, 1998: 218). "Its territory is our home; its people is marked by a common 'character,' much like the members of a family; its past is a 'heritage' passed down from our 'forefathers'" (Johansen, 1997: 171). The ties between family, nation, and state are further elaborated on by Anne McClintock (1995), who observes,

> [t]he term "nation" derives from *natio*: to be born—we speak of nations as "motherlands" and "fatherlands." Foreigners "adopt" countries that are not their native homes and are nationalized in the "national family." We talk of the "family of nations," of "homelands" and "native" lands. In Britain, immigration matters are dealt with at the Home Office; in the United States, the president and his wife are called the first family.

Home, then, is an idea that masquerades as a place. Having a home within a nation is not a geographical signpost but an ideology. Yet, even though "home is not necessarily a spatial concept, it is nonetheless often lived out as if it were such" (Morley, 2000: 8). Because of this, it profoundly shapes our consciousness of the relationship between place and "belonging." Its power rests in its ability to project nationalist formulations of home back through human history so that our current understanding of homelands is portrayed as being the outcomes of some supposedly natural need for roots.

It was only after the onset of European capitalist **colonization**, however, with its practices of mass displacement, that the social process of constructing boundaries between homes and between societies was intensified. Stronger insides and outsides were constructed as colonizers made contact with those they colonized and as profits were accrued from differentiating between the two. This, in turn, strengthened the association between family and nation. In the early 17th century, a period of great upheaval as the process of capitalist colonization intensified in many sites around the world, separate houses and households came to be more clearly demarcated from each other (Kumar, 1994). At the same time, a greater division of labour was implemented within the family home and boundaries between members and non-members of the family household became starker. Eventually, the household in Europe came to be imagined as the nuclear, patriarchal family with its fatherly head—at least ideologically. Similarly, European colonization gave shape to notions of discrete, ethnically bounded home(lands).

Indeed, a number of domestic metaphors have helped to organize the exclusion of those said to "not belong" within the national home (Cohen, 1996). It is not simply the physical borders of national home(lands) that are said to be in need of protection, but also the social boundaries between members and non-members of the national family. Looking at how European colonizers made themselves at home in particular colonies is instructive in this regard. The colonial doctrine of *Terra Nullius* asserted the idea that land not held as private property or as state territory was simply sitting "empty" and awaiting "improvement" by European colonizers. Within non-European colonies, this doctrine informed the large-scale transfer of land to either the imperial state, or to European settlers seen to be furthering the colonial project. Such a large transfer of wealth was, of course, enormously helpful in the "founding" of "white settler societies," such as Canada,

Let us consider the *kind* of human subject that nationalism has brought into being. The national subject is one who is intensely *possessive* of space that she or he imagines as national space, and is disconnected from others through feelings of national difference. Sociologist Ghassan Hage calls such feelings a sense of "governmental belonging," feelings based on the idea that national subjects are the rightful managers of a space that has become nationalized, a space that they also imagine as exclusively theirs. In nationalist practices, nationalists "assume, first, an image of a national space; secondly, an image of the nationalist himself or herself as master of this national space and, thirdly, an image of the racial or ethnic "other" as a mere object within this space" (Hage, 2000: 28). Their sense of "governmental belonging" allows nationalists to assume the role of the state for themselves. Perhaps this is what Foucault was getting at when he talked about the importance of "self regulation"?

The logics of nation-ness organize social relations so as to rationalize and legitimate discrimination against anyone constructed as an outsider. By accepting our status as national subjects, we accept the state's coercive activities against those we regard as "foreign." We accept as legitimate the nation state power to determine who stays, who moves, and under what conditions. Throughout the global North, there is a defence of border police, visas, passports, state classification schemes that separate good from bad, real from bogus migrants, induction centres, accommodation centres, detention centres—all in the name of the national community. The "nation," then, is not just a synonym for "community"; it is a very particular kind of community. Nationalism is a particular *style* of ruling (Anderson, 1991).

as well as to the privileged standing of Europeans within such spaces. The idea that the diverse people living on these lands for millennia prior to the arrival of European colonizers were never at home on these lands worked to de-politicize their homelessness after the advent of colonialism and the official redistribution of land to those imagined as being part of the colonizing regime.

The continuous displacement and forced assimilation of colonized people to make new home(lands), not only in white settler colonies but within each and every contemporary nation state, has not disrupted the notion that national communities are formed through shared characteristics. The nation is seen as rooted in blood and soil. The concept of ethnicity, reliant as it is on the idea that there exist a People that "naturally" belong to a given place, figures prominently in this.

ETHNICIZING BELONGING

When attached to ideologies of nationalism, *ethnicizing*—organizing people into ethnic groups—is a process that ties human cultures to particular places. Ethnicizing human societies has greatly informed our ideas of nations as natural homelands (Morley, 2000). Our imagination of contemporary "nations" has entailed the dividing of humanity along ethnic lines and arguing that each person belongs to one—and only one—such group. Doreen Massey (in Mackay, 1997) argues that "in that process the boundaries of the place, and the imagination and building of its 'character,' [become] part and parcel of the definition of who is an insider and who is not; of who is a 'local' and what that term should mean, and who is to be excluded." The exclusions that those with subordinated legal statuses ("migrant worker"; "illegal") are organized through such imaginations of belonging.

Thus, being at home in the nation is based on "mythic narratives, stories the telling of which has the power to create the 'we' who are engaged in telling them," as well as constructing the idea that "we" have a natural "right to a space (a country, a neighbourhood, a place to live) that is due us … in the name of the 'we-ness' we have just constructed" (Bammer, 1992: ix–x). Such a discourse "allows us to imagine that we do not have to share our space with anyone else unless they are of exactly our own kind by virtue of consanguinity" (or relationship by descent from a common ancestor) (Morley, 2000). What such a conflation allows is the identification of family-as-nation-as-race. This has had a particularly damaging effect on migrants, especially those who are racialized differently from those who are imagined as members of any given "nation." In the making of the "Canadian nation," the interlocking ideologies of nationalism and racism have helped to create the dominant belief that those racialized as white are the quintessential members of Canadian society.

As ideologies of highly ethnicized or racialized nations being "natural" homelands became dominant, understandings of people's geographical movements profoundly shifted. As borders became more fixed, migrants came to be increasingly portrayed as trespassers. In other words, as the nation became more "homey" to some (the national subjects), migrants became even more homeless. To be a "migrant" became tantamount to vagrancy.

Since vagrancy was portrayed as a moral (and often a criminal) offence, migrants came to be strongly associated not only with losing their homes but also their moral standing. Together, such ideologies worked to define the home space as that which stands against migrants.

This was strengthened as the nation-state system expanded in the mid-1800s. In Europe at this time, "the coupling of state sovereignty and nationalism with border control made the 'foreigner' an outsider" (Sassen, 1999: 78). Over time, the naturalization of xenophobia mobilized the idea that nations have some sort of right to preserve their presumed purity. Thus, unsurprisingly, anti-miscegenation discourses have, today, become the basis of asserting ethnic identities and has have often lead to virulent and highly violent forms of "homey racism." Such discourses are "a reactionary vocabulary of the identity politics of place and a spatialised politics of identity grounded in the rhetoric of origins, of exclusion, of boundary-making, of invasion and succession, of purity and contamination … [in short,] the glossary of ethnic cleansing" (Keith & Pile, 1993: 20). Racism is mobilized through the ideology of nationalism so that those conceived "foreigners" are scapegoated as the cause of the nation's problems and targeted for abuse.

Increasingly, goals of maintaining supposed homogeneity are fought for not just in the name of "race purity" but also in the name of preserving "cultural integrity." Indeed, recent practices of racism rely less on ideologies of race separation and more and more on ideas that sanctify culture. An impoverished view of "culture," one that sees it as an unchanging process of ethnicization, has come to overlay notions of biological race so that what connects identity to place is said to be the historical existence of certain "traditions." In this, "tradition [becomes] the cultural equivalent of the process of biological reproduction" (Morley, 2000: 65). This "new racism" has been called a "differentialist racism" (Taguieff, 1990) or, simply, "neo-racism" (Balibar, 1991).

This form of racism is heavily reliant on nationalist practices and is evident in some of the earliest attempts to debunk psuedoscientific rationales for racism. The United Nations agency UNESCO, in its 1951 "Statement on the Nature of Race and Race Differences," illustrates this well when it states, "Americans are not a race, nor are Frenchmen, nor Germans; nor *ipso facto* is any other national group.…" (cited in Guillaumin, 1995: 104). In the process of trying to shed light on the ideological character of ideas of separate and discrete "races," such statements, unfortunately, further naturalized the existence of "different nations."

This is not simply a shift in the meaning of race so that nation becomes collapsed into race. Rather, it signals the growing importance of nationalism and the maintenance of nationalized borders in the ongoing reconfiguration of racialized identities. In such "cultural fundamentalisms" (Stolcke, 1995: 5), the differences among nationals and immigrants are the most naturalized. Thus, instead of ordering different cultures hierarchically, cultural fundamentalism segregates them spatially, each culture in its place "[and] the 'problem' of immigration is constructed as a political threat to national identity and integrity on account of immigrants' cultural diversity" (1995: 8).

The assumption that any given culture is rooted in a particular geographical place "actively territorializes our identities, whether cultural or national … [and] directly enables a vision of territorial displacement as pathological" (Malkki, 1997: 42, 62). This leads to a suspicion of migration so that people's mobility is seen as only ever being caused by crisis and, for the "national subjects" of the places they move, as producing crisis (Sutcliffe, 2001). Consequently, "the common experience of the homeless and the migrant is to be made to feel out of place" (Bird, 1995: 119). As a result, since "foreigners" and "national subjects" in fact occupy the *same space*, the nation comes to occupy not only a territorial space but also an ideological space of belonging.

While such practices are often thought of as *racist* forms of discrimination, racist ideologies that mark people for exclusion because of their foreign standing rely on *nationalist* practices with their "categories of spatial management" (Hage, 2000: 38). Hage therefore cautions us to pay attention to the significance not only of racist practices but also of *nationalist* ones, for this will help us to uncover the *territorial* dimension of contemporary anti-immigrant politics. Indeed, *not* paying attention to the spatial character of how certain (im)migrants face oppression and **exploitation** has led to the serious understudying of new forms of racism. In this sense nationalism both organizes and helps to mask racialized forms of difference that organize inequalities. Even though Canada officially eliminated racist criteria for immigration selection in 1967, global inequalities between "the West and the Rest" continue to inform who is admitted to Canada and, just as importantly, what status they are assigned. For most of the world's population living in former colonies ("developing countries"), gaining access to Canada with the status of permanent resident remains out of reach. For those living in the so-called rich world, such access is far more secure.

Since "concepts of nation, people, and race are never very far apart" (Hardt & Negri, 2000: 103), examining nationalist practices helps to explain why within the homeland "not all strangers are equally strange" (Peter Fitzpatrick, cited in Morley, 2000: 249). Nationalist practices are concerned with issues of the supposedly "rightful" position of various differentiated people within nation states in ways that racist practices are not. Members of the nation have a sense of "empowered spatiality" in relation to Others who do not so that "in every [epithet of you] 'go home,' there is an 'I want to and am entitled to feel at home in my nation'" (Hage, 2000: 40).

There is, therefore, a particular kind of national subject that is important to construct and to maintain for power to be wielded within modern nation states. Michel Foucault's (1991) discussion of "self-regulation," or **self-government** (the process by which we come to regulate our own behaviour, including our beliefs, our emotions, and our practices, in accordance within the habits of power we live with), helps us to understand the crucial importance of the creation of a particular *subjectivity*, or sense of self, to the realization of nation-state power. Historically in Canada,

> [t]he entities being regulated were in the first instance the characters of individuals … but the nation was also seen as held together by a common subjectivity, whose constant recreation at the individual level ensured the continued survival of the collectivity. The collectivity thus organized had very specific class, gender and racial/ethnic characteristics" (Valverde 1991: 33).

The processes of national self-regulation is not only about constructing and regulating the proper national subject. Having the idea of the "nation" stand in for various levels of homeyness, whether that is the family, household, culture, or community, requires the existence of a "threat" to create a secure sense of Self. In this regard, Hage (2000), using insights from the psychoanalytic theories of Jacques Lacan, argues that nationalist discourses would fall apart if there were not Others against whom the nation could be defined. In the never-ending struggle to realize the goal of a "racially pure nation," Hage (1993: 99–100) notes that "in fact, the other is what allows the nationalist to believe in the possibility of that goal. It spares him the anxiety of having to face the fact that such a goal is impossible … by the very fact of being posited as that which threatens it." Opposition to foreigners, thus, becomes a way for those who self-define themselves as being at home within a nation state to argue for their more privileged access to much-needed life resources.

Hence, nationalist practices are based on ideas of *undesirability* rather than the ideas of *inferiority* that often underscore racism (Hage, 2000). While discourses of inferiority do not necessarily necessitate Self-defense, discourses of undesirability motivate *action* toward the neutralization, if not outright extermination, of whoever is presented as threatening the security of the homeland. Because the nation is a community of similarity, threats are defined as foreign, regardless of the actual location of the people so identified or the common traits that people may share across borders.

The sharp distinction between citizens and foreigners produces the image of migrants as polluting the home society. Excluding those who are deemed to be filthy and undesirable, as novelist Anne Michaels (1996) notes in her novel, *Fugitive Pieces*, comes to be seen as a national *obligation*. In writing about the Nazi policy of exterminating those constructed as being always outside of the German nation, she writes:

> Nazi policy was beyond racism, it was anti-matter, for Jews were not considered human. An old trick of language, used often in the course of history. Non-Aryans were never to be referred to as human, but as "figuren," "stücke"—"dolls," "wood," "merchandise," "rags." Humans were not being gassed, only "figuren," so ethics weren't being violated. No one could be faulted for burning debris, for burning rags and clutter in the dirty basement of society. In fact, they're a fire hazard! What choice but to burn them before they harm you?

Foreigners are perceived as weakening the bonds of community said to hold the national family together. Migrants, especially those arriving from places deemed as far (not necessarily only geographically but culturally) from the Self-identity of those claiming home ownership rights, challenge the very idea of the existence of national home(lands). Phil Cohen (1996) puts it this way: "[I]f immigrants put down roots, if ethnic minorities make a home from home, then they are perceived to threaten the privileged link between habit and habitat upon which the myth of indigenous origins rests."

The very mobility of those migrants deemed as "too strange to be Us" calls into question the segmentation of the world into separate zones of supposedly natural belonging. In this regard, such migrants are threatening because they "make our taken-for-granted identities visible as specific identities and deprive them of their assumed naturalness"; hence, "once we start thinking about them, becoming aware of them, we cannot feel "at home" any more" (Rathzel, 1994: 91). For this reason, the mobility of Others "becomes a basic form of disorder and chaos—constantly defined as transgression and trespass" (Cresswell, 1996: 87). A comment by a woman refugee from Cambodia living in Paris puts it succinctly: "we are a disturbance.... Because we show you in a terrible way how fragile the world we live in is" (in Morley, 2000: 152).

I turn now to the ways migrants have been made into strangers in nationalized homelands.

DEMONIZATION OF (CERTAIN) MIGRANTS

The strong association between migration and mayhem is a result of the inequalities created by European capitalist colonization. The supposed similarity of some people with one another (such as "The English") and the extraordinary "strangeness" of Others (such as "The Hindoos," as people in South Asia were once labelled) is an idea that formed through the global flow of capital, goods, and people and the gross inequalities that organized such movements. Many of the naturalized homelands of today (such as Canada) exist because of the forced dispossession, displacement, violent assimilation, and, sometimes, outright genocide of those whom the colonists called "the natives." This is most clearly understood in the case of the "New World," in which the path of nationhood for some of the world's First Nation states was paved by the severe reduction, and at times elimination, of the diverse groups of people through war, slavery, disease, genocide, and the forced adoption of capitalist social relations. Similar processes occurred in Africa, Asia, and even Europe, as nation states were violently erected on the ashes of many diverse preexisting societies. However, those living in societies defining themselves as "Western" set themselves apart from all others by arguing for their centrality in the advancement of "civilization" itself. Racializing themselves as white was a part of how this was accomplished (Hyslop, 1999).

Within this complexity of migration, displacement, and simultaneous homeyness and homelessness, we must not confuse the process of colonization with migration per se. Colonization is a relationship of exploitation and oppression. Colonization can be experienced both as dispossession and as displacement. The problem with colonization is not the "strangeness" of the colonizers, but their greed and the social relations they impose. Indeed, many groups who previously initiated practices of dispossession and displacement (the aristocracy and early capitalists in what we now call England, for instance) are now imagined as "related" to, or even the "same" as, those (commoners) whose lands they took and whose labour they exploited.

However, the migrations of people—displaced commoners, kidnapped Africans, indentured Asian labourers of the past, or, currently, professionals and their families, undocumented labourers, temporary foreign workers, or those fleeing political persecution—are not equivalent to the migration of colonizers. Instead, these movements of people were/are initiated and organized through processes of colonization that brought into asymmetrical relationship almost everyone on the planet and continue at a high rate today because of the long-term consequences of such asymmetries in power and wealth.

Ironically, the mayhem that results in people moving, or that ensues in the lives of those who migrate, is not at the forefront of discussions about the "problem" of migration. Instead, migrants are often scapegoated as the cause of mayhem for those who imagine themselves at home in nationalized spaces. Indeed, the association between migration and mayhem has become even more pronounced with the expansion of the power of nation states in our lives. Today, there is an almost complete collapse of the space between human society and nation states (Urry, 2000).

To more fully understand the relationship between state practices and social relations based on ideas of nation and race (or ethnicity) that allow some to claim exclusive homelands while leaving Others homeless in those same spaces, we need to challenge the separation of state from society that ideas of civil society put into place. In *The German Ideology*, Karl Marx and Friedrich Engels (1969) showed how the ideology that something called "civil society" *created* the state which was then seen to govern *for* the citizenry *was* in large part how working people were co-opted into the capitalist forms of state rule. Indeed, the idea that the state rules for the "Common Good" is a key part of its legitimacy in the eyes of those who imagine themselves as rightful members of national society.

The existence of a group of people who consider themselves to be part of the nation (or civil society) and therefore regard themselves not as ruled *over* but as ruled *for* helps to secure the continued existence of the nation state and the discriminatory practices against all those classified as "foreigners." In other words, the construction of a civil sphere becomes a way to naturalize the power of state rule. By claiming to represent the "national family" the state secures its power over not only those represented as "foreigners," but just as importantly, those represented as its national subjects.

However, these "foreigners" exist not only outside of the borders of the nation state but within it as well. This is not a new phenomenon. Throughout the history of nation states, the purported enemy/foreigner has never been limited to those *outside* of national space. In fact, the targeting of people represented as foreigners *within* the nation has often been more of a spur to nationalist activity than have outside threats (Hyslop, 1999).

One of the most recent examples in our post-9/11 world is how terrorism has been successfully represented as a *Third World import* carried in mainly by certain non-white migrants. Indeed, the Canadian border has been identified as the "first line of defense" against terrorists. With the intersection between the negative *racialization* of "terrorism" and its understanding as something *foreign* to Canada, it has been those with the status of *non-citizens* who have been made subject to the most coercive state actions—actions that would be unconstitutional were they to be carried out against citizens. The most notorious example of this has been the use of National Security Certificates that allow the Canadian state to indefinitely incarcerate non-citizens—and *only* non-citizens—without laying criminal charges or respecting the *habeas corpus* rights of the detainees to challenge their incarceration. Ideologically, the legitimacy of these Certificates rests on both the *racialization* of the threat of terrorism as embodied in those identified as "Muslims," "Middle-Easterners," and "South Asians" and on the *nationalization* of "terrorists" as "foreign." Indeed, the assumption "[u]nderlying much of the debate on security certificates … is the unspoken assumption that non-citizens are more dangerous than citizens" (Cleveland, Aiken & Crépeau, 2007). Legally, the use of these certificates rests on the modern practice of **national sovereignty**, in which those classified as "citizens" hold a higher value in spaces where they are seen by the state as its subjects.

Nancy Fraser (1993), in rejecting classical theories of national citizenship with their idea that those once left out will be progressively included in the nation, points out that the organization of civil society of capitalist liberal democracies is premised on many layers of separations and exclusions. There is both the separation of state from (civil) society and the existence of separate spaces of belonging for various "types" of people who are differently classified according to deeply entrenched ideologies of separate races and genders and, perhaps most legitimately, by the belief that there are different territorial spaces for differently nationalized people. The conclusion is that full inclusion is simply not possible within the logic of nation-state citizenship.

The notion of the nation as home for all who live there, then, is ideological. It conceals the fact that the exclusions organized through it are part and parcel to these processes, not simply coincidental or something that can be done away with through bureaucratic tinkering. In a global world, national borders are a major aspect of how the inequalities between "the West and the Rest" are maintained. In this respect, Avner Offer's (1989) argument that racist practices are *part of* the liberal "virtues of democracy, civic equality and solidarity" take on greater relevance, as does John Holloway's (1994) argument that because the state is formed through assertions of national sovereignty constructed through the organization of racialized differences between Us and Them, "the very existence of the [national] state is racist."

With regard to national styles of ruling, we need to pay more careful attention to Kobena Mercer's (1994) question: "*Why* the need for the nation?" Examining "*who* needs it, *who* manufactures the 'need' for it, and *whose* interests it serves" is an even more urgent task (Burton, 1997). In this sense, it is useful to understand that the state, like the nation, is *imagined*. This does not mean that the state does not exist. Rather, the state, like the nation, is a form of social relations. The legitimacy—and power—of the state is reliant upon the existence of the "imagined community" of the nation for whom it is said to operate (Anderson, 1991). That is, the state—and the set of social relationships organized through it—requires the existence of a group who understand themselves to be a "nation" to continue to make common sense to people.

Concepts of citizenship are the ideological glue that hold these nationalist ideas in place. Citizenship provides the legal framework through which the state performs its role as ruler *for* the nation. Citizens are given privileged standing within the nation state. It is not a coincidence, therefore, that the first *Canadian Citizenship Act* of 1946 was passed in the wake of World War II, when the idea of a distinct Canadian nation state became more accepted and full-fledged Canadian state sovereignty was secured. The ability of the Canadian state to bestow citizenship was a key marker of its sovereignty.

Together the ideas and practices of citizenship provide legitimacy to the state to legally subordinate those imagined as foreigners. Indeed, denying the rights, entitlements, and protections that citizens have to those made into non-citizens is a crucial feature of how dominant ideas of nations-as-homes operate within today's world. In this, citizenship and immigration policies are the key avenue through which nationalism is entrenched within social systems. Immigration policies have historically played a significant part in organizing and regulating the differences organized by nation states. This is why it continues to be onto the bodies of migrants that a "foreign" identity can most easily be grafted. In this process, citizenship plays a crucial part. Indeed, the closely related powers wielded by contemporary nation states and capitalists rest precisely on our acceptance of the citizenship divide. Moreover, "citizenship," along with conferring rights for some also works to deny these rights to many others who are deemed "non-citizens."

CITIZENSHIP AND THE MAKING OF DIFFERENCE

As discussed earlier, those imagined as foreigners live within nation states. In other words, in every nation state, many people who live and work within its territories are denied citizenship, and even immigration, status. In fact, within the hierarchy of citizenship and non-citizenship, people can hold a variety of statuses. These are arranged hierarchically with citizenship, and the rights it bestows, at the pinnacle. In Canada, the status of permanent resident (with which the category of "immigrant" is most associated) grants the recipient the right to stay within national territories under a certain set of conditions. Permanent residents can apply for citizenship status after years of residency. People may also be granted the status of refugee applicant, which accords them minimal rights and entitlements until they are given refugee status and the permanent residency that comes with it.

FIGURE 15.2 ■ Anytime and place where border controls have been erected, migrants have acted to protect their humanity and their rights. There is an active migrants-rights movement in Canada.

© Chris Wayatt/Alamy

Following these statuses there is a steep decline in the rights and entitlements available to migrants. People assigned "temporary foreign worker" or "non-immigrant" status are generally made to work for a particular employer. Their legal status in the country is wholly dependent upon their remaining employed. The vast majority of people falling in this category are expected to leave when their work visa expires. People working in temporary workers programs, including the Seasonal Agricultural Workers Program (SAWP) and the Live-in Caregiver Program (LCP), all face the threat of deportation if their employer is dissatisfied with them or if they work for an unauthorized employer. Those who are seen by the state as "illegal" have very limited rights to stay and no rights to work in Canada. Their ability to eke out a life in the country is dependent upon avoiding detection by immigration officials. Since anyone might potentially turn them in, including employers, teachers, doctors, neighbours, and even "friends," their "illegal" status makes them enormously vulnerable to those around them. As mentioned earlier, the vast majority of people entering Canada over the past three decades are no longer granted permanent resident status. Most new migrants to Canada are now either "non-immigrant" migrant workers or are illegalized.

In 2004, for instance, out of a total of about 354,000 people moving to Canada for work and residence, only 35 percent (about 125,000 people) were granted permanent residency, while 65 percent (about 229,000 people) were given temporary "foreign worker" status, tying them to their employers (Sharma, 2006). In addition, while it is difficult to definitively determine the number of people living and working in Canada without official state permission (those made "illegal" by the state), it is estimated that upwards of 500,000 migrants are without legal status.

This reveals that border controls and immigration restrictions are thoroughly *ideological*. First, they do very little to actually control people's movement across national borders. Second, because such borders are imagined as natural—and as a crucial part of state sovereignty—their operation as an integral feature of how national societies are shaped is confused if not completely concealed. Whether we talk about border control spectacles, such as the 3,200-kilometre steel fence being erected along the Mexico-U.S. border and patrolled by armed U.S. border control officers, or "Europe's new Berlin Wall" (the 8-kilometre fence between the Spanish-claimed enclave of Melilla and the rest of Africa), or the ever-more-restrictive immigration policies of every nation state in the global North, restrictions on who is legally able to enter with full status do very little to actually restrict migration itself. Nor are they intended to.

Restricting *immigration* (such as limiting permanent residency status) is not tantamount to restricting people's migration. Historically, many people have migrated to Canada only to live in the country under a subordinated legal status (including the status of "illegal"). Since the first *Immigration Act* in 1869, discrimination against the movement of certain people has been built into the immigrant process. Some migrants have been/are classified as "desirable" while others have been/are either denied entry outright or subordinated within Canadian society through restricted status. Over time, those on the "undesirable" list have included people considered physically or mentally ill or disabled, particular religious groups, those negatively racialized, sex workers and other independent women, those criminalized, political agitators (especially communists), homosexuals, and more.

This did not mean that people falling into these categories did not migrate to Canada or live their lives in the country. Rather, such people were legally subordinated members of Canadian society. For instance, while people racialized as Chinese were only granted Canadian citizenship status in 1947, there had been continuous Chinese presence in the territories now claimed by Canada since at least 1788. While many (but not all) of these restrictions were dropped in 1962, other forms of discrimination remain. Moreover, shortly after the opening up of the possibility of migration to Canada to people previously defined as undesirable, the process of closing down avenues of obtaining permanent resident status began.

Over the past 30 years, the majority of those moving to Canada have been denied permanent residency status. Instead, the majority of new migrants have either entered as "temporary foreign" workers or been forced to live as "illegals" (Sharma, 2006). Constructing people as foreigners has not resulted in outright exclusion of these people from Canadian society. Instead, placing state limits on their ability to migrate as permanent residents and eventually become Canadian citizens means that what is being restricted is their freedom, rights, and entitlements once they are living and working *within* Canada.

This can be seen in the changes made to Canadian immigration policy since the 1960s. By 1967, non-white people who had previously been placed in categories of "non-preferred races" or "non-preferred nations" and denied the ability to make a home in Canada were now deemed admissible to Canada as permanent residents. Unlike for the restrictions facing immigrants from Europe, however, there was a significant class dimension to this new admissibility of non-whites. Preference was given to immigrants with professional degrees and their families. Not only did this favour men, who had easier access to higher education than many women did, it also put in place severe barriers to immigration to Canada for those without professional accreditation. Even so, many "independent" class immigrants found that the degrees they earned outside Canada, especially in Third World countries, were not validated by Canadian professional associations. As a result, many were unable to find work in their chosen profession, and instead were situated in low-paying jobs with little benefits and security. In addition, despite the notion that many women in the "family" class of immigration were "housewives," a disproportionate number of them worked in the paid labour force, often in low-paying jobs. These realities continue to shape the experiences of immigrants today.

One of the significant post-1967 changes is the shift in Canadian immigration policy toward a greater emphasis on admitting people within a highly subordinated category of "non-immigrant." Despite living and working in Canada, these people are imagined as part of a "foreign" workforce. Since 1973, there has been a fundamental shift in the status accorded to new (im)migrants. Most are now admitted as **temporary foreign workers** (or **migrant workers**). For the vast majority, such a status precludes the possibility of permanent residency (and citizenship) status. Increasingly, many more people denied entry in any legal immigration channel are forced to live and work in Canada as "illegals."

Putting such restrictions on people's access to citizenship has been enormously beneficial to employers: those given less than permanent, legal status in Canada are generally cheaper and less able to organize to gain benefits than those with citizenship or permanent resident status. Their "cheapness" is legislated by the state to the benefit of employers. The simultaneous presence of anti-immigration political rhetoric that is highly evident within Canada and actual increases in the number of people migrating to Canada is not at all contradictory. In fact, as Hage (2000: 135) puts it, "anti-immigration discourse, by continually constructing the immigrants as unwanted, works precisely at maintaining [their] economic viability to … employers. They are best wanted as 'unwanted.'"

Border controls and restrictions on access to citizenship enable nation states to reorganize their nationalized labour markets to formally *include* a group of migrant workers made vulnerable to employers' demands through their lack of permanent and legal status. Today, when people's displacement and subsequent migration is occurring at a historically

While almost all "temporary foreign workers" are legally tied to their employer, some, like those regulated by Canada's Live-in Caregiver Program (LCP), the Seasonal Agricultural Worker Program (SAWP), or the even more restrictive Pilot Project for Occupations Requiring Lower Levels of Formal Training program introduced in 2002, face even further restrictions on their freedom and mobility within Canada. The LCP legally *requires* "temporary foreign workers" (mostly non-white women) to live in the same residence as their employers. Not only have there been well-documented cases of abuse arising from this condition, such a stipulation constitutes a clear violation of Section 6 of the *Canadian Charter of Rights and Freedoms* that protects the mobility rights of Canadian citizens, and to a lesser extent that of permanent residents. Persons regulated by the SAWP often have curfews imposed upon them, are prohibited from receiving visitors of the opposite sex, and are often fired if they become pregnant (Preibisch, 2010). In the case of those employed through the Pilot Project for Occupations Requiring Lower Levels of Formal Training program, the Canadian state has written itself out of its responsibility to intervene in the conditions of work for those recruited through it (largely persons from Guatemala). This leaves these persons with no official recourse if their employer reneges on his/her part of the contract. Moreover, the contract that is drawn up (by employers with the assistance the International Organization for Migration) and that potential recruits must sign, contains terms for employment that, again, should be considered unconstitutional. For the duration of their employment, workers are told they should "avoid" joining any group or association, showing any signs of what the employer considers "disrespect," or having sexual relations. The contract even contains a clause regarding the length of the person's hair (UFCW, 2010)! Clearly, Canada's "temporary foreign workers" programs create extra conditions to control workers and their entire personhood that are unavailable to the state or employers to act against "citizens" and "permanent residents."

unprecedented level—the United Nations (2005) estimates that every year over 190 million people migrate across national borders—nationalism, with its legitimization of differential treatment for citizens and foreigners, has become a motor force of capitalist development.

To better understand the significance of difference to such projects, we need to clearly distinguish between difference and diversity. Diversity is the tangible existence of heterogeneity within nature and within humanity. Difference, on the other hand, consists in socially organized inequalities between human beings and between humans and the rest of the planet. The social organization of difference is the effect of practices and beliefs founded upon hierarchies of differential value and worth.

When we say someone is "different," we are not simply recognizing that person's uniqueness. Instead, we are setting her or him aside as a member of a group that does not meet normative standards of being. Difference, then is a kind of relationship between people. "Difference" can only meaningfully be claimed in relationship to some other idea of "sameness." It is this **relational** aspect of difference that Stuart Hall talks about in his discussion about "the West and the rest." The norms constructed through such *binary codes* are always centred on the experiences, desires, and power held by those in the dominant half of Self/Other dichotomies.

The politics of constructing and maintaining such stark dichotomies in which one half of the equation is privileged is what constitutes the politics of identity of people with relative power (Bannerji, 1995). This is evident in everyday understandings of difference. People who are "different" are so identified because of the ways they are seen as standing apart from those with the power to define them. Someone's kinship and other social practices, the food they prefer, their appearance, and so on is deemed as being "different" only in relation to those who imagine themselves as representing the "norm" within any particular nationalized space. Such lines of difference between Self and Other are related to narratives of national belonging and to the global process of distinguishing "the West" from "the Rest."

In this, history and context matter. In Canada, the process of colonization prepared the groundwork for the contemporary organization of difference. The worldview of a select group of people profoundly shaped the social organization of relationships in Canada. The domination of capitalists over workers; of men over women and all of nature; the racialization and hierarchical organization of various racialized populations into "Natives," "Blacks," "Asians," "Whites," "Irish," "southern" and "eastern" "Europeans," "Latinos"; the demonization of non-Christian religions and of the non-religious; the classification of those whose sexuality is "queer" as deviant; the enclosure of the commons; and the creation of Europe and the colonization of its Others—all these have at various times been organized in opposition to "Canadian-ness." In short, it is through people's relationship to the Canadian self-identity of being white, Christian, heterosexual, and male that difference has been structured.

The central distinction between difference and diversity, then, is that unlike diversity, difference has *homogeneity* as its overarching goal. The organization of difference is about ensuring conformity to dominant beliefs and practices in an attempt to shape the world in the image of dominant groups. Difference is about universalizing a *particular* interest, of taking diversity and filtering it of any divergence from the norm to create a "monoculture of the mind" (Shiva 1997).

What to make, then, of current attempts to validate and valorize *difference* within contemporary politics (Young, 1989)? To start, it is important to note that the attempt to end oppressive and exploitative social relations, particularly those of racism, through an acknowledgement of *differences* has led to political solutions such as the official promotion of "tolerance" for "different" people. This kind of political practice has come to be called demonstrating a "respect for diversity." Of course, the stated aim of this respect is to secure the proper functioning of society as a singular, national body in the image of Self-defined rulers. In such rhetoric, the nation is thought to be able to simply transcend conflict through respect and celebration of difference without the elimination of any differentials in power and wealth and with no transformation at a systemic level.

This is the kind of diversity embraced by the state. It is one that enables those in positions of power over Others to "tolerate" people who have been differentiated. Yet, when those in positions of power are asked to be tolerant, their power to be intolerant is not taken away from them (Hage, 2000). It is, in fact, reasserted by the very request to have them not exercise it. In this regard, respect for diversity does not eclipse the social organization of difference but becomes a contemporary form of reproducing hierarchal social relations and re-centring the norms of the national subject.

This kind of **official diversity** needs to be distinguished from what I call forms of **radical diversity**. Official diversity is a co-opted form of diversity and has come to mean its exact opposite: the power of one group over the many others. Social systems based on radical diversity, on the other hand, depend on recognizing and maintaining heterogeneity. This is the kind of diversity that exists in healthy and sustainable ecosystems: each unique thing requires the uniqueness of other things for the continued existence of the whole. For instance, it is estimated that without bees, many of the crops that humans rely on could not grow and provide us with the food we need to survive.

The social organization of difference is therefore a highly ideological practice, one linked to the **material** production of unjust social relations. Within the conceptual carving out of differentiated zones of belonging lies concealed the interconnected relations between so-called different people. In particular, the idea that there exists two supposedly discrete spaces, the national one in which Canadians exist and a global or foreign one that contains Others, has structured the sense of Canadian-ness that legitimates the subordination of migrant workers within Canada.

The social organization of difference with regard to nationalized borders and the various state categories of citizenship works to create forms of **apartheid** whereby discrimination is organized through exclusionary inclusion. Nationalized differences, in particular, are consequential to the emergence and further entrenchment of **global apartheid**: the organization of an ever-widening differentiation between people in either wealthy or impoverished nation states through restrictive immigration policies that imprison impoverished people within zones of poverty (Richmond, 1994). We can see that a system of apartheid exists *within* Canada as well so that those with subordinated statuses, such as migrant worker or "illegal" live in zones of poverty inside the rich world. A system of apartheid can be said to exist when at least two different legal systems operate within the space of any given state. In the case of a contemporary global apartheid, it is an apartheid that has one set of laws that regulate those seen by the state as its national subjects and another set of laws (usually pertaining to citizenship and immigration) that regulate those classified as foreigners. While it is the legal system that puts the coercive force of the state behind such classifications, it is important to recognize that it is how we think of variously classified people within Canada that makes such a system appear to be legitimate for a large proportion of the population.

Nationalism, with its legitimization of nationalized borders and exclusionary practices of bestowing or denying citizenship, is an everyday practice that organizes discrimination within this global apartheid. For instance, many in Canada believe that if migrant agricultural workers were not forced to work for specific employers and were instead granted the freedom to work for whomever they choose, they would leave agricultural work altogether and look for better-paid and less dangerous, less backbreaking work. This is undoubtedly true, since this is precisely what those with Canadian citizenship status have done. To argue that one group (citizens) should have such rights while others (migrant workers) should not is, in part, what keeps the cost of food relatively affordable in the capitalist market. We tend not to see that the relative cheapness of our food is directly related to the low wages and lack of rights given to its direct producers, because this relationship has been hidden through nationalist ideologies that organize our belief in the right to do unto "foreigners" what we would not do to "citizens." In particular, the nation-state system has limited our sense of self and left us with an impoverished ability to empathize and connect to people beyond national borders and identities. The very practices that purportedly affirm our belonging in the nation are the same ones that allow the Canadian nation state to legitimately mark some Others who live there to be socially and legally inscribed as foreign bodies.

Challenging nationalized forms of "difference" and reconnecting to people across the boundaries created by national citizenship regimes, therefore, is one of the greatest political challenges of our time. This is because, today, nationalism provides one of the primary modes of self-identification. Challenging the legitimacy of national forms of discrimination, then, is a direct challenge both to the forms of subjectivity we hold and to the material organization of our lives. Doing so may lead us to ways of organizing human societies at the scales in which our lives are actually lived and with the affinities required to combat many of the major social problems we face, be they ecological disaster, growing poverty, wars over territory and "national honour," or hatred of the myriad Others who don't fit into dominant norms of national belonging. The challenge is clearly great. However, the fact that human societies are fundamentally *social* provides us with the hope for non-national forms of organization.

STUDY QUESTIONS

1. There is a deep relationship between ideas of "nation" and the power of states over people within the national territories it claims. Discuss the ways that the different identities of "national subject" and "foreigner" affect people's everyday lived experience of life in Canada.

2. What are some of the reasons that the Canadian nation state gives different legal and illegal statuses to people who move to Canada?

3. How are these different statuses legitimized (or normalized) within Canadian society?

4. What does it mean to contend that national border controls are ideological?

5. Do you think that national borders that empower states to regulate and limit people's mobility are ethical?

EXERCISES

1. *Ethical responses to global displacement.* There are a number of factors that cause people to migrate. These include: war; persecution; abuse; famine; inhabitability of a place (as a result of floods, earthquakes, tsunamis, droughts, etc.); loss of land and/or livelihood; poverty; a sense that there are better opportunities elsewhere; and the excitement of travel and a new life. How is the Canadian state at least partially responsible for the existence of these conditions in a number of places around the world? What is the ethical responsibility of a country like Canada to people who migrate as a result of its activities? Can we separate Canadian policy on immigration from its military policies, its international trade policies, or its policies on greenhouse gas emissions?

2. *Migrating to another nation state.* Think about the factors that might cause you to move from Canada to another nation state. How would you get there? What would you need? What legal channels would you have to follow? What would you do if you were not granted official permission to enter and reside in this new place? What would you miss about your life in Canada? How would you make a living in the new place? Remember, you need to find a place to live, food to eat, water to drink, and so on.

3. *Rights.* Go the websites of international bodies, such as that of the International Labour Organization (http://www.ilo.org/global/lang--en/index.htm) or the United Nations (www.un.org). Think about some of the other already existing ways that rights and entitlements are allocated and distributed in the world today. How do they compare to the rights granted "citizens" (and therefore denied "foreigners")? Are there even less exclusionary (or even nonexclusionary) ways to organize rights and entitlements? What are some other ways that we could allocate rights and entitlements to ensure that all human beings are able to live healthy and dignified lives?

REFERENCES

Anderson, Benedict. 1991. *Imagined Communities: Reflections on the Origin and Spread of Nationalism.* London: Verso.

Balibar, Étienne. 1991. Is there a neo-racism? In Étienne Balibar and Immanuel Wallerstein, eds., *Race, Nation, Class: Ambiguous Identities.* London: Verso.

Bammer, Anjelika. 1992. Editorial. *New Formations* 17 (Summer 1992): vii–xi.

Bannerji, Himani. 1995. *Thinking Through: Essays on Feminism, Marxism, and Anti-Racism.* Toronto: Women's Press.

Bird, John. 1995. Dolce domum. In J. Lingwood, ed., *House.* London: Phaidon Press.

Burton, Antoinette. 1997. Who needs the nation? Interrogating "British" history. *Journal of Historical Sociology* 10(3): 227–48.

Cleveland, Janet, Sharryn J. Aiken, and François Crépeau. 2007. The rights of non-citizens. *Ottawa Citizen*, October 31.

Cohen, Philip. 1996. Homing devices. In V. Amit-Talai and C. Knowles, eds., *Re-situating Identities.* Peterborough: Broadview Press.

Cresswell, Tim. 1996. *In Place/Out of Place*. Minneapolis: University of Minnesota Press.

Foucault, Michel. 1991. Questions of method. In G. Burchell, C. Gordon, and P. Miller, eds., *The Foucault Effect: Studies in Governmentality*. University of Chicago Press: Chicago.

Fraser, Nancy. 1993. Rethinking the public sphere. In B. Robbins, ed., *The Phantom Public Sphere*. Minneapolis: Minnesota University Press.

Guillaumin, Colette. 1995. *Racism, Sexism, Power and Ideology*. London: Routledge.

Hage, Ghassan. 1993. Nation-building-dwelling-being. *Communal/Plural* 1: 73–104.

Hage, Ghassan. 2000. *White Nation: Fantasies of White Supremacy in a Multicultural Society*. New York; Annandale, NSW, Australia: Routledge and Pluto Press.

Hardt, Michael, and Antonio Negri. 2000. *Empire*. Cambridge, MA: Harvard University Press.

Hobsbawm, Eric. 1991. Exile. *Social Research* 58(1) (Spring 1991).

Holloway, John. 1994. Global capital and the national state. In *Capital and Class* 52 (Spring): 23–50.

Hyslop, Jonathan. 1999. The imperial working class makes itself "white": White labourism in Britain, Australia, and South Africa before the First World War. *Journal of Historical Sociology* 12(4) (December): 398–421.

Irigaray, Luce. 1993. *An Ethics of Sexual Difference*. London: Athlone Press.

Johansen, Anders. 1997. Fellowmen, compatriots, contemporaries. In J. Peter Burgess, ed., *Cultural Politics and Political Culture in Postmodern Europe*. Amsterdam: Editions Rodopi.

Keith, Michael, and Steven Pile. 1993. The politics of place. In M. Keith and S. Pile, eds., *Place and the Politics of Identity*. London: Routledge.

Kumar, Krishan. 1994. Home: The nature of private life at the end of the twentieth century. In J. Wintraub and K. Kumar, eds., *Private and Public in Thought and Practice*. Chicago: University of Chicago Press.

Mackay, Hugh, ed. 1997. *Consumption and Everyday Life*. Milton Keynes, Buckinghamshire, UK: Open University Press.

Malkki, Lisa. 1997. National geographic. In A. Gupta and J. Ferguson, eds., *Culture, Power, Place*. Durham: Duke University Press.

Marx, Karl, and Friedrich Engels. 1969. Feuerbach: Opposition of the materialistic and idealistic outlook (Chapter 1 of *The German Ideology*). In *Selected Works, Volume 1*. Moscow: Progress Publishers.

McClintock, Anne. 1995. *Imperial Leather*. London, Routledge.

Mercer, Kobena. 1994. *Welcome to the Jungle: New Positions in Black Cultural Studies*. New York: Routledge.

Michaels, Anne. 1996. *Fugitive Pieces*. Toronto: McClelland and Steward.

Morley, David. 2000. *Home Territories: Media, Mobility and Identity*. London; New York: Routledge.

Offer, Avner. 1989. *The First World War: An Agrarian Interpretation*. New York: Oxford University Press.

Preibisch, Kerry. 2010. Pick-your-own labor: Migrant workers and flexibility in Canadian agriculture. *International Migration Review* 44(2): 404–441.

Rathzel, Nora. 1994. Harmonious "Heimat" and disturbing "Ausländer." In K. K. Bhavani and A. Phoenix, eds., *Shifting Identities and Shifting Racisms*. London: Sage.

Richmond, Anthony H. 1994. *Global Apartheid: Refugees, Racism, and the New World Order*. Don Mills, ON: Oxford University Press.

Sassen, Saskia. 1999. *Guests and Aliens*. New York: The New Press.

Sharma, Nandita. 2006. *Home Economics: Nationalism and the Making of Migrant Workers in Canada*. Toronto: University of Toronto Press.

Shiva, Vandana. 1997. *Biopiracy: The Plunder of Nature and Knowledge*. Toronto: Between the Lines.

Smith, Dorothy. 1990. *The Conceptual Practices of Power: A Feminist Sociology of Knowledge*. Toronto: University of Toronto Press.

Stolcke, Verena. 1995. Talking culture: New boundaries, new rhetorics of exclusion. *Current Anthropology* 36(1): 1–24.

Sutcliffe, Bob. 2001. Migration and citizenship: Why can birds, whales, butterflies and ants cross international frontiers more easily than cows, dogs and human beings? In Subrata Ghatak and Anne Showstack Sassoon, eds., *Migration and Mobility: The European Context*. New York: Palgrave.

Tabor, Philip. 1998. Striking home—The Telematic assault on identity. In J. Hill, ed., *Occupying Architecture*. London, Routledge.

Taguieff, Pierre-André. 1990. The new cultural racism in France. *Telos* 83: 109–122.

Thatcher, Margaret. 1989. Interview with Julie Cockroft. *Daily Mail*, May 4.

UFCW (United Farm and Commercial Workers Union). 2010. Guatemalan migrants. UFCW website, http://www.ufcw.ca/index.php?option=com_content&view=article&id=2161&Itemid=291&lang=en, accessed February 2, 2011.

United Nations Population Fund. 2005. *The State of World Population*. New York: UNFPA.

Urry, John. 2000. *Sociology Beyond Societies: Mobilities for the Twenty-First Century*. London; New York: Routledge.

Valverde, Mariana. 1991. *The Age of Light, Soap, and Water: Moral Reform in English Canada, 1885–1925*. Toronto: McClelland and Stewart.

Young, Iris Marion. 1989. Polity and group difference. *Ethics* 99(2): 250–274.

CONTRIBUTORS

Deborah Brock is an Associate Professor in the Department of Sociology at York University in Toronto. Her research and teaching address social, moral, and sexual regulation. The second edition of her book, *Making Work, Making Trouble: The Social Regulation of Sexual Labour* (1998), was released by the University of Toronto Press in 2009. She has edited one previous textbook for Nelson Canada: *Making Normal: Social Regulation in Canada* (2003).

Margot Francis is an Assistant Professor in the program of Women's Studies, cross-appointed to the Department of Sociology at Brock University. She teaches courses on queer communities and popular culture, the construction of race and gender in Canadian culture, and contemporary feminist methods. Her research interests include: feminist, queer, and postcolonial perspectives on settler societies, critical explorations of culture, arts, and identity, and integrative approaches to gender, sexuality, and the body. In the spring of 2007 she was awarded, along with Karl Hele, the Director of First Nations Studies at the University of Western Ontario, a Social Sciences and Humanities Research Council research grant for a project entitled Memory and History Through Performance at Garden River First Nation. She is currently completing a book titled *"Ghosts Trying to Find Their Clothes": Re-Imagining Icons and Identities of the Canadian Nation* (with UBC Press).

Gavin Fridell is an Associate Professor and Department Chair of Politics at Trent University and a research associate at the Center for Research on Latin America and the Caribbean (CERLAC) at York University. He is the author of *Fair Trade Coffee: The Prospects and Pitfalls of Market-Driven Social Justice* (University of Toronto Press, 2007) and several articles and book chapters on fair trade and international development, including contributions to *Historical Materialism*, *New Political Economy*, *Latin American Perspectives*, *Journal of Business Ethics*, and *Canadian Journal of Development Studies*.

Cynthia Levine-Rasky is Associate Professor in the Department of Sociology, Queen's University in Kingston, Ontario. She is editor of *Working Through Whiteness: International Perspectives* (SUNY Press, 2002). Her recent work appears in *Social Identities*, *British Journal of Sociology of Education*, *Canadian Ethnic Studies*, and *Journal of Education Policy*, and in Darren and Lund, eds., *The Great White North? Exploring Whiteness, Privilege and Identity in Education in Canada*. Her research interest in whiteness as it intersects with middle-classness and ethnicity in the subtle exercise of power is the subject of a monograph, *Whiteness Fractured*, in preparation for University of British Columbia Press.

Aryn Martin is Associate Professor at York University in the Sociology Department. Her teaching and research focus on the social studies of science, medicine, and technology, as well as feminist theory. Her work considers biomedical knowledge production and its incorporation into lived experience. She writes about genetic chimerism, microchimerism, and pregnancy as phenomena that trouble biological and political notions of the individual. Her work has been published in *Social Studies of Science*, *Osiris*, *Social Problems*, and *Body and Society*.

Zoë Newman's research examines the production of whiteness and heteronormativity in discourses of national culture and citizenship. Her current project looks at the multiple and ambivalent uses of spectacle, in particular the stories that get told in mainstream press about queer pride and Caribana/Carnival. As a guest editor of a recent special issue of *Resources for Feminist Research* entitled "Decolonizing Spaces," she continued investigations of how racial and sexual hierarchies are sustained and resisted through the organization of urban space. Zoë teaches in the Department of Sociology and the School of Women's Studies at York University, in the areas of critical sexualities, racialization, and transnational feminism.

Andrea Noack is an Assistant Professor in the Department of Sociology at Ryerson University. She specializes in research methods and social statistics, with a particular focus on how social processes inform the production of knowledge. In recent projects, she has investigated the working conditions of call centre workers in the federal government, the labour practices of local messengers (couriers) in Toronto, and the employment experiences of recent immigrants to Canada. Her ongoing interest in pedagogy and teaching is reflected in research investigating

students' conceptual learning in physics and her ongoing development and assessment of experiential and Service Learning components in courses for sociology students.

Joan Phillips is currently a Research Fellow at the Policy Studies Institute in the United Kingdom. A Barbadian national, she holds a B.Sc. and an M.Phil. from the University of the West Indies and a Ph.D. in tourism at the University of Luton, U.K. Her current research includes sex tourism and HIV/AIDS, and return migration to Caribbean.

Rebecca Raby is a sociologist housed in Child and Youth Studies at Brock University. She studies childhood and adolescence in terms of how they are produced as categories, experienced by children and adolescents, and intersected by gender, sexuality, race, and class. Her recent research on secondary-school discipline codes and their negotiation in schools has been developed into a book, *School Rules: Obedience, Discipline and Elusive Democracy*, forthcoming from University of Toronto Press. Currently she is co-investigator on a new SSHRC grant with Shauna Pomerantz on smart girls' negotiation of early high school.

Mary Beth Raddon is an Associate Professor in the Department of Sociology at Brock University, where she researches the political economy of institutions involving gift-giving, such as inheritance, charity, and philanthropy. She also engages in evaluation and action-research of various projects of municipal, activist, and nonprofit organizations for more socially just and livable communities, such as local currencies, transportation alternatives, and democratic public space. In addition, she is implementing and evaluating a pilot course in service-learning in which first-year students study, practice, and critically reflect on community engagement.

Heidi Rimke, Ph.D., teaches in the Department of Sociology at the University of Winnipeg. She specializes in the areas of social and political thought, criminology, cultural studies, and the history of the human sciences with a focus on psy discourses/practices. Some of her publications examine the role of popular psychology/self-help in neoliberalism, the medicalization of morality, the history of criminal sciences, the politics of (in)security, and cannibalism and mass-mediated crime consumption. She is a contributing author to *Racism and Borders: Representation, Repression, Resistance* (Algora, 2010) and *Criminology: Critical Canadian Perspectives* (Pearson, 2010). Her forthcoming book on the history of the doctrine of moral insanity documents the genealogy of "normal."

Nandita Sharma is an Associate Professor of Sociology at the University of Hawaii at Manoa. Her research interests address themes of human migration, migrant labour, national state power, ideologies of racism and nationalism, processes of identification and self-understanding, and social movements for justice. She is an activist scholar whose research is shaped by the social movements she is active in, including No Borders movements and those struggling for the commons. Sharma recently co-edited a special issue of *Refuge* entitled "No Borders as a Practical Political Project"

with Bridget Anderson and Cynthia Wright (2009).

Dennis Soron is an Associate Professor of Sociology at Brock University. His current teaching and research interests include contemporary social theory, cultural studies, the political economy of consumption, environmental sociology, radical ecology, automobility, critical animal studies, and the intersection of labour and environmental politics. He has published various book chapters, articles, and interviews on consumerism, globalization, work, the environment, automobile dependency, human–nonhuman relations, and the issue of depoliticization in advanced capitalist societies. He (with Gordon Laxer) is the co-editor of *Not for Sale: Decommodifying Public Life* (Broadview/Garamond, 2006).

Mark P. Thomas is an Associate Professor in the Department of Sociology at York University. His research interests are in the areas of political economy and economic sociology, with a primary focus on the regulation of labour standards at local, national, and transnational scales. He is the author of *Regulating Flexibility: The Political Economy of Employment Standards* (McGill-Queens, 2009) and co-editor with N. Pupo of *Interrogating the New Economy: Restructuring Work in the 21st Century* (University of Toronto Press, 2010). His most recent project, "From Labour Rights to Human Rights: Emerging Approaches to Labour Standards in the Global Economy," examines the economic, political, and social factors that shape the regulation of transnational labour standards.

GLOSSARY

A

accumulation by dispossession David Harvey's term for contemporary examples of Marx's concept **primitive accumulation**. We can see the results of "primitive accumulation" in a wide range of settings. At its base level, it refers to the introduction of market forces into spaces that were previously non-capitalist. This includes privatization of public resources, usurping foreign resources, and dispossession of land.

active texts a term coined by Dorothy E. Smith for written, visual, musical, and other forms of text that help organize the social relations in which they are embedded. Textual forms are therefore more than a mere medium through which ideas are transmitted; they actively participate in the constitution of knowledge.

advertising's "cultural role" relates not simply to its ability to sell individual products, but its ability to act as a myth-maker or "storyteller" in contemporary culture, exerting a more general influence on our collective values and aspirations. As Sut Jhally argues, the consistent message that cuts across all advertisements today is that happiness comes from the acquisition and consumption of marketplace commodities.

advertising's "marketing role" relates to its ability to increase demand for a particular good or service. For instance, executives at Pepsi might measure the success of a recent campaign by determining if it has contributed to an increase in Pepsi consumption in the target audience.

agency a capacity to make choices within the frames of reference and possibility available to us, and to act on those choices. The capacity of individuals for some degree of autonomous thought and action prevents their actions from being completely determined by existing circumstances.

age norms shared ideas about what is appropriate behaviour at certain times of one's life.

alienation loss by workers of much creative capacity, and their detachment from true productive capacities through engaging in wage labour, because working for a wage involves giving up control over the ability to decide what kind of work one will do, and how it will be done.

anthropocentric judging other forms of animal life according to human perceptions, values, and experiences.

apartheid the policy or practice of segregation of peoples through political, legal, and economic means. Apartheid is therefore a system of social and economic discrimination that maintains and perpetuates social inequalities. The most well-known system of apartheid was in South Africa, where from 1948 until 1993 the state enforced a system of racial segregation. Some social and political theorists now apply the concept of apartheid to international conflicts such as Israeli state policy toward the Palestinian people. The concept of **global apartheid** has also been developed to describe a global system of political, legal, military, and economic power that restricts the movements of people while facilitating the movement of capital.

archaeology of knowledge Foucault's term for the process of uncovering, or excavating, earlier patterns of thought and knowledge that guided people and shaped the times in which they occurred. See also **genealogy and history of the present**.

authoritarian populism   a concept developed by Stuart Hall in his analysis of the rise of conservativism in England during the 1970s. Hall revealed the cultural and policing mechanisms through which the organization of consent is secured, even where it may be against the best interests of many of those who lend their consent. Authoritarian populism is characterized by the attainment of broad public support for authoritarian forms of governing.

B

binary   a perspective in which being, thought, and action is conceptualized as being made up of a pair or two parts. The division of humans into females and males is one example. Binary categories are often presented as dichotomous, with little to no overlap between them. See **two-sex system**.

biological determinism   the claim that your bodily makeup (genetics and other inherited traits) determines who you are. It further postulates that certain social conditions (for example, poverty and criminal activity) are inevitable due to the inherent characteristics of individuals.

biologizing   refers to the Western rise of biology as a science in the late 18th century, and the claims made about biology being be able to "tell the truth" about the human body. These "truths" included the creation of sex, gender, sexuality, and race as categories that were said to be inherent, leading to biological determinism. These categories have often been used for the creation of social hierarchies, as biological science has been used to make claims about relative superiority and inferiority of people.

biopower   the name given by Michel Foucault to a form of power that arose in the 18th century, with the shift from hereditary, monarchical rule, to elected liberal democracy and the nation state. Its emergence marked the state's interest in the body and in how people lived. Biopower takes two main forms: disciplining of the body and intervention in the life of the population as a whole.

body politic   a group of which people may be considered members through a common political organization (such as a nation state) or collective unit (such as a gay identity and organization). The body politic embraces a vision of power through the way it includes and excludes members and non-members.

boundary work   the labour that goes into rendering certain kinds of knowledge, practices, and practitioners as legitimately scientific.

C

capitalism   a system of economic organization and production. It is based on ownership of private property, in which the few who own or control the **means of production** can accumulate capital through the sale of goods produced for a profit. Most people who live in capitalist societies must exchange their labour power for a wage and experience **exploitation** as the values of wages remain below the value of goods produced or services provided. While the exploitation of labour remains a fundamental form of capital accumulation, increasingly capital is also generated through financial speculation.

capitalist class according to Marx, one of the primary classes in capitalist society. The capitalist class are those who own and control the means of production, and through this accumulate capital.

cathedrals of consumption a term used by George Ritzer to refer to not only shopping malls, but also theme parks, hotels, cruise ships, casinos, sports facilities, airports, and other hypercommercialized settings for consumption. In spite of their seemingly "enchanted" character, Ritzer suggests, such environments are actually highly rationalized and carefully engineered to entice us to consume.

centre, the taken-for-granted, normative features of social organization, distinguished by the ability to confer privilege upon those who occupy it.

chromosomes an organized biological structure made up of tightly coiled DNA and proteins, of which every species has a characteristic number in all of its cells.

circuit of culture a concept of Stuart Hall that illustrates how meaning is produced at different sites and circulates through everyday social processes and practices. It has been used by Paul DuGay and his colleagues to describe and map the relationships between representations, people's identities, practices of social regulation, and practices of production and consumption. Analyzing these multiple facets of a cultural text or artefact provides a more comprehensive understanding of how everyday objects are related to larger social processes.

civilization on the assumption of evolutionary improvement, the endpoint on the evolutionary scale. For example, the so-called "civilized society" is usually assumed to be the most advanced and complex form of social organization.

class Max Weber used this term to describe those in the same "class situation," which referred to the likelihood of "(i) procuring goods; (ii) gaining a position in life; and (iii) finding inner satisfactions," leading to a set of shared interests. Marx developed a class analysis premised on a "relational" concept of class, defining classes in terms of their relation to the means of production. Within capitalism, the two primary classes are the working class and the capitalist class. The emphasis on class as being defined through exploitation, rather than simply income or status differences, is one of the fundamental points of distinction between Marxist and Weberian approaches to class relations.

classifying see **systems of classification**.

colonialism the conquest and control of other people's lands and resources, through: genocide, enslavement, and resistance; imposition of foreign governing structures and legal systems; immigration and settlement; and binary knowledge systems and representational forms. Colonial expansion and wealth extraction were part of European empire-building, but in later stages coincided with the development of capitalism and the nation state.

colonization see **colonialism**.

commodification expansion of the market, or commercialization, into areas not previously part of the market or commercialized. Not only material goods, but people, cultures, and places are increasingly drawn in to the global market.

commodity something produced as a generic or universal good specifically for sale on the market. Commodities are use values produced by labour for exchange. "Use values" are goods such as food, clothing, and houses and services such as education, and health care. In capitalism, commodity production primarily takes place for the purpose of exchange for profit rather than immediate use. Also, peoples' capacity to labour (labour power) is itself treated as a commodity, and is bought and sold through market exchanges (wage labour).

commodity fetishism   a term coined by Marx to refer to the condition of modern capitalism where the commodity itself becomes viewed as an independent object with its own intrinsic value, rather than being the end result of the work of other people. This is the process where the value of any commodity comes to be reflected in its price, obscuring the social relations of its production. Commodity fetishism refers to how the practices of exploitation and the power dynamics of class relations are made invisible.

commodity problem   the declining terms of trade of tropical commodities in relation to manufactured goods, and extreme price volatility. The problem generally impacts, to varying degrees, the international markets for most major tropical commodities exported from the South: coffee, tea, bananas, cocoa, sugar, etc.

communicative model of consumption   a model of consumer behaviour, predominant in the sociology of consumption since the 1980s, that holds that goods are valued not simply for their material or instrumental qualities, but also for their ability to symbolically communicate aspects of our own status and identity.

concept   a mental representation that groups things that are similar in some way.

Concepts enable us to cognitively hold on to the idea of something by giving it a name or a symbol we can incorporate into our thinking. They also give us a context for understanding the many people, objects, and events we encounter every day: she's another student, that's a chair, they are having an argument. We often use concepts to designate specific types of people in our society: deadbeat dads, terrorists, or the mentally ill. These designations are based on the presumption that we have a shared cultural understanding about who belongs in these groups.

conspicuous consumption   a term coined by Thorstein Veblen that refers to the acquisition and display of rare, expensive, and often frivolous goods by the wealthy in order to symbolically communicate their superior status and to arouse the envy and admiration of those less wealthy. While people from all classes generally struggle to demonstrate some level of conspicuous consumption to stave off feelings of inadequacy, ultimately those who have the greatest wealth are in the best situation to do so.

constitution/constituted   a postmodern term for the making up (or social production) of people, beliefs, and practices, as in the constitution of the **subject**.

consumer society   an umbrella term used to categorize relatively wealthy regions in the post–World War II era where material consumption rates rose dramatically, and consumption practices became a crucial site for broader processes of social integration, social reproduction, and identity-formation.

consumer sovereignty   a term used in mainstream economics and neoliberal political discourse, whose basic premise is that the consumer's self-defined needs and wants are ultimately what determines an economy's production priorities, regulates its allocation of resources, and decides what is and is not brought to the market for sale.

content analysis   a methodology that, when used by quantitative researchers, typically relies on creating a coding scheme and then systematically counting how often some symbolic content occurs in a series of texts or images.

contingent   something dependent on the chain of events that preceded it.

counter-hegemonic   said of forces that offer possibilities for resistance due to the fact that maintenance of **hegemony** is an uneven and difficult process, depending on the balance of social forces at a given time and place.

counter-history   a critical alternative approach to taken-for-granted or dominant histories.

creationism   the belief in the creation of biological life by a divine power.

cultural capital   a concept coined by Pierre Bourdieu to broaden the notion of capital beyond economic resources. It refers to access to material and symbolic resources, such as education, health care, social and intellectual networks, the arts, and languages. Young people who have access to significant cultural capital will be raised in homes that provide them with the conditions for economic and social success. According to Bourdieu, class position is therefore partly reproduced by maintaining and expanding one's cultural capital.

cultural economy   a field of study that examines the cultural dimensions of economic life.

cultural genocide   see **genocide**.

cultural hegemony   in Gramsci's thought, power maintained by a range of a complex and contradictory web of cultural practices. In this way domination can be accomplished without direct authoritarian rule. See also **hegemony**.

cultural studies   a broad field of study that bridges social science and literary analysis. Cultural studies aims to understand cultural practices, especially those of everyday life, from a critical perspective, attuned to how power constructs knowledge, and how cultural studies thinkers themselves are enmeshed in the social currents. Stuart Hall was one of the founders of cultural studies in England during the 1970s, an approach that blended Marx's materialism with the study of culture.

culture   the totality of socially transmitted ideas, behaviours, customs, and products of a group of people. There may be different cultures operating in a single place at any one time.

culture of recovery   describes contemporary Western societies, now characterized by a focus on the individual over the collective, which combine the human sciences with the climate of **neoliberalism**, and direct us toward an exploration of our inner selves and our relations with others, so that we can address our inadequacies and repair past emotional injuries. We may search for our "inner child," reveal our "co-dependency," insist on "tough love," recover our "true" or "real" selves, or blend popular psychology with Eastern, aboriginal, or "alternative" healing practices.

culture of therapy   the widespread acceptance of a particular psychotherapeutic ethos that shapes social practices, due to the now-pervasive presence of **psy discourses** in the everyday lives and practices of Westerners.

cybernetics   the study of communication systems (both animal and machine) for securing efficient operation, regulation, and control. The study of cybernetics may involve an interdisciplinary approach, involving both the human and physical sciences.

D

deconstruction   to take apart, or unpack, meaning by questioning the assumptions, revealing the contradictions, and so on, embedded in that meaning. Originating within literary theory, the concept of deconstruction is now used in various ways in a number of disciplines.

democratic racism   an ideology that permits and sustains two conflicting sets of values. One set of values consists of a commitment to a democratic society motivated by egalitarian values of fairness, justice, and equality. Conflicting with these liberal values are attitudes and behaviours consistent with racism.

developmentalism   an approach to understanding and studying children and adults that focuses on gradual, chronological, incremental biological, cognitive and/or psychosocial changes that people are thought to pass through as they grow up and grow old.

deviance   refers to any form of conduct that violates social norms, rules, or laws. To designate a person or a group as deviant is a proscriptive act; that is to say, it is to cast a negative judgement on those who engage in beliefs and practices outside of what is considered acceptable, right, and normal. One purpose of the deviant designation, then, is to define and regulate differences.

disciplinary power   a concept developed by Michel Foucault to describe the force that operates among people at the most micro levels of interaction, as people watch, assess, evaluate, and categorize, and are at the same time watched, assessed, evaluated, and categorized, creating and reproducing certain beliefs or knowledges about them. Disciplinary power entails the surveillance and correction of individual bodies and of populations of people. This form of power is much less visible than the exercise of **sovereign power**, and therefore much more difficult to identify and to resist.

disciplinary society   a society characterized by strategies to administer to and regulate populations and individuals (for example, through the creation of prisons, asylums, and workhouses), which according to Foucault arose in the 19th century.

discourse   a system of knowledge that uses elements of our shared cultural knowledge to produce a particular version of reality. Social constructionists argue that the material world only becomes meaningful to us through the concepts and systems of classification provided by language and discourses. This also applies to social practices; language and discourses limit what we can think and say, who we can be, what we can do, and what can be done to us. Discourses provide the framework people use to understand and interpret the everyday world.

Disneyfication/Disneyization   a process of **standardization** in commercial spaces such as tourist sites and shopping malls, and the transformation of urban centres, with a focus on homogenization, familiarity, efficiency, safety, and predictability. Social theorists created the terms in response to the fact that the Disney theme parks have become a model of this process.

diversity, official and radical   broadly, diversity describes heterogeneity within nature and within humanity. *Official* diversity is state-sanctioned, in which a range of specific cultures, identities, and practices are legitimated, under certain conditions (for example during multicultural celebrations); thus, an implicit normative centre is held in place. *Radical* diversity attempts to restore heterogeneity to diversity, throughout social life and the natural environment.

dividing practices actions that involve making value-laden distinctions between people, beliefs, and activities, typically in a hierarchical manner. Dividing practices are a key ingredient in the establishment of social inequality.

division of labour the organization of work into specific tasks, which are allocated according to gender or other social characteristics. While a social division of labour precedes the development of industrial capitalism, the division of labour now often refers to the segmentation and division of work under capitalist relations of production.

DNA a substance located within cells that contains genetic material that instructs the development and maintenance of components of living organisms. Often referred to as "the blueprint for building a body" or "a hereditary code."

domestic labour see **social reproduction**.

Drapetomania a diagnosis introduced by a Dr. Samuel Cartwright in 1851, defined as the pathological desire of African-American slaves to escape captivity from their natural and God-given masters.

E

economic determinism the theory that the structures and dynamics of capitalism shape social life and the course of economic history.

economic globalization describes the increase in global economic integration, characterized by an increase in the flow of goods, services, technology, and labour across national borders.

economic subjectivity modes of being, thinking, and acting in relation to categories within economic discourses (such as worker, owner, consumer, investor, debtor, saver, and so on).

ecotourism an approach to tourism that focuses on minimizing the environmental impact of tourism through preserving biodiversity and educating people in conservation. Ecotourism also often seeks to address social inequality.

emotional labour the manipulation of self-presentation while providing services to others. It is a key dimension of work in service-sector workplaces. Personal interaction with customers makes demands on the emotional energy of workers, since customers expect smiling, cheerful service. Moreover, customers play a key role in establishing control over emotional labour through channels for customer input and assessments of service provision. Thus, service with a smile becomes a form of self-governance for service-sector workers.

Enlightenment, the an era, well under way in Europe by the late 17th century, characterized by the radical new idea that people could use human reason to shape history. It was a period in which there was a transition to scientific thinking and a positivist approach to knowledge, with an emphasis on reason, logical thinking, and scientific experimentation as a legitimate means for making claims about the world.

entrepreneurs of the self a neoliberal interpretation of people as self-governing individuals who conduct themselves as though their lives are business enterprises and they are owners/managers responsible for developing their own human capital in order to produce maximal self-fulfillment.

environmental bubble   a "home away from home" atmosphere in tourist destinations, which it is a goal of most mass tourist enterprises to create.

epistemic privilege   the special status and credibility conferred upon the knowledge of the "critically conscious knower" whose subjective experience and social position reflect a critical perspective on the distribution of power in society.

epistemology   a branch of philosophy that focuses on what constitutes knowledge and how we come to know things. Epistemological perspectives inform us about what counts as "evidence," what criteria need to be met in order to develop new knowledge, and how knowledge is related to morals or values.

epistemology of ignorance   a concept described by C. W. Mills that refers to a particular and ironic rationality associated with a professed ignorance of racism. While "epistemology" always refers to knowledge, normalized racism involves an "epistemology of ignorance" in which ignorance- not knowledge- assumes the status of the rational. It is defended on the basis of its ability to perform as "a self- and- social shielding from racial realities."

essentialism   a position that assumes that human behaviours are rooted in some inherent, unchanging essence.

ethnocentrism   the belief that one's own nation and culture are superior to those of others.

ethnography   the study and systematic recording of human cultures. Ethnographic research is a branch of the discipline of anthropology and often focuses on cultures deemed more "primitive" than that of the scholar studying them.

ethnomethodology   an approach to research that focuses on the analysis of everyday talk in order to understand how people make sense of their lives and the world around them.

exchange value   a quantitative measure that can be used in the process of commodity exchange. In a capitalist market, the exchange value of a commodity is represented through money. Commodities in capitalism are both use values (based on an ability to meet a human need or want) and exchange values (a representation of its value in the form of money). To understand how a commodity comes to be exchanged, we need to look at its exchange value.

expert knowledge   a perspective that defines who people are, without direct input from those under observation. It expresses relations of power in which those at the centre can define and categorize social and material life.

exploitation   the commodification of people's labour power. The production of surplus value is based on the fact that wages paid in exchange for labour power are less than the value of the commodities produced or the services provided. According to Marx, this system of **wage labour** is not a fair exchange.

F

fair trade   rules and principles of trade practices that include the existence of democratic workplace organizations (of cooperatives or unions), no child labour, environmental sustainability, a minimum guaranteed price, and social premiums paid to producer communities to build community infrastructure.

feudalism a social, economic, and political system in which lords ruled over "serfs" who were compelled to pay tribute to the latter in the form of labour, military service, food, and other goods.

financial fitness a neoliberal discourse about the responsibility of individuals to participate in financial culture in prescribed ways, such as by using credit cards and repaying the monthly balance. A form of self-care, similar to diet and exercise, personal money management is thought to be important to individual and national financial health.

financial literacy individuals' ability to understand normalized financial concepts (such as money, credit, savings, compound interest, and investment risk), which makes them capable of participating in financial culture. Programs to enhance financial literacy are geared to making people better prepared for and inclined toward self-financing their education, leisure, housing, transportation, retirement income, etc.

financialization an economic and cultural shift that has taken place in the latter decades of the 20th century involving the expanding scale of financial markets and institutions (related to accounting, investment, insurance, pensions, savings, and debt) relative to other sectors of the economy; the increasing significance of financial knowledge in everyday life; and the growing importance of everyday financial activity, calculation and decision making among widening categories of people.

foreign worker in Canada, a person admitted with a Non-Immigrant Temporary Employment Authorization and who is usually legally obligated to work only for the employer listed on her/his work visa. Depending on the province, foreign (or *migrant*) workers are denied a number of rights and services that are accessible to permanent residents and Canadian citizens.

free market the notion that in order to be fully competitive capital must be allowed unfettered (unregulated) access to national and global markets.

free trade sociopolitical conditions reducing all forms of market regulation by such means as lessening or eliminating trade barriers and financial controls, devaluing local currencies to make exports more competitive, and severely cutting public spending and service provision.

free wage labour the sale of labour power for a wage. According to Marx, wage labour requires two specific forms of "freedom" experienced by the working class in capitalist societies: (1) freedom (separation) from the means of production; and (2) freedom any from legal constraints that would *prevent* one from selling their labour power (for example, slavery). These conditions create the need to sell labour power in exchange for a wage, which according to Marx leads to the exploitation of the working class. See **exploitation** and **surplus value**.

freeganism an anti-consumerist lifestyle that aims to refrain as far as possible to abstain from the purchase of consumer goods. Freegans, by engaging in dumpster diving, foraging for wild foods, reusing discarded items, and so on, aim to meet many of their needs in an ecologically friendly way, outside of the formal cash economy. The term is a play on "veganism," a philosophical and dietary practice based on abstaining from the use of products derived from nonhuman animals.

G

gender, gendering   in the West, refers to the label of "feminine" or "masculine" assigned to most of the world, from bodily behaviours and social practices to objects and places. Also refers to labels of "woman" and " man," and the social meanings assigned to them. Many feminists and other critical theorists have argued that "gender" is different from "sex," and that masculinity and femininity are socially constructed rather than biologically based. However, recent theorists turn this approach upside down by suggesting that the social meanings given to gender shape our understanding of anatomical sex, and that binary maleness and femaleness have a history and are socially constructed.

gender attribution   the socially shared methods we use in our everyday lives to assign gender to the people we come into contact with. Through the practices of gender attribution we transform a social world of vast gender diversity and variation into a world in which we can assign people into the binary categories of "women" and "men."

gender policing   one of the mechanisms through with gender binaries are enforced and maintained; monitoring of self and others to ensure gender conformity. This can occur at the level of the individual or in more organized, institutional forms, through verbal commentary on someone's appearance or body, through mockery of gender nonconformity, or through violence, often against someone seen as gender queer, or whose gender and sex are seen as ambiguous or not "matching." See **gender queer**.

gender queer   outside the limits of the range of potential identities set by the two-gender system. Seeing gender as fluid rather than fixed. Can also refer to disruptions of the sex-gender system, in which the assumption is that your anatomical "sex" determines or predicts your social "gender." Being "gender queer" can therefore mean presenting yourself socially in a way conventionally seen as incongruent with your sex. See **queer** and **transgender**.

genealogical method   a method that emphasizes the history of dominant paradigms of thought that pervade our culture, and which produce current "truths." Genealogy starts with the present, not to affirm or deny it, but to interrogate it, asking how the present has come to be constituted as it is, and how we create ourselves according to, or against, those truths. For Foucault, social life is the outcome of power–knowledge relations. See also **history of the present**.

generalizability   the extent to which knowledge can be extended to understand a group of people (or population) larger than the group (sample) from whom information was collected.

genocide   the intentional and systematic destruction of a people on the basis of their race, ethnicity, religion, or national origin, accomplished through the mass extinguishment of their actual physical beings. See also **cultural genocide**.

genre   a certain kind or type of representation, text, or story. For instance, we classify films into genres such as horror, romantic comedy, drama, action, pornography, and so on. Genres are also used as a shortcut that tells us what to expect in terms of the narrative, the people, and the setting. Whenever we encounter a representation, we assess it against our expectations for things of that genre (and are often disappointed when they do not match). The expectations we associate with a given genre help reveal our expectations about the organization of the social world and the types of people in it more generally.

gerontology the multidisciplinary study of aging, with a focus on late life. For some, gerontology's primary focus is biology; for others, gerontology encompasses a wide range of areas, including the body and social factors such as behaviour, attitudes, and the environment.

global apartheid see **apartheid**.

globalization the increasing economic, political, and cultural integration throughout the world as a result of economic, technological, and political forces. See also **economic globalization**.

global value chain a concept originally developed in World Systems Theory to describe how processes of production, distribution, and consumption are linked through transnational networks. Along the chain are a series of nodes where the original commodity is transformed, value is added, profits are generated through commodity exchange and consumption, and states, corporations, and households compete for their share of the wealth.

governmental power/governmentality an expanded conceptualization of government as, in effect, "the conduct of conduct," an idea introduced by Foucault. In this view, government occurs through organizations, through texts, between people, and even within ourselves. Foucault's concept had three main components: first, being governed; second, governing others; and third, governing the self. Governmental power is occurring when we are no longer aware of power's effects, because we have already embraced it, and reproduce it in relation to our selves and to others.

grand narratives grand or sweeping claims or stories about history. Examples are the explanations of history and knowledge provided by Christianity, capitalism, and socialism. Also known as *metanarratives*, a concept introduced by Jean-François Lyotard.

great confinement, the an unprecedented program of asylum building that was under way in 17th-century Europe. Foucault regarded the great confinement as a means for disciplining and regulating certain populations of people, in asylums, prisons, workhouses, and so on.

H

hegemony as described by Antonio Gramsci, "intellectual and moral leadership" that takes into account "the interests and tendencies of the groups over which hegemony is exercised" through compromises that may benefit many but do not ultimately threaten the rule of the dominant group. This is accomplished through both coercion (military and police) *and* the manufacture of consent (the production of popular knowledge). In this way, the ruling ideas of a society operate hegemonically through "common sense" shared by everyone but that reproduces dominant interests. See also **cultural hegemony**.

heliocentrism   the idea that the sun circles around the earth.

hermaphrodite   outdated mythological term that dates back to ancient Greece, and refers to a child of the Greek gods Hermes and Aphrodite, who combined attributes of the two parents. The two names were combined to identify someone thought of as two-sexed. In the late 19th century, "hermaphrodite" was used by some Western scientists in an expanded way, to also label people who were defined as sexually non-normative, and who might today be referred to as gay or lesbian. In the 20th century, "hermaphroditism" was treated as a medical problem, and a range of social and surgical treatments were used, usually without the knowledge or consent of the person involved. Such treatments aimed to keep sex categories distinct, and limited to two. Though hermaphroditism is still sometimes used in Western medicine to describe a condition of ambiguous genitalia, many activists argue that *hermaphrodite* is an outdated, inaccurate, and problematic term, and that **intersexed** is preferable.

heterogender   idea that dominant gender binaries not only teach separate and distinct ways of being masculine and feminine, but also involve a sexual dimension. "Normal" men and women are constructed as each others' opposites, and are expected to orient their desires toward their "opposites." For example, we can say that hegemonic masculinity is heteromasculinity, because the assumption is that "normal men" are sexually attracted to feminine women.

heteronormative   describing the idea or implication that heterosexual identity is the only normal and natural expression of human sexuality, to the exclusion of all non-heterosexual identities. Heteronormativity works in multiple ways, such as by representing heterosexuality as fulfilling and positive, by representing other forms of sexuality as dangerous and negative, and through absences and silences that make non-heterosexual practices seem rare and abnormal or nonexistent.

heterosexual   said of sexual attraction to a person of the "opposite" sex and "opposite" gender. Based on and intertwined with the binary sex-gender system, which assumes that men and women are dramatically different from each other. The dominant assumption is that heterosexuality is the natural and normal sexual state of affairs. The term only emerged in the late 1800s, first in German and then in U.S. medical discussions of sexual perversion, the definition of which included sexual acts not directed at reproduction.

historical materialism   the methodology for social research favoured by Marx, based on two essential assumptions. First, social relations can only be understood in historical context. While Marx saw class relations and class struggle as present throughout human history, he believed that the specific form these social relationships may take varied considerably across different historical periods. Second, to understand class relations, we must study the material conditions under which people live. In other words, we must look at how humans produce and reproduce themselves.

historicity   being place- and time-specific; identifying historical particularities.

historicize   to contextualize social phenomena within specific historical conditions.

history of the present an approach in which history is viewed as *contingent* meaning that for any event, other directions and outcomes were also possible rather than inevitable or determined by universal laws. Foucault developed this approach to interrogate the production of discourses, knowledge, and objects, and the meanings associated with them. He used it to avoid making universal claims, for example that there is such a thing as "truth" or "human nature." Instead, he undertook an analysis of how we come to believe in universal claims, seeking to discover how particular discourses come to be regarded as "truth." Foucault's later work referred to this as his **genealogical method**.

homosexual pertaining to sexual attraction to a person of the "same" sex and "same" gender. The term is based on and intertwined with the binary sex-gender system, which assumes that men and women are each other's opposites, and accordingly treats "heterosexuals" and "homosexuals" as opposing categories. It originates in medical literature of the 1860s describing "homosexuals" as people who are psychologically of the "opposite" sex. Because the term has a long history of use to describe something abnormal and pathological, and was not chosen by the people it describes, it is seen by many as outdated. Preferable terms include *gay, lesbian, queer*.

human deficit model the view that takes the individual person to be the source of problems due to inherent flaws, defects, or abnormalities. This perspective does not account for social processes and relations in understanding the human condition.

humanism an outlook predicated on the belief that there are essential inviolable truths about people (the humanist subject), most notably that individual consciousness and will shape human understanding and action.

hybridity the mixing and blurring of cultures and ideas, creating something entirely new.

I

ideology a broad prescriptive framework of beliefs, assumptions, and values furnishing people with an understanding of their world, and influencing how they interpret social, cultural, political, and economic systems and structures. The content of ideology is not neutral; it reflects the status quo, or "relations of domination," edging out alternative and competing ideas.

"illegal" migrant those without official state permission to visit, live, or work within territories claimed by the state.

immigrant in Canada, a person with the legal right of permanent residency in the state who has been granted official state permission to live and work in the country. Permanent residents who have resided in Canada for at least three years of the previous four, can speak English and/or French, and meet a number of other eligibility requirements can apply for Canadian citizenship status.

imperialism the extension of a nation state's authority or rule over other national territories through control over their economies. The development of imperialism often superseded direct colonial rule (see **colonialism**), rendering formal political and military control unnecessary for meeting the economic objectives of dominating nation states.

imperialist ideology   a set of beliefs about the "natural" right of an imperial power to expropriate land because of their cultural, economic, and religious superiority. In North America, the expropriation of land was often based on the inaccurate claim that Indigenous people did not farm and thus could not make efficient use of the territory.

indigenous   peoples considered to be the original occupiers of a land, usually prior to the incursion of a colonizing force.

infrastructure of consumption   the social, material, technological, and institutional framework that shapes and constrains the terrain of consumer choice, compelling us into certain types of patterned and predictable consumer behaviour.

inscriptions   written traces in two-dimensional space. These might be produced by humans or machines, and they might be text, images, graphs, maps, etc.

International Monetary Fund   an organization founded in 1947 as part of the United Nations, which works somewhat like a credit union with states putting money in and other states borrowing for development. The IMF has been critiqued for imposing certain politically oriented, restrictive conditions upon borrower nations.

interpretive flexibility   the concept that different people see different things despite the same visual information. This concept can include people or groups giving different meaning to the same symbol, object, or experience.

interpretive repertoire   a cluster of terms, descriptions, metaphors, and figures of speech that people use to understand the world around them. They provide a framework that people use to locate their own position in the world relative to others. Our interpretive repertoires help us establish our subject position, which we then use to give meaning to our experiences.

interpretivism   an approach to knowledge that emphasizes how people interpret their environment, assign meanings to things, and then act on the basis of their understanding of each situation. Interpretivism is strongly associated with symbolic interactionism. Interpretivists generally adopt a social constructionist perspective on reality.

intersectional analysis   an analytic perspective that accounts for how factors (including social locations and subject positions) such as race, gender, class, sexuality, dis/ability, and citizenship intersect, penetrate, and inform one another so that they become mutually constitutive and act together. It recognizes that vectors and patterns of oppression, such as racism, classism, and sexism ultimately cannot be separated from one other when examining the organization of power and inequality. See also **relational analysis**.

intersexed   said of bodies that cannot easily be constructed as male or female. This includes people who have primary or secondary sex characteristics that defy medical definitions of male or female. A significant proportion of human babies are born with genitals that do not obviously fit into "male" or "female," or whose genitals do not correspond to other (supposedly consonant) measures of biological sex such as chromosomes or hormones. See also **hermaphrodite**.

invisible hand   Adam Smith's metaphor to suggest that market forces have a self-regulating logic of their own.

J

juridical power a form of power that includes the rule of law, the techniques of the court, and the practices of policing. Juridical power has its roots in the exercise of sovereign power, and it retains the capacity for domination, repression, and control. However, much of the authority of juridical power is now governmentalized and normalized. There is general support for laws, courts, and policing as necessary aspects of ensuring democratic ordering.

K

Keynesianism the dominant economic theory in Western industrial capitalist countries in the period following World War II, according to which governments should take an active role in managing the national economy, especially through public-sector spending during periods of recession. Keynesian policies aim to achieve stable conditions for economic growth and employment by anticipating and moderating the disruptive effects of market cycles. States that have adopted Keynesianism have also instituted progressive taxation as a mechanism of downward wealth redistribution in order to support social welfare programs such as medical insurance, unemployment insurance, and old age pensions.

L

labour power people's capacity to engage in economically productive activity. Karl Marx stated that the working class are those who do not own means of production, and therefore must sell their labour power in order to earn wages to ensure their subsistence. The capitalist class purchases the labour power of the working class for a wage in order to generate profits.

liberalism a philosophical, political, and economic approach that focuses of the primacy of the individual, and on individual rights. Liberalism as a belief system was created simultaneous to the growth of capitalism and the notion of democracy.

life course a social understanding of the duration of our lives, from infancy to death, shaped by history, social institutions, practices, and beliefs.

literary technology a way of writing calculated to act on the readers in particular ways.

local currency money issued by community-based organizations or municipal governments that is designed to generate new circuits of earning and paying within a specific geographical region or among a particular network of participants. Local currencies may have a number of goals such as reducing dependence on large corporations, buffering local economies from global crises, fostering more personal relationships between producers and consumers, and reducing the separation between production and consumption.

looping effect the interaction between a classification and those people who are which classified. Humans inevitably respond to classification, which in turn alters their conduct, which will have an effect on the classification, and so on.

M

market populism a term coined by Thomas Frank, for the tendency in contemporary society to portray the capitalist marketplace as the ultimate expression of democracy and the popular will.

mass tourism large-scale tourism that is organized around specific predefined roles for both tourists and hosts, and that tends to commodify the tourist experience in an increasingly detailed way.

master narratives   dominant accounts of how the world operates which provide us with organizing principles for understanding events, behaviours, and beliefs. For instance, the archetypal struggle between the forces of good and evil is a prominent master narrative in North American discourses.

material   see **materialism**; **historical materialism**.

Matthew Effect   the cumulative nature of class-based inequalities as we age, over the life course.

McDonaldization   a term coined by social theorist George Ritzer for the process by which the principles of fast-food restaurants such as McDonald's are continually being extended to other areas of economic and social activity. These principles enforce standardization through predictability, efficiency, calculability, and control.

means of production   the materials, infrastructure, and natural resources needed to produce goods and provide services (including factories, technology, tools, etc.). Specifically, the capitalist class own and control the means of production, while the working class are forced to sell their labour power since they do not.

mechanical objectivity   the notion that machines are disinterested in outcomes, and therefore remove the subjective biases of humans.

medicalization   a broad sociological concept that refers to the social processes that define and categorize human conduct or experience as a medical problem, usually as an illness or a disorder requiring professional attention.

metaphor   describing one thing in terms of another in order to imply a comparison.

micro-processes   the detailed, contextual, contingent, and specific circulation of social meaning and practice.

migrant   any human being who moves across space. With the advent of nation states and their border regimes, the category of "migrant" is now used to label those who move across national borders.

mimetic play   the way people from one culture adopt another's culture (the process of *mimesis*) while distancing themselves from it.

mimicry   irony and visual spectacle in the portrayal of a people against type. For example, the portrayal of Indians intensifies specifically erotic representations. It suggests Euro-Canadian nostalgia and desire in relation to the Indian.

mode of production   the economic organization of a society; the ways people produce, distribute, and consume goods. Using the method of historical materialism, Marx suggested that human history is divided into identifiable periods, each characterized by a certain mode of production.

modern confessional   a **metaphor** coined by Foucault to characterize the use by residents of Western nations of such things as the therapist's office, the self-help group, and the blog, increasingly relying on the psy sciences (psychology, psychiatry, psychotherapy, etc.) rather than turning to the priest to confess our sins. Through the process of confessing we create our "self" rather than reveal it.

modernism   a mode of thought developed in the context of the **Enlightenment**, underlying which was the belief that through scientific exploration one could measure and understand not only the natural environment but also human behaviour. In other words, scientific method could be used to identify underlying structures or foundations that shape the organization of social life. Enlightenment thinkers embraced the hope that science could be a tool for human progress.

modernist   the modernist espouses the view that the physical world was not simply the creation of God, nor an unsolvable mystery beyond scientific understanding. See also **modernity** and **modernism**.

modernity   typically, the social, economic, political, and cultural conditions and beliefs that have arisen since the **Enlightenment** and the rise of capitalism.

moral insanity   a diagnosis introduced in the mid-19th century as part of the growing medical fixation on immoral or disrespectable conduct, particularly in response to what was perceived as increasing vices arising from industrialization and the growth of cities. Moral insanity linked perceived moral flaws to madness, as if one were the cause of the other.

moral regulation   Philip Corrigan's concept of a process that, first, establishes what is "right and proper," then encourages certain forms of conduct and expression while discouraging others. Finally, it establishes disciplinary regimes at both the symbolic and the institutional level.

N

nationalism   a modern ideology centred on the shared values and myths of the community of the nation state. This is a *relational process* in that the nation state relies on the complicity of those who make themselves at home in the nation in order to legitimize (or make "common sense" of) the highly differential treatment accorded those classified as the nation's non-citizens, particularly those placed in legal state categories.

nation state sovereignty   the legal right of nation states to act as if they have ultimate and independent authority over events within the territory claimed as theirs. In regard to issues of migration and citizenship, nation states have the "right," according to international law, to determine whether to admit persons seeking entry to their claimed territories. This is the basis for the existence of a legal distinction in rights and entitlements of either "citizens" of the state or "foreigners."

naturalization   a process of making social relations seem as though they are an inevitable and unchangeable part of nature.

neo-colonialism   what is happening when, through economic influence and global politics, more powerful countries maintain the control and domination of less powerful ones, particularly those that have freed themselves from formal colonial rule.

neoliberalism   a set of governing practices that came to rival Keynesianism starting in the 1970s, resulting in the reorganization of capitalist states and social life around the idea of markets as the most efficient and moral mechanisms for allocating social goods and shaping individual and collective behaviour. Neoliberal policies result in, and legitimize, upward redistribution of wealth. Although neoliberal philosophy decries government "interference" in the economy, neoliberal governments take an active role in negotiating the frameworks for global trade and financial activity, protecting private property, and converting public assets into private, for-profit businesses.

neurobiology   the study of the anatomy, physiology, and pathology of the nervous system.

normalization   Foucault's term for how a certain version of things takes on the appeal as standard, true, or "normal." Normalization has become a popular theoretical tool for identifying the arbitrariness of assigning "normal" status to many things most of us take for granted. Foucault believed that normalization is the most effective means of social regulation in contemporary Western societies.

normalizing power   a force in society that compares, differentiates, creates a hierarchy, homogenizes, and excludes. It is therefore also a **dividing practice**, because it clearly involves the making of value-laden distinctions between people.

norms   social expectations about attitudes, beliefs, and values.

O

objectivity   a research approach that strives to ensure that the researcher's own perspectives, biases, and opinions do not influence the research process. In theory, researchers should be interchangeable. Some researchers argue that objectivity is impossible to achieve.

official statistics   statistics collected or compiled by a government agency in order to find out more about a national population, usually with the goal of informing policy.

organization of consent   a process through which people come to identify the interests of the ruling group as synonymous with their own, making the exercise of power in Western, capitalist, and formally democratic countries much more effective.

Other   categories of exclusion through which certain groups of people are considered different and inferior. The process of othering simultaneously secures the otherer's own position.

P

panopticon   a type of prison envisioned by Jeremy Bentham in 18th-century England, which placed guard posts at the centre of a circular containment, so that the watchmen (prison guards) could not be seen, and would always be presumed by the inmates to be present and watching. Inmates would thus feel compelled to conduct themselves as if they were under constant surveillance. The panopticon thereby not only constrained prisoner's bodies but reconfigured their minds as well. Foucault adopted the model of the panopticon as illustrative of the growth of the **disciplinary society**.

paradigm   a conceptual framework that guides scientific work and determines what questions should be asked and what answers are allowable.

pathological approach   the view that some people are abnormal in their bodies/ minds/psyches, and that personal problems are individual and caused by biological and/ or psychological factors. This approach is a distinctly Western and recent historical phenomenon.

pathologize   to regard particular beliefs, feelings, habits, thoughts, and/or behaviours as rooted in physical or mental disease or dysfunction, as determined by scientific wisdom and truths.

patriarchy   a system in which social, economic, and political privilege and entitlement is conferred upon men, over women and children, regardless of the presence or absence of privilege in other areas of men's lives, and regardless of if/how they act upon that privilege.

performative   a concept employed by social theorist Judith Butler to explain how gender is something acquired or brought into existence through repetition. Repeated acts create an illusion of our core selves as gendered—"I *am* a woman"—and as always having been that way. Talking about gender as performative can help us to understand that dominant masculinity and femininity are not stable, universal, or biologically based.

pluralist states   the belief that nation states in liberal democracies function as a neutral arbitrator between competing social, political, and economic interests.

political economy   a field of study that seeks to understand the long-term history of, and prospects for, social change, especially the potential of emancipation from unjust and exploitative social relations under capitalism. As a methodology for understanding social organization, it puts emphasis on studying class relations, and interactions between capital and states. Many taking a political economy approach also adopt an **intersectional analysis** that recognizes class as inseparable from other social, cultural, and political relations. That is, in order to understand the everyday dimensions of class relations, we have to study the intersection of class with other social relationships including race, gender, sexuality, and citizenship.

politics of the image/politics of representation   analysis of how meaning is given to things, an understanding that reveals how knowledge and power intersect. Stuart Hall urged us to engage in an interrogation of the image, and uncover its political aspect. See also **representation**.

polysemy   in semiotics, a single sign can have more than one meaning or be interpreted in multiple ways. See **semiotics**, **sign**, **signified**, **signifier**.

positivism   an approach to knowledge that emphasizes the collection of information using the five human senses, the systematic analysis of data to identify general truths, and a clear distinction between facts and values.

postcolonialism   usually, scholarly research about the history and legacy of European colonialism, typically by scholars with origins within those former colonies. Postcolonial theorists have contributed significantly to the development of poststructuralist thought by introducing multiple and counter narratives that describe the ongoing effects of colonial rule.

postmodernism   an outlook rejecting the Enlightenment belief that, through human reason and research, humanity was on the road of progress. Instead, history was reconceptualized as fragmented, discontinuous, and without a larger purpose. From this perspective, while history should indeed be studied, researchers should pursue smaller-scale, localized studies in order to piece together the history of ideas and events, rather than making claims about broad swatches of human history and consciousness through the construction of **grand narratives**.

poststructuralism   a postmodern approach, as practised in the social sciences.

Poststructuralists reject **grand narratives**, and instead conceptualize social life as fractured and discontinuous. Research is best pursued through localized studies that reveal the minutiae of social meaning and organization. Identities are not considered fixed, but understood as relational, ever-changing, unstable, defined through difference, normalizing, and multiple across our lives.

power   at its most general level, the ability to put into place the definition of a situation, whether through consent or by force. Karl Marx believed that power is maintained through a system of domination, in which control is exercised by the ruling class over land, labour, and capital. Alternatively, Michel Foucault suggested that power does not work in one direction, from the top down, through direct coercion or physical violence. Rather, it comes from everywhere, and can have a positive character, creating new conditions of possibility. Nevertheless, the effects of power can also result in domination, and can be experienced by both the dominators and the dominated.

primitive accumulation   the expropriation and enclosure (privatization) of land that occurred when feudalism was transformed into capitalism. This situation created a mass of people who had no means to support themselves, since their access to land had been cut off (the working class).

primitivism   an implicitly racial concept that assumes precise stages in human racial evolution, so that "primitive" people are said to live in "savagery," and the "civilized" mark the endpoint on the evolutionary scale.

psychoanalytic theory   claims that individuals are motivated by strong and dynamic unconscious drives and conflicts arising in early childhood rather than biological functions of the brain and central nervous system. Psychoanalysis provided a non-biological theory of emotional and mental life alongside the dominating neurological, behaviourist, evolutionary, or hereditarian paradigms.

psychocentrism   the outlook that all human problems are pathologies of the individual mind and/or body.

psychopathic disorder   a recently abolished classification of personality disorders characterized by perceived antisocial behaviour.

psy complex   a heterogeneous network of agents, sites, practices, and techniques for the production, dissemination, legitimation, and utilization of psychological truths. The psy complex includes a loosely defined group of experts who possess a professional and moral status such as psychiatrists, psychologists, psychiatric nurses, counsellors, psychotherapists, criminologists, and social workers.

psy discourses   the perspective that all human problems are psychological or psychiatric in origin.

Q

qualitative research   an approach to research that emphasizes the collection of data in textual, auditory, or visual forms in order to describe the complexities and nuances of the phenomenon under investigation. Qualitative researchers often collect data using ethnographic methods, in-depth interviews, or focus groups or by analyzing cultural texts. The analysis of qualitative data often relies on discourse analysis or grounded theory approaches such as constant comparative analysis.

quantitative research an approach to research that emphasizes the collection of data in numerical form in order to quantify or make precise claims about the phenomenon under investigation. Quantitative researchers often collect data using experimental or survey methods and analyze data using statistical techniques.

queer sometimes used as an umbrella term to denote lesbians, gays, bisexuals, and transgendered people. the term is more appropriately used to convey the belief that sexual desires and identities are not determined by nature, and therefore are not fixed and unchangeable, but malleable and fluid. The term also reminds us that the boundaries between sexual categories are often blurred, meaning that binary-based categories like gay, lesbian, and heterosexual/straight are too rigid to accurately describe the range of people's sexual curiosities and desires.

R

race an arbitrary and socially constructed classification of persons on the basis of real or imagined physical characteristics. Race has no scientific meaning; there is only a singularity known as the "human race." The notion is a consequence of power relations, as it has been used to define and reinforce the unequal relations between dominant and subordinate groups.

racefulness the quality of "race" as an identity and social location.

racialization a process through which "race" is attributed to a population of people, facilitating the practice of racism against them.

racialized person(s), group(s), or racialized Others (an) individual(s) to whom "race" is assigned and to whom the process of racialization is applied. The term may refer to groups, for example "racialized immigrants." It may substitute for related terms that imply racial difference such as "people of colour," "visible minority," "Asian," "Native," "African-Canadian," and so on.

racism discrimination accorded to a group of people differentiated and evaluated on the basis of their alleged or real physical or social qualities. It is evident in its effects, as it affirms power relations and structural advantage and disadvantage. Racism is often attributed to institutional procedures, systemic inequities, or structural practices.

realism a perspective premised on the idea that there is a single reality that exists independently of human consciousness and is governed by unchanging natural laws.

realist someone who maintains there is a single reality that exists independently of society and is governed by unchanging natural laws.

recapitulation theory a theory popular in the late 19th and early 20th centuries that posited that the development of human beings from children to adults mirrors the evolution of "the race," which term might mean humanity itself or white or "civilized" people.

reductionism the practice of explaining complex events or processes in terms of isolated parts of it (for example, explaining crime exclusively in terms of genetics).

regime of truth a dominant system of knowledge that attempts to establish the limits of what is knowable and possible.

relational analysis builds on **intersectional analysis** to explain how social identities are constituted relationally, or in relation to one another, not independently of one another. Rather than simply adding one identity category to another (race + class), relational analysis takes into consideration the multiple, hybridizing, and shifting categories that inform and produce one another.

relational a way of explaining one belief or thing in relation to another belief or thing, so that they become constituents of one another.

relative autonomy the relationship of quasi-separation between the capitalist class and the state, achieved through some variation in the political programs advanced by the parties and leaders who hold office. The autonomy is only relative because all state programs in the industrialized capitalist nations defend the basic principles of the capitalist system.

representation traditionally, a re-presentation of something that has already happened or as "standing in" for something. Cultural theorists such as Stuart Hall argue that representation goes beyond this, that it becomes part of the thing itself, that is, representations become *constitutive*. It is in this wider sense that things are given meaning in the context of our shared culture. See also **politics of the image/politics of representation**.

reproductive labour see **social reproduction**.

responsibilization the process of transferring responsibility for peoples' needs (for education and training, health care, retirement income, and so on) from the collectivity, as organized through the state, onto individuals. Responsibilization requires that individuals adopt an ethic of self-improvement and self-care, and that they are provided with information about the risks associated with the choices available to them.

rhetorical devices linguistic techniques used to promote a particular understanding of a person, object, or event. Metaphors, alliteration, and hyperbole are commonly used rhetorical devices.

ruling apparatus or relations of ruling a notion developed by Dorothy E. Smith to explain how power in Western capitalist nations is held in place through knowledge production, and attendant managerial and administrative discourses and practices. This ruling apparatus is secured through the production and circulation of institutional, bureaucratic, and typically invisible active "texts." These texts include written, visual medium, and musical forms.

S

science a way of acquiring knowledge that depends on systematic observation and experimentation. Science is often considered to be outside of, and separate from, society and culture. However, it is a thoroughly social institution whose power is often invisible precisely because it is dismissed as extra-social, inevitable, and unchanging.

Scientific Revolution a revolution in meaning that began in the mid-16th century, through which scientific frameworks, analysis, and objectives reshaped how social and material life was understood and lived.

scientization the social processes that define and categorize human conduct or experience as a scientific problem to be solved in specifically objective and neutral terms.

semiotics the study of **signs** in systems of language, communication, and culture.

sex in the West, the label of female or male assigned to bodies, on the basis of supposedly binary genital and reproductive differences. A person's sex is often assumed to be biologically based or naturally occurring. Sex can also denote erotic practices. Since the late 19th century, sex acts have come to be seen as the basis of sexual identity, and are treated as who a person is, rather than just what a person does or desires.

sex-gender system the dominant assumption that sex and gender are naturally and inevitably linked. For example, the unquestioned belief is often that being gendered "feminine" follows from being a woman, and that, in turn, being a woman is the result of being born female.

sexual essentialism the idea that sexuality exists as a natural force independent of social relations. See also **essentialism**.

sexuality the representation of erotic practices; the social meaning given to sexual acts and identifications. The dominant assumption is that sexuality is part of your core identity.

sign something (a word, gesture, sound, etc.) that means something, and can be communicated to others. In semiotics, signs are historically and culturally produced in relation to both the **signifier** and the **signified**.

signified the concept or idea represented by a **signifier**.

signifier a symbol that calls up our conceptual understanding of an object, event, experience, feeling, or action. There is no guarantee that every person will interpret a signifier in the same way.

slow money a social movement for investment in small productive enterprises, especially organic farms, organic food products, heritage seed companies, restaurants that serve local food, and other elements of local food systems. Considerations other than short-term financial returns motivate investors, who may be equally concerned about supporting ecological sustainability, small-scale farming traditions, animal welfare, or social justice aspects of food production.

social construction the idea that what we understand as reality is constructed by, or socially made, through our shared culture. As a result, social constructionists attempt to identify the historically and culturally specific character of social beliefs and practices.

social control theory a sociological approach that analyzes social structures and beliefs that serve to dominate and constrain individuals and collectivities. Critics find that the social control perspective overstates the success of social control while understating the significance of human resistance to all forms of domination.

Social Darwinism application of Charles Darwin's research on evolutionary biology to human social life (Darwin himself only studied natural selection). Herbert Spencer (1820–1903) was among the first to do so; he coined the term "survival of the fittest" in his hypothesis that economic principles were similar to evolutionary principles.

social inequality unequal access to advantages and benefits among people in a society. Sociologists explore how unequal relations between individuals is linked to unequal relations between groups, with particular attention to inequalities organized by gender, race, class, sexuality, citizenship, and (dis)ability. Sociologists typically regard social inequality as a systemic feature of Western industrialized countries.

socialization a key concept in sociology, used to explain the process through which individuals come to acquire social habits, beliefs, and skills. **Postmodern** critics of the concept socialization are concerned that it assumes a high degree of homogeneity among social groups, and underemphasizes difference and resistance that result from people occupying multiple **subject positions**.

social reproduction in the broadest sense, the wide variety of interconnected processes that sustain a given social order over time and perpetuate its characteristic forms of power and inequality. For some feminist sociologists, this term refers to the day-to-day forms of domestic labour, care work, and familial responsibility that sustain the life of a society's current members and enable the emergence of new generations. The concept has been used by feminist political economists to illustrate the interdependent relationship between paid employment and unpaid reproductive labour by framing unpaid labour in the home as more than simply a private service that supports households. It also highlights the ways discourses and practices of masculinity and femininity become part of the class relations of capitalism by producing gendered norms about women's responsibilities in the home and men's role as "breadwinners," thereby sustaining feminized and masculinized norms of employment.

sociological imagination, the C. Wright Mills' reference to a "quality of mind" that uses information and reason to link personal biography to the broader social world.

sociology of consumption a subfield of sociology whose primary concern is with the social dynamics which drive consumer behaviour, and the complicated ways such behaviour interacts with prevailing structures and relations of power. This field of inquiry directly challenges the individualistic focus that has largely prevailed within discussions of consumer behaviour in economics and psychology.

sovereign power power exercised through direct political rule (for example, the rule over subjects by a monarch or the representatives of the monarch). It can also include other asymmetrical relationships, such as the patriarchal authority of men over their wives, children, and servants. Sovereign power is best described as power over groups and individuals, and it is generally negative and prohibitive ("You must *not*"). Sovereign power is expansive, and can be exercised as total control.

spaces of exclusion separate institutions to which, from the 18th century on, people considered mad or diseased, poor, criminal, unemployed, and idle began to be confined, which weakened their ties with their communities, and constituted them as outcast groups. See also **the great confinement**.

spectacle a striking or unusual public display.

staged authenticity the intentional production of attractions or experiences.

standardization the process through which diverse places or experiences become more and more alike and therefore predictable.

state, the   the set of political institutions that encompasses governments and their agencies (the police, military, courts, legislature, public service). The state is a political and administrative apparatus that claims legitimacy to manage or rule the affairs of a geographical and political territory. Within capitalist economic systems, it is fundamentally a *capitalist* state. It ultimately works in the interest of preserving a particular economic order that benefits foremost the owners of economic wealth. The modern state carried forward some of the features of sovereign power, particularly through its juridical authority.

statistics   aggregate data compiled on births, deaths, morbidity (patterns of illness), income, education, employment, housing, family size, and so on. With the growth of capitalism, industrialization, and urbanization, the administrative apparatus of governments became increasingly detailed and pervasive in producing new techniques of power linked to disciplinary power. As part of this trend, state administrators began to compile data in an increasingly detailed way about political subjects. This "science of the state" could only occur in the context of the production of new knowledges such as medicine, criminology, epidemiology, psychology, and so on.

status   social position in an economic hierarchy, in which status is connected not only to income, but also to occupation and education. For example, an occupation that affords one a high income and that requires a high level of formal education may be seen to reflect one's position in the "upper class," conferring a high social status. The concept emerged from Weber's writing on class.

stealth marketing   an "incognito" form of marketing in which the intended audience is not aware they are being targeted with commercial messages. Companies, for instance, might attempt to build up informal "buzz" around a commodity by hiring attractive models and actors to visibly use the good in a public place, talk up its features, and perhaps even have onlookers hold and use it themselves.

stereotypes   attempts to "fix" the meanings attributed to people and groups, according to Stuart Hall. By establishing narrow meanings for people and groups, stereotypes naturalize and limit how they can be understood.

structural adjustment programs   conditions for access to funds from the International Monetary Fund and for renegotiating loans. SAPs have tended to be controversial, (neo)liberalizing mechanisms, including: raise exports, cut imports, cut government spending, increase taxes, privatize formerly public services, deregulate prices, and remove trade controls.

structural functionalism   a theoretical position that conceptualizes society as based on consensus, with all parts functioning to serve the whole.

structuralism   the belief that there are underlying, unifying structures, or rules, shaping social life and communication, and that these structures can be studied through objective scientific method.

subaltern   those who possess knowledges subordinated by European colonial history and science.

subjectivity   how perspectives, experiences, and values shape each person's understanding of the world around them. Thus, our subjectivity is somewhat fluid, rather than a rigidly fixed aspect of who we are. As a research approach, subjectivity recognizes that the researcher's own perspectives and biases influence the research process. Researchers who adopt a subjective perspective often strive to disclose their personal perspectives and biases so that others can assess how they have influenced the research. See also **subject positions**.

subject positions   our understanding of who we are, achieved through both conscious and unconscious processes. We absorb social rules and meanings that originate externally to us, and understand who we are through this process. At the same time, we are always negotiating, and possibly reframing our subject positions, according to the distinct composition of multiple social locations that we occupy, and according to the ever-changing social world we live in. See also **subjectivity**.

subjugated knowledges   Foucault's reference to forms of knowledge that are hidden, disqualified, or masked by dominant knowledges.

surplus value   in the wage labour relationship, the difference between wages paid and the value of the commodities produced or the services provided. The production of surplus value is the key to the condition of exploitation experienced by the working class and how the capitalist class generates profit through wage labour.

sustainable tourism   tourism practices seeking equity through an improvement of life for people in host areas, including their participation in decision making; sustainability, through protecting natural resources; and meaningful visitor enjoyment and connection with others.

symbolic attributes   qualities attributed to a given commodity and often embedded in geographical indications, trademarks, and sustainability labels. Along the **global value chain**, power is distributed not solely on the basis of market share, but also on the basis of the ability to define a given commodity's identity, norms, reference values, and quality standards.

symbolic system   an interconnected group of symbols that have acquired a widely understood cultural meaning. The most prominent of our shared symbolic systems is language, in which a series of letters stand in for an idea or a concept.

symmetry   a way of looking at beliefs on both sides of a controversy using the same explanatory resources.

system of classification   placement of concepts in relation to one another to extend our models of the social world. It tells us what types of things are alike and what types are different. Concepts such as "race" and "gender" rely on complex systems of classification.

T

taxonomy   a **system of classification**.

technoscience   the combination of science and technology. Often (and inaccurately) theorized as a sphere that is autonomous, inevitable, and beyond human control.

textual practice   a way of producing social reality through the everyday activities of reading, writing, and interpreting words, images, and artifacts.

theory-laden observation   the action of scientists who bring preexisting theories about what the world ought to be like to their interpretation of sensory information.

tourism   the whole realm of leisure travel distinct from one's regular work, including the expectations and adjustments made by host residents; the employment of a very large number of people that make such travel possible; the involvement of numerous tourism-related agencies and institutions; the production of particular ways of seeing and understanding the world; and the inequalities embedded in all of these dimensions. See also *mass tourism*.

tourist bubbles   areas preserved and remade expressly for **tourism**, for example famous historical and architectural sites integrated into new facilities such as pedestrian malls and markets.

tourist gaze   a specific way of seeing the world that distinguishes a place, thing, or experience from the tourist's everyday. The tourist gaze is fostered by brochures, books, and tour guides that instruct people on what is an important site to examine, how to look at it, and how to interpret it as tourists.

transgender   an umbrella term used to describe the various categories of people who do not fit into the **binary** gender system. This includes cross-dressers, transvestites, female and male impersonators, drag kings, drag queens, non-, pre-, and postoperative **transsexuals**, and those whose perceived **gender** or anatomical **sex** may conflict with their gender expression. See also **gender queer**.

transitions   pivotal points of change from one life stage to another. For example, high school graduation is often considered a key life course transition.

transsexual   said of people who experience a conflict between their gender identity and their assigned, anatomical **sex**. This group includes individuals who seek to have, or have had, sex reassignment surgery. Some transsexuals seek a combination of surgical and hormonal treatment to correct their inappropriate anatomy.

trope   a familiar and repeated symbol, pattern, character, or theme used as a shortcut for communicating information.

two-sex system   a European way of seeing and categorizing human bodies, dating back to the late 18th century and the emergence of biology as a science, as either male or female, with dramatic differences between the two. The two-sex system became the basis for a pervasive sexual division of the world, dualistically shaping labour, identities, architecture, fashion, family relations, and so on the basis of the bodily differences named as male and female. Despite some broad social recognition of the existence and experiences of transgendered, **transsexual**, **gender queer**, and **intersexed** people, the two-sex system persists in the West.

U

upscale emulation   a term coined by Juliet Schor to describe the comparative process by which consumers of even relatively humble means come to derive their material aspirations by looking upward to the extravagant, largely unattainable lifestyles and consumption patterns of the "rich and famous," as opposed to simply striving to "keep up with the Joneses" and other reference groups closer to their own socioeconomic status.

use value   the ability to satisfy a human need (or want). Every commodity—including goods like food, clothing, and houses and services like education, health care, and personal services—has a use value.

V

volunteer tourism　**tourism** that involves people doing volunteer work while away on holidays.

W

whiteness　a position of structural advantage and social dominance facilitating the practice of power over the inclusion and exclusion among different groups. This set of practices can involve differential access to resources, rewards, and futures and more subtle inequities experienced in the everyday quality of life.

white solipsism　the assumption that only white values, interests, and needs are important and worthy of attention. It involves the achievement of an emotional and structural distance from its interdependence with racialized Others, creating psychic distance between a population identified as "us" and another identified as "them." It ensures an abdication of responsibility for the problem by dismissing the relevance of economic and cultural inequalities organized on the basis of race.

working class　a fundamental class in capitalist society, along with the **capitalist class**. The working class are all those who do not own the means of production and thus must sell their labour power in exchange for a wage in order to survive.

■ INDEX

Note: Page numbers with italicized *f*'s refer to figures

A&P, 284
Abyssinia, 279
Accumulation by dispossession, 117, 347
Active texts, 347
Acupuncture, 172
Adams, Mary Louise, 7, 24, 59
Adolescence, 135, 141–143
Adulthood, 59, 135–138
Advertising, 210–211. *See also* Consumption
   cultural role of, 212, 347
   global expenditures, 211
   marketing role of, 212, 347
Advertising and the End of the World (film), 211
African-Canadians, 99
Age norms, 135, 347
Age of Reason, 193
Agency, 5, 62, 149, 347
Ages of Man, 134*f*
Alienation, 119–121, 347
Al-Jazeera, 49
Alternative medicine, 172
Anishinaabec people, 252
Anthropocentric, 163, 347
Anti-racism, 88
Anti-Terrorism Act of 2001, 87
Apartheid, 338, 347
Apple Corp., 45
Arab stereotypes, 97–98*f*
Arbenz, Jacobo, 281
Archaeology of knowledge, 347–348
Argentina, 227
Ariés, Phillipe, 138–140
Arrighi, Giovanni, 228
Assadourian, Erik, 210
Assembly of First Nations, 268
Astral Media, 37
Asylum, 191–193
Authoritarian populism, 26, 348
Authority, 48–49
Automobiles, 215

Baby Boomers, 146
Back, Brian, 263–264
Bank of Canada, 232
Barter exchanges, 239
Bauman, Zygmunt, 205
Beauvoir, Simon de, 62
Bederman, Gail, 262
Bell, Daniel, 111
Bentham, Jeremy, 21, 364
Bhabha, Homi K., 13
Biased science, 164
Binary, 348
Biological determinism, 348
Biologizing, 348
Biopower, 22, 62, 76–78, 348
Birch Bark Roll of Woodcraft, The (Seton), 261
Bisexuality, 59
Blacks, 91–92
Bly, Robert, 267
Body politic, 95, 348
Boundary work, 171–172, 348
Bourdieu, Pierre, 351
Bourgeoisie, 117
Boyle, Robert, 169
Brahe, Tycho, 166
Brazil, coffee production in, 280–281
Bread riots, 16
Bretton Woods Agreement, 230
British Crime Survey, 304
British North American, 116
Burundi, life expectancy in, 277
Bush, George W., 203, 223
Business tourism, 304
Butler, Judith, 24, 72, 365

Caffeine, 285
Calello, Paul, 117*f*
Calgary Dollar, 239*f*, 240
Calvert, Karen, 140
Canada
   colonial expansion in, 116
   consumer spending, 232

   economic polarization in, 125–126
   illegal migrants, 333–334
   immigration policy, 335
Canadian Centre for Policy Alternatives (CCPA), 41
Canadian Charter of Rights and Freedoms, 66, 336
Canadian Citizenship Act, 332
Canadian dollar, 240
Canadian Muslims, racial profiling of, 104
Canadian Race Relations Foundation, 253
Canwest Global, 37
Capitalism
   class relations in, 115–121
   definition of, 348
   political economy of, 225
   primary features, 115
   social relations of, 4, 110
Capitalist class, 15, 117, 126–127, 349
Carlson, Kris, 196
Carlson, Richard, 196
Cartier, Jacques, 258
Cartwright, Samuel, 189–190, 353
Casino capitalism, 235
Cathedrals of consumption, 214, 349
Celebrity Rehab (television show), 195
Central banks, 223
Centre, 4, 59–60
   adulthood, 59
   advocacy for young and old, 149–150
   consumption and, 147–148
   definition of, 349
   dependency and, 148–149
   heterosexuality, 59
   intersections and, 146–147
   middle class, 60
   production and power, 147–148